D0439221

Zambia
& Malawi

Alan Murphy

Nana Luckham, Nicola Simmonds

DEMOCRATIC
REPUBLIC OF
THE CONGO
(ZAÏRE)

Bukama
Kinda
Luena
Lubudi

Sandoa
Kafakumba
Kasaji
Nasondoye
Tenke
Kolwezi
Mutshatsha
Kambove
Malonga
Massibi
Luashi
Sacuunda
Benwa
Jimbe
Ikelenga
Cazombo
Mwinilunga
Mumena

LUSAKA (p65)
Chow down amongst the region's
best selection of restaurants and let
loose amidst the thumping nightlife
of Zambia's multicultural capital

**CHIMFUNSHI WILDLIFE
ORPHANAGE (p95)**
The largest chimpanzee sanctuary
in the world – a unique place to interact
with our closest cousins in the wild

Kipushi
Lubumbashi
Musoshi
Kasumbalesa
Kansanshi
Solwezi
Mutanda
Chilumbulwa
Chimfunshi
Wildlife
Orphanage
Chingola
Mufuli
Kalulushi
Kitwe
Ndola

ANGOLA

Zambezi River

T5
Lumwana
Chibwika
Kanyilombi
Ntambu
Nyamwana
West Lunga
National
Park
Katala

KAFUE NATIONAL PARK (p174)
Explore a classic African wilderness
area with the best chance of
spotting leopard in Southern Africa

Karangua
Matuxziadonba Range
Saint Mary's
The Copperbelt
Luanshya
Chilo
Caripande
Chavuma
Mutumbwe
Kawana
Ingwe
Kasempa
Mpongwe
Walamb
Munkumpu
Kashitu
Chouka Hills
Kabompo
ZAMBIA
North-Western
Province
M8
Kangondi
Mwinuama
Kapiri Mposhi
Shamputa
Zambezi
Chitokoloki
Chipepo
Kabv
Nyama
Mushima
Busanga
Plains
Kaindu
Lukanga
Swamp
Chibombo
Chisam
Liuwa Plain
National Park
Lukulu
Lungubu
Luena Flats
Kaoma
M9
Kafue
National
Park
Mafungabusi Plateau
Mumbwa
Kungulu
Chongw
Kalabo
Mongu
M8
Katobo
D769
Kapanda
Blue Lagoon
National Park
Sokola
LUSA
Lus
Provi
Nalolo
Western
Province
Itezhitezhi
Namwala
Kafue
Kafue River
Central
Province
Kafue
Chitongo
Lochinvar
National
Park
Magoye
Mugoto
A1
Chirun
Senanga
Kataba
M11
Magunza
Monze
Changa
Kalongola
Pemba
Chisekesi
Gwembe
Shangombo
Sioma
Mulobezi
Kalomo
Batoka
T1
M10
Choma
Sioma Ngwezi
National Park
Southern
Province
Sinazongwe
Bumi
Hills
Dane
Chete
Safari
Area
Siabuwa
Imusho
Seseke
Kongola
Katima Mulilo
Mwande
Kazungula
Binga
NAMIBIA
Chobe River
Livingstone
Mwiri Range
Lake Kariba

VICTORIA FALLS (p149)
Revel in the spray of this
humongous, thundering waterfall –
one of the world's natural wonders

Victoria Falls

LAKE KARIBA (p136)
Explore remote and wild islands on on
of the largest artificial lakes in the wo

Luana
Kib
Isla
Kashib
Mbere
Mwense
Chem
Mwenda
Pe
Sal
Chin
Kab

KASANKA NATIONAL PARK (p100)
Search for shy sitatungas in the rich swamps of this little-visited national park

MUTINONDO WILDERNESS (p104)
Explore whaleback hills, clear rivers and waterfalls in this untouched slice of northern Zambia

NYIKA NATIONAL PARK (p224)
Hike, bike or ride on horseback amongst zebra and antelope on a vast grassy plateau

LIVINGSTONIA (p221)
Learn about the history of Malawi's early missionaries in this colonial hilltop town

VIPHYA PLATEAU (p241)
Hike or bike through the cool mountain air and spend the night in a cosy forest resthouse

KUNGONI CENTRE (p252)
Delve into Malawi's cultural history, and watch craftsmen at work at this art co-operative, museum and educational centre

CAPE MACLEAR (p253)
Snorkel and kayak the clear waters of Lake Malawi and enjoy the laid-back traveller lifestyle of this pretty beachside resort

SOUTH LUANGWA NATIONAL PARK (p119)
Tiptoe through the bush on a walking safari in Zambia's best park, awash with wildlife and fantastic scenery

LIWONDE NATIONAL PARK (p263)
Cruise the Shire River in Malawi's premier wildlife park – the perfect place to spot hippos, elephants and crocs

LOWER ZAMBEZI NATIONAL PARK (p142)
Admire the stunning landscape on a canoe safari with elephants swimming in the river and fish eagles soaring overhead

MULANJE (p280)
Scale Malawi's highest peak, then relax in an old planter's house on a vibrant green tea estate lining the mountain's lower slopes

TANZANIA

ZIMBABWE

MOZAMBIQUE

MALAWI

Northern Province

Central Province

Eastern Province

Lilongwe

Blantyre

HARARE

On the Road

ALAN MURPHY Coordinating Author

I'm in my element here. Right in the midst of colossal Kafue National Park (p174) watching a bull elephant with huge tusks in the distance (yes, my foot doesn't hover far from the accelerator). In the foreground are puku, impala and some rather skittish baboons. Kafue really surprised me, I had no idea just how good the wildlife watching would be and how accessible. For me, this is the reason to come to Africa and it always holds me spellbound, such a rare privilege; it feels like a window into a time on this planet long before man was leaving his footprint.

NANA LUCKHAM Deep in the heart of the northern Zambian wilderness is Shiwa Ng'andu (p106) – a stately old manor house built in the 1920s by former British army officer Sir Stewart Gore-Browne. I have just finished a tour of the 10,000 hectare estate and am standing on the house's perfectly manicured lawns with the owner's very friendly Rhodesian ridgebacks.

For full author biographies see p320

BEST OF ZAMBIA & MALAWI

Zambia and Malawi have some magnificent wild places, encapsulating unforgettable African landscapes. In this varied and special countryside is an astonishing variety and density of wildlife that will captivate and mesmerise you. You're practically guaranteed to see plenty of hoofed, tusked, winged and other creatures, not to mention the fabled big cats and great herd animals. And if this all seems a bit exhausting, then lazing around Malawi's twinkling lake, finding your own patch of paradise off the beaten track, or indulging in a luxury safari are other ways to experience one of Africa's finest corners.

1

Wildlife

The beauty of the wildlife is not just the Big Five (lion, leopard, buffalo, rhino and elephant). You may be entertained by the clownish antics of the dwarf mongoose, captivated by the speed and grace of a cheetah, in awe at the beauty of a sable antelope, outraged at the cheek of a curious baboon or startled at the rippling power of a hippo.

4

❶ Elephants
As in many parts of Southern Africa, elephant numbers are on the rise and you've an excellent chance of spotting these magnificent creatures in both countries.

❷ Lions
Zambia is fertile ground for spotting lions, especially in Kafue (p174) and South Luangwa National Parks (p119), and there are opportunities to track lions in the wild with expert guides.

❸ Leopards
Kafue National Park (p174) in Zambia is surely one of the best places on the continent to see a leopard – notoriously shy creatures and unique amongst the big cats for pulling their kill up trees.

❹ Hippos
Zambian and Malawian river systems are full of grunting hippos who haul themselves onto grassy banks around sunset to spend the night foraging for food, sometimes miles inland.

❺ Antelopes
The graceful antelopes of the region are a real highlight for visitors with puku, bushbuck, waterbuck and impala commonly seen on open grasslands and many other, rarer species deep inside the parks.

❻ Birds
Both Malawi and Zambia are studded with a wonderful array of feathered creatures. Rainbow-flecked kingfishers, rollers and bee-eaters are commonly seen, as are African fish eagles.

Wild Places

Densely wooded national parks, which include some of the best on the continent, combined with natural features such as thundering waterfalls, mighty mountains and vast plateaux provide simply breathtaking landscape. Watching wildlife in these habitats is a powerful and heady experience.

① Victoria Falls

One of the most awesome natural spectacles on the planet, just viewing the thundering waters close up provides an adrenaline rush; if that's not enough there's always rafting or a microflight (p149).

② South Luangwa National Park

Zambia's best national park (p119), this unforgettable wilderness with its majestic landscapes and variety and density of wildlife is regarded as one of the finest in Africa.

③ Lower Zambezi National Park

Independent travel here (p142) is a logistical challenge but the rewards are immense. A canoe trip along the pristine waters of the Zambezi River is an adventure you'll long remember (p143).

④ Kafue National Park

This vast park (p174) (about the size of Belgium) has a thousand different landscapes and is classic African safari territory. Leopards – famously elusive – are regularly spotted here on night drives (p175).

⑤ Liwonde National Park

The Shire River dominates this beautiful park (p263) where crocs, hippos and elephants are commonly seen but birds are the real highlight: more than 400 of Malawi's 650 species have been spotted here.

⑥ Mt Mulanje

This huge hulk of twisted granite towers over 3000m, making it the highest point in the region (p281). With its beautiful scenery and easy access, the 'Island in the Sky' is very popular with hikers.

⑦ Nyika National Park

Explore this wilderness in northern Malawi (p224) by foot, mountain bike, on horseback or vehicle and you'll find gently sloping hills, broad valleys, and grasslands interspersed with pockets of thick pine trees and crystal clear streams.

Chilling Out

Zambia and Malawi are made for sitting back and soaking up the wildlife and the wild places. You can chill out in style on safari, otherwise make the most arduous thing you do putting your feet up and relaxing beside breathtaking views and enormous, shimmering lakes.

4 Lake Kariba
This gigantic artificial lake (p136) deserves a few low-key days on sunset cruises, walking the dam wall and watching the storms roll in over the jagged peaks of Zimbabwe across the waters.

5 Likoma Island
A jewel in the middle of Lake Malawi (p237), with sublime crescent bays, views over to Mozambique and a pace of life even slower than the mainland.

1 Nkhata Bay
Chill out in a reed hut on the beach at one of Malawi's favourite relaxation outposts (p232), where lazing on the sand and taking a dip in the sparkling waters are mandatory.

2 Cape Maclear
A long piece of golden beach with islands bobbing offshore in the glassy-blue waters of the bay, this is a place where plans are forgotten as visitors are lulled into life on the lake (p253).

3 Walking Safari
Although your first walking safari can be challenging you'll soon be lulled into the rhythm of the African bush and its wild inhabitants.

6 Livingstonia
Stroll around the old stone buildings, which provide a snapshot of Malawi's colonial past (p221), and especially the influence of the missionaries, while drinking in the views across to Lake Malawi.

7 Shiwa Ng'andu
Staying at this peaceful yet incongruous country manor (p106) is all about four-poster beds, roaring log fires, poking around dusty family heirlooms and sipping gin on manicured lawns.

Three men in a boat, in the late afternoon sun, Lake Malawi

Contents

Regional Map Contents

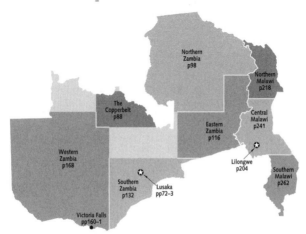

Destination Zambia & Malawi

Zambia and Malawi perfectly complement each other as travel destinations, for both first-time visitors to the continent and experienced travellers. Zambia, known as the 'real Africa', holds myriad opportunities for exploring true African wilderness. Peeling away its layers reveals a throbbing heart of natural wonders that are a real adventure to discover under your own steam – getting off the beaten track here means leaving Lusaka. Intrepid travellers will discover an astonishing diversity and density of wildlife, from the fleet-footed grazers to the rippling power of the stalking hunters. And there are plenty of waterfalls, including one of the planet's great natural wonders...no-one should miss the thundering torrent that is Victoria Falls.

Malawi is much easier to navigate earning it the slogan, 'Africa for Beginners'. Its attractions are pretty well organised and bundled into compact, neat packages. The country relies on the crystal-clear waters of its pristine lake, full of rainbow-coloured fish, to draw visitors for serious chilling, or any number of water-based activities including canoeing and diving. It also offers national parks like Nyika, actually more reminiscent of the Scottish highlands, genuine wilderness areas teeming with birdlife, mountainous retreats such as Mulanje, and the historic outpost of Livingstonia.

One thing for which both countries are renowned is the warmth of their people and their friendliness towards visitors. In more remote areas they may be astonished to see you – but don't mistake staring for antagonism; most people would move heaven and earth to ensure a visitor to their country is comfortable, safe and happy.

Zambia's people are known for being docile – probably because of the country's relatively peaceful political scene in a region historically surrounded by civil war and unrest. However, corruption they don't like and there is concern that the country is sliding back into bad habits under its new president, who is proving to be unpopular.

In Malawi the president is riding on a wave of popularity. However, because his party won more than a two-thirds majority in recent parliamentary elections, some people are worried that this may hand the government too much power. The Madonna adoption row has also been a hot conversation topic – many locals feel that Malawi's orphans should be helped in their own community and that the negative international press coverage is damaging.

There's a certain joy about travel in these countries. Whether it comes from the people, the wild landscapes or the astounding animal population it is difficult to tell, but this indefinable quality will probably hit you when you first set foot here. Now is the time to go as both countries gear themselves up for the influx of visitors the 2010 World Cup in South Africa is expected to bring – an influx who will get the chance to live out their dreams of Africa if they set even a toenail inside Zambia and Malawi.

Getting Started

Together, Zambia and Malawi present far-reaching opportunities for all types of trip, regardless of budget, experience or interest, although individually the two countries are very different. Malawi is easy to get around via public transport or driving your own car because distances are short, roads are in good condition and there is accommodation aimed at all budgets – especially backpackers. Malawi is also a good place for first-time visitors in Africa, and for solo travellers, as it provides a gentle introduction to travel in the region, without many of the more challenging aspects that may be encountered in some other countries.

Zambia, on the other hand, can present more logistical problems and the sheer size of the country and the time it takes to get anywhere can be daunting. Zambia is less developed (the roads, even major highways, are often in a shocking condition), is expensive to travel around and has far fewer options for budget travellers – but its wealth of wildlife and landscapes make it worth spending that bit extra. It has some of the finest national parks and wildlife-viewing opportunities in Africa, and a genuine chance to cut away from the popular tourist trail. Zambia is one of the best destinations in Africa, both for midrange visitors and the highly exclusive top end of the market. Camps and lodges in national parks are highly regarded by safari cognoscenti, and in Zambia you can enjoy fine food and wine, skilful guides, good-quality vehicles and privately chartered planes.

Anyone with limited time will want to plan their trip carefully, while those with more time may prefer to just follow their whims and take life at a leisurely pace, stopping whenever something takes their fancy. (Although in Zambia in particular you'll benefit from a bit of forward planning.) Don't run around trying to fit too much into your time – Zambia and Malawi need to be approached with a sense of fun and laid-back nonchalance: before long you'll find yourself in tune to the rhythm of their friendly people, wild landscapes and majestic wildlife.

WHEN TO GO

The best time to go to Zambia and Malawi can largely be determined by the weather. If you're driving, it's worth noting that in the rainy season, or just afterwards, access roads in the parks (and other minor roads

---

DON'T LEAVE HOME WITHOUT...

- A sense of fun and a relaxed attitude about African travel
- Binoculars for wildlife-watching and a decent camera for taking great wildlife shots
- Reading the Malaria section of the Health chapter (pp309–10) in this book
- A basic medical kit that includes a preparation to relieve itchy bites and stings; and anything to repel pesky tsetse flies
- Warm, waterproof clothing, a hat and warm socks for cold highland areas in Malawi and for national parks such as Kafue in Zambia
- Reading a few of the books listed on p20, or bringing one with you for long bus rides
- A tent, sleeping bag, sheet liner (which may also come in handy at budget hotels) and other equipment for camping

around the country) are often impassable unless you've got a rugged 4WD vehicle; this is especially the case in Zambia.

Also weather patterns all over Southern Africa have become less predictable in the last decade or so with the onset of climate change. Some years the rainy seasons have arrived later and some years they have finished earlier.

Zambia

See Climate Charts (p184) for more information.

Zambia has three main seasons: May to August is dry and warm; August to October is dry and hot; November to April is the rainy season. The climate is a major consideration because it affects wildlife watching (called 'game viewing' in Zambia). The rains end around May, when conditions become dry and the landscape is beautifully lush but animals are relatively hard to see. Through June and July temperatures are cool and the bush starts to thin out. By August the weather is warmer again and the bush has died back to allow very good wildlife viewing. Rising temperatures through September and October (the 'suicide month') result in very dry and dusty conditions, but with excellent wildlife viewing as the animals cluster around precious water holes. The rains break in November, and the new grass starts to grow. Plentiful food and water allows most animals to produce their young; true wildlife aficionados enjoy this period, but in the rains many dirt roads become impassable and some national park lodges close (although those that stay open give good discounts).

If you're heading for Victoria Falls, or looking for white-water rafting and other activities, the water level of the Zambezi River will be a factor to consider: in 2009 the Zambezi was at its highest level in about 60 years and the Falls were at their thundering best.

Malawi

Malawi's wet season runs from October/November to late April, and its dry season is from April/May to October/November. Climatic conditions are similar to those in Zambia.

When you go to Malawi will also be determined by your reason for coming. Late in the dry season is the best time for wildlife viewing as the vegetation is not so dense and animals converge at reliable watering holes but the heat can be unpleasant – especially in the lowland areas. May to July is not so good for seeing wildlife but the landscape itself is much more attractive and conditions less oppressive. August is a busy period, mainly because the weather is good but also because it is school holiday time in both Malawi and South Africa, from where many visitors come.

If you come only to take landscape photographs, the later months of the dry season may not be the best time as the views, especially from the highland areas (such as Livingstonia and the Nyika Plateau) can sometimes be obscured by haze and smoke from burning grass on the lower plains. Views are at their sharpest during the wet season (when it isn't actually raining) or in the first few months of the dry season.

Although the views might be good, it's best not to consider hiking or trekking in the highlands during the wet season. Showers, which may be short on the lowlands, can last for longer on the higher ground, and stream crossings (particularly on Mt Mulanje) can be treacherous. Another factor to consider if you intend to travel in southern Malawi, especially if you plan to visit Mt Mulanje, is a heavy mist called a chiperone (chip-er-own-ee), which occurs during the early months of the dry season, sometimes lasting up to five days at a time.

OSTS & MONEY

Generally speaking, prices in Zambia and Malawi are around 50% to 75% of what they are in Europe, Australasia or North America. In general, locally produced items (such as food and beer) will be good value wherever you go, while imported goods may be twice what they cost in the West (thanks to import duties).

Serious backpackers may get by on an average of US$15-20 per day, including accommodation, food and transport. For a bit more comfort, US$30 to US$40 per day is a reasonable budget for day-to-day living expenses. To stay in midrange hotels, eat well and travel in comfort when possible, you're looking at around US$75 per day or more. Top end travellers should expect to pay at least US$100 per day, but upward of this is more realistic, while those on safari in top end lodges and camps in the national parks should be looking at about US$300 to a whopping US$900 a day.

If you're travelling in both countries you'll find Zambia more expensive overall than Malawi, especially for accommodation. Malawi offers a wide range of options, from dirt cheap to exceptionally expensive, while Zambia caters much more for the midrange and top end market, with a very under-developed market in budget tourism.

Getting around Zambia by public transport seems expensive compared to Malawi, but that's mainly because the distances are so long. Car rental starts at about US$45 per day for city driving, plus costs such as kilometre charge and insurance – see p198. For travel around the country 4WDs are at least US$120 per day (older second-hand Landrovers), but usually closer to US$200. Internal flights are also expensive, eg Lusaka to Mfuwe (South Luangwa National Park) is US$500 return.

In Malawi car rental for city driving also starts at around US$45, while 4WD hire is about US$150.

See the Transport sections of individual country chapters, and the Money sections in country-specific directories, for more information on costs.

HOW MUCH?

4WD car hire US$120-200

Bunch of bananas or mangoes at roadside US$1

Walking safari US$45

Hourly internet access US$2-3

Traditional dance performance US$10-20

TRAVELLING RESPONSIBLY

Travelling responsibly in Zambia and Malawi means taking a keen interest in the country you're visiting and actively thinking about the consequences of your visit. In both countries tourists pay to visit national parks and other popular tourist areas (such as Victoria Falls), and this provides employment for the people and income for the country. Some schemes distribute money earned from tourism to local communities located around national parks; this is particularly the case around South Luangwa National Park in Zambia. This in turn provides an incentive to conserve the wilderness areas and the animals they contain.

However, tourism can also have a negative effect. In those very national parks and wilderness areas that attract large numbers of tourists, the building of new camps and lodges (and the number of guests they contain) is restricted, but sometimes not as tightly as it could be because the government body issuing the licenses wants more revenue or the tour companies want more visitors to improve the bottom line on their balance sheet. The end result is too many tourists in too small an area, which puts a strain on the local environment and also dilutes the 'wilderness' experience that tourists have paid to enjoy. This scenario has already occurred in several national parks in other African countries, but so far Zambia and Malawi have pretty much avoided it, mostly because tourist numbers are relatively small and because in Zambia, in particular, the safari industry is fairly exclusive.

'take a moment to consider where the money goes'

You can make a difference by deciding where to spend your money. Try to make sure that as much money as possible stays inside the country, and near to the bottom of the economic ladder. Travellers with cars and on public transport have many opportunities to buy local goods and services, from soft drinks and market produce to souvenirs and nights in locally run hotels. If you take a tour or safari, or even have your whole holiday organised by an agent, take a moment to consider where the money goes. If you want to support tour companies with a good environmental record, you have to look beyond vague 'ecofriendly' claims and ask what they are really doing to protect or support the environment and its local inhabitants (and remember that includes local people just as much as wild animals).

Here are some suggestions to get you thinking:

- Consider staying in community-run guesthouses (such as Tikondane, p117) or in local villages (such as Kawaza Village, p125 or Njobvu Cultural Village, p264) where possible.
- If you're travelling around independently be upfront about asking your accommodation about their 'green' credentials.
- Many lodges and camps in national parks claim to be helping local communities – ask how they are achieving this.
- Stick to marked trails and tracks in national parks and other protected areas, whether walking or driving.
- Consider very seriously a donation to a reputable development organisation or charity as part of your trip (see p59).
- Many businesses are run by Europeans and South Africans: take note of how they treat their local staff, and channel your money accordingly.
- Be prepared to bargain, sure, especially when shopping for carvings and other souvenirs, no-one likes to get ripped off. But remember that a US dollar or two means a lot more to them than it does to you.
- Don't give money or sweets as gifts for children. If you want to help them, find the village school and donate some pens or schoolbooks, or seek out the clinic and donate unwanted first aid items. Don't allow schoolkids to guide you during school hours as this encourages them to play truant.

Organisations with information on responsible travel and sustainable environmental practices include: **Tourism Concern** (☎ 020-7133 3800; www .tourismconcern.org.uk; Stapleton House, 277-281 Holloway Rd, London N7 8HN); and **Action for Southern Africa** (☎ 020-3263 2001; www.actsa.org; 231 Vauxhall Bridge Rd, London SW1V 1EH), which campaigns for (among other things) sustainable tourism throughout the region.

TRAVEL LITERATURE

In *Scribbling the Cat: Travels with an African Soldier*, Alexandra Fuller journeys with a companion through Zambia, Zimbabwe and Mozambique, revealing a legacy of conflict and its effects on themselves and the region's indigenous peoples.

Zambia: Safari in Style by David Rogers is an indispensable guide for those considering an upmarket safari in Zambia. It reveals in detail 25 of the country's top wildlife lodges, peeling apart their unique ambience.

In *The Ukimwi Road*, Dervla Murphy, the famously eccentric Irish grandmother, recounts her adventures as she cycles through Africa (including Malawi and Zambia), downing beers and observing life – most notably the harrowing effects of AIDS.

TOP PICKS

MALAWI
Angola   ZAMBIA   Lilongwe   Mozambique
Lusaka

FESTIVALS

The numerous tribes and ethnic groups of Zambia and Malawi enjoy a diverse and fascinating collection of traditional festivals. These folk know how to party. Most festivals include drumming and other music, and many feature dancing. The most popular dance form in Zambia is called *makishi*; it originated in western Zambia, but is now popular among tribes all over the country. *Makishi* is performed by troupes of energetic dancers wearing brightly coloured skirts and leg tassels, with equally colourful face masks surrounded by a mane of feathers. Most festivals also involve a lot of drinking; the aim of any festival is to give everyone a good time!

- N'cwala (Zambia), near Chipata, February (p185)
- Kuomboka (Zambia), near Mongu, March/April (p172)
- Kungoni Festival (Malawi), Mua, August (p252)
- Kusefya Pangwena (Zambia), near Kasama, August (p185)
- Lake of Stars (Malawi), Senga Bay, October (p251)

ADRENALINE SPORTS

The range of energetic, adventurous and downright scary activities in Zambia and Malawi is growing, and the choice is bound to be even bigger by the time you arrive. This is the place to blow those hard-earned dollars on a few hours, or even a few seconds, of total excitement.

- Abseiling (Zambia), Batoka Gorge (p150), near Victoria Falls, year round; (Malawi), Livingstonia (p222), year round
- Bungee jumping (Zambia), Victoria Falls (p150), year round
- Gorge swing (Zambia), Batoka Gorge (p150), near Victoria Falls, year round; (Malawi), Livingstonia (p227), year round
- Kayaking safari (Zambia), Lake Kariba (p139), year round
- Microlight flight (Zambia), Victoria Falls (p151), year round
- Rock climbing (Malawi), Mulanje and Viphya Plateau (p281), year round
- White-water rafting (Zambia), Batoka Gorge (p151), near Victoria Falls, mid-June to October

A fun and fascinating collection of stories from Africa about cars, bars, rebellions and other diverse subjects, *Mr Bigstuff and the Goddess of Charm* by Fiona Sax Ledger includes some insightful conversations with Zambian politicians.

In Quest of Livingstone by Colum Wilson and Aisling Irwin is the story of two British travellers who followed the explorer's footsteps through Tanzania and Zambia, combining contemporary observations with flashbacks to Livingstone's own journals.

Laurens van der Post's poetic descriptions of his 'exploration' of Malawi's Mt Mulanje and Nyika Plateau in *Venture to the Interior* are augmented by his report of the quaint workings of the British colonial administration.

Zambezi – Journey of a River by Michael Main is a slightly rambling but immensely fascinating study of Zambia's mighty river; a combination of history, geography, geology, anthropology, careful observation, humour, rumour and myth.

BEST BOOKS

Here's a selection of some of our favourite books about Zambia and Malawi.

The Africa House, by Christina Lamb, relates the story of Stewart Gore-Brown and his grand plans for a utopian fiefdom in a remote part of Zambia during the 1920s. His country mansion at Shiwa Ng'andu still stands (see p106).

Challenging the effectiveness of aid in Africa, Zambian-born Dambisa Moyo explodes the myths in *Dead Aid*, arguing that aid is actually a major cause of poverty.

The Jive Talker: Or, How to Get a British Passport: by Samson Kambalu is a memoir about growing up in '70s and '80s Malawi.

Although a personalised selection of observations on wildlife and humans, *Kakuli* by Norman Carr also raises deeper issues and suggests some practical solutions to current conservation problems. The author spent a lifetime working with animals and people in the South Luangwa National Park (see p119).

My Malawi Journal by Bea Buckley is a travelogue telling the story of a Peace Corps volunteer in a rural village in Malawi.

On the Wild Side, by Outi Maattanen-Bourke, is a pictorial detailing the history of Liwonde National Park and conservation issues facing it.

Mark and Delia Owens (authors of the famous *Cry of the Kalahari*) based *Survivor's Song* in the North Luangwa National Park. They launch themselves single-mindedly into the hard fight against elephant poachers, putting their lives and relationship seriously on the line.

In *Wisdom of the Yawo People*, Ian Dicks has collected traditional proverbs and stories from Malawi's Yawo people. Simple and humourous they often have a poignant meaning, such as 'Under the Elephant's Belly, You Can't Pass Twice'.

The compelling *Zambian Myths and Legends of the Wild* by Kenneth Kangende is a detailed examination of good and bad omens and explains how manifestations of evil are often the strange or unexplained amongst a superstitious people.

The well-written and entertaining *The Scramble for Africa: White Man's Conquest of the Dark Continent from 1876 to 1912*, by Thomas Pakenham is the standard work that details both sides of the colonial story.

INTERNET RESOURCES

Lonely Planet (www.lonelyplanet.com) Everything travel related you need to kick off a trip.

Malawi Tourism (www.malawitourism.com) The official site for Malawian tourism promotion.

Malawi Tourism Association (www.malawi-tourism-association.org.mw) Lots of practical info, car hire, places to stay, buses, safari operators etc.

Zambia Online (www.zambia.co.zm) This lively site has webzines, news summaries and links to many other sites.

Zambia Tourism (www.zambiatourism.com) Detailed and comprehensive site by the Zambia National Tourist Board.

Zamnet (www.zamnet.zm) Zambia's main service provider has good news and business information, with links to useful sites.

Itineraries
CLASSIC ROUTES

NATURAL DELIGHTS & MAN-MADE WONDER

**One Week /
Lusaka to Livingstone**

Start your trip in **Lusaka** (p65), the gateway to Zambia, and then zip straight down to **Siavonga** (p138) on sparkling **Lake Kariba** (p136), one of the largest artificial lakes in Africa, and relax on a boat cruise. Retrace your steps and head for **Monze** (p132), staying at one of the most beautifully landscaped **campsites** (p132) in the country; consider a side trip to entrancing **Lochinvar National Park** (p133), part of a huge World Heritage Wetland Site called the Kafue Flats and a haven for many species of antelope and bird. Then head further south and drop into the **Choma Museum** (p135) with its interesting exhibits on the local Tonga people and a great crafts shop. Now it's time to see one of the greatest natural sights on the planet – the last leg of your trip takes you into **Livingstone** (p153), the gateway to the **Victoria Falls** (p149), whose mighty spray can be seen from 50km away. There's a plethora of activities including serene canoe trips on top of the falls or rafting down the churning Zambezi.

This 1000km trip serves up a delightful variety of watery treats, and if you're not in a hurry you could slow the pace down and include some time wildlife-watching in the Game Management Area (GMA) around the Lower Zambezi on your way to Lake Kariba.

MAGNIFICENT WILDLIFE & MIGHTY LAKE MALAWI

One Month /
Lower Zambezi to Livingstonia

The **Lower Zambezi National Park** (p142) is spectacular, and an excellent place to see elephants and other wildlife. Tear yourself away from here and mosey down the Great East Road to Zambia's premier park, **South Luangwa National Park** (p119), with its incredible density of game. After getting that photo of a stalking leopard, head for the Malawi border, overnighting at **Tikondane Community Centre** (p117) in the Katete district, perhaps seeing the legendary **Ghost Dance** (p117) in a local village. The next day make a beeline for **Chipata** (p118), cross the border and then it's only a couple of hours to sleepy **Lilongwe** (p203). Head north for the lake, passing through historic **Nkhotakota** (p245), and if you've wildlife withdrawal symptoms, duck into **Nkhotakota Wildlife Reserve** (p247). And now for the lake: **Nkhata Bay** (p232) with its Caribbean vibe and clutch of water-based activities is a stone's throw north and the perfect place to laze by the shimmering waters of Lake Malawi. From here grab the ferry to beautiful **Likoma** (p237) and **Chizumulu** (p239) islands for a chance to explore the lake's crystal waters and admire the panorama of Mozambique's wild coast, a few kilometres away. Trek north, passing through **Mzuzu** (p228), a useful service town, and on to **Rumphi** (p223). Make a side trip to one of Malawi's best-kept secrets, **Vwaza Marsh Wildlife Reserve** (p228) with its hippo-heavy river. Then end your trip with a vertical drive or walk up to **Livingstonia** (p221) – with its grand architecture, intriguing museum and sweeping lake views, it provides a captivating glimpse into the man himself and Malawi's colonial past.

This mammoth trek takes you through breathtaking landscapes; some of the best Zambia and Malawi have to offer. You could zip through the 2500km in three weeks, but we recommend taking at least a month to enjoy the incredible wildlife and Africa's third-largest lake.

MALAWI SNAPSHOT   Three to Four Weeks / Blantyre to Livingstonia

Whether you start north or south, this is the ultimate journey, taking in beaches, safari parks and mountains.

Fly into **Blantyre** (p270) and after a day's acclimatisation head down to **Mulanje** (p280) for a three-day hike across the country's highest peak. Recover by spending a day or two in an old planter's house on one of Mulanje's many **tea estates** (p286). Then on to colonial gem, **Zomba** (p266), and a day or two of gentle walking on the misty **Zomba Plateau** (p267), perhaps finding time for a riding lesson as well. Now it's wildlife time! Make your way to nearby **Liwonde National Park** (p263), basing yourself at the excellent **Mvuu Camp** (p265), for a few days of hippo and elephant spotting by car, boat and on foot. Now head for the lake and the small resort village of **Cape Maclear** (p253). You'll need a good three or four days here to recover – spend them lolling on the sand and swimming with the brilliantly coloured fish.

Next, it's time to board the Ilala Ferry for a classic Lake Malawi experience. Sleep out on deck on a mattress underneath the stars and disembark at **Nkhata Bay** (p232), Malawi's other famous lakeshore resort, where you can snorkel, kayak or even take a PADI course at local dive school **Aqua Africa** (p232). When you've had enough of the water, move on to **Nyika National Park** (p224), the country's largest, where you can explore wild grasslands, strangely reminiscent of the Yorkshire Moors, on foot or on horseback. Finally, it's time for a history lesson at nearby **Livingstonia** (p221), an isolated colonial hilltop town.

Mountains, wilderness, the lake, historical riches – tracking across the length of this marvellous country you'll see the very best of Malawi. We'd recommend taking a month, as side trips could always be on the cards, but you could squeeze it into three weeks at a canter.

ROADS LESS TRAVELLED

MALAWI'S SOUTHERN WILDERNESS

Two Weeks /
Blantyre to Elephant Marsh

Head south from the commercial hub of **Blantyre** (p270) and the road plunges down the Thyolo Escarpment into the heat of the Lower Shire, a region little visited by travellers. It may be Malawi's most densely populated area but you'll also find empty national reserves and wild marshland. On the journey, take in the magnificent views across the Shire River floodplains; perhaps stop at the **Fisherman's Rest nature reserve** (p279) for a coffee with a view. Make your way west to **Majete Wildlife Reserve** (p287) and check into **Thawale Camp** (p287), from where you can watch elephants, buffalos and waterbuck around the floodlit waterhole. Also, make sure to go on an exciting **elephant tracking trip** (p287) as well as the traditional safari drives. There's no big game at the next stop, **Lengwe National Park** (p288), but it's famous for its nyalas – you won't find them any further north in Africa. This is a good place for walking safaris and there are several tree hides with views of the watering holes. Further south, on Malawi's southernmost tip is **Mwabvi Wildlife Reserve** (p289), the smallest, least visited and least accessible reserve in the country – don't even think about visiting without a 4WD. There may be no big game at present but hikers can see antelopes and buffaloes, and there's a dreamy campsite.

Elephant Marsh (p288) is your final destination. Forming the eastern floodplain of the Shire River, its lush swamps are studded with flowers and rich in birdlife. A boat trip amongst the crocodiles, hippos and, of course, elephants, can be arranged through the local villages.

The distances may be short, but put aside time to go off the beaten track into the untamed wilderness of this forgotten corner of Malawi. Although not known for its big game, the area has majestic landscapes and plenty of antelopes, elephants, birds and hippos.

THE UNTAMED NORTH
Two Weeks / Lusaka to Kalambo Falls

Zambia's vast north is a landscape of sweeping hills, untamed parks and secret waterfalls as yet undiscovered by most visitors, so you're likely to have it all to yourself.

Leaving **Lusaka** (p65) head north on the Great North Road. It's a long journey, so you may have to stop off at **Serenje** (p99) for the night. The next day head for **Kasanka National Park** (p100) to see sitatunga antelopes, rich bird life, and in season, millions of fruit bats. An arduous drive away are the **Bangweulu Wetlands** (p103), huge, wild swamps and grasslands where you'll fine the endemic black lechwe, the rare shoebill and a rustic island camp.

Make your way back to the Great North Road now – it will take a day or so. Then head further north to **Mutinondo Wilderness** (p104). You could easily spend a week here, exploring the bush, plains and whaleback hills, horse riding, swimming and canoeing in croc-free rivers, and sleeping in semi-open chalets with astounding views. Next, and further on up the Great North Road is **Shiwa Ng'andu** (p106), a magnificent manor house built by **Sir Stewart Gore-Browne** (p107). You can tour the house and estate, or get out your binoculars and go birdwatching. Nearby, on the same estate, is **Kapishya Hot Springs** (p107) where you can take a dip in a steaming, palm-fringed lagoon. Back to the road and you can make **Kasama** (p108) your next stop – an excellent jumping-off point for exploring the nearby waterfalls and ancient rock paintings. Push further north still to the border with Tanzania and you'll come to the spectacular **Kalambo Falls** (p111) – the second-highest single-drop waterfall in Africa.

If you want to visit some of Zambia's best untrodden wilderness, with rarely another tourist in sight, then this northern route is for you. Go now, before the government opens the area to mainstream tourism, but take your time (the dilapidated roads will help you).

TAILORED TRIPS

MAJESTIC WILDLIFE & AFRICAN LANDSCAPES

In Zambia the inspirational landscapes of **South Luangwa National Park** (p119) contain an astonishing abundance and variety of wildlife. But if size matters, the gigantic **Kafue National Park** (p174) is one of the best places in Africa to see leopards. The **Lower Zambezi National Park** (p142) in the south has elephants in profusion, browsing on the lovely acacia trees and in the thick miombo woodland. To get really wild, head for **North Luangwa National Park** (p129) where walking safaris are the only way to explore this pristine wilderness. And in the rarely visited Copperbelt you'll find the world's largest chimpanzee sanctuary, **Chimfunshi Wildlife Orphanage** (p95). In Malawi hippos, elephants and colourful kingfishers dominate the lush surrounds and tranquil Shire River at **Liwonde National Park** (p263), while the **Nyika National Park** (p224) has antelopes, endless views and clean, crisp air. **Vwaza Marsh Wildlife Reserve** (p228) with its open swamps and dense woodlands has plenty of waterbuck, eland, zebras and elephants. Further south the cool slopes of **Mt Mulanje** (p281) are excellent for hiking. A series of remote wilderness areas in the south include **Elephant Marsh** (p288), where spectacular birdwatching (not elephants) is the draw, and the beautiful wilderness of **Majete Wildlife Reserve** (p287). And, of course, you can't forget Lake Malawi …

CULTURE & CRAFTS

Zambia and Malawi present some excellent opportunities to scratch the cultural surface of their varied ethnic groups, as well as benefit from wonderful arts and craftwork. In Zambia **Kawaza Village** (p125) and **Tikondane Community Centre** (p117) both provide accommodation and cultural experiences including watching traditional dancing. **Malambo Womens Centre** (p133) offers the opportunity to purchase knitted and sewn arts from a textile collective run by AIDS widows. Rummage through the largest collection of woodcarvings, textiles and other artisanal goods in the country at the **Sunday market at Arcades** (p81) in Lusaka; there are some fine pieces of work for sale. The **Mumwa Craft Association** (p171), a network of local craft producers in far-flung Mongu, has some of the best basket-weaving in Africa and it's very cheap. In Malawi at **Njobvu Cultural Village** (p264) you stay in traditional huts, participate in everyday village life and are offered the chance to watch dancing and drumming. **Kungoni Centre of Culture and Art** (p252) offers traditional dance displays, a museum describing the Yao, Ngoni and Chewa cultures, and a carving workshop, where you can see artisans at work and purchase their products. You'll find excellent examples of woodcarvings, jewellery and woven baskets at small **craft markets** (p214) in Lilongwe (Kamuzu Procession Rd) and Blantyre (Chilembwe Rd).

History

The pre-colonial history of Zambia, Malawi and the wider area of Southern Africa is a compelling, interwoven web of peoples on the move throughout this vast region – the original travellers on our planet. It's also a story of technology and its impact on our early ancestors. Although Southern Africa's history stretches far back into the mists of time, the only records today are intriguing fossil remains and an extraordinary human diary of Stone Age rock art, with good examples still seen in Northern Zambia.

A copy of the skull of Zambia's most celebrated early inhabitant, Broken Hill Man – a Neanderthal human thought to be about 100,000 years old – can be seen in the museum at Livingstone.

Over 2000 years ago the Bantu moved from West Africa into the Congo Basin, and over the next thousand years spread across present-day Uganda, Kenya and Tanzania and migrated south into Zambia, Malawi, Mozambique and other parts of Southern Africa. The term 'migration' here refers to a sporadic and very slow spread over many hundreds of years. Typically, a group would move from valley to valley, or from one water source to the next. This process inevitably had a knock-on effect, as weaker groups were constantly being 'moved on' by invaders from other areas.

Zambia

The first of the 'modern' (ie still found today) ethnic groups of Zambia to arrive were the Tonga and Ila peoples (sometimes combined as the Tonga-Ila), who migrated from the Congo area in the late 15th century. By 1550 they had occupied the Zambezi Valley and plateau areas north of where Lake Kariba is now – still their homeland today. Next to arrive were the Chewa. Between the 14th and 16th centuries they followed a long and circuitous route via Lakes Mweru, Tanganyika and Malawi before founding a powerful kingdom covering much of present-day eastern Zambia, as well as parts of Malawi and Mozambique. Today, the Chewa are still the largest group in eastern Zambia.

After Livingstone's death, his African companions carried his body over 1000km across present-day Zambia, Malawi and Tanzania to Zanzibar. From here it was shipped back to Britain, and buried in Westminster Abbey.

The Bemba (most notably the ruling Ngandu clan) had migrated from Congo by crossing the Luapula River into northern Zambia by

---

THE BANTU

The Bantu peoples could more accurately be called 'Bantu-speaking peoples' since the word 'Bantu' actually refers to a language group rather than a specific race. However, it has become a convenient term of reference for the black African peoples of Southern and Eastern Africa, even though the grouping is as ill-defined as 'American' or 'oriental'. The Bantu ethnic group is composed of many subgroups, each with their own language, customs and traditions.

TIMELINE

100,000 BC	2000–500 BC	1616
Zambia's most celebrated early inhabitant, Broken Hill Man, lives and dies. Evidence unearthed by archaeologists in Malawi suggests that Early Stone Age settlements existed along the shore of Lake Malawi at this time.	Iron-skilled Bantu migrate through the Congo basin into present-day Zambia, Malawi and other parts of East and Southern Africa. This is a gradual movement of people rather than a migration tidal wave.	Portuguese explorer, Gaspar Bocarro journeys from Tete (on the Zambezi River) through the Shire Valley to Lake Chilwa (south of Lake Malawi), then through the south of what is now Tanzania and back into Mozambique.

The oldest hominid remnant found in Malawi is a single jawbone of the species *Homo rudolfensis*, which palaeontologists calculate to be 2.5 million years old.

around 1700. Meanwhile, the Lamba people migrated to the area of the Copperbelt in about 1650. At around the same time, the related Lala settled in the region around Serenje.

Meanwhile, in western Zambia, the Lozi people established a dynasty and the basis of a solid political entity that still exists. The Lozi's ancestors may have migrated from what is now Angola as early as AD 450.

Malawi

Migration into the area of Malawi stepped up with the arrival of the Tumbuka and Phoka groups, who settled around the highlands of Nyika and Viphya during the 17th century, and the Maravi people (from whom the modern-day Chewa are descended), who established a large and powerful kingdom in the south.

The early 19th century brought with it two more significant migrations. The Yao invaded southern Malawi from western Mozambique, displacing the Maravi, while groups of Zulu migrated northward from Southern Africa, to settle in central and northern Malawi (see below).

THE DIFAQANE

The name 'Malawi' was officially inspired by the Chichewa word malavi, which means reflected light, haze, flames or rays, and is thought to describe the vision of the sun rising over the lake.

The *difaqane* (meaning 'forced migration' in Sotho, or *mfeqane*, 'the crushing', in Zulu) was a period of immense upheaval and suffering for the indigenous peoples of Southern Africa. It originated in the early 19th century when the Nguni ethnic groups in modern KwaZulu-Natal (South Africa) changed rapidly from loosely organised collections of chiefdoms to the more centralised Zulu nation. Based on its highly disciplined and powerful warrior army, the process began under Chief Dingiswayo, and reached its peak under the military commander Shaka Zulu.

Shaka was a ruthless conqueror and his reputation preceded him. Not surprisingly, groups living in his path chose to flee, in turn displacing neighbours and causing disruption and terror across Southern Africa. Ethnic groups displaced from Zululand include the Ngoni who fled to Malawi and Zambia; and the Makololo who moved into southern Zambia, around the towns of Kalomo and Monze, and eventually were forced further west into southwest Zambia, where they displaced more Tonga people. To this day Makolo is the dominant language of much of western Zambia.

THE RISE OF SLAVERY

Slavery, and a slave trade, had existed in Africa for many centuries, but in the early 19th century demand from outside Africa increased considerably. Swahili-Arabs, who dominated the trade on the east coast of Africa, pushed into the interior, often using the services of powerful local ethnic groups such as the Yao to raid and capture their unfortunate neighbours. Several trading centres were established in Malawi, including Karonga and Nkhotakota – towns that still bear a strong Swahili-Arab

1790s	1830–50	1855
First Europeans, intrepid Portuguese pioneer explorers, reach Zambia, coming into the country from Angola. Although the Portuguese explore part of the country they don't lay claim to its territory.	The *difaqane* (forced migration) or *mfeqane* (crushing); ethnic groups scatter across Southern Africa in the face of Zulu expansion and aggression; Makololo people migrate from Southern Africa to Zambia.	David Livingstone explores large parts of Zambia and discovers a magnificent waterfall, never before seen by a European. He coins it 'Victoria Falls' in homage to royalty back home.

THE HORRORS OF SLAVERY

At the height of slavery in the 19th century, one of Africa's busiest slaving areas was in present-day Malawi and eastern Zambia. During this time the Swahili-Arabs together with dominant ethnic groups are reckoned to have either killed or sold into slavery 80,000 to 100,000 Africans per year. Those taken from the areas now called Malawi and Zambia would be brought to one of the Arab trading centres, such as Nkhotakota, Karonga or Salima, where they would be sold to 'wholesalers'. They were crammed into dhows and taken across Lake Malawi. On the other side they were marched across Mozambique to the east coast, usually chained or tied to poles of wood to prevent escape. Many also carried elephant tusks, as ivory was another major commodity. Any slaves too ill to make the journey were simply abandoned, and died of dehydration or were killed by wild animals.

At the coast, the slaves were once more loaded back into dhows for the hazardous journey north to Zanzibar. They would be packed tightly, lying down in several layers in the hold of the boat and jammed in place by the deck holding the layer above. For the duration of the voyage they would have no food or water, and would lie in their own excrement. Those who died – and there were many, particularly if journeys took longer than anticipated because of poor winds – could not be removed until the journey ended. Those who managed to survive all this were sold once more in the large slave market in Zanzibar and then shipped to places such as Arabia or India. Estimates vary, but it's believed that of all the slaves captured in the interior of Africa, two in every three died before reaching their final destination.

influence today. The slave-traders also captured many people from Zambia and took them across Lake Malawi and through Mozambique or Tanzania to be sold in the slave markets of Zanzibar.

EARLY EUROPEANS

The first Europeans to enter Zambia and Malawi were Portuguese explorers who generally followed routes established many centuries earlier by Swahili-Arab slave-traders. In Malawi they came from Mozambique and in Zambia the Portuguese entered from Angola as well – in the 1790s several of them travelled as far as the headwaters of the Zambezi River. Around the same time, another group of Portuguese pushed inland from Mozambique to Lakes Mweru and Bangweulu.

The masks that Chewa people make are an integral part of ceremonies. They represent cultural ideals, with themes such as wisdom, sickness, death and the ancestors.

Livingstone & the First Missionaries

The most famous explorer to reach this area was David Livingstone from Scotland, whose exploration heralded the arrival of Europeans in a way that was to change the nature of the region forever, and would leave an indelible footprint on Malawi and Zambia.

Livingstone travelled up the Zambezi in the early 1850s in search of a route to the interior of Africa and hoped to introduce Christianity and the principles of European civilisation to combat the horrors of the slave

1859	**1873**	**1878**
Livingstone discovers Lake Malawi, naming it Lake Nyasa and providing fodder for thousands of tourist brochures to come by reportedly dubbing it the 'lake of stars'.	Livingstone dies while searching for the source of the Nile in northern Zambia. His heart is buried under a tree near the spot where he dies, in Chief Chitambo's village, southeast of Lake Bangweulu in Zambia.	In Scotland, the Livingstonia Central African Mission Company is formed by private enterprise. Its object is to introduce trade into Malawi and surrounding areas, working alongside the Livingstonia missionaries.

trade. His first foray into Malawi was unplanned. Returning to Africa in 1858, after a short spell drumming up missionary support back home, he found his planned route up the Zambezi was blocked at Cahora Bassa, so he followed a major Zambezi tributary called the Shire into southern Malawi. He reached Lake Malawi shortly after, naming it Lake Nyasa. He returned in 1861 with some fellow missionaries to establish a mission in the Shire Highlands, and later on the Lower Shire. In 1864, ravaged by malaria and other illnesses, and plagued by conflict with slave-traders and local people, the surviving missionaries withdrew to Zanzibar. In 1866 Livingstone returned to Malawi again, on his quest to find the source of the Nile.

The Tumbuka are known for their healing practices, which combine traditional medicine and music.

Livingstone's legacy inspired a legion of wannabes to come to Africa and help save the 'poor natives'. In 1875 a group from the Free Church of Scotland built a new mission at Cape Maclear in Malawi, which they named Livingstonia; and in 1876 the established Church of Scotland built a mission in the Shire Highlands, which they called Blantyre. Cape Maclear proved to be malarial, so the mission moved to Bandawe, then finally in 1894 to the high ground of the eastern escarpment. This site was successful; the Livingstonia mission flourished and is still there today (see p221). The early missionaries blazed the way for adventurers and pioneer traders.

THE COLONIAL ERA

Like in many parts of Southern Africa, Zambian and Malawian history was largely influenced by the British South Africa Company (BSAC) during the colonial period.

Zambia

This 'new' territory did not escape the notice of entrepreneur Cecil John Rhodes, who was already establishing mines and a vast business empire in South Africa. Rhodes' BSAC laid claim to the area in the early 1890s and was backed by the British Government in 1895 to help combat slavery and prevent further Portuguese expansion in the region.

Go to http://news.bbc .co.uk and search for Timeline: Zambia or Timeline: Malawi — it gives useful chronological timetables of events in the two countries.

Two separate territories were initially created – North-Western Rhodesia and North-Eastern Rhodesia – but these were combined in 1911 to become Northern Rhodesia. In 1907, Livingstone became the capital. At around the same time, vast deposits of copper were discovered in the area now called the Copperbelt. The indigenous people had mined there for centuries, but now large European-style opencast pits were dug. The main source of labour was Africans, who had to earn money to pay the new 'hut tax'; in any case, most were driven from their land by European settlers.

In 1924 the colony was put under direct British control and in 1935 the capital was moved to Lusaka. To make them less dependent on colonial rule, settlers soon pushed for closer ties with Southern Rhodesia and

1884–85	1890s	1907
Claims over African territory by European powers are settled at the Berlin Conference. The continent is split into colonies and spheres of influence – Britain claims Rhodesia (Zambia and Zimbabwe) and Malawi.	Envoys of Cecil Rhodes' British South Africa Company (BSAC) sign protection treaties with local chiefs; territories of North-Western Rhodesia and North-Eastern Rhodesia come under BSAC control.	The British Central Africa Protectorate becomes the colony of Nyasaland, with all responsibility transferring to the British Colonial Office. These moves lead to an increase in the number of settlers from Europe.

Nyasaland (Malawi), but various interruptions (such as WWII) meant the Federation of Rhodesia and Nyasaland did not come about until 1953.

Malawi

In 1878 the Livingstonia Central African Mission Company (later renamed the African Lakes Corporation) was formed and built a trading centre in Blantyre. The company then established a commercial network along the Shire River and the shores of Lake Nyasa. As intended, this had a serious effect on the slave trade in the region and after several clashes many slave-traders were forced to leave the area.

By the 1880s the competition among European powers in the area was fierce. Colonial rule brought with it an end to slave-traders and interethnic conflicts, but it also brought a whole new set of problems. As more and more European settlers arrived, the demand for land grew, and the hapless local inhabitants found themselves labelled as 'squatters' or tenants of a new landlord. The 'hut tax' was introduced here too and traditional methods of agriculture were discouraged. Increasing numbers of Africans were forced to seek work on the white-settler plantations or to become migrant workers in Northern and Southern Rhodesia (present-day Zambia and Zimbabwe) and South Africa. By the turn of the 18th and 19th centuries some 6000 Africans were leaving the country every year. (The trend continued throughout the colonial period: by the 1950s this number had grown to 150,000.)

The *Zambian Chronicle*'s take on Zambia's most controversial politician – Kaunda – including some interesting photos is at http://kenneth-kaunda .blogspot.com

NATIONALIST RESISTANCE & THE TRANSITION TO INDEPENDENCE

Meanwhile, African nationalism was becoming a more dominant force in the region. In Malawi the first serious effort to oppose the Nyasaland colonial government was led by the Reverend John Chilembwe, who protested in his preaching about white domination, and later about the forced conscription of African men into the British army at the outbreak of WWI. In January 1915 Chilembwe and his followers attacked and killed the manager of a large estate. His plan had been to trigger a mass of uprisings but these failed or didn't materialise, and the rebellion was swiftly crushed by the colonial authorities. Chilembwe was executed, his church was destroyed and many supporters were imprisoned. Today Chilembwe is remembered as a national hero, with many streets named in his honour.

After WWI the British began allowing the African population a part in administering the country, although it wasn't until the 1950s that Africans were actually allowed to enter the government. The economic front was similarly sluggish; Nyasaland proved to be a relatively unproductive colony with no mineral wealth and only limited plantations.

An attempt to boost development in 1953 led to Nyasaland being linked with Northern and Southern Rhodesia in the Federation of Rhodesia and

History of Southern Africa by JD Omer-Cooper provides an excellent, highly readable account of the early peoples of Southern Africa, including fascinating cultural detail that differentiates the many Bantu-speaking groups.

1920s	1953	1958
Northern Rhodesia is put under direct British control; large copper deposits are discovered in the area now know as the Copperbelt, and mines are established.	The Rising power of Africans worries the white settlers, resulting in the formation of the Federation of Rhodesia and Nyasaland (also known as the Central African Federation).	Elections in Zambia but few Africans are allowed to vote; the Northern Rhodesia African National Congress (NRANC), led by Kenneth Kaunda, boycotts the election and Kaunda is imprisoned.

An Introduction to the History of Central Africa – Zambia, Malawi and Zimbabwe by AJ Wills provides a comprehensive account of the region and is considered one of the best around.

Nyasaland. But the federation was opposed by the pro-independence Nyasaland African Congress (NAC) party in Malawi, led by Dr Hastings Kamuzu Banda. The colonial authorities declared a state of emergency and Banda was jailed.

Banda was eventually released, and returned to head the now renamed Malawi Congress Party (MCP), which won elections held in 1962. The Federation was dissolved in 1963 and Nyasaland became the independent country of Malawi in 1964. Two years later, Malawi became a republic and Banda was made president.

In Zambia the United National Independence Party (UNIP) was founded in the late 1950s by Dr Kenneth Kaunda, who spoke out against the Federation on the grounds that it promoted the rights of white settlers to the detriment of the indigenous African population.

Through the 1960s, as many other African countries gained independence, Zambian nationalists opposed the colonial forces. This resulted in a massive campaign of civil disobedience and a small but decisive conflict called the Chachacha Rebellion.

Northern Rhodesia became independent a year after the Federation was dissolved and changed its name to Zambia. While the British government had profited enormously from Northern Rhodesia, the colonialists chose to spend a large portion of this wealth on the development of Southern Rhodesia (now Zimbabwe). Zambia still suffers from the effects of this staggering loss of capital and the difference between the development of the two countries during and since colonial times is obvious.

THE DICTATORS
Kaunda

Although many poets and novelists were jailed for criticising President Banda, it wasn't only fictional works that angered him. Some contemporary history books were also banned, including, perhaps not surprisingly, *Malawi – the Politics of Despair*.

After gaining independence, Zambia inherited a British-style multiparty political system. Kaunda, as leader of the majority UNIP, became the new republic's first president. The other main party was the African National Congress (ANC), led by Harry Nkumbula. But Kaunda disliked opposition. In one swift move during 1972, he disbanded the Zambian ANC, created the 'second republic', declared UNIP the sole legal party and made himself the only presidential candidate.

Consequently, Kaunda remained in power for the next 27 years. His rule was based upon 'humanism' – his own mix of Marxism and traditional African values. The civil service was increased, and nearly all private businesses (including the copper mines) were nationalised. But corruption and mismanagement, exacerbated by a fall in world copper prices, doomed Zambia to become one of the poorest countries in the world by the end of the 1970s. The economy continued to flounder while Zambia's trade routes to the coast through neighbouring countries (eg Zimbabwe and Mozambique) were closed in retaliation for Kaunda's support for several liberation movements in the region.

1960–62	1962–64	1971
Kaunda is released and becomes leader of United National Independence Party (UNIP). Chachacha Rebellion campaign of civil disobedience. Elections with every adult allowed a vote; UNIP wins a clear majority.	The Federation of Rhodesia and Nyasaland is dissolved and Malawi becomes independent. Northern Rhodesia also becomes independent, taking the name Zambia.	With the opposition muzzled, Banda continues to strengthen his dictatorial powers in Malawi by having himself declared 'President for Life' and waging vendettas against any group he regards as a threat.

By the early 1980s two important events occurred that had the potential to significantly improve Zambia's economy: Rhodesia gained independence (and had become Zimbabwe), which allowed Kaunda to take his country off a war footing; and the Tazara railway to Dar es Salaam (Tanzania) was completed, giving Zambia unencumbered access to the coast. Yet the economy remained on the brink of collapse: foreign exchange reserves were almost exhausted, serious shortages of food, fuel and other basic commodities were common, and unemployment and crime rates rose sharply.

In 1986, an attempt was made to diversify the economy and improve the country's balance of payments. Zambia received economic aid from the International Monetary Fund (IMF) but the IMF conditions were severe and included cutting basic food subsidies. Subsequent price rises led to country-wide riots in which many people lost their lives. Kaunda was forced to restore subsidies.

The Early History of Malawi and *Malawi – the History of a Nation* by B Pachai are two academic histories that cover the country from the Iron Age to colonial times.

The winds of change blowing through Africa during the late 1980s, coupled with Zambia's disastrous domestic situation, meant something had to give. Following another round of violent street protests against increased food prices in 1990, which quickly transformed into a general demand for the return of multiparty politics, Kaunda was forced to accede to public opinion.

He announced a snap referendum in late 1990 but, as protests grew more vocal, he was forced to legalise opposition parties and announce full presidential and parliamentary elections for October 1991. Not surprisingly, UNIP (and Kaunda) were resoundingly defeated by the Movement for Multiparty Democracy (MMD), led by Frederick Chiluba, a former trade union leader. Kaunda admirably stepped down without complaint, which may have saved Zambia from descending into anarchy.

Banda

President Banda began consolidating his position after being made Malawian president in 1966 and demanded that several ministers declare their allegiance to him. Many resigned rather than do so and took to opposition. Banda forced them into exile and banned other political parties. He continued to increase his power by becoming 'President for Life' in 1971, banning the foreign press and waging vendettas against any group regarded as a threat. He established Press Holdings, effectively his personal conglomerate, and the Agricultural Development and Marketing Corporation, to which all agricultural produce was sold at fixed rates, and thus gained total economic control. In a blow to travellers all over the region, miniskirts, women in trousers, long hair for men and other such signs of Western debauchery were outlawed.

Livingstone by Tim Jeal is often reckoned to be the best of the great explorer's biographies. It presents a complete picture of the man, describing his obsessions, jealousies and weaknesses as well as his achievements.

Alongside this move towards dictatorship, Banda remained politically conservative, giving political support to apartheid South Africa, which, in

1972	1986	1991
Kaunda disbands Zambian ANC, creates the 'second republic', declares UNIP the sole legal party and himself sole presidential candidate; economy spirals downwards for the next two decades.	Zambia receives loans from the International Monetary Fund; conditions include cutting food subsidies, leading to serious riots. In future the IMF changes its loan conditions as a consequence of these experiences.	Full presidential and parliamentary elections are held in Zambia; Kenneth Kaunda and UNIP are defeated by Frederick Chiluba and the Movement for Multiparty Democracy (MMD).

turn, rewarded Malawi with aid and trade. This angered the Organisation of African Unity (OAU), which was furious at Banda's refusal to ostracise the apartheid regime.

Nyasa – A Journal of Adventures by ED Young was written in the 1870s, reprinted in 1984, and is a missionary's account of his journey to help establish the original Livingstonia mission at Cape Maclear.

As well as the dictator-like behaviour of living it up at the expense of his citizens and clamping down on freedom of expression, Banda had a bizarre range of habits. He was fond of wearing jaunty gangster-style hats and carrying an African fly-whisk; and at public appearances he was often accompanied by a group of women who danced and chanted words of praise, clad in customised outfits with his face printed all over them.

With the end of the East/West 'cold war' in the 1990s, things began to get dicey for Banda. South Africa and the West no longer needed to support him, and inside the country opposition was swelling. In 1992 the Catholic bishops of Malawi condemned the regime and called for change, and demonstrations, both peaceful and violent, added their weight to the bishops' move. As a final blow, donor countries restricted aid until Banda agreed to relinquish total control.

In June 1993 a referendum was held for the people to choose between a multiparty political system and Banda's autocratic rule. Over 80% of eligible voters took part; those voting for a new system won easily, and Banda accepted the result.

THE 1990s
Zambia

President Chiluba moved quickly to encourage loans and investment from the IMF and World Bank. Exchange controls were liberalised to attract investors, particularly from South Africa, but tough austerity measures were also introduced. Once again, food prices soared. The civil service was rationalised, state industries privatised or simply closed, and thousands of people lost their jobs.

By the mid-1990s, the lack of visible change in Zambia allowed Kaunda to confidently re-enter the political arena. He attracted strong support and soon became the UNIP leader. Leading up to the 1996 elections, the MMD panicked and passed a law forbidding anyone with foreign parents to enter politics (Kaunda's parents were from Malawi). Despite intercessions from Western aid donors and world leaders like Nelson Mandela – not to mention accusations that Chiluba's parents were from the Democratic Republic of the Congo (Zaïre) – the law was not repealed. The UNIP withdrew all its candidates in protest and many voters boycotted the election. Consequently, Chiluba and the MMD easily won, and the result was grudgingly accepted by most Zambians.

A collection of reminiscences from the chief ranger, and others of Malawi's Nyika National Park in colonial times, can be found in *The Nyika Experience* by F Dorwood (ed).

Malawi

At Malawi's first full multiparty election in May 1994, the victor was the United Democratic Front (UDF), led by Bakili Muluzi. On becoming

1994	1997	2002
At Malawi's first full multiparty election, the victor is the United Democratic Front (UDF), led by Bakili Muluzi. Much needed change quickly follows, including new freedom of speech and print rights.	A bungled coup attempt allows Chiluba to announce a state of emergency in Zambia and many opposition figures are arrested. Kaunda, claims the coup is a set-up, and is placed under house arrest until March 1998.	Levy Mwanawasa is elected president in Zambia. The opposition allege fraud in the elections but a few years later the supreme court rejects this challenge, although it finds that the ballot had flaws.

President, Muluzi moved quickly – political prisons were closed, freedom of speech and print was permitted, and free primary school education was to be provided. The unofficial night curfew that had existed during Banda's time was lifted. For travellers, the most tangible change was the repeal of that notorious dress code.

The Muluzi Government also made several economic reforms with the help of the World Bank and the IMF; these included the withdrawal of state subsidies and the liberalisation of foreign exchange laws.

In April 1995 former president Banda was brought to trial accused of ordering the murder of three government ministers who died in a mysterious car accident in 1983. He was acquitted and the result was greeted with general approval, especially when Banda went on to apologise publicly. As the population warmed once more to Banda, it became clear that the UDF's honeymoon period was well and truly over.

By 1996 the economic reforms were hitting the average Malawian citizen very hard. Food prices and unemployment soared. There were reports of increased malnutrition, and crime, particularly robbery, increased in urban areas. Matters were made worse by a slow resumption of international aid, after it had been frozen in the final years of Banda's rule.

In November 1997 Dr Banda finally died. His age was unknown, but he was certainly over 90.

Zambia Shall be Free by Kenneth Kaunda is the former president's political manifesto – a classic of 1960s African nationalism.

IN THE 21ST CENTURY
Zambia
The political shenanigans continued unabated at the start of the new millennium: in mid-2001, Vice-President Christon Tembo was expelled from parliament by Chiluba, so he formed an opposition party – the Forum for Democratic Development (FDD). Later, Paul Tembo, a former MMD national secretary, joined the FDD but was assassinated the day before he was due to front a tribunal about alleged MMD corruption.

Chiluba was unable to run for a third presidential term in December 2001 (though he badly wanted to change the constitution so he could). He anointed his former vice-president, Levy Mwanawasa, as his successor, but Mwanawasa only just beat a coalition of opposition parties known as the United Party for National Development (UPND). Again, allegations from international observers about the MMD rigging the results and buying votes fell on deaf ears. To Chiluba's horror, Mwanawasa stripped his predecessor of immunity from prosecution and proceeded to launch an anti-corruption drive, which targeted the former president. In August 2009, after a long-running trial, Chiluba was cleared of embezzling US$500,000 by Zambia's High Court. His wife, however, was not so lucky, having been given a jail term earlier in the year for receiving stolen funds while her husband was in office. In a separate case, the High Court in Britain ruled Chiluba and four of his aides conspired to rob Zambia of

A fascinating collection of short and highly readable essays, Tales of Zambia by Dick Hobson, covers Zambian history, landscape, people, myths, and more.

2004	2005	2006
Bingu wa Mutharika is elected president in Malawi bringing new hope as he sets about stemming corruption, stepping up the fight against HIV/AIDS, and attempting to attract greater foreign investment.	As Zambia is deemed to be a Heavily Indebted Poor Country, most of its US$7 billion international debt is eliminated but the country is still heavily dependant on world copper prices.	In Malawi Vice-President Cassim Chilumpha is arrested and charged with treason, while ex-president Bakili Muluzi is arrested and charged with corruption. The charges against Muluzi are dropped suddenly.

about US$46 million, but it remains to be seen whether this judgement will be enforced within Zambia.

Though Zambia is still a poor country, its economy experienced strong growth in the early part of the 21st century with GDP growth at around 6%. However, the country is still very dependant on the world prices of its minerals (copper and cobalt). Knocking Zambia off its feet in the early '70s, the whim of the market then brought about huge gains in wealth early in the new millennium as world copper prices rose steadily. However, with the global economic slump of 2008/09, and with the price of minerals such as copper falling rapidly, Zambia is on the same merry-go-round. There has been large foreign investment in the mines (especially from China), and South African-owned businesses are exploding in towns across the country, as there is finally a local demand for their businesses.

In 2005, under the Highly Indebted Poor Country Initiative, Zambia qualified for debt relief to the tune of US$6 billion.

As well as combating global markets, natural disasters play a significant role in the country's fortunes. Although a bumper harvest was recorded in 2007, floods in 2008/09 that killed tens of people were declared a national disaster – the Zambezi River which flooded much of Western Zambia was said to be at its highest level in 60 years, and crops were severely affected.

Poverty continues to plague Zambia, but the economy has strengthened with inflation down to single digits, its currency relatively stable and increased levels of trade. Hopefully, the current global economic crisis will be merely a blip on its continued progress.

Parts of a 1981 film, *The Grass is Singing*, were shot in Zambia, although the original story by Doris Lessing, about the loneliness of a white-settler farmer's wife, is set in Southern Rhodesia (Zimbabwe).

Malawi

In July 2002 Muluzi attempted to change the constitution by proposing an Open Terms Bill to parliament, which would have given him life presidency. When it was defeated, he aired the idea of proposing a Third Term Bill instead, which would have extended his presidency for one more term.

When this failed, Muluzi chose Bingu wa Mutharika as his successor, and in 2004 he duly won the election. Many thought he would simply follow in Muluzi's footsteps, but he soon declared his independence by quitting the UDF and setting up his own party, the Democratic Progressive Party (DPP). Controversially, he set about restoring Banda's reputation as a great African hero, although he has also led an anti-graft drive.

The massive famine in 2005 put the pressure on, with Malawi bearing the brunt of crop failure and drought in the region – and a power struggle between the president and his predecessor curtailed efforts to deal with the most pressing of humanitarian issues. In 2006, under the Highly Indebted Poor Country Initiative, Malawi qualified for debt relief.

The recent resounding re-election victory for President Mutharika was not before there were arrests of opposition figures, as Mutharika accused ex-president Muluzi of trying to depose him.

2008	2009	2009
President Mwanawasa dies in Paris. Rupiah Banda has a narrow election victory in Zambia and is sworn in as president; the main opposition candidate alleges fraud.	President Mutharika is returned to power in Malawi when he wins a decisive victory in the election, defeating John Tembo, who was backed by former president, Bakili Muluzi.	Chiluba is cleared of embezzling US$500,000 by Zambia's High Court, however a British High Court decision that he conspired to rob Zambia of millions still hangs over the ex-president's head.

The Culture

DAILY LIFE

Local community and family life is very important in both Malawi and Zambia, and most people, even more affluent urbanites, will live at home until they are married. Families are large by Western standards and many couples have several children. The extended family, and the idea of kinship, is also very important. People will keep in touch with uncles, aunts and distant cousins, and feel a bond even if they meet only occasionally. Close cousins are often called 'brother' or 'sister', and regarded as such, especially if they are the children of an uncle related by blood. However, the children of a father's sister are more likely to be called cousins.

As in most traditional societies, older people are treated with deference. Teachers, doctors, and other professionals (usually men) often receive similar treatment.

Zambia

Zambia has one of the world's most devastating HIV and AIDS rates. More than one in every seven adults in Zambia is infected, and there are funeral processions on a daily basis, as the disease has claimed enough lives to lower the average life expectancy at birth to just over 40 years. AIDS hasn't just affected households and communities. The public sector, the economy and national development have been weakened. A new population of 'street kids' has emerged, who live in roadside sewers and on central reservations in urban centres.

Almost half of all Zambians now live in urban centres. Crowded housing compounds, water shortages and overstretched sewage systems are causing all sorts of health problems, including cholera during the rainy season. Most unskilled city labourers work six to seven days per week, with their families sometimes living on less than US$1 per day.

In rural Zambia, life has not changed much. Traditional religions mixed with Christian beliefs, subsistence agriculture and village hierarchies are the mainstays of rural life. Many subsistence farmers eke out a living at the whim of crop success or failure.

Malawi

Malawi remains one of the world's poorest countries, with a per capita GNP of less than US$250. Nearly half the population is chronically malnourished and life expectancy is only 43 years, owing in large part to the HIV/AIDS infection rate in Malawi, which is estimated to run at almost 12%.

The vast majority of Malawians, over 80% of the population, live in rural areas. Yet Malawi is urbanising rapidly and the rate of population growth in the cities is far higher than that in rural areas. As in Zambia, the poorer suburbs and urban areas are becoming overcrowded. Natural resources struggle to support the burgeoning population, and schools, hospitals and other social institutions are overflowing.

According to the UN's human development index of 2008, Malawi and Zambia rank 162nd and 163rd respectively, out of a list of 179 countries.

ECONOMY
Zambia

Zambia's economy is dependent on the mining industry, relying on copper sales in particular for an estimated 70% of revenue. Other important sources of revenue are manufacturing and agriculture. After years of rampant deflation and a copper industry in freefall, Zambia's economy enjoyed a period of resurgence in the mid noughties. The full privatisation of the industry in 2001 led to increased output and revenue, and in 2005 Zambia qualified for US$6 billion in debt relief under the Highly Indebted Poor Country (HIPC) initiative. A successful harvest in 2007 boosted GDP and agricultural exports, and Zambia's economic growth reached the 6% to 7% needed to significantly reduce poverty.

However, the government didn't take advantage of the boom time to diversify the economy for the future and in 2009 the global financial crisis was having a serious impact on Zambia's economy. Foreign investors were pulling out of mines, Zambians who had enjoyed a brief period of prosperity were out of work, consumer spending was down and there were concerns that the country could not cope with a collapse of copper prices.

Malawi

Malawi is one of the world's poorest and least developed countries. Its economy depends on agriculture, which accounts for some 35% of GDP and 80% of export revenues. Tobacco is the main cash crop, accounting for over 70% of exports. Also important are tea, sugar and coffee.

ZAMBIAN ETHNIC GROUPS

The government of Zambia officially recognises 73 different ethnic groups. This section gives a brief overview of some of the larger or more significant groups, listed roughly in order of population size.

Bemba

The Bemba are the largest ethnic group in Zambia, forming about 20% of the population. Their traditional homeland is in northern Zambia, a large area around the town of Kasama, and spreading southwest around Lake Bangweulu. Many also live in the Copperbelt, having migrated for work, and Bemba is now the dominant language there.

As with most ethnic groups in Zambia, the Bemba migrated from the Congo in the 16th century, as a breakaway group from the powerful Lunda-Luba empire. Even today the Bemba and their associated groups share many cultural features and traditions with the people of what is now the Democratic Republic of the Congo (formerly Zaïre).

Tonga

The traditional homelands of the Tonga people are the Zambezi Valley and much of the higher country to the north, thus dividing them into two groups: Valley Tonga and Plateau Tonga. The Valley Tonga's traditional territory once spread into Zimbabwe, but largely disappeared when Lake Kariba was formed.

Closely related groups are the Ila (found north of the Zambezi around the town of Namwala) and the Lenje (around the town of Kabwe). The Tonga, Ila and Lenje are sometimes grouped together as the Bantu Botatwe – literally 'the three people'. Other related Tonga groups and subgroups include the Toka, who inhabit the western plateau areas; the Leya, a small group located near Livingstone; and the Soli, the traditional inhabitants of the area around Lusaka.

All together, speakers of Tonga as a first language make up about 15% of Zambia's population. Most are farmers and cattle herders, while those along the rivers catch fish. Traditionally, Tonga people also survived by hunting. The Ila particularly took great advantage of the massive herds of lechwe that inhabit the flood plains of the Kafue River.

Chewa/Nyanja

The term Nyanja is used more to describe a language than a particular people, and covers several different groups. People speaking Nyanja as a first language make up about 15% of the

In 2006, after years of poor harvests and a serious famine, the Malawian government drew up a programme of fertilizer subsidies with the aim of boosting crop production. This programme has been very popular, and largely successful. Spurred on by good weather conditions and better macroeconomic management, the economy has grown steadily over the past few years, with growth rates of almost 10% in 2008 and a decline in interest rates from 40% in 2004 to 15% in 2008. There is increasingly interest in exploiting the country's mineral potential and a uranium mine started production at Kayelekera in northern Malawi in 2009.

The impact of the financial crisis on Malawi has so far been limited, though Malawi's agricultural sector could be affected through reduced demand for the country's main exports of tobacco, sugar and tea.

POPULATION
Zambia

Zambia's population is about 11.8 million, with a growth rate of around 1.7%. The country has an area of 750,000 sq km, giving a population density of about 15 people per square kilometre, making Zambia one of the most thinly populated countries in Africa. But these figures give

total Zambian population. The Chewa people make up about a third of the Nyanja-speakers in Zambia, and the terms Nyanja and Chewa are often used interchangeably. The Chewa people are found in Eastern Province around the town of Chipata, and many more live over the border in Malawi.

Ngoni

The Ngoni, found in southeast Zambia around the town of Chipata, form about 6% of the population. They are descended from Zulus who migrated here in the early 19th century (see the History section). They still maintain some Zulu traditions, notably the ceremonial leopard-skin dress of the chief, and the spears and shields carried by the men at festivals, but they have adopted Nyanja as their language.

Nsenga

In the southeast of Zambia, the Nsenga people inhabit the lands around the town of Petuake, along the lower Luangwa River and along the Great East Road, making up about 5% of population. There are many more over the border in Mozambique. Along with the Chewa and the Ngoni, their language is Nyanja.

Lozi

The Lozi have their own distinct nation called Barotseland, a significant part of Zambia's Western Province, and with about 650,000 people they make up roughly 6% of the population. The heart of Barotseland is the vast Zambezi flood plain. The annual inundations provide good soil for crops and good grass for cows, so naturally the Lozi are farmers and herders, although when the flood plain is covered in water, they often have to move to villages on higher ground.

The Lozi are also particularly noted for their expertise in basketry. Maybe it's because they move house twice a year and need to carry things, maybe it's because the grass is good. Whatever, Lozi craftwork is among the finest in Africa.

Lala & Bisa

The Lala people inhabit the area around Serenje, in central Zambia, and the area to the east towards the Luangwa River, while the closely related Bisa are found north of here in a large area around Mpika. Both groups are also related to the Bemba. Between them they make up about 5% of the population.

the wrong impression. The population is not evenly distributed, almost 40% live in two compact urban areas – in and around Lusaka and the cities of the Copperbelt. This is noticeable as you travel through rural areas; you can go for hours without seeing more than a couple of small villages.

Malawi

Malawi is one of the most densely populated countries in Africa, and southern Malawi is the most densely populated part of the country. Over 50% of Malawians live in that region.

According to the 2008 census, Malawi's total population is around 13.1 million. This is growing by around 2.4% a year. Because the county is small, this creates one of the highest population densities in Africa. About 85% of the people live in rural areas and are engaged in subsistence farming or fishing, or working on commercial farms and plantations. Around half the population is under 15 years of age.

Malawi's main urban centres are Lilongwe, the political and administrative capital in the centre of the country; Blantyre, the commercial capital (with its sister city, Limbe) in the south; Mzuzu, the main town in the north; and Zomba, a major trading centre and the former political capital, situated between Lilongwe and Blantyre.

PEOPLE
Zambia

The population of Zambia is made up of between 70 and 80 different ethnic groups. The final count varies according to your definition of ethnicity, but the Zambian government officially recognises 73 groups in the country.

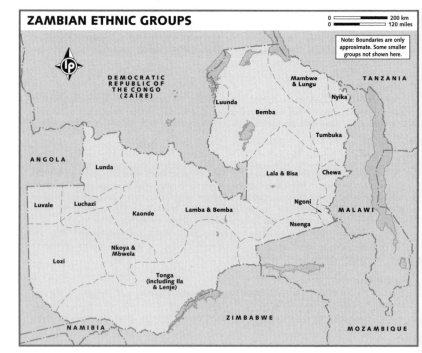

ZAMBIAN ETHNIC GROUPS

There is considerable homogeneity among the tribes of Zambia. This is partly due to a long history of people moving around the country, settling new areas or looking for work, and also because after independence President Kaunda fostered national unity, while still recognising the disparate languages and cultures. There are interethnic rivalries in Zambia, but they are not as overt as they are in some other countries.

Intermarriage among the officially recognised groups is common, and Zambia is justifiably proud of its almost complete lack of ethnic problems. For more information on Zambia's peoples see pp40–1.

The vast majority (99%) of Zambians are indigenous Africans. The final 1% are people of Indian or European origin (mostly involved in business, commerce, farming and the tourist industry). These are Zambian citizens; many white and Asian families have lived here for generations – although race relations are still sometimes a little strained.

Relative newcomers to the country include South African businesspeople and Zimbabwean farmers who lost their land thanks to Robert Mugabe. There are also many people from Europe and North America; some (such as mining consultants) live in Zambia for decades, others (such as aid workers) stay for only a few years before moving on.

> Zambia has seven official languages and Malawi has two. English is the official language of government in both countries.

Malawi

Malawi's main ethnic groups are: Chewa, dominant in the central and southern parts of the country; Yao in the south; and Tumbuka in the north. Other groups include the Ngoni (also spelt Angoni), inhabiting parts of the central and northern provinces; the Chipoka (or Phoka) in the central area; the Lambya; the Ngonde (also called the Nyakyusa) in the northern region; and the Tonga, mostly along the lake shore.

There are small populations of Asian and European people living mainly in the cities and involved in commerce, farming (mainly tea plantations) or tourism.

Malawi's small Indian population first came to the country when they were brought in by the British in the early 1900s to help construct a railway line between Malawi and Mozambique. During the Banda regime they were not allowed to participate in politics and certain sections of the economic sector, and many were forced to leave the country.

Most Westerners in Malawi are here on a short-term basis and involved in business, aid or the diplomatic service.

THE CHEWA

The Chewa are the largest ethnic group in Malawi, although their ancestors hail from the Congo. During the first millennium, they migrated through Zambia and then on to central Malawi, conquering land as they went and eventually establishing a powerful kingdom in 1480 that covered southern Malawi as well as swathes of Mozambique and Zambia. During the 17th century, Malawi experienced an influx of diverse cultures and dynasties, but the Chewa kept their ethnicity distinct through language, tattoos and secret societies.

The Chewa believe that God (Chiuta or Chautu) created all living things during a thunderstorm, at a mountain range that straddles the Malawi and Mozambique border. They also believe that contact between spirits and the living is achieved through a dance called Gule Wamkulu, (see p252). Today, however, Chewa culture is a mixture of traditional beliefs and European influences; although Christianity is the dominant religion, it's common practice to consult a witch doctor in times of trouble.

To really experience Chewa culture, it's best to immerse yourself in a village. There is a cultural village offering overnight stays near Liwonde National Park (see p264).

SPORT

Football (soccer) is without a doubt the most popular sport in both Zambia and Malawi. Most supporters are into the English Premier League with Manchester United attracting the most support. People aren't just spectators though, it's also played throughout both countries, from young boys on makeshift pitches to the national teams. Unsurprisingly, the 2010 World Cup, the first to be held on the African continent, was generating a great deal of excitement at the time of research, with both countries vying for a spot in the finals. Other sports played in Zambia and Malawi include golf (there are more than a few courses). In Zambia polo and polo-cross – a mixture of polo and lacrosse – are also popular, and polo games can be seen at the Showgrounds in Lusaka on weekends between May and August.

RELIGION

Around 75% of Malawians and Zambians are Christians. They are usually members of one of the Protestant churches originally founded by the missionaries who came to this part of the world in the late 19th century. There are also some Catholics, and many Malawians and Zambians follow indigenous Christian faiths that have been established locally, ranging from small congregations meeting in a simple hut to large branches of the African Zion churches that are based in Zimbabwe and South Africa.

Both Zambia and Malawi also have significant Muslim populations of around 20%. The Yao people along Lake Malawi's southern shores are the most closely associated with Islam – a legacy of the Swahili-Arab slave-traders who once operated in this area.

Alongside the established churches many Zambians and Malawians also follow traditional religions. As with such faiths all over Africa, there are no great temples or written scriptures. Most traditional religions are animist – based on the attribution of life or consciousness to natural objects or phenomena, and many accept the existence of a Supreme Being with whom communication is possible through the intercession of ancestors. The principal function of ancestors is to protect the group or family, and they may on occasion show their pleasure (such as a good harvest) or displeasure (such as a member of the family becoming sick). Thus ancestors play a particularly strong role.

WOMEN IN ZAMBIA & MALAWI

Both Malawi and Zambia's constitutions uphold the principle of equal rights for men and women and prohibit any discrimination based on gender or marital status. Yet they are both still very traditional societies and gender inequality is evident in all walks of life. It is particularly reflected in the disproportionate amount of work that women do. For example, as well as doing most of the work around the home, women also undertake the bulk of farm work. An African man on a bus might give his seat to an older man, but not normally to a woman, never mind that she is carrying a baby and luggage and minding two toddlers.

Women are often the most vulnerable and poorest members of society in Malawi and Zambia and are not offered the same opportunities as men. Accepted social practice often makes it difficult for girls to gain an education. Girls drop out of school far more often than boys, and the literacy rate is also lower amongst women.

Women find it difficult to own property as access to land usually comes through men; rural women find it difficult to gain access to credit because of the need for security. Some financial institutions will ask women to provide a man as a guarantor for a loan, or for their husband's consent, even though this is illegal.

Representation by women in Zambia and Malawi's parliament still stands below the 30% recommended by the South African Development Community (SADC). In 2009, out of 150 Zambian MPs only 22 were women. Women's representation in Malawi's parliament stood at 22%.

ARTS

Dance

The most notable traditional dance in Zambia is the *makishi*, which features male dancers wearing masks of stylised human faces, grass skirts and anklets. It probably originated in the Democratic Republic of the Congo (Zaïre) and was brought to northwestern Zambia by the Luvale or Luchazi people, before being adopted by other ethnic groups. *Makishi* is now found in many parts of Zambia, mainly at boys' initiation ceremonies. But any local celebration seems to be a good excuse for the men to boogie down.

Dance is an important social element across Malawi, and most dances are rooted in traditional beliefs and customs. The most notable traditional dance in Malawi is Gule Wamkulu (see p252), indigenous to the Chewa people (the largest and most dominant group in the country), but also enjoyed by some other tribes. The dance reflects traditional religious beliefs in spirits and is connected to the activities of secret societies. Leading dancers are dressed in ragged costumes of cloth and animal skins, usually wearing a mask, and occasionally on stilts.

Other groups have their own music and dance traditions. For example, among the Tumbuka, in northern Malawi, the *vimbuza* is a curative dance performed by traditional healers ('witch doctors') to rid patients of sickness.

Music

ZAMBIA

All of Zambia's ethnic groups have their own musical traditions. The Lozi are famous for the large drums played during the remarkable Kuomboka ceremony (see the boxed text, p172), while the Bemba are also renowned drummers. Other traditional musical instruments used by most groups include large wooden xylophones, often with gourds underneath the blocks for resonance, and tiny thumb pianos with keys made from flattened metal.

Contemporary Zambian musicians who have achieved some international fame include Larry Maluma, who blends traditional Zambian beats with reggae, and had just released his 9th album *Tusekelele* (Let's Celebrate) at the time of writing. Younger Zambians prefer reggae – both the old-school Jamaican style and the softer version popular in Southern Africa – and contemporary Zambian RnB and hip-hop. C'Millian is a hugely popular Zambian RnB artist. Also well loved is JK who plays a mixture of hip-hop, reggae and traditional Zambian beats. Zambians love Congolese *soukous* (termed rhumba in Zambia), which is always blasted at deafening levels at local bars and nightclubs.

MALAWI

Traditional music and dance in Malawi, as elsewhere in Africa, are closely linked and often form an important social function, beyond entertainment. In Malawi there are some countrywide traditions, and also some regional specialities where local ethnic groups have their own tunes and dances.

'any local celebration seems to be a good excuse for the men to boogie down'

Featuring local, regional and international acts, Malawi's 'Lake of Stars' festival takes place on the shores of Lake Malawi in September or October of every year. See www .lakeofstars.org for details.

Malawian musical instruments are similar to those found in other parts of East and Southern Africa, with local names and special features. These include various drums, from the small hand-held *ulimba*, made from a gourd, to ceremonial giants carved from tree-trunks, and the *mambilira*, which is similar to the western xylophone, but with wooden keys, and sometimes played over hollow gourds to produce a more resonant sound.

Modern home-grown contemporary music is not a major force in Malawi as it is in, say, Zimbabwe or South Africa. However, it has increased in popularity, due largely to influential and popular musicians such as Lucius Banda, who performs soft 'Malawian-style' reggae, and the late Evison Matafale. Other reggae names to look out for are the Black Missionaries and Billy Kaunda.

Theatre

Once thriving, Lusaka's theatre scene has taken a turn for the worse, though many Zambian writers still produce plays and other works, from slapstick comedy through to hard political comment. From time to time, the Lusaka Playhouse has a show worth seeing (see p81). Both the Umunthu Theatre (see p213) in Lilongwe and the Warehouse Cultural Centre (see p277) in Blantyre actively promote the Malawian arts scene and theatre and put on regular performances.

Literature

ZAMBIA

Well-known Zambian poets and novelists are very thin on the ground. The most notable home-grown literature still dates from the 1960s and 1970s – Fwanyanga Mulikita's collection of short stories *A Point of No Return*, and writer-politician Dominic Mulaisho's novels *The Tongue of the Dumb* and *The Smoke That Thunders*.

Although big names are rare, Zambia has its share of local writers; you can find their works in shops selling school textbooks. Although some are aimed at older children and young adults, they're a useful insight into Zambian life and thinking. Also aimed at young adults is *Dawn is Coming* by Zambia-based novelist Timothy Holmes, a pertinent study of an African family facing a society riddled with disease, crime and corruption. Similar themes are explored in *The Changing Tides* by Michael Mulilo, in which a Western-educated writer returns to his home country and, shocked by all-pervading poverty and government oppression, attempts to alter things through his writing, with cataclysmic results.

MALAWI

Like most countries in Africa, Malawi has a very rich tradition of oral literature. Since independence, a new school of writers has emerged, although thanks to the despotic President Banda's insensitivity to criticism, many were under threat of imprisonment and lived abroad until the mid-1990s. Not surprisingly, oppression, corruption, deceit and the abuse of power are common themes in their writing.

Poetry is very popular. Steve Chimombo is a leading poet whose collections include *Napolo Poems*. His most highly acclaimed work is a complex poetic drama, *The Rainmaker*. Jack Mapanje's first poetry collection, *Of Chameleons and Gods,* was published in 1981. Much of its symbolism was obscure for outsiders, but not for President Banda – in 1987 Mapanje was arrested and imprisoned without charge; he was eventually released in 1991.

Most critics agree that Malawi's leading novelist is Legson Kayira, whose semi-autobiographical *I Will Try* and *The Looming Shadow* earned him acclaim in the 1970s. A later work is *The Detainee*. Another novelist is Sam Mpasu. His *Nobody's Friend* was a comment on the secrecy of Malawian politics – it earned him a 2½-year prison sentence. After his release he wrote *Prisoner 3/75* and later became minister for education in the new UDF government.

A more modern success story is Samson Kambalu, whose autobiography *The Jive Talker: or, how to get a British Passport* tells of his transition from schoolboy at the Kamuzu Academy to conceptual artist in London.

Painting & Sculpture

ZAMBIA

Zambia has a thriving contemporary art scene. One of the country's most famous and respected painters is the late Henry Tayali. His works – described by critics as 'crowded social realism' – have inspired many other Zambian painters and enjoyed a popular following among ordinary folk.

Other internationally recognised artists include Agnes Yombwe, who works with purely natural materials and uses traditional ceramics and textile designs in her striking sculptures; Shadreck Simukanga, arguably the finest painter working in Zambia; and the country's best-known artist, Stephen Kapata. Prominent sculptors include Eddie Mumba and the prolific Friday Tembo.

Zambian artistry includes skilfully woven baskets from Barotseland (Western Province) and Siavonga; malachite jewellery from the north; and woodcarvings and soapstone sculptures from Mukuni village, near Livingstone. Most of these crafts are sold in markets around the country, along the roadsides of intercity highways and in souvenir shops in touristy areas.

See Shopping in the Zambia Directory (p188) for more information about buying crafts, curios and souvenirs.

MALAWI

All over the country visitors will see hand-produced items for sale in curio shops, markets and roadside stalls. If you're looking for cheap souvenirs, there's plenty to choose from: animals carved from wood or soapstone, clay figures, mats and baskets, model cars and bicycles made from raffia or wire, and Malawi's famous chief's chairs.

Malawi's leading artists include Kay Chirombo, Lemon Moses, Willie Nampeya, Berling Kaunda, Charley Bakari or Louis Dimpwa, many of whom have exhibited their work overseas. Possibly the best-known artist is Cuthy Mede – he is also actively involved in the development and promotion of Malawian art within the country and around the world.

FOOD & DRINK

The staple diet for most Malawians and Zambians is unquestionably *sima* (Malawi) or *nshima* (Zambia), a thick, doughy maize porridge that's bland but very filling. It's eaten with your hands and always accompanied by beans or vegetables and a hot relish, and sometimes meat or fish.

Fish is particularly good in Malawi, and *chambo*, the popular, bream-like variety, can be found on every menu, from cheap cafes to top-end restaurants. *Kampango*, a lake fish from the catfish family, is also often served.

To peruse the thoughts of UK-based Malawian author and artist Samson Kambalu, visit his website at www.holyballism.com.

To check out the work of local Zambian artists head for the Henry Tayali Visual Arts Centre at the Showgrounds, Lusaka.

COMING HOME FOR DINNER

While you're in Malawi or Zambia you might get the chance to eat in somebody's home and will usually be given royal treatment and a seat of honour. Table manners in these parts are probably different from what you're used to, although you'll probably be let off for the odd gaffe because you're a foreigner.

Before eating, a member of the family may pass around a bowl of water, or jug and bowl, for washing hands. The African staple, maize meal (*nsima or nshima*), or sometimes sorghum meal, is the centre of nearly every meal. It is normally taken with the right hand from a communal pot, rolled into balls, dipped in some sort of sauce – meat gravy or vegetables – and eaten. As in most societies, it is considered impolite to scoff food; if you do, your hosts may feel that they haven't provided enough. In fact, for the same reason, it may be polite *not* to be the one that takes the last handful from the communal bowl. If your food is served on separate plates and you can't finish it, don't worry; again this shows your hosts that you have been satisfied. Often containers of water or home-brew beer may be passed around from person to person. However, it is not customary to share coffee, tea or bottled soft drinks.

Most other cheap meals are an unimaginative and unhealthy choice of fried eggs, fried sausages, and fried chicken, and burgers usually accompanied with chips.

Tea, coffee, bottled mineral water and soft drinks are widely available and inexpensive. If you like lagers, the local beer is good. In Zambia the local beer is Mosi, and in Malawi it's Kuche Kuche. Many travellers to Malawi prefer the beer produced by Carlsberg at its Blantyre brewery. There are three main types of beer: 'greens' (lager), 'browns' (like a British ale) and 'golds' (a stronger brew). If you're a beer fan, you can visit the brewery (see p274).

Traditional 'opaque' beer made from maize is sold commercially in cardboard cartons (they look deceptively like milk cartons). It's thick and sour and tastes pretty nasty. Make sure you shake the carton before drinking.

Where to Eat & Drink

Hungry for a quick and unusual bite? Try a portion of fried caterpillars. These delicious delicacies can be found at roadside stalls throughout Malawi and Zambia.

Markets and bus stations usually harbour a collection of food stalls where you can get tea with milk for around US$0.50, a bread cake or deep fried cassava for US$0.30, or a simple meal of beans or meat and *nsima, nshima* for about US$1.

Local restaurants in small towns provide simple meals for around US$2. In cities and larger towns, cheap restaurants serve traditional food as well as chicken or fish with rice or chips for around US$3.

Most midrange hotels and restaurants serve European-style food such as steak, chicken or fish, which is served with vegetables and chips or rice – usually around the US$5 mark.

If you're hankering for something different, in Malawi and Zambia's major cities you can find restaurants serving Ethiopian, Indian, Korean, Chinese and Portuguese food. Main courses range from around US$5 to US$10. More elaborate French and Italian cuisine is also available from better hotels, and you'll also find several steakhouses. At most top-end establishments, main courses start from about US$12.

In Zambia some of the best food you'll taste is at the lodges and camps in and around national parks. Dishes are usually Western or Asian in origin and often exquisitely prepared.

Environment

THE LAND
Zambia

Landlocked Zambia is one of Africa's most eccentric legacies of colonialism. Shaped like a mangled butterfly, its borders don't correspond to any tribal or linguistic area. And Zambia is monstrous. At some 752,000 sq km, it's about the size of France, England and the Republic of Ireland combined.

Zambia is chock full of rivers. The Luangwa, the Kafue and the mighty Zambezi (see boxed text below) dominate western, southern and eastern Zambia, flowing through a beautiful mix of flood plains, forests and farmland. In the north, the main rivers are the Chambeshi and the Luapula – sources of the Congo River. Northern Zambia has many smaller rivers too, and the broken landscape helps create stunning scenery of lakes, rapids and waterfalls.

Of course, Zambia's most famous waterfall is the Victoria Falls, where the Zambezi plunges over a mile-wide cliff before thundering down the long, zigzagging Batoka Gorge. The Zambezi flows into Lake Kariba, created by a dam but still one of the largest lakes in Africa. In northern Zambia is the even larger Lake Tanganyika – 675km long, second deepest in the world, and holding one-sixth of the earth's fresh water.

In the south and east, Zambia is cut by deep valleys – some of them branches of the Great Rift Valley. The Zambezi Valley is the largest, and defines the county's southern border, while the 700km-long Luangwa Valley is lined by the steep and spectacular Muchinga Escarpment.

Even the flat places can be stunning: The endless grassy Busanga Plains in Kafue National Park attract fantastic wildlife, while the Liuwa Plain – part of the even larger Upper Zambezi flood plain that makes up much of western Zambia – is home to Africa's second-largest wildebeest migration.

Some of Zambia's other geographical big hitters include the high, rolling grasslands of the Nyika Plateau, the seasonally flooded wetlands

Writing about the area surrounding Victoria Falls in 1857, David Livingstone described scenes 'so lovely' that they must have been 'gazed upon by angels in their flight'.

One of the most popular activities on the Zambezi is white-water rafting in the area around Victoria Falls. The first commercial rafting expeditions took to the Zambezi's waters in 1981.

THE ZAMBEZI – RIVER OF AFRICA

The Zambezi is the fourth-longest river in Africa, after the Nile, the Congo and the Niger, and has a long and varied course through Zambia. It rises in the far northwestern corner of the country and flows through a short section of Angola before re-entering Zambia and creating the huge flood plains around Mongu. Further downstream, the river becomes the border between Zambia and Namibia, and then between Zambia and Zimbabwe, before plummeting over the world-famous Victoria Falls and forcing its way down the Batoka Gorge to Lake Kariba.

Beyond Kariba Dam, the major Kafue River adds its waters to the flow, and the Zambezi runs between Zimbabwe's Mana Pools and Zambia's Lower Zambezi National Park. It is joined by another large tributary, the Luangwa River, before entering Mozambique and another dam-created lake – Lago de Cahora Bassa. Downstream from here the giant river crosses the last few hundred kilometres of coastal plain, finally flowing into the Indian Ocean north of Beira.

Most of the river is wide, deep and slow-moving – ideal for canoes and even large boats. But these lazy sections are interrupted by the odd waterfall, where the river crosses bands of harder rock. These mere specks on the map were enough to prevent navigation between the interior and the coast, as the explorer Livingstone discovered to his cost in the 19th century. Later, the colonial powers in Zambia were also unable to develop the Zambezi for serious transportation.

of the Kafue Flats, the teak forests of the Upper Zambezi, and the Kariba and Mpata Gorges on the Lower Zambezi.

Malawi

Pint-sized Malawi is no larger than the US State of Pennsylvania. It's wedged between Zambia, Tanzania and Mozambique, measuring roughly 900km long and between 80km and 150km wide, with an area of 118,484 sq km.

Malawi has no access to the sea, but no matter – almost one-fifth of the country is covered by that great 'inland sea', Lake Malawi. Lying in a trough formed by the Rift Valley, it makes up over 75% of Malawi's eastern boundary. A strip of low ground runs along the western lakeshore, sometimes 10km wide, sometimes so narrow there's only room for a precipitous footpath between the lake and the steep wall of the valley. The lakeshore is sandy in many places, with natural beaches, particularly in the south. Beyond the lake, escarpments rise to high, rolling plateaus covering much of the country.

Malawi's main highland areas are the Nyika and Viphya Plateaux in the north and Mt Mulanje in the south, and the country's highest point is the summit of Sapitwa (3002m) at the centre of Mt Mulanje. There are also several isolated hills and smaller mountains dotted around, the largest being the Zomba Plateau, near the town of the same name.

Though it's dominated by Lake Malawi, there are three other lakes in this tiny country, the largest of which is Lake Chilwa, southeast of Lake Malawi. North of here is the remote Lake Chiuta, which spreads across the border into Mozambique. Less than 10km south of Lake Malawi is Lake Malombe.

Malawi's main river is the Shire (pronounced *shir-ee*); it flows out of the southern end of Lake Malawi, through Lake Malombe and then southwards as the plateau gives way to low ground, to flow into the Zambezi River in Mozambique. In this area, the lowest point is a mere 37m above sea level.

Lake Malawi is the third-largest lake in Africa after Lake Victoria and Lake Tanganyika, and the second-deepest lake in Africa after Lake Tanganyika. It has more fish species than any other lake in the world.

WILDLIFE

If you're hoping to see the 'Big Five' for which Africa is famous, you can't go wrong in Zambia. It is one of the continent's best destinations for going on safari (Swahili for travel), with plenty of national parks that will provide wonderful opportunities for viewing lions and elephants in action. Neighbouring Malawi's parks aren't known for their big stars, and those seeking a classic African safari will be disappointed, but it does rate highly as a destination for birdwatchers.

Animals

ZAMBIA

Because of Zambia's diverse landscape, plentiful water supplies, and position between Eastern, Southern and Central Africa, the diversity of animal species is huge. The rivers, of course, support large populations of hippos and crocs, and the associated grasslands provide plenty of fodder for herds of zebras, impalas and pukus (an antelope common in Zambia but not elsewhere).

Huge herds of rare black lechwe live near Lake Bangweulu, and endemic Kafue lechwe settle in the area around the Kafue River. Kasanka National Park is one of the best places on the continent to see the rare, water-loving antelopes called sitatungas. South Luangwa and Lower Zambezi National Parks are good places to see tall and stunningly graceful giraffes, and

Zambia has its own subspecies – Thornicroft's giraffe. South Luangwa has its very own subspecies of wildebeest too – the light-coloured Cookson's wildebeest – but the best place to see these creatures is the Liuwa Plain, a remote grassland area in western Zambia where thousands converge every year for Africa's second-largest wildebeest migration.

These animals naturally attract predators, so most parks contain lions, leopards, hyenas (which you'll probably see) and cheetahs (which you probably won't). Wild dogs were once very rare but are now encountered more frequently. Another big drawcard – elephants – are also found in huge herds in South Luangwa, Lower Zambezi and some other national parks. Zambia's herds of black rhino were destroyed by poachers in the 1970s and 1980s, but over the past few years reintroduction programmes have seen rhino transported to North Luangwa National Park.

Bird lovers can go crazy in Zambia, where about 750 species have been recorded. Twitchers used to the 'traditional' Southern African species listed in the *Roberts* and *Newman's* field guides will spend a lot of time identifying unusual species – especially in the north and west. Most notable are the endangered shoebill storks (found in the Bangweulu Wetlands); fish eagles (Zambia's national bird); and endemic Chaplin's barbets (mostly around Monze).

Good safari companions include *Field Guide to the Mammals of Southern Africa* by Chris and Tilde Stuart, and for twitchers, *Birds of Southern Africa* by Ian Sinclair.

MALAWI

Malawi is not often thought of as a great place to see wildlife so if you're looking for a stereotypical safari experience, this is not the country to choose. However, for those less concerned with simply ticking off the 'Big Five', the country has plenty to offer. Most people head for Liwonde National Park, noted for its herds of elephants and antelopes including impalas, bushbucks and kudu. Liwonde is also a good place to see hippos and crocodiles, and the only park in the country where you might see rhinos.

Elephants are also regularly seen in Kasungu National Park, as are buffaloes, zebras, hippos and several antelope species. Elephants are also regularly seen in Nkhotakota Wildlife Reserve, as are lions. Nyika National Park is renowned for roan antelope and reedbucks, and you'll also see zebras, warthogs, jackals, and possibly leopards. Nearby Vwaza Marsh is known for its hippos as well as elephants, buffaloes, waterbucks and other antelopes. In southern Malawi, Majete Wildlife Reserve is another good place to see elephants and Lengwe National Park supports a population of nyalas – at the northern limit of their distribution in Africa.

Lake Malawi has more fish species than any other inland body of water in the world, with a total of over 600, of which more than 350 are endemic. The largest family of fish in the lake is the *Cichlidae* (cichlids). For more information see the boxed text, p255.). In some areas like Cape Maclear, the fish are so accustomed to being fed that they flock towards any swimmer and nibble anything that moves – including your toes. Other fish families in the lake include *usipa*, or lake whitebait, *mpasa* (lake salmon) and *kampango* (catfish), which you'll see on quite a few menus.

For birdwatchers, Malawi is rewarding; over 600 species have been recorded, and a visit to any of the parks or wildlife reserves will please serious ornithologists, tourists and everyone in between with a diverse and colourful array of species. Birds rare elsewhere in Southern Africa but more easily seen here include the African skimmer, Böhm's bee-eater and the wattled crane.

Carnivore Conservation Malawi (www.carnivore conservationmalawi.org) is a non-profit NGO whose aim is to preserve large carnivores – including wild dogs, lions and cheetahs – in Malawi.

To learn more about Lake Malawi's inhabitants, pick up a copy of the *Guide to the Fishes of Lake Malawi* by D Lewis or *Cichlids and other Fishes of Lake Malawi* by A Koning.

Plants
ZAMBIA

About 65% of Zambia, mainly plateau areas and escarpments, is covere in miombo woodland, which consists mainly of broad-leaved deciduou trees, particularly various species of *Brachystegia* (another name for thi type of vegetation is Brachystegia woodland.) Some areas are thickly wooded, others are more open, but the trees never form a continuou canopy, allowing grass and other plants to grow between them.

In the dryer, hotter valleys, much of Zambia's vegetation is mopan woodland. Dominant trees are the species *Colophospermum mopane* usually around 10m high. The baobab tree also grows here. You'll se this landscape in Zambia's best-known national parks, Lower Zambez and South Luangwa.

With its many rivers and lakes, Zambia has some of the most extensive wetlands in Southern Africa. These include the Bangweulu Wetlands along the southern and eastern shores of Lake Bangweulu; and the vas plains of the Kafue Flats downstream from Kafue National Park, which i dotted with seasonally flooded marshes, lagoons and oxbow lakes.

Most grassland in Zambia is low, flat and flooded for part of the year - with hardly a tree in sight. The largest flood-plain area is west of the Upper Zambezi – including Liuwa Plain National Park – where thousand of square kilometres are inundated every year. Another is the Busang Plains in Kafue National Park. Both are excellent wildlife areas.

Along many of Zambia's rivers are riverine forests. Tourists will se a lot of this type of landscape as national park camps are often built o riverbanks, under the shade of huge trees such as ebony, winter-thorr and the unmistakable 'sausage tree' (*Kigelia africana*).

Evergreen forest, the 'jungle' of Tarzan films, is found only in isolate pockets in northwest Zambia – a remnant of the larger forests over the border in Angola and the Democratic Republic of Congo.

MALAWI

Miombo woodland is the dominant vegetation in Malawi, originally covering 70% of the land, although much of it has now been cleared for farming or plantations. It occurs up to an altitude of about 1500m in areas where the rainfall is reliable. The relatively poor soil that cover much of Malawi encourages the growth of small-to-medium height well-spaced trees that produce open-canopy woodland. Enough sunligh penetrates through this to the ground to allow the growth of grasses an shrubs. Good examples can be seen on the slopes of Nyika Plateau and in Kasungu National Park. The dominant trees of the open canopy miombo are *Julbernadia globiflora* and several types of *Brachystegia*.

Mopane woodland occurs in hot lowland areas that have relatively low rainfall, including the middle parts of the Shire Valley, the plains along the southern shores of Lake Malawi and some of the smaller lakes. More than half of Liwonde National Park is covered by mopane woodland This vegetation zone derives its name from the mopane tree, a tal multi-stemmed tree that characteristically grows well on soils with high clay content. The baobab tree, which favours the same dry conditions frequently occurs in mopane woodland areas.

There isn't much forest left in Malawi (most has been cleared), but areas do exist that are thought to be remnants of the extensive evergreer forests that once grew all over the country, as well as in southern Tanzania northern Zambia, and Mozambique. There are two main types – montane evergreen forest and semi-evergreen forest.

Montane grassland occurs generally above 1800m and is predominantly found on the Nyika Plateau in northern Malawi, where the rolling hills are covered in grass. These grasslands are maintained by the annual fires, both natural and intentional, which sweep through and discourage the growth of shrubs and trees.

Along the shores of the lakes and the banks of the rivers that flow into them, the natural vegetation consists of dense riverine woodland or long reeds and grasses. In various parts of Malawi, wide and marshy river courses where reeds and grasses grow are called *dambos*.

Africa's first walking safaris took place in the Luangwa Valley in the 1950s. Conservationist Norman Carr would lead visitors single file into the bush, with an armed scout bringing up the rear.

NATIONAL PARKS
Zambia

Zambia boasts 19 national parks and reserves, and some 30% of the land is protected, but after decades of poaching, clearing and general bad management, many are just lines on the map that no longer protect (or even contain) much wildlife. However, some national parks do accommodate healthy stocks of wildlife, and these are among the best

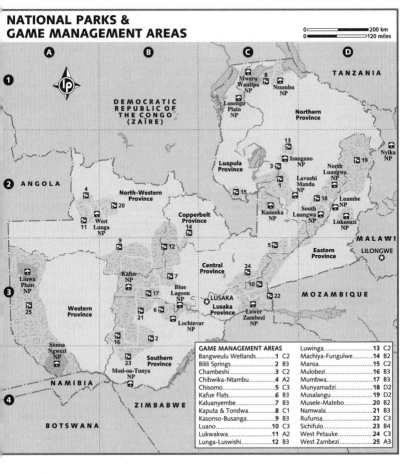

NATIONAL PARKS & GAME MANAGEMENT AREAS

GAME MANAGEMENT AREAS			
Bangweulu Wetlands	1 C2	Luwinga	13 C2
Bilili Springs	2 B3	Machiya-Fungulwe	14 B2
Chambeshi	3 C2	Mansa	15 C2
Chibwika-Ntambu	4 A2	Mulobezi	16 B3
Chisomo	5 C3	Mumbwa	17 B3
Kafue Flats	6 B3	Munyamadzi	18 D2
Kaluanyembe	7 B3	Musalangu	19 D2
Kaputa & Tondwa	8 C1	Musele-Matebo	20 B2
Kasonso-Busanga	9 B3	Namwala	21 B3
Luano	10 C3	Rufunsa	22 C3
Lukwakwa	11 A2	Sichifulo	23 B4
Lunga-Luswishi	12 B3	West Petauke	24 C3
		West Zambezi	25 A3

NATIONAL PARKS & WILDLIFE RESERVES

Zambia's Most Important National Parks

Park	Size	Features	Activities	Best time to visit
Bangweulu Wetlands (p103)	9800 sq km	floodplain; black lechwes, shoebills, waterbirds	walking, canoe trips, birdwatching	Dec-Mar
Kafue National Park (p174)	22,400 sq km	miombo woodland, open grasslands, Kafue River; red lechwes, leopards, cheetahs, lions	game drives, birdwatching, fishing	May-Oct
Kasanka National Park (p100)	390 sq km	woodlands, plains, rivers, swamps; sitatunga, wattled cranes, hippos, blue monkeys, bats	boat trips, walks, game drives	Jul-Nov
Lower Zambezi National Park (p142)	4092 sq km	Zambezi River, sandy flats, mopane woodland; crocs, hippos, elephants, buffaloes, lions	canoeing, boating, birdwatching, game drives	May-Nov
North Luangwa National Park (p129)	9050 sq km	Luangwa River, miombo woodland, plains; buffaloes, elephants, hippos, Thornicroft's giraffes, leopards, lions	walking safaris	May-Oct
South Luangwa National Park (p119)	9050 sq km	mopane & miombo woodland, grasslands; Thornicroft's giraffes, Cookson's wildebeest, lions, leopards, elephants, pukus	day & night game drives, walking safaris	Apr-Oct

Malawi's Most Important National Parks & Wildlife Reserves

Park	Size	Features	Activities	Best time to visit
Kasungu National Park (p243)	2100 sq km	mopane woodland; elephants, hippos, zebras, buffaloes,	game drives, walking safaris, birdwatching	May-Oct
Lake Malawi National Park (p254)		glittering waters; over 1000 species of, colourful fish	snorkelling, kayaking, scuba diving	May-Oct
Lengwe National Park (p288)	900 sq km	thick undergrowth: nyalas, warthogs, buffaloes	nyala spotting, birdwatching	Jul-Nov, Dec-Jan for birdwatching
Liwonde National Park (p263)	580 sq km	grassland, marshes, mopane woodland; elephants, hippos, crocodile-filled Shire River	game drives, walking safaris, boating, birdwatching, rhino sanctuary	Sep-Dec
Nyika National Park (p224)	3200 sq km	cool, sweeping, grasslands; antelopes, zebras, leopards	hiking, horse riding, birdwatching	Sep-Oct for mammals, Oct-Apr for birds
Vwaza Marsh Wildlife Reserve (p228)	1000 sq km	wetlands: buffaloes, elephants, hippos, antelopes	wildlife walks. day & night drives	Jun-Nov for mammals, year round for birdwatching

n Southern Africa: South Luangwa, Lower Zambezi, Kafue and North
.uanga.

Kasanka National Park has been leased to a private operator since 1990.
This park is now fully funded by donations and tourism, and functions very
vell. Another example of successful cooperation between an ecofriendly
institution, the government and the Zambian park authorities is the rehabilitation of the previously neglected Liuwa Plain National Park (p173).

Zambia also has 35 vaguely defined game management areas (GMAs).
These mainly act as buffer zones around the major national parks, and
re mostly used for commercial hunting. The semi-autonomous Zambia
Wildlife Authority (ZAWA) administers all the GMAs and national
parks/reserves (except Kasanka and Bangweulu Wetlands) – see p68 for
contact details.

Admission fees to the parks vary, so they're listed in the appropriate
ections later in this chapter. Each ticket is valid for 24 hours from the
ime you enter the park, but if you're staying inside the park at official
accommodation this admission fee is valid for seven days.

Malawi

Malawi has five national parks. These are (from north to south) Nyika,
Kasungu, Lake Malawi (around Cape Maclear), Liwonde and Lengwe.
There are also four wildlife reserves – Vwaza Marsh, Nkhotakota, Mwabvi
and Majete. Over 16% of Malawi's land is protected.

Traditionally the wildlife reserves have been less developed than the
national parks, with fewer accommodation options and a more limited
network of roads and tracks (if they exist at all), but this is changing as
.ccess is improved, new camps built and wildlife stocks increased.

All national parks and reserves have accommodation; this ranges
from simple campsites and rustic rest houses to self-catering chalets
and comfortable (even luxurious) lodges. In most parks and reserves,
accommodation – lodges, chalets and campsites – is run by private
companies.

As well as national parks and wildlife reserves, Malawi has almost
'0 forest reserves across the country. The largest forest reserves, and
the most famous for tourists, include Mt Mulanje, the Zomba Plateau,
Ntchisi and Dzalanyama. On Mulanje there's a series of huts especially
or hikers and trekkers.

Apart from Majete (admission MK2000) and Mwabvi Wildlife Reserves
admission MK750) all parks and reserves cost US$5 per person per day
(each 24-hour period), plus US$2 per car per day. Citizens and residents
pay less. All fees are payable in kwacha.

> Lake Malawi National Park was proclaimed a Unesco World Heritage Site in 1986 (p254).

ENVIRONMENTAL ISSUES
Zambia

Although the population is growing rapidly, it is still relatively sparse, so
Zambia doesn't suffer many of the environmental problems encountered
by its neighbours. That being said, Zambia faces the daunting challenge
of deforestation and consequent soil erosion and loss of productivity.
Land is regularly cleared for agricultural purposes, local people chop
down wood for charcoal fires, and the timber industry clears vast tracks
of trees to meet the demand for wood from China. The government
has banned the export of raw timber to other countries in the Southern
African Development Community (SADC) but illegal logging and timber
smuggling continues.

FIND OUT ABOUT CONSERVATION IN ZAMBIA

To learn more about conservation in Zambia, or to help, contact the **Kasanka Trust** (www.kasanka .com) or the **Wildlife and Environmental Conservation Society of Zambia** (www.conservation zambia.org), both of whom accept volunteers to help with their conservation projects.

The Wildlife and Environmental Conservation Society of Zambia (www .conservationzambia.org) is a leading environmental advocacy organisation, creating environmental awareness amongst local people and lobbying for sustainable environmental policies.

Hunting has greatly damaged Zambia's wildlife. In the past, people moved into some protected areas, chopped down trees, grew crops or hunted the animals. Who could blame them? They were poor, and good land and food were scarce elsewhere. Even outside the parks, on areas of land shared by people and animals, there was conflict. The same is still true today. To a poor rural subsistence farmer, wildlife is nothing but a problem: lions will kill cattle, and an elephant takes an hour to polish off a field of crops that took all year to grow.

Under pressure from international organisations, however, the government started to take conservation more seriously and introduce serious anti-poaching and development measures. Despite successes in some parks, notably South Luangwa and Lower Zambezi, poaching and poor management remain major problems.

The detrimental impact of tourism is also a problem and most obvious along the Zambezi River (particularly near Victoria Falls), where lodges continue to be built unabated. As in the national parks, locals are attracted by work opportunities and in the poor suburbs and townships around Livingstone the population has increased massively. There are frequent water shortages, leading to health problems, and sewage systems can't cope with the increased usage so waste ends up in the river. The increase in river activities such as white-water rafting, canoeing and booze cruises is damaging natural vegetation and disturbing wildlife.

Malawi

Generally speaking environmental issues relevant to Malawi are similar to those faced by other parts of East and Southern Africa, and many countries elsewhere in the world. These include population growth, air and water degradation, industrial pollution, deforestation, soil erosion, urban encroachment, habitat and wildlife destruction and the conservation of resources.

In Malawi the population is growing rapidly. Malawi has more people than Zambia, Namibia and Botswana combined, and is far smaller than any one of them, giving it one of the highest population densities in Africa. The ever-increasing human population puts great demands on the land and other natural resources – the vast majority of Malawians live without electricity and therefore the use of wood as a source of fuel in Malawi is very high. It's estimated that 30% of the country's forests have disappeared over the past 10 years, with over 50,000 hectares being cleared each year mostly for fuel. Although some replanting is taking place, at this current unsustainable rate the woodlands and forests will eventually disappear.

FIND OUT ABOUT CONSERVATION IN MALAWI

To learn more about environmental issues facing Malawi, or to help, get in touch with **Project African Wilderness** (www.projectafricanwilderness.org), the **Wildlife Action Group of Malawi** (www .wag-malawi.org) or **Ripple Africa** (www.rippleafrica.org). All three are admirable conservation projects, and accept volunteers.

Another environmental challenge faced by Malawi is overfishing. Population growth over the years means that the demand for fish has grown, to an extent that stocks are now taken from the lake at an unsustainable level. An initiative launched by the government in early 2009 and funded by the African Development Bank hopes to discourage fishermen from fishing in shallow waters – the breeding ground where many fish lay their eggs – by providing them with the necessary equipment to fish in deeper waters.

Malawi's protected areas have suffered heavy wildlife reductions due to poaching, especially in the 1980s and 1990s. Although many problems still remain, the situation is better managed than it once was – the government has increased the number of rangers and improved infrastructure and funding for the country's parks, and some of the country's wildlife reserves have come under private management.

Grassroots Development in Zambia & Malawi

Sub-Saharan Africa is the poorest region in the world, containing some 50% of the world's poor. Both Zambia and Malawi reflect this widespread impoverishment – almost 70% of Zambians live below the poverty line while Malawians don't fare much better at 50%. In a broad measurement of human well-being, the UN Human Development Index ranked Malawi and Zambia 162 and 163, respectively, out of 179 countries, in 2008.

Zambia and Malawi's public debt was 26% and 49% of GDP respectively in 2008.

To put it starkly, poverty has been and continues to be a huge problem in Zambia and Malawi, stubbornly defying the predictions of the optimists and seemingly intractable to the pessimists. The economies in both countries are heavily dependent on overseas aid from international institutions such as the World Bank and the IMF, as well as individual donor nations.

GRASSROOTS DEVELOPMENT ORGANISATIONS

In Eastern Zambia, near South Luangwa National Park, **Tikondane Community Centre** (www.tikondane.org) has a wide-ranging programme of development projects in local villages. These include a focus on adult and child education, a village outreach programme, teaching improved agricultural methods and training home-based carers for AIDS victims. It's an innovative place that is looking to many future programmes to improve the long-term sustainability of local communities.

Donor countries to Zambia and Malawi include the US, Canada, Germany, Japan, the Netherlands, Norway, Sweden, Ireland and the UK.

The Katete district where Tikondane is located has a catchment area of over 20,000 people: unemployment runs at about 80% with most people dependent on subsistence farming. Tikondane began as a grassroots enterprise in 1993 – a small initiative born out of St Francis hospital next door. It was formally established as a community-based organisation in 1999 and is currently run by local volunteers who receive a small allowance. The centre attempts many income-generating activities such as weaving, craftwork, a hair salon, animal husbandry, managing a restaurant and guesthouse (see p117), and an internet cafe is planned.

THE COST OF LIVING

In simple terms, wages and salaries, for those lucky enough to have a job, are very low. The following figures, for example, were compiled a few years ago and would still be reflective today: in urban areas in Zambia an unskilled labourer or security guard earns around US$25 per month. A farmer who manages to sell a few chickens or vegetables makes only half that. A skilled manual worker, such as a bricklayer or a waiter in a city restaurant, earns about US$60 per month. To put this into perspective, you have to look at the cost of living. The baseline measure for most Zambians is a 25kg bag of maize meal, which a small family can just about survive on each month. Eating more comfortably, two adults and five children would get through three bags a month. A bag of 'breakfast meal' (the good stuff) costs about US$6, and 'roller meal' (the rough stuff) about US$4.50. Of course, added to this is the cost of other food – another US$5 to US$10 per month. On top of this comes rent – the cheapest two-room concrete hut in a poor city suburb is US$25 per month. Then there are clothes, shoes, school fees... It's easy to see that the money doesn't go far.

AID & GOOD GOVERNANCE

In the 21st century Western nations are demanding much more stringent accountability in the form of good governance from African nations in exchange for future delivery of aid. US President Obama seemed to draw a line in the sand in 2009 when, on a visit to Africa, he condemned tyrannical African leaders who enrich themselves, promising new partnerships only with states that were well governed: 'development depends on good governance, and that is the ingredient which has been missing in far too many countries. That's the change that can unlock African potential.'

This view of good governance was most recently felt in Zambia where the Swedish and Dutch governments shut off the aid taps to the country's health sector in 2009 in response to allegations of a multi-million dollar corruption scandal in the Ministry of Health. And recent investigations into former President Chiluba resulted in the High Court in Britain ruling in 2007 that he and four of his aides conspired to rob the country of US$46 million (p37). In 2009 Zambian courts cleared Chiluba of corruption charges.

Its mission is simple: economic empowerment through the offering of education, basic health and development courses, and skills training.

The free community school, which has educated hundreds of local people, is the backbone of Tikondane. As well as running literacy classes, the centre also runs workshops on the basic principles of hygiene, the prevention of HIV transmission and the importance of maintaining a balanced diet.

Dead Aid by Zambian economist Dambisa Moyo is a compelling book arguing that aid simply does not work in Africa and that market economics is the answer.

Tikondane carries three messages to local villages in its many workshops and seminars:

- It is not witchcraft but microbes (and other things) that cause illness.
- Nshima (maize) is fine but a balanced diet is essential.
- For peace of mind, voluntary counselling and testing for HIV/AIDS are needed.

Despite its income-generating activities Tikondane remains partly reliant on overseas donors, and child- and family-sponsorship schemes. Cash donations from visitors go towards, for example, the building of a pit toilet or a pump for a well. Donations of items such as secondhand clothes, schoolbooks, pens and pencils, and linen are accepted.

Tikondane also actively encourages volunteers from overseas. It's a unique opportunity to get involved with the local community here. A minimum of two weeks is required, but really volunteers should consider at least three months to get the most out of the experience. In particular, Tikondane is looking for people with skills in writing grant applications; fundraising; teaching; computing; agriculture, such as environmental awareness and animal husbandry; and for those with hospitality experience. See the boxed text, p60, for more information on volunteering here.

Tikondane Community Centre is located in the town of Katete, about 500km east of Lusaka on the Great East Road, and 90km west of Chipata, the gateway town to South Luangwa National Park. It's about a six-hour drive from Lusaka or slightly longer on a bus – any Lusaka–Chipata service (p82) will stop here.

The World Bank has invested around US$3.6 billion in Zambia since the mid-1960s to support development projects.

Another grassroots initiative in Zambia is the **Malambo Women's Centre & Craft Shop** (www.malambo-moorings-zambia.com; marylee@zamnet.zm; 7am-5pm Mon-Fri, 7am-noon Sat, closed last weekend of month), born out of the work of the Canadian, English and Dutch families of Zambian farmer Tom Savory and his Dutch wife, Dr Thea Savory, at their farm near Moorings Campsite (see p132). It's a women's textile collective with offshoots of basketry and papier mâché run by Tonga women from the farm and nearby villages, many of them AIDS widows who themselves look after orphans. The collective is walking distance from the campsite, and for sale is a colourful myriad of bedspreads, wall hangings, quilts and other knitted and sewn arts. The fine textiles capture scenes of Zambian life, often incorporating oral culture by representing traditional folk tales. Purchases contribute directly to the community.

Workshops are held at the centre for the local community giving participants the opportunity to discuss issues such as AIDS, alcohol, nutrition, healthcare, environmental awareness, gender imbalance and many local development issues. A local radio station interviews the women

ELKE KROEGER-RADCLIFFE

Elke has poured her heart and soul into Tikondane over the last 16 years and believes passionately in the work the centre does for the local communities in Eastern Zambia.

How did Tikondane begin? We started with a mud hut on a plot of land next to the hospital given to us by the local chief. We also had an unfinished building on the property and we thought we need money, so we better make it a guesthouse. Would you believe that in those days I didn't even think of water toilets – our ideas were so small and so local. We started off with adult literacy classes, but what we found in the beginning was that the villagers thought they didn't really want literacy, they wanted a job, a skill, an income. So, for instance, we had these sewing classes and when you learn to sew, all of a sudden you think gee, it would be good to write down an order, good to write down measurements…in the long run we would hope to have a skills training centre to give people the chance to have an income. And that's really it – we want to make our own income at Tikondane to become self-sufficient, and teach people to make their own income.

Could you tell me about a particular highpoint in your time at Tikondane? I tell you when my heart jumps it's for little things. For example, we have a certain scheme from St Francis Church where we get a little money to help discharged patients from St Francis who don't have money to go back home. They look like the people hardest hit by fate, the worst of the worst, and that smile on their face is one of the better things in life. Also it still touches me when our Doris (a local volunteer at the centre) reads – she is one of our best people here, she is one of the pillars of the establishment. She was completely illiterate; she went through the course and was one of the first to read. And she is still so proud.

Could you tell me about a particular lowpoint in your time at Tikondane? We did have a young man that I sort of discovered and who was educated as a chartered accountant and he ran Tikondane when I was away – for two years he was with us and then he left and did not explain why. It turned out that he stole money from us. I was very upset at the time.

What are the kinds of things volunteers can help with around the centre? Well we've had people constantly here for the last few years volunteering from overseas – they have worked on the computers and the website or written up various schemes and programmes, using skills no one here has, yet. We have also had people playing with the kids – they have no toys at home – and giving them regular reading lessons. We've had groups who have painted and helped with building. We are keen for volunteers to spend time with the people and make them feel good, so it's not a structured eight-hour day.

What kind of money should volunteers be looking at to live on per week? About US$15 would cover people for accommodation and simple meals that our restaurant provides. And anything on top of that would be extra such as buying a Coke, or telephone calls or transport if they're going somewhere.

Any special treats in store for volunteers? Volunteers can see the local Ghost Dance (p117) and we can take our volunteers to the Chief's palace – on Fridays he holds court and you can go and see that: the guys still lie themselves longways on their bodies in front of him.

Elke Kroeger-Radcliffe is the founder and director of Tikondane Community Centre.

and the discussions are broadcast around the province, reaching a wide audience. The centre's stated goals are economic growth, individual skills training, community development and cultural preservation.

Through the help of individual donors and donor organisations, the Savorys also run a health clinic on their farm for locals, subsidise high school education, and facilitate a food-for-work programme where locals work on small projects beneficial to the community and receive food in exchange. The centre's website has information on current projects – many requiring funding – mainly building projects after the 2007/08 floods, as well as on many innovative and exciting initiatives in the pipeline.

Malambo is located on Moorings Farm, right next to Moorings Campsite and is open to visitors. Moorings Campsite is well signed off the main Great South Road, about 11km north of Monze. Buses (p82) between Lusaka and Livingstone can drop you off at the turn-off.

The **Billy Riordan Memorial Trust** (www.billysmalawiproject.org) in Malawi was inaugurated in 2002 in honour of a young man who drowned in Cape Maclear. Identifying the need for a clinic in the area (the nearest hospital is four hours away), founder Maggie Riordan decided to raise money to build a clinic, which opened in 2004. In 2007 a second building was completed, and in 2009 they received delivery of a second ambulance. Together they provide primary medical care for some 12,000 people in the local area and, to date, have treated over 80,000 people. Malaria, bilharzia, chest infections and HIV/AIDS are among the most common conditions treated. In fact, a new initiative at the clinic is a HIV/AIDS treatment programme – providing counselling and testing services as well as prescribing anti-retroviral drugs to those in need in the community.

They also offer English lessons to children in Chembe Village and there are plans to construct a primary school. At the moment, a temporary school exists where children can take English lessons outside regular school hours.

The trust doesn't receive aid from donor organisations so most funds raised are from private individuals or from charity fundraising events. The clinic is staffed by local workers as well as a number of international health workers. It is able to survive through the help of volunteers, and the trust welcomes qualified doctors, nurses and other medical personnel to come and devote their time to the project. It also needs administrative staff and teachers to help run its other projects. A minimum commitment of three months is needed. Donations to the trust are always welcome.

Based in and around the village of Mwaya in Malawi's Nkhata Bay district is **Ripple Africa** (www.rippleafrica.org), set up in 2003 by British couple Geoff and Liz Furber. All of their projects are directed in-country by Malawian managers and they employ some 80 local staff working on a variety of different development projects. Target areas include education, healthcare and the environment. For example, they support, run and stock a community library, raise salaries so that Malawian teachers can be trained at local schools, sponsor local students to attend secondary schools and finance the construction of new classrooms around the area. They are also heavily involved in conservation and have set up over 170 nurseries – run by local communities – which combat deforestation by planting trees. Over three million have been planted so far. This project also engages local people in environmental awareness training programmes.

Ripple Africa accepts donations to fund its many projects and welcomes volunteers to work on them. Especially welcome are trained teachers and doctors, but they also accept general volunteers to assist in

As of December 2008, the World Bank had 14 active projects in Malawi with a total commitment of US$407.9 million.

Jonathan Glennie's *The Trouble with Aid* assesses the positive and negative consequences of aid arguing that now is the time to reduce aid dependency.

MS ActionAid Denmark has a very interesting article about the effectiveness of development aid at www.ms.dk/sw101683.asp, based on an international conference in 2008.

their environmental, teaching and other projects (though they only take volunteers over the age of 21, and prefer you to have a university degree). Volunteers are based at Mwaya beach and work alongside and support the Malawian staff: they are careful to ensure that volunteers don't take away jobs from local people. They ask that volunteers make a minimum commitment of three months.

OTHER ORGANISATIONS IN ZAMBIA & MALAWI

The following organisations are involved in helping disadvantaged people and communities in the region:

Children in Need Network (Zambia; www.chin.org.zm) A national network of NGOs, community-based organisations and churches working for children's rights. Volunteers welcome.

Children in the Wilderness (Malawi; www.childreninthewilderness.com) Vulnerable children living alongside Malawi's parks and reserves are taught environmental and life skills, and are educated on the importance of conservation – with the aim that they become environmental leaders in the future.

Flip Flop Foundation (Zambia; www.flipflopfoundation.com) Works to support Zambian children through the supply of basic necessities and the provision of skills training.

Friends of Mulanje Orphans (Malawi; www.fomo.co.uk) Runs 13 centres for orphaned children in the Mulanje district.

Habitat for Humanity (Zambia; www.habitatzam.org.zm) Building houses for the nation's poor; over 1600 houses have been built since 1984.

Malawi Education Project (Malawi; www.malawieducationproject.com) Supplies books, stationery and other educational resources and has established a primary school library in Cape Maclear.

Vinjeru Malawi (Malawi; www.vinjerueducationmalawi.com) Set up by a Malawian author living in the UK, Vinjeru advances learning in Malawi by donating books and educational materials as well as sponsoring schools.

World Vision (Zambia; www.worldvision.org) One of the bigger NGOs in Zambia with a presence for almost 30 years working in many different community areas including nutrition, education, healthcare, agriculture and child immunisation.

Zambia

Snapshot Zambia

The landlocked country of Zambia may well be plucked from your dreams of Africa: mesmerising landscapes encapsulating the very best of African wilderness; an astonishing diversity of wildlife; and a people with genuine friendliness and warmth. As you venture into this wonderland, however, your dream may soon start to evaporate after that first bone-crunching pothole, probably on the outskirts of Lusaka. Zambia is a logistical challenge, make no mistake about it. But the rewards are unrivalled in the region.

The remoteness of the parks and protected areas, together with a network of well-run, unfenced camps and lodges, makes the African bush experience here quite simply magical and unique. At least that's how it feels when you gaze across a wide, shimmering, perfectly still river watching grunting hippos haul themselves up on the grassy bank, just as the blood-red sun sinks below the horizon. It really is that good – actually, much better.

Independent travel is a challenge, however. The country – with its dilapidated infrastructure, crumbling roads and lack of signage – simply isn't set up for it. For some that may be off-putting, but for others it's the reason to come here. Zambia is the preferred viewing point of the mighty Victoria Falls, and the 2010 World Cup kicking off not far south will certainly put the region firmly in the spotlight, but the country is a long way from becoming another tourist mecca. And that makes us breathe a sigh of relief, and look forward to our dreams…

HIGHLIGHTS

- Sharing the turf with the incredible diversity of winged, hoofed and furred creatures during a walking safari in **South Luangwa National Park** (p119)
- Staring dazedly at the thundering might of **Victoria Falls** (p149), truly one of the continent's awe-inspiring sights
- Kicking back at **Lake Kariba** (p136), and watching a storm roll in over the jagged peaks of Zimbabwe across the waters
- Spotting leopards in **Kafue National Park** (p174), a behemoth wilderness area where wildlife dreams unfold amid stunning landscapes
- Watching the spectacle of **Kuomboka** (p172), probably one of the last great Southern African ceremonies, around Mongu, a place of endless flood plains

Lusaka

LUSAKA

In this part of the world, all roads lead to Lusaka. Like it or not there's no easy way of bypassing Zambia's capital and largest urban zone, with its mishmash of dusty tree-lined streets, bustling African markets, Soviet-looking high-rise blocks and modern commerce. If that doesn't sound appealing it's because Lusaka does not easily lend itself to superlatives. There are no real attractions, grand monuments to drool over or historical treasures to unearth. Lusaka, like the rest of the country, is not set up for independent tourism and you're more likely to find schoolkids than other tourists at the city's one museum. For some, this is an attraction in itself and it's certainly an easy enough place to spend time, with its genuine African feel, cosmopolitan populace, some excellent restaurants and quality accommodation options (including two of the few backpackers in the country, a smattering of midrange options and luxury hotels). It's a good spot to snoop around markets too, with the best range of woodcarvings and other artisanal goods in the country; and, if you feel like letting loose, expat bars and the home-grown nightclub scene will see you through to the wee hours.

HIGHLIGHTS

- Being enthralled by the pulse of Africa in Lusaka's chaotic **markets** (p70)

- Leaving behind urban grime and experiencing the country's extraordinary wildlife at **Munda Wanga Environmental Park** (p70) and **Kalimba Reptile Park** (p70)

- Indulging in the local brew and showing the locals your latest moves in the city's thumping **bars** and **clubs** (pp80–1)

- Finding that perfectly carved hippo while **shopping** (p81) for traditional arts and crafts

- Chowing down in the city's **restaurants** (p78), Zambia's most diverse culinary scene

| ■ TELEPHONE CODE: 0211 | ■ POPULATION: 1.2 MILLION | ■ ELEVATION: 1300M |

ORIENTATION

The main street, Cairo Rd, is lined with shops, cafes, fast-food outlets, travel agencies, banks and bureaux de change. To the north is a major traffic circle and landmark, the North End Roundabout; to the south is the creatively named South End Roundabout. East of Cairo Rd, across the railway line and near the train station, is the Inter-City Bus Station. Further east are the wide jacaranda-lined streets of the smarter residential suburbs and the area officially called Embassy Triangle (not surprisingly, home to many embassies and high commissions). West of Cairo Rd are the busy streets of Chachacha Rd and Freedom Way, home to small shops selling everything from maize meal to auto spares. North and northwest of here is the industrial area, and beyond that are the poorer suburbs, generally called 'the compounds' (read 'townships').

See p83 for more information on getting around Lusaka.

Maps

The dusty government-run **Map Sales Office** (Map pp72-3; 8.30am-3.30pm Mon-Fri; maps ZK20,000-30,000) is beneath the Ministry of Lands and Natural Resources building, southwest of the junction of Independence Ave and Nationalist Rd. Note that while the topographical maps can be very useful, most maps sold here are no newer than 1986 so many road networks are out of date. Many maps are out of print anyway – try your luck; we found an old moth-eaten map of South Luangwa, damaged but useable.

Modern commercial maps of Zambia (ZK70,000) and Southern Africa are available at bookshops and supermarkets at the **Manda Hill Shopping Centre** (Map pp72-3; Great East Road) and **Arcades Shopping Centre** (Map pp72-3; Great East Road).

INFORMATION

Petrol stations are dotted around town – the Total petrol station located at the north end of Cairo Rd is open 24 hours.

Bookshops

Book Cellar (Map pp72-3; ☎ 255475; Manda Hill Shopping Centre, Great East Road; 9am-6pm Mon-Sat, 9am-2pm Sun) Great selection of regional travel guides, novels and some useful road maps of Zambia. Also decent selection of books on African and Zambian subjects.
Bookworld Downtown (Map pp72-3; ☎ 225282; Cairo Rd; 8.15am-5pm Mon-Fri, 8.15am-1pm Sat); Manda Hill (Map pp72-3; ☎ 255470; Manda Hill Shopping Centre, Great East Road) Mainly stationery and educational books but a few titles on Zambia by Zambian writers – from the copper mines in the north to the scourge of AIDS.
Planet Books (Map pp72-3; ☎ 256714; Shop 12b, Arcades Shopping Centre, Great East Road; 9am-7pm Mon-Fri, 9am-6pm Sat, 9am-2pm Sun) Interesting for its collection of books about Zambia and useful for its Zambian maps.

Emergency

Ambulance (☎ 992)
Police (Map pp72-3; ☎ 991; Church Rd)
Specialty Emergency Services (☎ 273303; www.ses-zambia.com) For evacuations. Has bases in Lusaka, Livingstone and Kitwe but operates throughout the country. Also has ambulances and in-patient care.

ON THE ROAD TO CAIRO

Lusaka started life as a dusty railway siding and storage depot on the new line that empire-builder Cecil Rhodes was constructing from South Africa. This was the first stage of his grand design for a Cape Town to Cairo railway that would pass through British territory all the way. The nearest village to the siding was called Lusaakas, after the name of its chief, and the title was simplified to Lusaka and attached to this point on the railway.

In the 1920s copper was discovered in the highlands north of Lusaka, and the railway became important for transporting goods to Southern Rhodesia (in present-day Zimbabwe), South Africa and the industrial markets of Europe and America. At Lusaka, a small station was built, and nearby a few shops were established to serve settlers farming in the surrounding area. Then came some houses, a ramshackle hotel and even a main street, running parallel to the railway line.

By the 1930s Lusaka had developed into a sizeable town, and in 1935 the capital was moved here from Livingstone, to take advantage of Lusaka's central position. The railway never reached Egypt, but Rhodes' dream was remembered when the name of the main street was formally changed to Cairo Rd – the name it still has today.

Internet Access

Wireless internet is all over Lusaka now – at many cafes, restaurants and hotels. Look for the 'I Spot' sign. Connections are usually good and ZK5000 will buy you a 30-minute voucher. You buy vouchers onsite at I Spot locations but note they are only good for that particular cafe, restaurant or hotel – they are not transferable.

Computer Lab (Map pp72-3; ☎ 238375; Nkwazi Rd; per min ZK150; ☺ 8.30am-4.30pm Mon-Thu, 8.30-11.45am & 2-4.30pm Fri, 8.30am-12.30pm Sat) High-speed internet cafe – best in the city centre.

Corner Internet Cafe (Map pp72-3; Heroes Pl; per min ZK150) Next to the British Council. Nice people – not the best connections.

Global.com Internet Cafe (Map pp72-3; 2nd fl, cnr Cairo & Nkwazi Rds; per min ZK150) Slow connections.

Microlink I Zone (Map pp72-3; Arcades Shopping Centre, Great East Road; per min ZK200; ☺ 9am-9pm Mon-Sat, 10am-7pm Sun) Reliable, fast internet access, plus wireless facility.

TheCafé@la.com (Map pp72-3; Longacres Roundabout; per 15/30min ZK4500/6000; ☺ 8am-9.30pm Mon-Thu & Sun, to 10.30pm Fri & Sat) This place is popular and modern with good internet speeds.

Media

The monthly *Lowdown* magazine (ZK5000) is available at bookshops and supermarkets at the Manda Hill Shopping Centre and Arcades Shopping Centre. It has a calendar of what's happening around town, lists restaurants, has a small classifieds section and advertises lodges around the country.

Medical Services

There are well-equipped private clinics around town catering for Lusaka's affluent populace. If you fall sick you should have no problems getting an appointment at one of these – ask your hotel or embassy for further information. Pharmacies are also located at both Manda Hill and Arcades Shopping Centres.

Care for Business (Map pp72-3; ☎ 256731, 255728; Addis Ababa Rd)

Corpmed (Map pp72-3; ☎ 222612, 226983; Cairo Rd) Behind Barclays Bank. Has a doctor on duty 24 hours and is probably the city's best-equipped facility. Also runs its own ambulance service.

Hilltop Hospital (☎ 263407; Plot 148, Kabulonga Rd, Ibex Hill)

Greenwood Pharmacy (Map pp72-3; ☎ 227811; 680 Cairo Rd; ☺ 8am-8pm)

Money

Along Cairo Rd, Barclays Bank, Indo-Zambian Bank, Stanbic Bank and Standard Chartered Bank have branches with ATMs. These banks also have ATM branches elsewhere in Lusaka, such as on Haile Selassie Ave, and at the Manda Hill Shopping Centre and Arcades Shopping Centre. Keep in mind that the only debit and credit cards ATMs accept are those bearing the Visa logo.

Remember that changing travellers cheques is very difficult in Zambia (see p187) and usually not possible at bureaux de change. To change cash, try the following, which don't charge commission, and bear in mind that when changing US dollars you often get a better rate for US$50 and US$100 bills:

Fx Foreign Exchange (Map pp72-3; Cairo Rd; ☺ 8am-4pm Mon-Fri, 8am-noon Sat) At least three branches along Cairo Rd.

Stero Bureau de Change (Map pp72-3; ☎ 255765; Manda Hill Shopping Centre, Great East Road; ☺ 9am-6pm Mon-Fri, 9am-5pm Sat, 10am-2pm Sun)

Zampost Bureau de Change (Map pp72-3; cnr Cairo & Church Rds; ☺ 8am-5pm Mon-Fri, 8am-12.30pm Sat) Inside the main post office.

Bullion, APT and Choice are all bureaux de change located at South End Roundabout on Cairo Rd – compare rates here within an easy strolling distance.

Post

Main post office (Map pp72-3; cnr Cairo & Church Rds; ☺ 8am-5pm Mon-Fri, 8am-12.30pm Sat) Contains Zambia's only reliable poste restante.

Telephone & Fax

A dozen telephone booths (using tokens and phonecards) can be found outside the post office. 'Phone shops' and 'fax bureaux' are dotted along Cairo Rd.

Zamtel (Map pp72-3; cnr Cairo & Church Rds) International calls can be made and faxes sent at the telephone office upstairs from the main post office.

Tourist Information

Zambia National Tourist Board (Map pp72-3; ☎ 229087; www.zambiatourism.com; Century House, Cairo Rd; ☺ 8am-1pm & 2-5pm Mon-Fri, 9am-noon Sat) The head office has friendly enough staff but information is limited to Lusaka and its environs. No map of Lusaka is available, although you can buy the *Street Guide: Lusaka and Livingstone* (ZK35,000) here. It's located next to the

Shoprite Supermarket, down a lane on the southern side; look for the sign.

Zambia Wildlife Authority (ZAWA; off Map pp72-3; ☎ 278524; info@zawa.org.zm; Kafue Rd; ☽ 8am-5pm Mon-Fri) In Chilanga, about 16km south of the city centre, facing Munda Wanga. It's a labyrinth of offices with no signage and not really worth visiting as it's hard for foreigners to get much help with making arrangements to visit national parks. Try calling or emailing first – theoretically it is in regular contact with parks management and should be able to get up-to-date information on road conditions, lodge closures etc. The ZAWA office is accessible on the minibus to Chilanga or Kafue town from the City Bus Station or South End Roundabout.

Travel Agencies

Airmasters Travel & Tours (Map pp72-3; ☎ 250000; 34 Omelo Mumba Rd; ☽ 8am-5.30pm Mon-Fri) This Rhodes Park agency books flights and hires cars and 4WDs. A car with driver around Lusaka is approximately ZK400,000 a day, plus petrol.

Bimm Travel Agency (Map pp72-3; ☎ 234372; www .bimmtourszambia.com; Shop 3, Luangwa House, Cairo Rd; ☽ 8am-5.30pm Mon-Fri, 8am-1pm Sat) Just south

of the post office, it's reliable and locally run. It can also arrange car hire.

Bush Buzz (Map pp72-3; ☎ 256992; www.bush-buzz .com; 4169 Nangwenya Rd; ☽ 9am-5pm Mon-Fri, 9am-1pm Sat) This agency is especially popular for trips to Kafue and Lower Zambezi National Parks. It also organises a range of trips to South Luangwa and Livingstone.

KNP Promotions (off Map pp72-3; ☎ 266927; www .knp-promotions.com; 13 Chindo Rd Ext; ☽ 8am-5pm Mon-Fri, 8am-noon Sat) This agency, located in the Woodlands neighbourhood, arranges accommodation for every lodge and camp in and around Kafue National Park.

Steve Blagus Travel (Map pp72-3; ☎ 227739; www .steveblagus.com; 24 Nkwazi Rd; ☽ 8am-4pm Mon-Fri, 8-11.30am Sat) This is *the* agency for Amex and a dozen upmarket lodges/camps. Also organises regional and domestic tours.

Travel Shop (Map pp72-3; ☎ 255559; www.travel shopzambia.com; Arcades Shopping Centre, Great East Road) Another agency for lodges/camps, tours and safari companies, and it sells discounted airline tickets. Another branch is at Manda Hill Shopping Centre.

Voyagers (Map pp72-3; ☎ 253082; www.voyagers zambia.com; Suez Rd) Perhaps the most popular agency in Zambia, it arranges flights, hotel reservations and car hire.

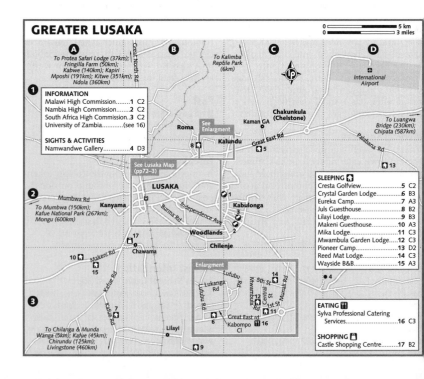

Zambian Safari Company (Map pp72-3; ☎ 231450; www.zambiansafari.com; Farmers House, Cairo Rd; ☻ 8am-5pm Mon-Fri, 9am-1pm Sat) Also a booking agency for upmarket lodges/camps and safaris throughout Zambia. Very professionally run.

DANGERS & ANNOYANCES

Like most African cities, pickpockets take advantage of crowds, so be alert in the markets and bus stations and along the busy streets immediately west of Cairo Rd. At night, most streets are dark and often empty, so even if you're on a tight budget, take a taxi. It would be foolish to wander the streets after dark, especially in and around Cairo Rd. The corner of Church and Cairo Rds, and around the railway line, are currently hotspots for pickpockets and local thugs. Locals advise 'stand on your foot', which means don't back down if approached and hassled – tell them to get lost and they usually will. Take this advice with a grain of salt though if someone pulls a knife or other weapon (although this is not common).

The suburb of Rhodes Park, between Cairo Rd and Embassy Triangle, which is quite upmarket during the week, takes on a sleazy twist at weekends when prostitutes display their wares at night, especially along Mwilwa Rd.

Lumumba Rd, parallel to and just west of Cairo Rd, has a bad reputation for robbery, especially from cars at a standstill in traffic jams, and especially from foreigners. Keep your windows up and doors locked if driving down this road.

Zambian markets are organised chaos – some more organised than others. For any market, watch your belongings and be aware of pickpockets. Don't flash a mobile phone around and don't carry a bag. Take only the cash you need in your pockets. Soweto Market in particular is notorious for robbery and pickpockets (if in a car, wind windows up and lock doors); there is a township nearby with a very bad reputation, so be careful around here.

SIGHTS & ACTIVITIES

Taking a walk down Cairo Rd (during the day) is an important part of acclimatisation to Lusaka and interesting for the hustle and bustle of Zambia's modern commercial district. The streets are often packed with people and traffic – if it gets a bit overwhelming try walking down the central strip of Cairo Rd, a surprisingly pleasant and well-tended garden area; just be careful crossing the road to get there.

The downstairs galleries in the **National Museum** (Map pp72-3; Nasser Rd; adult/child US$2/1; ☻ 9am-4.30pm), a big square box of a building with plenty of natural light, offer a snapshot of Zambia, both past and present. Highlights are the displays of contemporary Zambian paintings and sculpture – there are some striking paintings of Zambian life and some fine carvings. Upstairs are exhibits of cultural, ethnographical and archaeological interest; don't miss the display about witchcraft and initiation ceremonies. Artefacts include masks and musical instruments and exhibits relate to Zambia's various ethnic groups. The museum is currently working on a new plan to create a modern exhibition showcasing Zambia's cultural history. Hopefully it will go ahead as this place could really do with a facelift. Access the museum off Independence Ave.

The **Freedom Statue** (Map pp72-3; Independence Ave), just around the corner from the museum, is dedicated to freedom fighters and those who lost their lives in the struggle for Zambia's independence. The depiction of a man breaking his chains symbolises the country's break with colonial bondage and was erected to celebrate Zambia's independence in 1964. It's a popular place for celebrations on Africa Freedom Day (25 May).

Check out **Henry Tayali Visual Arts Centre** (Map pp72-3; ☎ 254440; Showgrounds; admission free; ☻ 9am-5pm Mon-Fri, 10am-4pm Sat & Sun) if you're in the mood for buying local contemporary art. It's a small collection but well worth a look. There are scenes of everyday Zambian rural life as well as abstract pieces. If you're keen on buying you can pick up an oil painting for between ZK1,000,000 and ZK2,000,000. We liked the paintings depicting traditional village life and portraying wildlife against some of the country's dramatic landscapes the best. It's better to come here during the week when it's more likely someone will be in attendance. Ask about the **studio** nearby for working artists where you can see these artists sharing workspaces and learning from each other. There's painting, sculpture and lots of visual arts going on, and it makes for a fascinating insight into the creative process of many art forms – come here on weekdays only.

Some of the best contemporary Zambian art is at **Namwandwe Gallery** (Map p68; ☎ 096 6750694; Leopards Hill Rd; admission free; 🕑 9am-4.30pm Tue-Fri, 9am-noon Sat & Sun). This gallery is home to the impressive private collection of John Kapotwe, businessman and patron of the arts. There are works by both established and budding Zambian painters and sculptors, plus items such as masks and fabrics from other parts of Africa. The gallery is about 15km southeast of the city centre. A return taxi from the city costs at least ZK100,000, depending on waiting time.

The **Town Centre Market** (Map pp72-3; Chachacha Rd; 🕑 7am-7pm) is chaotic and, frankly, malodorous, but fascinating. Zambians get their bargains here, whether it's fruit or veggies, new or secondhand hardware, tapes or clothes. The market is pretty relaxed and probably a good first venture for visitors unfamiliar with African markets.

The **Lusaka City Market** (Map pp72-3; Lumumba Rd; 🕑 7am-5pm) is large and lively, but not as atmospheric (or smelly) as the Town Centre Market. The nearby **Soweto Market** (Map pp72-3; New City Market; Los Angeles Rd; 🕑 7am-7pm) is the largest market in Lusaka (and Zambia). This is one place where you are most likely to be relieved of your valuables – so be careful (see p69). The sheer scale of the market and the amount of goods on offer and people buzzing around can be overwhelming – consider a visit on a Sunday when things are quieter and it's easier to move about. Note that the **New Soweto Market** is about to open and will attempt to bring some order with designated market stalls under a covered roof. The current market spills out into surrounding streets in a haphazard fashion but New Soweto Market will hopefully accommodate a lot of the current street traders.

The **Dutch Reform Market** (off Map pp72-3; Kabulonga Rd; admission ZK4000; 🕑 8am-5pm last Sat of month) is more like a bazaar and is very busy and popular with embassy people; it focuses mainly on plants, furniture, books and a few crafts. It's also a good place for a snack and a cup of coffee.

Munda Wanga Environmental Park (off Map pp72-3; ☎ 278456; www.mundawanga.com; Kafue Rd, Chilanga; adult/child ZK20,000/10,000; 🕑 8am-5pm) rehabilitates all sorts of animals for re-entry into the wild, unless they are too injured. The park features plenty of regional fauna, including cheetahs, lions, banded mongoose, wild dogs, jackals, warthogs and baboons; feeding time is 2pm Friday to Sunday, but get here early if you want to get a good view. Oddly there is also a Bengal tiger and a brown bear – throwbacks to the days when the place was a zoo. The wildlife park is a little shabby in parts with slightly dilapidated enclosures, but the animals mostly seem well cared for, and it makes for a casual introduction to the local wildlife. The lovely **botanical gardens** alongside the wildlife park have been redeveloped, and there are plans for an indigenous forest.

Munda Wanga was established in 1950 by a Rhodesian civil servant, who sold it to the government in 1968. After falling into disrepair, it was taken over by a private trust in 1998 and is much better for it. Besides the wildlife park and gardens, there's a 'recreational village' with a pool and kids' playground, plus a bar/restaurant serving simple food. Munda Wanga is about 16km south of central Lusaka and accessible by any minibus heading towards Chilanga or Kafue from the City Bus Station or South End Roundabout.

A bit of a trek northeast from town, **Kalimba Reptile Park** (off Map pp72-3; ☎ 213272; off District Rd; adult/child ZK20,000/10,000; 🕑 9am-5.30pm) is not only a crocodile and snake zoo (not

---

ON THE MARKET

Apart from food, none of the major city markets have much of interest for visitors (in terms of goods) as they sell mostly clothes, food, housewares and spare parts (especially Soweto Market). For carvings, textiles, curios and other artisanal goods head to Northmead, Kabwata Cultural Village or Arcades Shopping Centre on a Sunday (see p81). However, if you want to see a slice of Zambian life including everyday people going about their business, haggling for goods, spruiking their wares and looking for a bargain, then the markets present a unique insight as well as an authentic African experience.

for petting!) but is also a pleasant place to grab a beer and a crocodile sandwich, though you'll need a 4WD to get here. There's also a fishing pond, crazy golf and a children's playground. Go east on the Great East Road 13km from Arcades Shopping Centre, then make a left at the Caltex petrol station, take the road to the end (11km) and the park is on the right. Note that this route can be a tortuous journey pitted with potholes and deep ruts, especially after the rainy season. There's an alternative access road signposted from the airport.

The spotlessly clean Olympic-sized **public swimming pool** (Map pp72-3; off Nangwenya Rd; admission US$1; ⏰ 9am-5pm Tue-Sun) is surrounded by a pleasant shaded area and is a great place to relax and unwind.

Horse riding among wildlife can be arranged at Lilayi Lodge (see p77) for US$25 per person (two hours).

SLEEPING

Lusaka's sleeping options are pretty spread out, although if you're looking for a hostel that's easy as there are only two and they're right next to each other. In central Lusaka midrange and top-end options are peppered around Rhodes Park and Embassy Triangle with a couple on Cairo Rd; in Greater Lusaka most accommodation tends to be in the east off Great East Road, in the direction of the airport.

Budget

Pioneer Camp (Map p68; ☎ 096 6731420; www.pioneer campzambia.com; Palabana Rd, off Great East Road; campsite per person ZK25,000, s/d chalets with shared bathroom US$45/60, s/d/tr 2-room chalets US$55/70/90, d luxury chalet US$120) A marvellous, isolated 25-acre camp, surrounded by bird-rich woodland, this makes a great alternative to staying in central Lusaka. The luxury chalets have flagstone floors, verandas and sunken baths, and are removed from the main chalet grouping. Its seclusion and tranquillity make it very popular and, if you don't want to self-cater, there's a bar and restaurant. It's signposted 5km south of Great East Road and 17km east of the Manda Hill Shopping Centre. If you don't have a car, contact the camp beforehand for current advice about how to reach it by minibus.

Lusaka Backpackers (Map pp72-3; ☎ 977 805483; www.chachachasafaris.com; 161 Mulombwa Cl; campsite

per person ZK27,500, dm ZK66,000, s, d, tw with shared bathroom ZK137,5000; 🖥 🛏) When there are so few hostels around it's unsurprising that this place is popular with young backpackers. It's a fairly relaxed hostel and a good spot for meeting independent travellers. Camping is on a small patch of grass that can fill up quickly, so get in early. Dorms have four to six beds and decent mattresses while rooms are simple, clean and bare. Chachacha can help with travel throughout Zambia as it organises trips to Kafue National Park, Lower Zambezi National Park and Livingstone (which is handy as the national parks can be very expensive to visit independently). The courtyard, pool and bar are inviting, and other facilities include a restaurant (serving basic meals); a tub for doing laundry; a communal, dilapidated kitchen and baggage store. Note that it can be a bit of a party place, particularly at weekends, so watch your stuff. Airport transfer available.

Eureka Camping Park (off Map pp72-3; ☎ 272351; eureka@zamnet.zm; Kafue Rd; campsite per person ZK28,000, chalets ZK275,000-358,000; 🛏) The campsite here is grassy and shaded by big trees. The security is good, while the swimming pool and bar (which sells snacks) are nice touches. Chalets are cool and comfortable and modelled on the traditional thatched hut. Firewood is for sale and there is an abutting walkable safari area with animals that don't want to eat you. It's about 12km south of the city centre. Minibuses from the City Bus Station or South End Roundabout go past the gate.

Kuomboka Backpackers (Map pp72-3; ☎ 222450; kvkirkley@zamtel.zm; Makanta Cl; dm ZK45,000, d with shared bathroom ZK125,000) A labyrinthine-style place, with colourful murals depicting Zambian life. Accommodation is around one big main building here; there are three dorms, each with 10 beds and low ceilings, which feel a bit cramped, especially when they get crowded. In fact the whole compound feels like it could get pretty packed out when it fills up. Plain but serviceable rooms come with clean, shared bathrooms. There's no self-catering kitchen but meals are provided and it will do laundry for ZK20,000 per bag. Staff are laid-back, and it's recommended by readers. Airport transfer available.

YWCA (Map pp72-3; ☎ 252726; Nationalist Rd; tw with shared bathroom/cooking facilities ZK150,000/180,000) The Y offers budget accommodation with a

LUSAKA

To Kapiri
Mposhi (200km);
Ndola (325km);
Kitwe (385km)

To Eureka Camping Park (10km);
Zambia Wildlife Authority (14km);
Munda Wanga Environmental Park (15km);
Lilayi Lodge (30km); Kafue Town (50km);
Chirundu (135km); Livingstone (470km)

To Kafue National
Park (275km)

North End
Roundabout

Central Park

Train
Station

South End
Roundabout

Comesa
Market

Kamwaia
Market

Rhodes
Park

FedEx
Roundabout

Government
Area
(Ministries)

See Enlargement

Chakaluka Rd
Mandi Hill Rd
Manchichi Rd
Sibweni Rd
Chitemene Rd
Limbe Rd
Pasili Rd
Nchenja Rd
Libambe Rd
Mukosa Rd
Wamulwa Rd
Rhodalakishi Rd
Great North Rd
Chandwe Musonda Rd
Washama Rd
Chishango Rd
Kutwa Rd
Mwayi Rd
Luanshya Rd
Panganini Rd
Katambo Rd
Musonda Ngosa Rd
Freedom Way
Limumba Rd
Mumbwa Rd
Kalundwe Rd
Chiparamba
Nkwazi Rd
Katondo Rd
Los Angeles Rd
Ben Bella Rd
Kafue Rd
Katunjila
Cairo Rd
Sadzu Rd
Dedan Kimathi Rd
Independence Ave
Chilumbulu Rd
Obote Rd
Nasser Rd
Dushambe Rd
Chilubi
Muchisha
Nyakaseya Runa Rd
Tito Rd
Lagos Rd
Lagos Rd
Katemo Rd
Mahambuli Rd
Mulombwa Cl
Bwinjimfumu Rd
Mwilwa Rd
Chingalika Rd
Masansa Close
Provident Rd
Makishi Rd
Tuleteka Rd
Kabelenga Rd
Broads Rd
Parirenyetwa Rd
Church Rd
Nyimba Rd
Mwembeshi Rd
Lubwa Rd
Mwaimwena Rd
Addis Ababa Dr
Sue Rd
Chikwa Rd
Chimanga Rd
Mogadishu Rd
Kombe Rd
Nsunzu Rd
Burma Rd
Burma Rd
Independence Ave
Great East Rd
Chozi Rd
Lumbe Rd
Ndeki Mumba Rd

1
5
6
15
17
19
20
23
28
30
31
32
38
40
42
44
45
47
48
49
51
52
54
56
58
60
63
64
66
67
73
76
77
78
81
83
87
89
90
92
93
94
95
96
97
98
99

A B C D
1 2 3 4 5 6

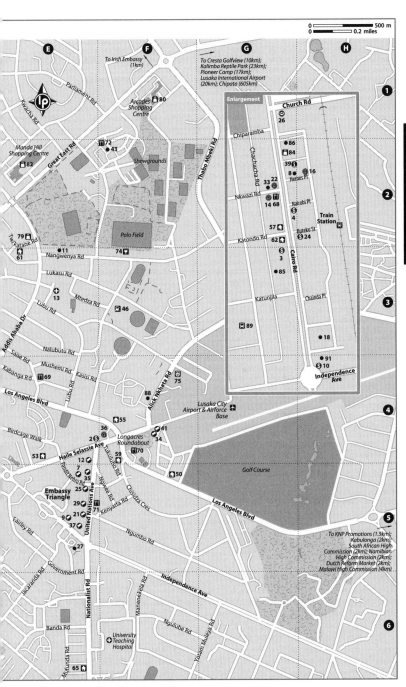

LUSAKA

INFORMATION
Airmasters Travel &
   Tours **1** C3
Barclays Bank **2** E4
Barclays Bank .... (see 80)
Barclays Bank **3** G3
Barclays Bank .... (see 7)
Barclays Bank **4** G2
Barclays Bank **5** A3
Bimm Travel Agency .... (see 86)
Book Cellar .... (see 82)
Bookworld **6** A3
Botswanan High
   Commission **7** E5
British Council **8** G2
British High Commission **9** E5
Bureau de Change
   outlets (Bullion, APT,
   Choice) **10** H4
Bush Buzz **11** E3
Canadian High
   Commission **12** E4
Care for Business **13** E3
Computer Lab **14** G2
Congo (Zaïre) Embassy **15** C4
Corner Internet Cafe **16** H2
Corpmed **17** A3
Department of
   Immigration **18** H3
French Embassy **19** D5
Fx Foreign Exchange **20** A4
German Embassy **21** E5
Global.com Internet Cafe **22** G2
Greenwood Pharmacy **23** A3
Indo-Zambian Bank **24** H2
Kenyan High
   Commission **25** E5
Main Post Office **26** G1
Map Sales Office **27** E5
Microlink I Zone .... (see 80)
Mozambican High
   Commission **28** C3
Netherlands Embassy **29** E5
Planet Books .... (see 80)
Police Station **30** B4
Stanbic Bank **31** B4
Standard Chartered Bank **32** A3
Stero Bureau de Change .... (see 82)
Steve Blagus Travel **33** G2
Swedish Embassy **34** F4
Tanzanian High
   Commission **35** E5
TheCafé@la.com **36** F4
Travel Shop .... (see 82)
Travel Shop .... (see 80)
US Embassy **37** E5

Voyagers **38** D4
Zambia National Tourist
   Board **39** G2
Zambian Safari Company **40** B4
Zampost Bureau de Change ...... (see 26)
Zamtel .... (see 26)
Zimbabwean High
   Commission **41** F4

SIGHTS & ACTIVITIES
Freedom Statue **42** C5
Henry Tayali Visual Arts
   Centre **43** F2
Lusaka City Market **44** A5
National Museum **45** C5
New Soweto Market .... (see 47)
Public Swimming Pool **46** F3
Soweto Market **47** A5
Town Centre Market **48** A4

SLEEPING 🏠
Chita Lodge **49** D1
Chrismar Hotel **50** F5
Endesha Guest House **51** C4
Fairview Hotel **52** C4
InterContinental **53** E4
Kuomboka Backpackers **54** B4
Longacres Lodge **55** F4
Lusaka Backpackers **56** C4
Lusaka Hotel **57** G2
Marble Inn **58** B4
Ndeke Hotel **59** F4
Nena's Guesthouse **60** C3
Pearl Haven **61** E3
Protea Hotel **62** G2
Southern Sun Ridgeway **63** D5
Taj Pamodzi Hotel **64** D4
YWCA **65** E6
Zamcom Lodge **66** D4

EATING 🍴
Arabian Nights .... (see 80)
Cattleman's Grill .... (see 50)
Chit Chat **67** C3
Coffee Talk Cafe .... (see 40)
Creamy Inn, Chicken Inn,
   Pizza Inn, Food Palace **68** G2
Debonairs .... (see 82)
Diane's **69** E4
Kilimanjaro .... (see 82)
LA Fast Foods .... (see 36)
La Gondola .... (see 80)
La Mimosa Coffee Shop .... (see 80)
Marlin **70** F4
Mint Cafe .... (see 80)
O'Hagans .... (see 82)

Oriental Garden
   Restaurant **71** E5
Rhapsody's .... (see 80)
Sichuan **72** F2
Zebra Crossing .... (see 79)

DRINKING 🍸
Brown Frog **73** B4
O'Hagans .... (see 82)
Polo Grill **74** F3
Rhapsody's .... (see 80)
Times Cafe .... (see 80)

ENTERTAINMENT 🎭
Alliance Française **75** F4
Chez-Ntemba **76** B6
Cinema .... (see 80)
Johnny's **77** D3
Lusaka Playhouse **78** D4

SHOPPING 🛍
Ababa House **79** E2
Arcades Shopping Centre **80** F1
Kabwata Cultural Village **81** D6
Manda Hill Shopping
   Centre **82** E2
Northmead Market **83** C3
Shoprite **84** G2
Shoprite .... (see 82)
Spar .... (see 80)
Sunday Market .... (see 80)

TRANSPORT
Air Zimbabwe **85** G3
Avis .... (see 63)
Bimm Travel Agency **86** G2
British Airways **87** D5
British Airways Office **88** F4
City Bus Station (Kulima
   Towers) **89** G3
Cycle Mart **90** A4
Ethiopian Airlines **91** H4
Game .... (see 82)
Juldan Motors Bus Station **92** A4
Kenya Airways **93** A5
Lusaka City Market Bus
   Station **94** A5
Lusaka Inter-City Bus
   Station **95** B5
Millennium Bus Station **96** A4
New Soweto Minibus
   Station .... (see 47)
South African Airways .... (see 53)
Soweto Market Bus Station **97** A5
Tazara House **98** B5
Total Petrol Station **99** A3

a local feel for men and women. It's tatty, the premises are quite dingy and the rooms need fixing up, but staff try to keep it clean. Simple and decrepit it may be but, at these prices, it's a good option if you don't want to stay at the hostels. The restaurant serves basic meals (dinner served Monday to Friday only) and is open to the public. Note that reception is in a building out the back.

Midrange
All rooms in the places listed below contain a private bathroom, at least a fan (air-con is indicated) and a TV; all rates include at least a continental breakfast unless otherwise stated.

CENTRAL LUSAKA
Endesha Guest House (Map pp72-3; ☎ 225780; 095 5550532; Parirenyetwa Rd; r with/without bathroom

ZK220,000/180,000) A cosy pension (guesthouse) with eight rooms, this place is set in an unattractive concrete compound and the rooms are sparse, but it's pretty good value, especially for the excellent location. The 'standard' rooms have unattached but private bathrooms, while the more expensive rooms have a private bathroom inside. All rooms have a TV and fridge, and mosquito nets drape over the beds. The staff are very friendly; the biggest drawback is the worrying number of cockroaches scurrying around the bathrooms.

Marble Inn (Map pp72-3; ☎ 230617; marbleinn.lusaka @gmail.com; Makanta Cl; r ZK200,000) This place is a motel-style arrangement, which is unusual for Lusaka. Each room is big, airy and scrupulously clean with huge tiled showers. There's not much in the way of decor, but for the space and cleanliness this is a good Lusaka deal. An extra bed in the room raises the price to ZK250,000. It may be noisy from the backpackers next door, so you'll do well to keep this in mind when choosing your room. The entrance is the gate to the right of Kuomboka Backpackers.

Nena's Guesthouse (Map pp72-3; ☎ 239541; www. nenaguesthouse.co.zm; 126 Masansa Cl, Rhodes Park; s/d ZK200,000/250,000; ☒) Nena's has four clean rooms, which can, however, be slightly dingy with a rundown look, so peruse more than one if possible (keeping in mind that some have a shower, others a bath). There's an onsite restaurant and some good chill-out areas including a lounge under a tree beside the pool and a grassy bar area. It has an excellent location in the Rhodes Park district, close to Cairo Rd and the shopping centres.

Zamcom Lodge (Map pp72-3; ☎ 251811, 097 8953019; doreen@zamcom.ac.zm; Church Rd; d ZK250,000-300,000; ☒ ☎) The spick-and-span rooms in this motel-style complex are devoid of charm, but they also have no dirt or mosquitoes. There's a spacious, shady courtyard/car park with resident turkeys strutting their stuff out the front. It's mainly used for conferences and wedding receptions so, if you're staying here at the weekend, check there's no reception on the Saturday night as these can be extremely loud and raucous affairs, and will mean little sleep (although you may score some cheap drinks). Rooms are simple but good

value for what you get, and the lodge is in a great location. Room 20 is the best double.

Longacres Lodge (Map pp72-3; ☎ 254847; Los Angeles Blvd; s/d ZK250,000/300,000, ste ZK350,000; ☒) This absolute warren of a place with its institutional feel and low-slung ceilings is a revamped government hostel with functional rooms. It's very spread out with lots of paved courtyard, but not many trees. Though friendly and spotless, it's not the most interesting place to stay. Rooms are pretty good though, with the bedroom separate from the small living areas that contain comfy chairs and TV. A suite buys you a bigger bed and slightly more space.

Lusaka Hotel (Map pp72-3; ☎ 229049; www.lusaka hotel.com; cnr Cairo & Katondo Rds; s/d from ZK295,000/ 315,000, d with air-con ZK365,000; ☒ ☒) Given the central location of Lusaka Hotel on the maddening Cairo Rd, it has a surprisingly serene entry set back from the road, with the sound (and sight) of water trickling through a lush little swamp as you approach reception. A good start. The longest-standing hotel in Lusaka, it's been open since 1914 and features plenty of black-and-white pictures on the walls as a reminder of yesteryear; it has a rather dark and sombre feel to it. Hallways are somewhat institutional too but the rooms are a good size, all with bathroom; the more expensive ones come with kingsize beds and armchairs. It would suit business travellers although anyone can take advantage of the excellent central location.

Pearl Haven (Map pp72-3; ☎ 252455; Twikatane Rd; s/d ZK300,000/350,000; ☒ ☒) In the shady Rhodes Park suburb, just off Addis Ababa Dr, this is an interesting place with flamboyant rooms featuring heavy curtains, plush carpets and carved wooden furniture. It also boasts a second-storey bar on stilts, which although a drawcard, can get noisy on weekends. Pearl Haven is a particularly good option if you want to be within a short walking distance of Manda Hill Shopping Centre.

our pick **Fairview Hotel** (Map pp72-3; ☎ 222604; www.fairview.co.zm; Church Rd; s/d ZK312,000/339,000; ☒ ☒ ☎) The Fairview is an old-style hotel with dated rooms that could really do with sprucing up (and a few repairs). It's a very friendly, convivial place to stay though and there's a regimental routine to cleaning the rooms and changing the beds. The standard

LUSAKA

twin rooms are a reasonable size, but you should check if your shower works before taking a room. Although staff jump to be of service, a story related to us about the safes (in all the rooms) being inoperable because management doesn't have a master key perhaps sums up a feeling of disarray. Ask for a room facing away from the casino, which gets noisy, even during the week. The suites are the best deal, more like small flats with separate bedroom, living room with couches, balcony and fridge. The terrace bar is perfect on a warm evening and a nightly barbecue is also held here. The location is great, within walking distance of Cairo Rd, Embassy Triangle and associated restaurants.

Ndeke Hotel (Map pp72-3; ☎ 251734; cnr Chisidza Cres & Los Angeles Blvd; d or tw with 1/2 persons ZK350,000/ 400,000; 🖫) With its attempted villa-inspired look, Ndeke has pokey but very clean rooms that are somewhat overpriced. Adorned with modern artwork including some contortionist carvings in the foyer, it's a strange place that's not really sure what it's trying to do. It has a great location though if you want to be around Embassy Triangle, there's rampant bougainvillea in the courtyard giving it a slightly Mediterranean sensibility, and for solo travellers there are two single rooms (book in advance) for ZK150,000 each – a bargain.

GREATER LUSAKA

Mwambula Garden Lodge (Map p68; ☎ 292826; mwambulagardenlodge@yahoo.com; Mwambula Rd, Jesmondine; s/d ZK120,000/150,000, d executive ZK250,000, ste ZK350,000; 🖫) There's a range of rooms in this garden lodge in Lusaka's east. The main building is quite dark with its timber-panelled ceilings and parquetry floor, and inside are mostly executive rooms that come with a lounge area and a balcony. A couple of standard rooms, which are plain but quite serviceable, are also in this building. More rooms are beyond a bamboo patch and a rather unnecessary pond; the best ones overlook the garden.

Makeni Guest House (Map p68; ☎ 274667; sikazinga@zamtel.zm; Plot 57, Makeni Rd, Makeni; r ZK140,000-180,000) A simple, homely place set in a small compound, Makeni is low on security but big on friendliness. There are half a dozen rooms, which vary markedly in size and bed arrangement, but all are clean and comfortable. Two rooms share an external bathroom. A cooked breakfast is ZK20,000, and other meals can be arranged with plenty of notice.

Reed Mat Lodge (Map p68; ☎ 293426; reed matlodge@yahoo.com; 5th St, Chudleigh; s/d ZK200,000, 275,000, chalet ZK375,000; 🖳 🖫) In a big garden plot, the rooms here are jazzed up with African patterned fabrics, prints and textiles which gives them a great feel, particularly in the rondavel-style chalets. Chalets also have stone-walled showers, another nice touch, although the whole compound is pretty crammed with the chalets stuck between the rooms. Overall it's a bit crowded but very clean, and the African stylistic touches and strong cultural ethic really differentiate this place. There's also a gym here with simple equipment (ZK15,000 per day). Children are welcome.

Crystal Garden Lodge (Map p68; ☎ 290044; crystalgarden2020@yahoo.com; Kabompo Cl, Kalundu; s/d ZK225,000/250,000; 🖫) This place feels a bit like it's been put out to pasture – past its best – but it's good value, in a quiet part of town and has helpful staff. There are 10 rooms in a white, weathered building; the compound contains several other buildings around a small pool and a garden, and these are rented out to local students. Rooms are clean but old and a bit frail, with dark wood furniture and fridges; some have a bath, others a shower. Meals are available at their restaurant but don't just wander in – advance notice is required.

Mika Lodge (Map p68; ☎ 291494; mika@coppernet .zm; cnr Central & 1st Sts, Jesmondine; r ZK350,000-400,000; 🖳 🖫) Run more like a hotel, there's an absence of charm at this antiseptic, sterile place, with its wall-to-wall tiles that have been scrubbed to within an inch of their life. The modern approach combines with lots of facilities but not much atmosphere, meaning it's all very pristine but any personality has been long snuffed out. If you want to spoil yourself go for a presidential suite, which comes with a separate lounge and a Jacuzzi. The executive and standard rooms are similar, although you can stretch out on a queen bed in the executive. If you're suffering culture shock, this place may be good for providing refuge.

Juls Guesthouse (Map p68; ☎ 293972, 097 7759326; www.julsafrica.com; Libala Rd, Kalundu; s/d US$77/95; 🖫 🖫) In the smart northeastern suburbs, this converted villa is several guesthouses in one, with its rooms spread over several buildings; it also has self-contained cottages. Rooms vary in size and layout, some with small balconies, that have either tiled or parquetry floors and are maintained to a high standard. There are also comfortable guest lounges. The associated travel agency and car-hire operation is very efficient (with discounts for guests). Credit cards are accepted. The amount of repeat business here is a good sign.

Wayside Bed & Breakfast (Map p68; ☎ 273439, 272736; www.wayside-guesthouse.com; 39 Makeni Rd, Makeni; s US$80-90, d US$100-120; ☎ ⌨) This upmarket guesthouse is one of the best in Lusaka, with only a handful of snug, en suite rooms. It used to be a farm and today the sizeable grounds are devoted to the owners' love of gardening, and really are magnificent (and ever-growing); a place where you can wander well away from other guests. Staying here is very peaceful. There's no TV in the rooms but there is a TV lounge. There's also an impressively (or disconcertingly) high level of security.

Chita Lodge (Map pp72-3; ☎ 293779; www.chita .co.zm; 25 Chakeluka Rd; d/f ZK450,000/550,000; ☎ ⌨) This impressive accommodation option is in a beautifully designed place with paintings and sculptures adorning the walls and passageways. It has 10 sumptuous rooms; eight doubles and two family rooms, which come with bath and shower. If you want to stay here book ahead as it caters for lots of conferences. The whole place is set in a delightful landscaped compound and Chita comes highly recommended. Airport transfer is ZK100,000 for the bus, one way, making it a great deal for groups.

Top End

All rooms in the hotels listed here have a bathroom, air-con and TV, and all rates include breakfast.

Lilayi Lodge (Map p68; ☎ 279024; www.lilayi.com; s/d from US$105/120, incl all meals & activities approx US$235/280; ☎ ⌨) This is one of Lusaka's finest options. The bungalows in this private wildlife reserve are very comfortable, and the gardens and pool are lovely. It offers horse riding and the chance to learn to play (horse) polo. The lodge is about 8km east off Kafue Rd and about 12km south of the city centre, and is only accessible by taxi or

private/rented car. It's very popular with the Zambian military.

Chrismar Hotel (Map pp72-3; ☎ 323141; www .chrismarhotels.com; Los Angeles Blvd; r US$120-150; ☎ ⌨ ⌨ ⌨) This contemporary offering doesn't present much in the way of individuality, but its features and comfort level stand as a bridge between the midrange and top-end markets in Lusaka. Standard rooms are in the old part of the hotel, while suites are in a newer wing and have African-style prints and wall hangings. The restaurant and bar are popular with expats, and the hotel's facilities do a roaring trade with conferences and weddings; note that it can get noisy, particularly at weekends. It's simple, modern and good value, especially if you're looking for an oasis away from Lusaka's perpetually busy streets.

Protea Hotel (Map pp72-3; ☎ 238360; reservations @phcairoroad.co.zm; cnr Katondo & Cairo Rds; s/d ZK695,000/790,000; ☎ ⌨) All that you'd expect from this South African chain – large bland rooms with modern furniture, inoffensive decor and a range of services aimed towards the business traveller. It has reliable facilities and may lack charm but the location is excellent, and it is only one of two options on Cairo Road. If you're missing the comforts of home and don't want to blow the budget it could even be ideal. Another branch is at the Arcades Shopping Centre.

Cresta Golfview (Map p68; ☎ 290718; reservations @cresta.co.zm; Great East Road, Chudleigh; s US$130-150, d US$190, 2-bedroom ste US$280; ☎ ⌨ ⌨) The Cresta is a modern business hotel, comfortable but lacking stylistic touches (though perhaps the rather unnecessary water feature in the pool counts as one). Its low-ceilinged corridors are lined with plain rooms, while set away from the main building are chalets. The sizeable landscaped grounds are adjacent to a golf course (the real reason to stay here) – hotel guests pay card fees only. Large bar-restaurant onsite.

Lion House (off Map p68; ☎ 097 7207996; nikkicolvin @iconnect.zm; Kyindu Game Ranch, Leopards Hill Rd; full board per person US$175; ⌨) Just 20km outside of Lusaka, this is the ideal wildlife retreat if city life is getting a bit much for you. Wildlife walks and horse riding are available and the ranch here has much to see including kudus, impalas, zebras, warthogs, buffaloes, elands, waterbucks and many lovely birds.

Accommodation is in a small five-bedroom guesthouse, which is filled with nostalgia from the old hunting and fishing days in Zambia; with hunting trophies decorating the walls. Full board includes accommodation and meals but excludes transfers and alcohol.

Southern Sun Ridgeway (Map pp72-3; ☎ 251666; res@southernsun.co.zm; cnr Church Rd & Independence Ave; s/d US$180/200; 🗷 🛜 🐖) This hotel group has taken over from the old Holiday Inn, and the hotel offers a more affordable top-end, city-centre option. The expected muted tones in the foyer decor give way to an outdoor sitting area around a fishpond with resident baby crocs (keep that in mind while you enjoy your G&T). Rooms are what you'd expect, with a high level of comfort, but are fairly bland and some furniture is surprisingly dated. The newly renovated wing is the plushest and has the best furniture. If you can, try to nab rooms 315, 317, 319 or 321 for the best views in the house.

InterContinental (Map pp72-3; ☎ 250000; www .ichotelsgroup.com; Haile Selassie Ave; s/d from US$275/ 300; 🗷 🖳 🛜 🐖) Renovated in 2008, this swish place offers the sort of bling-bling amenities and rooms found in most of the hotels run by this chain throughout the world. If you're after a hairdryer, ironing board, a newspaper delivered to your room and a bit of pampering then it could be the place for you.

Taj Pamodzi Hotel (Map pp72-3; ☎ 254455; pamodzi.lusaka@tajhotels.com; Church Rd; s/d from US$300/325; 🗷 🖳 🛜 🐖) Specialising in inoffensive muted creams and browns, fountains and plenty of greenery as you walk in, this is by far the fanciest of the slick hotels in Lusaka. It's a large multi-storey complex with surprisingly personal touches, and an impressive level of service. Rooms have balconies and you should grab one near the top floor for striking views. The onsite gym is one of the best in town. Call for discounted room prices.

EATING

Lusaka's eating scene has improved considerably and there's now a range of decent cafes and restaurants in which to enjoy a meal. The better places tend to congregate either inside or fairly close to the two main shopping centres: Manda Hill and Arcades. It

can be a bit weird going to a shopping centre for a candlelit dinner, but what the setting lacks in ambience is usually made up for in the quality of the cuisine. Other options reside in the suburbs, especially around Embassy Triangle and Rhodes Park.

Restaurants

Sylva Professional Catering Services (Map p68; ☎ 290344; University of Zambia, Great East Road; mains ZK10,000; 🕙 lunch & dinner) This is a unique place to sample quality Zambian food. It's a simple dining hall at the university, a couple of kilometres on from Arcades Shopping Centre. You'll find dishes like goat or chicken (and *nshima* of course), but it's the vegetable dishes that are particularly recommended by locals. If you can, give them some notice for a wider variety of dining possibilities. This excellent catering service can also provide entertainment such as traditional Zambian singing and dancing, for groups that are dining.

Diane's (Map pp72-3; ☎ 097 7847157; 5018 Saise Rd; mains ZK20,000-35,000; 🕙 11.30am-2pm & from 6pm; 🍽) Diane's has a great feel to it with a lovely garden (go for a table on the terrace) and an excellent selection of Asian foods, although the emphasis is on Korean dishes. It has a superb cook-at-the-table Korean barbecue which goes down a treat. It's a cosy spot for dinner, very welcoming and also has a good range of vegetarian offerings.

[our pick] Oriental Garden Restaurant (Map pp72-3; ☎ 252163; United Nations Ave; mains ZK25,000-40,000; 🕙 lunch & dinner; 🍽) This place surely serves some of the best Indian food to be found in the country. The spices are a sophisticated and subtle blend while the marinades are spicy and very tasty: all evidence of a superior chef who maintains an extensive menu. Forget the Chinese and grill dishes at the back of the menu and stick to their speciality – Indian. There's a small bar terrace area, or a spacious indoor restaurant, offering excellent service. Good veggie options are on the menu, such as a tasty masala kofta. It's located opposite the Dutch embassy.

La Gondola (Map pp72-3; ☎ 291244; Arcades Shopping Centre, Great East Road; mains ZK30,000-50,000; 🕙 lunch & dinner) You might wonder if the interior designer of this pizza and pasta joint was on acid when they put together the confused Cubist decor, which looks like a cross between a backgammon and a chequerboard. Sit outside for visual relief. The menu doesn't try to do too much and the pizza in particular is excellent.

Cattleman's Grill (Map pp72-3; ☎ 253036; Chrismar Hotel, Los Angeles Blvd; mains ZK30,000-70,000; ☺ lunch & dinner) Under a high thatched roof, next to the pool at the Chrismar Hotel, this restaurant brings in the city's expats as well as foreign business people. As the name suggests, the menu is very meat focused with pride of place going to the flame-grilled barbecue selections. Live music will often accompany your meal. If you're looking for a quiet candlelit offering or a light salad for dinner this probably isn't the place.

our pick Rhapsody's (Map pp72-3; ☎ 256705/6; www.rhapsodys.co.za; Shop 41, Arcades Shopping Centre, Great East Road; mains ZK30,000-70,000; ☺ from 11.30am; **V**) This is one of the best places to eat in Lusaka: mind you, it can take a while to get used to fine dining, Zambian style – in a shopping centre with a nice view over to the green fluoro lights of the BP service station. But don't let that bother you; the food is excellent. It has huge eating areas, inside and outside under an industrial-style roof, and the international menu does everything from steaks to Thai chicken, salads and even nasi goreng. There are also lots of seafood dishes and the prawns are recommended. Try the chicken Espetada, a delicious Portuguese-inspired chicken dish whose presentation will have you playing hangman in minutes – tip: go easy on the jalapeno. Finish off with a hot chocolate brownie and a decent, strong coffee.

Sichuan (Map pp72-3; ☎ 253842; Showgrounds, off Nangwenya Rd; mains ZK35,000-50,000; ☺ 11am-2.30pm & 7-10.30pm Mon-Sat, dinner Sun; **V**) The best Chinese restaurant in Lusaka, which is bizarrely situated at the back of a warehouse at the Showgrounds. It's an excellent place with a cosy dining area employing subtle partitions to give diners a sense of space and privacy. Wood-panelled ceilings and lots of Chinese decoration contribute to the ambience. The usual suspects are on the menu and are well prepared in record time from the kitchen – don't miss their crocodile offerings.

O'Hagans (Map pp 72-3; ☎ 255555; Shop 42, Manda Hill Shopping Centre, Great East Road; mains ZK35,000-60,000; ☺ breakfast, lunch & dinner) A South African chain pub, O'Hagan's can provide temporary

transportation to more Western-style entertainment and dining. The large outdoor terrace is its best feature and the pub focuses on pub faves such as steak-and-Guinness pie, and loads of other red-meat delights designed for the mainly Afrikaner clientele, whose weighty proportions spill over most of the bench space here.

Marlin (Map pp72-3; ☎ 252206; Longacres Roundabout, Los Angeles Blvd; mains ZK50,000-70,000; ☺ lunch & dinner Mon-Sat) Housed in the colonial-era Lusaka Club, this perennial, wood-panelled favourite is the best steakhouse in Zambia. While it does serve gargantuan portions of every cut of meat under the sun, most guests come for the aged fillet with mushroom or pepper sauce. It has an old-style, easy-going dining ambience. Reservations are strongly recommended.

Arabian Nights (Map pp72-3; ☎ 257085; Shop 37, Arcades Shopping Centre, Great East Road; mains ZK70,000-95,000; ☺ lunch & dinner Mon-Sat) With a fairly authentic, exotic Middle-Eastern feel, complete with hookah pipes and brass artefacts, it's nice to be transported beyond African borders for a couple of hours of fine dining. This refined place attempts a head-spinning variety, although quality Pakistani dishes are the mainstay. Try the Kenyan coriander lamb, Parmesan meatballs or Pakistani barbecue. Middle-Eastern spiciness is combined with Zambian friendliness.

Cafes
Coffee Talk Cafe (Map pp72-3; Central Park, Cairo Rd; mains ZK15,000-30,000; ☺ 7am-8pm Mon-Fri, 7am-5pm Sat, 9am-5pm Sun) This cafe churns out bakery items such as pies and sausage rolls; pizzas and burgers are also served. It's a pleasant Cairo Rd spot for a sit down and a cuppa over the newspaper. More substantial meals are sometimes available.

La Mimosa Coffeeshop (Map pp72-3; Arcades Shopping Centre, Great East Road; mains ZK20,000-35,000; ☺ breakfast, lunch & dinner) Spreading out onto the mall, this cafe is populated with expats and South Africans during the day and Zambians at night. It serves basic, good-value nosh such as salads, sandwiches, light meals and savoury crêpes, although it seems popular mainly as a place to natter. There are plenty of ads for local businesses and it certainly has a more Zambian flavour than neighbouring cafes.

LUSAKA

LA Fast Foods (Map pp72-3; Longacres Roundabout, Haile Selassie Ave; meals ZK20,000-50,000; 10.30am-9pm Mon-Thu & Sun, to 10pm Fri & Sat) An ideal place to grab a meal if you have to wait for your visa from any of the nearby embassies. Allow some time to plough through the confusing array of menus on the counter offering Chinese food, burgers, steaks and a hundred variations of 'chicken and chips'.

Zebra Crossing (Map pp72-3; Ababa House, cnr Addis Ababa Dr & Twikatane Rd; breakfast & light meals ZK25,000-30,000; 9am-5pm Mon-Sat) At this small boutique you can eat at shaded tables overlooking a garden surrounded by wood-carvings and African artwork. Tuck into carrot-and-marmalade muffins, wraps and sandwiches. A children's playground makes it popular with families and it's a very pleasant stop for fuel after a browse through the nearby shop and gallery.

Mint Cafe (Map pp72-3; Arcades Shopping Centre, Great East Road; mains ZK25,000-45,000; breakfast & lunch; V) The garish lime-green decor does not appear appetising, but Lusaka's expats and business visitors flock here to indulge in expertly prepared Western-style creations such as tortilla wraps or freshly made open sandwiches for lunch. There's an impressive selection for breakfast too: good coffee and even smoothies – try the mango madness. It sits within the shopping centre, just outside the entrance to the Protea Hotel. It won't win awards for ambience, but its culinary creations are some of the city's best.

Kilimanjaro (Map pp72-3; 255830; Manda Hill Shopping Centre, Great East Road; mains ZK25,000-50,000; breakfast & lunch; V) The drab entrance here belies the eclectic, cluttered interior, chock-a-block full of African curios, textiles and artworks, and souvenirs all for sale. It's definitely a local hotspot with its fair selection of African and expat cool-cat clientele. There's an impressive range of breakfasts and bakery items, even muesli. Sandwiches, rolls, salads, pastas and burgers with scores of different combos feature for lunch, and there's lots of old faves such as BLTs and Caesar salad. The coffee is very good, including the double espresso. There's also an internet cafe, expat noticeboard and a play area for kids, making it popular with families. Easily the best hang-out at this shopping centre.

our pick Chit Chat (Map pp72-3; 097 7774481; 5A Omelo Mumba Rd; mains ZK30,000-50,000; noon-3pm Mon, 8.30am-midnight Tue-Sat, hours variable Sun;) A popular place for lunch or dinner in a relaxed, open-air atmosphere, Chit Chat has an eclectic menu featuring burgers, tortilla wraps, salads, pastas, kebabs, Mexican food and a variety of breakfasts served on colourful African tablecloths. It's on a lovely tree-shaded street, and there's playground equipment and a grassed area for kids. Grab a comfy couch and while away an afternoon with the newspaper as you check your emails and sip a cold beer.

Quick Eats

For local meals, the food stalls at the **Town Centre Market** (Map pp72-3; Chachacha Rd) serve cheap local food, but the scavenging dogs roaming the increasing piles of rubbish around the market may affect your appetite, it's not a sight for the squeamish. Sausages and steaks are grilled before your eyes and served with a generous portion of veg and *nshima* for ZK10,000 or less. Cleaner food stalls are at the **Lusaka Inter-City Bus Station** (Map pp72-3; Dedan Kimathi Rd). Alternatively, jump on a minibus to one of the two modern shopping centres: **Manda Hill** (Map pp72-3; Great East Road) and **Arcades** (Map pp72-3; Great East Road), where you'll find a range of Western-style fast-food outlets such as **Debonairs** (Map pp72-3; Manda Hill Shopping Centre; pizzas ZK30,000-45,000; lunch & dinner, 24hr Fri & Sat). If you're desperate and on Cairo Rd, pop into **Creamy Inn**, **Chicken Inn**, **Pizza Inn** or **Food Palace** (Map pp72-3; Cairo Rd) – all offering fast-food meals for around ZK30,000.

DRINKING

Rhapsody's (Map pp72-3; 256705/6; www .rhapsodys.co.za; Shop 41, Arcades Shopping Centre, Great East Road) This place, combined with a large restaurant (see p79), is a more upmarket option for a drink. It has stools at the bar and a good selection of South African wine and spirits. It's mainly frequented by well to-do Zambians and NGO workers.

our pick Polo Grill (Map pp72-3; 2374 Nangweny Rd; 8am-midnight) A large, open-air bar under an enormous thatched roof overlooking a huge, well-kept polo field (where you can occasionally catch a live match); it's all rather incongruous for Lusaka, but an exceedingly pleasant place to knock back a few Mosi's. It livens up at night when bands (mostly local acts) strut their stuff on the stage and there's no cover charge.

Times Cafe (Map pp72-3; Arcades Shopping Centre; ☉ till late nightly) For a drink in trendy, semi-industrial decor with a clubby feel, try this place, which also shows English Premier League football matches. Better to come here with friends: it's not much of a solo drinker's haunt.

O'Hagans (Map pp72-3; ☎ 255555; Shop 42, Manda Hill Shopping Centre) This South African chain pub is ideal if you like fake Irish pubs and a more Western drinking experience. It's very popular with South Africans and Brits. There are decent beers and a great outdoor terrace, even if it does overlook a car park.

Brown Frog (Map pp72-3; Kabelenga Rd; ☉ 11am-1pm) Popular with NGO workers who come to dance at weekends, this British-style pub is a bit of an institution. At weekends when there's a DJ or local band, you'll have to shell out at least ZK10,000 to enter. It's a barn of a place where you'll most likely spot locals practising their dance moves during the week – propping yourself at the bar is a good opportunity to meet Zambians, or go for a booth if you're after seclusion.

ENTERTAINMENT

Johnny's (Map pp72-3; ☎ 252197; 9 Lagos Rd; ☉ 7pm-late Fri & Sat; ⓐ) An extremely popular nightclub with a ramshackle feel, Johnny's is the only disco in Zambia with an indoor pool, into which the occasional drunken dancer jumps.

Chez-Ntemba (Map pp72-3; Kafue Rd; admission K20,000; ☉ till late Wed, Fri & Sat) This traditional nightclub in the downtown area usually blasts out loud rhumba and the folk in here shake their booty until the wee hours on weekend nights. It's a good place to party and is in a convenient downtown location.

Lusaka Playhouse (Map pp72-3; cnr Church & Nasser Rds; tickets ZK20,000-50,000) From time to time local performers put on a good show. Check signs outside to see what's playing.

Alliance Française (Map pp72-3; ☎ 253467; ☐@microlink.zm; Alick Nkhata Ave, Longacres; tickets free-ZK20,000) The Alliance brings in performers, exhibitions and films from Europe and Francophone Africa. The programmes are advertised on posters around town and mentioned in *Lowdown* magazine.

The **cinema** (Map pp72-3; Arcades Shopping Centre; adult/child ZK24,000/17,500) at Arcades Shopping Centre shows all the blockbusters and even rolls out the red carpet on occasion.

SHOPPING

If you're looking for a cheap, local souvenir consider a *chitenje*. This is the brightly patterned cotton cloth that you'll see all over the place, often wrapped around local women to hold their bubs in place. You should be able to pick one up for roughly ZK50,000, and the best places to look are in local shops and the markets (see p70).

Northmead Market (Map pp72-3; Chozi Rd; ☉ 9am-5pm) The best place for kitschy souvenirs, local traders here will appreciate your business. The choice is limited but the carvings, fabrics and pottery on offer are reasonably priced.

Kabwata Cultural Village (Map pp72-3; Burma Rd; ☉ 9am-5pm) You'll find a scruffy collection of thatched huts and stalls at this place southeast of the city centre, near some decrepit white apartment blocks. Prices are cheap, however, because you can buy directly from the workers who live here. The specialities are carvings, baskets, masks, drums, jewellery and fabrics. No signage.

Ababa House (Map pp72-3; cnr Addis Ababa Dr & Twikatane Rd; ☉ 9am-5pm Mon-Sat) This place is a smart boutique full of imaginative creations from Zambian and Zimbabwean artists, furniture-makers and weavers. Most items are made for Western tastes and are not the sort of things you'll see in the markets. If you're a chocoholic you'll be in heaven as there's also a shop selling handmade Belgian chocolates.

Sunday Market (Map pp72-3; Arcades Shopping Centre, Great East Road; ☉ 10am-6pm Sun) This weekly market at the Arcades Shopping Centre features Lusaka's best range of artisanal goodies, especially wood carvings, curios made from malachite and African prints. Sellers from other markets, such as Northmead and Kabwata, also come here to display their wares. Note that while the range is extensive this market is also the priciest, so be prepared to bargain hard.

The swish **Manda Hill Shopping Centre** (Map pp72-3; Great East Road) and **Arcades Shopping Centre** (Map pp72-3; Great East Road) are easy to reach by minibus from along Cairo Rd or from the Millennium Bus Station, or by taxi (ZK25,000). As well as banks, bookshops, internet cafes, furniture stores, restaurants and fast-food outlets, the two shopping centres boast huge Shoprite and Spar supermarkets. Another Shoprite is located along Cairo Rd.

For the rest of Lusaka's markets, see p70.

GETTING THERE & AWAY
Air
For details about international and domestic flights to/from Lusaka, see p192 and p196.

Bus & Minibus
To avoid some inevitable confusion and frustration, take a taxi to whichever station your bus/minibus leaves from.

DOMESTIC
From in front of the massive and chaotic **Lusaka City Market Bus Station** (Map pp72–3; Lumumba Rd) buses and minibuses leave for nearby towns such as Kafue (ZK10,000, one hour, 10 to 15 daily), Chirundu (ZK30,000, 2½ hours, five to seven daily), Siavonga (ZK45,000, three hours, three to five daily) and Luangwa Bridge (ZK50,000, four hours, one or two daily) and destinations are more or less signposted.

Public transport to nearby towns, especially minibuses, also leaves from the **Soweto Market Bus Station** (Map pp72–3; Los Angeles Rd), but here *nothing* is signposted, so you're better off avoiding it if possible, otherwise you'll have to ask again and again for the bus/minibus you want. Note though that the New Soweto Market (see p70) will also incorporate a new bus station in front of it, so buses/minibuses should start to leave from there and (fingers crossed) the signposting may be improved.

To add to the confusion, minibuses to places not far south of Lusaka also leave from the **City Bus Station** (Map pp72–3; off Chachacha Rd), also called the Kulima Towers Station. So it's possible to get to Kafue, Chirundu and Siavonga from here too. Minibuses heading to the north (eg the Manda Hill Shopping Centre) depart from the **Millennium Bus Station** (Map pp72–3; Malasha Rd).

All long-distance public buses (and most private ones) use the **Lusaka Inter-City Bus Station** (Map pp72–3; Dedan Kimathi Rd), where there is a left-luggage office and inquiries

counter. A range of buses from different companies usually cover the destinations listed here (all leaving from this bus station unless otherwise stated) – we've quoted the highest prices because they represent the best companies, with the most comfortable buses (two-storey with reclining seats) and are generally only between ZK10,000 and ZK20,000 higher in price (and well worth the extra). Note too that buses operated by CR Holdings, which used to be the best bus company in Zambia, are getting pretty old and standards are falling, although there are rumours of new buses being purchased.

From this terminal, buses go to Copperbelt destinations such as Ndola (ZK65,000, four hours, five daily), Kitwe (ZK70,000, five hours, five daily) and Solwezi (ZK110,000, two daily). Euro Africa Bus Services is the best company on this route, although it doesn't travel as far as Solwezi. Kapiri Mposhi (ZK50,000, 2½ hours, five daily) is also reached along this route.

Tracking northeast, Germins and Jordan are the best companies, making a beeline for Kasama (ZK130,000, 14 hours, four daily) and Mpulungu (ZK150,000, 18 hours, four daily).

Heading southwest, as you'd expect there are plenty of buses to Livingstone (ZK100,000, seven hours, at least seven daily), but we'd recommend travelling with Mazahandu Family Bus or Booker Express. Both these bus companies travel on to Kazungula (for Botswana; ZK105,000, four daily) and Sesheke (for Namibia; ZK115,000, four daily).

Travelling east, many companies operate services to Chipata (for South Luangwa or Malawi; ZK115,000, eight hours, eight daily); all operate from Lusaka Inter-City Bus Station except one service, which leaves from Juldan Motors on Freedom Way.

Heading west, 10 buses a day go through Kafue National Park and on to Mongu (ZK115,000, seven hours).

It's certainly worth double-checking the schedules and booking your tickets one or two days before you leave.

Another option worth considering is the post bus, which is normally less crowded and carries mail (and passengers) to Chipata (ZK80,000, 7am Tuesday and Saturday), Ndola (ZK40,000, 7.30am Monday to Saturday) and Kasama (ZK85,000, 6.30am Monday, Wednesday and Friday) from ust behind the **main post office** (Map pp72-3; cnr Cairo & Church Rds). Tickets are available in advance at the post bus counter inside the post office.

INTERNATIONAL

All buses mentioned here (unless stated otherwise) leave from the **Lusaka Inter-City Bus Station** (Map pp72-3; Dedan Kimathi Rd).

To Botswana, Zambia-Botswana has buses to Gaborone (ZK180,000, 22 hours, three weekly) via Kasane and Francistown.

For South Africa, City to City has buses leaving every day for Johannesburg (ZK300,000, 26 hours, one daily). Trans Africa, however, is far more comfortable with services to Jo'burg (ZK360,000) three times a week. All buses between Lusaka and Jo'burg travel via Harare, Masvingo and Pretoria.

To Zimbabwe, take any bus going to South Africa, or Pioneer, Zupco or First Class buses go directly to Harare (ZK70,000, nine hours, one daily each).

For Malawi, there's no direct service to Blantyre, but there are three services a week to Lilongwe (ZK150,000, 12 hours), where you can change buses.

Zambia-Tanzania and Takwa Bus Services both make the run to Dar es Salaam (ZK250,000, 27 hours, six weekly), but services can be a bit haphazard (and the train is a lot more fun).

Hitching

Although we don't recommend hitching, many locals do it. There are several recognised places to wait for lifts: for Eastern Zambia, including Chipata, wait just beyond the airport turn-off; for places to the south, go to the Chirundu–Livingstone junction 0km past Kafue town; to the north, try at the junction north of Kapiri Mposhi.

Train

The *Zambezi Express* travelling to Livingstone (economy class ZK40,000, 14 hours), via Choma, leaves Lusaka at 11.50pm on Monday and Friday and no longer has 1st or sleeper class. Tickets are available from the reservations office inside the **train station** (Map pp72-3; btwn Cairo & Dedan Kimathi Rds). Get there early and be prepared for hustle and bustle. Slow, 'ordinary' trains to Ndola (standard class ZK25,000, 12 hours), via Kapiri Mposhi (ZK17,000, eight hours), depart Tuesday and Saturday at 1.20pm.

For information about the Tazara train between Kapiri Mposhi and Dar es Salaam (Tanzania) see p199.

GETTING AROUND
To/From the Airport

The international airport is about 20km northeast of the city centre. Taxis to and from the airport to central Lusaka cost ZK120,000 (although many drivers will charge ZK150,000). There's no airport bus, but the upmarket hotels send courtesy minibuses to meet international flights, so you may be able to arrange a ride into town with the minibus driver (for a negotiable fee).

You should also check to see if the **Platinum airport shuttle service** (☎ 096 6249299; one-way ticket ZK50,000) is running; it travels between the airport, Cresta Golfview, Arcades Shopping Centre, InterContinental, Taj Pamodzi Hotel and the Southern Sun Ridgeway.

Car & Motorcycle

The roads can get really clogged around Lusaka at peak traffic times, and you should always be alert on the road as accidents happen pretty regularly. Speed limits are enforced in and around the city; take note

---

DEPARTURE TAX & AIRPORT SERVICES

There's a departure tax of US$25 per person applicable to all flights departing Lusaka international airport. Before you make your way to the relevant counter to pay, check with your airline, as it's sometimes included in the price of your ticket (no sense in paying twice!).

The international airport has slim pickings as far as services are concerned. Remember to buy any books/mags at the bookshops in Lusaka before you get to the airport, as the selection in the shop here is very poor. If you've got a laptop, the wireless internet access now available at the airport is a welcome addition. If you have time on your hands, make your way upstairs to the bar, which is surprisingly good with large, wide booths to sit in – ideal for escaping the madness below.

of the speed signs on the way to the airport as this is a favourite area for police to nab unwary drivers. Do not park your vehicle on the streets unless you have someone to keep an eye on it for you; hotels, restaurants and shopping centres all have guarded car parks. If you drive around at night you raise the risk of an accident or carjacking a lot higher – after dark leave the car at your hotel and take a taxi.

Several international car-rental companies have counters at the airport, such as **Avis** (Airport ☎ 271303; Lusaka Map pp72-3; ☎ 251652; Southern Sun Ridgeway, cnr Church Rd & Independence Ave) – who also have an office in the city – and **Imperial** (☎ 271221).

Bimm Travel Agency (Map pp72-3; ☎ 234372; www .bimm.co.zm; Luangwa House, Cairo Rd) offers the cheapest hire-car rates. Vehicles cost from US$45 per day and US$0.30 per kilometre, plus US$10 per day for insurance, but the company inexplicably charges extra for keeping the car outside of Lusaka overnight.

If you want a car and driver to help get you around Lusaka, you're better off hiring a taxi for the day, although travel agencies do offer this service – see p68. One of the official blue taxis should charge around ZK300,000 to ZK350,000 for a day, but an unofficial taxi would be cheaper.

Public Transport

Local minibuses run along Lusaka's main roads, but there are no route numbers or destination signs, so the system is difficult to work out. See p82 for explanations about the confusing array of bus and minibus stations.

Otherwise, it is possible to flag down a minibus along a route. For instance, from the South End Roundabout, the 'Kabulonga' minibus goes along Independence Ave to Longacres Roundabout and then heads back towards the city along Los Angeles Blvd and Church Rd; the 'Chakunkula' or 'Chelston' minibus shuttles down Kafue Rd to Kafue town; and the 'Chilanga' minibus heads to Chilanga, via Kafue Rd. The standard fare is ZK2000 to ZK3000.

Taxi

Official taxis can be identified by the numbers painted on the doors and their colour – light blue – but hundreds of unofficial taxis also cruise the streets (you'll

hear them beep their horn as they go past you on the street, looking for business). Some unofficial taxis are really decrepit vehicles (we had the overwhelming smell of petroleum in the back seat of one we caught) so have a good look before jumping in one. Generally they'll be ZK5000 to ZK10,000 cheaper for a single journey within the city.

Official taxis can be hailed along the street or found at ranks near the main hotels and markets, and outside the Shoprite supermarket on Cairo Rd. Fares are negotiable, but, as a guide, ZK30,000 will get you between Cairo Rd and Manda Hill Shopping Centre during the day in an official taxi. If you're unsure, official taxis should carry a price list for journeys around the city – ask to have a look.

AROUND LUSAKA

If you feel like a bit of space and don't want to stay in the city (and have your own wheels), or you want to stay out of town so you can get an early start tracking north in the morning, consider the following accommodation options.

Protea Hotel Safari Lodge (off Map p68; ☎ 212843; www.proteahotels.com; 7km off the Lusaka-Kapiri Mposhi Rd; r US$200 🗙 🖳 🕿) This large and luxurious place in its own private game reserve has a relaxed country-club feel. The bar and restaurant are both excellent here; meals in particular are renowned among Lusaka's more affluent residents, especially Sunday lunch. The stylish, original rooms are striking, with soaring thatched roofs and a high degree of comfort. In the reserve you'll find warthogs, zebras and lots of antelope species including reedbuck, kudu, sable and eland. There's also a lion enclosure and a rescued baby elephant wandering around. Note that during the rainy season the entrance road can be in very bad condition. This unique Protea Hotel is 37km north of Lusaka.

Fringilla Farm (off Map p68; ☎ 213885; www .fringillalodge.com; Lusaka–Kapiri Mposhi Rd; campsite ZK25,000, r from ZK150,000, chalets ZK300,000-500,000 🖳 🕿) About 50km from Lusaka, Fringilla is a working farm offering a friendly welcome and a good range of accommodation. It comes across as a bit helter skelter, but

taff are friendly and helpful. There's a
good range of accommodation including
halets, huts and simple rooms with fans;
nd a restaurant selling snacks and meals.
The grounds are really lush, with verdant
greenery and large shady grassed areas. It's
ust off the main road, and is a very handy
lternative to Lusaka if you want some
peace and quiet.

KABWE

This is a dusty, but well-laid-out service
centre about 150km north of Lusaka. It
makes a good stop for lunch, with plenty
f parking, if you're driving between Lusaka
nd the Copperbelt, although watch for
drunken youths roaming the near-empty
treets at weekends.

Try **Zamchick Inn** (Main Rd; 2 pieces chicken &
chips ZK13,000; ☺ lunch & dinner) for something
quick and filling. Bottled water is available
on the opposite side of the road at the
takeaway place (Hot or Not?) next to the
petrol station. For more relaxed dining,
however, try **Fig Tree Cafe** (☎ 097 7872966; Main
Rd, 4km south of Kabwe; snacks ZK15,000-30,000; ☺ 6am-
6pm). Providing a welcome break from the
road, this cafe, set in manicured gardens,
has breezy outdoor bench seating or comfy
tables and chairs inside. It does burgers,
toasted sandwiches, tea, coffee and cold
drinks. There's even a selection of desserts.
It makes a great pitstop between Lusaka and
the Copperbelt, and there are swings and
trampolines for the kids. Fig Tree is well
signed off the road in both directions.

LUSAKA

The Copperbelt

Not on the radar for most visitors, the Copperbelt Province is the industrial heartland of Zambia and the main population centre outside of Lusaka. The region is rarely visited by tourists but unique attractions, such as the largest chimpanzee sanctuary in the world, make it well worth the trip. It's also the only place in the country (outside of Lusaka) where you can see the urban side of Zambia, and Ndola in particular makes that a very pleasant experience. Solwezi, a long way off the beaten track – even for the Copperbelt – is quickly becoming the hotspot for copper mining in the region and there's a real buzz about this once-languid town.

The world copper market slumped during the 1970s, so vast opencast mines cut back production, thereby creating high unemployment in the area. The cost of copper and cobalt went through the roof in the early 21st century; however, the global economic crisis of 2008/09 has seen demand, and therefore prices, plummet once again.

THE COPPERBELT

HIGHLIGHTS

- Hanging out with the cousins at **Chimfunshi** (p95), the largest chimpanzee sanctuary in the world
- Enjoying the peaceful surrounds and learning the fascinating story of **Dag Hammarskjöld** (p90) at his memorial, a World Heritage Site
- Strolling the well-kept streets of **Ndola** (p87), a refreshing change to Zambia's other urban spaces

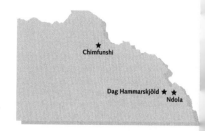

KAPIRI MPOSHI

☎ 0215

This dismal town, about 200km north of Lusaka, is at the southern end of the Tazara railway from Dar es Salaam (Tanzania) and at the fork in the roads to Lusaka, the Copperbelt and the Northern Province. If you're driving, there are plenty of petrol stations: providing a one-stop shop is Continental Oil, which has toilets (ZK500), bakery items (ZK7000) and a useful little store. It's a good place to refuel yourself and the car. If you're looking to kill time there are plenty of internet cafes around town to check your emails.

If you get stuck at Kapiri Mposhi, there are some local resthouses along the main street, such as **Eros Lodge** (Main Rd; s/tw/d ZK50,000/70,000/90,000). Only the doubles have a private bathroom, and it's well worth spending the extra kwacha to get one – No 5 is probably the best. Overall it's pretty dreary lodgings, although OK for a cheapie; at least the rooms are out the back, off the main road and set around a quiet grassed area.

If you're coming from Tanzania, there's a passport check before you can get out of the station, then from outside the station there's a mad rush for buses to Lusaka and elsewhere. Thieves and pickpockets thrive in the crowds and confusion, so take great care of your belongings.

Buses and minibuses from Lusaka (see p82) leave regularly and are a quicker and more convenient option than the local train from the capital. Note that the train station for the daily Lusaka–Kitwe service (Lusaka; ZK17,000, twice weekly), which stops at Kapiri Mposhi, is 2km from New Kapiri Mposhi station, the official name of the Tazara station. Refer to p199 for details about the trains from Kapiri Mposhi to Dar es Salaam.

NDOLA

☎ 0212 / pop 500,000

Ndola, the capital of the Copperbelt Province, is a peaceful, prosperous little city that provides relief from the pace, pollution and chaos of its larger cousin, Lusaka. In comparison it is clean, well kept and has some excellent facilities with little of the annoyance and no real evidence of its industrial base. In addition there are lots of shady trees on the streets and minimal traffic congestion, making it very pleasant to wander around.

Ndola's football stadium is being redeveloped in time for the 2010 World Cup in South Africa.

Information

Mixed Doubles Internet Cafe (Buteko Ave; per min ZK200; ☉ 8am-8pm Mon-Sat, 8am-6pm Sun) Wireless service and slow internet access. Upstairs next to the Copperbelt Museum. Serves cold drinks too (no alcohol).
Voyagers (☎ 097 7860647; Arusha St; ☉ 8am-1pm & 2-5pm Mon-Fri, 9am-noon Sat) The ever-reliable Voyagers can organise car rental and other travel arrangements.

Sights

While you're in town, drop into the **Copperbelt Museum** (☎ 617450; Buteko Ave; adult/child ZK15,000/10,000; ☉ 9am-4.30pm) at the north-eastern end of the main road. It showcases the local industry and downstairs are billboards with displays on Zambia's mining history, gemstones and the processing of copper. The upstairs section begins rather strangely with an exhibit of local toys and models of vehicles made mainly from wire. Beyond this is the interesting bit: artefacts

---

DRIVING IN THE COPPERBELT

The roads around the Copperbelt are generally very good and it's one of the best regions in the country for driving (with, of course, a few notable exceptions). It's understandable given the importance of the copper industry.

The road from Lusaka to Ndola is in excellent condition. It should take about four to five hours to drive with a stop for lunch. The road between Ndola and Kitwe is perhaps the best in the country: a dual carriageway in very good condition. In Kitwe itself, there are some shockingly potholed roads, especially in the cross streets in the north of town. From Kitwe through to Chingola is OK, but watch out for the heavy traffic including trucks. The Chingola–Solwezi road is full of human traffic, but there's not many vehicles. The road itself is in fair condition, but watch for potholes: they are a fairly frequent occurrence. This road is 180km, roughly a 2½- to three-hour drive.

THE COPPERBELT

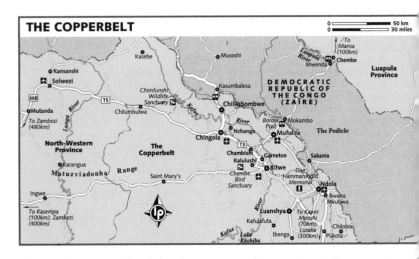

THE COPPERBELT

that include items used in witchcraft, personal ornaments, smoking and snuffing paraphernalia and musical instruments such as talking drums. It's this section that makes this small museum worth a visit. At the entrance is a well-stocked craft shop.

A short walk from the museum, the old **Mupapa Slave Tree** (Makoli Ave) is of great historical importance, although there's not really much to see and the tree sits behind locked gates. The shade from this ancient pod mahogany tree was used as a meeting place by Swahili slave-traders and slaves were also bought and sold here in the late 19th century. It's a bit neglected nowadays but can easily be spotted by the steel fence surrounding its girth. Have a read of the plaque at the foot of the tree.

Sleeping

our pick New Ambassador Hotel (☎ 097 7773909/374396; President Ave; s/tw/d ZK100,000/130,000/210,000; 💻 🛜) OK, so there's nothing 'new' about it, but this place is the best value in town. Sure, staff are a bit surly and have unusual hairdos but, at this price, who cares. The New Ambassador's wood-panelled lobby gives way to creaking hospital-ward hallways, but rooms are clean, as are the bathrooms, and you get plenty of space. Try to get a light and airy room on the 3rd floor; some of these have great views. The en suite rooms are a lot better than those that share a bathroom; the shared bathrooms make some terrifying

screeching noises. A decent continental breakfast awaits in the morning.

Royal Hotel (☎ 621840; royhotel@zamnet.zm; Vitanda St; s/d incl breakfast ZK145,000/250,000; 🛜) This huge old hotel sits languidly in the city centre, languishing perhaps in past glory. Today, however, it's not bad value as the rooms and en suite bathrooms are a decent size and kept nice and tidy. The whiff of stale tobacco may assault your nostrils as you enter a room, so ask to see a few. The service is fairly indifferent but if you're a Manchester United fan you'll be in good company as the attached bar seems to be a hang-out for local supporters and screen games. Note that Visa cards are no longer accepted despite the sign. It's 1km north of the public bus station and 200m southwest of the train station.

Endesha Guest House (☎ 617815; 6 Tusha St; ZK150,000-280,000, chalet ZK380,000) With a range of excellent options, this guesthouse has straightforward double rooms with shared facilities and chalets that are equipped with kitchens. There's a lovely grassed area with tables and chairs, and the restaurant and bar are kind of homely. It's a friendly and professional place and a classier option than its sister place of the same name in Lusaka.

Kaps Villa & Lodge (☎ 097 7117747; www.kaps villalodge.com.zm; Mulobezi Rd; r ZK300,000-350,000 🛜 💻) With a slightly ramshackle feel, this place makes a good alternative to Ndola's more expensive guesthouses. Cheaper

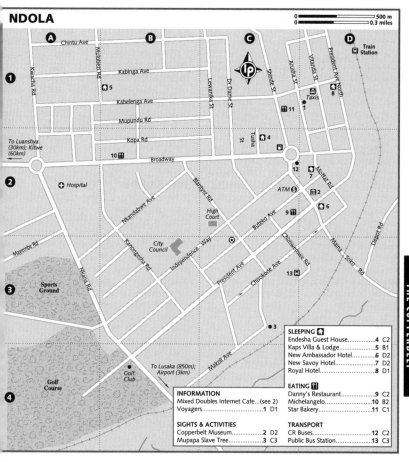

NDOLA

INFORMATION
Mixed Doubles Internet Cafe...(see 2)
Voyagers...............................1 D1

SIGHTS & ACTIVITIES
Copperbelt Museum..................2 D2
Mupapa Slave Tree.................3 C3

SLEEPING
Endesha Guest House...............4 C2
Kaps Villa & Lodge..................5 B1
New Ambassador Hotel............6 D2
New Savoy Hotel.....................7 D2
Royal Hotel..............................8 D1

EATING
Danny's Restaurant..................9 C2
Michelangelo...........................10 B2
Star Bakery.............................11 C1

TRANSPORT
CR Buses................................12 C2
Public Bus Station..................13 C3

THE COPPERBELT

rooms are far better value; more expensive rooms have a separate sitting room but are over-crammed with furniture, leaving little room to move about. The pine-and-cane decor in many rooms doesn't work that well, but this is compensated for with modern gadgets and a shiny tiled floor almost clean enough to eat your dinner off. Quiet location.

New Savoy Hotel (☎ 611097; savoy@zamnet.zm; Buteko Ave; s/d incl breakfast ZK425,000/475,000, executive r/ste ZK505,000/545,000; ✄ ☐ ☒) This grand old lady in the centre of town is holding up standards well. Old-fashioned yes, but not without charm and plenty of smiles from helpful staff. Its 154 rooms mean it's the largest hotel in the Copperbelt. The standard rooms are

fine, but executive rooms buy you a lot more space for not a lot more kwacha. Suites, on the other hand, are not that much better than executive rooms. The executive rooms are very spacious and many come with nice views from the upper floors, although they do vary a bit so it's worth seeing a few. A band serenades you over dinner nightly in the restaurant, and there's a great bar area broadcasting CNN news on big-screen TV. It practically faces the museum and is 600m north of the public bus station.

Eating

If you're in need of a quick snack, try **Star Bakery** (Arusha St; bakery items ZK2000-5000), just north of the town centre.

Danny's Restaurant (☎ 621828; President Ave; starters ZK17,000, mains ZK36,000; Ⓨ lunch & dinner) The reception area is a bit more inviting than the garish green of the restaurant, but the chandeliers and Indian handicrafts splashed around the dining area are a nice touch. Importantly, the food at this Indian favourite has an excellent reputation. Ignore the Chinese offerings at the back of the menu – stick to the Indian dishes. Try the lamb saag waala – lamb in a decadently rich gravy.

ourpick Michelangelo (☎ 620325; 126 Broadway; mains ZK38,000-60,000; Ⓨ 7am-3pm & 7-10pm Mon-Fri, 8am-2pm & 7-10pm Sat, residents only Sun but takeaway available) The wood-fired pizzas at this Italian place are excellent. The restaurant is cheerful and gaudy with a mock Italianate interior and is crammed full of Mediterranean furnishings and themes. It's lots of fun, and the plastic-wrapped chairs finish off the theme nicely! This is actually refined dining Zambian-style and the best place in the region for Italian food, including 'real' coffee; it even does a full English breakfast for ZK42,000.

Getting There & Away

Ndola is about 325km north of Lusaka. Every day, **Proflight Zambia** (☎ 0211 271032; www.proflight-zambia.com) flies between Lusaka and Ndola (US$60 one way), while **South African Airlink** (☎ 0211 254350; www.saairlink.co.za) has daily flights to Johannesburg for around US$280. The airport is 3.5km south of the public bus station.

See p82 for information about buses and trains between Lusaka and Ndola. From the **public bus station** (the southern end of Chimwemwe Rd), three blocks south of Buteko Ave, minibuses and buses run every few minutes to Kitwe (bus; ZK14,000, 45 minutes); there are also regular buses to Solwezi (ZK60,000). **CR Buses** depart from the stand next to the Broadway–Maina Soko roundabout and run to Lusaka (ZK60,000, four hours, up to seven buses daily). The **train station** (☎ 617641; off President Ave North) is 700m north of the museum.

Avis (☎ 620741) and **Voyagers/Imperial Car Rental** (☎ 620604) both have offices at the airport.

AROUND NDOLA

Shamilimo Lodge (☎ 097 9548001; Ndola-Kabwe Rd, 40km south of Ndola; rondavel ZK150,000-250,000; 🖳) is an excellent alternative to staying in Ndola,

and helpful if you want to get an early start on the road south to Lusaka: the thatched roofs are distinct from the roadside. Accommodation is in very affordable rondavels that are a good size (especially the more expensive ones) and are nice and airy (great in hot weather); some of them are extravagantly furnished with plump beds and huge en suites. The only minus is that they can be a bit dark inside. The restaurant here sells local food (mains ZK15,000) and there's even a butchery that sells local bushmeat.

Lake Kashiba

West of Mpongwe is this sunken lake, which was created millions of years ago when surface rock collapsed into underlying limestone caves. Popular with private divers and swimmers, the lake is strangely rectangular and is more than 100m deep *on the sides* (no one is really sure how deep it is in the centre), giving the water a strange aquamarine colour.

Kafue Lodge (chalets per person sharing US$70) located along the bank of the Kafue River arranges trips to the lake for US$30 per person. Contact the lodge through Voyager (p87) in Ndola. The lodge itself is on a game farm with loads of antelopes and good birdwatching.

To get to the lake or the lodge, head southwest to Luanshya from Ndola, and take a good map. Ask in Ndola about the state of the roads before attempting to drive out to either place.

NDOLA TO KITWE

If you're driving from Ndola to Kitwe you'll have the pleasure of cruising along Zambia's only rural dual carriageway. On the side of the road, close to Ndola, are African artwork and crafts for sale and it's worth pulling over and having a browse if you're interested in picking up a souvenir from the region.

A bit further along the road is the turn off to the **Dag Hammarskjöld Memorial,** national monument and World Heritage Site that commemorates the UN secretary general, whose plane crashed here in the 1960s during a peace mission to the Congo. It's a simple plinth with memorial stones from different countries and organisations topped by a globe and surrounded by a circle of trees in the shape of a plane. The site itself is very peaceful. The caretaker-guide really brings the place to life as he presents a vivid account of the plane crash while showing you around the attached **museum** (☎ 097 7685331; adult/child US$3/2; ☑ 8.30am-4.30pm). There are lots of pics from the crash site and diagrams of the route the plane took. Apparently the UN also sent a decoy plane (to fool Congolese rebels who may have been plotting to target the flight). One person survived the crash but died a few days later – he recounted the plane accelerating near Ndola, an explosion and then the plane crashing. Whether the plane was shot down or mechanical failure was to blame is still unclear.

There's also a useful map in the museum showing the location of historic monuments around Zambia – there's a concentration in the Copperbelt proving the area's long history of human occupation.

To get here, travel about 10km from Ndola on the main highway towards Kitwe and turn north (signposted), following a minor gravel road (good condition) for about 7km to reach the memorial.

KITWE
☎ 0212 / pop 700,000

Zambia's second-largest city and the centre of the country's mining industry, Kitwe feels far more urban than quiet Ndola. It's larger and rougher around the edges, with an African feel and an air that can be slightly intimidating, especially around the market and bus stations. Don't walk around with valuables. Not kept as clean as Ndola, the streets are noisy and dirty, although nice parks such as City Sq can be found. The main reason to stop here is the excellent selection of accommodation and eating places. The condition of roads north of the centre, running east to west, such as Mpenzi Ave, is very bad, rough and potholed, so drive carefully.

To change money check out **Dondou Bureau de Change** (cnr Independence & Obote Aves), in a mobile phone shop, which seems popular with expats.

There are no real attractions in Kitwe, although it has an extensive **market** (Chisokone Ave; ☑ 7am-7pm) one block west of the main street (Independence Ave). It *may* be possible to organise a **mine tour**, although be prepared

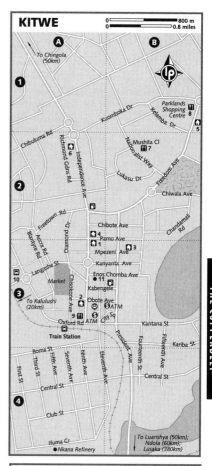

INFORMATION	
Dondou Bureau de Change	(see 2)

SLEEPING ⌂	
Africaza Guesthouse	(see 7)
Dazi Lodge	**1** A3
Hotel Edinburgh	**2** A3
Mukwa Lodge	**3** B3
Pamo Lodge	**4** A2
Town House Lodge	**5** B1
YMCA	**6** A2

EATING ⊞	
Arabian Nights	**7** B2
Courtyard Cafe	(see 3)
Dazi Lodge	(see 1)
Mona Lisa	**8** B1
Shoprite Supermarket	**9** A3

TRANSPORT	
Public Bus Station	**10** A3
Voyagers	**11** A3

THE COPPERBELT

as this will probably be a protracted and bureaucratic process. If you're keen and you've time on your hands, ask at Voyagers (p93) for advice.

Sleeping

YMCA (☎ /fax 218108, 097 9898588; Independence Ave; s with shared bathroom ZK75,000, d with bath/shower ZK160,000/220,000; ☐ ☎) Although it has an institutional feel, and the state of the rooms does vary, this is a genuine cheapie – something that's difficult to find in Zambia. The dark rooms can be a bit grim and the shared facilities are not great, but it's friendly enough and rooms have mozzie nets (fortunate as there is no netting over the windows), TVs and good space (including singles). It's 1.5km north of the city centre.

Pamo Lodge (☎ 222769; Pamo Ave; s ZK160,000, d ZK200,000-250,000) This place spends more money and tender-loving-care on its garden and conference facilities than its rooms. However, it would do if you were short of alternatives. The single is very pokey while the larger doubles are pretty good and come with fan, TV and fridge. All rooms have private bathrooms.

ourpick Dazi Lodge (☎ 095 5460487; Pamo Ave; r ZK180,000-260,000; ☎ ☒) This place has a wonderful kitschy air about it, as evidenced by the apricot-coloured bedcovers embroidered with love-hearts. Targeting wedding parties and other groups, the rooms are all different sizes – in the main building and out the back. Some rooms have en suite bathrooms, others come with shared facilities and all are spick and span. One bonus is that new mattresses on the beds ensure a good night's kip. There are two bars including a bamboo bar near the swimming pool – near the pool that has a little stone water fountain that is! Most requests can be met – including washing; just name your own price (around ZK30,000 for a full load is fair). Note that rooms overlooking the swimming pool can be noisy from the adjacent bar.

Hotel Edinburgh (☎ 222188; cnr Independence & Obote Aves; s/d ZK340,000/440,000, business d ZK475,000, ste ZK500,000-750,000; ☎) With its Scottish theme and central location, consider splashing out on the presidential suite here, which comes with two bathrooms! Try to get a room on or close to the 5th floor –

they have terrific views and heaps of light from large windows. Bathrooms are the usual standard, with showers in particular rather suspect, but they are generally clean, and the upstairs reception feels slightly regal with bars and restaurants leading off in all directions. Top patio for a sundowner.

Town House Lodge (☎ 221855; 65a Mabvuto Ct; d ZK400,000; ☎) With manicured lawns, trees and space, this place has a nice feel to it. Rooms reflect modern motel standards but are a bit pokey, although the beds look comfy and inviting, and en suites are a good size. The plus is the quiet, spacious location. The lobby has a rather corporate approach with leather couches and a TV screening African wildlife documentaries.

Africaza Guesthouse (☎ 229530; dcole@iconnect .zm; 11 Mushita Cl; s incl breakfast ZK450,000-500,000, d ZK500,000-550,000; ☒ ☎) This fancy guesthouse adjoining Arabian Nights (opposite) has eight rooms, each with its own theme. The large, warm rooms are beautifully furnished with heavy drapes, deep bedcovers and eastern trinkets mingling with African art and carvings. The expensive rooms are worth paying a bit more for – you get a huge room in a private building out the back of the main premises with a modern shower.

ourpick Mukwa Lodge (☎ 224266; www.muka lodge.co.zm; 26 Mpezeni Ave; s/d incl breakfast ZK500,000-600,000; ☒ ☒) This lodge has gorgeous rooms with stone floors that are beautifully furnished – the bathrooms are as good as you'll find in Zambia. Even mosquito nets are moulded into the design of the place. The owner's meticulous touch is apparent as soon as you walk into Mukwa, with fountains, sprouting greenery and an aviary full of parrots and parakeets fronting the property alongside its impressive Courtyard Cafe (opposite). It's a delightful place to stay that's well worth splashing out on. Look out for the artwork out the front – tortuous, rusting metallic sculptures.

Eating

Dazi Lodge (☎ 095 5460487; Pamo Ave; mains ZK25,000-40,000) The extensive menu in the small restaurant at this guesthouse has local African goodies, Spanish/Peruvian food and the usual steak and chicken dishes. Without notice some dishes are unlikely to be available, and the food is a bit hit and miss as the chef is still learning her trade, but the signs are good so check what's currently being served from the menu. The attempted variety is at least refreshing.

Mona Lisa (☎ 229677; Parklands Shopping Centre, Freedom Ave; pizza & pasta ZK35,000-50,000, other mains ZK75,000) A popular spot for a drink, this is also the place for pizza – pasta, steaks and grills are available too. It's a cross between a sports bar and a snug, warm, brick eatery. You'll probably be hassled from street vendors on the way in – be polite and firm.

ourpick Courtyard Cafe (☎ 224266; 26 Mpezeni Ave; mains ZK55,000-75,000; ☺ 10am-2.30pm & 6-10pm) The well-laid-out restaurant here has a flagstone floor, heavy wood furniture, French doors onto the garden, plenty of windows and exposed red brick. The combination creates a soothing dining sensation, especially with the sound of trickling water in the courtyard garden. It's a lovely uncluttered environment to have a meal. Service can be a bit hit and miss but the food is on the money. There are Western-style steak, chicken, fish and shellfish dishes. The Lisbon-style prawns in particular are delicious.

Arabian Nights (☎ 229530; dcole@iconnect.zm; 11 Mushita Cl; mains ZK70,000; ☺ noon-2.30pm & 6-10.30pm) With a constantly changing menu and a reputation for rich desserts, this is one of the top restaurants in the region, featuring lots of Middle Eastern and Asian creations. Try the green masala lamb shank. Dining in the atrium is by a fountain and a beautiful garden – a perfect accompaniment to fine food. The ambience here is much better than the Lusaka branch. It's off Nationalist Way; look for the salmon-coloured wall and gate, and the sign 'Heer LTD' on the gate; it's well signposted.

Getting There & Away
Kitwe is about 60km northwest of Ndola. Refer to p82 for details about buses and trains to Kitwe from Lusaka. The public bus station is situated 500m west of Independence Ave, and the **train station** (☎ 223078) is at the southern end of Independence Ave.

Frequent local minibuses and buses run to Ndola (ZK14,000, 45 minutes) and Chingola (ZK13,500, 30 minutes).

Voyagers (☎ 617062; Enos Chomba Ave) is very helpful and can arrange car hire and other travel arrangements.

AROUND KITWE
The **Chembe Bird Sanctuary** (adult/child K10,000/ 1000) has a rather spooky and deserted feel to it and is a bit of an expedition, even though it's not far from Kitwe. Unless you can get a boat out onto the water there's not much to do here, except perhaps have a picnic lunch – if it's solitude you're after though, you'll at least find that. Otherwise it's for hardcore bird-lovers only. There's a dilapidated, run-down lodge on the lake, picnic tables and a lovely shaded area. Watch out for crocs around the lake.

From Kitwe, it's 20km to Kalulushi (follow the road past the market in town, turn right at the T-junction, and then left at the sign to Kalulushi, crossing the rail tracks) and it's about another 12km from there to the sanctuary.

From Kalulushi, go through the town down President Ave (the main street) and turn left at the first roundabout (before the Catholic University). Go through one roundabout, and turn hard right at the second roundabout (at the bus station). Go straight through until the T-junction, turn right and from there it's 11km down a shocking, potholed road to the turn-off into the sanctuary, which is clearly signed.

CHINGOLA
☎ 0212
An intelligently laid-out town that has come along in leaps and bounds, Chingola is basically a huge mine with a settlement wrapped around it. On the Solwezi Rd you'll get a look at the enormous, open-pit mine, and you may even get a glimpse of the giant dumper trucks ferrying back and forth. The reason to come here is because it's the closest town to Chimfunshi (see p95) and has a decent range of accommodation, making it a good place to base yourself. Streets generally follow a grid pattern feeding off central roundabouts.

There are three petrol stations on Kabundi St, as well as Dondou Bureau de Change. Shoprite supermarket is on Kwacha St, and a Stanbic with an ATM is on Independence Dr.

Sleeping & Eating
Nchanga Hotel (☎ 096 6840081; cnr Kabundi St & Independence Ave; s/d ZK120,000/140,000) This is the town cheapie and the good news is that

it's central and…cheap. The bad news is that rooms are pretty grim. Probably best to bring your own bedsheet and use the room to crash briefly; it'll do at a pinch. The attached restaurant does very cheap meals.

Mica's (☎ 097 7188782; 5th St; r incl continental breakfast ZK200,000) Mica's rooms are neat as a pin and come with TV, fan and mosquito net. It's a good, reliable option. A cooked breakfast is an extra ZK25,000, and there's a great bar area on warm evenings. It's located close to the hospital in the north of town.

Hibiscus Guest House (☎ 313635; 33 Katutwa Rd; r per person incl breakfast ZK250,000) Traditional bed and breakfast is served up at this homely, English-style guesthouse. Decent rooms come with en suite and there is cheerful if slightly dated decor in the clean rooms. Judy has been doing hospitality in these parts for many years and really knows her stuff. It's good, old-fashioned warmth – you're made to feel welcome without being smothered by the owners.

Protea Hotel (☎ 310624; proteachingola@zamtel .zm; Kabundi St; s/d ZK616,000/688,000; ☒ ☎ ☒) Characterless rooms are set around a swimming pool with manicured grass verges at this branch of the ubiquitous chain. The foyer has a large chandelier, fireplace and decadent, black leather sofa – an attempt to create an air of sophistication that is not really delivered. However, rooms do sparkle with modern amenities, including an enormous showerhead in the en suites. There's also a breezy outdoor restaurant providing patio dining.

Golf Club (☎ 313765; snacks ZK10,000-20,000; mains ZK30,000-40,000; ☒ breakfast, lunch & dinner) Overlooking the manicured grounds of the golf course, and often getting a gentle breeze around the 18th fairway, outdoor tables here are an excellent place to sit. Inside, the building is sparse and fairly functional with enough dark wood to be mildly soothing. The cooked breakfasts are well done: tasty and filling. For dinner there is a limited menu including a couple of stir-fry options, pasta dishes or steak. Or it would make a decent pitstop for coffee and cake.

Mona Lisa (☎ 314762; Kabundi St; pizza & pasta ZK35,000-50,000; ☒ lunch & dinner) This branch of the Copperbelt pizza chain has a more African feel with plenty of locals taking advantage of the cheap bar. What doesn't change is the excellent wood-fired pizza. Seating is on stools around large chunky tables or outside on the patio – both suffer from noise: inside, bad pop music; outside, traffic. Consider takeaway if you're looking for peace and quiet.

Getting There & Away

Chingola is 50km northwest of Kitwe. The **bus station** (13th St) is in the centre of town. There are frequent buses and minibuses to Solwezi (ZK26,500, 2½ hours); and to Kitwe (ZK13,500, 30 minutes).

THE CHIMPS OF CHIMFUNSHI

The Chimfunshi Wildlife Orphanage was founded in the early 1980s by cattle farmers David and Sheila Siddle. The whole thing was an accident: Sheila was well known for nursing sick calves, so an orphan chimpanzee confiscated from poachers in neighbouring Congo (Zaïre) was brought to her for help. The young chimp recovered, the word got around, and over the following years increasing numbers of chimps rescued from poachers, zoos and circuses all over the world were brought to Chimfunshi. Many were sick, traumatised and unused to the company of other chimps.

Meanwhile, the farm became a sanctuary, the cattle were sold and the Siddles forgot all ideas of retirement. Along the way, they also became experts in chimpanzee behaviour and rehabilitation techniques. Contrary to the advice of primatologists, chimps from different backgrounds (eg the jungle of Cameroon, a zoo in Russia and the private house of an Arab millionaire) were placed together in enclosures. This proved successful, as many chimps settled down happily and formed cohesive family groups.

It was not possible or safe to release the chimps back into the wild, so to cope with the growing numbers the sanctuary expanded. Two 200-hectare enclosures of natural forest and grassland – the largest of their type in the world – were established in April 2000, giving groups of 20 to 30 chimps huge areas of secure 'virtual wilderness' where human contact is kept to a minimum. A third enclosure is on the drawing board subject to funding.

CHIMFUNSHI WILDLIFE ORPHANAGE

On a farm in a beautiful location, deep in the African bush approximately 70km northwest of Chingola, is this magnificent **chimpanzee sanctuary** (chimfunshiwildlife@iwayafrica .com; day visit project area adult/child ZK50,000/25,000, orphanage ZK25,000/10,000; ☺ 9am-3pm daily). It's home to nearly a hundred adult and young chimps; most have been confiscated from poachers and traders in neighbouring Congo or other parts of Africa; it's the largest of its kind in the world. This is not a natural wildlife experience, but it's still a unique and fascinating opportunity to observe the chimps as they feed, play and socialise. It could well be one of the highlights of your trip to Zambia.

The sanctuary was started by Sheila and David Siddle (Sheila and her daughter still run the orphanage here) on their farm. Visiting the sanctuary provides much-needed income and your entry fees go directly into helping it remain financially viable. *Please* do not come though if you're sick; the chimps can easily die of a simple disease like the flu. Visitors can come to the sanctuary for the day and spend some time at the orphanage where there are chimps being rehabilitated and other wildlife such as a beloved hippo. The highlight though is observing the chimps feeding in their wild enclosures in the project area; the best time to visit is their 1.30pm feed when they are out in the open (not in the concrete blocks they enter for their morning feed). It's a delightful time to observe their behaviour – we saw a dominant alpha male performance that made us happy we were on the other side of the fence! Bring a packed lunch and drinks; there's also a braai area available.

Your other option is to overnight at the **campsite** (per person US$10, coal for fires extra) or in the **self-catering cottage** (per person sharing US$25, whole cottage US$200) at the education centre, which has 10 beds, self-catering facilities and bed linen. Note that the accommodation is about to undergo a serious overhaul. Planned is a new safari camp aimed at the midrange to top-end market, (ie probably US$100 to US$120 per night). There will also be a new campsite by the river.

A very special way to experience this place would be to do a chimpanzee bush walk (US$100) with some of the younger

---

VOLUNTEERING AT CHIMFUNSHI

Chimfunshi Wildlife Orphanage presents a unique Zambian opportunity to help look after some of our closest cousins: a chance to observe, understand and interact with a diverse bunch of chimpanzees. Ninety days is the maximum time you can volunteer here and the cost is US$30 per day or US$600 for 21 days. It's an opportunity to get involved in all facets of the project; just be prepared to roll your sleeves up and get your hands dirty (tasks include fencing, cleaning out the chimps' feeding areas and helping out at feeding times).

---

chimps. Listen closely to your guide and don't take anything the chimps can easily grab (like a watch).

By car, take the Solwezi Rd for about 43km northwest from Chingola, then turn right at the signposted junction and follow it for 18km to the orphanage; it's then a further 12km to the project area. Note that the road is in bad condition, after the wet season in particular. However, a new road that has been built and is currently being graded is much better and shorter (it's about 20km off the main road straight to the project area), and is 55km from Chingola and well signposted. Although buses between Chingola and Solwezi can drop you off at the junction, you really need your own car to visit Chimfunshi.

SOLWEZI

☎ 0218

Solwezi is not exactly a pretty town, but one with good facilities if you need to stock up – ie if you're heading west, or south towards Kafue National Park. Get advice before attempting the road to Kafue though, as conditions will change depending on the season. The town is strung out along the main road and there are lots of administrative buildings and people milling around. It's the new centre of Zambia's copper industry, as evidenced by the opening of the Lumwana Copper Mine in 2009 – the largest open-pit copper mine in Africa.

There are lots of internet cafes in town and banks with ATMs. A Shoprite supermarket is in the process of being built and there's a local food market on your

THE COPPERBELT

right at the beginning of town (as you enter from Chingola).

Not far from the centre of town is **Kifubwa Stream Rock Shelter** (admission ZK20,000; ☺ 9am-6pm) where visitors can view rock carvings under an overhang dating back to the Stone Age. The engravings aren't in good condition but it's a lovely spot to visit. Turn off the main road heading south – look for the National Monument sign – towards the Teachers' College, which is 3km away. After another 3km you'll come to a boon across the road where you pay the admission fee.

Sleeping & Eating

Anina's Guest House (☎ 097 7615582; r ZK160,000) The best value in town, this place is also barely in town, although it's well signed off the main drag – you'll need at least a high-clearance 2WD to access it. The guesthouse mixes traditional with modern, and African carvings and artwork abound. The rooms are fantastic – very clean, and well furnished with stone floors and large, inviting beds and huge bathrooms. The best thing though is the location, well off the scrappy main road; it has a very rural feel to it. The beautifully kept lawns and garden are perfect for an evening drink and the gazebo provides lovely views of the surrounding country.

our pick Floriana Lodge Trust (☎ 821130; Independence Ave; r ZK250,000-500,000; ☒) This place is a real treat. It's a huge resort, including a health club, with lovely grassed areas and large shady trees, and it exudes a feeling of relaxation. The rooms are beautifully done. Each one is themed differently using pine or dark wood and metal framing; most are airy with great light. The VIP deluxe (ZK320,000; No 21 is a good one) is a terrific room category with heaps of space

and a nice cottagey feel. Guests can use the health club for free, which includes the gym and sauna. Massage is also available. This really is one of the best guesthouses in the region and is very professionally managed. Visa accepted.

Royal Solwezi (☎ 821620; www.solwezi.com; s/c US$130/140; ☒ ☒) The finest hotel in the region, this place has an enviable setting best enjoyed from the luxury rooms or the terrace adjoining the restaurant. Inside the main building large, black chandeliers wood panelling and whitewashed walls give a warm and slightly gothic feel. The two carved 'walking' hippos you see as you enter are a lovely greeting. Double rooms have two double beds – they are simply furnished and have very classy fittings, especially in the en suites. Staff are attentive if inexperienced. Visa accepted.

Yummylicious Bakery (Independence Ave; mains ZK12,000-35,000) If you're after something quick and filling, drop into this clean fast-food place doing burgers, kebabs and pies. It's easy to spot at the northern end of the main street. Their soft ice creams are particularly popular.

Bush Fire Restaurant & Bar (mains ZK20,000-40,000; ☺ 7am-11pm) Serving standard nosh such as burgers, pizzas and steaks, this is a good place if you want to meet a few local Zambians – as long as you don't mind the colossally loud pop tunes pumped out by the bar. It's just off Independence Ave, opposite the police station.

Getting There & Away

Solwezi is 180km from Chingola. There are regular buses and minibuses to Chingola (ZK26,500, 2½ hours), Kitwe and Lusaka (see p82). The bus station is at the western end of town near the market.

Northern Zambia

People with a spirit of adventure who love wild, open spaces will have a blast in Zambia's untamed north. Yes, it can be difficult to get around: distances are long and the tracks often rough once you get off the main drag, but that can all be part of the fun. It makes a visit here feel like an adventurous voyage.

Northern Zambia starts once you've passed the 'Pedicle' – the thin slice of the Democratic Republic of the Congo territory that juts sharply into Zambia, almost splitting it in two. From here onwards the Great North Road shoots its way straight up to Tanzania, passing national parks, vast wilderness areas and waterfalls along the way. If you're in a car (and you'll need a 4WD) there's a lot to be discovered here and you won't meet too many other travellers while you're doing it. On public transport you'll have to miss out on the smaller and more out-of-the-way destinations, but with some perseverance you can make it to this region's major attractions – and they are all worth the effort.

Topping the list are Kasanka National Park, where you can camp by the side of a river and listen to the sound of hippos without another soul in sight, or watch sitatungas splashing in the swamps at dawn from high up in a mahogany tree; Mutinondo Wilderness – a vast area of whaleback hills, rivers and valleys so still and untouched you feel almost transported to a prehistoric era; and startling Shiwa Ng'andu – a grand English mansion buried deep in the Zambian bush. And hidden on the rocks and in caves of this vast, beautiful landscape are thousands of ancient rock paintings, some of the most important in Southern Africa.

HIGHLIGHTS

- Discover a soul-stirring landscape of granite hills, clean rivers and endless vistas at **Mutinondo Wilderness** (p104)

- Visit an incongruous English-style mansion in the middle of the bush at **Shiwa Ng'andu** (p106)

- Look for shy sitatungas and fall asleep to the grunting of hippos at **Kasanka National Park** (p100)

- Drift through the wetlands in search of the elusive shoebill at **Bangweulu Wetlands** (p103)

- Hike to the top of majestic **Kalambo Falls** (p111)

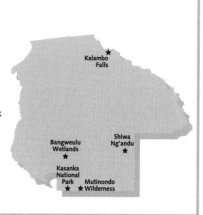

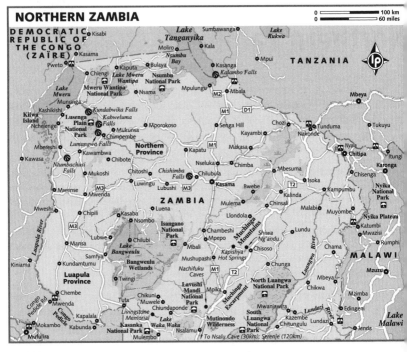

NORTHERN ZAMBIA

MKUSHI

☎ 0215

Deep in the heart of farming country, this prosperous small town serves as the 'big smoke' for surrounding farms and villages, and people come from miles around to use the town's banks and shops. Just 1km north of the Great North Road, it is also a handy stop-off point for travellers heading to and from northern Zambia who need to stock up on provisions and fuel or get to an ATM. There are also a couple of decent hotels here.

Sleeping

Forest Inn (☎ 362003/362188; www.forestinn-zambia .com; campsite per person ZK30,000, s/d/tr chalets ZK190,000/255,000/340,000). Just off the Great North Road, this is a convenient stop-off if driving up or down from northern Zambia's attractions. It's a pretty setting, with massive leafy gardens dotted with funky wire sculptures. Comfortable chalets have stone floors, local artwork and ethnic print bedspreads, and some of the bathrooms have wall-mounted candleholders for romantic bathing. There's also a campsite with clean, hot showers, a dining area, barbecues, plenty of electric lights for the evening and power points to charge your electronics. Birdwatchers will be kept happy with birding trails and nature walks in the surrounding forest. Don't expect tranquillity though. This place is right on the road and at night (particularly if camping) you can hear trucks whizzing past and distant thumping from the local bar down the road. Forest Inn is on the Great North Road, 30km south of Mkushi and 65km from Kapiri Mposhi, and is well signposted on both sides.

Shalom Lodge (☎ 096 6694764; r/chalets from ZK90,000/110,000) Like the nearby Marian Hotel, the owner seems to have a penchant for animal statues, but this time the A-frame chalets are pink. Rooms are a bit of a mixed bag, ranging from rundown singles to brand new, spacious brick chalets, so ask to see a selection. The owners are very friendly and there's a good bar and restaurant blasting out loud '80s Western pop music. It's behind Chibefwe Upper Basic School; turn off just before the Mariana and it's 1.6km from the main road (not 900m as the sign says!)

Mariana Hotel (☎ 362513; tw/chalet ZK100,000/ 120,000) The first thing you'll notice here are the large gardens dotted with all kinds of animal sculptures from swans to giraffes, and the numerous little nooks to sit out in the sun. The rooms aren't particularly well designed though – the twin rooms are spartan, some with bare corrugated iron roofs while the A-frame chalets are crammed with far too much stuff – including heavy sofas and fridges – so that they appear poky. The Mariana is on the main road into town, on the left-hand side if you're driving in from the Great North Road.

Eating

There are some cheap cafes around Mkushi town centre as well as a couple of supermarkets. The best restaurant in town is at the **Mariana Hotel** (ⓨ breakfast, lunch & dinner). It's large and airy and serves hearty plates of chicken and T-bone steak from ZK22,500.

The restaurant at the **Forest Inn** (breakfast ZK20,000-30,000, mains from ZK50,000 ⓨ breakfast, lunch & dinner) is excellent and even if you're not staying here makes a good rest stop on a long drive. You can eat in the cool dining room or out on the terrace overlooking the gardens, and food includes full English breakfasts, as well as burgers, grills and pasta dishes.

Getting There & Away

There are regular CV Transport and Juldan Motors buses to Lusaka (ZK50,000, three to four hours), Mpika (ZK70,000, four hours) and Kasama (ZK110,000, six hours) from the bus station in Mkushi town. There is also a Tazara train station here, just south of town, for trains to/from Tanzania (p199).

SERENJE
☎ 0215

Serenje is a pretty nondescript town, spread out west from the Great North Road. The only reason for travellers to pass through is as a convenient refuelling stop (both petrol and food) on the way to more exciting destinations. There are two main hubs in the town: the turn-off at the junction, which has a petrol station, a couple of shops

and a few basic restaurants; and the town centre, 3km north of the Great North Road, which has a bank, a market, a bus station and a couple of places to stay.

Sleeping & Eating

Mapontela Inn (☎ 382026; r US$65) This charming guesthouse is hidden from the heat of the street behind a green and brick façade, and its courtyard provides welcome respite, with a touch of greenery and a chilled-out bar. Opening out onto the courtyard are a number of bright, homely rooms with fans and spotless bathrooms, and there's also a good restaurant attached. It's the best place to stay in town.

Government Resthouse (d with shared bathroom ZK45,000) By government resthouse standards this isn't too bad if you're looking for dirt-cheap but reasonably clean rooms in a central location. It's on the right-hand side as you enter the town centre.

Mapontela Restaurant (☎ 382026) Plates of grilled meat, nshima, chips, sandwiches and breakfasts are available here, all served on a patio overlooking the street, with plenty of umbrellas for shade.

Siga Siga Resthouse (☎ 382362; d with shared bathroom ZK50,000) This is a useful option if you're travelling by public transport as it's right by the junction with the Great North Road. Rooms here are pretty basic and share acceptable bathrooms but on the plus side there are a couple of OK places to eat nearby.

For other eats there are a few cheap supermarkets and cafes in the town centre as well as at the junction with the Great North Road, including the interestingly named Human Filling Station, where you can pick up cheap samosas, pastries and other snacks. Near the Siga Siga Resthouse is the Siga Siga Restaurant, serving basic plates of nshima and beans or meat, and the Siga Siga Supermarket operates as a bar (with pool table) as well as a store.

Getting There & Away

All buses between Lusaka (ZK60,000, five hours) and Kasama (ZK90,000, four to five hours) pass through Serenje. Most of the big buses stop beside the petrol station at the junction with the Great North Road, while minibuses stop at the station in town. You can buy tickets for Juldan Motors and CV

Transport at the Siga Siga Supermarket. The Tazara train (p199) also stops at the Serenje train station, 3km north of the town centre.

KASANKA NATIONAL PARK

☎ 0214

One of Zambia's least known wilderness areas and a real highlight of a visit to this part of the country is the privately managed **Kasanka National Park** (www.kasanka.com; admission US$10; ☺ 6am-6pm). At only 390 sq km, it's pretty small compared with most African parks, doesn't have many facilities and sees very few visitors, and this is what makes it special. There are no queues of jeeps to get a look at a leopard here – instead you'll discover great tracts of miombo woodland, evergreen thicket, open grassland and rivers fringed with emerald forest, all by yourself.

Kasanka is perhaps most famous for its swampland though – as it's here that you'll see the park's shy and retiring star – the sitatunga, a semi-aquatic antelope distinguished by its long splayed hooves and oily coat. Other common antelope species include bushbuck, duiker, reedbuck and puku. Between July and October you'll most likely see sable antelopes and hartebeests, and may also be treated to a glimpse of a roan antelope. Hippos and crocodiles inhabit the lakes and rivers here and there's a small population of elephants, though these aren't often seen. Night time brings out jackals, civets and porcupines, and during the months of November and December, this park is home to five *million* migratory fruit bats – the biggest such gathering anywhere in the world – which can blanket the sky for several minutes at dusk. Bird spotters will also love Kasanka. There are over 412 species here, including the wattled crane, African fish eagle and Ross's lourie.

Kasanka is a privately managed national park, run by the Kasanka Trust. Revenue is reinvested in the park, and the trust is also involved in conservation and local community projects.

Sights & Activities

A trip to Kasanka isn't complete without viewing the park from the heights of the **Fibwe Hide**, a 15-minute drive from Wasa Lodge (right). It's not for those with a fear of heights, though. You climb 20m up an old mahogany tree via a rickety wooden ladder, and lo and behold there's a platform where you can sit and watch the swamps below. Come at dawn and dusk for the best chance of spotting sitatungas. It's also a good spot for birdwatching, or, in season, for watching the hordes of fruit bats heading off from the nearby trees to feed.

Game drives can be arranged at the main lodge for wildlife viewing in comfort. Drives cost US$15 per person (minimum two people). They also arrange walking safaris, anything from a one-hour jaunt near the camp, to a five-day extravaganza with an armed ranger, camping out in the bush. There are plans to introduce mountain-bike hire and organised cycling safaris in the near future.

Finally, gliding along the Luwombwa River in a canoe or a motorboat surrounded by bustling forest on either side is a wonderful way to get a different spin on the park, and see crocodiles, otters and even the rare blue monkey. Fishing on the river can also be arranged and, if you make a decent catch, the guys at the lodge can cook it for you.

Just inside the camp is a **conservation centre** that it is worth passing through on the way in or out of Kasanka. It is mostly used as an educational centre for local children, and also runs re-education programmes for poachers, but there's a small museum that's open to all and is particularly interesting for kids. There's a display of animal skulls, information on the birds and bats of Kasanka, interactive wildlife Q&As and there are weighing and measuring stations where you can compare your height and bulk to that of the park's larger beasts. There's no fee to enter the centre, but donations are appreciated.

The Kasanka team also runs excellent tours of northern Zambia, using vehicles or planes, linking the park with visits to the Bangweulu Wetlands, Shiwa Ng'andu and North Luangwa National Park. This is well worth considering if you want to cover this area in a limited period; rates depend on group size, duration and interests.

Sleeping

Wasa Lodge (☎ 873 76 2067957; www.kasanka.com self-catering chalets per person US$50; full board incl all activities per person US$360) This doubles as the park headquarters. Accommodation consists of thatched bungalows in two sizes. The smaller ones are a little poky with no outside space and shared facilities. Larger chalets are airy and cool with wide balconies and lovely stone showers. The real advantage of a stay here is the setting. The lodge overlooks Lake Wasa and you can look out over the swamp and spot hippos and puku and sometimes even sitatungas. There are several vantage points for this, including stone benches lining the edge of the lake, a small hide up in the trees and the deck of the large bar and dining area. If you don't want the full-board option you bring your own supplies and the camp staff will cook for you.

Luwombwa Lodge (☎ 873 76 2067957; www kasanka.com; self-catering chalets per person US$50; full board incl all activities per person US$360) This lodge is on the western side of the park and is popular for fishing, as it sits on the banks of the Luwombwa River. Like at Wasa Lodge, there's a choice between smaller and older chalets with shared facilities or larger family-style affairs with more space and balconies with a view. Luwombwa is more likely to be closed during the wet season.

Conservation Centre (campsite per person US$10, r per person US$30) Just inside the park is a small conservation centre with a campsite as well as basic twin rooms in thatched chalets. There's a shared bathroom for every pair of rooms. School groups often book these out, but if they're empty then visitors are most welcome to stay. It's convenient but lacks the atmosphere or the views of the other places inside the park.

There are three basic campsites in Kasanka, where you'll be surrounded by the noise of animals, the stars and little else. The **Pontoon Campsite** (per person US$10) and the **Kabwe Campsite** (per person US$10) both look out over the Kasanka River, and the **Fibwe Campsite** (per person US$10) is a short walk from the Fibwe Hide. All are around 10–12km from the main Wasa Lodge and all come equipped with long-drop toilets and bucket showers (staff will prepare hot water for you if you let them know in advance). Kabwe is the smallest site, sleeping only six.

Getting There & Away

From Lusaka, take a bus in the direction of Mansa, or take any bus from Lusaka to Serenje and change onto a minibus for Mansa. After turning off the Great North Road, ask the driver to drop you at Kasanka National Park (near Mulembo village), not at Kasanka village, which is much further away. The journey should cost you about ZK100,000 from Lusaka or ZK30,000 from Serenje. From the gate to Wasa Lodge is 12km; you can radio Wasa Lodge for a lift.

If you have your own vehicle, continue north along the Great North Road from Serenje for 36km, then turn left onto the road towards Mansa. It's then 55km on a good road to the Kasanka entrance gate – clearly signposted on your left. The guards at the gate will then direct you to Wasa Lodge where you must pay your entry and accommodation fees. There is no fuel available in the park so stock up at Serenje.

There are two airstrips in the park and charter flights are available through **Skytrails Charters** (☎ 216 245268; www.skytrailszambia.com), which is based there. For further information and prices contact the **Kasanka Trust** (www.kasanka.com).

AROUND KASANKA
☎ 0214

Drivers with 4WD and high clearance may like to take the 'back route' from Kasanka direct to the Great North Road, which winds past several attractions.

History buffs can go in search of the **David Livingstone Memorial** – a simple stone memorial topped with a cross – which honours the famous explorer's death here in 1873 while he was searching for the source of the Nile. The local villagers buried Livingstone's heart under a mupundu tree before his body was sent home to the mother country, and the memorial marks the spot, though the tree is no longer there. To get here, pass the Kasanka National Park gate and continue 11km to the Livingstone Memorial turn-off, which will be on your right. Take the first left, from where it's another 25km to the memorial.

This route also winds past beautiful little **Lake Waka-Waka**, with glassy, croc-free waters (though always check the situation locally before jumping in) encircled by miombo woodland. Accommodation is in the form of a small community **campsite** (per person US$5) with basic bucket showers, barbecues and long-drop toilets. Local villagers will collect clean water for you and prepare fires.

To get here, pass the Kasanka gates and take the turn-off to the Livingstone Memorial, but this time continue straight on for 35km, leaving the Livingstone Memorial road on your left.

In between Kasanka National Park and the Bangweulu Wetlands is the **Nakapalayo Tourism Project** (contact via Kasanka Trust; campsites incl village tour & entertainment per person US$20 huts incl village tour & entertainment per person US$40

WATERFALL COLLECTING

Northern Zambia is packed full of rivers and sweeping hills. Put these together and you get an incredible collection of waterfalls – you should try and visit at least a couple. There are about 20 falls scattered about these parts and keen collectors try to 'bag' them all in a large circuit. The following list, organised roughly clockwise, should help you decide which ones to go for. For more inspiration see *Waterfalls of Zambia* by François d'Elbee, a large-format book with evocative descriptions and a collection of stunning photos.

It has to be said that this is mainly a task for drivers, as nearly all the falls are off the main routes, away from public transport, but for backpackers, Chisimba and Kalambo waterfalls are reachable – fortunately, these are among the best.

Most waterfalls are protected as heritage sites or National Monuments, and even at the most remote locations a caretaker may appear from the bush to collect a fee (usually US$3) while you sign a visitors book. At some waterfalls, camping is permitted (US$10), although facilities are usually limited to a long-drop toilet.

Kundalila Falls

These are the most southerly falls, about 15km south of the Great North Road, between Serenje and Mpika. Here, the Lukusashi River tumbles about 60m, almost diagonally over steeply tilting rock strata, before rushing away down a narrow ravine. The name means 'cooing doves' in the local language, which could refer to the sound of the water, although when you scramble down the cliffs opposite for excellent views, the noise is much louder. There's a campsite here.

Ntumbachusi Falls

About 15km west of Kawambwa, between Mansa and Lake Mweru, Ntumbachusi is a small but very picturesque waterfall, with little cascades and pools upstream and down. You can camp here.

Lumangwe Falls

Often called 'mini Victoria Falls', Lumangwe does look like a smaller version of the famous Zambezi waterfalls. But it's not that miniature – in fact, it's a surprisingly large (30m high and 100m wide) curtain of water, broken into several separate streams by rocks and miniature islands at the lip of the falls. There's even a bit of mist and a patch of rainforest. Camping is possible.

Kabweluma Falls

About 8km downstream from Lumangwe – a beautiful walk – Kabweluma is actually three separate waterfalls. The highest is a small, perfectly formed horseshoe, and the lowest is a more gently angled cascade flowing over grass and moss-covered rocks. You can hear the falling water as you approach, but the thick vegetation hides the view until the last moment. The caretaker at Lumangwe will show you the way.

Kundabwika Falls

On the Kalungwishi River, about 40km downstream from Kabweluma Falls, Kundabwika Falls is reached from the (pretty bad) road between Mporokoso and Lake Mweru. The river flows through a gorge over two small falls, then plummets over the main waterfall, which is about 25m high, before thundering off down the gorge again.

Kalambo Falls

By far the highest falls in Zambia, and the second highest in Africa, Kalambo can be reached by road from Mbala or by boat from Mpulungu. For full details see Kalambo Falls later in this chapter (p111).

Chishimba Falls

Chishimba is a series of three waterfalls, shaped into a wide curtain of water pounding over rocks in a thickly wooded amphitheatre. Camping is permitted nearby and buses and minibuses run daily between Kasama and Mporokoso, passing close to the falls. For full details see p110.

huts incl village tour, entertainment & meals per person US$60), a community initiative that allows tourists to experience life in a real Zambian village. Visitors can camp, or stay in specially made huts with double beds and mosquito nets. Activities revolve around village life and include learning how to pound cassava, meeting local healers and bush walks where you're taught about traditional uses for plants and trees. Meals are local fare, eaten with the villagers. Day visits are also available for US$20 per person. To get here, continue just past Lake Waka-Waka, where the road will fork. Take the left-hand fork and continue for 35km to Chiundaponde, where you'll find the project.

BANGWEULU WETLANDS
☎ 0214

Some 50km to the north of Kasanka are the Bangweulu Wetlands – a watery wilderness of lakes, seasonally flooded grasslands, swamp and unspoilt miombo woodland. This rarely visited part of Zambia is the only place in Africa where you'll see major numbers of black lechwes (antelopes with long, curved antlers). There are estimated to be some 100,000 here – few places in the world contain such large antelope herds – and the endless sound of thousands of lechwe hooves clattering and splashing through the marshes could be one of your strongest memories of Zambia. The wetlands are also home to the swamp-dwelling sitatunga and many other antelope species, including oribi, tsesebe, bushbuck and reedbuck. Attracted by rich pickings, jackals are often seen and hyenas often heard at night, and, when the floodwaters have receded, herds of elephant and buffalo venture here.

Bangweulu is also known for its birds. Some 400 species have been noted, and a particular highlight for twitchers is the strange and rare shoebill stork – cruising silently through the papyrus and lilies in a dugout canoe searching for this elusive evolutionary misfit is a magical experience. Other birds found here include egrets, Denham's bustard, herons, ibis, storks and pelicans; and when the floodwaters are high, huge numbers of birds, including flamingos and geese, migrate here from elsewhere in Africa.

The best time to see the lechwe herds is June to July as the waters have begun receding, leaving vast plains of fresh green grass. September to November is great for general birdwatching, though you may not see shoebills at this time. The best time to see shoebills is when the water levels are still high but starting to recede – from March to April. After the waters have retreated you can still see shoebills on canoe trips up to around August.

The wetlands are surrounded by small villages living mainly by subsistence fishing and hunting. The running of the Game Management Area (GMA) was passed to the **African Parks Network** (www.african-parks.org) in 2008, though Shoebill Island Camp (see below) is still managed by the Kasanka Trust.

Sleeping

Nsobe Camp (www.kasanka.com; campsite per person US$10) This is a basic campsite with braai area, bucket showers, long-drop toilets and a couple of thatched cooking shelters.

Shoebill Island Camp (www.kasanka.com; self-catering chalets with shared bathroom per person US$50, chalets incl meals, transfers from the nearest airstrip & several activities per person US$360) This camp rests in the heart of the wetlands and is splendidly positioned on a tiny permanent island with only birds, hippos, lechwes and the occasional passing fishermen for company. Booking is essential, especially if you want meals and need to be taken to the camp by boat. Guests are put up in safari tents and reed cottages and there's a dining area and lookout point. Most activities revolve around dugout canoes, but drives are also on offer in the drier areas and in the surrounding woodlands. When there's not enough water for the canoes, you can take guided walks over the spongy floating reed beds. The camp aims to stay open year round but is sometimes not accessible in January and February.

Getting There & Away

The only way into the wetlands is by vehicle and chartered plane. Dirt roads lead here from Kasanka via Lake Waka-Waka and the Nakapalayo Tourism Project (opposite). The Chikuni ranger post and Nsobe Camp are 65km on from Nakapalayo, and from here it's another 10km to Shoebill Island

---

THE SHOEBILL STORK

One of the rarest birds in Africa, the shoebill stork (*Balaeniceps rex*) is found only in the Bangweulu Wetlands, in some parts of Uganda, and possibly in Sudan and Congo (Zaïre). This bird has a body pretty much like that of any other large stork (about 1m high), but its bill (or beak), as its name implies, is bizarrely shaped like a shoe – and a big shoe at that. In fact, it's more like a clog. Another name for this species is the whale-headed stork and that's even nearer the mark. Technically, it's not even a stork – its nearest relative is thought to be the pelican. Whatever, for ornithologists it's a big tick on the list. These weird birds can usually be seen perched high on palm trees or wading through the reeds searching for fish. They are extremely shy, and fly surprisingly well for such top-heavy giants, so seeking them out takes silence and patience.

Camp if it's dry. In the wet, you'll have to travel this last stretch by boat. You will definitely need a fully equipped 4WD to attempt this trip as the going is tough. Set off from Kasanka in the early morning in order to reach Bangweulu before it gets dark. The folks at Kasanka can provide you with a detailed information sheet about getting to the wetlands.

There is an airstrip 3km from Shoebill Island Camp and charters are available through Skytrails Charters, based at Kasanka National Park.

SAMFYA

☎ 0214

Perched on the western shore of Lake Bangweulu, about 10km east of the main road between Mansa and Serenje, is Samfya, a small and dusty trading centre with little going for it except for its excellent position on the western shores of beautiful Lake Bangweulu. The hub of transport on the lake, it has a couple of resthouses, restaurants and bars. In the local language bangweulu means 'where the water meets the sky' and if you watch the lake at sunset, when the lake and hazy clouds both turn the same shade of blue, it's not hard to see why. Just outside town is a long strip of blinding-white beach bathed by startling blue waters. Don't jump in here though unless you fancy being a crocodile's dinner.

Sleeping

Samfya Beach Hotel (campsite per person ZK40,000, s, d ZK120,000) Sits along Cabana Beach. This place has a pretty good location, but the rooms are poky with basic bathrooms and the food isn't much cop. If you have a tent you might be better off camping. To get here take the first turning on the left (it's

the turning before the port road) as you enter the town – it's about 2km north of the town centre.

Samfya Sun and Sand Resort (s/d ZK90,000/110,000) Just a short walk down the beach from the Samfya Beach Hotel, it has basic thatched huts on the beach, a restaurant and also camping.

Getting There & Away

Samfya is regularly served by minibuses from Serenje (ZK60,000, four to five hours). Buses from Lusaka (ZK95,000, nine to ten hours) may drop you in town or at the junction 10km away, from where local pick-ups shuttle passengers to and fro.

MUTINONDO WILDERNESS

☎ 0214

This is perhaps the most stunning place in northern Zambia: a beautiful 10,000-hectare wilderness littered with whaleback hills or *inselbergs* – huge, sweeping hulks of stone in varying shades of black, purple, green and brown. The landscape here feels unspoilt and somehow ancient. Scramble to the top of one of those great granite beasts (and they do look like they could be giant animals who've been asleep for so long they've sunk back into the earth) and you can easily imagine a time when Stone Age hunters wandered the endless valleys, woodland and rivers below.

You are unlikely to see many mammals on a stay here, though there are plenty of vervet monkeys, tree squirrels, klipspringers and other critters lurking around out of sight. Mutinondo is more viable as a birding destination and there are almost 300 species here including plenty of rare specimens that are difficult to find outside the country. Notable are the long-toed fluff tail and the bar-winged weaver. The lounge at the camp has a list of all the mammal and bird species recorded so far at Mutinondo.

Sights & Activities

Maps are available at the Mayense Camp lodge (see below) for the vast number of wilderness trails (over 60km of them) around the area. It's beautiful walking country and you could easily spend your time here just gently taking it in. If you can get a group as big as six together, then more formal guided hiking and camping experiences of several days are also available at around US$50 per person per day, including all food and equipment.

They have nine horses at Mutinondo (they are stabled at night but during the day you'll see them wandering around free as you like) and short rides of a couple of hours (ZK50,000 per hour) can be arranged, as can short sundowner rides.

The network of rivers and waterfalls at Mutinondo are incredibly clear and calm, safe to swim in (and to drink) and lazily swimming upstream and listening to the sounds of nature all around you is a wonderful way to spend a day. If you're not so keen on swimming you can also hire canoes (ZK40,000 for half a day).

During the mushroom-friendly rainy season (December to March), you could go in search of the largest edible mushroom in the world, and the area also contains newly found rock paintings and Iron Age workings.

Next to reception is a small shop selling jewellery designed and made by local people, as well as cards, books, paintings and photographs of Mutinondo.

Sleeping

our pick **Mayense Camp** (www.mutinodozambia.com; s/d per person incl meals & activities from ZK350,000/420,000) It's tough to design accommodation that fits in with the splendour of this setting but the folks at Mayense have managed it. Built into the hillside are a handful of individually designed chalets, which, while not fancy, are beautiful in their simplicity and blend in seamlessly with their natural environment (including one built into the granite rocks, with a huge handmade bath with a view). They are far enough apart from each other to give a real sense of privacy and all have outstanding views. The majority are open to the elements so it feels as if you're sleeping out in the middle of the wild.

Mayense campsite (campsite per person ZK40,000, s/d tent with bedding ZK150,000/180,000) This is a fantastic campsite, they've really thought about making a user-friendly and fun spot to pitch your tent. Each camping spot has cooking areas and raven-proof cupboards to protect your stuff. The large, open-air showers (constructed out of sustainable materials, of course) have plenty of changing and clothes hanging space (and hot water). The sinks have framed pieces of information to read while you brush your teeth, and the eco-toilets have magazines to browse and strategically placed viewing slots, so you can look out into the bush while you pee.

Kankonde (campsite per person ZK50,000, chalets per person ZK70,000) Around 10km from the main camp, this basic bush campsite sits alongside the Mutinondo River. It's a beautiful spot but you'll have to be fully self-sufficient, though there is a caretaker to help you out should you need him. The friendly and energetic owners are keen to protect the environment and the camp uses a number of alternative sources of energy such as solar panels, a wind generator and sun stoves. The food here uses as much locally sourced produce as possible and campers can arrange to have meals at the main Mayense Camp (breakfast ZK55,000, packed lunch ZK30,000, three-course dinner ZK90,000).

Getting There & Away

The turn-off to Mutinondo is 164km past Serenje heading north on the Great North Road. It's signposted to the right; Mutinondo is 25km down a 2WD-friendly track.

Road transfers for a maximum of five people can be arranged from Mpika (US$100) or Lusaka (US$500). If you'd like to charter a plane there's also an airstrip.

MPIKA

☎ 0214

Mpika is a busy crossroads just east of the Great North Road. Like many of the other towns along this stretch, there's not a great deal to distinguish it and the only reason travellers end up here is to change money or stock up on supplies. There are two petrol stations just outside of town on the Great North Road itself, including a BP station with a Barclays Bank ATM, plus several well-stocked shops and a large market in the town centre. If you want to change money there's a Zambia National Commercial Bank and a Finance Bank.

Sleeping & Eating

Musakanya Resthouse (r with/without bathroom ZK30,000/25,000) You can't miss this bright green and pink place. It has basic rooms, including a couple of self-catering units that are run-down but clean. There are mosquito nets in the rooms but no fans.

Melodies Lodge (☎ 097 6381135; r with/without bathroom ZK60,000/45,000) Simple, clean rooms with fan are decent value for the price, grouped around a large gravel courtyard. There's no hot water on tap but they will prepare it for you. There's a small restaurant with meals from ZK18,000.

CIMS Restaurant (☎ 370058; ☺ 24 hr) Just outside of town opposite Melodies Lodge is this large restaurant and cafe. Order at the counter for decent meals of *nshima*, chips and rice with pork, beef or chicken. If you're feeling adventurous you can also sample fried caterpillars. There's a cake stall in the corner selling cupcakes, bread and fresh juice as well as ice cream.

Getting There & Away

Buses and minibuses stop at the junction where the Kasama road and the Great North Road divide. Destinations include Lusaka (ZK100,000, eight hours) and Kasama (ZK60,000, two hours).

Mpika's Tazara train station is about 7km southwest of the town centre, and reachable by minibus when trains are due.

The Power Tools Coach has a daily service to Nakonde (ZK90,000, five to six hours) from outside CIMS Restaurant.

AROUND MPIKA

Keen fans of pre-colonial art may want to see the rock paintings at **Nachikufu Cave** (admission per person US$3; per car US$3; campsite per person US$10; ☺ daily), a heritage site signposted 2km west of the Great North Road, 56km south of Mpika and 180km north of Serenje. The paintings here were discovered in 1948 and are estimated to be up to 15,000 years old. Sadly most of the paintings are worn away or have been defaced. Inside, the

black silhouette paintings are badly defaced and faded – only one figure (an elephant) is discernible. Above the main cave a smaller rock shelter contains a red geometric design, but again it's rather faded. The top cave has no paintings at all, but does have nice views. The caretaker who lives nearby, will unlock the gate to the main cave. You can camp near the caves but facilities are limited to a long-drop toilet.

At **Nsalu Cave** (admission per person US$3, per car US$3; campsite per person US$10; ☺ daily) are much older paintings – thought to be at least 20,000 years old. Instead of the stick figures and animals usually associated with Bushmen's paintings there are abstract patterns, lines and outlines. As with the paintings at Nachikufu, these paintings have been vandalised and neglected in the past, but Zambia's Heritage Department is involved in the cave's protection and things have improved somewhat with many of the paintings now visible. The cave is signposted on the stretch of the Great North Road between Serenje and Mpika, about 60km north of Serenje. After the turn-off it's another 20km to the cave.

SHIWA NG'ANDU
☎ 0214

Deep in the northern Zambian wilderness sits **Shiwa Ng'andu** (www.shiwangandu.com), a grand country estate and labour of love of eccentric British aristocrat Sir Stewart Gore-Brown. The estate's crowning glory is **Shiwa Ng'andu manor house**, a glorious brick mansion. Driving up to the house through farm buildings, settlements and workers' houses it almost feels like an old feudal domain – there's a whole community built around it, including a school and a hospital, and many of the people now working at Shiwa Ng'andu are the children and grandchildren of Sir Stewart's original staff. Today Gore-Brown's grandchildren live on and manage the estate, which is a working farm.

Sights & Activities

Shiwa House itself is the main draw here and visitors can go on guided **tours** (US$20; ☺ 9-11am Mon-Sat, 10-11am Sun). The great house is full of old family heirlooms, photographs and stories, and standing out on the perfectly manicured lawns in front of it you could almost forget that you're in Southern Africa and imagine instead that you're at a 1920s garden party on an English summer's day.

Guided tours of the estate, in a car or on foot, are also possible (though you are also free to wander) and on the estate are puku, kudu, zebra and wildebeest, among others. Shiwa is also an important birdwatching area with over 370 species recorded here. You could see long-toed fluff tails or palm-nut vultures, and, by the lake, pygmy geese, herons and kingfishers.

Kapishya Hot Springs is about 20km west of Shiwa House, but still on the Shiwa Ng'andu estate. The setting is marvellous – a blue-green steaming lagoon of bath-hot water, surrounded by thick palms. If staying at Kapishya Lodge (right), then you can use the springs for free; otherwise the cost for day visitors is US$5. From the lodge, **walking**, **fishing** and **canoeing** trips are also offered, as well as trips to Buffalo Camp in North Luangwa National Park (p129).

Sleeping

Kapishya Lodge (☎ 0211 229261; www.shiwasafaris .com; campsite per person US$10, self-catering chalets per person US$90, dinner, bed & breakfast per person US$130, full board meals & activities per person US$175) This is a beautiful spot. The chalets are light and spacious, with wide wooden decks complete with fireplaces and views down over the river and the gardens. Bring your own food for the staff to prepare, or meals (and very good ones at that) can be provided with enough notice. There's a good campsite here with free firewood, hot showers and barbecue areas. For self-caterers and campers, meals

THE SHIWA STORY

In 1914, a young British colonial officer called Stewart Gore-Brown was helping establish the border between Rhodesia and the Belgian Congo, when he stumbled across a lake that the local Bemba people called Shiwa Ng'andu – the place of the royal crocodiles. For years he'd harboured dreams of his own kingdom in Africa, and with characteristic verve he decided Shiwa Ng'andu was the ideal spot, swiftly buying about 10,000 hectares from the local chief and returning to the spot after the end of WWI to build his little piece of England in the bush.

The heart of the estate was the great mansion of Shiwa House, made from materials found locally, or transported on foot by porters from the nearest town of Ndola – an eye-watering 110km and three weeks' walk away. Items such as chairs and tables were made locally in an antique style, but essentials such as grand pianos and fine wines were shipped from London. The house sat overlooking the lake, complete with manicured lawns and servants clad in white gloves and pillbox hats. Around the house grew an estate, which included workers' houses for his 2000 employees, schools and a post office.

All of this upkeep was expensive and Gore-Brown tried many money-making schemes including growing flowers from which to extract and export oils for perfume, but none succeeded, and Shiwa was constantly bankrolled by his wealthy aunt in Britain.

Gore-Brown was a stickler for discipline in his attempts to create a utopian fiefdom, and his violent temper was legendary. Beatings measured out on hapless workers earned him the nickname Chipembere (Rhinoceros). But unusually for the time, he believed in African independence. Gore-Brown became a well-known figure in Northern Rhodesia and in Britain. He was knighted by George VI and was close friends with early nationalists including Kenneth Kaunda, Zambia's first president. When he died in 1967 he was, unusually for a foreigner, given a full state funeral and is buried on the hill overlooking the lake at Shiwa.

Through the 1980s, Gore-Brown's daughter and son-in-law continued struggling to run the estate, and were actively involved in the campaign against poachers, especially in nearby North Luangwa National Park. In 1992 they were mysteriously murdered; it's assumed because they knew too much about senior government figures connected to the illicit ivory trade. Shiwa House stood empty for several years, and rapidly disintegrated, but in 2001 Gore-Brown's grandsons began a major renovation and opened the house to visitors again.

Stewart Gore-Brown's story is described (or perhaps romanticised) in *The Africa House* by Christina Lamb (p22).

are also available (full breakfast ZK75,000, packed lunch ZK45,000, three-course dinner ZK100,000).

Shiwa House (bookings through Kapishya Lodge; full board from US$350) This old place is suitably attired for a grand old English manor, with fireplaces, four-poster beds, oil paintings and big old roll-top baths. There's also a glorious guest sitting room looking out onto the front lawn, which is even more atmospheric at night when lit by candles and a crackling fire. Tasty dinners are taken in the rather splendid dining room. The hosts (the grandchildren of Sir Stewart Gore-Brown) are happy to chat and to give you personal tours of the house. If you're staying here you could even browse the Gore-Brown archives – a fascinating collection of Sir Stewart's journals, letters and old photographs.

Getting There & Away

To reach Shiwa House, head along the highway by bus (or car) from Mpika for about 90km towards Chisoso. Look for the signpost to the west, from where a 13km dirt road leads to the house. Kapishya Hot Springs and the lodge are a further 20km along this track. You can also get to Shiwa from the Mpika to Kasama road – this time look for the signpost pointing east and it's then 30km down the dirt track to Kapishya. There is no public transport along this last section but vehicle transfers are available from the Great North Road turn-off for US$40 per vehicle (maximum four people). Transfers can also be arranged from Mpika (US$300 per vehicle) or from Kasama (US$400 per vehicle). Transfers are also available between Kapishya and Shiwa House for US$30 per vehicle.

KASAMA

☎ 0214

Kasama is the capital of the Northern Province and the cultural centre of the Bemba people. With its wide, leafy streets and handsome, old, tin-roofed colonial houses, it is the most appealing of the northern towns. There's a laid-back, friendly feeling here, a number of good guesthouses, decent shops and good bus connections. While there's not much for tourists to do in the town itself, Kasama's surroundings are home to ancient rock paintings and a beautiful waterfall.

Information

There are Zambia National Commercia Finance, and Barclays Banks with ATMs i town as well as an internet cafe (per min ZK1C ✆ 8am-5pm Mon-Fri, 8am-noon Sat) on Luwing Rd. **Thorn Tree Safaris** (www.thorntreesafaris.cor based at Thorn Tree Guesthouse organise tailor-made trips all around Zambia northern region.

Sleeping

J.B. Hotel (☎ 221452 or 0977 844149; Golf Rd; s with bathroom ZK120,000/140,000, s/d without bathroo ZK50,000/55,000) A quality, friendly hotel rigl in the heart of town near the bus statio Rooms are spic and span with nets and ver clean, well-kept shared bathrooms. Room with bathrooms also have TVs and mir fridges. There's a veranda bar where yo can sit outside for a drink and look out a the pleasant courtyard garden.

Sahel Lodge (☎ 0977 815190; per person wit shared bathroom ZK50,000, s/d with bathroom per persc ZK75,000/95,000) Yes, the walls might be brigh orange and covered in brown squiggles bu considering the garden is overflowing wit stork statues it all seems to fit. Inside, th rooms are a much calmer shade (thoug they do share bright green, plant-strew verandas) and are cool and spacious wit fun touches like wardrobes made out c woven reeds. It's about 800m out of tow on the Luwingu Rd, in the direction c Chishimba Falls. Look for the signpost t the right.

Dauson Lodge (☎ 221440; s/d/ste ZK10,00 160,000/320,000) TVs, fridges and fans ar standard in this lodge's bland, clean room They are rather at odds with the incredibl chintzy lounge room that comes with gigantic TV, leather sofas, doilies and fau marble aplenty. Be warned that the (rathe corridor-like) suite shares a wall with th lounge TV so can get quite noisy. Meal like fish, spaghetti and T-bone steak are o offer from ZK20,000. It's just east of tow off the Luwingu Rd. Look for the signpos on the left.

Kasama Lodge (☎ 04 221039; fax 222825; Zamb Rd; s/d/ste from ZK130,000/220,000/400,000) Opposit the Thorn Tree Guesthouse, this join is run by Zambia's Hostels Board c Management. It's pretty comfortable, an rooms are spacious with fridges and free te and coffee, but at the time of research th bathrooms were already looking a bit rough even though it was only a year or so old. There's a quiet restaurant here that charges ZK25,000 for a full breakfast, or you can order pizzas (order well in advance) for ZK15,000. A three-course dinner costs ZK60,000.

Thorn Tree Guesthouse (☎ 221615 or 096 951149; www.thorntreesafaris.com; 612 Zambia Rd; r per person from US$30) The Thorn Tree is family run, homely and very popular – you should definitely book before turning up. Rooms are either in the main house sharing spic and span facilities or in their gardens there are traditionally made huts with bathrooms. There's a bar and a restaurant serving fresh farm produce. As you reach Kasama from Lusaka, turn left at the first crossroads, keep right at the forks and continue past the Heritage Centre for 1km. They also run a safari company specialising in tours of the little visited northern region.

Also recommended is **Kalambo Guest House** (☎ 222221; Luwingu Rd; s/d from ZK50,000/60,000) on the town's main drag. The welcome is warm and there are spotless rooms, a TV lounge and a restaurant.

Eating

Kasama will be a welcome change to people who've been travelling in the north for a while. There's a large Shoprite here with everything a self-caterer could ask for, as well as a very good market. There are plenty of cheap cafes on Luwingu Rd, and the J.B. Hotel has a good restaurant at the back which serves local dishes such as *nshima* and chicken as well as more exotic dishes like sea bream curry and chicken schnitzel (meals from ZK25,000).

Getting There & Away

Buses and minibuses leave for Lusaka daily. CV Transport departs for Lusaka (ZK120,000, ten hours) at 3.30pm from its stop opposite the main bus station on Golf Rd, via Mpika (ZK60,000, two hours), Serenje (ZK90,000, four hours) and Mkushi (ZK110,000, six hours). Northbound buses go to Mbala (ZK40,000, two hours) and Mpulungu (ZK50,000, three hours). Minibuses run on a fill-up-and-go basis to a variety of destinations including Mpulungu, Mbala and Mpika.

THE ROCK PAINTINGS OF KASAMA

Archaeologists rate the **Kasama rock paintings** (admission adult/child US$3/2, campsite per person US$10) as one of the largest and most significant collections of ancient art in Southern Africa, although it has to be said that in terms of quality, pictures found in Zimbabwe or Namibia are easier for casual visitors to appreciate. But if you've got an interest in Zambia's creative heritage, a visit is highly recommended.

The paintings are attributed to Stone Age hunter-gatherers (sometimes known as Twa) and are up to 2000 years old. Many are abstract designs but some of the finest pictographs show human figures and animals – often capturing a remarkable sense of fluidity and movement, despite being stylised with huge bodies and minute limbs.

The paintings (about 700 in all) are in caves and overhangs spread over a very wide area of bush about 7km east of Kasama, on the road towards Isoka. The most famous site is called Sumina, and here you scramble up a steep path and squeeze between boulders to reach a well-preserved picture of a hunter chasing a lion and a buffalo. At the Mwela site, the pictures are mainly geometric patterns: spirals, circles, 'ladders' and rows of dots, although one picture shows an antelope and four figures, supposedly in a trance. The Mwankole site has a mix of designs, including a group of dancing people, plus the famous – and remarkably lifelike – penis image. Other patterns have been likened to female genitalia, leading archaeologists to propose that these paintings were connected to fertility rites, while the dots and stipple may symbolise hope for good rains.

If you don't have a vehicle, the easiest way to reach the paintings area is by taxi (ZK30,000 each way, plus waiting time). About 4.5km from Kasama is a signpost for 'Mwela Rocks National Monument'. Here there's a kiosk where you pay the caretakers the entry fee. One of them will then take you round as many or as few of the paintings as you like. For further information, there's a small information panel at the kiosk telling the story of the paintings.

The Postbus departs from outside the post office on Luwingu Rd. On Tuesday, Thursday and Saturday it leaves at 6am for Lusaka (ZK110,000) via Mpika (ZK60,000) and Serenje (ZK80,000). On Wednesday, Friday and Sunday the bus heads for Ndola (ZK100,000, ten hours), also leaving at 6am. You can buy tickets in advance inside the post office.

The Tazara train station is 6km south of the town centre. The express train to Nakonde (for the Tanzanian and Malawian border) and Dar Es Salaam leaves in the small hours of Wednesday and Saturday mornings. The 1st-class fare to Dar Es Salaam is about ZK120,000 and to Nakonde ZK60,000.

AROUND KASAMA
☎ 0214

About 35km west of Kasama are the stunning **Chishimba Falls** (adult/child US$2/3, campsite per person US$10) – a series of three waterfalls, two natural and one formed by a small hydro-electric power station. The main falls are the furthest from the entrance and are an impressive torrent of water tumbling into a deep canyon, thought to be inhabited by spirits. There are walkways and thatched picnic spots all around the site as well as a campsite near the entrance. The only facilities at the time of research were two long-drop toilets but they are improving facilities and building a reception area and gift shop. To get here, take the Luwingu Rd west of Kasama. After 25km there is a gravel road to the right heading to Mporokoso. The falls are signposted 10km down this track. If you don't have a car you could find a minibus headed for Mporokoso and ask to be dropped at the turn-off to the falls, where it's about a 1km walk to the falls car park.

Keen historians should stop at the bridge over the **Chambeshi River**, about 80km south of Kasama, and walk a few hundred metres to the painted WWI field gun commemorating the spot where the German forces of General Von Lettow-Vorbek surrendered at the end of the war. The caretaker lives near the bridge and will show you the way; there's no charge but a small tip is appreciated. In a more recent conflict, the old bridge just downstream was destroyed by Southern Rhodesian commandos in the 1970s.

MBALA
☎ 0214

This sleepy town sits on the periphery of the Great Rift Valley, from where the road drops over 1000m down to Lake Tanganyika. It was once a colonial centre called Abercorn and a few relics from this time remain. Today the only reason to visit is the Moto Moto Museum, or as a stop-off point for Kalambo Falls. Other than that the town is pretty gloomy and lacks any decent places to stay. Practicality-wise, there's a Barclays Bank ATM, a post office, a fuel station and a couple of small supermarkets.

Sights & Activities

Moto Moto Museum (admission US$3; ☺ 9am-4.45pm daily except Christmas & New Year's Day) This museum is well worth a visit if you're in the area. It's a large and diverse collection, much of which details the cultural life and history of the Bemba people. You pay your entry fee at the small gift shop and then walk through a very pleasant courtyard garden (and a small room containing lots of jars of pickled snakes and other reptiles!) to get to the main event. Items on display here include old Bemba drums, traditional musical instruments and an array of smoking paraphernalia. Particularly noteworthy is an exhibition detailing how young Bemba women were traditionally initiated into adulthood. It includes a life-size, walk-in example of an initiation hut, and small articles on the wall explain the initiation process. (There's a particularly interesting extract from an old problem page entitled, 'My betrothed is just eight – do I leave her?')

The only problem is that it's quite dark so exhibits are not displayed at their best and some are without sufficient explanation. Better set out is the new gallery opposite the gift shop/reception. It covers everything from the lives of hunter-gatherers to the early economic activities of the Bantu, and Zambia during the slave trade. There's also a display on rock art, including a map pointing out the country's key sights.

The gift shop sells baskets, sculptures and masks, as well as a surprisingly large number of hoes and spades (which you'll have less use for). To get here, follow the road north out of town for about 500m and turn left just before the prison. The museum is about 3km from the main road.

Sleeping

Arms Hotel (r with shared/private bathroom ZK25,000/30,000) Although conveniently located right on the main street, there's not a great deal else to recommend this place. The rooms are very basic and there's a loud bar that appears to be open all hours. Ask to see a couple of rooms – some of them don't have mosquito nets.

Grasshopper Inn (☎ 0977 504580; r with/without bathroom ZK40,000/30,000, campsites ZK50,000) The inn is set in large grounds about 750m off the main street. Rooms here are in serious need of an upgrade – they are run-down and scruffy. There's a small restaurant onsite and a big, loud bar, which could prove to be an irritation. They will let you camp on the grounds but they'll charge you even more than the full room price (because they also give you a key to a room so you can have use of a bathroom).

Makungo Guest House (s/d with bathroom K40,000/45,000) This is the best place to stay in town. Rooms are clean and good value and are centred on a courtyard that also doubles as a minibus garage. The guesthouse is about 100m off the main road; take the turning opposite the fuel station. Note that this is different to the Makungo Rest House on the main street, which is not recommended.

Getting There & Away

Minibuses owned by the Makungo Guest House run a couple of times a day to Kasama (ZK35,000, two hours) and Mpulungu (ZK15,000, fifty minutes), leaving from the main street. CV Transport buses leave at 1pm daily to a number of destinations including Lusaka (ZK130,000, twelve hours), Mpika (ZK70,000, four to five hours) and Kasama (ZK40,000, two hours). Juldan Motors, on the opposite side of the street next to Makungo Rest House, has a similar service, also departing at 1pm. They also have a daily 6pm service to Mpulungu (ZK10,000, one hour).

KALAMBO FALLS
☎ 0214

About 40km northwest of Mbala on a good tarmac road, and along the border between Zambia and Tanzania, is the 221m-high **Kalambo Falls** (admission adult/child US$3/2, per car US$3, campsites US$10). Twice as high (but nowhere near as expansive) as Victoria Falls, Kalambo is the second-highest single-drop waterfall in Africa (the highest being Tugela Falls in South Africa). From spectacular viewpoints near the top of the falls, you can see the Kalambo River plummeting off a steep V-shaped cliff cut into the Rift Valley escarpment down into a deep valley, which then winds towards Lake Tanganyika. There is a campsite here, with stunning views out over the Great Rift Valley. Facilities are basic (there's only a long-drop toilet) but there is a caretaker.

The best way for travellers without a car to get here is from Mpulungu. A thrice-weekly taxi boat service (open wooden craft built for about 20 people, often carrying more, that serve villages along the lake shore) stops at villages east of Mpulungu. It moves quite slowly and makes plenty of stops so just getting to the base of the

---

LAKE TANGANYIKA

Spreading over a massive 34,000 sq km, and reaching 4700ft deep, cavernous Lake Tanganyika is the second-deepest lake in the world, and is thought to be up to 15 million years old. Lying in the Great Rift Valley, the shores of the lake reach Tanzania, Burundi, the Democratic Republic of the Congo and Zambia. The climate here is always very hot – especially at the end of the dry season. This makes a swim very tempting, but there are a few crocodiles and hippos around, as well as the poisonous Tanganyika water cobra, so take advice locally before plunging in.

Other notable inhabitants of Lake Tanganyika are the many species of colourful cichlid fish, which specialist operators catch and breed for export to aquariums all over the world. There are over 350 species here, most of which are endemic and many are similar to those found in Lake Malawi. Snorkelling and diving can be good here because of the plentiful brightly coloured fish – for professional scuba equipment and lessons contact Ndole Bay Lodge (p113).

Fishing is also popular on the lake, especially around Nsumbu National Park, which is well known for its excellent angling. The best time of year to get a good catch is November to March.

NORTHERN ZAMBIA

falls can take all day – you don't want to risk arriving in the dark as it's two to three hours walking uphill to the viewpoint near the top of Kalambo Falls (and the campsite). It's also possible to hire a private boat from Mpulungu harbour, which will cost around ZK300,000 a day including fuel. Ask around at the market near the lake in Mpulungu.

Another alternative would be to stay in one of the lakeshore lodges near the falls, from where you could hike to the falls or visit on an organised boat trip. Charity, the manager at Nkupi Lodge in Mpulungu, can also help you out with boats to the falls.

MPULUNGU
☎ 0214

Resting at the foot of mighty Lake Tanganyika, Mpulungu is a crossroads between Eastern, Central and Southern Africa. As Zambia's only international port, it's the terminal for the ferry across the lake to Tanzania. It's also a busy commercial fishing port and several fisheries are based here (some of them export tropical fish to aquariums around the world). The streets are fairly lively and busy, especially at night, and if you are arriving (or planning to leave) on the ferry to Tanzania or are on your way to one of the lakeshore lodges then Mpulungu makes an OK stopover for the night, but don't make a special trip here. Although it's always very hot, don't be tempted to swim in the lake in this area because there are a few crocs.

Sights & Activities

Worth a look is the **Niamkolo Church**, a five-minute walk up the hill from Nkupi Lodge. It's an old stone ruin that you can walk inside and around. It was built in 1895–96 by the London Missionary Society, who had arrived in the town some ten years earlier to establish a mission. It was abandoned in 1908 when the missionaries all got sleeping sickness and moved away from the lakeshore.

Sleeping

Nkupi Lodge (☎ 455166; campsite per person ZK40,000, chalets from ZK80,000) By far the best place for independent travellers, this shady campsite and lodge is a short walk out of town and has plenty of soft, grassy earth for erecting tents as well as a number of rondavels,

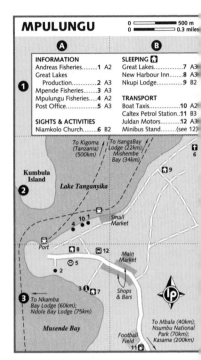

including a huge place with fresh ston floors, its own bathroom and a large comf bed. Showers and toilets are spotless an there's plenty of hot water. There's also self-catering kitchen and a bar (food can b prepared if they're given plenty of notice and the very friendly manager can arrang onward transport to Tanzania or help out you want to see the falls.

New Harbour Inn (☎ 0978 571331; r from ZK80,00 This is a simple, friendly place just a shor walk from the centre of town. The room of this small inn are in little cottages in th grounds. They are large, clean and simpl with separate sitting areas, large fans, DST and huge tiger-face rugs. There is a smal restaurant too.

Great Lakes (☎ 0977 173874; chalets ZK150,00 Sharing large grounds with Great Lake Products are a few large thatched rondave which are spacious and comfortable if little sparse. You get a view of the lak from here but unfortunately you can walk down to it because the area aroun the lodge is fenced off, and the rondavel don't have outside space so there's no really anywhere to sit and enjoy the view. There's a decent restaurant here, though breakfast ZK10,000, lunch ZK17,500, dinner ZK17,500).

Getting There & Away

Most buses/minibuses connect with the Lake Tanganyika ferry. To/from Lusaka, Juldan Motors departs at noon daily (ZK130,000, thirteen hours) via Kasama (ZK50,000, three hours) and Mbala (ZK10,000, one hour). Minibuses also depart from near the BP petrol station in Mpulungu for Mbala (ZK15,000, fifty minutes). The drive can be a bit bumpy as the road between Mbala and Mpulungu is very potholed.

AROUND MPULUNGU
☎ 0214

Along Lake Tanganyika are a couple of lodges that can only be reached by boat. All of them can arrange to pick you up from Mpulungu harbour.

For a beautiful lodge try **Isanga Bay Lodge** (☎ 096 646991/992; www.isangabay.com; campsite per person US$15, full-board chalets per person US$150). It's the perfect place to make like Robinson Crusoe for a few days. There are breezy thatched and wood chalets right on the beach, with small terraces and fabulous views of the lake, as well as smaller stone rondavels in the gardens. Food is good and includes lots of fish pulled freshly from the lake. For the active there's beach volleyball, snorkelling, fishing and kayaking, and trips can be arranged to Kalambo Falls (per person ZK60,000). Road access was not possible at the time of research, though the road was being upgraded. Transfers can be arranged from Mpulungu (if you've a car you can park it at Mpende Fisheries) for ZK380,000 per round trip. It's a 30-minute boat ride.

Another beachside option is **Mishembe Bay** (☎ contact via Thorn Tree Safaris 0214 221615; www.thorntreesafaris.com; full board per person US$150). Run by Luke Powell, the son of Ewart and Hazel Powell, who run Thorn Tree Safaris in Kasama, this rustic lodge also goes by the name of Luke's Beach. You can stay in a little stone hut up in the hills or in en suite reed chalets set on wooden platforms overlooking the bay. The price includes tasty meals baked in their bush oven, and a hefty three courses are dished up in the evenings. On the activities side of things,

---

> **GETTING TO TANZANIA**
>
> The MV *Liemba*, a hulking ex-German warship, leaves from Mpulungu harbour every Friday, arriving in Kigoma, Tanzania, on Sunday. Fares for 1st, 2nd and economy class are US$60, US$45 and US$35, respectively. Visas can be issued on the ferry and cost US$50 single entry.

Kalambo Falls is only an hour's hike away and you can snorkel in front of the lodge. Transfers (ZK500,000 return) are available from Mpulungu, which is a half-hour boat ride away.

NSUMBU NATIONAL PARK
☎ 0214

Hugging the southern shores of Lake Tanganyika, little visited **Nsumbu** (admission US$10; ☷ 6am-6pm) is a beautiful 2020 sq km of hilly grassland and escarpment, interrupted by rivers and wetlands. Like other remote parks in Zambia, Nsumbu was virtually abandoned in the 1980s and 1990s and poaching seriously affected wildlife stocks here. Conditions have improved over the past decade, though. Poaching has come under control, and animal numbers have increased, in part thanks to a buffer zone created by two Game Management Areas that adjoin the park.

Herds of elephants and buffaloes are seen here once again, often coming to the lake to drink. There are also plenty of antelope, including roan and sable antelope, waterbuck and sitatunga. You might also see zebras. All of these animals attract predators and these days lions and hyenas can often be heard at night. In the lake itself are hippos as well as some of the largest crocodiles in Africa. For anglers, Lake Tanganyika offers top-class sport: Nile perch, tigerfish and nkupi (yellow belly) are plentiful, while golden perch and giant tigerfish all exist in the waters.

There is decent birdwatching here, too, with some 300 species recorded, including red bishop and Pel's fishing owl.

Sleeping

Ndole Bay Lodge (☎ 096 6780196 or 0212 711150; www.ndolebaylodge.com; campsite per person US$10; chalets with full board per person from US$100; 🖫)

Set back from a pretty beach just outside Nsumbu National Park, this lodge has several spacious (mostly en suite) thatch chalets dotted around the grounds, all made from natural local materials. There is also a campsite right under the trees on the sandy beach and a large communal area right by the beach with plenty of comfy chairs and hammocks, perfect for a day of lazing. Meals are taken in the communal dining room and there's tons of fresh Lake Tanganyika fish on the menu. All kinds of activities are on offer here including snorkelling (per person US$20), water-skiing (per person US$25), bush walks (per person US$40) and fishing trips (per boat US$120-335). Ndole Bay also has a PADI dive centre where you can take half-day discover scuba diving courses as well as a PADI open-water course. For trips further afield you could try one of their 4WD waterfall tours or go on a sailing trip up Lake Tanganyika in a wooden dhow.

Nkamba Bay Lodge (☎ 027 73 690 2992; www .nkambabaylodge.com; full board incl activities per person US$400; 🏊) This exclusive private lodge is currently the only accommodation operating within Nsumbu National Park itself. It's set in a gorgeous, pristine cove, and has nine luxurious but understated chalets, decorated with African prints and art. The chalets all have bathrooms and balconies overlooking either the lake or the bush. There's also a small swimming po with views of the lake (you can't swim in th lake here because of crocodiles and hippos the latter of which sometimes wander arour the lodge at night). Food here is excellen and plentiful and, for romantics, dinn is candlelit. Game drives, birdwatchin and fishing are the main activities but yo could also go on canoe trips or walks in th surrounding rainforest. There are discoun for locals.

Getting There & Away

Each lodge will arrange transfers for gues from the airstrip at Kasaba Bay, or acro the lake from Mpulungu. The only wa to fly to Kasaba Bay is by charter. **Profligh Commuter Services** (☎ 0211 271032; www.proflig -zambia.com) arranges flights to Kasaba Ba on a five-seater plane, from US$470 for the plane for the round trip. Hard overlanders can drive, but aim to com from the southwest, where the roads a in better condition. There are good roa up to Mporokoso, followed by a rough di road to Nsumbu for which you'll need 4WD. Many maps will show a road goin directly from Mbala to Nsumbu Nation Park but you cannot safely access the par by this route at present. Some of the roa in the north were being upgraded at th time of research though, so check with th lodges for up-to-date information.

Eastern Zambia

This part of the country contains one of Zambia's finest attractions – South Luangwa National Park, often considered one of the greatest parks in Africa for the density and variety of its game and for the beauty of the landscape. Sitting further north is wild North Luangwa, more difficult to access than its southern cousin and far less developed, but also notable for its density of game.

The Eastern Zambia chapter covers the Great East Road – and sections around it – extending east of Lusaka to the border with Malawi, some 600km. This stretch contains few towns, a scattering of villages, and includes one of the country's genuine opportunities to find volunteer work at a grassroots level and experience traditional Zambian culture. There are several buses a day up to Chipata and through to Malawi and frequent flights between Lusaka and South Luangwa National Park.

HIGHLIGHTS

- Identifying the incredible diversity of winged, hoofed and furred creatures along the dreamy landscapes in **South Luangwa National Park** (p119)

- Tracking wildlife via poo and tracks during a walking safari in Zambia's premier wilderness, **South Luangwa National Park** (p123)

- Discovering the wildlife and revelling in the remote nature and wild feel of **North Luangwa National Park** (p129)

- Meeting local villagers and observing the benefits of grassroots work at a local NGO at **Tikondane Community Centre** (p117)

- Experiencing genuine village hospitality and a **traditional dancing ceremony** (p117)

★ North Luangwa
National Park

★
South Luangwa
National Park

Katete &
Tikondane
Community Centre
★

- TELEPHONE CODE: 0216

EASTERN ZAMBIA

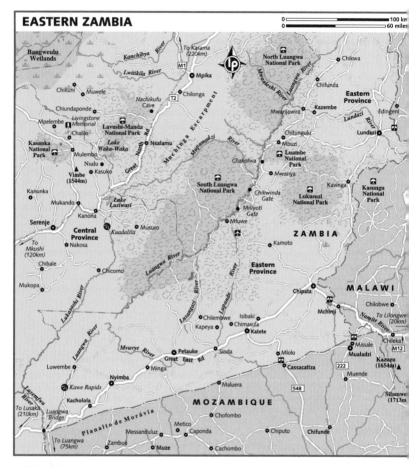

EASTERN ZAMBIA

LUANGWA BRIDGE

The Great East Rd crosses the Luangwa River on a large suspension bridge about halfway between Lusaka and Chipata. It's unusual to see such a construction in Zambia, and there's a permanent security checkpoint manned by the army. The nearby settlement of Luangwa Bridge is near the eastern end of the Lower Zambezi National Park, and far from the South and North Luangwa national parks. It serves as an ideal place to break up a journey. There's no petrol station but there's a lively little market, which seems to specialise in weaved products.

Luangwa Bridge Camp (☎ 097 7197456; www .bridgecampzambia.com; Feira Rd; campsite per person ZK40,000, chalets per person ZK85,000-205,000; ⊠)is on the western side of the river, about 3km south of the mainroad. This place does make a convenient stop between Lusaka and Chipata; the food is very good and the stone chalets are simple and comfortable. However, the pricing system for the accommodation is confusing and it's overpriced (especially when the single supplement kicks in). The owners, while friendly enough, have probably been in the bush too long – you'll most likely hear constant bickering between them. Shared ablution blocks are clean, there's also a book exchange and, best of all, a great upstairs deck with views over the muddy river.

Get off any bus between Lusaka and Chipata at the place called 'Luangwa station' from where it's a 3km walk to the camp.

PETUAKE

On the main road between Lusaka and Chipata, about 180km east of Luangwa Bridge, Petuake is where people with rugged 4WDs and plenty of time can turn off to reach South Luangwa. Make sure you have good maps, GPS and plenty of advice on the tracks you need to take. Apart from that, the town makes a good place to break a journey.

The enclosed grassy areas, with plenty of shade, make an ideal area to pitch your tent at **Zulu's Kraal Camping** (campsite per person US$4). It offers cooked meals or else you can bring your own food and prepare it in the kitchen. The campsite is on the way into town from Lusaka, is very well signed and, although a bit rundown, would do for a night to break from the road.

With its sculpted gardens and manicured lawn, the signs are all good on the way into the well-looked-after **Chimwemwe Lodge** (☎ 371543; campsite ZK50,000, chalet ZK200,000-300,000, mains ZK30,000). Chalets are excellent value and very clean. You get more mod cons (such as DSTV) the more you pay. The chalets have pleasingly high thatched roofs, giving them an airy feel when it's hot outside. It's a little gem in this fairly nondescript little town. The restaurant here prepares local cuisine too at reasonable prices, including game meat.

The town is on the main highway – get off any bus between Lusaka and Chipata.

KATETE

About 90km from Chipata and 500km from Lusaka, Katete is a small town just south of the Great East Rd. On the main road, 4km west of Katete, **Tikondane Community Centre**, next to St Francis Hospital, is a grassroots initiative that works with local villages. Among its many activities, it focuses on adult and child education, agricultural initiatives, and trains home-based carers for AIDS victims. Tikondane also accept volunteers to work at their centre and on their projects (p60).

If you're interested in having a look at what this place offers, or just wanting a break from the road, consider staying at their **Guest House** (Tiko Lodge; ☎ 252122; www.tikondane.org; Great East Rd; s without bathroom ZK60,000, d with bathroom ZK90,000, tr ZK105,000). The simple rooms here come with bed, and small chair and table. They are cool inside and monastic in size and feel. It's simple digs but very good value for the price. Simple meals, such as chicken and nshima, are provided. The lodge is community-run with all proceeds going back into the local villages. It's very friendly and staying here is a real boost for the local economy, as well as a good chance to interact with rural Zambians. If you intend staying here over the weekend you should enquire about the local traditional dances (below). An internet cafe and further guest accommodation is planned.

CULTURAL EXPERIENCES AROUND KATETE

Tikondane Community Centre can organise a very unique Zambian experience – watching traditional dances in the nearby village of Kachipu. This is a very authentic opportunity to see African culture up close; there's nothing 'put on' or 'staged' about these events.

There's a women's initiation dance undertaken before they are married called Chinamwali; men are not usually allowed into these events, but white men are considered 'honorary women'. The other traditional dance held in the village, normally most frequently in the months leading up to August, is the Ghost Dance. Elaborate masks are worn as are grass costumes; mythological creatures may be present and huge drumbeats are employed to assist the stomping of men from the village. It's not to be missed. When it's running, the Ghost dance normally takes place on a Saturday.

You'll need to give Tikondane a few days notice if you'd like to attend, and the cost is ZK80,000 per trip (not per person) to Chinamwali and ZK120,000 per trip (not per person) to the Ghost Dance. Transport is by oxcart (ZK35,000 one way) and a guide (ZK25,000) is available, as is dinner (ZK25,000).

Tikondane can also organise visits to the local market and shops of the nearby township, as well as to St Francis Mission Hospital, one of the best in the country, and the cathedral at Msoro, site of the first missionaries from Malawi.

CHIPATA

Chipata is a large, busy town and, despite its size, has a rural feel – it's the primary urban space though in this district. There are some decent and affordable accommodation options, making it a very useful stop between Zambia and Malawi (30km from the border), as well as a launching pad into South Luangwa National Park. If you're stuck for transport into the park make enquiries with the owner of Dean's Hill (below), who may be able to arrange something.

There are petrol stations and banks with ATMs along the main road.

Sleeping

our pick **Dean's Hill View Lodge** (☎ 221673; deanmitch@zamtel.zm; campsite ZK25,000, dm or tw per person ZK50,000) This lodge is a great little place run by an affable British chap. It features upstairs dorms, twin rooms and camping, a nice big sloping garden, spacious and spotless shared ablutions and grand views over Chipata and the hills. Good, simple meals can be provided with prior notice and a new dining area was being built when we came through. It's the best budget option in town. Coming from Lusaka, take the first right after the welcome arch, just before the Total petrol station.

Mama Rula (☎ 097 7790226; mamarula@iwayafrica .com; campsite US$8, r incl breakfast per person US$75; 🖳 🕏) There's a huge grassy garden campsite here with a large bar that's very popular with the overland crowd. Next door is the bed and breakfast, which really does have some lovely, cosy rooms; each one is themed a little differently and only some come with TV. There's also a resident parrot. At the campsite are some cheaper rooms with shared ablutions. It's a great place to stay, 4km out of Chipata along the Mfuwe Rd to South Luangwa.

Katuta Lodge (☎ 221210; katutalodge@iwayafrica .com; campsite per person ZK50,000, r ZK100,000-250,000; 🕏) This sprawling place is the closest accommodation in Chipata for the run to Mfuwe, for those headed into the park. It's situated just before the tarmac runs out. There's a big range of spacious rooms and, although (as usual) the bathrooms aren't all that great, there are varying degrees of luxury (such as cane couches, fridges and satellite TV); note that only some rooms come with shower (most with bath) so request that if you want it. There's an

DRIVING IN EASTERN ZAMBIA

Generally the Great East Rd from Lusaka to Chipata, near Malawi, is in a fair condition. However it can get very narrow, with drops into gravel on either side, and in places has potholes, so keep a sharp eye out when driving. When you have a bus or truck heading from the other direction, be particularly vigilant. The section between Nyimba and Petauke is quite bad with potholes so be careful here, while the road after Petauke and on through to Chipata is probably the best section. For road conditions and the best route into South Luangwa National Park, see p128.

excellent grassed area for camping, and there were extensions being built, adding more rooms, when we passed through.

Crystal Springs Hotel (☎ 222006; Umodzi Hwy r ZK90,000-250,000; 🛜 🕏) This is a pretty good option, on the edge of town near a mosque. The huge rooms in this African-style hotel are pretty much the same, just looking a bit more weary the cheaper you go. Most rooms are twins, and it's all fairly clean. Note that there are baths only in the en suites, no showers. The bar area around the back of the hotel is a bit more welcoming than the sparse lobby.

Ndanji Lodge (☎ 097 6656460; r with/without bathroom ZK120,000/100,000) If you prefer more of a guesthouse vibe then this locally run place makes an excellent choice. Ask to see a few rooms because they do vary – some are much larger than others, and all should be hooked up to satellite TV. Rooms are reasonably basic but have a homely feel, reflecting the rest of the house. It's a friendly, local place and meals are available although self-catering is also possible as they will let you use their kitchen. It's a good Chipata experience.

Chipata Motel (☎ 221846; tw/exec ZK100,000/ 150,000) This place is worth a look if you're after a cheapie, and a springboard into South Luangwa National Park the next morning. Rooms are pretty bland; the exec rooms are far superior though and well worth the extra kwacha. If you've a fetish for sparkling bathrooms, perhaps give this place a miss, but it's friendly enough and a bit out of town, so nice and quiet.

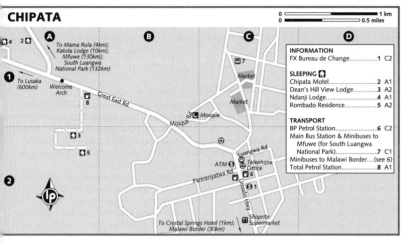

Rombado Residence (☎ 097 7227048; r ZK150,000) This brand-spanking-new place has four large, double rooms and a bar-restaurant perched high up on a hill overlooking Dean's, the rest of Chipata and the hills beyond. The views are quite superb and there's a real feeling of solitude up here. If you fancy a bit of 'me' time and have your own car it's a great alternative. Just be aware that there's not much to do once you actually get here – you'll have to suffice with a cold beer or two. Rooms are large, clean and very comfortable with sparkling floor tiles underfoot, and the en suites have hot water. It's the same turn-off you use to Dean's Hill – follow the signs.

Getting There & Away

There are currently five different bus companies in Lusaka offering services to Chipata, so buses are frequent – refer to p128 for details. The main bus station and departure point for minibuses to Mfuwe (for South Luangwa National Park) is located in the tangle of streets about 1.5km north of the town centre. See p128 for details about travelling between Chipata and South Luangwa National Park. Minibuses for the Malawi border depart from the BP Petrol Station on the main drag in town.

THE LUANGWA RIVER

The Luangwa River, along with the Kafue and Zambezi, is one of the largest rivers in Zambia. It rises in the far northeast of Zambia, near the border with Malawi, and flows southward for 800km through the broad Luangwa Valley – an offshoot of the Great Rift Valley, which cuts through East and Southern Africa.

Although this whole area is sparsely populated, the northern part of the Luangwa Valley is the homeland of the Tumbuka people, while the central area is inhabited mainly by the Kunda and Bisa. Further south, where the Luangwa meets the Zambezi, the people are predominantly Nsenga. But most tourists to the Luangwa Valley come for the animals: in this part of Zambia are the national parks of North Luangwa and South Luangwa – quite simply, two of the finest wildlife areas in all Africa.

SOUTH LUANGWA NATIONAL PARK

For scenery, variety and density of animals, accessibility and choice of accommodation, **South Luangwa** (admission per person/non-Zambian reg vehicle US$25/15, Zambian-reg vehicle ZK15,300; ☉ 6am-6pm) is the best park in Zambia and one of the most majestic in Africa. In fact when the best parks in Africa are being considered experts often have South Luangwa in their top handful on the continent. Impalas, pukus, waterbuck giraffe and buffaloes wander on the wide-open plains; leopards, of which there are many in the park, hunt in the dense woodlands; herds of elephants wade through the marshes; and hippos munch serenely on Nile cabbage in the Luangwa River. The bird life is also tremendous: about 400 species have been recorded – large birds like snake eagles, bateleurs and ground hornbills are normally easy to spot.

The quality of the park is reflected in the quality of its guides – the highest in Zambia. The local professional guide association sets standards, and anyone who shows you

CROSSING THE ZAMBIA–MALAWI BORDER

Getting into Malawi from Zambia is generally a pretty straightforward process with little hassle – especially if you know the procedure. In this box we provide some tips and advice, as well as practical detail about making the journey by public transport or in your car. When we passed through we saw a well-to-do Malawian and his Zambian wife get a grilling at Zambian immigration because they didn't have their paperwork in order – to avoid any hassles always be polite and (especially if you have a car) ensure you have the correct paperwork prepared.

The Zambian border post is around 30km from Chipata (on the Malawian side the town of Mchinji is closer to the Malawian border post). At both border posts you'll need to get your passport stamped and at the Malawian border post you'll need to fill in an entry card (exit card if you're leaving). There are plenty of moneychangers hanging around if you need to change kwacha. However, FX Bureau de Change in Chipata is the best place to change before you cross the border. Note that visas into Malawi are free for most nationalities.

By Car

At the Zambian Border Post enter the immigration/customs building (park your car before the gate), complete the vehicle ledger at the customs window, and request a Temporary Export Permit (TEP). Complete this (note that you'll need lots of detail about your car such as engine number, chassis number, vehicle weight etc, which your hire company should have provided you with) and take your copy with you. Then ask the customs officer where to purchase insurance (sometimes called COMESA) for Malawi. This is *very* important! You should not enter Mchinji (in Malawi) without insurance, as the police prey on unsuspecting tourists. You have the options of buying the insurance at the Zambian border post (ZK55,000 for one month, valid for one country), or just after you've gone through the formalities on the Malawian side (MK5500). Try to buy it on the Zambian side as it's much cheaper and the office in Malawi is sometimes closed.

Go back to your car and drive through the gate to the nearby Malawian immigration/customs building (just up the road). Here, go to the customs window and request and complete a Temporary Import Permit (TIP), after, of course, filling in the obligatory ledger for vehicles. After receiving your copy of the TIP, move to the cashiers' window and pay MK1200 for the TIP. Proceed through the gate and, if you have your Malawian insurance, on into Malawi. If not, stop 100 metres up the road at Prime Insurance Company (on the right-hand side of the road). There, purchase your insurance – again, do not proceed into Malawi without this insurance – this is your last opportunity to purchase it. In the town of Mchinji, up the road, there will be a police checkpoint for sure, and if you don't have your insurance they'll slap you with a big fine.

When you're re-entering Zambia from Malawi, at the Malawi border post remember to fill in the vehicle ledger once again for the car, and hand back your copy of the TIP while retaining the payment receipt for it. At the Zambian border post fill out the vehicle ledger, and hand back your copy of the TEP. This is important – if you don't hand back the TEP, the vehicle is technically still out of the country and this could cause real headaches for the owner. Note also that Zambia charges a carbon tax (any excuse!) for non-Zambian registered vehicles; it's usually about ZK150,000-200,000 per vehicle.

By Public Transport

From Chipata regular minibuses and shared taxis go to the Malawi border crossing, 30km east of the town (ZK20,000). Once you've passed through Zambian customs, it's a few minutes' walk to the Malawian entry post. From the border post you can catch a shared taxi to nearby Mchinji (MK300) before getting a minibus all the way to Lilongwe.

around this park should have passed a set of tough examinations. This cuts out the cowboys but, of course, the end result is higher costs. Believe us, it's worth it.

The focal point is Mfuwe, a village with shops, as well as a petrol station and market. Around 1.8km further along is **Mfuwe Gate**, the main entrance to the park, where a bridge crosses the Luangwa River and several cheaper lodges/camps and campsites are set up. This part of the park can get quite busy with vehicles in the high season, but only because it's the best wildlife-viewing area. But in Zambia everything is relative: compared to the rush-hour, rally-style safaris in South Africa's Kruger National Park, for example, it's positively peaceful around Mfuwe. (Note that lots of wild animals in this area makes walking around at night *very* dangerous.)

Away from Mfuwe, in the northern and southern parts of the park, the camps and lodges enjoy a quieter and more exclusive atmosphere. The animals may be less used to vehicles and slightly harder to find, but there are fewer visitors in these areas and watching the wildlife here is immensely rewarding.

Although South Luangwa is hard to visit on the cheap, there are more options for the budget-conscious here than at most other parks in Zambia.

Most of the park is inaccessible between November and April (especially February and March), so many lodges close at this time.

Flora & Fauna

The wide Luangwa River is the lifeblood of the park. It flows all year, and gets very shallow in the dry season (May to October) when vast midstream sandbanks are exposed – usually covered in groups of hippos or crocodiles basking in the sun. Steep exposed banks mean animals prefer to drink at the park's numerous oxbow lagoons, formed as the river continually changes its course, and this is where wildlife viewing is often best, especially as the smaller waterholes run dry. Thus boat trips are not a major feature of South Luangwa, as they are in other Zambian parks.

Vegetation ranges from open grassy plains to the strips of woodland along the river bank, dominated by large trees including ebony, mahogany, leadwood and winterthorn, sometimes growing in beautiful groves. As you move away from the river onto higher ground, the woodland gets denser and finding animals takes more patience.

Not that you'll ever be disappointed by Luangwa's wildlife. The park is famous for its herds of buffaloes, which are particularly large and dramatic when they congregate in the dry season and march en masse to the river to drink. Elephant numbers are also very healthy, even though ivory poaching in the 1980s had a dramatic effect on the population. Elephants are not at all skittish as they are very used to human activity and game vehicles, especially around Mfuwe.

NORMAN CARR & SOUTH LUANGWA

The history of South Luangwa National Park is inextricably linked with the story of Norman Carr, a leading wildlife figure whose influence and contribution to conservation has been felt throughout Africa.

One year after the North and South Luangwa Game Reserves were created in 1938 to protect and control wildlife populations, Carr became a ranger there. With the full backing of the area's traditional leader, Carr created Chief Nsefu's Private Game Reserve in 1950 and opened it to the public (until this time reserves had been for animals only). All visitor fees were paid directly to the chief, thus benefiting the wildlife and the local community.

Carr was years ahead of his time in other fields too: he built Nsefu Camp, the first tourist camp in Zambia, and developed walking safaris. In the following decades, other game reserves were created, more tourists came to Luangwa parks and more camps were built along the river.

In 1972 Nsefu and several game reserves were combined to form the South Luangwa National Park, but poaching of elephants and rhinos soon became an increasing problem. So, in 1980 Carr and several others formed the Save the Rhino Trust, which helped the government parks department to deter poachers.

In 1986 Carr opened yet another camp, Kapani Lodge, and continued operating safaris from this base. He retired from 'active service' in the early 1990s, and died in 1997, aged 84.

This park is also a great place to see lions and leopards (especially on night drives), and local specialities include Cookson's wildebeest (an unusual light-coloured subspecies) and the endemic Thornicroft's giraffe, distinguished from other giraffes by a dark neck pattern.

Even the zebras here are unusual; called Crawshay's zebras, their stripes are thin, numerous and extend down to the hooves, under the belly, with no shadow stripe – they are an intermediate form between the 'standard' East African form and the extra-stripy subspecies in Mozambique.

There's a stunning variety of 'plains game'; the numerous antelope species include bushbuck, waterbuck, kudu, impala and puku. Roan antelopes, hartebeests and reedbucks are all here, but encountered less often.

An exciting development for wildlife fans, Luangwa's population of wild dogs seems to be increasing. This is one of the rarest animals in Zambia (and Africa), but sightings have taken place near Mfuwe, and there has been a resurgence in numbers around the Nsefu sector as well. An organisation that is putting a lot of work into protecting and increasing wild dog populations is **African Wild Dog Conservation** (www.awdczambia.org): healthy packs require huge areas to roam for their nomadic lifestyles, and it is trying to open up a viable corridor for the dogs between South Luangwa and the Lower Zambezi national parks.

SOUTH LUANGWA CONSERVATION SOCIETY

This society, partly funded by lodges in and around the park, supports and works closely with the Zambian Wildlife Authority (ZAWA; www.slcs-zambia.org) by pursuing ways to conserve local wildlife and resources. Specifically it spearheads anti-poaching and anti-snaring initiatives and also trains and supports ZAWA scouts. The South Luangwa Conservation Society does much good work for both conservation and education in the area and acts as an umbrella organisation for local projects. You may be able to visit while you're in South Luangwa – ask at Flatdogs Camp (p124).

The birdlife in South Luangwa is also tremendous. As small lagoons dry out fish writhe in the shallows and birds mass together as 'fishing parties'. Pelicans and yellow-billed storks stuff themselves silly and become so heavy they can't fly. Herons, spoonbills and marabou storks join the fun, while grasses and seeds around the lagoons attract a moving coloured carpet of quelea, and Lilian's lovebirds. Other ornithological highlights are the stately crowned cranes and the unfeasibly colourful carmine bee-eaters, whose migration here every August is one of the world's great wildlife spectacles – some visitors come just to see these flocks of beautiful birds busy nesting in the sandy river banks.

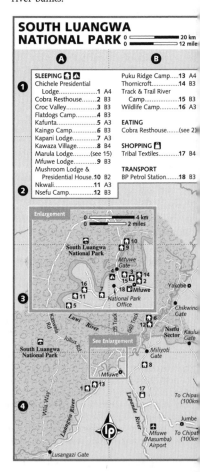

SOUTH LUANGWA NATIONAL PARK

0 — 20 km
0 — 12 miles

A **B**

SLEEPING
Chichele Presidential
Lodge....................1 A4
Cobra Resthouse........2 B3
Croc Valley.................3 B3
Flatdogs Camp...........4 B3
Kafunta.....................5 A3
Kaingo Camp.............6 B3
Kapani Lodge.............7 A3
Kawaza Village...........8 B4
Marula Lodge.....(see 15)
Mfuwe Lodge.............9 B3
Mushroom Lodge &
Presidential House.10 B2
Nkwali.....................11 A3
Nsefu Camp.............12 B3
Puku Ridge Camp....13 A4
Thornicroft...............14 B3
Track & Trail River
Camp...................15 B3
Wildlife Camp..........16 A3

EATING
Cobra Resthouse.......(see 2)

SHOPPING
Tribal Textiles...........17 B4

TRANSPORT
BP Petrol Station.......18 B3

Activities

Unlike other parks in Zambia, boat trips are not available in South Luangwa, but all lodges/camps run excellent day or night **wildlife drives** (called 'game drives' in Zambia) and some have **walking safaris** (June to November). These activities are included in the rates charged by the upmarket places, while the cheaper lodges/camps can organise things with little notice. A three-hour morning or evening wildlife drive normally costs around US$40 to US$45, and the evening drive in particular offers the chance to spot an elusive leopard and shy nocturnal creatures such as a genet or a serval. You also have to pay park fees on top of this, but only once every 24 hours, so you can have an evening drive on one day and a morning drive on the next. A walking safari (US$45) is perhaps the best way of all to experience the park, offering the chance to break out of the confines of the vehicle and experience the African bush first hand with an expert guide, see below.

Theatre may not be the first thing to pop into your mind when thinking about South Luangwa National Park but that may be because you haven't heard of Seka (www seka-educational-theatre.com; it stands for Sensitisation and Education through Kunda arts). Seka is a local NGO that organises and conducts performances for the local Kunda people on important issues such as poaching, AIDS/HIV, malaria etc; pressing issues in the community. Have a look on their website, and ask your lodge about any performances going on while you're in the area.

Sleeping

Most lodges/camps in South Luangwa are along the banks of the river or at an oxbow lagoon. Several lodges/camps also have smaller 'bush camps' deep in the park, where they operate walks or drives away from the busier areas. Despite the rustic title, most 'bush camps' are very comfortable, with large tents, private bathrooms and excellent food. Joining a walking safari for a few days from one bush camp to the next is a popular and wonderful way to really experience the sights, sounds and smells of the bush.

Several budget places are just outside the park boundary, so you don't pay admission fees until you actually enter the park. Note that some lodges/camps open only in the high season (April to November), but those in and around Mfuwe are open all year. Places that open in the low (or 'green') season offer substantial discounts – often up to 40%. However, at this time of year, the grass is high, walking safaris are for the most part unavailable, and many tracks are impassable; so, while it's cheaper, you mightn't actually see that much wildlife.

The rates listed here are per person during the high season for double/twin rooms; single supplements usually cost 30% more. The camping rates are also per person. All-inclusive rates include accommodation, meals, snacks, laundry, activities such as game drives, and park fees. Local alcohol and house wine, and transfers are also usually included, but you should double check when booking. None of the lodges or camps described here are fenced.

WALKING SOUTH LUANGWA

Unexpectedly, a walking safari in South Luangwa presents an opportunity to learn more than you probably ever wanted to know about poo! A walk is a completely different way of experiencing the park, and focuses on picking up the little things (such as tracks and poo) you otherwise miss, whizzing past in a vehicle. It's a breathtaking opportunity to get close to grazers such as pukus, waterbucks, zebras and impalas, and there will probably be baboons around too. Hyenas are fairly common sightings, and the birdlife, which you'll undoubtedly become much more attuned to, is a real highlight: look out for bateleurs, hawks, vultures and eagles circling the skies above or perched imperiously on branches. It's also a chance to learn a lot more about the native flora, including its medicinal and cultural uses.

A trek through the bush is a fascinating way to discover the park, giving a completely different perspective from the game drives. Even sitting under a tree and feeling the breeze whip through your hair while looking over a plain filled with grazers munching their way through the morning is very special. It's an authentic African bush experience providing a greater understanding of the park and its inhabitants, and, of course, of poo...

BUDGET & MIDRANGE

All places mentioned here are outside the park and open all year.

Cobra Resthouse (Mfuwe; s/d with shared bathroom ZK30,000/40,000; mains ZK16,000) The rooms of this very budget resthouse in Mfuwe village are rather hopefully named after animals. Inside, pretty dismal concrete boxes are for the extremely budget conscious only, or if you're on a crack-of-dawn minibus early in the morning. At least try and get a room with a working fan.

ourpick Flatdogs Camp (☎ 246038; www.flatdogs camp.com; campsite US$7.50, safari tent US$35-40, self-catering chalets US$50; 🖳 🏊) This large, spread-out camp has a wide choice of affordable accommodation, great facilities and is very popular, so you should book well ahead in high season. Wildlife drives and walking safaris can be organised at affordable rates. The safari tents are our favourites, perched right on the river's edge with outside tables and chairs for enjoying the view. The camping pitches in the riverside campsite all have barbecues, washstands and wastebins and, even better, there are several platforms high up in the trees, where the dextrous among you can pitch your tent. They're perfect for spying on the wildlife below and a night sleeping among the branches and the swinging monkeys should not be missed. The chalets are enormous and surprisingly luxurious, with large, mosaic-tiled bathrooms and self-catering facilities – very good for families or small groups (they sleep six). No 4 is the best with a brilliant upstairs deck overlooking the river. There's a terrific bar area serving your choice of cocktail and here you can sit on bench seating in a grassy area overlooking the water. The restaurant has an excellent menu – it does the best food in the valley. Even with a crowd in residence, the spread out nature of the camp and its accommodation gives a good feeling of space to enjoy the wild surrounds. This is a very professionally run operation – the staff here are some of the best we came across in Zambia. Payment is by Visa or even travellers cheques!

Croc Valley (☎ 246074; crocvalleycamp@iwayafrica .com; campsite US$7.50, dm US$25, chalets US$50; 🏊) Set under a tangle of trees on a large grassy area, this place has a slightly ramshackle feel, mostly due to extensive building and renovations going on. There's an excellent range of accommodation though and it's probably the best deal for budget travellers with backpacker rooms that are surprisingly good value and very comfortable. (If you're on the bone-crunching minibus from Chipata, try asking the driver to take you straight here instead of dropping you in Mfuwe village.) There's a separate camping area for independent campers, the chalets have a vogue look with sunken bathrooms and safari tents sitting under thatched roofs are also a good option. Chalets with a decent set-up for families are being built and an internet cafe is planned. There's a bar-restaurant and plenty of hammocks and shaded chill-out spots. Wildlife drives and walking safaris can be arranged and, in the dry season, you can play beach volleyball on the river bed.

Wildlife Camp (☎ 246026; www.wildlifecamp -zambia.com; campsite US$10, safari tents US$40; chalet US$60; 🏊) If you want a classic safari-camp atmosphere without breaking the bank, this place is ideal. A spacious, secluded spot about 5km southwest of Mfuwe village, the chalets here sleep up to three people and there's a shared kitchen, but they don't have great views. The safari tents and spacious campsite are much better situated, with their own bar and pool and perfect sundowner views. Wildlife drives and walks are available in the park and in the area round the camp, which is rich in wildlife (and outside the park, so you don't pay fees). There's also a bushcamp, which makes a great overnight safari walking option (US$220 per person, all inclusive). The camp operates in association with the Wildlife & Environmental Conservation Society of Zambia, so you know that part of your money is going directly into conservation and development projects.

Marula Lodge (☎ 246073, 097 6676757; www .marulaluangwa.com; r per person US$40, full board US$155; 🏊) Marula has new owners who are making extensive refits to their elderly chalets. The refurbishments were taking place when we dropped by so it's early days but the signs are good, and this place could become one of the best budget options in the area. The range of accommodation is limited to chalets, but they are a good size, en suite, and very comfortable – the only downside is that the tin roofs will heat them up in summer. There are nine twins and two family chalets; all have mosquito nets and ceiling fans. The swimming pool area is very inviting, although it could do with a bit more shade, and there's a large fire pit right by the river for storytelling in the evening over a few cold ones. There's also a self-catering kitchen: you can even bring your own food and they'll cook it for you. It needs a minimum of five people and it costs US$15 per day in total. Bring *all* the food you need as nothing is supplied.

Kawaza Village (www.kawazavillage.co.uk; full board US$70; day visits US$25) This enterprise is run by the local Kunda people and gives tourists the opportunity to visit a real rural Zambian village while helping the local community. The village has four rondavel huts (each sleeps two) reserved for visitors and there are open-air reed showers and long-drop toilets. Visitors are encouraged to take part in all aspects of village life, such as learning how to cook nshima and other traditional food, attending local church services, visiting local schools and perhaps participating in a lesson. Other activities include visits to the local healer or to the chief's palace, and bushwalking. Traditional meals are eaten in the *chitenge* – a thatched, open-sided shelter with traditional wooden chairs and reed mats; and evenings are filled with dancing, drumming and storytelling around the fire. Many visitors describe a visit here as the

highlight of their trip to South Luangwa. Transfers can be arranged from Flatdogs Camp; if you have your own wheels, enquire at Flatdogs as to the state of the track (and the level of the water at the river crossing) to the village before heading off.

TOP END
South of Mfuwe Gate

ourpick **Track & Trail River Camp** (☎ 246020; www .trackandtrailrivercamp.com; full-board chalet/safari tent $190/170; 🏊) This place is a great choice; set in extensive grounds, there are many riverside nooks to park yourself – including hammocks and a fantastic pool area – to observe the wildlife on the opposite bank (where you've a good chance of spotting hippos, crocs and buffaloes) or simply laze the afternoon away. There are four fairly luxurious chalets sleeping up to four, each with a deck overlooking the river. There is also a large safari tent raised on a wooden platform (three more planned) a bit further back in the bush – baboons like playing on its roof. Camping is also available (US$12.50). The grounds are just lovely with a bridge walk over a former home to crocs (when this was a croc farm) shaded by a giant African fig. The area along the river and especially around the pool (which has the best location here) has mahogany and winterthorn trees casting shadows in the heat of the day. The food is excellent too, and vegetarians, as well as gluten-free and diabetic diets, are catered for. The bar and restaurant are built around a lime tree so, unsurprisingly, lime cocktails are its speciality! There's also a 'wellness area' where you can indulge in an aromatherapy massage and other such treats. It's located about 400m east of Mfuwe Gate.

Thornicroft (☎ 265 01-757120; full board & game drives US$250; 🏊) This new camp is operated by Land & Lake Safaris, which are based in neighbouring Malawi. There are 10 stone-and-wood chalets, all with verandas overlooking the Luangwa River. The decor is earthy and the chalets are quite stylish inside with mod cons and newish fittings. The central bar-restaurant area is great for relaxing, and this place represents good value. It's located along the river to the east of Track & Trail River Camp, not far from the confluence of the Luangwa and Lupande rivers.

SOUTH LUANGWA ON THE CHEAP

If you're in either Zambia or Malawi, on a budget and looking for ways to see South Luangwa without breaking the bank, consider organising a safari, which will also sort out those pesky transport logistics. You should definitely shop around before deciding which is the best for you, but two budget operators that have been recommended are: **Jackalberry Safaris** (www.jackalberrysafaris.net; 3/4/5-day safaris per person US$425/545/645) in Zambia, which grew out of Lusaka Backpackers in Lusaka and operates small, personalised safaris with a diversity of activities departing from Chipata; and **Kiboko Safaris** (www.kiboko-safaris.com; 4-day safari per person US$410) who operate from Lilongwe, from where transfers are organised. Accommodation is in tents.

Kafunta (☎ 246046; www.luangwa.com; all-inclusive US$430; ⊙ all year; ☒) Kafunta has a nice set-up with a vast bar-dining area offering a wonderful open view of the river and adjacent flood plains, built around a mango tree. The open-air deck to the front is great for game viewing, and it's the perfect spot for a candle-lit dinner. Apart from a swimming pool there's also a hot tub whose waters come from a local hot spring – not a bad spot to relax while you feast on the views. The accommodation itself is unusual: thatched wooden chalets built on stilts with four-poster beds and white-tiled bathrooms – it provides airy digs but makes you feel somewhat disconnected from the land. It's located about 1.5km from the Nkwali pontoon and 9km southwest of Mfuwe.

Kapani Lodge (☎ 246015; www.normancarrsafaris .com; standard suite all-inclusive US$550; ⊙ all year) The most famous of the top-end lodges is this classic Luangwa camp built by Norman Carr (see the boxed text, p121) in Lupande GMA. The 10 thatched cottages and large circular houses all have private verandas, set among neat lawns and colourful gardens overlooking a beautiful green lagoon frequented by birds and weed-munching hippos. Accommodation is among the most comfortable and roomy of the smaller camps in and around South Luangwa. Communal areas include a large wooden deck with inbuilt fireplace that hangs over the river and a cosy sitting area for those chilly evenings. The staff here are incredibly friendly and the lodge runs highly rated walking safaris, usually to and between four smaller rustic bushcamps, ideal for experiencing the African bush. It's located about 4km southwest of Mfuwe Gate.

Nkwali (☎ 246090; www.robinpopesafaris.net; all-inclusive US$550; ⊙ all year; ☒) A long-standing classic Luangwa lodge, run by Robin Pope Safaris, Nkwali has just six small cottages with delightful open-air bathrooms. They're all very comfortable but with no unnecessary frills, which gives a feel of the bush – rustic, but also quite classy. If you're after privacy the two-bedroom Robin's House has traditional African decor and a private guide, hostess and chef! The bar-restaurant, built around an ebony tree, overlooks the river and a small waterhole that attracts game right into the camp. It is located in the Lupande GMA overlooking

the park, incorporating acacia and ebony woods, making it a favourite spot for elephants and giraffes. Walking safaris are conducted throughout the year.

Puku Ridge Camp (☎ 27-11-438 4650 in South Africa; www.sanctuarylodges.com; safari tent all-inclusive US$600; ☒) Drop-dead luxurious. The voluminous safari tents, of which there are only six, are a travel agent's dream – they have massive mahogany beds, separate seating areas, sunken corner baths, indoor and outdoor showers (complete with puku-skull towel rails) and expansive balconies. There's a small, sumptuous open lounge and bar area with a curved infinity pool below and a deck for wildlife watching. And the views are incredible – the plains stretch on for miles and there's so much wildlife on display that you hardly need to go on a safari drive. You can just have a relaxing drink in the pool while watching the elephants prance around in front of you. It doesn't get better than that.

Chichele Presidential Lodge (☎ 27-11-438 465 in South Africa; www.sanctuarylodges.com; r all-inclusive US$650; ☒ ☒) In the south of the park, near Puku Ridge, this used to belong to Kenneth Kaunda back in the day, and, with its white brick chalets and green-tiled roof, provides a breath of fresh air if you're sick of all the canvas and thatch. The lodge is built on a hill – President Hill – and has some breathtaking views. It has solid hotel-like rooms decked out in white and mahogany with four-poster beds and large roll-top baths. The large lounge with its wraparound veranda, grand piano, old gramophone and fireplace gives the place the feel of a colonial hunting lodge.

North of Mfuwe Gate

North of the main gate are several other options; each is inside the park. Again, rates are per person.

Mfuwe Lodge (☎ 245041; www.mfuwelodge.com; all-inclusive US$420; ⊙ all year; ☒) This impressive lodge has a central restaurant and bar area with a gigantic thatched roof and open sides, leading out onto a deck with swimming pool and splendid views over a lagoon where numerous animals come to drink. The 18 separate cottages have large and airy hotel-style rooms, imaginatively designed with private verandas and colourful bathrooms with big windows. Who needs a wildlife drive when you can watch the animals from your bathtub? Suites and family rooms are available, and there's a well-stocked library. This lodge is ideal if you're nervous about the wilder nature of the smaller camps. Ask about special deals such as five nights for the price of four. Rates don't include the bar.

Mushroom Lodge & Presidential House (☎ 246117; www.mushroomlodge.com; all-inclusive US$425; 🛜 🏊) This historic lodge was built at the whim of former president Kaunda about 40 years ago. Reddish chalets with thatched roofs are very comfortable and, as with the rest of the place, overlook Mfuwe Lagoon. Children are well catered for here with a babysitting service and meals and games available especially for them. As well as the usual array of activities, tours of local villages are also on offer, and a massage is a good way to wind down after a day spent tensing at the sight of elephant trunks swinging precariously close to your game vehicle. Accommodation in Presidential House is also usually available in five bedrooms, but this was undergoing renovations at the time of research. Mushroom is in the park just north of Mfuwe Lodge.

Kaingo Camp (☎ 245190; www.kaingo.com; all-nclusive US$650; 🕙 mid-May–Oct) Run by highly respected safari guide, Derek Shenton, in the northern part of the park, Kaingo is relaxed, understated and exclusive with five delightful cottages surrounded by bush overlooking the Luangwa River. The honeymoon suite has a huge skylight – ideal for bedtime star-gazing – and a private section of river bank, complete with hammocks and outside bathtub. A highlight is the camp's three hides, popular with photographers: called elephant, hippo, and carmine bee-eater. The camp is in a prime game-viewing area and a good distance from other camps, meaning you get to see wildlife without other safari vehicles crowding around. Leopards are their speciality and it claims about 95% of visitors will spot one – good odds! Other attractions include excellent food, with fresh supplies from the lodge's own garden near Mfuwe, a floating deck for eye-to-eye views of the hippos, and wildlife walks through the enchanting grove of ebony trees just a short distance from the camp.

Nsefu Camp (☎ 246090; www.robinpopesafaris.net; ll-inclusive US$650; 🕙 most of the year) Luangwa's first tourist camp (now protected as a historic monument) has an excellent location smack bang in the middle of the Nsefu sector, which is awash with wildlife. Although the rondavels have been completely renovated, they retain a 1950s atmosphere (along with the rest of the camp), complete with brass taps in the bathrooms and a wind-up gramophone (which works) in the bar – which is perfectly placed for sunrise *and* sunset. Inside, rondavels are stylishly furnished with dour colours and superior fabrics, while good-size windows provide river views. We'd rate this as one of the valley's better choices; it's run by the reputable Robin Pope Safaris.

Eating

All the lodges/camps and camping grounds provide meals – from simple snacks to haute cuisine at the top-end lodges/camps. Flatdogs Camp probably has the best food of the 'drop in' lodge restaurants. There are also a couple of basic eateries in Mfuwe village.

Cobra Resthouse (Mfuwe; meals ZK16,000) serves up local Zambian food – it's a good place to sample nshima. It claims to have the best food in Mfuwe (maybe true); Cobra is a basic restaurant for the budget conscious and those looking to escape the sanitised nature of the lodges.

Shopping

Most of the lodges/camps have souvenir shops selling the usual array of carvings. Other locally made mementos include ceramics and elephant-dung paper (mostly made in Malawi, however).

Tribal Textiles (☎ 245137; www.tribaltextiles.co.zm; 🕙 7am-4.30pm) Along the road between Mfuwe village and the airport is a large enterprise that employs a team of local artists to produce, among other things, bags, wall hangings, bed linens and sarongs, much of which are sold abroad. Tribal Textiles have some striking original designs and it's quite a refined place for a shop, better suited perhaps to couples and families. Short (free) tours around the factory are good fun. Local craftspeople outside in the car park sell animal carvings, jewellery and even the odd carved wooden mask. It's a relaxed place to have a browse with no hassle, but the range is limited.

Getting There & Away

AIR

Most people reach South Luangwa by air. Mfuwe (Masumba) airport is about 20km southeast of Mfuwe Gate and served by chartered flights from Lusaka and, occasionally, from Lilongwe (Malawi). **Proflight** (☎ 0211-271032; www.proflight-zambia .com) offers regular flights between Lusaka and Mfuwe every day for US$250 one way (during high season there are two to three flights a day). There are also regular daily flights to/from Livingstone for US$230. **Nyassa Air Taxi** (www.nyassa.mw) flies from Lilongwe in Malawi to Mfuwe for US$320 by charter with a minimum of two people.

Most lodges will meet clients who have made reservations. The airfare may seem steep (it is), but it beats the hell out of two days of torture on buses and minibuses from Lusaka, which may cost you about US$60 anyway (with bus fares, food and accommodation). Some travellers who endured the torturous trip from Lusaka bit the bullet, found the credit card and bought a flight out of Mfuwe back to Lusaka.

BUS & HITCHING

Minibuses leave when *really* full one or two times a day between Chipata and Mfuwe village. Fares are squarely priced for foreigners (about US$8). From Mfuwe village, it's easy to walk (about 1km) to Flatdogs and Croc Village, or hitch to the Wildlife Camp – but, we repeat, do *not* walk at night. Otherwise, offer some extra kwacha to the minibus driver to take you to one of these three campsites or to Mfuwe Gate. It may also be possible to arrange a private shared lift in Chipata for about US$25 – ask at Dean's Hill (p118).

Some travellers have hitched all the way from Chipata – but start at dawn. The junction by the Chipata Motel is the best place to wait for a lift; in Mfuwe, wait outside the BP petrol station.

If you're in a group, consider chartering your own minibus from Chipata for a negotiable US$70 to US$80 one way.

CAR

To get to Mfuwe Gate and the surrounding camps from Chipata you definitely need a 4WD, high-clearance vehicle. In the dry season the dirt road is usually poor and the drive

takes about three hours. In the wet season, however, the drive can take all day (or be impassable), so seek advice before setting off.

In 2009 the road was in a pretty bad way in places, so be patient and alert, especially as people and animals frequently wander over it. From Chipata take the turn-off to the left just before you cross under the welcome arch into town (this is also the road to Mama Rula's). The tar soon runs out and after you travel 70km on a fairly decent gravel road you'll come to a Zambian Wildlife Authority (ZAWA) checkpoint where you can turn left and follow the ZAWA sign to South Luangwa National Park (some lodges such as Flatdogs are signed as well); or go straight ahead on a single track road that runs back into the main road some 18km on. The advantage of taking the track straight ahead is avoiding some of the worst parts of the main road. However, you should check locally before you do this (Dean's Hill in Chipata is a good place to ask) as conditions of both tracks do vary each year. After you are back on the main road you travel about 20km before another ZAWA sign directs you left (this road takes you to the airport – a much better route than going straight to Mfuwe as the road is in really bad condition here). At the airport a right-hand turn (just before you enter the airport) will take you onto tarmac from where it's a straight drive (around 25km) into Mfuwe village and onto Mfuwe Gate and into the national park. This route information may become redundant if the planned upgrade to the Chipata–Mfuwe road actually takes place. It's been rumoured for years now – fingers crossed…

Getting Around

For independent drivers, South Luangwa is probably the easiest park to access (with the exception of Kafue, which has a main highway cutting through it) and drive around. There's a limited section of all weather gravel roads in excellent condition near Mfuwe Gate and then lots of smaller tracks. You should be able to pick up a very basic map at the gate. Driving yourself can be very rewarding as the bush opens up off the side of the roads (even early after the rainy season in May), making wildlife spotting fairly easy, especially along the river. If you're in doubt in the park you can always tail an official wildlife drive

GETTING THE BEST OUT OF THE LUANGWA VALLEY

Eastern Zambia contains a couple of the country's wilderness gems. It's a sparsely populated region with one long highway, the Great East Rd, meandering out to the border with Malawi and onto Lilongwe. South Luangwa (p119) and North Luangwa (below) national parks complement each other beautifully: stunning South Luangwa is the most 'set-up' park for tourism in Zambia, as well as being one of the best in the region for wildlife watching; while North Luangwa is wild, difficult to access and spectacular for watching wildlife on foot.

South Luangwa suits all types of wallet sizes but is the best park for budget tourists in Zambia; North Luangwa, on the other hand, would suit those who prefer to arrive by private charter and sip their cocktails by the pool.

How Long & How to Get There

We found South Luangwa simply magnificent and you could easily spend a week exploring the fabulous bush here – especially if you have your own wheels. If you're short on time you'd still see plenty over two or three days of jam-packed wildlife watching. The lodges in North Luangwa recommend at least four days to absorb the unique and exclusive nature of that park.

Having your own wheels is the best option. South Luangwa is fairly easily accessed from Chipata (p118) via a rough three-hour drive, while you can reach Mano Gate in the north of North Luangwa from the Great North Rd near the village of Luana, about 60km north of Mpika. Note that for both parks you'll need a 4WD and, for North Luangwa in particular, you need to be well set-up with a fully equipped, high-clearance 4WD (see p130), preferably GPS, good maps and advice on the state of the route into the park.

How Much?

South Luangwa has the most flexibility in terms of expense of any park in Zambia. The cheapest, easiest way to see the park would be to do a budget tour (see p125). For independent travellers you probably won't get much change out of US$100 a day and US$120 would be more comfortable (beers are expensive in the park!), although if you really want to do it on the cheap you could probably bring this down to US$80 if you stayed in a dorm and curtailed your time spent on organised activities such as game drives (but then what's the point in coming), and it would be cheaper again if you were camping. For visitors who are feeling flush you could easily burn US$300 to US$600 a day in either park on an all-inclusive package deal at a luxury lodge. However you do things, the standards in the lodges and the camps in South and North Luangwa national parks is generally very high; they are often run by wildlife lovers and committed conservationists.

Tips

Take a night drive in South Luangwa – the type of wildlife you can see changes considerably with genets on the prowl and hippos grazing on the grasslands. Both parks offer walking tours – don't miss that, it's a unique opportunity to experience the African bush.

---

although try to keep your distance (unless of course it has just spotted a pride of lions by the side of the road!).

NORTH LUANGWA NATIONAL PARK

This **park** (admission US$20, vehicle US$15; 6am-6pm) is large, wild and spectacular, but nowhere near as developed or set-up for tourism as its southern counterpart. The big draw of North Luangwa is its walking safaris, where you can get up close to the wildlife in a truly remote wilderness.

The bush in North Luangwa is dense in places, so the animals are slightly harder to see, and there are very few tracks for vehicles, so the emphasis is firmly on walking. The range of wildlife is similar to South Luangwa's, except there are no giraffes, and the park is particularly famous for its huge buffalo herds (sometimes up to 1000-strong), which in turn attract large numbers of lions and hyenas. Ask anyone who's visited the park to sum it up and you'll inevitably hear words like 'true Africa' or 'total wilderness'.

EASTERN ZAMBIA

North Luangwa's eastern boundary is the Luangwa River, but the heart of the park is the Mwaleshi River – a permanent watercourse and vital supply for wildlife. Dotted along the river, specialised camps and lodges cater for enthusiasts and aficionados. These are open only in the dry season, usually June through to November, as access is very restricted in the rains.

It's important to note that most of the southern part of the park has been set aside as a wilderness area. There are not many roads and only three smallish camps that mainly run walking safaris. The only way to access this part of the park is to arrange your stay with one of these operators. However, to the north is a zone that allows wider self-drive access with one main track and several smaller tracks running off it. Note though that you'll need to have a fully-equipped 4WD vehicle to attempt this.

If you'd rather have a look through an organised tour, the team at Kasanka National Park run excellent tours here – see p100.

Sleeping

Natangwe Community Camp Site (natwangw@yahoo.com; campsite US$10) Run by the Mukungule Community and set in woodland by the northern park entrance gate. The campsites are very pleasant with recently upgraded hot showers and flush toilets. There are also barbecue spots (you need to be fully self-sufficient) and you can sometimes arrange to visit one of the villages in the area.

Chifundu Community Bushcamp (☎ 0211-226082; www.itswild.org; campsite per person US$10, chalet per person US$40; ☺ May-Sep) A local initiative with profits split between nearby villages, it offers a great value alternative to the camps in the park. Near the Luangwa pontoon in a game management area, just outside the eastern boundary of the park, the campsite is set in shady woodlands. Besides camping, simple thatched chalets with open-air bathrooms are available and guests can self-cater or meals can be arranged. Walking safaris are on offer.

Buffalo Camp (☎ 0211-229261; www.shiwasafaris.com; self-catering chalets per person US$100, all-inclusive per person US$300, game drives US$30, game walks US$15; ☺ Jun-Oct) Located in the south of the park, Buffalo Camp is a quiet, secluded place run by knowledgeable and helpful staff. It's good value and the chalets have been rebuilt

here in recent times in traditional style with thatched roofs overlooking the river. Book ahead for the 'self-catering rates': these are normally only available when there's a pau city of big-spending guests on the all-inclusive package. Transfers for those without vehicles are usually possible from Kapishya Lodge (see p107) or Mpika (maximum four people).

Mwaleshi Camp (www.remoteafrica.com; all-inclusive per person US$520) A relaxed and luxuriou bushcamp with accommodation in fou simple chalets made from reeds and thatch with open-roofed bathrooms. Walking i the main activity and that's a fortunate thing once you've tasted their excellent food Spotted hyenas are commonly seen in thi area as are buffaloes and, of course, lions The spectacular Mwaleshi Falls is anothe highlight. Most guests on organised tours fly in and out on chartered planes.

Kutandala Camp (www.kutandala.com; all-inclusive per person US$500; ☺ Jun-Oct) The hospitality i first rate at this small bushcamp with it four chalets, each with a nice big verand fronting the Mwaleshi River. A four- to five-night stay gives the opportunity for a thorough exploration of the area on foot and the camp only caters for six guests a a time so solitude is not hard to find. The food is also first rate.

Getting There & Away

If you are coming into the park independently remember that you need to be well set-up with a fully-equipped, high-clearance 4WD and your accommodation prebooked unless you're staying at a campsite (even then, be prepared to be fully self-sufficient). Also get advice regarding the state of the road into the park and make sure you've go maps that cover the area (and GPS); they should be supplemented by a map of the park, usually available at Mano Gate and detailing where you're allowed to drive.

Despite the proximity of North and South Luangwa National Parks, driving between them is long, hard and rarely attempted Guests on exclusive tours fly in on chartered planes. By car, you can reach Mano Gate i the north of North Luangwa from the Grea North Rd near the village of Luana, abou 60km north of Mpika – it's well signposted The road can be rough, rarely travelled and drops steeply down the Muchinga Escarp ment into the Luangwa Valley.

Southern Zambia

This region is a real highlight of Zambia with some wonderful natural attractions. There are national parks, with the Lower Zambezi in particular highly regarded for both its wildlife (especially elephants) and its scenic landscape. The area is also home to the remote Lochinvar National Park, a World Heritage Wetland Site with pristine wetlands well worth a visit. Then there's the massive Lake Kariba, with Siavonga's sandy beaches and Chikanka Island (smack in the middle of the lake) providing fascinating views of the night sky and a glimpse of the 60 elephants that make their way between the islands. If you're lucky enough to see a storm roll in over the steely waters from Zimbabwe, it'll be an experience you'll long remember. Siavonga itself offers the chance to experience the more rural side of the country, including an opportunity to go on a traditional village tour.

This section covers the following areas in relation to Lusaka: southwest down to Livingstone, south to Lake Kariba and southeast to incorporate the Lower Zambezi National Park. See the Victoria Falls chapter (p149) for detailed information about Livingstone, the Zambezi waterfront and the magnificent falls.

HIGHLIGHTS

- Discovering the **Lower Zambezi National Park** (p142), one of Zambia's most stunning wilderness areas

- Motoring out to remote islands on sparkling **Lake Kariba** (p136), one of Africa's largest artificial lakes

- Peering down at the gargantuan engineering feat of **Kariba Dam** (p139), from atop the mighty wall

- Going right off the beaten track to discover a World Heritage Wetlands Site at **Lochinvar National Park** (p133)

- Camping at one of the most beautifully landscaped sites in Zambia and buying crafts from a women's cooperative at **Moorings Campsite** (p132)

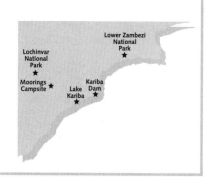

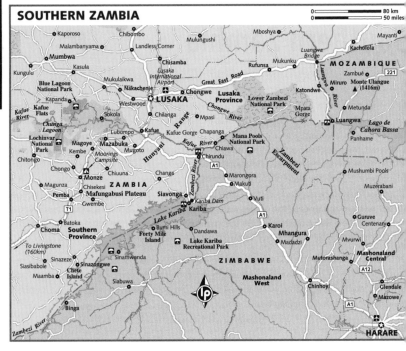

SOUTHERN ZAMBIA

MAZABUKA

☎ 0213

You'll likely spot sugarcane swaying in the breeze around this town as it's the epicentre of the surrounding farming district. It's a fairly large, spread-out place about 125km south of Lusaka with dusty streets and trees shading scurrying pedestrians.

It can make a good spot to take a break from the road and there are a couple of decent accommodation options. **Namusa Lodge** (☎ 097 9932866; r ZK120,000-200,000) is a basic, friendly guesthouse close to the centre of town. A more expensive room buys you a fridge and a bit more space. (No 3 is a good room.) Take the second road after Shoprite (which should be on your left), and note that it's a dirt road; Namusa is on your right. Or try **Mazabuka Motel** (☎ 097 7860702; r ZK100,000), a sun-drenched group of buildings 3km north of town – it's a nice, quiet option. The basic rooms come with bathroom, fan and TV. Note too that there may be a couple of more upmarket accommodation options opening around town by the time you read this: have a look near Shoprite for signs, and on your way north out of town.

MONZE

☎ 0213

Monze is a small town with a nearby campsite that makes one of the best places to break a journey between Lusaka and Livingstone. It's also a great base from which to make a foray into nearby Lochinvar National Park.

our pick Moorings Campsite (☎ 250049; www .mooringscampsite.com; campsites ZK30,000, s/d chalet ZK180,000/260,000) Located 11km north of Monze on an old farm, this is perhaps the most beautifully landscaped campsite in Zambia. It's a lovely secluded spot with plenty of grass and there are open-walled thatched huts spotted around the campsite with a light for reading and a braai next to them for cooking. Chalets have two single beds and are a simple, practical affair; if you don't like spiders though, you're better off camping! There's plenty of shade, and a large thatched-roof bar area with a stone floor where simple meals are available. A

MWANACHINGWALA CONSERVATION AREA

This fairly new conservation area protects an area of wetlands on the Kafue Flats about 25km north of Mazabuka, between Lochinvar and Blue Lagoon National Parks. This is one to keep an eye on – at the moment there are no facilities for visitors so you really need your own vehicle and to be prepared to drive in and out the same day. It consists of land donated by the local community and some private farms in the area and attracts a wealth of birdlife, especially water birds, as well as being home to the semi-aquatic Kafue lechwe and sitatunga antelopes. You can walk, fish or possibly hire a boat to explore some of the lagoons. Information is supposedly available at the Mwanachingwala Conservation Area office in the municipal offices in Mazabuka. However, it may not be staffed. Try checking here before you go, though, for access information and to pay an entrance fee if required.

Access is in the dry season only by 4WD: head south from Mazabuka towards Livingstone for about 5km, take a right onto Ghana Rd, then a few kilometres along it's another right to Etebe School. Another 4km or so takes you to a turn-off to a fishing camp; now you're on the flats.

sunset this is a particularly beautiful place with nothing but the sound of birdsong in the African bush. Day visitors are welcome to use braais and the grassed area for a picnic (ZK5000/2500 for adult/child). Proceeds are used to support an onsite clinic and the Malambo Women's Centre (see p59).

LOCHINVAR NATIONAL PARK

This small (410 sq km) **park** (admission US$10, vehicle US$15; ☉ 6am-6pm), northwest of Monze, consists of grassland, low wooded hills and the seasonally flooded Chunga Lagoon – all part of a huge World Heritage Wetland Site called the Kafue Flats. You may see buffaloes, wildebeests, zebras, kudus and some of the 30,000 Kafue lechwes residing in the park. Bushbuck, oribi, hippo, jackal, reedbuck and common waterbuck are also here. Lochinvar is also a haven for birdlife, with more than 400 species recorded. Its mudbanks and shallows are a treat for wading birds and a big draw for birdwatchers. An excellent selection of wetland birds (including wattled cranes) occur near the ranger post along the edge of Chunga Lagoon.

For history and geology fans, **Gwisho Hot Springs** is the site of a Stone Age settlement, today surrounded by palms and lush vegetation with steaming water far too hot to swim in. Nearby Sebanzi Hill was the site of an Iron Age settlement inhabited last century. Keep an eye out for an enormous baobab tree with a hollow trunk big enough for a small number of people to sleep in. The tree apparently had special powers that would protect travellers passing by from animals.

Lochinvar was virtually abandoned in the 1980s. By late 2001, a tour operator, Star of Africa, had started to redevelop the park. It also built the superb Lechwe Plains Tented Camp, under a clump of acacia trees along the shores of the Chunga Lagoon. The camp, now called **Lochinvar Camp** was taken over by **Sanctuary Lodges & Camps** (www.sanctuarylodges.com); it's currently closed

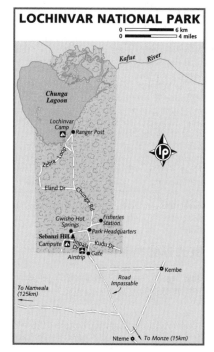

LOCHINVAR NATIONAL PARK

0 ———— 6 km
0 ———— 4 miles

Kafue River

Chunga Lagoon

Lochinvar Camp
● Ranger Post

Zebra Loop

Eland Dr

Chunga Rd

Gwisho Hot Springs
Fisheries Station
● Park Headquarters
Sebanzi Hill ▲
Campsite ▲ Impala Dr
Kudu Dr
● Gate
Airstrip

● Kembe

To Namwala (125km)

Road Impassable

Nteme ◊ \ To Monze (15km)

DRIVING IN SOUTHERN ZAMBIA

Lusaka–Livingstone road: from Lusaka to Mazabuka this road is poor in parts, narrow and with heavy traffic, so drive carefully. The Munali Hills (not far from the turn-off to Chirundu) give lovely vistas north and south. From Monze heading south, the road is generally in good shape (although narrow in parts) until the south side of Zimba, approximately 50km outside of Livingstone, where a new road is being put through – there's a diversion in rough gravel, and then there's a very poor section of potholed tarmac to negotiate before the last short leg to Livingstone: allow for extra time (perhaps an extra hour) when planning the last stretch of this drive.

Kafue town down to Siavonga on Lake Kariba: from the Livingstone turn-off, for a few kilometres down this road, the condition of the bitumen is shocking with plenty of potholes to look out for. But then there's an excellent 34km section navigating through the worst of the twists and turns of this hilly country. Before this new road it was a nightmare run with trucks broken down everywhere and accidents a frequent occurrence. Unfortunately the road is already showing signs of wear and poor craftsmanship; hopefully it will hold up for a few years yet. From the turn-off to Siavonga, you're on pretty good tar all the way (last 60km or so), though it's a narrow road with livestock about so be alert. Rewarding views of the lake appear over the last 20km or so and are well worth a picture from the side of the road.

If you're continuing down to Chirundu, about 20km from the Siavonga turn-off, watch out for the potholes – some are axle-breakers.

---

until 2010. When reopened it should offer the usual game drives along with *mokoro* (canoe) trips and walking safaris. Cultural trips visiting nearby fishing villages should also be available.

Otherwise, provided you bring all your own gear, you should be able to camp – ask the scouts at the gate for the latest on viable campsites within the park. Remember that facilities will be poor, and don't forget to bring your own food.

The network of tracks around the park is still mostly overgrown, with only the track from the gate to Chunga Lagoon reliably open. By car from Monze, take the dirt road towards Namwala. After 15km, just past Nteme village, turn right and continue north along the narrow dirt road for 13km. Near Kembe village, turn left (west) and grind along the road for another 13km to the park gate. A 4WD with high clearance is recommended for getting to and around the park, though you may get stuck if you don't also have a winch.

BLUE LAGOON NATIONAL PARK

On the north side of the Kafue Flats, small **Blue Lagoon** (admission US$5, plus US$15 per vehicle) was one of many national parks abandoned in the 1980s, then overlooked through the 1990s. It was owned by the Critchleys, a conservationist farming couple (the old farmhouse is now the park reception).

For years it was then used by the Zambian military; animals were handy for target practice, then ended up in the soldiers canteen. Today, thankfully, things have changed and the park is open to visitors (you need your own vehicle), although there are no real facilities. This is one to keep an eye on though – if a big operator can be attracted, then facilities could improve rapidly, and the park be rehabilitated. The same wildlife seen in Lochinvar can be seen here too, and one unusual sight is the huge river pythons which are attracted by the large numbers of lechwe and birds.

To get here, take the Mumbwa–Mongu road from Lusaka, turn left at the sign for Nampundwe Konkola Coppermine opposite a store called the Farmers Supermarket, about 28km from Lusaka. Along this road you'll see a sign on the left: 'Blue Lagoon National Park' – Nakenda Lodge. Drive a further 7km to find the entrance gate, and then it's into the park until you reach the old farmhouse. A 4WD with high clearance is highly recommended to reach and get around the park.

CHOMA
☎ 0213

This busy market town 188km northeast of Livingstone is the capital of the Southern Province. Most visitors zip through on their way to Lusaka or Livingstone, but Choma is a pleasant stopover and staging post for trips to Lake Kariba and Kafue National Park. There's not much to the town itself, although the museum is worth a look; otherwise it's a small town strung out along the highway. Services include a Spar supermarket and banks with ATMs (including Barclays and Standard Chartered).

Sights & Activities

For anyone interested in regional history, **Choma Museum** (adult/child US$2/1; ☑ 8am-5pm) is well worth a visit. Based in a former school dating from the 1920s (one of the oldest preserved colonial buildings in Zambia) and in beautiful landscaped gardens, the exhibits concentrate on the Tonga people, most of whom were forcibly displaced when the Kariba Dam was built. There are displays on the traditional life of Tonga women and men, including Possession Dances, and craftwork with some lovely beadwork exhibited (check out the horn flutes). There's also lots of info on Zambia's Southern Province, including some interesting old black-and-white photos – check out Livingstone last century: unrecognisable! It also houses an art gallery with exceptionally good carvings (although it's only small and actually closed when we came through); and a craft centre selling basketry, crafts, textiles and carvings; don't miss the very cute helmeted guinea fowl. The museum is about 1.5km east of the town centre along the road to Lusaka.

Sleeping & Eating

Gwembe Safari Lodge (☎ 220169; www.gwembe safaris.com; campsite per person ZK30,000, s/d with breakfast ZK180,000/260,000) There's a lovely shaded area at this lodge, complete with thick grass, tables and chairs and a braai. Adjoining is a large camping area with spotless ablutions. Chalets with shared bathrooms have modern fittings and are very clean. This place does big business with tour groups but when it's not busy makes a very restful place to lay your head. The lodge is signposted 1km southwest of town and is a further 2km north off the tar road.

New Choma Hotel (☎ 097 9311997; Main Rd; r ZK85,000-130,000) 'New' is probably an exaggeration at this basic place, with its range of rooms that are all pretty similar. It's worth paying a bit more for the extra space

though, as well as a fan and a less decrepit en suite. The rooms upstairs are the best; ask to see a few and compare bathrooms. The hotel is very central to town (next to the Total service station), and has a bar, restaurant and pool table.

our pick **Leon's Lodge** (☎ 0978666008,0955799756; r ZK180,000-200,000, chalets ZK250,000-350,000) This lodge is currently being refurbished and the results look terrific. Just off the main street (and clearly signposted) with two enormous stone carved lions out the front, it feels quite grandiose. But importantly the hospitality is welcoming and warm. Rooms are huge, spotlessly clean, and come with DSTV, fridge and en suite – they're a real bargain. Chalets have traditional thatched roofs and are a step up in luxury. There's a small bar and restaurant onsite and a tiny outdoor circular bar area. It's very central to town and quiet as it's off the main drag.

Kozo Lodge & Lituwa Fast Foods (☎ 225347; kozolodge@zamtel.zm; s/d ZK200,000/300,000, deluxe ste ZK410,000; sandwiches ZK15,000, chicken & chips ZK30,000) About 7km south of Choma this place with a large fast-food outlet is designed as a stop for tour groups. It does lots of chicken combinations, specialising in *kozo* (smoked) chicken. There are outdoor tables with loud pop music or you can sit inside and enjoy a real coffee. Around the back is Kozo Lodge, which has fairly ramshackle chalets, but being this far south of town they are quiet and convenient for getting on the road the next morning. Chalets have en suite bathroom and the deluxe versions come with Jacuzzi. Fridge, fans and limited satellite TV is standard. Check your chalet for mozzies; if they're bad, alert reception and they'll give your room a spray.

Getting There & Away

All daily buses and trains between Livingstone and Lusaka stop at Choma. The bus to either Lusaka or Livingstone is ZK65,000 or ZK50,000 and there are many departures every day. The bus company ticket offices (including CR Holdings) are in the Star Snacks building on the main road.

NKANGA RIVER CONSERVATION AREA

This rudimentary **conservation area** (admission ZK30,000) covers a few local farms and is a tourism venture aimed squarely at birdwatchers, but welcoming everyone. It protects many different varieties of antelope too, including eland, sable, wildebeest and kudu. It's an excellent area for birdwatching with in excess of 400 species recorded, including the Zambia (Chaplin's) barbet, Zambia's only endemic species.

Bruce-Miller Farms (☎ 0213-225592, 097 7863873; nansaibm@zamtel.zm; campsites ZK30,000, d full board ZK300,000; ☻) has a tranquil campsite set on the banks of the Nkanga River, surrounded by birdlife, and where bushbuck are commonly seen. Otters and marsh mongoose are common here too but shy. The campsite facilities are basic with flush toilets, cold showers, fireplaces and an open dining/cooking area. Make sure you bring your own food and utensils. Three double rooms at the farmhouse – an old classic, colonial house boasting a beautiful garden – are also available. Kids are welcome. Game drives are available or pick up a guide and head off in your own wheels. Fishing for bream and barbel, canoeing and bird walks are all on offer from the farmhouse.

Masuku Lodge (☎ 0213-225225; www.masukulodge zambia.com; s incl breakfast US$85, full board US$105) Nestled in the Nkanga River Conservation Area, a birdwatcher's paradise, this comfortable lodge has six spacious rondavels with luxury fittings in an attractive, remote area. There are beautiful shaded grounds with plenty of grass and this makes a nice place to spoil yourself; it's all very civilised. You'll probably be greeted by a horde of friendly motley pooches on arrival.

The turn-off to Nkanga River is about 3km north of Choma, and then it's about 20km on a decent gravel road to Masuku Lodge and another 5km to Bruce-Miller Farms. It's not a bad idea to call or email for exact directions as a new tarred road may be up and running by the time you read this.

LAKE KARIBA

Beyond Victoria Falls, the Zambezi River flows through the Batoka Gorge then enters the waters of Lake Kariba. Formed behind the massive Kariba Dam, this is one of the largest artificial lakes in Africa. The lake is enormous and spectacular with the silhouettes of jagged Zimbabwean peaks far across its shimmering waters. The Zambian side of Lake Kariba is not nearly as developed or as popular as the southern and eastern shores in Zimbabwe. On the Zimbabwean side are national parks and wildlife areas, and some tourist development, while the Zambian side remains remote and rarely reached by visitors. For those who make it here, this remote-

---

THE PLIGHT OF THE TONGA

The Zambezi Valley between Victoria Falls and the Kariba Gorge is the homeland of the Tonga people – known as the Tonka or Batonka in Zimbabwe, and the Valley Tonga in Zambia, to distinguish them from their Plateau Tonga cousins who live on the high ground further north.

Unlike many Bantu peoples of Southern Africa, the Tonga did not have a tradition of powerful chiefdoms, but instead established a more decentralised and less warlike society. In precolonial days they were frequent targets for slave hunters, or raids from more aggressive tribes. The Makololo, a Zulu offshoot who migrated to the Zambezi Valley in the 1830s, subjugated the Tonga before moving upstream to lord it over the Lozi for 40 years.

Towards the end of the 19th century, the Lozi overthrew the Makololo, then it was their turn to oppress the hapless Tonga. Through the colonial period the Tonga remained largely ignored and among the least developed of Zambia's ethnic groups.

In the 1950s the Tonga received the toughest blow of all when the creation of Lake Kariba put a big slice of their territory underwater. A huge and expensive project called Operation Noah rescued rhinos, lions and other species trapped on islands by the rising waters, and brought them to the mainland – mostly on the Zimbabwean side of the lake. At the same time, the Tonga were virtually forgotten, their land submerged with no one to rescue them, and nowhere else to go.

Some groups were allocated new land, but it was 'spare' precisely because it was no good for farming. Many people were forced to move on, and look for work in the cities. Those who resisted the longest were simply rounded up, loaded into trucks and relocated with nothing (or very little) in the way of compensation. The International Rivers' Mission estimates that about 57,000 Tonga were displaced from their ancestral lands – an issue that remains unresolved today.

ness is the very attraction.The main base for adventures on and around the lakeshore is Siavonga, which is a small town with accommodation set up mainly for the business market, although tourist activities do exist.

History

Lake Kariba was formed in the 1960s, its waters held back by the massive Kariba Dam, built to provide electricity for Northern and Southern Rhodesia (later Zambia and Zimbabwe) and as a symbol of the Central African Federation in the days before independence. Today, Kariba measures 280km long by 12km to 32km wide, with an area of over 5500 sq km, making it one of the largest artificial lakes in the world. Underground power stations on both sides of the dam produce over 1200 megawatts between them.

As well as being a source of power, Lake Kariba is an important commercial fishing centre. Small sardine-like fish called kapenta were introduced from Lake Tanganyika, and they thrived in the new mineral-rich waters. During the 1970s and 1980s the fishing industry flourished, with many 'kapenta rigs' – floating pontoons – on the lake. Lights were used to attract the fish at night; the fish were then scooped up in large square nets on booms. In recent years, overfishing has led to a decline in catches, but some rigs still operate, and you'll often see their lights twinkling on the horizon.

The fishing industry was always part of the plan, so while the dam was being constructed, vegetation in the valley was cleared by bulldozers pulling battleship chains through the bush, tearing down everything in their path. The chains were held off the ground by huge steel balls – three of which are now on display in Choma Museum (p135). When the dam was complete, the waters rose faster than expected and covered huge areas of woodland before the trees could be cleared. Scuba divers today tell stories of enchanted forests under the water – swathes of large trees, still with every leaf and twig intact, frozen in time – a poignant reminder of the valley now covered by the lake.

Chikanka Island

This beautiful private island (actually an archipelago of three islands since a rise in water levels), 8km from Sinazongwe, is privately owned and is mostly wooded. There are impala, kudu, zebra and bushbuck with elephants dropping in occasionally too. Crocs and hippos patrol the shores so don't even think about popping in for a dip.

Chikanka Island Camp (☎ 097 9493980; reservations @lakeview-zambia.com; full board per person US$100) on one of the islands here has A-frame chalets built in their own private space and looking out towards Zimbabwe, providing great early morning views. They are built of stone and thatch with a pretty simple setup inside that includes mosquito nets. For groups there are good self-catering options available too. There's a minimum of four people and a maximum of 10, in which case you'd have the island to yourself. Fishing, canoe trips and wildlife walks can all be arranged. Transfers are arranged by boat (US$100 for up to 10 people) from Lake View (p138). Note that Chikanka was closed in early 2009 for renovations, and due to rising water levels in the lake from the rains in western Zambia.

Chete Island

The largest island on Lake Kariba (27 sq km), Chete has a good wildlife population. The island is actually much closer to Zimbabwe than Zambia and imbues a feeling of wilderness and seclusion – Sinazongwe on the mainland is a long 17km away across the water. There is a breeding herd of elephants on the island and the bigger game (especially elephants) migrates to and from Zimbabwe – 150m away. There are also lion, leopard, eland, waterbuck, bushbuck, impala and kudu, and of course hippos and crocs lurking in the shallow waters. The astonishing variety of birds in the area can also provide many hours of wonderful wildlife viewing. There are no roads, and only one lodge, so a walk into the rugged, wooded interior, which opens out across large flood plains, is a real highlight.

The island's only accommodation, **Chete Island Safari Lodge** (☎ 097 7415594; www.chete island.com; all-inclusive per person US$385) was unfortunately closed until further notice in 2009; check their website for the latest. It's a luxurious tented camp, usually offering a range of activities including boating safaris, fishing and wildlife viewing by boat or on foot. The lodge is reached by boat from Sinazongwe; the transfer is included in the tariff.

Sinazongwe

☎ 0213

Near the southwestern end of Lake Kariba and far from its cousin on the water at the other end of the lake, Sinazongwe is a small Zambian town used by *kapenta* fisherman as an outpost. The centre of town is actually up on a hill away from the lake's edge. If Zambian tourism to the lake does pick up, this town is well placed to become a major hub on the lakeshore. However, at the moment things are a touch quieter.

A kilometre from town and easy to find is **Lake View** (☎ 097 9493980; reservations@lakeview -zambia.com; s/d ZK200,000/300,000), where simple chalets with ceiling fans have a secluded terrace overlooking the lake. There's also a small beach area and a braai. Meals are ZK40,000 and you can hire a boat for ZK300,000 per hour. This would make a good spot to do the washing and chill out for a few days.

A lot further away, but with an excellent array of accommodation options, is **Kariba Bush Club** (☎ 097 9493980; www.siansowa.com; campsite per person US$10, dm US$15, d US$40, 6/10-bed guesthouse US$200/250; ⬛), a beautifully landscaped site. Traditional buildings have dorm accommodation as well as a double, twin and family rooms with shared bathrooms; and there are two very comfortable guesthouses for groups with DSTV, brilliant locations and gobsmacking views. You can self-cater or meals are available including local specialities such as crocodile curry and lake bream. Activities include walking safaris on their private islands. To get to the club, take the road to Maamba from Batoka on the main Lusaka–Livingstone Highway – about 2km before Maamba take the dirt road to the left and follow the signs.

Ask in Choma for minibuses that can take you to Sinazongwe. By car, head to Batoka, just north of Choma. From here take the turn-off to Maamba. After about 50km look for the turn-off to Sinazongwe the town is a short distance down this dirt road.

Siavonga

☎ 0211

Siavonga, the main town and resort along the Zambian side of Lake Kariba, has a location to be envied. Set among hills and verdant greenery, just a few kilometres from the massive Kariba Dam, views of the lake pop up from many vantage points especially from the lodges. Although set up primarily for the conference/business market, Siavonga is popular with urban Zambians (especially from Lusaka) who tear down here towing their sleek boats. A rather strange place, it's more accommodation than town with just a market, a few shops, bank, post office and that's about it. The accommodation is spread out, so you're better off with your own wheels. It's a good place to kick back and relieve some hard days on the road. Accommodation is affordable and there are some adventurous water activities available such as canoeing through Zambezi Gorge, as well as a civilised sunset cruise to the dam wall.

The tiny **Zanaco Bank** (Government Rd) has an ATM that theoretically accepts Visa cards and changes US dollars after 10am. There's also a **post office** (Government Rd) nearby and a **bakery** (Government Rd; snacks ZK2000-5000; ⏰ 6am-7.30pm Mon-Sat, 6am-6.15pm Sun). The Caltex Service Station in town was closed when we came through – but there are two petrol stations on the turn-off into Siavonga.

ACTIVITIES

A visit to the dam wall is a must while you're here. Some lodges organise boat trips (see opposite), otherwise you can take your own wheels (see boxed text opposite).

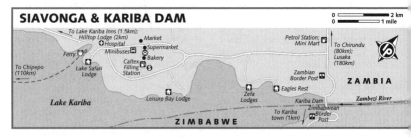
SIAVONGA & KARIBA DAM

The lodges organise activities in and around the lake and Eagles Rest (right) has the greatest variety of options. It organises the following (all should be booked in advance, especially the canoe safari and village tour).

Sunset cruise (per person min 8 people ZK60,000, 2 hr) On the lake – if less than eight people it's ZK480,000 for the boat to yourself.

Boat trip and village tour (per person min 2/8 people ZK580,000/ZK265,000) Includes a lake cruise to Village Point, visiting a small lodge that focuses on ecotourism, lunch, a tour of a working village to see traditional life, including women pounding maize and men repairing fishing nets, and finally a lake cruise back to Eagles Rest or sunset.

Fishing rod hire (ZK40,000 plus ZK150,000 deposit) You'll need your own lures.

Canoe (3hr hire ZK60,000) On the lake.

There are also one-day to four-night **canoe safaris** on the Zambezi where you'll canoe through the gorgeous Zambezi Gorge. You have a choice of standard safari where everything is done for you, or DIY with everything supplied. A DIY safari works out to be roughly ZK500,000 per day per person (food included).

Leisure Bay Lodge (p140) also rents out **canoes** (per person per hr ZK30,000) and Lake Safari Lodge organises **boat trips** (banana boat/ suncruiser/ fast boat per hr ZK290,000/ZK400,000/ZK340,000) on the lake.

Lake Kariba Inns (p141) organises lots of different **boat trips** on the lake. They range from a trip to the dam wall to a longer distance motor around to Lottery Bay ZK1,540,000). The price of dam wall trips depends on the size of the boat and ranges from ZK135,000 to ZK530,000.

SLEEPING & EATING

our pick Eagles Rest (☎ 511168; www.eaglesrestresort .com; campsite per person ZK40,000, with tent supplied ZK90,000, chalets ZK200,000; 🞢 🞢) With the only campsite around town, this place is directed more towards tourists than its counterparts who look to conferences as their main trade. It's the best value in Siavonga with large, spacious chalets that boast stone floors, a double and single bed and great decking outside with patio furniture overlooking the lake. The camping ground is nice and grassy and well landscaped. Ablutions are reasonable, although the showers could be better. Just watch for the hippos at night and don't even think of putting your big toe in the water – crocs lurk around the lakeshore. The owners are savvy about the local area, and are experienced in organising lake-based activities. The food here is excellent too as the restaurant is a branch of Lusaka's Chit Chat (p80), which ensures quality meals are available.

Hill Top Lodge (☎ 097 7404115; r ZK150,000) Come up here for the views not the luxury. Basic rooms have newly tiled floors, TV, hot water, en suite and sparse furnishings. It's super friendly and there's a simple bar with pool table and million dollar views across the lake. Rooms 4 and 5 are the best – very spacious. It's a very rough but short road with a massive, crater-like pothole to negotiate up to the lodge.

Lake Safari Lodge (☎ 511148; www.lake-safari .com; s/d incl breakfast from ZK195,000/255,000; 🞢

VISITING THE DAM WALL

A visit to the dam wall with your own wheels is quite straightforward. Head down to the Zambian border post; it's a few kilometres from the wall. Enter the immigration building (on the right-hand side down some stairs as you face the border gate). Tell them that you just want to visit the wall, that you are coming back to Zambia and not going on to Zimbabwe. They will give you a stamped pass to the dam wall and ask you to leave some ID behind (driving licence or passport are OK). At the gate, show them your pass and you'll be let through. From here it's a short drive or long walk to the wall. Once there, park your car, and walk out over the wall; the views are spectacular, and it's well worth the trip – particularly if you admire gargantuan engineering projects. You should be allowed to take pictures of the wall, but not the power station. Remember that the authorities don't like cameras around here and have a fear of terrorism or sabotage to the dam. So, do what they tell you, but be firm about reminding them that it's only a picture of the wall you want. On the way back, surrender your pass at the border gate, and don't forget to pick up your ID from immigration.

🖳 🛜 🖳) Slightly upmarket and nicely situated on the shore, it's the longest-standing lodge in town and has more of a resort feel. Accommodation options enjoy an elevated position over the lake providing wonderful views. Basic rondavels pull off a cute look quite successfully (mind your head). The twin rooms are also pretty basic (although they have revamped bathrooms), but it all gets a bit flash from here with the premier room (ZK385,000) the pick of the bunch. This lodge is a more luxurious option – not exactly cutting edge, but catering for the tastes of urban-weary Zambians, especially those with their own boat (only ZK40,000 launching fee). There are lovely elevated outdoor areas under palm trees, giving the whole set-up a tropical vibe. Lake Safari can also organise paragliding.

Leisure Bay Lodge (☎ /fax 511136, 097 7755531; s/d with breakfast ZK240,000/320,000, executive ZK350,000; 🖳 🖳) The rooms at this large lodge right on a lovely piece of the lakeside are quite homely. African prints and cane furniture give them warmth and character. The executive room buys you more space and furniture, although the fittings (especially in the bathroom) are looking a bit worn. The rooms are actually in free-standing huts and there's a large chunk of lawn overlooking the lake with a swimming pool in the middle: a great spot for a sundowner. The only real downside is the indifference from staff, who can be a bit uninterested.

Zefa Lodges (☎ 511480; r ZK250,000-400,000; 🖳) The rooms at this guesthouse are of a high standard – superior to other guesthouses in town. Spotlessly clean and with plenty of space, the rooms come with fan, TV and hot water; some even have a fridge. Rooms 1 to 6 are probably the best, and the executive and VIP are huge – try negotiating a rate on one of these. Note that the ceilings are a bit low which means the smaller rooms can seem slightly claustrophobic and the collection of furniture in each is also a bit motley. There's a comfortable bar and restaurant area, and six new spacious chalets are being built

---

THE CURSE OF KARIBA

Kariba Dam was constructed at the head of Kariba Gorge, and both are named after a huge rock buttress called Kariba, which the local Tonga people believe is the home of their river god – fish-headed and serpent-tailed Nyaminyami. When the Tonga learnt that the new lake would flood Nyaminyami's residence they were understandably angry, but when they found out their own homes and ancestral lands would also be submerged it was the last straw, and they called on their god to step in and destroy the white man's interference.

Did the god deliver? Oh yes. In July 1957, about a year into the dam's construction, a torrential storm on the Upper Zambezi sent flood waters roaring through the work site, breaching the temporary 'coffer' dam and damaging equipment. The following March, there was an even greater flood – the sort expected only once in a thousand years, and never two years running – again destroying the coffer dam and causing major damage, as well as washing away a bridge that had been constructed downstream.

The engineers may have had a grudging respect for Nyaminyami by this time (they did increase the number of spillway gates from four to six), but the building continued and the dam was officially opened in 1960. Meanwhile, the justifiably disgruntled Tonga were forced to leave their homeland.

But Nyaminyami still had a final trick up his sleeve. No sooner had the lake begun to fill, than a destructive floating weed called *Salvinia molesta* began choking the lake's surface. A native of South America, its arrival in Kariba remains a mystery, but the Tonga no doubt assumed divine intervention. At one stage, a third of Lake Kariba was covered in this green carpet, rendering boating impossible and threatening to block the dam's outflow.

Finally, for reasons still not fully understood, the weed started to disappear, but other problems continued: in the early 1990s, a drought caused water levels to drop so low that there wasn't enough to generate power. The rains returned and through 2000 and 2001 the lake was mostly full again, but with rumours of earth tremors and cracks in the concrete, and concern over the dam's long-term strength and design, not to mention another dam proposed at Batoka Gorge below Victoria Falls, it remains to be seen whether Nyaminyami will rise in wrath again.

It's on the road down to Eagles Rest and everything is negotiable when it's quiet.

Lake Kariba Inns (☎ 511290/249; www.karibainns.com; s/d from ZK305,000/420,000; 🅿 🖵 🛜 🏊) This fine establishment is good value for the added bit of Zambian luxury that guests receive. Executive rooms have a bit more space, can be set up for kids and have a veranda, with some looking over the lake. The restaurant is a grandiose affair, ablaze with African carvings and decoration. It overlooks the pool area, which is itself perched way up above the lake. There's a sense of space up here and a certain refinement, not to mention some good freebies, such as use of the gym, sauna and pedal boats. Lunch and dinner buffets are ZK75,000 each and full-board deals are available.

GETTING THERE & AWAY

Drivers should see the earlier boxed text (p134) for information on the roads down to Siavonga. Minibuses from Lusaka (ZK45,000, three hours, three to five daily) leave when bursting to capacity for Siavonga and the nearby border. Alternatively, get a bus towards Chirundu and get dropped off at the Siavonga turn-off, from where a local pick-up the rest of the way costs ZK15,000. From the makeshift bus stop in Siavonga, you can easily walk to Leisure Bay Lodge or Lake Safari Lodge. Leaving Siavonga, minibuses depart from near the market. There are no taxis in Siavonga, but your hotel may be able to arrange a private car to the border; otherwise, take the Lusaka minibus, which detours the border.

Around Siavonga

West of Siavonga are a number of alternative lake accommodation options. They provide solitude and a more personalised way to experience a stay by the lake. Take the turn-off to the west about 2km north of Siavonga. The track is very rough and a 4WD is recommended (in the dry season a high-clearance 2WD would probably suffice).

Sandy Beach Safari Lodge (☎ 095 5824444; sandybeachzm@gmail.com; campsites ZK40,000, chalets ZK240,000; 🏊) A quiet, secluded camp which does indeed have a wonderful sandy beach, as long as the lake waters aren't too high! The owner, Herman the German, is a relaxed character and this place definitely has a laid-back approach. A plethora of activities are on offer such as windsurfing, abseiling and canoeing. It's 8km from the Siavonga turn-off.

Butete Bay (☎ 097 7713752; campsite/chalet per person US$10/50) Located further on from Sandy Beach, this is a popular camp for groups. It's a small place that overlooks a bay that has the skeletal remnants of drowned trees. Thatched chalets are a simple set-up with views of the lake and it's possible to self-cater here or meals can be provided. Fishing, bush walks and visits to local villages are all on offer.

Village Point (☎ 097 9278676; www.village-point.com; campsite per person ZK30,000, tent hire ZK40,000, chalets incl brunch & dinner ZK300,000; 🏊) This eco-lodge is in a gorgeous bush setting on a peninsula in Lotri Bay, 40km west of Siavonga. It's ideal for washing away urban grit and offers local village tours, fishing, walks or just plain lazing about (resident hippos and plenty of birds provide distraction at the bar). Very comfortable thatched chalets have an upper storey open to the lake and the breeze, and couples should note the open-air bathtubs strategically located for sunsets.

Mango Grove (self-catering chalets ZK160,000) If you and your wallet prefer your surroundings a bit more basic, Mango Grove has traditional African rondavels, brightly decorated and also with thatched roofs. There are two doubles and one dorm that can accommodate up to four people. There's also a campsite where you can even hire your own tent. Transfers are available from Eagle's Rest in Siavonga (US$40).

CHIRUNDU
☎ 0211

This border town is on the main road between Lusaka and Harare. The only reason to stay here is if you're going on to Zimbabwe or planning to explore the Lower Zambezi National Park. The town isn't up to much – there are a few shops and bars, as well as a bank (Barclays with ATM) and a number of moneychangers, but that's about it. What's more, the roads are permanently clogged with snaking queues of heavy-duty trucks, all heading for, or coming from, the Zimbabwean border.

There is no petrol station in town. Gwabi Lodge has a couple of fuel pumps but there is a limited supply, so it's safer to stock up in Lusaka or Kafue. If all else fails, there are always a few people selling black-market fuel in the street.

Sleeping

Gwabi Lodge (☎ 515078; www.gwabiriverlodge.com; campsite per person US$5, s/d chalets incl breakfast US$60/ 100; 🛜 🔌) This renovated lodge is spacious with a large grassy and well-equipped camping ground, and solid chalets with stone floors. With a lovely elevated outlook over the river, take advantage of the decking in front of the à la carte restaurant here to observe birds and wallowing hippos along the riverfront. The benched seating nearby makes a great spot for a sundowner. At this part of the river the main activity is fishing or just having a poke around on a boat for half a day. Boat rides are available (half/ full day US$50/100 plus fuel). The lodge is located 12km from Chirundu towards the Lower Zambezi National Park. Head north through the truck park just before the border, then along the dirt road. Unless you've got your own wheels, you'll have to hitch or walk.

Zambezi Breezers (☎ 097 9279468; campsites ZK40,000, s/d tented chalets with full breakfast ZK300,000/ 500,000, block rooms ZK150,000; 🔌 🚿) This friendly lodge has some great accommodation options including a huge grassed area for camping along the riverbank. There are also six tented chalets overlooking the water that have great decks and are simple, clean set-ups inside. If you're on a budget take a block room, a concrete box with beds that take a max of two people; nothing flash, but there are few alternative cheapies around (especially if you aren't camping) near the park. This place is good for kids and there are activities such as boat trips (ZK50,000 per hour or ZK200,000 per half day, plus petrol). There's a very pleasant bar, and à la carte restaurant where dinner mains (ZK60,000) include stirfries, chicken, fish and steak dishes. The staff can also organise multi-day canoeing trips on the Zambezi through Zambezi River Adventures: it uses this place as a base. Zambezi Breezers is 6km from Chirundu along the same road as Gwabi Lodge.

Nyambadwe Motel (s/d ZK65,000/70,000, standard tw ZK120,000, executive ZK150,000) Right on the border in Chirundu, this motel is noisy and unappealing, but certainly convenient. Standards are pretty ordinary, but would do at a pinch. The overly weary rooms are only just passable – splash out for a larger room; you may even get a TV and air-con. Ask when you want hot water. Watch yourself around here as it's friendly enough but a bit seedy. The entrance is up a road off to the left-hand side just before the border.

Getting There & Away

Minibuses leave regularly for Chirundu from Lusaka (ZK30,000, 3½ hours, five to seven daily). To reach Siavonga (on Lake Kariba) from Chirundu, catch a minibus towards Lusaka, get off at the obvious turn-off to Siavonga and wait for something else to come along. See p195 for more on getting to Zimbabwe from Chirundu.

AROUND CHIRUNDU

West of Chirundu, near the Siavonga turn-off, is the **Fossil Forest** where ancient trees have petrified. From a sign on the main road, paths lead through the bush. At first, things are pretty uninspiring, but as you go further it gets more impressive, with huge trunks of solid rock perfectly preserved with age rings and grains of bark still visible.

LOWER ZAMBEZI NATIONAL PARK

Zambia's newest **national park** (admission US$25, vehicle US$15; 🕒 6am-6pm) covers 4092 sq km along the northwestern bank of the Zambezi River. This is now one of the country's premier parks, with a beautiful flood plain alongside the river, dotted with acacias and other large trees, and flanked by a steep escarpment on the northern side, covered with thick miombo woodland. Several smaller rivers flow through the park, and there are also some pans and swamp areas.

On the Zambezi are several islands. Some are large rocky outcrops covered in old trees, which feature in the writings of explorers such as Livingstone and Selous. Others are nothing more than temporary sandbanks with grass and low bush. Along the riverside grow the largest trees – jackleberry, mahogany and winterthorn. On the opposite bank, in Zimbabwe, is Mana Pools National Park, and together the parks constitute one of Africa's finest wildlife areas.

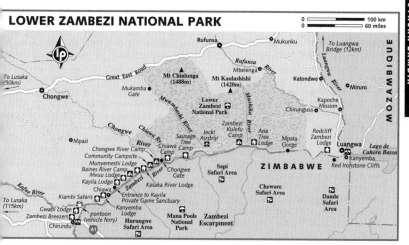

The best wildlife viewing is on the flood plain and along the river itself, so **boat rides** are a major feature of all camps and lodges; doing a boat trip down the river (about US$30) is certainly a rewarding activity and it won't be long before you're lulled into the majesty of the Zambezi. The elephant population was ravaged by poaching until the early 1990s, but is making a strong comeback now with the surrounding Game Management Area (GMA) particularly dense with elephants. Other mammal species include puku, impala, zebra, buffalo, bushbuck, lion and cheetah, and more than 400 bird species have been recorded, including the unusual African skimmer and narina trogon, and there's plenty of water birds such as plovers and egrets on the reed islands. Seeing elephants swim across the river, or hundreds of colourful bee-eaters nesting in the steep sandy banks, could be the highlight of your trip. The best time to visit is May to December.

The main entrance is at **Chongwe Gate** along the southwestern boundary. The southwestern sector of the park is the easiest to reach and the most scenic, and has excellent wildlife viewing, so as you might expect it's a popular area. As you go further into the central part of the park the surroundings become wilder and more open and there's more chance of having the place to yourself. Although the park is technically open all year, access is impossible in the rainy season.

The eastern part of the park is different in character, as here the hills are close to the Zambezi and there's virtually no flood plain. The park's eastern boundary is the dramatic Mpata Gorge where the steep hillsides plunge straight into the river, and the only access is by boat. There are gates along the northern and eastern boundaries for hardy travellers.

Sights & Activities

One of the best ways to see the Lower Zambezi is by canoe safari. Drifting silently past the riverbank you can get surprisingly close to birds and animals without disturbing them. Nothing beats getting eye-to-eye with a drinking buffalo, or watching dainty bushbuck tiptoe towards the river's edge. Excitement comes as you negotiate a herd of grunting hippos or hear a sudden 'plop' as a croc you hadn't even noticed slips into the water nearby.

Most of the camps and lodges have canoes so you can go out with a river guide for a few hours. Longer safaris are even more enjoyable; ask your lodge what is available.

Sleeping

The rates listed here are per person during the high season (April to October) staying in twins/doubles unless mentioned otherwise; single supplements are usually 30% extra. (The rates for camping are also per person.) Also, add on transfers if you haven't got your own wheels. None of the

NEW OFFERINGS

There have recently been murmurs about Protea Hotels possibly opening up a 74-room hotel next door to Mvuu Lodge. Protea is a chain with upmarket hotels throughout Southern and Eastern Africa. The enormous positive of this is that such a hotel may come with the building of a tar road into the GMA. Given the horrendous state of the tracks and lack of road signs this could signal a real improvement to park access. The real negative, as espoused by local lodge owners, is potentially altering the special feel and remote nature of the park. Generally, lodge owners are not in favour of development such as the Protea; they don't want *their* valley being altered and they feel it would affect the 'exclusive' nature of their business. After battling the tracks into the park, personally we think that anything that improves access is a good thing!

lodges described in this section are fenced and all offer wildlife-viewing activities by boat or by safari vehicle.

There is a line of lodges running through the Chiawa GMA before the Chongwe Gate, a few in the park itself and one to the east of the park boundary. See p147 for the distances of the lodges from Chirundu; this should assist independent drivers in getting around.

IN THE GMA

Community Campsite (campsite US$5; year-round) A basic place a few kilometres before Chongwe Gate, don't expect any frills here. It's mainly set up for travellers with their own vehicles. Run by local people, the modest profits are put back into the community.

Kiambi Safaris (097 7186106; www .kiambi.co.za; campsite US$17, full board from US$126;) This well-run operation at the confluence of the Zambezi and Kafue Rivers has a smattering of different, affordable accommodation options – a rare thing in this part of the world. Tented chalets here are a soothing, airy option – elevated and very comfy. The air-con chalets are a luxurious option, good if the humidity is getting a bit much. Flintstone-esque inside

with a stone bathroom, they are quite stylish with even the mosquito nets acting as design feature. Self-catering cottages round out the options and make a great choice for families – they're very well equipped Campers maybe get the best deal of all with a separate bar (with pool table) and upstair viewing platform: perfect at sunset with cold drink from below. And don't worry i you've forgotten a tent; they'll provide on with bedding for an extra US$7. If you'r not on an all-inclusive deal, note that mea are set choice, but prices are comparatively reasonable: US$23 for dinner.

Mvuu Lodge (27-12-660 5369 in South Africa; www .mvuulodge.com; campsite US$20, safari tents US$16(Mvuu has comfortable tented rooms over looking the Zambezi River, with balconie and sandy outdoor fireplaces that are li outside your tent every night. Tales by th communal campfire are popular here an the hosts look after their guests very wel staff are also attentive and efficient. There' a superb decking area overlooking the rive that makes a perfect spot for a sundowner with grunting hippos below. The camp ground is a mix of grass and hard dirt area but there are private ablution facilities. Th cost of camping is steep for what you ge but there's not that much choice this fa into the GMA. Relatively new owners ar still feeling their way here, but the signs ar good. Note the rate above is for the safar tent and is not per person, making it a goo deal. All-inclusive rates in a safari tent ru from about US$210 per person.

Kayila Lodge (bookings through Safaris P Excellence 0213-320606; www.safpar.com; full board US$18 year-round;) This is a beautiful lodg with chalets smack bang on the river. Th chalets have mosquito screen walls so yo have a fantastic feeling of space all aroun you – at night it's as if you're sleeping unde the stars – but there are curtains to draw you feel you need more privacy. There is range of options including the honeymoo suite with its large stone bath; and the fis eagle chalet is good for families; but the bes is the tree-house suite, a chalet accessed b ladder, high up in a sausage tree, with massive shower room constructed aroun its base. You could spend all day on th deck looking over the river with a ligh breeze in your face. The dining and bar are also has one of the funkiest toilets aroun built inside the hollow of a baobab tree – great fun, and you'll also have the odd bat for company. Note that new managers here mean that there could be changes at this place – it may go more upmarket.

Kanyemba Lodge (☎ 097 7755720; www.kanyemba .com; full board around US$330; ⚡) This lodge has phenomenal river views and proximity to big wildlife, as well as authentic, homemade Italian food and a cappuccino machine that's ready to roll 24 hours a day. The chalets are an excellent option if you're after a slice of luxury but don't want to burn too big a hole in the hip pocket. They're simply but stylishly furnished with carved wooden pieces from their own workshop. Families can stay in rondavels and have their own deck on the water. The well-developed verdant garden puts plenty of shrubbery between you and your neighbouring chalet, meaning privacy is valued here. The lodge has an enviable, elevated spot above the river – the island you can see offshore is owned by the lodge and it also runs a luxury camp there (see below). Make sure you take a guided canoeing safari or try your luck at tigerfishing while you're here. You're sure to see more wildlife than in many of the big parks. If you don't have your own wheels, take a bus to Chirundu and someone will collect you there.

Kanyemba Island Bush Camp (☎ 097 7755720; www.kanyemba.com; full board around US$400; ⚡) Kanyemba owns the island just across the water from its lodge. In a secluded corner it has built a very comfortable bushcamp utilising native vegetation (such as shower heads stuck onto the branches of trees protruding into the bathrooms). The island itself is crammed with wildlife and the owner is trying to get it made into a wildlife sanctuary. Walking safaris are a highlight – you're sure to see loads of animals: at any one time there are 40 to 100 elephants on the island. They often wander through the bar/restaurant area while you may be nibbling at your main course; this area is raised above marshland giving fine views over hippo grazing areas. The chalets themselves are simple but very comfortable and filled with stylish wood furniture made by Kanyemba. What you get here is the seclusion and the pleasure of totally private African wildlife and bush experience. There's no kids allowed, and

plenty of staff are on hand to ensure you are escorted around the camp due to the extensive wildlife.

Kasaka River Lodge (☎ 0211-256202 in Lusaka; www.kasakariverlodge.com; all-inclusive US$500) Kasaka has excellent staff and is quite innovative within the valley. It caters especially for children, with a Bush Programme for Kids, which includes specifically designed safaris. Cultural visits to a local community and local schools are a good way to break up the wildlife viewing. Tented chalets on stone platforms are very luxurious and there's even a honeymoon suite with Ottoman-style bed and open-air bath. The hippo pod caters for families and has its own viewing deck while the luxury acacia suite caters for four in two separate chalets done in a Bedouin style and linked by a central covered outdoor lounge area.

Chongwe River Camp (☎ 0211-286 808; www .chongwe.com; all-inclusive US$650; ⚡ Apr-Nov; ⚡) Right on the Chongwe River that marks the boundary between the GMA and the national park, and overlooking the river crossing to Chongwe Gate, this camp has an enviable position with plenty of game around the camp but without the park fees. There are tented chalets with twin beds, shaded verandas and open-air bathrooms well spaced along the edge of the river. A laid-back place with elephants wandering between the tents, it's also a good spot for birdwatching and staff are very helpful. Chongwe also has other options in the area, such as the **Albida Suite**, a private set-up ideal for families with exclusive en suite tents near the confluence of the Zambezi and Chongwe rivers; and **Bushbuck Bushcamp**, a small, rustic bushcamp where walking safaris are the focus.

Baines River Camp (☎ 27-33-342 7793 in South Africa; www.bainesrivercamp.com; all-inclusive US$660; ⚡ Apr-Dec) This sumptuous 16-bed camp offers luxury suites with large verandas under giant tamarind and jackalberry trees and is set at a point on the river where the Zambezi Escarpment curls in close to the river, making it a very scenic spot. Inside the suites, fittings are very classy with quality fabrics and natural hardwoods. There are plenty of activities on offer including a fly-fishing clinic and photographic workshops, and good deals if you stay three nights or more. A lodge area was under construction when we passed through – in 2010 when it opens it will comprise a bar and dining area with fireplaces, covered verandas facing the river and a library.

Munyemeshi Lodge (☎ 0211-286961 in Lusaka) This place is set on old hunting grounds, which are being turned into a conservation area by a couple of entrepreneurs. Chalets on stilts with self-catering facilities are undergoing repair and being upgraded – they are large and airy; the decks catch the breeze lightly whipping off the Zambezi. The dining/bar area is set over plenty of grass, ideal for spotting some hippo munching. Get in touch for rates, which were not available at the time of research.

INSIDE THE PARK

Ana Tree Lodge (☎ 0211-250730; www.anatreelodge .com; all-inclusive US$575) On the Mushika River near an airstrip (the lodge has its own small plane for transfers), this lodge is a good way into the park and, as such, is quieter and feels more isolated. It has a good spread of tented chalets on concrete pads that are a bit dated inside but still very comfortable. Ana Tree is popular with anglers and especially noted for its nearby catches of tigerfish – rods for beginners are available at the camp. Note that drinks purchased at the bar and fishing permits are not included in the tariff.

Zambezi Kulefu Camp (☎ 27-11-438 4650 in South Africa; www.sanctuarylodges.com; all-inclusive US$820; 🐾) Deep inside the park, this lavish camp has seven safari tents facing the riverfront. It is shaded by huge winterthorn acacias and has a large bar-restaurant area adjoining the lounge in the style of a Bedouin tent, giving it an open, airy feel. Teak is the wood of choice for the furniture and there are quality touches around this place. Kick back on the decking by the pool and watch the best of Africa fly, grunt, whistle and stomp past your very eyes.

Sausage Tree Camp (☎ 0211-845204 in Lusaka; www.sausagetreecamp.com; all-inclusive US$895; 🕑 May–mid-Nov; 🐾) Overlooking the Zambezi, deep inside the national park, Sausage Tree is exclusive and slightly unconventional. Traditional safari decor is rejected in favour of cool and elegant Bedouin-style tents completely rebuilt in 2008, each in a private clearing, with minimalist furniture, cream fabrics and vast open-air bathrooms,

which continue the North African theme Each tent has a discreet *muchinda* (butler) while other features are the library tent with couches and cushions, and the airy dining tent with a Paris-trained chef. The famous and eponymous sausage tree unfortunately toppled over during the floods of 2000–0 and is now home to bee-eaters and monitor lizards, as well as serving as the base for an observation deck extending out from the riverbank. The tariff includes internal park transfers, fishing and the butler.

Chiawa Camp (☎ 0211-261588 in Lusaka; www.chiaw .com; all-inclusive US$895; 🕑 Apr-Oct) In a spectacular position at the confluence of the Chiawa and Zambezi Rivers, inside the park, this luxurious lodge was one of the first in the Lower Zambezi. As pioneers in this area the owners know the park intimately and their expertise is highly regarded. The large walk-in tents feature pine-clad private bathrooms. The bar-lounge has an upstair deck with majestic views over the river and there's a viewing platform high up in the trees. The food is top notch and for the romantics among you, candlelit private tables can be set up in the bush, on a boat or, when the full moon is out, on a sand bar in the middle of the river. The tariff includes internal park transfers and fishing.

EAST OF THE PARK

Redcliff Zambezi Lodge (☎ 27-12-653 2664 in South Africa; www.redcliff-lodge.com; all-inclusive US$275; 🐾) This lodge is east of the park, about 20km upstream from Luangwa town on the Mozambican border. Accommodation is in tented chalets (both twin and family) that are simply furnished with indigenous teak and are spaced along the bank of the Zambezi, under shady trees. Fishing (especially for tigerfish) is a major feature here and tackle is provided. You can take boat trips to Mpata Gorge, with a good chance of seeing elephants and other animals, or to the towering red ironstone cliffs that give the lodge its name – absolutely stunning at sunset. Cultural tours to a nearby village and a one-day slave trail around the confluence of Zambia, Zimbabwe and Mozambique are also available. Access is by boat or plane from Luangwa, which in turn can be reached via a turn-off (and very bad road) from the Great East Road. Charter flights from Lusaka or Livingstone are also possible. Note the ransfers, drinks at the bar and entry fees into the park are not included in the tariff.

Getting There & Away

There's no public transport to Chongwe Gate, nor anything to the eastern and northern boundaries, and hitching is very difficult. Most people visit the park on an organised tour, and/or stay at a lodge that offers wildlife drives and boat rides as part of the deal.

If you have your own vehicle (you'll need a high-clearance 4WD), head down to Chirundu (p141). As you enter the town, you are looking for a left-hand turn to Gwabi Lodge and from there into the GMA and on to the Chongwe Gate into the Lower Zambezi (all the same route). The turn-off can be tricky to spot as there are often trucks parked in front of it, and it's an unmarked track. It's basically at the bottom of the hill before the green-roofed police station. If you reach the police station (look out for the distinctive roof), you know you've gone too far. The other landmark to look for is a sign to 'Zanaco – Chirundu

---

DRIVING TO CHONGWE GATE IN THE LOWER ZAMBEZI NATIONAL PARK

The often bad condition of the road makes driving from Chirundu to Chongwe Gate an adventure in itself and hopefully the following will help you find your way (it would have helped us as we got lost plenty of times!).

The road from the pontoon up to Chiawa village is mostly excellent graded gravel road. The track from Chiawa village to the Gate, however, is in very poor condition – and generally worse just after the rainy season (ie April/May). Check with locals before you set off and make sure you have a high-clearance 4WD. When you reach the entrance to Kayila Private Game Sanctuary the track is in better shape, apart from a few steep dry riverbed crossings. However, be aware that finding your way from here to the Chongwe Gate is difficult as there are unmarked turn-offs and T-junctions with no signage. Also the route can change slightly from year to year depending on the condition of the track. Try to bring the best maps you can get your hands on, as well as a compass. Note that Kasala Lodge provides a free map from their place to the Gate (mainly because many 'lost' drivers end up at their lodge – it's easy to do!) and it's very useful as from there is the trickiest bit to navigate. Ask for directions and advice along the way – especially at lodges, as they are using the track into the park all the time and should have up-to-date information. Be aware that it's a long and potentially frustrating drive to the Gate; leave plenty of time. Your last hurdle into the park is crossing the Chongwe River. There are three crossings – again ask which is the best to use (ie where the river is at its lowest) and have a look at where the vehicle tracks head (ie what crossing the wildlife drives are using). Across the river is Chongwe Gate into the park.

To help you keep on track, the following are distances from Chirundu to most of the lodges:

Destination	Distance (km)
Zambezi Breezers	5.7
Gwabi Lodge	9.1
Pontoon	11.6
Kiambi Safaris	21.4
Chiawa Village (bad rd) turn-off	37.1
Kayila Private Game Sanctuary	55.4
Kayila Lodge	58.3
Mvuu Lodge	63.7
Baines River Camp	65.7
Munyemeshi Lodge	68.7
Kasaka River Lodge	74.3
Community Campsite	79.9
Chongwe River Camp	83.4
Chongwe Gate (Chongwe river crossing)	83.4

Branch' which is very clearly in the middle of the road – the turn-off is almost opposite on the left.

There are also tracks via the north for those heading to the eastern side of the park but these are far less used: there's an approach road accessed from the Great East Road, 100km east of Lusaka, that will take you to Mukanga Gate; and there's a track from Leopards Hill in Lusaka. Seek local advice before attempting either of these routes.

For budget travellers, ask at Lusaka Backpackers (p71) in Lusaka or Jolly Boys (p156) in Livingstone for deals on budget safaris into the Lower Zambezi.

Getting Around

Remember that you'll need a well-equipped 4WD to access and get around the park. You must drive slowly in the GMA area and the park itself – watch especially for elephants along the roadside at all times! the vegetation is thick against the roadside be particularly vigilant. There are sever loops inside the park for wildlife viewing but these change from year to year especially after the rainy season, so pick u a guide at any of the gates. Routes depen mostly on the work that the lodges do t the tracks, ie which ones they repair fc game drives.

Not far from Gwabi Lodge in the GM is a pontoon which you'll need to tak to cross a river; it costs ZK40,000 for Zambian registered vehicle, or US$20 for non-Zambian registered vehicle, while foe passengers go free.

One adventurous way to visit the par is by canoe along the Zambezi. Most c the lodges listed previously offer two- c three-day canoe trips, with stops at season camps along the river or makeshift camp on midstream islands.

Victoria Falls

Victoria Falls is the largest, most beautiful and most majestic waterfall on the planet, and is the Seventh Natural Wonder of the World as well as being a Unesco World Heritage Site. A trip to Southern Africa would not be complete without visiting this unforgettable place. But it isn't just the one million litres of water that fall – per second – down a 108m drop along a 1.7km wide strip in the Zambezi Gorge that makes Victoria Falls so awesome; it's the whole natural context in which the falls are located that makes Victoria Falls so special.

Jump into the gorge, get drenched by the spray of the falls, raft along the rapids or cruise gently along the great Zambezi River. Whether it's wildlife that attracts you or the chance to fill your life with wildness, this place is rare and extraordinary and yet easy and unspoilt. Victoria Falls is to be seen, heard, tasted and touched: it is a treat that few other places in the world can offer, a Must-See-Before-You-Die spot.

Victoria Falls has a wet and dry season: when the river is higher and the falls fuller it's the Wet and when the river is lower and the falls aren't smothered in spray it's the Dry. The falls are spectacular at any time of year, except if all you want to do is ride those famous rapids, in which case you want the river low, the rocks exposed and the rapids pumping. The weather is never too hot or too cold, and all else on offer – from fine dining to zipping across a border on a high wire – are also there year round. The high seasons are June to August and Christmas, but April, with all the spray, is special too. Although Zimbabwe and Zambia share it, Victoria Falls is a place all of its own, which is why we give it its own chapter.

HIGHLIGHTS

- Gazing in amazement at Victoria Falls from the **Zambian** (p159) or **Zimbabwean** (p165) side (or preferably both)
- Visiting the falls during the full moon and seeing the enigmatic **lunar rainbow** (p160 and p166)
- Drinking a cocktail at the **Royal Livingstone Hotel** (p158) on a deck on the river near the lip of the falls
- Enjoying a spot of high tea at the **Terrace** (p164) at the elegant Victoria Falls Hotel
- Getting your **adrenaline kicks** (p150) with bungee jumping, microlighting, white-water rafting, jet-boating or a Gorge Swing

ACTIVITIES: A–Z

Face fear and enjoy the rush: Victoria Falls has got it all! Activities listed in this section can be booked through your accommodation and started from either Livingstone (Zambia) or Victoria Falls (Zimbabwe) for about the same cost. Confirm any extra costs such as park or visa fees, at the time of booking. All operators give package prices too and for around US$125 you can sample all the adrenalin leaps. The operators usually offer photos and videos of your escapades as well (US$35 for videos, US$15 for single shots, US$45 for both). Note that rates given in this section are approximate and subject to change.

Abseiling

Spend the day rappelling down cliffs and swinging across the canyons and gorges the rushing Zambezi cuts through in the scenic Batoka Gorge. Half-/full-day excursions cost US$80/100.

Bird Walk

Check out the amazing birds that inhabit the area around the falls for around US$70.

Botswana/Chobe Day Trip

Located a mere one-hour's drive from Victoria Falls, this day trip includes a breakfast boat cruise, a game drive in Chobe National Park, lunch and transfer back to Victoria Falls by 5pm. Wildlife viewing is excellent: lions, elephants, wild dogs, cheetahs, buffaloes and plenty of antelopes. The price is US$150 per person.

Bungee Jumping

Tackling the third-highest jump in the world (111m) costs single/tandem US$105/$130. There are two main spots, and both jumps are from the same height.

Canoeing & Kayaking

Half-/full-day trips along the Zambezi River cost US$60/75; overnight jaunts cost US$150, and three-night trips start at US$300.

Clay Pigeon Shooting

Morning, lunch and afternoon sessions are available, the latter with dinner, which you eat in a boma with panoramic views over the rolling African bush. Situated only 3km from Victoria Falls, these sessions are of

an international standard with instructor and are good for both beginners and the experienced. Costs start at US$55.

Elephant-Back Safaris

Take a journey on the back of an elephant through stunning national parkland or nature reserves. See the boxed text, p152, for information on some issues with wild animal encounters.

Fishing

Tackle the mighty tiger fish of the Zambezi with a half-day trip including tackle, rods, lures and bait, all for around US$90.

Fixed-Wing Flights

Whether you fly in a modern Cessna or a vintage Tiger Moth, you'll have amazing views of the falls, the spray and the river from above. Flights range from US$80 to US$160 depending on the type of craft and the route.

Flying Fox

Zip across the Batoka Gorge for just US$25.

Game Drives & Walks

Take a morning or evening guided safari in a national park, either in a 4WD or on foot. Enjoy the African landscape at its best in the gentle morning or early evening light. Costs are from US$50 per person or game walks US$70. Note that this is for group bookings only.

Golf

Enjoy scenic game drives between rounds on immaculate fairways on both sides of the border, in Zimbabwe at The Elephant Hills Hotel or in Zambia at Livingstone Royal Golf & Country Club. A game of nine holes costs US$10 (equipment hire US$10) and 18 holes costs $US20 (equipment hire US$20). Caddy fees are US$5 extra.

Gorge Slide

This is a lot like the Flying Fox but you whiz down into the Batoka Gorge and back up the other side (single/tandem $35/45) – an adrenalin rush for starters.

Gorge Swing

For those who want to be brave enough to bungee jump but never will be, this is perfect. It's located at the Batoka Gorge.

ump

ump feet first, free fall for four seconds ut you'll end up the right-way-up, swing-ng but not upside down. There are tandem options of this too. There are two main spots, one right off the Victoria Falls Bridge, and the other a bit further along he gorge. Costs are US$75.

Helicopters

The 'Flight of the Angels' is a 15-minute oy ride (US$115 excluding park fees) over he falls or 30 minutes (US$260) across he falls and Zambezi National Park.

Hiking

Embark on a hike with guides around the Zambezi National Park (Zimbabwe) or Mosi-oa-Tunya National Park (Zambia). Day hikes cost US$50, while overnight camping is an additional US$10.

Horse Riding

Tracks go alongside the Zambezi, and you an indulge in a bit of wildlife spotting rom horseback. Two-/three-hour rides ost about US$45/60, while half-/full-day ides are about US$85/160.

Hwange Day Trips

Don't miss the park with one of the largest number of elephants in the world. A day trip will cost around US$250.

Interactive Drumming

Spend an evening by a campfire drumming under the southern African sky. A ne-hour session followed by a traditional meal costs US$25.

NATIONAL PARK FEES

You can pay your park fees at the national park entrances and national park offices inside the parks.

- US$10 Victoria Falls Entrance – from the Zambian side
- US$20 for overseas residents in Zimbabwe
- US$15 for regional residents in Zimbabwe
- US$20 Victoria Falls Entrance – from the Zimbabwean side

Jet Boats

Go straight into whirlpools! This hair-raising trip costs US$90, and is combined with a cable-car ride down into the Batoka Gorge.

Microlights & Ultralights

These motorised hang-gliders offer fabulous aerial views, and the pilot will take pictures for you with a camera fixed to the wing. Prices are US$104 for 15 minutes over the falls and US$185 for 30 minutes for the falls and Zambezi National Park.

Night Game Drives

Only available on the Zimbabwean side, these take place in the Zambezi National Park, and cost US$90 for a full night drive.

Quadbiking

Discover the spectacular landscape surrounding Livingstone, Zambia, and the Batoka Gorge, spotting wildlife as you go on all-terrain quad bikes. These ultimate adventure vehicles allow all riders to go at their own pace, under supervision of qualified guides. Trips vary from eco trail riding at Batoka Land to longer range cultural trips in the African Bush. A one-hour spin costs US$60.

Rafting

There are high-water runs through rapids 11 to 18 (or 23), which are relatively mild and can be done between 1 July and 15 August, though in high rainfall years they may begin as early as mid-May. Wilder low-water runs operate from roughly 15 August to late December, taking in the winding 22km from rapids 4 to 18 (or 23) if you put in on the Zimbabwean side, and from Rapids 1 to 18 (or 23) if you put in on the Zambian side. Half-/full-day trips cost about US$110/125, and overnight trips about US$165. Longer jaunts can also be arranged.

Retail Therapy

You'll find markets located in Victoria Falls town and on the Zambian side of the bridge after immigration, near the entrance to the National Park and the falls.

Rhino Walks

These and other nature walks are done on the Zambian side, through the Masi-oa-Tunya National Park. It must be noted

VICTORIA FALLS

that, as with all safaris, although guides do their best, viewing of particular animals cannot be guaranteed. Walks costs $US85 per person, for groups of up to eight. Organised by Bwaato Adventures, you can book online through www.zambiatourism.com, but this can also be booked through your hotel or hostel.

River-Boarding
How about lying on a boogie board and careering down the rapids? 'Waterfall surfing', as it's sometimes called, costs from US$135/150 for a half/full day. The best time of year for river-boarding is February to June.

Sitting
Not to be underestimated is the fine art of sitting while at Victoria Falls and soaking up the atmosphere, gazing about you while watching the world go by. You can sit either at a restaurant (Zambezi Waterfront for example; see p156) or bar (Royal Livingstone for preference; see p158) with the river rushing underneath you, or have the falls and bungee jumpers plummeting in front of you (Drop Zone Viewing Platform) on the Zambian side of the bridge. In Zimbabwe you can make like a local and sit on The Rock, which is near The Big Tree – stunning! And absolutely free.

Steam Train Trips
A variety of steam train tours ranging from the Royal Tea Run to the Victoria Falls Bridge, to an *Out of Africa* Bush Breakfast or

---

> **ANIMAL ENCOUNTERS: SHOULD YOU AVOID THEM?**
>
> There are some dodgy operators out there, so do think about what they are offering in terms of the welfare of the animals. For example, what happens to the young lion cubs or elephants when they get older? If elephants are to be used for commercial purposes, there are a few good operations in Africa that are 'using' elephants in the right way, ie by doing walks with elephants rather than riding them. This serves to educate the public about elephants and satisfies the desire for tourists to have close contact with elephants, which is after all an extraordinary privilege.

> **ZAMBEZI RIVER: HIGHS & LOWS**
>
> During the rainy season (March to May), the Zambezi's flow can be 10 times higher, while in the dry season (September to December), the volume of water can be as low as 4% of the peak flow.

---

sunset steamer (only for prebooked groups a minimum of 25) cost about US$95.

Traditional Dancing
Great as a spectator sport or you can join in for US$40.

Victoria Falls Tour
The best way to see the falls is on the Zimbabwean side. You enter through the National Park gates (open from 6am to 6pm), show your passport and pay a US$20 fee per person. Hire a raincoat and umbrell just inside those gates if you go in April or you may as well walk in your swimming suit – you *will* get drenched! The walk i along the top of the gorge on a path, which is signposted with the best vantage point and can sometimes be shared with monkey and warthogs. The former are cheeky and the latter are shy. Note that you can get to the bridge, but not onto it, from this path

Wildlife Drives
Head out on a guided safari in Mosi-oa Tunya Game Park, Zambia, which is a grea place to see white rhinos. Wildlife drive here cost around US$50. Or choose a rive safari on the Zambezi. River cruises along the Zambezi range from civilised jaunts on the *African Queen* to full-on, all-you-can drink sunset booze cruises. Prices rang from US$30 to US$60. Great for spotting wildlife, though some tourists get just a much enjoyment out of the free drinks!

TRAVEL & ADVENTURE COMPANIES
What's so easy is that 99% of all booking for activities in the falls are done through the lodge, hotel or backpacking hostel you are staying in. Prices for activities are all basi cally the same, and arranging it from where you stay means transfers are included.

You can also go directly to tour operator who have activities operators on their book too. Try **Wild Horizons** (☎ 44571; www.wildhorizon

VISAS

You will need a visa to cross sides from Zim to Zam or vice versa. These are applicable to most nationalities and they are available at the border posts.

■ Day visit: US$20 for 24 hours

■ Single entry: US$50

■ Double/multi-entry: US$80

■ Multi-entry: on application

).zw) with an office in Victoria Falls town, **frican Horizons** (☎ 323432; www.adventure-africa om) in Livingstone, or **Safari Par Excellence** ☎ in Zambia 326629, 421190, 011205306; www.safpar et) which all cover activities on either side.

If you want independent advice, visit **ackpackers Bazaar** (Map p162; ☎ 013-45828; bazaar@ web.co.zw; off Parkway; ⏰ 8am-5pm Mon-Fri, 8am-4pm t & Sun) in the town of Victoria Falls.

‍AMBIA

/hile Zimbabwe is working hard to rekin- le its economy, Zambia is stable; the 73 ibes coexist peacefully and the currency he kwacha) is strengthening. The recent)urist swing to the Zambian side of Vic-)ria Falls due to Zimbabwe's troubles has litiated a construction boom. Local busi- ‍ess owners are riding the tourism wave nd are building and renovating for even ore expected growth. The Zambezi River aterfront is rapidly being tastefully devel-)ed as one of the most exclusive destina- ons in Southern Africa.

IVINGSTONE

☎ 0213

he historic town of Livingstone, named fter the first European to set eyes on Vic-)ria Falls, sprung to life following the)nstruction of the Victoria Falls Bridge 1 1904. During the remainder of the 20th ‍entury, Livingstone existed as a quiet pro- ‍incial capital. However, during the politi- al and economic troubles in Zimbabwe, ivingstone quickly lifted its game and was)le to cater for a new wave of tourists. His-)ric buildings got much-needed facelifts, ‍ew construction projects began and plans ‍ere hatched for increased transport links.

Today, Livingstone is the preferred base for backpackers visiting Victoria Falls. The town is not much to look at but it is a fun place for backpackers: It's set 11km away from the falls and unless you've gone for the option of staying on the Zambezi riverfront, you are not staying in a natural setting, but an African border town. That said, it has excellent (read: fun, cheap and well-organised) hostels, all with internet access and the full gamut of activities on offer within, plus restaurants and bars in town catering to every type of traveller – from those on a shoestring to those on a once in a lifetime event such as a honeymoon.

History

Although several explorers and artists visited the area following its 'discovery', Victoria Falls were largely ignored by Europeans until the construction of Cecil Rhodes' railway in 1905. During the British colonial era and the early years of Zambian and Zimbabwean independence, the falls emerged as one of the most popular tourist destinations in southern Africa. However, tourist numbers plummeted in the late 1960s in response to the guerrilla warfare in Zimbabwe, and the climate of suspicion aimed at foreigners under the rule of Zambian President Kenneth Kaunda.

During the 1980s, tourism surged once more as travellers started flocking to the region in search of adrenaline highs. The town of Victoria Falls (p161) in Zimbabwe billed itself as a centre for extreme sports, while sleepy Livingstone absorbed some of the tourist overflow. By the end of the 20th century, Victoria Falls was receiving over a quarter of a million visitors each year, and the future (on both sides of the falls) was looking bright.

In a few short years however, the civil unrest resulting from Zimbabwean President Robert Mugabe's controversial land reform programme brought tourism in the town of Victoria Falls to a halt. Although foreigners safely remained on the sidelines of the political conflict, hyperinflation of the currency, lack of goods and services and the absence of commodities such as petrol all served as significant deterrents to tourism.

On the Zambian side of the falls however, business is booming. After years of playing second fiddle to the town of Victoria Falls,

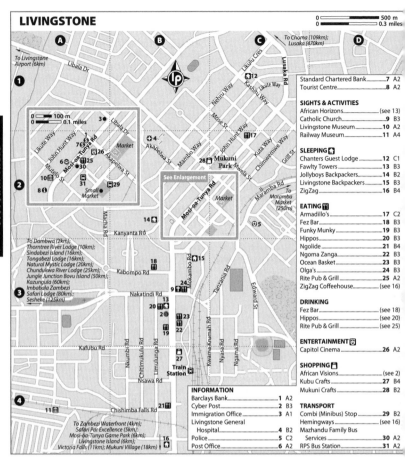

Livingstone has been reaping the benefits of Zimbabwe's decline. New hotels, restaurants and shopping malls are popping up all over town and along the Zambezi riverfront, while increased flights and bus routes are making it easier for travellers to arrive en masse. While Zimbabwe still has political tensions, the dollarisation and other moves to revitalise the economy will no doubt have their effect here on Livingstone.

Orientation
Livingstone is a small African town that has taken on the role of a backpacking mecca. The town centres itself around one main road, Mosi-oa-Tunya Rd, meaning 'The Smoke That Thunders', which is exactly what the falls look like from Livingstone. The tow centre itself is 11km from the entrance to th falls. Several establishments are set right o the Zambezi River, but most of the action i set a bit back from the waterfront.

Information
Barclays Bank (cnr Mosi-oa-Tunya Rd & Akapelwa St) Accepts major brands of travellers cheques, offers cash advances on Visa and MasterCard and changes money.
Cyber Post (216 Mosi-oa-Tunya Rd; per hr US$4) Also offers international phone calls and faxes. All the hostels now have wi-fi or at least internet access.
Livingstone General Hospital (☎ 321475; Akapelwa St)
Police (☎ 320116; Maramba Rd)

ost office (Mosi-oa-Tunya Rd) Has a poste restante and x service.

tandard Chartered Bank (Mosi-oa-Tunya Rd) Accepts ajor brands of travellers cheques, offers cash advances on sa and MasterCard and changes money.

ourist Centre (☎ 321404; Mosi-oa-Tunya Rd; 🕒 8am-1pm & 2-5pm Mon-Fri, 8am-12pm Sat) is is mildly useful and has a few brochures and maps, but ally, the hostels are heaving with all the information u need.

angers & Annoyances

on't walk from town to the falls as there ave been a number of muggings along this retch of road – even tourists on bicycles ave been attacked. It's a long and not a terbly interesting walk anyway. Take a blue xi for US$10.

ights & Activities

ne of the most popular sights is **Livingstone land** (Map pp160-1), in the middle of the ambezi River at the top of the falls, so you n literally hang your feet off the edge. A ip to the island costs about US$45 and can e arranged at your hotel or hostel.

African Culture, Language and Meals Experi- nces (☎ 323432; www.adventure-africa.com; 559 akambo Rd), which can be organised through awlty Towers, is an African experience at goma Zanga with a meal, singing, drum- aing and dancing. It's good value.

Mukuni Village (admission US$3; 🕒 dawn-dusk) is a raditional' Leva village that welcomes tour- ts on guided tours. Although the village can e inundated with tourists at times, the ad- mission fee does fund community projects.

The **Capitol Cinema** (Mosi-oa-Tunya Rd), located uite close to the Jollyboys, caters for trav- llers, and at the time of writing it was

showing a James Bond Film Festival. They also screen football matches.

The stately **Livingstone Museum** (Mosi-oa-Tunya Rd; adult US$2; 🕒 9am-4.30pm) is divided into five sections covering archaeology, history, ethnography, natural history and art, and its highlights are Tonga ritual artefacts, a life-sized model African village, a collec- tion of David Livingstone memorabilia and historic maps dating back to 1690.

The **Railway Museum** (Chishimba Falls Rd; admis- sion US$5; 🕒 8.30am-4.30pm) features a charming but motley collection of locomotives, roll- ing stock and rail-related antiques. Unless you're a ravenous railway buff however, it probably isn't worth visiting.

Sleeping

Accommodation on the Zambian side of Victoria Falls is located either in Livingstone or along the Zambezi waterfront. In town you are within walking distance of all the bars and restaurants; along the riverfront you can relax in seclusion along some gor- geous stretches of the Zambezi. It is certainly stunning to be able to be simultaneously on the edge of the river and on the lip of the falls where the river rushes at great speed and you can see the spray. Or if you're staying further away, it's just as amazing to be down the river where it opens up more and you can see extraordinary amounts of elephants and other wildlife including hundreds of species of birds, right from the hotel.

TOWN CENTRE
Budget

Livingstone Backpackers (☎ 323432; www.adventure -africa.com; 559 Makambo Rd; campsite US$3; dm from US$5, private room US$20; 🖳) This is a brand new

VICTORIA FALLS

VISITING ZAM FROM ZIM (OR VICE VERSA)

From Victoria Falls you can walk, take a taxi, or a complimentary bus service from your hotel to the Zimbabwean immigration post, and then continue 1.3km on foot over the Victoria Falls Bridge. Enjoy the thrilling atmosphere of the bungee jumpers, and their audiences, halfway across the bridge. Just past the bridge is the Zambian border crossing, and 100m beyond it, the entrance to Mosi-oa-Tunya National Park.

Take a blue taxi (US$10) to Livingstone, about 11km away. Mugging is common along this route and it's too far to walk.

Most travel agencies and hotels in Victoria Falls and Livingstone charge about US$25 for minibus transfers between the two towns. If you're crossing into Zambia for the day, advise the Zimbabwean officials before leaving the country so you won't need to buy a new visa when you return later in the day.

VICTORIA FALLS

offering; it's Fawlty Towers Mark II set in a nearby location, only this is bigger, better and cheaper than ever. It has an outdoor bar, nice pool, Jacuzzi, snazzy open-air living room, climbing wall, pool table, DSTV (digital satellite television) with all the sport channels and self-catering kitchen. In total it offers 78 beds, and is a great deal for both groups or individuals.

Jollyboys Backpackers (☎ 324229; www.backpack zambia.com; 34 Kanyanta Rd; campsite per person US$6, dm from US$6, d from US$25; 🔊) Located behind the museum, this place won the prize for the best hostel in Zambia in 2008. From the sunken pillow lounge to the pool, cheap restaurant, bar, barbecue, DSTV and lofty observation tower, everything has been carefully designed by the fun-loving owners. At night, management will not let you bring in people who are not staying at the hostel.

Midrange

Fawlty Towers (☎ 323432; www.adventure-africa.com; 216 Mosi-oa-Tunya Rd; s/d half board US$25/45; 🖳 🔊) This backpacking institution has been renovated into a guest house, full of upmarket touches: free internet and wi-fi, hip bar, shady lawn, a great pool plus a well-organised, on-the-pulse vibe, which comes directly from its owner, Richard Sheppard, a campaigner for bringing back budget travel. There is also a towering thatched bar-restaurant on the premises called Hippos (p158) which is one of the hottest nightspots in town.

ZigZag (☎ 322814; www.zigzagzambia.com; Mosi-oa-Tunya Rd; s/d US$45/70, f US$90; 🖳 🔊) This place consists of 12 motel-style rooms, a lovely swimming pool and a small craft shop. Comfortably and peacefully set in a 1.5 acre garden, this very friendly family-run business has all the mod cons such as air-con and wi-fi. Lovely baking really takes the cake here, though. It also has ZigZag Coffee House (p158).

Chanters Guest Lodge (☎ 323412; www.chanters-livingstone.com; Likulu Cres; s/d incl breakfast US$55/65, f incl breakfast US$85; 🔊) This lodge has 10 motel-style rooms in suburban Livingstone, a pool and restaurant and is set in quiet surroundings. This is a good option for families.

ZAMBEZI RIVERFRONT

Prebooking for hotels along the riverfront is necessary.

Budget

Jungle Junction Bovu Island (☎ 323708; www.jungl junction.info; campsite per person US$10-15, huts pe person $20-30; 🔊) Hippos, hammocks an harmony. Located on a lush island in th middle of the Zambezi River, Jungle Junc tion attracts travellers who want to do noth ing more than lounge beneath the palm trees, or engage in some fishing. Meals ar available (from US$7 to US$12).

Midrange

All prices include meals and transfers from Livingstone.

Zambezi Waterfront (☎ 320606; www.safpar.ne campsite per person US$10, s/d pre-set tents US$30/20 s/d incl breakfast per person from US$125/110, f US$20⁰ 🔀 🔊) Accommodation is varied, and in cludes luxury tents, standard and riversid chalets as well as executive rooms and fam ily suites. It includes a great open-air bee garden right on the Zambezi River.

Natural Mystic Lodge (☎ 324436; www.naturalmyst lodge.com; s/d from US$85/95; 🔊) The atmospher at Natural Mystic is significantly less lavis than at some of the more upmarket lodge though it makes for a peaceful retreat. It 20km from Livingstone and 30km from th falls. Transfers are usually provided.

Top End

Chundukwa River Lodge (☎ 324452; info@maplanᶜ .co.za; campsite per person US$10, huts per person US$12 🔊) This simple but rustic lodge consists thatched huts perched directly on the wate Sightings of elephants and hippos from th rooms are commonplace, there is a coo ing plunge pool right on the riverbank an yummy home-cooking Zambian style.

Imbabala Zambezi Safari Lodge (☎ in Sou Africa 27 11 921 0225; per person from US$157) Set on riverine fringe of the Zambezi River wher Zimbabwe, Botswana and Zambia converg 80km west of Victoria Falls, this lodge offe amazing game viewing and birdwatching. is set in a national parks concession borde ing the Chobe Forest Reserve – a park r nowned for its massive elephant population

Thorntree River Lodge (☎ 324480; www.safpar.co /thorntree.htm; chalets per person US$250; 🔀 🔊) Th Thorntree River Lodge is located within th borders of Mosi-oa-Tunya National Par and features rustic chalets with panoram views of elephants frolicking along th Zambezi River. Prices include full board.

THE MAN, THE MYTH, THE LEGEND

David Livingstone is one of a few European explorers who is still revered by modern-day Africans. His legendary exploits on the continent border on the realm of fiction, though his life's mission to end the slave trade was very real (and ultimately very successful).

Born into rural poverty in the south of Scotland on March 19, 1813, Livingstone began working in a local cotton mill at the age of 10, though his first passion was for the classics. After studying Greek, medicine and theology at the University of Glasgow, he worked in London for several years before being ordained as a missionary in 1840. The following year, Livingstone arrived in Bechuanaland (now Botswana) and began travelling inland, looking for converts and seeking to end the slave trade.

As early as 1842, Livingstone had already become the first European to penetrate the northern reaches of the Kalahari. For the next several years, Livingstone explored the African interior with the purpose of opening up trade routes and establishing missions. In 1854, Livingstone discovered a route to the Atlantic coast, and arrived in present-day Luanda. However, his most famous discovery occurred in 1855 when he first set eyes on Victoria Falls during his epic boat journey down the Zambezi River.

Livingstone returned to Britain a national hero, and recounted his travels in the 1857 publication *Missionary Travels and Researches in South Africa*. Livingstone's oft-cited motto was "Christianity, Commerce and Civilization", and he believed that navigating and ultimately controlling the Zambezi was crucial to this agenda.

In 1858, Livingstone returned to Africa as the head of the 'Zambezi Expedition', a government-funded venture that aimed to identify natural resource reserves in the region. Unfortunately for Livingstone, the expedition ended when a previously unexplored section of the Zambezi turned out to be unnavigable. The British press labelled the expedition as a failure, and Livingstone was forced to return home in 1864 after the government recalled the mission.

In 1866, Livingstone returned to Africa, and arrived in Zanzibar with the goal of seeking out the source of the Nile River. Although the British explorer John Hanning Speke had arrived on the shores of Lake Victoria in 1858, the scientific community was divided over the legitimacy of his discovery (in actuality, the Nile descends from the mountains of Burundi halfway between Lake Tanganyika and Lake Victoria).

In 1869, Livingstone reached Lake Tanganyika despite failing health, though several of his followers abandoned the expedition en-route. These desertions were headline news in Britain, sparking rumours regarding Livingstone's health and sanity. In response to the growing mystery surrounding Livingstone's whereabouts, the *New York Herald* newspaper arranged a publicity stunt by sending journalist Henry Morton Stanley to find Livingstone.

According to Stanley's published account, the journalist had once asked the paper's manager how much he was allowed to spend on the expedition. The famous reply was simple: "Draw £1000 now, and when you have gone through that, draw another £1000, and when that is spent, draw another £1000, and when you have finished that, draw another £1000, and so on – but find Livingstone!"

After arriving in Zanzibar and setting out with nearly 200 porters, Stanley finally found Livingstone on November 10, 1871 in Ujiji near Lake Tanganyika. Although Livingstone may well have been the only European in the entire region, Stanley famously greeted him with the line 'Dr Livingstone, I presume?'.

Although Stanley urged him to leave the continent, Livingstone was determined to find the source of the Nile. Livingstone penetrated deeper into the continent than any European ever had. On May 1, 1873, Livingstone died from malaria and dysentery near Lake Bangweula in present-day Zambia. His body was carried for thousands of kilometres by his attendants, and now lies in the ground at Westminster Abbey in London.

VICTORIA FALLS

Zambezi Sun (Map pp160-1; ☎ 321122; www.sunint .co.za; s/d from US$275/300; ✷ ✭) The closest Zambian hotel to the falls, this huge complex, with restaurants, bars and a casino, is Moroccan-inspired, and designed to simulate a north African kasbah. It contains a great playground for kids.

Royal Livingstone (Map pp160-1; ☎ 321122; www.sunint.co.za; s/d from US$415/450; ✷ ✭) Very stylish colonial accommodation with a manicured lawn leading to the river, the hotel has an atmosphere of indulgence and yesteryear glamour, and is absolutely fab for a honeymoon.

Tongabezi Lodge (☎ 323235; www.tongabezi.com; cottages/houses per person US$430/530; ✷ ✭) Here you'll find sumptuous spacious cottages and open-faced 'houses', with trees as part of the structure and private dining decks. Guests are invited to spend an evening on nearby Sindabezi Island (per person per night US$350), selected by the *Sunday Times* as the best remote place to stay in the world.

Eating & Drinking

Livingstone is home to a number of high-quality tourist-oriented restaurants, including a batch of excellent newcomers.

Royal Livingstone (Map pp160-1; ☎ 321122; www .sunint.co.za; cocktails US$4) Try a refreshing beverage on the extraordinary drinks deck on the water not far from the lip of the falls.

Funky Munky (216 Mosi-oa-Tunya Rd; snacks & mains US$5) This laid-back bistro is a popular backpackers' hang out and prepares baguettes, salads and pizzas in a comfortable setting.

ZigZag Coffee House (Mosi-oa-Tunya Rd; mains US$5) This place offers an eclectic range of dishes, from tacos to tandoori, and is ideal for a coffee or milkshake.

Olga's (cnr Mosi-oa-Tunya & Nakatindi Rds; mains US$5-10) This new place is a good bet for pizza. It's opposite Fawlty Towers and behind the Catholic church.

Armadillo's (Mosi-oa-Tunya Rd; mains US$5-10) Located in the centre of town, this is a new and homey but nice place, with 'international' dishes cooked by an internationally trained chef: fish as well as local food. It can cater for large groups.

Ngolide (Mosi-oa-Tunya Rd; mains US$5-10) This place is a very popular Indian tandoori restaurant which also sells spicy chicken, so is popular with the locals as well as tourists. The chef is from India and it is good value

for money. Groups are welcome and takea ways are available.

Ocean Basket (82 Mosi-oa-Tunya Rd; mains US$5 10) This popular South African restauran specialises in (not surprisingly) fish. Sure you're dining in a landlocked country bu the quality and selection here is good.

Fez Bar (Kabompo Rd; mains US$6) This Moroc can-inspired bar and lounge serves tasty and eclectic meals throughout the day, though things really get kicking here once the sur goes down.

Hippos (Limulunga Rd; mains US$6) This raucou but newly renovated bar-cum-restaurant a the back of Fawlty Towers is housed under neath a soaring two-storey thatched roof.

Rite Pub & Grill (Mosi-oa-Tunya Rd; mains US$7) Thi centrally located pub draws in a good mi> of travellers and locals, and serves tasty pul grub amid a kitschy Wild West setting.

Ngoma Zanga (Mosi-oa-Tunya Rd; meal US$25) Thi restaurant allows you to release your inne tourist! It has comparatively expensive but ex cellent African cuisine, in a typical 'traditiona scenario, from the welcoming routine to the performances while you eat the local fare.

Shopping

African Visions (216 Mosi-oa-Tunya Rd) Near the Livingstone Adventure Centre, this is a charming place selling quality fabrics and crafts from all over Africa.

Kubu Crafts (Mosi-oa-Tunya Rd) This shop offer a vast selection of classy souvenirs. You ca admire your purchases while sipping a tea or coffee in the shady tea garden.

Mukuni Crafts (Mosi-oa-Tunya Rd) The craf stalls in the southern corner of this park are a pleasant, and relatively hassle-free place to browse for souvenirs.

Getting There & Away
AIR
Proflight Zambia (☎ 0211-271032; www.proflight-zambi .com) connects Livingstone to destinations throughout Zambia, Botswana and Namibia **South African Airways** (www.flysaa.com) and **British Airways** (www.britishairways.com) both have daily flights to and from Johannesburg, and the cheapest economy fare starts at around US$450 return.

BICYCLE
Bikes can be ridden to/from Zimbabwe do be cautious as cyclists have been mugged

while riding to/from the Zambian border and Victoria Falls.

BUS & COMBI (MINIBUS)

Domestic

RPS (Mutelo St) has two bus services a day travelling to Lusaka (ZK65,380 to ZK84,060), seven hours). **CR Carriers** (cnr Mosi-oa-Tunya Rd & Kapelwa St) runs four services a day to Lusaka (ZK65,380 to ZK84,060, seven hours). Buses to Shesheke (ZK32,690, five hours) leave at around 10am from Mingongo bus station next to the Catholic church at Dambwa village, 3km west of the town centre. Direct buses to Mongu (ZK51,370, nine hours) leave at midnight from Maramba market, though you might feel more comfortable on a morning bus to Sesheke, and then transfer to a Mongu bus (ZK23,350, four hours).

Combis (minibuses) to the Botswana border at Kazungula (ZK18,680, one hour) depart from Dambwa, 3km west of the town centre, on Nakatindi Rd.

International

For information about travelling to Botswana, and crossing the Zambia–Botswana border at Kazungula, see p166. For information about travelling to Namibia, and crossing the Zambia–Namibia border at Katima Mulilo, see p179. For information about crossing into Zimbabwe along the Victoria Falls Bridge, see p155.

CAR & MOTORCYCLE

If you're driving a rented car or motorcycle, be advised that the vast majority of companies do not insure their vehicles in Zambia.

HITCHING

With patience, it's fairly easy to hitch from Kazungula, Botswana, and Katima Mulilo, Namibia, to Livingstone. The best place in all three towns to arrange a lift is at any petrol station.

TRAIN

The *Zambezi Express* leaves Livingstone for Lusaka (economy/standard/1st class/ sleeper US$4/5/7/8, 15 hours), via Choma, on Tuesday, Thursday and Sunday at 7pm. Reservations are available at the **train station** (☎ 320001), which is signed off Mosi-oa-Tunya Rd.

Getting Around

TO/FROM THE AIRPORT

Livingstone Airport is located 6km northwest of town, and is easily accessible by taxi (US$10 each way).

CAR & MOTORCYCLE

If you're planning on renting a car in Zambia, consider using **Hemingways** (☎ 320996, 323097; www.hemingwayszambia.com), based in Livingstone. They have new Toyota Hi-Lux campers, fully kitted.

COMBIS & TAXIS

Combis run regularly along Mosi-oa-Tunya Rd to Victoria Falls and the Zambian border, and cost US$0.50 for 15 minutes. Taxis, which are blue, cost US$10.

MOSI-OA-TUNYA NATIONAL PARK

Zambia's smallest national park is located 11km from Livingstone, and is divided into two sections – the Victoria Falls World Heritage National Monument Site and Mosi-oa-Tunya Game Park.

Victoria Falls World Heritage National Monument Site

The entrance to the **park** (admission US$10, ☉ 6am-6pm) is located just before the Zambian border post. From the entrance, a path leads to the visitor information centre, which has modest displays on local fauna, geology and culture as well as a healthy number of craft stalls.

From the centre, a network of paths lead through thick vegetation to various viewpoints. You can walk upstream along a path mercifully free of fences – and warning notices (so take care!) – to watch the Zambezi waters glide smoothly through rocks and little islands towards the lip of the falls.

For close-up views of the **Eastern Cataract**, nothing beats the hair-raising (and hair-wetting) walk across the **footbridge**, through swirling clouds of mist, to a sheer buttress called the **Knife Edge**. If the water is low, or the wind is favourable, you'll be treated to a magnificent view of the falls as well as the yawning abyss below. Otherwise, your vision (and your clothes) will be drenched by spray. Then you can walk down a steep track to the banks of the great Zambezi to see the huge whirlpool called the **Boiling Pot**.

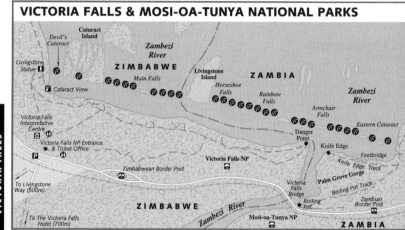

VICTORIA FALLS & MOSI-OA-TUNYA NATIONAL PARKS

Like its counterpart on the Zimbabwean side, the park is open again in the evenings during (and just before and after) a full moon in order to see the amazing **lunar rainbow**. The tickets cost an extra US$10 – hours of operation vary, though you can inquire through your accommodation.

Mosi-oa-Tunya Game Park
Upriver from the falls, and only 3km southwest of Livingstone, is this tiny **wildlife sanctuary** (per person US$10; 6am-6pm), which has a surprising range of animals including rhinos, zebras, giraffes, buffaloes, elephants and antelopes.

Getting There & Away
The Zambian side of the falls is 11km south of Livingstone and along the main road to the border with Zimbabwe. Plenty of minibuses and shared taxis ply the route from the minibus terminal along Senanga Rd in Livingstone. As muggings have been reported, it is best to take a taxi.

ZIMBABWE

Although Zimbabwe was long the preferred base for visiting Victoria Falls, in recent years travellers have been reluctant to cross the border. In all fairness, there were plenty of reasons to be alarmed, especially since the international media held a glaring spotlight on stories of petrol rationing, hyperinflation, rampant land reform and food shortages. At the time of research, the US-based *Foreign Policy* magazine ranked Zimbabwe second (after Somalia) in their top 10 list of failed states.

As a testament to their resilience, however, Zimbabweans always believe this will get better and fortunately tourists and tourist locations are not targets for political violence. So foreign tourists continue to remain safely on the sidelines of the majority of Zimbabwe's ongoing problems.

Despite the threat of nation-state collapse, Zimbabwe has always been on the map for certain groups of intrepid travellers. For the luxury-seeking international jet setters, the generator-fuelled power in the five-star lodges has never flickered and the imported fine wine has never stopped flowing. For shoestringers looking to bolster their travel resumes with a bit of street cred, travelling around Zim has always had undeniable appeal. But Victoria Falls is good for Granny, adrenaline junkies, nature freaks and everyone in between.

While it is recommended that you monitor the situation closely before visiting Zimbabwe, at the time of research, the recent introduction of the US dollar means shortages are not an issue in Vic Falls, and that the town is safe to visit. The farcical Zim dollar is now being sold just as a souvenir, and while dollarisation hasn't helped everyone in the country, food is

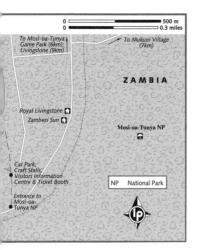

To Mosi-oa-Tunya
Game Park (6km);
Livingstone (9km)

To Mukuni Village
(7km)

ZAMBIA

Royal Livingstone
Zambezi Sun

Mosi-oa-Tunya NP

Car Park,
Craft Stalls;
Visitors Information
Centre & Ticket Booth

NP   National Park

Entrance to
Mosi-oa-
Tunya NP

0 ——————— 500 m
0 ——————— 0.3 miles

VICTORIA FALLS

☎ 013

Unlike Livingstone, the town of Victoria Falls (or simply Vic Falls) was built for tourism. It is right upon the falls with neat, walkable streets lined with hotels, bars, shops and craft markets. These days, however, Vic Falls feels like a resort in off-season. The off-season for this side has been long and tragic, but it's no longer deserved. The Zimbabwean side is a safe, calm and fully functional tourist resort.

Remote in terms of the rest of Zimbabwe, Vic Falls remained largely untouched by the violent troubles elsewhere in the country. And with road access to and from Zambia, Namibia and Botswana, the lodges and smart hotels remained relatively well-stocked even in the hard times. Dollarisation happened in Vic Falls years ahead of the rest of the country. And yes, there was a Z100 trillion dollar note.

The people of the town are passionate about their home and boy have they got some generous hospitality to offer too. However, it isn't all-paradise here and visitors can expect to be approached by touts.

All this, together with an active organisation of community-minded and resourceful tourism operators leading a campaign called gotovictoriafalls.com, means tourism should/could be *the* economic anchor for Zimbabwe. Social responsibility is ingrained in their plans and, being entirely dependent on tourism, Victoria Falls

back in the stores, and petrol is back in the pumps. And, although it remains to be seen whether or not newly elected Prime Minister Morgan Tsvangirai can continue to share power with the country's big man, President Robert Mugabe, a coalition government was a fascinating development in Zimbabwean politics.

Walking through the streets of Vic Falls can make you wonder how it looked when it was heaving. Locals eke out a meagre living by tending to the few remaining tourists. As when making plans to visit any African country, remember that situations can change. Zimbabwe is the path less travelled right now, yet it is extraordinary and unforgettable.

ZIM OR ZAM?

Victoria Falls straddle the border between Zimbabwe and Zambia, and are easily accessible from both countries. However, the big question for most travellers is: do I visit the falls from the town of Victoria Falls, Zimbabwe or from Livingstone, Zambia? The answer is simple: Visit the falls from both sides and, if possible, stay in both towns.

From the Zimbabwean side, you're further from the falls, though the overall views are better. From the Zambian side, you can almost stand on top of the falls, though your perspective is narrowed. Admission is cheaper on the Zambian side, though the Zimbabwean side is less-touristed and much quieter.

The town of Victoria Falls was built for tourists, so it's easily walkable and located right next to the entrance to the Falls. It has a natural African bush beauty.

Livingstone is an attractive town with a relaxed ambience and a proud, historic air. Since the town of Victoria Falls was the main tourist centre for so many years, Livingstone feels more authentic, perhaps because locals earn their livelihood through means other than tourism. Livingstone is bustling with travellers year round, though the town is fairly spread out, and located 11km from the falls.

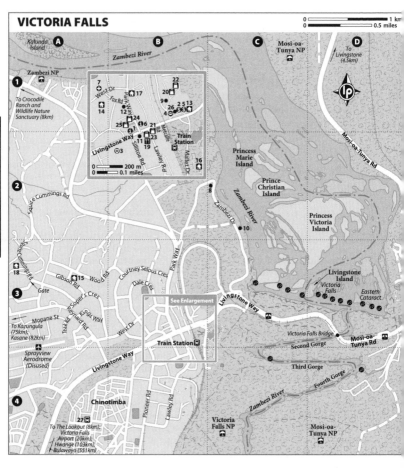

residents are very mindful of the need for safety, quality and stability and to ensure all visitors take away positive memories of this stunningly beautiful destination.

Orientation

Vic Falls was designed to be walkable – it's just over a kilometre from the town centre to the entrance to Victoria Falls National Park.

Information

EMERGENCY

Medical Air Rescue Service (MARS; ☎ 44764)
Police (☎ 44206; Livingstone Way)
Victoria Falls Surgery (☎ 43356; West Dr)

INTERNET ACCESS

Telco (☎ 43441; Phumula Centre; per hr US$1; ☒ 8am-6pm) Surprisingly reliable internet access.

MONEY

Barclays Bank (off Livingstone Way)
Standard Chartered Bank (off Livingstone Way)

POST

Post office (off Livingstone Way)

TELEPHONE

Telephone calls can be made at telephone offices and travel agencies upstairs in Soper's Arcade. To dial Livingstone you don't need the country or city code – simply dial ☎ 8, then the local number.

TOURIST INFORMATION

Zimbabwe Tourism Authority (☎ 44376; zta@vicfalls .tzatim.co.zw; 258 Adam Stander Dr; ⏰ 8am-4.30pm Mon-Fri) gives away a few brochures and can book accommodation throughout the country.

Dangers & Annoyances

Mugging is not such a problem in Victoria Falls any more, but at dawn and dusk wild animals such as lions, elephants and warthogs do roam the streets away from the town centre, so take taxis at these times. Although it's perfectly safe to walk to and from the falls, it's advisable to stick to the more touristed areas.

Sights & Activities

The **Big Tree**, which is a huge baobab tree with a 20m circumference and historical importance, is on Zambezi Dr heading north from near the entrance to the falls. This was the main trading spot for Zimbabweans and Zambians – the latter canoed across the river before the bridge was built.

Further on from there, take the first road and clear path leading to the river. It leads to a spot called **The Rock**, a wonderful place to watch the wildly rushing water right at the lip of the falls. Local guides can take you. Ask them also about **The Lookout**, 8km out of town, another local secret, where you really hear the sound of the Smoke That Thunders.

The **Falls Craft Village** (☎ 44309; Adam Stander Dr; ⏰ 8am-5pm) is a touristy mock-up of a traditional Zimbabwean village. Souvenirs start at US$20. It offers the chance to watch craftspeople at work, consult with a *nganga* (a fortune teller) and see some remarkable

'pole dancing' (but not the sort you might find in a Western strip joint).

The **Crocodile Ranch and Wildlife Nature Sanctuary** (☎ 40509-11; Parkway; admission incl guided tour US$10; ⏰ 8am-5pm) offers lots of crocs, lions and leopards.

The impressive **Victoria Falls Aquarium** (Livingstone Way; admission US$5; ⏰ 9.30am-5.30pm) is apparently the largest freshwater aquarium in Africa. It's worth a visit for the bright and imaginative displays about the aquatic life in the Zambezi River.

The **Elephant's Walk Museum** (Elephant's Walk Shopping Village, off Adam Stander Dr; admission free; ⏰ 8am-5pm) houses a small but worthwhile private collection detailing the cultural heritage of local ethnic groups.

The **Zambezi Nature Sanctuary** (☎ 44604; Parkway; admission incl guided tour US$5; ⏰ 8am-5pm) offers lots of crocs, as well as lions and leopards. It shows informative videos, and houses a museum, aviary and insect collection. Try to get there for the lion and croc feeding, which takes place around 4pm daily.

Sleeping

There are budget and midrange places in Zimbabwe but on the whole, accommodation in Zimbabwe is expensive.

BUDGET & MIDRANGE

Victoria Falls Backpackers (☎ 42209, www.victoria fallsbackpackers.com; 357 Gibson Rd; camping per person US$4, dm US$8, s/d with shared bathroom US$10/20; 💻 📶) Although it's a bit further out than other places, Victoria Falls Backpackers is superbly set up for independent and budget travellers.

VICTORIA FALLS

VICTORIA FALLS

Shoestrings Backpackers (☎ 40167; 12 West Dr; campsite per person US$6, dm US$9, d US$35; ☲) Shoestrings is a popular stop for the overland truck crowd, though the laid-back ambience also draws in a good number of independent travellers.

Victoria Falls Restcamp & Lodges (☎ 40509-11; www.vicfallsrestcamp.com; cnr Parkway & West Drs; campsite US$10, dm US$11, s/d chalets with shared bathroom US$25/34, fitted dome tents US$60, s/d cottages with bathroom US$67; ☲) Now run by the same people who do the sumptuous Ilala Lodge Hotel. This institution still has a great pool and the restaurant, In-Da-Belly (right), but is doing well under new management. The rooms are very clean and you can now book all your falls activities here. Everything under one roof.

TOP END

Victoria Falls Safari Lodge (☎ 43201; www.vfsl.com; Squire Cummings Rd; s/d incl breakfast from US$315/395; ☒ ☲) If you were only coming to Victoria Falls on your Africa trip, staying here would give you it all: set in a national park you get the bush experience of a tented camp complete with waterhole where wildlife drink at sunset (as you drink your sundowner or dine on gourmet bush cuisine), on top of your trips to the falls and the river.

Victoria Falls Hotel (☎ 44751; www.victoriafalls hotel.com; Mallet Dr; s/d incl breakfast from US$216/232; ☒ ☲) This historic hotel (the oldest in Zimbabwe) oozes elegance and sophistication, and occupies an impossibly scenic location. Looking across manicured lawns to the gorge and bridge, you can't see the falls as such but, they are just there, and you do see the spray. High tea here is an institution.

Ilala Lodge (☎ 44737; www.ilalalodge.com; 411 Livingstone Way; s/d incl breakfast from US$256/320; ☒ ☲) This hotel is situated just 300m from the main entrance to the mighty Victoria Falls and is a truly magnificent hotel. A colonial relic, it is adorned with mounted rifles, hunting trophies and oil paintings; classically decorated rooms face out towards the manicured lawns and elaborate gardens.

Matetsi Water Lodge (☎ 04731295; www.andbeyond .com; per person sharing US$435; ☲) Situated 30km from the falls, along the banks of the Zambezi, this shows Zimbabwean finesse in hospitality at its best. Each uber-luxurious bungalow has its own pool yet is set in the wild. There are very good specials throughout the year so contact them for cheaper rates.

Eating

In-Da-Belly Restaurant (☎ 332077; Victoria Falls Rest camp & Lodges; meals US$5-8) The name is a pla on Ndebele, one of the two major popula tion groups in Zimbabwe, and it serve good bistro-style cuisine.

Mama Africa (☎ 41725; meals US$5-8) Thi perennial tourist haunt behind the Landel. Centre specialises in local dishes, steaks an game meats when available.

River Cafe (☎ 42994; Landela Centre) This caf serves a variety of cafe-style meals. It's a nic spot to hang out and have a meal or drinks You can shop for curios in the complex too

Terrace (Victoria Falls Hotel, Mallet Dr; meals US$20 The Terrace at the stately Victoria Falls Hote overlooks the hotel gardens and the Victori Falls Bridge, and brims with English colonia ambience. High tea here is a must – just do it

Boma (☎ 43201; Victoria Falls Safari Lodge, Squir Cummings Rd; meals US$40 buffet) Boma is the plac to release your inner tourist without bein tacky and enjoy a taste of Africa: do interac tive drumming or get your fortune told b a witch doctor.

Drinking

There's unfortunately not much life in Vi Falls after sunset, though the bar at **Shoe strings Backpackers** (☎ 40167; 12 West Dr; drinks from US$3) is the place to go. Here you can mee the local guides off duty, and they can giv you local knowledge on places to visit.

Shopping

The **craft market** (Adam Stander Dr) has loads o curios, while the nearby Elephant's Wall Shopping Village complex stocks mainly up market crafts. The craftsmen eke out a mea

---

THE MIGHTY ZAMBEZI RIVER

The Zambezi River emerges from the north-western tip of Zambia, one of the greatest rivers of Africa. It descends from 1500m above sea level and traverses six countries before its epic 2574km journey ends. The Indian Ocean receives its largest fresh water discharge through this incredible catchment. The Zambezi has a basin of more than 1,570,000 sq km and is the lifeblood of the people that reside on the river. The life it supports – from people to vast populations of animals – is as wild as it is captivating.

FURTHER READING

Want to know a bit more about Victoria Falls? We suggest having a read or a look at:

- *Exploring Victoria Falls* by Prof Lee Berger and Brett Hilton-Barber
- *Mosi-oa-Tunya: Handbook to the Victoria Falls Region* by DW Phillipson
- www.wildzambezi.com
- www.gotovictoriafalls.com
- www.africaalbidatourism.com
- www.africanencounter.com
- www.zctf.mweb.co.zw – Zimbabwe Conservation Task Force
- www.zimbabwe-art.com – Zimbabwe Conservation Art Programme

are living by selling to tourists, so it would be good for lots of reasons to go shopping! African items are often made from recycled items and they do look good at home.

The **Phumula Centre** is a small mall of shops for locals and tourists, supermarkets and small restaurants.

Getting There & Away

AIR

Check out www.flightsite.co.za, where you can search all the airlines including low cost carriers (and car-hire companies) for the cheapest flights and book yourself. **South African Airways** (☎ 011-808678; www.flysaa.com) and **British Airways** (www.britishairways.com) fly every day to Johannesburg from around US$320 return. **Air Namibia** (www.airnamibia.com) flies to Windhoek for around US$530 return.

BICYCLE

Bikes can be ridden to/from Zambia, however, bear in mind that cyclists have been mugged while riding to/from the Zambian border and the falls.

BUS & MINIBUS

Minibuses or combis are no longer recommended to travellers as they become so neglected and overused that they break down and are frequently involved in fatal accidents.

For information about crossing into Zambia along the Victoria Falls Bridge, see p155.

CAR & MOTORCYCLE

If you're driving a rented car or motorcycle from Zambia, you'll need a letter from your rental company stating that you are permitted to enter Zimbabwe.

HITCHING

It's fairly easy to hitch between Victoria Falls and Kazungula, Botswana. If you head to the petrol station in both towns you'll have the best chance of a lift.

TRAIN

The *Mosi-oa-Tunya* train leaves Victoria Falls daily at 6.30pm for Bulawayo, Zimbabwe (economy/2nd/1st class, US$1/3/4, 12 hours). Make reservations at the **ticket office** (☎ 44391; ⏱ 7am-12pm & 2-4pm Mon-Fri, 7am-10am Sat & Sun) inside the train station.

Getting Around

TO/FROM THE AIRPORT

Victoria Falls Airport is located 20km southeast of town, and is easily accessible by taxi (US$20 each way).

CAR & MOTORCYCLE

When planning your trip, find out what the situation is with petrol availability, as this is an issue that has cycles all of its own. At the time of writing, petrol was readily available in petrol stations but this may change.

TAXIS

A taxi around town costs about US$10 and slightly more after dark. Taxis don't use meters, so you'll have to bargain. The taxi cabs themselves are all pretty shabby, but they get you from A to B.

VICTORIA FALLS NATIONAL PARK

The entrance to the **national park** (Map pp160-1; admission US$20, ⏱ 6am-6pm) is located just before the Zimbabwean border post. The admission price must be paid in US dollars. One of the most dramatic spots is the westernmost point known as **Cataract View**. Another track leads to the aptly named **Danger Point**, where a sheer, unfenced 100m drop-off will rattle your nerves. From there, you can follow a side track for a view of the **Victoria Falls Bridge**.

Like its counterpart on the Zimbabwean side, the park is open again in the evenings during (and just before and after) a full moon in order to see the amazing

CROSSING THE BORDER FROM ZAMBIA INTO BOTSWANA

Coming from Livingstone, it's about 60km west to Kazungula, the Zambian border town, and across the river, a short pontoon ride away, is Botswana. There are one or two buses (ZK20,000, 35 minutes) here daily from Livingstone, departing from Nakatindi Rd in the morning. The Zambian side of the border is disordered and frankly, at times, chaotic. There are huge lines of trucks on the road leading up to the border and then a mess of trucks near the pontoon.

Heaps of guys at the Zambian border post will hassle you to change money; and you will need Botswanan pula if you're bringing a car across the border into Botswana. Give the sharks a wide berth and change at the Stero Bureau de Change (a clearly visible shack on your left as you approach the border – it should be open even if the sharks tell you that it's closed). Keep in mind that you need around 200 pula, and whatever sum you require for a visa (if you need one). Note that US dollars and other currencies are not accepted at the Botswanan border post.

To avoid the sharks and touts trying to 'steer' you through formalities, follow these simple steps. If driving, park your car just before you go through the border gate and go to change money. Then walk through the gate and around to the back of the building immediately on your left. Go inside and get your passport stamped. If you have a vehicle go to the last window on your left and fill out a Temporary Export Permit (TEP), as well as filling in the register with details of your vehicle. This costs nothing – make sure you get a copy of the TEP form (after it's stamped). Then proceed down to the departure point for the pontoon. Walk into the pontoon company building and pay ZK30,000/40,000 for an ordinary/large vehicle (ZK4000 for foot passengers, or US$20 for a non-Zambian registered vehicle). Leave this building, turn right, and go into the next building to see if you are required to make a customs payment for departing Zambia (ZK10,000; tourists should be exempt, but it's a good idea to check). Then go back to your vehicle, and drive through to the pontoon departure point and wait to be directed onto the pontoon.

At the border post in Botswana, it's a huge contrast: orderly with no hassle. Proceed to the immigration/customs building up the road from the pontoon, a short drive or walk away. Fill in an entry card, get your passport stamped (or a visa if you require one), and then fill in a Temporary Import Permit for your vehicle if you're driving, and get that stamped. Go to the payment window and pay for the permit (120 pula), insurance (50 pula) and road duty (20 pula). This is all very straightforward, and the immigration/customs staff are helpful.

Lastly if you're in a vehicle, drive through a puddle of water and get out of the car to stamp your feet on a mat – it's a foot & mouth disease control measure. The town of Kasane is only 12km west and is the jumping-off point for excursions into Chobe National Park.

Heading back into Zambia don't forget to hand back your copy of the TIP at the Botswanan border post; and get your copy of the TEP stamped and then hand it in at the gate on your way out at the Zambian border post. Note that you'll get hassled from Zambians on the Botswanan side of the border trying to sell you insurance – you don't need this if you're in a Zambian registered vehicle. If you are in a non-Zambian registered vehicle then you also have to pay a carbon tax (about ZK150,000, depending on the size of your vehicle) payable on the Zambian side of the border. Pay for the pontoon at the same office on the Zambian side of the border once you've crossed.

lunar rainbow. The tickets cost an extra US$10 – hours of operation vary, though you can inquire through your accommodation.

ZAMBEZI NATIONAL PARK

This **national park** (Map p162; admission US$10; ◷ 6am-6.30pm) consists of 40km of Zambezi River frontage and a spread of wildlife-rich mopane forest and savannah. The park is best known for its herds of sable antelopes but it is also home to lions, giraffes and elephants. The entrance to the park is situated only 5km northwest of the Victoria Falls town centre, and is easily accessible by private vehicle. If you don't have your own wheels (or your petrol is running low) tour operators on both sides of the border offer wildlife drives, guided hikes and fishing expeditions in the park.

Western Zambia

Western Zambia is at the bottom of some travellers' itineraries and at the top of others': if you're after easy access, lots of other tourists and well-known attractions look elsewhere. But if you're after a real wild Africa experience then you're heading in the right direction. This western area is dominated by two huge rivers, the Kafue and the upper waters of the Zambezi, and the woodlands of central Zambia thin out here as the soil becomes sandy – this area is an extension of the Kalahari Desert in neighbouring Namibia.

Kafue National Park is the biggest single park in Africa, and is truly magnificent with all the big mammals, marvellous birdwatching and a thousand different landscapes that include river systems offering the chance to float past a leopard stretched out on the shore, a fish eagle perched imperiously on a branch above the water or a 500-strong buffalo herd lapping noisily at its cool waters. It's the only place in the country where you can track lions on foot and have a great chance of finding them.

Other highlights are thundering waterfalls and tremendous views of flood plains; a chance to experience even more remote wilderness areas such as Liuwa Plain National Park, which sees few visitors but is a majestic patch of Africa; an exploration of Barotseland, home of the Lozi people and site of the colourful Kuomboka, Zambia's best-known traditional ceremony; and easy access to Botswana and Namibia with world-class national parks such as Chobe to explore.

WESTERN ZAMBIA

HIGHLIGHTS

- Figuring out where to begin in **Kafue National Park** (p174), a colossal wilderness and one of the best places on the continent to spot leopards

- Popping into wildlife-rich **Botswana** and travel-friendly **Namibia** (p178)

- Getting up close to thundering **Ngonye Falls** (p169), an off-the-beaten-track rival to Victoria Falls

- Staring across the expansive flood plains from far-flung **Mongu** (p170)

- Heading out to remote **Liuwa Plain National Park** (p173) to see staggering numbers of great herd animals

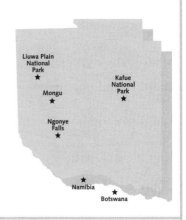

Liuwa Plain National Park ★

Kafue National Park ★

Mongu ★

Ngonye Falls ★

Namibia ★

Botswana ★

TELEPHONE CODE: 0217

SESHEKE

Sesheke consists of two towns on either side of the Zambezi River linked by a new bridge. They are 200km upstream from Livingstone (virtually opposite the Namibian town of Katima Mulilo) – and it makes a handy gateway to Barotseland if you're coming from the southeast. The major part of town is on the eastern side of the river, before you cross the bridge. There's not much to actually see or do here and it's really used as a transit point between Zambia and Namibia. The smaller section of town, on the western side of the river, is centred around the Zambian border post, with the Namibian border a few hundred metres down the road (opposite).

ourpick **Brenda's Best & Baobab Bar** (☎ 097 9011917; campsite per person ZK30,000, chalets ZK150,000-250,000) This is the best place to stay in Sesheke. It is friendly, and offers homely and airy chalets with thatched roofs and a relaxing but basic campsite with a popular bar built around a massive baobab. The more expensive chalets come with DSTV and a fridge, not to mention a huge armchair.

DRIVING IN WESTERN ZAMBIA

The road from Livingstone to Sesheke is in very good condition and sees little traffic; it's tar all the way, and about 200km in distance. From Sesheke north to Mongu, you need to check road conditions before you set off. During the wet season and in the month or two afterwards this road can be impassable due to flooding.

Along the Great West Road, the stretch from Lusaka to Nasalunga Gate (Kafue National Park) is excellent, and it's also in very good condition through the park. From the western gate (Tateyoyo) to Kaoma road conditions worsen considerably, so keep your speed down: it's bumpy; there are dips and hiding-in-the-shadows potholes. The road then, from Kaoma to Mongu, is quite good, with few potholes.

The doors to the four chalets have intri cate carvings of different animals instea of numbers, and there are other attractiv woodcarvings around the place. There's als

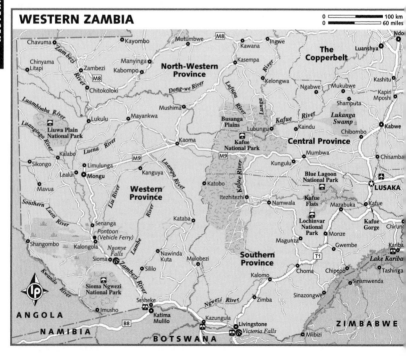

WESTERN ZAMBIA

a grassed area along the riverfront with bench seating that makes a lovely place to camp: watch for hippos and monitor lizards! A restaurant should be open by the time you read this. The entrance to Brenda's (which is well hidden from the main drag) is 200m on the western side of the church on the main street, down an unmarked road towards the river.

Not the most beautiful place to stay, **Sisheke Lodge** (☎ 481086; main road; tw/d/queen ZK180,000/200,000/220,000) is nevertheless functional and practical – and rooms, that come with a TV, fridge and fan, reflect this. Twin and double rooms come with a shower, while a queen room comes with a shower and bath. Service is polite and professional and a continental breakfast is included.

Small buses link Sesheke with Natakindi Rd in Livingstone (ZK45,000, two hours,

two or three daily), usually in the morning, and minibuses also make this journey. Occasional minibuses also link Sesheke with Katima Mulilo.

SIOMA & NGONYE FALLS

The village of Sioma is about 60km southeast of Kalongola. It has a large mission, a row of shops, and that's about it. The only reason to come here is **Ngonye Falls** (also called Sioma Falls) (admission free; ☉ 24hr), a 1km-wide chain of waterfalls, rapids and rocky islands cutting across the Zambezi River. It's beautiful and very impressive and would be a major attraction if it wasn't so difficult to reach. Imagine something almost as majestic as Victoria Falls, but with almost no other person (local or foreign) in sight.

If you can, stop at the National Parks & Wildlife Service office near the falls who can

WESTERN ZAMBIA

CROSSING THE BORDER INTO NAMIBIA

Coming from Livingstone, it's around 200km west to Sesheke, the Zambian border town, and here, a short distance away across the bridge, is Namibia. See above for details of bus services from Livingstone.

If you have a vehicle, drive straight through Sesheke and over the bridge that spans the Zambezi River. Note that the formalities for leaving Zambia are over this bridge (not before you cross it). Curve right after the bridge and the immigration/customs building is on your left (last building on your left). Go in and get your passport stamped at immigration. Customs is out the back of this building – it's an unmarked door hidden among boxes of confiscated alcohol piled almost to the roof; ask at the immigration desk for directions. This is where you fill in a Temporary Export Permit (TEP) for your vehicle. Before you leave the Zambian side ensure that you have enough Namibian dollars or SA rand to pay for your visa (if you require one) and for the Cross Border Charge Permit for your car/4WD (180 Namibian dollars) or motorbike (110 Namibian dollars). For help in changing money, ask in the immigration/customs building. A black market in currency exchange does exist; know your exchange rates, though, before you do this.

Cross the border and Namibian formalities at Wenela border post are just up the road. Here, go into the immigration/customs building, fill in an arrival card and get your passport stamped. If you have a vehicle, complete a Cross Border Charge Permit and you'll be given a certificate to take with you confirming it has been paid. Don't forget to walk over the mat for foot and mouth disease control, just outside of immigration. You may also need to stop at the military checkpoint on your way out to fill in a register with details of your vehicle. The Namibian town of Katima Mulilo is then only a few kilometres away.

On your way back out of Namibia, fill in a departure card and get your passport stamped at Wenela. If driving, surrender your Cross Border Charge Permit and you'll be given a tax invoice for your records. At the gate on your way out, sign the exit register.

On the Zambian side, fill in an entry card and get your passport stamped, or buy a visa. Slide past the mountains of alcohol and surrender your TEP at customs. Here you may be asked some penetrating questions such as, 'What's the colour of your car?' Drive back over the bridge into the main town of Sesheke if heading towards Livingstone, or continue on towards Mongu in the far-flung west (but check with locals regarding the state of this road first, especially after the rainy season as it can get flooded/washed away).

advise on the best way to visit and point out a local **campsite** (campsite US$10). You should be able to engage an official guide here. While it's easy to get a view of the falls, getting a really good view is much harder as you need to get out onto an island in front of the falls – ask at the National Parks office if there are any boats that might take you there.

Situated 8km south of Ngonye Falls, **Maziba Bay Lodge** (☎ 0927-11 234 1747; www.mutemwa.com /maziba.htm; all-inclusive per person US$320) has large wooden chalets with bathrooms and comfortable furnishings, overlooking an idyllic sandy beach on the Zambezi. Bookings are necessary for the chalets, but campers can just turn up; no large trucks are permitted. This place organises visits for its guests to the falls. Tariff does not include drinks.

The falls are less than 1km east of the main road, about 10km south of Sioma. For drivers, access is not difficult from Sesheke, but far more problematic from Senanga (p170). Otherwise, hitch a ride and ask to be dropped by the turn-off (look for the 'Wildlife Department' sign).

SIOMA NGWEZI NATIONAL PARK

This undeveloped, very remote and rarely visited 500 sq km **national park** (per person/vehicle per day US$5-15) is one to watch for future developments. It's in the southwestern corner of Zambia, bordering Angola and the Caprivi Strip in Namibia; it's also only 50km from Botswana. The park is dry, quite flat and forested with miombo and acacia woodland with areas of teak forest. It's unfenced and there is free movement of animals between the park and the surrounding Game Management Area (GMA). The park has a history of cross-border poaching problems, though, and wildlife is scarce, although elephants still do occur in reasonable numbers. There are very few roads and no permanent settlements. It is hoped that a big operator will come in and repopulate the park with animals, and given its proximity to Livingstone it has enormous potential. If you want to visit, it's worth contacting **Mutemwa Lodge** (☎ 0927-11 234 1747; www .mutemwa.com), located not far from the park, which sometimes runs safaris here.

An independent trip is possible but very difficult – you need to be completely self-sufficient and have a fully equipped 4WD.

Begin by heading to Sioma and picking up a scout from the National Parks & Wildlife Service office.

SENANGA

If you're coming from Lusaka, Senanga has a real 'end of the line' feel – the tar runs out and the dusty dirt road that continues south is quiet and rarely travelled – although the main street can be surprisingly lively especially in the evening, and the views of the Zambezi are beautiful. It is the best place to break up a journey between Mongu and Ngonye Falls or Sesheke.

The best accommodation option is **Senanga Safaris** (☎ 230156; campsite per person ZK30,000, d incl breakfast US$60). It offers comfortable rondavels with splendid views over the Zambezi plains – spoilt only by the giant satellite TV dish in the garden. The bar sells cold beer and the restaurant serves expensive meals. Several cheaper restaurants are dotted along the main street nearby. Be warned that you may have difficulty getting accommodation when it hosts an annual fishing competition over a few days in the dry season.

Minibuses and pick-ups run between Senanga and Mongu (US$4.50, two to three hours) several times a day. About 30km south of Senanga (and accessible by minibus) a pontoon (vehicle ferry) carries passengers (normally free) and vehicles (US$20/30 for 2/4WD) across the Zambezi to the tiny settlement of Kalongola (on the west bank of the river) from where the sandy road continues south towards Sesheke and Namibia. Often the ferry doesn't operate between February and June and the road between Senanga and Kalongola is flooded and impassable, so passengers take a small boat, but car drivers may have to charter a larger, different pontoon. Kalongola is marked as Sitoti on some maps, but this is a separate village about 5km south of Kalongola.

MONGU

The largest town in Barotseland, and the capital of the Western Province, is on high ground overlooking the flat and seemingly endless Liuwa Plain. This is a low-key town with plenty of activity on the streets but doesn't feel as hectic as other Zambian towns. It's quite spread out with no real centre, and the highlight is the view over the flood

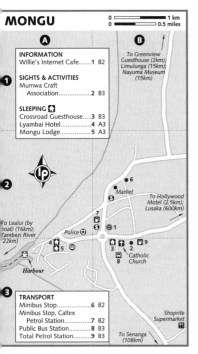

MONGU

0 ———— 1 km
0 ———— 0.5 miles

INFORMATION
Willie's Internet Cafe......1 B2

SIGHTS & ACTIVITIES
Mumwa Craft
    Association................2 B3

SLEEPING
Crossroad Guesthouse....3 B3
Lyambai Hotel...............4 A3
Mongu Lodge.................5 A3

To Greenview
Guesthouse (2km);
Limulunga (15km);
Nayuma Museum
(15km)

• 6
Market

To Hollywood
Motel (2.5km);
Lusaka (600km)

To Lealui (by
boat) (16km);
Zambezi River
(22km)

Police

Catholic
Church

Harbour

TRANSPORT
Minibus Stop.................6 B2
Minibus Stop, Caltex
    Petrol Station............7 B2
Public Bus Station..........8 B3
Total Petrol Station........9 B3

Shoprite
Supermarket

To Senanga
(108km)

plains – the town has an enviable position, making for spectacular panoramas. From harbour on the southwestern outskirts of town, an 8km canal runs westwards to meet a tributary of the Zambezi. The river port is a fascinating settlement of reed and thatched buildings, where local fishermen sell their catch, and it's a good spot for people watching as longboats glide down the river transporting people and goods to nearby villages.

Mongu really comes alive once a year when thousands of people flock there for the annual **Kuomboka ceremony** (p172). Not surprisingly, the prices for rooms (if you can find one) skyrocket at this time.

There are a few internet cafes around town including **Willie's Internet Cafe** (per min K300; 8am-8pm), which has modern facilities and decent speeds.

Sights & Activities

The non-profit **Mumwa Craft Association** (221623; Lusaka Rd) is well worth dropping into while you are in town. It represents a network of local craft producers throughout

the province with proceeds from sales being ploughed back into the communities. The basket weaving in particular is something special and the woodcarving is also very high quality. It's a great place to shop because of the low prices and high standard of workmanship. It's located right next to the Total petrol station on the road to Lusaka.

VISITING THE PALACES

The village of **Limulunga** is 15km north of Mongu. Here you can see the palace of the *litunga* – the king of the Lozi. It's a large traditional house, occupied by the *litunga* from around April to June, when his main residence at Lealui is flooded. You cannot go inside, and photos are not allowed. Of more interest is the **Nayuma Museum** (admission ZK5000; 8am-5pm daily), with its colony of bats in the roof, and exhibits about the Lozi, *litunga* and Kuomboka including a large model of the *nalikwanda* boat used in the ceremony. There are also some fascinating shots of royal pageantry, Zambian-style, in a black-and-white photo exhibition titled, 'A Retrospective in the Forties' by Max Gluckman. Otherwise, various artefacts and cultural exhibits including a potted history of snuffing are pretty old and dusty, but there are some interesting pictures of the historical line of the Lozi *litungas*. Minibuses run between Mongu and Limulunga throughout the day.

The village of **Lealui**, on the flood plain 15km northwest of Mongu, is the site of the *litunga*'s main palace; he lives here for most of the year (July to March), when the waters are low. The palace is a large single-storey Lozi house, built with traditional materials (wood, reeds, mud and thatch) and meticulously maintained. Around the palace are smaller houses for the *litunga*'s wives and family, and a tall reed fence surrounds the whole compound. It's not easy to reach, but the journey by boat (along a canal from Mongu to a branch of the Zambezi, then upstream to Lealui) is spectacular, passing local villages and plenty of birdlife. Avoid visiting at weekends, when *litunga*'s *kotu* (court) is closed, because you need permission from his *indunas* (advisors) to get a close look at the palace and even to take photos – and the *kotu* is only open from Monday to Friday.

WESTERN ZAMBIA

KUOMBOKA CEREMONY

The Kuomboka (literally, 'to move to dry ground') is probably one of the last great Southern African ceremonies. It is celebrated by the Lozi people of western Zambia, and marks the ceremonial journey of the *litunga* (the Lozi king) from his dry-season palace at Lealui, near Mongu, to his wet-season palace on higher ground at Limulunga. It usually takes place in late March or early April, and sometimes ties in with Easter. The dates are not fixed, however; they're dependent on the rains. In fact, the Kuomboka does not happen every year: in 1994, 1995 and 1996 the floods were not extensive enough to require the *litunga* to leave Lealui.

In 1933, a palace was built by Litunga Yeta III on permanently dry ground at the edge of the plain at a place called Limulunga. Although the Kuomboka was already a long-standing tradition, it was Yeta III who first made the move from Lealui to Limulunga a major ceremony.

Central to the ceremony is the royal barge, the *nalikwanda,* a huge wooden canoe, painted with black-and-white stripes, that carries the *litunga.* It is considered a great honour to be one of the hundred or so paddlers on the *nalikwanda,* and each paddler wears a head-dress of a scarlet beret with a piece of a lion's mane and a knee-length skirt of animal skins. Drums also play a leading role in the ceremony. The most important are the three royal war drums, kanaona, munanga and mundili, each more than 1m wide and said to be at least 170 years old.

The journey from Lealui to Limulanga takes about six hours. The *litunga* begins the day in traditional dress, but during the journey changes into the full uniform of a British admiral, complete with regalia and ostrich-plumed hat. The uniform was presented to the *litunga* in 1902 by the British King, Edward VII, in recognition of the treaties signed between the Lozi and Queen Victoria.

Public longboats between Mongu harbour and Lealui (US$2, one hour) leave once or twice a day. Alternatively, charter a boat to Lealui for about ZK500,000 return, which could take six people: the price includes fuel and is usually negotiable. There are many more options for boats around the time of the Kuomboka festival; then it's possible to get a ride for around ZK70,000 per person if you ask around. Make inquiries at the shed on the left as you enter the harbour. Buses do the trip in the late months of the dry season.

Sleeping & Eating

Sleeping options in Mongu are surprisingly good value – perhaps some of the best value for a town in the country. You'll easily find a comfortable option which won't make too great a demand on your wallet. Standard Zambian fare is available from most accommodation places and basic restaurants in town, and includes chicken, steak or fish with *nshima* or rice.

Lyambai Hotel (☎ 221138; Lusaka Rd; r ZK80,000-100,000) Yes, the Lyambai has seen better days – much better. It's ragged around the edges, not to mention in the middle. However, this beat-up place does have character, shade, sublime views over the flood plain and

friendly staff. We like it! ZK100,000 will buy you a bedroom and a separate sitting room complete with tatty furniture. Check the en suite bathroom though before you agree to a room. The hotel is 1.2km west of the public bus station and past the post office.

Crossroad Guesthouse (☎ 221649; Lusaka Rd; ZK100,000; 🗶) This place has a bar at the front of the building with rooms out the back that are a good distance from the road outside. Although it doesn't look much from the outside, the en suite rooms here are actually pretty good, kept very clean and will do nicely for a night or two, though maybe it's not the friendliest place around.

Mongu Lodge (☎ 221501; Mwanawina St; s/d inc breakfast ZK150,000/200,000; 🗶) In a nice, quiet location not far from the post office, this business-style lodge attracts Zambian business folk. It's worth paying extra for the renovated rooms with a bathroom and air-con. All room have fans and TV and the prices include breakfast. The outdoor bar is a nice touch.

Greenview Guesthouse (☎ 221029 Limulunga Rd; chalet ZK165,000) Next to the church, chalets here sleep two people and are fantastic value. Shiny tiled floors, fans DSTV and en suites make staying here a winning choice. Spacious inside and se in nice, grassy grounds with views of the flood plains, it may well be the best deal in Mongu. It belongs to the new Apostolic church next door, so partying is probably not a great idea. To find it, head up the road to Limulunga and keep an eye out for the sign on the left.

Getting There & Away

The public bus station is on the southeastern edge of town, behind the Catholic church. Several companies offer buses between Lusaka and Mongu (ZK115,000, eight hours).

A daily bus operates between Livingstone and Mongu (ZK120,000, 10 hours) via Sesheke, Kalongola and Senanga, but you're advised to break up this tough journey in Senanga. Better still, go to Lusaka from Livingstone and take the bus along the tarred road from Lusaka.

Minibuses and pick-ups leave on a fill-up-and-go basis from near the Caltex petrol station in Mongu for Senanga (US$4.50, three hours). From there, minibuses head to Sesheke.

LIUWA PLAIN NATIONAL PARK

About 100km northwest of Mongu, **Liuwa Plain National Park** (☎ 097 7158733; liuwa@african parks.co.zm; per person per day US$40; campsite per person

US$10, scout per day US$10) is 3600 sq km of true African wilderness on the Angolan border. A remote and rarely visited wild grassland area, it's where vast numbers of wildebeests and other grazing species such as lechwes, zebras, tsessebes and buffaloes gather at the beginning of the wet season. Although their gathering is often called a migration, it's more of a meander, but the wall-to-wall herds are nonetheless spectacular. Roan antelope, wild dogs, cheetahs and, in particularly high numbers, hyenas can be found in the park (lions are scheduled to be reintroduced in 2009) and birdwatching is also a highlight with water birds such as wattled cranes, marabou, saddle-billed storks, herons, pelicans and egrets, among others, making an appearance when the pans fill with water.

Although it became a national park in 1972, for years the park was in decline with no government funds to rehabilitate it. However, an organisation called African Parks (www.african-parks.org), which assists African governments in funding conservation projects, signed a lease agreement in 2004, and now manages the welfare and facilities of the park.

Liuwa Plain is accessible from June to November but the best time to go is

BAROTSELAND

For many Zambians, Western Province is Barotseland – the kingdom of the Lozi people who settled the fertile flood plains of the Upper Zambezi, and established a stable system of rule and administration, under the power of a paramount chief or king, called the *litunga*.

In the early 19th century, the effects of the *difaqane* disrupted Lozi culture. Barotseland was occupied by the Makololo people for around 40 years, but the Lozi regained control in the mid-19th century, and reinstated the *litunga*. At around the same time, the explorer Livingstone came through, blazing the trail for other Europeans, including a trader called George Westbeech who settled and became an adviser to the *litunga*.

During the 'Scramble for Africa' of the 1880s, Portugal wanted the Upper Zambezi region to link the colonies of Angola and Mozambique, but the British South Africa Company had designs on the mineral rights in the area. The incumbent *litunga*, whose name was Lewanika, felt threatened by the neighbouring Matabele people, so he requested British support, and in 1900 Barotseland became a British protectorate. It was later incorporated into the colony of Northern Rhodesia, despite Lozi hopes that they might retain some autonomy.

When Zambia became independent in 1964, the new government of Kenneth Kaunda maintained control over Barotseland, further fuelling Lozi bitterness and separatist aspirations. After the change of government in 1992, President Chiluba declined to address the Barotseland issue, and through the late 1990s the Lozi people found themselves supporting the main opposition party – the UNIP, led, ironically, by Kenneth Kaunda.

A new *litunga*, Lubosi II Imwiko, came to the throne in 2000. The Lozi independence issue remains unresolved and calls for self-rule continue.

November, just after the rains start (the later the better). Make sure you leave before the flood waters rise, however, or you'll be stuck for months.

Getting here independently, via the park headquarters at Kalabo, is restricted to well-equipped and completely self-contained vehicles and is a real expedition, hence the small visitor numbers (only 25 vehicles are allowed in at any one time; and a GPS is advisable). Otherwise the best way to see Liuwa is on an organised safari – one company that offers quality safaris is **Robin Pope Safaris** (www.robinpopesafaris.net); a trip out to Liuwa Plains will cost about US$2500 for four nights.

Sleeping

There are three campsites in the park, **Kwale**, **Lyangu** and **Katoyana**, that are open to independent travellers and run by the local community in partnership with African Parks. Remember that you must be totally self-sufficient, including bringing all your food for yourself and your guide. Each campsite can take up to five vehicles only and is situated among the densest game areas in the park along the wildebeest migration path. Campsites have two cold-water showers, two flush toilets and a craftshop with local souvenirs. Guided walks, boat trips and even traditional fishing trips can be organised at the campsites.

Getting There & Around

Access to Liuwa Plain National Park is restricted to the dry season and even then you should seek information about the state of the roads from Mongu through to the park before attempting the run.

It's about a 70km drive from Mongu northwest to Kalabo. The road from Mongu to the ferry across the Zambezi River is rough and for 4WD vehicles only. From here the road improves but access depends largely on the severity of the rainy season so it is best to contact the national park for up-to-date information. From Kalabo, you need to cross another river via a pontoon (per vehicle ZK40,000). From that point it's 12km to the park boundary.

Despite a network of tracks, Liuwa is serious 4WD territory; a lot of the tracks are very sandy, wet or both and it's easy to get yourself into trouble here. Although the

trackless, featureless, endless plains appear benign, it's also very easy to get lost. Taking a scout with you is highly recommended and also financially assists the national park; this can be organised at the park headquarters.

KAFUE NATIONAL PARK

This stunning **park** (per person/vehicle US$15/15 ☼ 6am-6pm) is about 200km west of Lusaka and is a real highlight of Zambia. Covering more than 22,500 sq km (nearly the size of Belgium), it's the largest park in the country and one of the biggest in the world. This is the only major park in Zambia that's easily accessible by car, with a handful of camps just off the highway.

The main road between Lusaka and Mongu runs through the park, dividing it into northern and southern sectors. (You don't pay park fees if you're in transit.) There's an incredible amount of animals to be seen just from the main road – wildlife watching doesn't get much easier than this! There are several gates, but three main ones: **Nalusanga Gate** along the eastern boundary

KAFUE NATIONAL PARK

0 ————— 50 km
0 ————— 30 miles

for the northern sector; **Musa Gate**, near the New Kalala Camp, for the southern sector; and **Tateyoyo Gate** for either sector if you're coming from the west. Rangers are also stationed at the two park headquarters: one at Chunga Camp and another 8km south of Musa Gate.

Flora & Fauna

Kafue is classic wildlife country. In the northern sector, the Kafue River and its main tributaries – the Lufupa and Lunga – are fantastic for boat rides to see hippos in great grunting profusion, as well as crocodiles. The forest along the water's edge conceals birds such as Pel's fishing owls and purple-crested louries, while you can't miss the African fish eagles perched on top of palm trees. Away from the rivers, open miombo woodlands and dambos (grassy, swampy areas) allow you to spot animals more easily, especially the common antelope species such as waterbuck, puku and impala, and the graceful kudu and sable antelope. This area is one of the best places in Zambia (maybe even in Africa) to see leopards – they are regularly spotted on night drives.

To the far north is Kafue's top highlight, the Busanga Plains, a vast tract of Serengeti-style grassland, covered by huge herds of near-endemic red lechwes and more solitary grazers such as roan antelopes and oribis. (Note that this area is accessible only between late July and November.) Attracted by rich pickings, lions (which climb the local sycamore figs to keep cool and away from the flies) and hyenas are plentiful, and during the dry season there are buffaloes, zebras and wildebeest herds that move onto the plain from the surrounding areas. There are also at least two packs of wild dogs. It's a simply superb place to watch wildlife.

In the southern sector of the park, the vegetation is more dense, and early in the season the grass is very high, making animals harder to locate, although the thick woodland around Ngoma is the best place to see elephants. **Lake Itezhi-Tezhi**, a vast expanse of water, is both tranquil and beautiful, especially at sunset. In the far south, the Nanzhila Plains support an abundance of red lechwes, while other species include oribi, roan and sable antelope, hartebeest, wildebeest and puku. Large buffalo herds are sometimes seen,

and there are lions and leopards around. The southern sector is less visited (not that the north is crowded); you're unlikely to see another vehicle all day.

For birdlovers, Kafue is a dream; the wide range of habitats means that over 400 species have been recorded. The south of the park is the best place for spotting Chaplin's barbet – Zambia's only endemic species – and the equally rare black-cheeked lovebird.

Staying a few days in Kafue allows you to explore different habitats and to experience the great diversity of wildlife that this beautiful park has to offer.

Activities

All camps and lodges arrange wildlife-viewing drives (called game drives in Zambia) in open-top cars. Night drives, in vehicles armed with powerful spotlights, can be especially exciting as lions and leopards are often most active at night. Foot safaris (also called game walks) are available too, but you can't walk in the park without an armed scout (ranger). Activities are included with accommodation at top-end lodges, or available as extras at budget and midrange places. It's worth noting that the evenings in Kafue can be surprisingly cold from May until September, and you'll need a coat, a hat and gloves for the night drives.

Sleeping

We list a selection of the numerous campsites and lodges/camps offered in and around the park. Several lodges/camps

---

BACK TO SCHOOL

If all this wildlife viewing is getting a bit much and you'd like to inject some variety into your trip, how about taking the opportunity to visit a community school for Years one to seven and pre-school. The whole school only has five teachers! With the help of some Dutch donors, Mukambi Safari Lodge (p176) has built and now runs a school on its property, which is very well attended by children from the local area. One of the teachers will be happy to show you around, and you can even go into a classroom and say hello to the very excitable kids. It's a welcome you won't forget!

are just outside the park boundaries, which means that you don't have to pay admission fees until you actually visit the park. The inexplicable 'bed levy' (US$10) charged to tourists is usually included in the rates charged by the upmarket lodges, but elsewhere the levy is added to your accommodation bill (unless you're just camping). Rates here are per person per night based on two people sharing.

JUST OFF THE LUSAKA–MONGU HIGHWAY

The following places are very accessible – just off the main road – and feature some excellent accommodation in a very good area for wildlife.

our pick **Mukambi Safari Lodge** (☎ www.mukambi .com; contact for rates; ☉ year round) This very accessible lodge along the northeastern bank of the Kafue River is a great place to stay and very easy to reach from Lusaka. As it's outside the national park there are no park fees associated with a stay here. There are chalets set along the river's edge that are extremely comfortable and simply but elegantly furnished including sink-in-and-smile beds. Close by in its own private setting is their bushcamp (available as full board or on a self-catering basis), which consists of seven very comfy tents (No 6 has the best views) and a shared ablutions block in pristine condition. The restaurant, bar and lounge area are intelligently built over the river and there's a roaring log fire awaiting guests who come in from their night drive. It's very tastefully designed and somehow lulls visitors into a happy vibe. The food is outstanding, especially dinner; your three courses will rarely disappoint. There's no official camping here, but inquire at the lodge as it may be possible out of season. See their website for rates (it's in the midrange bracket) and contact details.

Busanga Plains Camp In a wetland area in the north of the park, this luxury, tented camp is also run by Mukambi. It is set on huge flood plains with islands of palms and there are plenty of animals to be seen including lions. It's usually open from July to October and is a five-hour drive (160km) from Mukambi; most visitors first stay at Mukambi for a couple of days and then the lodge organises a transfer to Busanga for a couple of nights.

Mayukuyuku (www.kafuecamps.com; campsit US$12, tents US$60, full board US$150) A rustic bush camp, small and personal, in a gorgeou spot on the river. Although there's a lacl of shade around, it's a well-designed plac with wash basins and showers built int tree branches in ablution areas – a nic touch. Mayukuyuku has a camping area and three safari tents with a fourth planned You can just rock up and camp in the well landscaped areas, but if you book you'll ge the best sites. It's possible to self-cater or t stay full board, or even on an all-inclusiv deal (which includes accommodation, meals game drives, fishing permits, transfers pick-up from airport etc). An all-inclusiv six-night package is US$1800. This plac is also a great option for backpackers an budget or independent travellers. The cam does pick-ups (US$30 per vehicle) from th nearby Hook Bridge on the main highwa (jump off from any Lusaka–Mongu bu or minibus). If you don't have your ow camping gear, you can even rent tents her (US$15/25 small/large tent). Mayukuyuk is accessible by 2WD and is only 5km of the main road on decent gravel.

Zamlodge (☎ 0211-295204; www.zamlodge.con campsite ZK85,000) This place is another optio just off the main road (about 7km) in th northern part of the park on the banks o the Kafue River. The turn-off is not fa from Mayukuyuku and at the moment it i still under construction with just the shad campsite open (no booking required). It' in a beautiful spot with camping right o the river's edge and firewood is supplied fo the braais. When the traditional chalets ar finished they should be about ZK200,00C Activities and meals should be booked i advance.

SOUTHERN SECTOR

The places listed here are outside the par. and south of the main road between Lusak and Mongu.

Puku Pan (☎ 0211-266927; www.pukupan.con campsites US$10, chalets with full board & one activi US$195; ☉ year round) A low-key spot that i beautifully situated with eight cottages wit verandas overlooking the hippo- and croc filled river. There's also a campsite her with hot showers and clean ablutions. It Zambian managed and is a straightforwar place that is comfortable but with n rills. There's a comfortable viewing area overlooking the swamps at the back of the lodge. Walking safaris, boat trips and visits to local villages are available as well as the usual wildlife drives. For independent drivers, take the road to Itezhitezhi, which is clearly signposted; after 45km you'll need to sign in at the Mwengagwa scout post, and a couple of kilometres after that there's a clearly marked turn-off to the lodge. Then it's about another 40km through woodlands and past an airstrip before you reach the lodge.

New Kalala Camp (☎ 0213-263179; www.newkalala .com; campsite US$10, s/d US$90/140, s/d full board US$120/200; 🖳)) Just outside the park boundary, in mountainous terrain, this low-key place has large, well-furnished chalets with bathrooms, in a rocky setting overlooking beautiful Lake Itezhi-Tezhi. Keep an eye out for the occasional too-cute rock dassie scurrying about. There's a bar and a charming little restaurant serving breakfast (US$6) and other meals (around US$12). The campsite is separate from the lodge in a patch of shady trees. Fishing, boat rides, wildlife drives and village visits can all be arranged.

KaingU Safari Lodge (☎ 0211-256992; www .kaingu-lodge.com; campsite US$25, full board & two activities US$355; 🖳 year round) Set on an absolutely beautiful stretch of the Kafue River, about 10km south of Puku Pan in the GMA, the waterway just outside your tent here is definitely the highlight of a stay. The river is quite broad and there are vegetated islands among the rapids providing lots of nooks and crannies to explore, with large numbers of birds making for some delightful birdwatching. The Meru-style tents raised on rosewood platforms with

---

BUDGET SAFARIS INTO KAFUE

For a budget safari into the park, check with **Jolly Boys Backpackers** (p156) in Livingstone and **Lusaka Backpackers** (p71) in Lusaka. In 2009 there was the possibility of safaris being organised with accommodation at Hippo Lodge (p180). Also check with **KNP Promotions** (☎ 0211 266927; www.knp-promotions.com; 13 Chindo Rd Ext; 🖳 8am-5pm Mon-Fri, 8am-noon Sat) in Lusaka to see if it has any good deals.

---

stone bathrooms overlook the river and have large decks to enjoy the view. They are tastefully furnished and thoughtfully set up, including their incorporation into the surrounding landscape. There are also two campsites, each with its own ablution and braai facilities. To get here take the road to Itezhitezhi, which is clearly signposted; after 45km you'll need to sign in at the Mwengagwa scout post, and a couple of kilometres after that there's a clearly marked turn-off to the lodge. From there it's a run of just over 40km.

NORTHERN SECTOR

Several lodges/camps are inside the northern section of the park, north of the main road from Lusaka.

Leopard Lodge (☎ 027-82 416 5894 in South Africa; www.leopard-lodge.com; campsite US$12.50, all-inclusive US$260; 🖳 year round) Situated on the Kafue River, in a GMA at the edge of the park, Leopard Lodge is very secluded, some 25km north of McBrides Camp. It's a small, family-run camp in an enviable location, about 4km from one of Zambia's best hot springs. There are stunning views from the hill behind the camp, and this is where lions come to mate, usually in May. In 2007 the camp underwent a wide-ranging refurbishment and the five brick chalets with thatched roofs are very comfortable with cotton linen and ceiling fans. There's a newly built bar and restaurant onsite, although private lunches and dinners in the bush are the way to go, and a picnic on a river island is a highlight. Boat trips and fishing trips feature alongside walking safaris and game drives.

our pick **McBrides Camp** (www.mcbridescamp.com; mcbrides.camp@uuplus.net; campsites incl park entry fees US$45, all-inclusive US$370) This is one of the best places to stay in Kafue. It's designed to give visitors maximum exposure to the bush, so a few nights here is about as genuine as it gets. There's lots of open space around and animals such as lions, elephants and hippos all wander through the camp. It is cleverly built around wildlife paths, assuring the regular presence of these animals. It's a real bushcamp, surprisingly comfortable but not luxurious. The six chalets (called shallets; another three are planned) are spacious and simple – built of thatch and wood. The campsite is the

EXCURSION INTO BOTSWANA AND NAMIBIA

Both Botswana and Namibia are short drives away if you're in the southwest of Zambia, and both make excellent excursions, even for a few days, although a week or longer would be ideal. The two countries are also easily accessible from Livingstone. For info on how to cross the borders, especially if you're driving, see the boxed text on p166 and p169.

BOTSWANA

After crossing into Botswana, travellers will soon find themselves in the pleasant town of Kasane in northeastern Botswana – about 12km from Kazungula, the Zambian border crossing. This is the northern gateway to one of the country's gems: magnificent Chobe National Park. Having your own vehicle here is very handy for accessing Chobe and this will probably be one of the wildlife highlights on your trip. The Chobe River and surrounding bush pulse with some of the best wildlife concentrations in Southern Africa. Here, life and water dance a perennial duet, and the end result is a rich, velvet landscape where you're practically guaranteed good animal spotting.

Kasane

Kasane lies in a riverine woodland at the meeting point of four countries – Botswana, Zambia, Namibia and Zimbabwe – and the confluence of two major rivers – the Chobe and the Zambezi. There are plenty of accommodation options in town including **Garden Lodge** (☎ (267) 625 0051; www.thegardenlodge.com; President Ave; r incl breakfast & dinner from US$180; 🖳), which is a simple but charming lodge built around a tropical garden, and features a number of well-furnished rooms that exude a homely atmosphere. It's a little more quirky than the average lodge in these parts, and it also has 'walk-in rates' for as cheap as US$60 per person.

Chobe Safari Lodge (☎ (267) 625 0336; www.chobesafarilodge.com; President Ave; campsite US$14; r from US$134; 🖳 🖳) is one of the more affordable upmarket lodges in Kasane, and is excellent value, especially if you're travelling with little ones. Understated but comfortable rooms are priced according to size and location, though all feature attractive mosquito-netted beds and modern furnishings. The outdoor dining and bar areas perched over the river are a real treat, and their buffet dinners are not to be missed.

Chobe National Park

Chobe National Park (per person/vehicle/campsite per day P120/50/30), which encompasses nearly 11,000 sq km, is understandably one of the country's greatest tourist attractions. Along the northern boundary of the park is the Chobe riverfront, which flows all the year round and supports the largest wildlife concentration in the park. The town of Kasane is built along the riverbank and the entrance to the park is a few miles out of town (or accessible directly from your accommodation if it's on the river and it has a boat).

The Chobe riverfront rarely disappoints. Whether you cruise along the river in a motorboat (highly recommended), or drive along the banks in a jeep, you're almost guaranteed an up-close encounter with some of the largest elephant herds on the continent. The elephant population at Chobe numbers in the thousands and, although they're fairly used to being gawked at by camera-wielding tourists, being surrounded by a large herd is an awesome (and somewhat terrifying) experience.

With the exception of rhinos, the riverfront is home to virtually every mammal found in Southern Africa. The river brims with hippos, and cheetahs and lions are frequently sighted along the banks. During the dry season (April to October), herds of antelopes, giraffes, zebras, buffaloes and wildebeests congregate along the river, providing plenty of nourishment for the local crocodiles.

Although exploring Chobe properly and independently requires more of a 4WD expedition than a casual drive, the proximity of Kasane to the national park means that it's fairly easy to visit the Chobe riverfront by day, and spend the night at any of the well-developed lodges or campsites in town. The riverfront is extremely easy to navigate, and allows independent travellers with their own 4WD vehicle to enjoy a short 'on-road' wildlife drive from Kasane. The best time to go on safari along the riverfront is in the late afternoon when hippos amble onto dry land and elephants head to the banks for a cool drink and a romp in the water.

NAMIBIA

After crossing into Namibia, travellers will soon find themselves in the far-flung town of Katima Mulilo in the Caprivi Strip, Namibia's spindly northeastern appendage. This area is typified by expanses of mopane and terminalia broadleaf forest and there are some unique wildlife areas that are really off the beaten path: hidden gems such as Mudumu, Mamili and Bwabwata National Parks. Bwabwata is the easiest and quickest to access if you've not much time, and it's also perhaps the most rewarding.

Katima Mulilo

You'll probably find yourself staying in this town for at least a night or two. It's a thriving little border town and minor commercial centre.

There are a couple of decent accommodation options in town including **Mukusi Cabins** (☎ (264) 066-253255; Engen petrol station; campsite N$50, s/d from N$300/350; ✕) Although it lacks the riverside location of other properties in the area, this oasis behind the petrol station has a good range of accommodation from simple rooms with fans to small but comfortable air-con cabins. The lovely bar-restaurant dishes up a range of unexpected options – including calamari, snails and kingklip – as well as steak and chicken standbys.

Protea Hotel Zambezi Lodge (☎ 066-253149; http://namibweb.com/zambezilodge.htm; campsite per person N$50; s/d from N$650/955; ✕ ❑ ❑), a stunning, riverside lodge, is perched on the banks of the Zambezi, and features a deck where you can watch the crocs and hippos below. The camping ground is a beautiful grassy stretch, while accommodation is in classy refurbished modern rooms that open up to small verandas and ample views.

Bwabwata National Park

Just over an hour away (about 100km) from Katima along a good tar road, **Bwabwata** (per person/ vehicle N$40/10; ☾ sunrise-sunset) was only very recently recognised as a national park, and was established to rehabilitate local game populations. If you're looking to get off the beaten path, this is a great area to explore while it's still relatively undiscovered. Coming from Katima, you'll pass through Kongola, just before the park, after which is a police checkpoint. From there it's a couple of hundred metres to the park entrance. A left-hand turn will take you into the park, or take a right to go to park headquarters and pay the entry fee (you should do this first). You can also pick up a map at headquarters. The best wildlife viewing is at the Horseshoe where big herds of elephants can be seen coming to drink late in the day. It makes for a lovely drive and is an easy way to see a chunk of the park in a relatively short time (day trip from Katima Mulilo).

If you've got a bit more time on your hands, nip down to Mahango Game Reserve, a small but diverse 25,000-hectare park occupying a broad flood plain in Bwabwata. It attracts large concentrations of thirsty elephants and herd animals, particularly in the dry season. With a 4WD, you can explore the 20km Circular Drive loop, which offers the best wildlife viewing. Don't miss the chance to stop beside the river in the afternoon and watch the elephants swimming and drinking among hippos and crocodiles.

If you're camping, **Nambwa Camp Site** (campsite per person N$50), 14km south of Kongola, is in a beautiful spot with spacious sites and is the only official camp in the park. It provides easy access to the wildlife-rich oxbow lagoon, about 5km south. Book and pick up a permit at the Susuwe ranger station, about 4km north of Kongola (4WD access only) on the west bank of the river. To reach the camp, follow the 4WD track south along the western bank of the Kwando River.

budget alternative and is simple, shady and has two clean ablution blocks.

The other side of the river is where walking safaris are conducted. This is a wild part of the park and you've a good chance of spotting lots of wildlife, but Chris and Charlotte's passion is lions. Chris has written three books on them (with the *White Lions of Timbavati* the only one still easily available) and is a fountain of knowledge. These guys have spent many years in the bush and really know what they're doing; they're absolutely passionate about wildlife. The whole set-up is quite informal so activities can take place sporadically, according to what you feel like doing, but it's the chance to go walking with lions that is really special. If roaring has been heard in the night you'll be woken early in the morning and carted off for a walk to locate the king of the felines. It may end up being the highlight of your trip to Africa. Alcohol, transfers and ZAWA vehicle fees are not included in the tariff.

Lufupa Tented Camp (www.wilderness-safaris.com; campsite US$10, all-inclusive US$450; 🗓 May-Jan; 🚘) At the confluence of the Lufupa and Kafue Rivers this large camp is the epicentre of the northern part of the park. Accommodation is in en suite Meru-style tents, each with wooden decking overlooking the water. Although help is on hand, this is not the kind of place where you'll be waited on hand and foot, despite the tariff. It's an unassuming spot that serves decent buffet-style meals in a convivial atmosphere. The lodge offers boat rides, walking safaris and wildlife drives, and the guides are reportedly adept at spotting elusive leopards, which makes a

night drive a real highlight. It's probably th best chance you'll have of spotting a leopar in Zambia. Lufupa also has a **campsite** nearb with a slipway for launching boats.

Hippo Lodge (☎ 0211-295398 in Lusaka; ww .hippolodge.com; all-inclusive chalets around US$42 🗓 year round) This place has a good set-u with individual stone chalets spaced we apart and a great riverside dining roon and bar to enjoy the views. Chalets featur quirky, deep baths (from the honeymoo chalet you can watch the river ripple past a you rejuvenate weary bones) and bathroom include the branches of trees in their design it's all very innovative. Alternatively, basi but comfortable safari tents are more o a budget option. It's worth checking th website of this place to see what special (including budget options) are available.

Busanga Bushcamp (www.wilderness-safaris.com all-inclusive US$500; 🗓 Jun-Nov) The Busang Plains, an enormous area of seasonal floo plains, has a reputation for teeming wildlif and is perhaps one of the best places i Zambia to see lions. This small camp, with four luxury tents, is well placed to take advantage of the wildlife viewing, cleverl hidden among sycamore figs on a verdan island in the middle of the open plain. Th lounge-bar area has terrific views over th plains and meals are served in the open, li by lanterns – it's a great bush experience Game drives are the main activity, althougl walking safaris can be provided with notice Sunsets here can be really spectacular.

Lunga River Lodge (www.wilderness-safaris.com all-inclusive US$580; 🗓 Jun-Nov; 🚘) There's plenty of quality about this remote camp, perchec on the shores of the Lunga River. The

---

DRIVING TO MCBRIDES, HIPPO LODGE & LEOPARD LODGE

If you want to drive from Lusaka to one of these lodges, take the Mongu road for 150km. Turn right into the Mumbwa road, then turn left at the roundabout (with Total Garage) in town. Go 1km up a very bad road, then turn right onto an unsigned, excellent graded gravel road. (If you're unsure, ask a passer-by if it's the road to the pontoon.) This is one of the best gravel roads in Zambia; despite this, though, there has been a number of accidents in recent times along here, so be careful, especially around corners. From here it's 67km to Kabulushi Gate (often unmanned). From the gate it's a further 20km to the turn-off for Hippo Lodge and McBrides camps. After another 7km you'll reach another fork (left for McBrides, right for Hippo Lodge). From here, it's 6km to Hippo Lodge and about 14km to McBrides. Both camps are clearly signed.

For Leopard Lodge ignore the turn-off for Hippo Lodge and McBrides and continue along the gravel road until you reach the Kafue River. Cross the river via the pontoon, drive for a further 3.5km and then turn off (signposted to Leopard Lodge); it's another 1.5km to the lodge.

rick-and-thatch chalets have walk-in mosquito nets and are tastefully furnished, aking advantage of local lumber. There's a bar with sundeck that extends over the iver and is ideal for a sundowner; and an outdoor covered lounge area, where meals are sometimes served, sits on top of a termite mound. The river is the focus of activities such as boat trips or walks along the grassy banks, and game drives are offered to explore surrounding woodland. Many guests combine a stay here with Busanga Bushcamp and Wilderness has a helicopter for quick and easy transfers.

Getting There & Away
Most guests of the top-end lodges/camps fly in on chartered planes. Transfers from the airstrip to the lodges/camps are often included in the rates.

For drivers, the main route into Kafue National Park is along the road between Lusaka and Mongu. It's about 200km from Lusaka to Nalusanga Gate, and then 50km west of Nalusanga Gate a road leads southwest towards Lake Itezhi-Tezhi. The road is in very bad condition, with a small part graded only. The rest is terrible – it's only accessible by a 4WD with high clearance. Note the tsetse flies are bad down here too – so air-con is a big comfort. Just past Itezhitezhi village is Musa Gate, from where the road crosses Lake Itezhi-Tezhi to the New Kalala Camp and Musungwa Lodge.

If you're staying at Mukambi Safari Lodge, continue west along the main road from Lusaka until about 10km before Kafue Hook Bridge (or 82km from Nalusanga Gate) and look for the signposted turn-off to the south. On the western side of the bridge, a main track leads into the northern

sector of the park, and a dirt road leads southeast to Puku Pan. See the box on p180 for details on driving to Hippo Lodge, McBrides and Leopard Lodge.

Note that there are rumours that Kafue will become more easily accessible from Livingstone with the road between Livingstone and Itezhitezhi set to become tarmac.

There's no public transport in the park, but you could get off the bus between Lusaka and Mongu and reach Mukambi Safari Lodge on foot, or get off at the Kafue Hook Bridge and Mayukuyuku will pick you up. Alternatively, take the slow daily bus, or one of the more regular minibuses, from Lusaka to Itezhitezhi village (US$12, six hours). From the village bus stop wait around for a lift (because of the number of wild animals it may not be safe to hike).

KAOMA
Kaoma is a busy little town about 80km west of Kafue National Park. It's a good place to fill up with petrol (two stations) and not a bad spot to break a journey from Lusaka out to the far west of Zambia. A simple, basic set-up that's clean and friendly, **Kaoma Cheshire Orphanage Guesthouse** (r ZK55,000, chalet ZK100,000) overlooks the Luena Valley and has some gorgeous views, especially early in the morning. There are clean twin rooms with shared bathrooms (sporadic running water) or en suite chalets available. If you give them notice a simple dinner can be prepared (ZK15,000) and breakfast is available in the morning. You can also self-cater: it costs ZK6000 to cook for yourself or for ZK10,000 they'll cook your food for you. Your patronage here supports a local orphanage, which has ever-increasing numbers of AIDS orphans.

Zambia Directory

CONTENTS

ACCOMMODATION

Prices for all accommodation listed in this book are for the high (dry) season – ie April/May to October/November – and are based on the 'international rates'. Often, lodges offer resident rates that are at an unfairly and far reduced rate, sometimes cut by as much as half.

Accommodation has been listed in budget order throughout the Zambia chapters, from cheapest to most expensive. The parameters for dividing accommodation into categories by price is budget up to ZK150,000, midrange between ZK150,000 and ZK350,000, and top end upwards of ZK350,000. This is a guide only, however, and lodges and camps in and around national parks are considerably more expensive due to their remote locations and, in some cases, their exclusive nature. It's also worth noting that prices for rooms with private bathrooms (called self-contained rooms in Zambia) are about 40% higher than rooms without, and that all accommodation in Lusaka is about 50% higher than anywhere else in Zambia. Most midrange and top end hotels include either a continental or cooked breakfast in their rates.

Budget

Most cities and larger towns have campsites where you can pitch your tent, but most are way out in the suburbs. Camping is also possible at privately run campsites at the national parks, though most are located just outside the park boundaries to avoid admission fees (until you actually want to visit the park). No campsites are run by the national wildlife authority. Many lodges around national parks will accept independent campers – this can be a great deal as you have access to the lodge's facilities while paying a pittance for accommodation.

The (*very*) few youth hostels around Zambia are not part of any international organisation, so hostel cards are useless. But hostels in Lusaka and the major tourist areas are well set up with swimming pools, bars, restaurants and travel agencies offering organised tours.

Some of the cheapest hotels in the cities are actually brothels. The better budget hotels charge by the room, so two, three or even four people travelling together

---

BOOK ACCOMMODATION ONLINE

For more accommodation reviews and recommendations by Lonely Planet authors, check out www.lonelyplanet.com/hotels. You'll find the true, insider lowdown on the best places to stay. Reviews are thorough and independent. Best of all, you can book online.

PRACTICALITIES

- The *Daily Times* and *Daily Mail* are dull, government-controlled rags. The independent *Post* (www.postzambia.com), featuring a column by Kenneth Kaunda, continually needles the government. Published in the UK but printed in South Africa, the *Weekly Telegraph,* the *Guardian Weekly* and the *Economist* are available in Lusaka and Livingstone.

- The monthly *Lowdown* magazine (www.lowdown.co.zm; ZK5000), aimed at well-off residents in Lusaka, has useful information for visitors such as restaurant reviews and lists of upcoming events in the capital, as well as handy adverts for package deals for lodges around Zambia.

- Both of the Zambian National Broadcasting Corporation (ZNBC) radio stations can be heard nationwide; they play Western and African music, as well as news and chat shows in English. ZNBC also runs the solitary government-controlled TV station every evening, but anyone who can afford it will subscribe to South African satellite TV. *BBC World Service* can be heard in Lusaka (88.2FM) and Kitwe (89.1FM); *Radio France Internationale* (RFI) can also be heard in Lusaka.

- Televisions use the PAL system.

- Electricity supply is 220V to 240V/50Hz and plugs are of the British three-prong variety.

- The metric system is used in Zambia.

---

an get some real (if crowded) bargains. ingle travellers may find some prices steep, hough negotiation is always possible.

idrange to Top End

his is the main budget for accommodation n Zambia. All national parks are dotted ith expensive privately operated lodges nd 'camps' (a confusing term often used o describe expensive lodges). They offer he same sort of luxury and exclusivity as ther lodges and camps in Southern and ast Africa – all from US$150 (but usually nuch more) per person per night (twin hare). Foreigners usually pay 'international ates' for lodges/camps, while tourists rom Southern Africa get a 'regional rate' f 25% less, and Zambians pay about half he 'international rates'. These rates usually nclude all meals, drinks, park fees and ctivities, such as wildlife drives, but not ransfers by road, air and/or boat. Lodges/ amps should be booked in advance, either irectly by phone, fax or email, or through n agent in Lusaka or abroad. Some lodges/ amps close in the wet season (November o April); if they're open, discounts of up to 0% are common.

Lusaka and other large towns have a ood number of midrange hotels, lodges nd guesthouses, while real top end hotels re less common (although easily found n Lusaka and Livingstone). Facilities and standards in midrange places can vary a great deal, and they are often set up for the conference trade and not tourists.

ACTIVITIES

Companies in Livingstone (and Victoria Falls town in Zimbabwe) offer a bewildering array of activities (see pp150–2), such as whitewater rafting in the gorge below the falls or river boarding and canoeing on the quieter waters above the falls. Those with plenty of nerve and money can try bungee jumping or abseiling, or take a ride in a microlight or helicopter. The less adventurous may want to try hiking and horse riding.

Canoeing is also a great way to explore the Zambezi River and can be arranged in Siavonga (p138). Fishing along the Zambezi, and at several lakes in northern Zambia, is also popular; the tigerfish are almost inedible but provide a tough contest for anglers. Fishing and boating are also possible on Lakes Kariba, Bangweulu and Tanganyika.

Most national parks, such as Kasanka (p100), Kafue (p174), Lower Zambezi (p142) and South Luangwa (p119) have activities for visitors, with wildlife drives and walks the main focus of these places, and the main drawcard for visitors to Zambia.

Many tour companies in Livingstone offer short wildlife drives in Mosi-oa-Tunya National Park near Victoria Falls, while companies in Lusaka and Livingstone can also arrange longer wildlife safaris to more remote national parks. In some parks (eg Kafue and South Luangwa), you can turn up and arrange wildlife drives or walking safaris on the spot.

BUSINESS HOURS

Government offices are open from 8am or 9am to 4pm or 5pm Monday to Friday, with an hour for lunch sometime between noon and 2pm. Shops keep the same hours but also open on Saturday. Supermarkets are normally open from 8am to 8pm Monday to Friday, 8am to 6pm Saturday and 9am to 1pm Sunday (although some are open 8am to 10pm daily at the big shopping centres in Lusaka). Banks operate weekdays from 8am to 2.30pm (or 3.30pm), and from 8am to 11am (or noon) on Saturday. Post offices open from 8am or 9am to 4pm or 4.30pm weekdays. Restaurants are normally open for lunch between 11.30am and 2.30pm and dinner between 6pm and 10.30pm, though bar-restaurants in Lusaka are often open until 11pm on Friday and Saturday. Reviews in this chapter generally won't list business hours unless they deviate from these standards.

CHILDREN

While most people do not travel with children in Zambia, lodges, such as Mushroom Lodge & Presidential House (p127) in South Luangwa National Park, and Kasaka River Lodge (p145) in the Lower Zambezi National Park will specifically accommodate them with activities and facilities set up for kids, and perhaps even offer lower rates for them.

In Lusaka many upmarket cafes and restaurants such as Chit Chat (p80) have play areas for kids, either outside on the grass with swings, slides etc or inside, set up as a soft-play area with toys, such as Kilimanjaro (p80).

CLIMATE CHARTS

As Zambia is in 'the tropics' (the part of the world between the tropics of Cancer and Capricorn), you might expect it to have a tropical climate. However, the country's altitude, much of which is between 1000m and 1500m above sea level, takes the edge off the extreme heat or humidity that other parts of Africa may experience. Having said that, heat and humidity are features

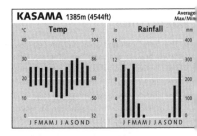

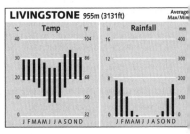

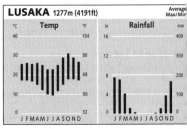

in the lower areas such as the Zambez and Luangwa Valleys – two of the mos visited parts of the country. Conversel temperatures are a few degrees lower tha average on the high ground of northeas Zambia or the Copperbelt. For more detai about the best times to visit see p17.

CUSTOMS REGULATIONS

There are no restrictions on the amount foreign currency tourists can bring in o take out of Zambia. Import or export Zambian kwacha, however, is technicall forbidden, but if you bring in/out a sma amount (say, US$25 worth), it's unlikely be a problem.

DANGERS & ANNOYANCES

Generally, Zambia is very safe, though the cities and tourist areas there is always chance of being targeted by muggers or co artists. As always, you can reduce the ris onsiderably by being sensible. In Zambia, hieves are known as *kabwalalas* universally.

For as long as the seemingly endless civil trife continues in the Democratic Republic f the Congo (Zaïre), avoid any areas long the Zambia–Congo (Zaïre) border, specially around Lake Mweru. Foreign mbassies in Zambia warn of landmines left over from the Rhodesian civil war) in he Sinazongwe area on the shores of Lake Kariba. Avoid trekking off the beaten track n this area.

The possession, use and trade of ecreational drugs is illegal in Zambia and enalties are harsh.

It's also worth noting that some ravellers who have an Asian background ave reported annoying glares and racial lurs from Zambians. See p69 for specific nformation about keeping safe in Lusaka.

Visitors hiring a car and travelling ndependently should take sensible recautions such as carrying a mobile hone, getting the best maps they can find nd letting someone know where they ntend travelling (for those getting more ff the beaten track, a satellite phone and GPS may be advisable).

DISCOUNT CARDS

Hostel cards and senior cards are useless, hough student or youth cards may be useful or buying tickets on major international irlines and the Tazara railway between Zambia and Tanzania.

EMBASSIES & CONSULATES

The following countries have embassies or high commissions in Lusaka (area code ☎ 0211). The British high commission ooks after the interests of Aussies and Kiwis as the nearest diplomatic missions or Australia and New Zealand are in Harare. Most consulates are open from 8.30am to 5pm Monday to Thursday and from 8.30am o 12.30pm Friday, though visas are usually only dealt with in the mornings.

Botswana (Map pp72-3; ☎ 250555; fax 253895; 5201 Pandit Nehru Rd)
British (Map pp72-3; ☎ 423200; http://ukinzambia.fco gov.uk/en; 5210 Independence Ave)
Canada (Map pp72-3; ☎ 250833; fax 254176; 5119 United Nations Ave)
Congo (Zaïre; Map pp72-3; ☎ 235679, 213343; fax 29045; 1124 Parirenyetwa Rd)

France (Map pp72-3; ☎ 251322; fax 254475; 74 Independence Ave, Cathedral Hill)
Germany (Map pp72-3; ☎ 250644; 5209 United Nations Ave)
Ireland (off Map pp72-3; ☎ 291298; 6663 Katima Mulilo Rd)
Kenya (Map pp72-3; ☎ 250722; 5207 United Nations Ave)
Malawi (Map p68; ☎ 265764; fax 260225; 31 Bishops Rd, Kabulonga)
Mozambique (Map pp72-3; ☎ 220333; fax 220345; 9592 Kacha Rd, off Paseli Rd, Northmead)
Namibia (Map p68; ☎ 260407/8; fax 263858; 30B Mutende Rd, Woodlands)
Netherlands (Map pp72-3; ☎ 253819; fax 253733; 5208 United Nations Ave)
South Africa (Map p68; ☎ 260999; 26D Cheetah Rd, Kabulonga)
Sweden (Map pp72-3; ☎ 251711; fax 254049; Haile Selassie Ave)
Tanzania (Map pp72-3; ☎ 227698; fax 254861; 5200 United Nations Ave)
USA (Map pp72-3; ☎ 250955; http://zambia.usembassy. gov; cnr Independence & United Nations Aves)
Zimbabwe (Map pp72-3; ☎ 254006; fax 254046; 11058 Haile Selassie Ave)

FESTIVALS & EVENTS

One remarkable festival to look out for is **Kusefya Pangwena**, practised by the Bemba people of northern Zambia. This programme of music, drama and dance, which is held near Kasama over four days in August, commemorates the victory of the Bemba over the marauding Ngoni in the 1830s.

N'cwala is a Ngoni festival held near Chipata in eastern Zambia on 24 February. At this time, food, dance and music are all enjoyed by participants who celebrate the end of the rainy season and pray for a successful harvest.

Refer to the boxed text for details about the remarkable **Kuomboka Ceremony** (p172).

Information about these and other festivals are on the official Zambian tourism website: www.zambiatourism.com; also see p21.

FOOD

Although food is generally not a highlight of travel in Zambia, lodges and camps in and around the national parks usually offer the highest standards of culinary options. Perhaps the opportunity to taste local game (kudu is very good) is the standout. For more see p47.

ZAMBIA DIRECTORY

We've listed eating places in the regional Zambia chapters of this guide in order of price, starting with the cheapest first. Generally a budget meal is under ZK20,000, midrange is between ZK20,000 and ZK50,000, while a top end feed is upwards of ZK50,000. Remember that this is a guide only and prices will be considerably more in many lodges and camps in national parks. Also note that we've used a (V) symbol to denote places that serve vegetarian dishes.

GAY & LESBIAN TRAVELLERS

Male homosexual activity is illegal in Zambia. Lesbian activity is not illegal, but that's only due to it not being recognised. (Zambia's legal code is based on Victorian England's.) In traditional African society, same-sex relationships are cultural taboo, so most Zambians are very conservative in their attitudes towards gays and lesbians, and homosexuality is rarely discussed sensibly in public. In Zambia public displays of affection, while possibly not being illegal, are insensitive to local attitudes and are very much frowned upon, whatever your orientation.

HOLIDAYS

During the following public holidays, most businesses and government offices are closed:
New Year's Day 1 January
Youth Day 2nd Monday in March
Easter March/April
Labour/Workers' Day 1 May
Africa (Freedom) Day 25 May
Heroes' Day 1st Monday in July
Unity Day 1st Tuesday in July
Farmers' Day 1st Monday in August
Independence Day 24 October
Christmas Day 25 December
Boxing Day 26 December

INSURANCE

A travel-insurance policy to cover theft and medical problems is very highly recommended. Although having your camera stolen or your backpack eaten by hippos can be a problem, the medical aspect of the policy is most important; good hospitals in Zambia are not cheap. Getting from an accident to a hospital can also be expensive, so ensure the policy covers ambulances (land and air) and emergency flights home.

Many policies are available, so shop around carefully and read the small print to make sure your type of trip is covered. Som policies exclude 'dangerous activities', which can include white-water rafting or canoeing

Some policies pay doctors or hospital directly. For others, you pay on the spo and claim later – so ensure you keep al documentation. You may be required t call the insurance company for an on-the spot assessment.

INTERNET ACCESS

Zamnet is the country's largest interne service provider. Internet centres are i Lusaka (p67), Livingstone (p153), and th bigger towns such as Mongu (p170) an Ndola (p87) and are spreading rapidly. A few upmarket lodges allow guests (only) t use their internet facilities for a small charge Access at internet centres is cheap – abou ZK150–200 per minute – but connections ca be horribly slow depending on equipmen and, importantly, the provider used. Eve in Lusaka using the internet can be lik watching grass grow, although this book list the places with the fastest connections.

Wireless is becoming more common particularly as most accommodation place outside of the national parks are set up fo business folk and conferences. If you trave with a laptop that has wireless connectivit you'll be surprised at how useful it can be even in remote towns. In Lusaka (p67) loo for the I Spot zones, which can be found a accommodation and eating places.

Throughout the Zambia chapters of thi guide we've used the 🖳 icon to denot accommodation options that have interne access and the 🛜 icon to denote places tha also offer a wireless service.

LEGAL MATTERS

Zambia's legal code is based o Victorian England's and is therefore ver conservative, outlawing things such a male homosexuality. The buying, selling possession and use of all recreational drug are illegal. Having said that, 'grass' an other drugs can be fairly easily found i Lusaka, Livingstone and other large towns If this is your scene, though, take great care In 1999, two New Zealand travellers got si months in jail with hard labour after bein caught with a relatively small amount.

The only place you'll find moneychanger in Zambia is at borders, where there's ofte no bank. Although using them is technically illegal, moneychangers – invariably young wise-guys in trendy gear and carrying huge wads of cash – operate in full view of customs officers, so trouble from this angle is unlikely.

Note that it is illegal to wear camouflage clothing.

MAPS

The German *Zambia Road Map* (ZK70,000) by Ilona Hupe Verlag is currently the best available map for touring around Zambia – it shows petrol stations and important wildlife areas. Also easy to find is Globetrotter's *Zambia and Victoria Falls* map, which includes regional and national park insets (with a guidebook from the same company it costs ZK120,000), and *Street Guide Lusaka and Livingstone* (ZK35,000), which is a book-form collection of blow-ups of the two cities. All are available at bookshops in Lusaka.

See if you can get your hands on the South African Boraro map of *Inside Zambia*, available from www.discovering-africa.com – it has some detailed insets of the national parks, such as Lower Zambezi. If you're trekking or driving into more remote regions, detailed survey maps at various scales from 1986 (ZK20,000 to ZK30,000) are sometimes available from the government-run Map Sales office in Lusaka (p66).

MONEY

Zambia's unit of currency is the kwacha (k), sometimes listed as 'ZMK' (Zambian kwacha) or 'kw'. In this book it is noted as ZK to distinguish it from Malawian kwacha. Bank notes come in denominations of ZK50,000, ZK20,000, ZK10,000, ZK5000, ZK1000, ZK500, ZK100, ZK50 and ZK20, the last of which are extremely rare and virtually worthless. One hundred ngwee equals one kwacha so, not surprisingly, ngwee coins have become souvenirs.

Inflation is high in Zambia (around 14%) and some prices in the regional chapters are quoted in kwacha and others in US dollars (US$), as different businesses base their rates on the different currencies.

Most tourist-oriented places in Zambia quote prices in US dollars, but you must by law pay in kwacha – except for international airfares, top end hotels/lodges, visas and

most organised tours. In reality however, US dollars are commonly (and gratefully) accepted by most hotels, budget campsites, tour operators and national park scouts.

See also inside front cover for exchange rates and p19 for information on costs while you're in Zambia.

Cash & ATMs

You can obtain cash (kwacha and sometimes US dollars) over the counter at Barclays, Stanbic and Standard Chartered banks in the cities and larger towns with a Visa card. It can take most of the day, however, and you may be slugged a fee of about US$10. Larger branches of these banks have ATMs that accept Visa, but only kwacha can be withdrawn, and although ATMs have had a patchy record, malfunctioning on occasion, they are usually OK to use and reliable enough. ATM cards bearing the MasterCard mark are fairly useless.

Credit Cards

Some shops, restaurants and better hotels/lodges accept major credit cards, though Visa is the most readily recognised. A surcharge of 4% to 7% may be added to your bill if you pay with a credit card, so you're probably better off using it to draw cash and paying with that.

Moneychangers

The best currencies to take to Zambia (in order of preference) are US dollars, UK pounds and South African rands. Euros have yet to take off and the currencies of most neighbouring countries are worthless in Zambia, except at the relevant borders. The exception is Botswanan pula, which can also be exchanged in Lusaka.

In the cities and larger towns, you can easily change cash at branches of Barclays Bank, Stanbic and Standard Chartered Bank. In smaller towns, try the Zambia National Commercial Bank. Theoretically these banks also change travellers cheques, however they are generally loathe to do so. Infuriatingly and inexplicably they usually require you to have your original purchase sales receipt in order to change (defeating the purpose of travellers cheques) and even then they will only recognise some kinds of sales receipt!

Foreign-exchange offices – almost always called bureaux de change – are easy to find in all cities and larger towns. Their rates for cash and travellers cheques (rarely accepted) are around 5% better than the banks' rates; the service is also faster and there are no additional fees.

There is no black market. You might get a few kwacha more by changing money on the street, but it's illegal and there is a chance that you'll be ripped off, robbed or set up for some sort of scam. However, moneychangers at the borders are more or less legitimate, but may take (slight) advantage of your ignorance about the current exchange rates. If you can't change cash at a bank or bureau de change, try a hotel or a shop that sells imported items.

Tipping

While most restaurants add a 10% service charge, rarely does it actually get into the pockets of waiters. Therefore, you may choose to tip the waiter directly.

Travellers Cheques

It's worth avoiding travellers cheques for several reasons: they are not accepted at most bureaux de change; banks are loathe to change them (see above); and they attract high charges and lower exchange rates (5% to 8% lower than for cash). Commission rates vary, so it's always worth shopping around. The standard commission charged by Barclays and Standard Chartered banks is about 1%, but often with a minimum of US$15. If you're likely to be charged a ridiculous commission – eg US$15 (!) on a US$20 travellers cheque – try negotiating a lower commission.

You can pay for some items (such as tours, activities, hotels and lodges) directly with travellers cheques, but a few hotel and tour operators have a nasty habit of adding a surcharge (up to US$20) for this.

Barclays, AmEx, Thomas Cook and Visa are by far the most accepted brands.

PHOTOGRAPHY & VIDEO

In Lusaka and Livingstone it costs ZK10,000/ 12,000 for a roll of 24-/36-exposure print film, while a roll of 36-exposure slide film is about ZK30,000 (without processing). Developing and printing 24-/36-exposure print film costs about ZK25,000/35,000, but developing slide film is almost impossible. It costs ZK10,000 to burn a CD of your digital photos, and around ZK1500 to ZK3000 per

digital image, to develop. Bring everything you need for video cameras.

Zambian officials do not like foreigner photographing any public buildings bridges, dams, airports or anything else tha could be considered strategic. If in doubt ask; better still, save your camera for the national parks.

POST

Normal letters (under 20g) cost ZK2700 to send to Europe and ZK3300 to the USA, Canada, Australia and New Zealand while postcards are a flat rate ZK1650 Sending international letters from Lusaka is surprisingly quick (three or four days to Europe), but from elsewhere in the country it's less reliable and much slower. Parcel up to 1kg to Europe cost ZK55,500 by airmail and ZK60,600 to the USA, Canada Australia and New Zealand. The cost i about half this for surface mail.

Poste-restante service is available a the main post office in Lusaka (p67) for a negligible fee.

SHOPPING

For intrepid shoppers, Zambia offers a wide range of curios and souvenirs, with differen parts of the country producing distinctive localised crafts. For example, the Lozi people of western Zambia are famed for thei basketwork, while the Leya of Livingstone make excellent wooden carvings.

The wooden carvings are mostly representational animals and figures, o ornaments such as bowls, stools and chess sets. In your average curio stall you'll be faced with row upon row of carvings. Don't be pu off. If possible, take your time when browsing because quality varies immensely. In among the stuff that's hammered out in a hurry you can find pieces that have been created by artists of better-than-average talent, with traders often making no distinction when it comes to setting a price. As well as the conventional souvenirs, some craft-worker. produce abstract or contemporary carvings the smooth and rounded Zimbabwe-style soapstone figures are especially good.

You can buy traditional items such a gourd containers decorated with beads and cowrie shells, which originate from Western Province. In sharp contrast are the mode bikes, buses and aeroplanes made from wire alled 'jouets' in the Copperbelt (a franco-phone Congolese import); simple models made by children are cheap and fun, but you can also find very intricate works, complete with opening doors and moving engine parts.

At the other end of the price market, collectors of modern art can find pieces by some of Zambia's best-known artists in galleries in Lusaka (p69).

On a more practical note, in shops and markets all over Zambia you can buy *chitenjes* – sheets of brightly coloured cloth that local women use as wraps, cloaks, scarves and baby carriers. They make nice souvenirs and are useful items for female travellers, especially if heading for conservative rural areas.

The best places to buy your souvenirs are roadside stalls or curio stalls in markets. Prices here will not be fixed, and you have to bargain.

SOLO TRAVELLERS

Solo travel in Zambia, whether you're male or female, is straightforward. While you will probably be a minor curiosity in rural areas (so will visitors in pairs or groups), especially solo women travellers, it's likely that in most urban centres nobody will even bat an eye. Times when you'd likely want to find a group to join would be for a safari (to cut costs and because they often have minimum numbers) and at night. Solo women should always exercise extreme caution at night and avoid isolating situations. If you're hitting the pubs and bars in Lusaka it's much wiser and safer to go with a group.

TELEPHONE

Almost all telecommunication services are provided by the government monopoly, Zamtel. Public phones operated by Zamtel use tokens, which are available from post offices (ZK500) or local boys (ZK1000) hanging around phone booths. These tokens last three minutes but are only good for calls within Zambia. Phone booths operated by Zamtel use phone cards (ZK5000, ZK10,000, ZK20,000 or ZK50,000) available from post offices and grocery shops. These phone cards can be used for international calls but it's often easier to find a 'phone shop' or 'fax bureau', from where all international calls cost about ZK12,000 per minute.

International services are generally good, but reverse-charge (collect) calls are not possible. The international access code for dialling outside of Zambia is ☎ 00, followed by the relevant country code. If you're calling Zambia from another country, the country code is ☎ 260, but drop the initial zero of the area code.

Mobile Phones

MTN, Celtel and Zain (best coverage) all offer mobile (cell) phone networks. It's almost impossible to rent mobile phones in Zambia, though if you own a GSM phone, you can buy a SIM card for around ZK8000 without a problem. In Lusaka the best place to buy a cheap mobile phone is around Kalima Towers (cnr Chachacha Rd and Katunjila Rd); a basic Zain model is about ZK80,000 to ZK100,000.

Scratch cards come in denominations of ZK1000, ZK2000, ZK5000, ZK10,000, ZK20,000, ZK50,000 and ZK100,000. Numbers starting with ☎ 095, ☎ 096, ☎ 097 and ☎ 099 are mobile phone numbers.

Mobile phone reception is getting better all the time; generally it's very good in urban areas and surprisingly good in some rural parts of the country with reception now possible in South Luangwa National Park! Companies have been erecting mobile radio signal towers all over the place.

Phone Codes

Every landline in Zambia uses the area code system; you only have to dial it if you are calling outside of your area code. Remember to drop the zero if you are dialling from outside of Zambia.

Area Code	Province(s)
☎ 0211	Lusaka
☎ 0212	Copperbelt
☎ 0213	Southern
☎ 0214	Northern
☎ 0215	Central
☎ 0216	Eastern
☎ 0217	Western
☎ 0218	Northwestern

TIME

Zambia is two hours ahead of Greenwich Mean Time (GMT/UTC). There is no daylight saving.

ZAMBIA DIRECTORY

TOILETS

There are two types of toilet in Zambia: the Western style, with a toilet bowl and seat; and the African style – a hole in the floor that you squat over. Standards of toilets can vary tremendously, from pristine to nauseating. Some travellers complain that African toilets are difficult to use, but it only takes a little practise to accomplish a comfortable squatting technique.

In rural areas, squat toilets are built over a deep hole in the ground. These are called 'long-drops', and the waste matter just fades away naturally, as long as the hole isn't filled with too much non-biodegradable rubbish (such as plastic bags and tampons – these should be disposed of separately).

TOURIST INFORMATION

The regional tourist offices in Lusaka and Livingstone are worth visiting for specific inquiries, but provide limited information about Zambia in general. Refer to the relevant sections for contact details.

The **Zambia National Tourist Board** (ZNTB; www .zambiatourism.com; UK ☎ 020-7589 6655; zntb@aol.com; 2 Palace Gate, Kensington, London W8 5NG; South Africa ☎ 012-326 1847; zahpta@mweb.co.za; 570 Ziervogel St, Hatfield, Pretoria) is worth contacting for some guidance with your planning. The official website is outstanding, and provides links to dozens of lodges, hotels and tour agencies.

The **Tourism Council of Zambia** (tcz@zamnet.zm) is an umbrella group of private companies throughout the country involved in the promotion of tourism.

TRAVELLERS WITH DISABILITIES

Although wildlife safaris are ideal for those in wheelchairs or on crutches, you'll need to be intrepid in Zambia, as there are very few facilities for the disabled – even though there are more disabled people per head of population here than in the West. It has to be said that most disabled travellers find travel in Zambia much easier with the assistance of an able-bodied companion.

Part of the whole safari ethos in Zambia is being adaptable and flexible, so most camps and lodges in national parks have no problem catering for disabled guests – with notice. Safari lodges are single storey, and getting around is fairly easy, although gaps in slatted wooden decking can easily trap a wheel or walking stick. Another great advantage at upmarket lodges is room outdoor bathrooms.

In cities and towns, midrange and upmarket hotels have lifts, ramps and private bathrooms attached to the room. A few of the smart hotels in Lusaka and Livingstone have rooms with specific disabled facilities. Getting around urban areas is much harder for people with wheelchairs or walking difficulties, though. Footpaths (where they exist at all) are often in bad condition with cracks or damaged sections, and crossing the road can be hard because curbs don't have ramps and traffic rarely stops for pedestrians anyway.

A final factor to remember, which goes some way to making up for the lack of facilities and infrastructure, is the friendliness and accommodating attitude of Zambians towards disabled people. In most situations people will be more than happy to help if you politely explain to them exactly what you need.

VISAS

All foreigners visiting Zambia need visas but for most nationalities tourist visas are available at major borders, airports and ports. But it's important to note that you should have a Zambian visa *before* arrival if travelling by train or boat from Tanzania.

Citizens of South Africa and Zimbabwe can obtain visas on arrival for free. For all other nationalities, tourist visas are issued on arrival; the prices have been standardised with most nationalities paying US$50 for single entry (up to one month) US$80 for double entry (up to one month) and US$160 for multiple entry (up to three months). Note that only a single- or double entry visa is available from Lusaka airport. Make sure you request how long you want as you may not automatically be given the maximum time for any type of visa.

Payment can be made in US dollars, and sometimes UK pounds, although other currencies such as euros, South African rand, Botswanan pula or Namibian dollars, may be accepted at borders, but don't count on it.

Tourist and business visas can also be obtained from Zambian diplomatic missions abroad, and application forms can be downloaded from the websites run by the **Zambian high commission** (London www.zhc .org.uk; USA www.zambiaembassy.org).

VISAS FOR ONWARD TRAVEL

If you're travelling to neighbouring countries here's some information about getting that all-important visa (see p185 for contact details). It's always best to visit any embassy or high commission in Lusaka between 9am and noon from Monday to Friday. You will probably need two passport-sized photos.

Your chances of obtaining a visa for Congo (Zaïre) or Angola are extremely remote in Lusaka, so get it before you arrive in Zambia.

Botswanan High Commission (☽ for visa applications 8am-12.30pm & 2-3.30pm Mon, Tue & Wed) Visa ZK358,000; ready in seven days; bring two passport photos.

Malawian High Commission (☽ 8.30am-noon Mon-Thu, 8.30-11am Fri) Transit visa US$70, single US$100, multiple for 6/12 months US$220/300; takes three days to process; bring one passport photo and photocopy front of passport.

Namibian High Commission (☽ 10am-3pm Mon-Fri) Visa US$50; takes two days to issue; bring two passport photos and photocopy front of passport.

Tanzanian High Commission (☽ apply 8am, ready 2pm same day, Mon-Fri) Visa US$50 (no kwacha); bring two passport photos.

If you come to Zambia from Zimbabwe on a free-visa transfer from Victoria Falls, make sure you keep all your paperwork, because you may be asked later why there is no indication on your passport that you have paid for a Zambian visa, and then be forced to buy one.

Visa Extensions

Extensions for all types of tourist visas are possible at any Department of Immigration office in any main town in Zambia, though you're likely to be more successful in **Lusaka** (Map pp72-3; Memaco House, Cairo Rd) and **Livingstone** (Map p154; Mosi-oa-Tunya Rd). A month extension normally costs up to US$100 (depending on your nationality).

If the paperwork seems overwhelming, and the fees exorbitant, simply cross into Zimbabwe, Mozambique, Namibia, Botswana or Malawi (the easiest options) and pay for a new visa when you return to Zambia.

WOMEN TRAVELLERS

Generally speaking, women travellers in Zambia will not encounter gender-related problems any more than they might in other parts of the world. In fact, women travellers say that compared with North Africa, South America and many Western countries, Zambia is relatively safe and unthreatening; friendliness and generosity are encountered far more often than hostility.

Due to Zambia having a small population of people of European origin, it is one of few places in the developing world where women travellers can meet and communicate with local men – of any race – usually without being misconstrued. That's not to say that sexual harassment never happens, but local white women have done much to refute the image that females of European descent are willing to hop into bed with the first taker.

Be aware, though, that when it comes to evening entertainment, Zambia is a conservative, male-dominated society. Even in bars where women are 'allowed', cultural conventions often dictate that you don't go in without a male companion.

Generally speaking, local Zambian women (like most Zambian men) are friendly and approachable, once initial surprise at being greeted or addressed by a foreigner is overcome. Nevertheless, because of prevailing attitudes, it can be hard to specifically meet and talk with local women in Zambia.

Transport in Zambia

CONTENTS

The main way to get to Zambia is by land or air. Overland, travellers might enter Zambia from Malawi, Botswana, Namibia, Zimbabwe or Tanzania. There are no direct flights to Zambia from mainland Europe or the US. The easiest way to reach the country by air is via Kenya or South Africa. Flights, tours and rail tickets can be booked online at www.lonelyplanet.com/travel_services.

GETTING THERE & AWAY

ENTERING ZAMBIA

See p190 for full information on visa requirements for entering Zambia.

A yellow fever certificate is not required before entering Zambia, but it *is* often requested by Zambian immigration officials if you have come from a country with yellow fever. It is certainly required if you're travelling from Zambia to South Africa (and, possibly, Zimbabwe).

AIR
Airports & Airlines

Zambia's main international airport is in Lusaka, though some international airlines fly to the airport at Livingstone (for Victoria Falls), Mfuwe (for South Luangwa National Park) and Ndola. The major domestic an international carrier was Zambian Airway but it suspended operations in early 200 citing high fuel costs, although its high det was probably the real reason.

Zambia is well connected with Souther Africa. **Zambezi Airlines** (www.flyzambezi.con flies to regional destinations such a Johannesburg in South Africa (from Lusaka and Ndola) and to Dar es Salaar in Tanzania, while **South African Airway** (www.flysaa.com) is the major regional airlin flying regularly to Lusaka from its hub i Johannesburg; it also connects with the res of the region and continent.

Air Malawi (www.airmalawi.com) connects Lusak with Lilongwe three times a week, and wit Blantyre twice a week; while **Air Zimbabw** (www.airzimbabwe.com) also flies to Lusaka fron Harare on the way to Nairobi.

There is also an increasing number o flights to Livingstone for Victoria Fall: both South African Airways and Britisl Airways fly from Johannesburg.

AIRLINES FLYING TO/FROM ZAMBIA
Air Malawi (code QM; ☎ 0211-228120 in Zambia; www.airmalawi.com)
Air Zimbabwe (code UM; ☎ 0211-221750; www.airzimbabwe.com)
British Airways (code BA; ☎ 0211-254444; www.britishairways.com)
Ethiopian Airlines (code ET; ☎ 0211-236402/3; www.flyethiopian.com)
Kenya Airways/KLM (code KQ; ☎ 0211-228886; www.kenya-airways.com)

THINGS CHANGE...

The information in this chapter is particularly vulnerable to change. Check directly with the airline or a travel agency to make sure you understand how a fare (and a ticket you may buy) works and be aware of the security requirements for international travel. Shop carefully. The details given in this chapter should be regarded as pointers and are not a substitute for your own careful, up-to-date research.

DEPARTURE TAX

The departure tax for all international flights is US$20. This tax is *sometimes* included in the price of your airline ticket, but if not must be paid at the airport (in US dollars only).

outh African Airways (code SA; ☎ 0211-254350; www.flysaa.com)
ambezi Airlines (code ZJ; ☎ 0211-257606; www.flyzambezi.com)

frica
Many travellers on trans-Africa trips fly some ections, either because time is short or simply because the routes are virtually impassable.

The overland route between East Africa and Southern Africa is extremely popular, but it's also easy to find a flight between Nairobi (Kenya) and Johannesburg (or even straight to Lusaka). Alternatively, it's a short hop between Dar es Salaam (Tanzania) and Lusaka, which avoids a gruelling overland stretch. Coming from Cairo (Egypt) or Ethiopia, most flights to Southern Africa go via Nairobi.

If you're travelling from West Africa, you have to fly as the overland route is blocked by turmoil in Democratic Republic of Congo (Zaïre). Travellers also tend to avoid Nigeria and Congo-Brazzaville. Options include from Accra (Ghana) or Dakar (Senegal) to Johannesburg and then to Lusaka or Livingstone.

Australia & New Zealand
Airlines flying from Australia to Zambia go via South Africa and include Qantas and South African Airways; both fly to Johannesburg where you can connect with Lusaka or Livingstone (flying time from Perth to Johannesburg is about 10 hours). If flying between New Zealand and Zambia you must go via Australia. The best place to start looking for cheap deals is the ads in major weekend newspapers.

Two well-known agencies that are good for offering cheap fares in Australia are:
Flight Centre (☎ 131 600; www.flightcentre.com.au) Offices throughout Australia.
STA Travel (☎ 1300-733 035; www.statravel.com.au) Offices in all major cities and on many university campuses.

TRANSPORT IN ZAMBIA

CLIMATE CHANGE & TRAVEL

Climate change is a serious threat to the ecosystems that humans rely upon, and air travel is the fastest-growing contributor to the problem. Lonely Planet regards travel, overall, as a global benefit, but believes we all have a responsibility to limit our personal impact on global warming.

Flying & Climate Change
Pretty much every form of motor travel generates CO_2 (the main cause of human-induced climate change) but planes are far and away the worst offenders, not just because of the sheer distances they allow us to travel, but because they release greenhouse gases high into the atmosphere. The statistics are frightening: two people taking a return flight between Europe and the US will contribute as much to climate change as an average household's gas and electricity consumption over a whole year.

Carbon Offset Schemes
Climatecare.org and other websites use 'carbon calculators' that allow jetsetters to offset the greenhouse gases they are responsible for with contributions to energy-saving projects and other climate-friendly initiatives in the developing world – including projects in India, Honduras, Kazakhstan and Uganda.

Lonely Planet, together with Rough Guides and other concerned partners in the travel industry, supports the carbon offset scheme run by climatecare.org. Lonely Planet offsets all of its staff and author travel.

For more information check out our website: lonelyplanet.com.

These agencies are also represented in New Zealand:

Flight Centre (☎ 0800-243 544; www.flightcentre. co.nz) Many branches throughout the country.
STA Travel (☎ 0508-782 872; www.statravel.co.nz) Main office in Auckland and branches in Hamilton, Palmerston North, Wellington, Christchurch and Dunedin.

In addition, the following agencies specialise in Africa travel:

Africa Travel Company (☎ 02-9264 7661; Level 1, 69 Liverpool St, Sydney 2000, NSW)
African Wildlife Safaris (☎ 1300-363 302, 9249 3777; www.africanwildlifesafaris.com.au) Cobbles together custom tours to Zambia and the entire region. The focus is on wildlife safaris.

Continental Europe

You can fly to South Africa from any European capital, but the main hubs are Amsterdam and Frankfurt. The most popular routes are generally the cheapest, which means that Johannesburg or Cape Town will normally be destinations of choice. From Johannesburg flights leave regularly for Lusaka, Ndola and Livingstone. Specialist travel agencies advertise in newspapers and travel magazines, so check there before ringing around.

There are bucket shops by the dozen in cities such as Paris, Amsterdam, Brussels and Frankfurt. Many travel agents in Europe have ties with STA Travel, where you'll find cheap tickets. STA Travel and other discount outlets in major transport hubs include:

Anyway (☎ 08 92 30 23 01; www.anyway.fr) France.
Airfair (☎ 0900-7717 717; www.airfair.nl) Netherlands.
Alternativ Tours (☎ 030 21 23 41 90; www.alternativ-tours.de) Germany.
Barcelo Viajes (☎ 902 200 400; www.barceloviajes.com) Spain.
CTS Viaggi (☎ 06 462 0431; www.cts.it) Italy; specialising in student and youth travel.
STA Travel Germany (☎ 069 743 032 92; www.statravel.de) Switzerland (☎ 0900-450 402; www.statravel.ch)

UK & Ireland

Numerous airlines fly between Britain and Southern Africa, and you'll occasionally find excellent rates. The least-expensive point of arrival to reach Zambia will probably be Johannesburg, although an increasing number of flights arrive in Cape Town. British Airways, however, do have three direct London-to-Lusaka flights a week but fares can be pricey.

London is normally the best place to buy a ticket, but specialist agencies elsewher in the UK can provide comparable value Also check ads in the travel pages of the weekend broadsheet newspapers, in *Tim Out*, the *Evening Standard*, in the free online magazine *TNT* (www.tntmagazine.com and in the free *SA Times*, which is aimed at South Africans in the UK. Some place worth checking out:

Africa Travel Centre (☎ 0845-450 1520; www.africatravel.co.uk)
North-South Travel (☎ 01245-608291; www.northsouthtravel.co.uk) At this experienced agency profits support development projects overseas.
Quest Travel (☎ 0871-423 0135; www.questtravel.com)
STA Travel (☎ 0871-230 0040; www.statravel.co.uk) Branches in London, Manchester, Bristol and most large university towns.
Trailfinders (☎ 0845-058 5858; www.trailfinders.co.uk This popular company has several offices in London, as we as Manchester, Bristol and several other cities.
Travel Bag (☎ 0871-703 4698; www.travelbag.co.uk)
Travel Mood (☎ 0800-011 1945; www.travelmood.com

USA & Canada

SAA flies direct from New York to Johannesburg (17½ hours), and this i generally one of the least-expensive routings To reach Lusaka you can get a connection from Johannesburg. It may be cheaper to fly on an economy hop from the USA to London (on British Airways or Virgin Atlantic) or Amsterdam (on KLM), and then buy a discount ticket from there to Southern Africa. Canadians also will probably find the best deals travelling via Atlanta or London.

North Americans won't get the great deal that are available in London, but discoun agencies to watch out for:

Air Brokers (☎ 800-883 3273 or 415-836 8718; www.airbrokers.com) A consolidator that can come up with good rates on complicated itineraries.
High Adventure Travel/Airtreks (☎ 877-247 8735; www.airtreks.com) Specialises in round-the-world travel including Southern Africa stops.
Premier Tours & Travel (☎ 800-545 1910; www.premiertours.com)
Spector Travel (☎ 617-351 0111; www.spectortravel .com) Combines tours with discounted airfares.
STA Travel (☎ 800-781 4040; www.statravel.com) This organisation, which isn't limited to students, has offices all over the USA.

ivel Cuts (☎ 866-246 9762; www.travelcuts.com)
 Canadian student-travel association.

AND
order Crossings

imbia shares borders with eight countries,
 there's a huge number of crossing points.
ll are open daily from 6am to 6pm,
ough the border closes at 8pm at Victoria
lls and at 7pm at Chirundu. The
llowing borders issue visas to foreigners
 arrival:

tswana Zambia and Botswana share what is probably
 world's shortest international boundary: 750m across
 Zambezi River at Kazungula. The pontoon (car ferry)
oss the Zambezi is 65km west of Livingstone and 11km
uth of the main road between Livingstone and Sesheke.
u can buy a Botswana visa at the border, when you get
 the ferry there.

ngo (Zaïre) The main border is between
lilabombwe (Zambia) and Kasumbalesa (Congo).
as are issued to tourists in Lusaka but can be difficult
 obtain.

alawi Most foreigners use the border at Mchinji, 30km
utheast of Chipata, because it's along the road between
saka and Lilongwe.

ozambique The main border is between Mlolo
imbia) and Cassacatiza (Mozambique), but most
vellers choose to reach Mozambique through Malawi.

amibia The only border is at Sesheke (Zambia), on the
rthern and southern bank of the Zambezi, while the
mibian border is at Wenela near Katima Mulilo.

nzania The main border by road, and the only crossing
 train, is between Nakonde (Zambia) and Tunduma
anzania).

mbabwe There are three easy crossings: at Chirundu,
ong the road between Lusaka and Harare; between
avonga (Zambia) and Kariba (Zimbabwe), about 50km
stream from Chirundu; and between Livingstone
imbia) and Victoria Falls town (Zimbabwe).

otswana

or detailed information about crossing
e border into Botswana from Zambia
a your own vehicle or public transport,
d advice on what permits and currency
change you need, see p166.

A quicker and more comfortable (but
ore expensive) way to reach Botswana
om Zambia is to cross from Livingstone
 Victoria Falls (in Zimbabwe), from where
uttle buses head to Kasane.

Buses to Gaborone, via Kasane and
rancistown, leave several days a week from
usaka (see p82).

Malawi

See p120 for detailed information about
crossing the border into Malawi via the
main border post near Chipata on the
Lusaka–Lilongwe road.

Further north is another border crossing
at Nakonde. Going either way on public
transport is very difficult; you really need
your own wheels. Coming from Malawi into
Zambia the Malawi border post is at Chitipa,
a 60km drive along a very bad road from
Karonga (which takes about four hours).
There are some matola and minibuses that
go along that route (about MK500) but they
are very infrequent. Once you get there, the
Malawi border post is five kilometres out
of town. Then it's another 80km (three- to
four-hour drive) to the Zambia immigration
post at Nakonde. The only way to get past
this bit without a car is to hitch on a truck,
but vehicles are infrequent on this road. At
Nakonde you can get a bus to Mpika for
around ZK100,000.

Mozambique

There is no public transport between
Zambia and Mozambique and the only
common border leads to a remote part of
Mozambique. Most travellers, therefore,
choose to visit Mozambique from Lilongwe
in Malawi.

Namibia

See p169 for detailed information about
crossing the border into Namibia from
Zambia via your own vehicle or on
public transport. Alternatively, cross from
Livingstone to Victoria Falls (in Zimbabwe)
and travel onwards from there – see p165
for details.

See p82 and p169 for information about
buses to Sesheke, the Zambian border town,
from Lusaka and Livingstone respectively.

From the Namibian side, it's a 5km walk
to Katima Mulilo, from where minibuses
depart for other parts of Namibia.

South Africa

There is no border between Zambia and
South Africa, but several buses travel daily
between Johannesburg and Lusaka (see
p82 for details) via Harare and Masvingo
in Zimbabwe. Make sure you have a
Zimbabwean visa (if you need one before
arrival) and a yellow fever certificate for

entering South Africa (and, possibly, Zimbabwe).

Tanzania

Although travelling by bus to the Tanzanian border is quicker, the train is a better alternative.

See p82 for details about buses from Lusaka to Dar es Salaam. Alternatively, walk across the border from Nakonde, and take a minibus from Tunduma to Mbeya in Tanzania.

The Tazara railway company usually runs two international trains per week in each direction between Kapiri Mposhi (207km north of Lusaka) and Dar es Salaam. The 'express train' leaves Kapiri Mposhi at 5.15pm on Tuesday, while the 'ordinary train' leaves Kapiri Mposhi at 5.15pm on Friday. The journey time for both trains is 48 hours. The fares on the express train are ZK237,000/198,000/145,000 in 1st/2nd/3rd class (1st and 2nd class are sleeping compartments) and ZK187,000/151,000/125,000 on the ordinary train. A discount of 50% is possible with a student card.

Tickets are available on the spot at the New Kapiri Mposhi (Tazara) train station in Kapiri Mposhi and up to three days in advance from **Tazara House** (Map pp72-3; ☎ 0211-222280; Independence Ave, Lusaka). If there are no more seats left at the Lusaka office, don't despair because we've heard from travellers who easily bought tickets at Kapiri Mposhi, and upgraded from one class to another while on board.

It's prudent to get a Tanzanian visa in Lusaka, see p191, (or elsewhere) before you board the train; at least, contact the Tanzanian high commission in Lusaka about getting a Tanzanian visa on the train or at the border. You can change money on the train but take care because these guys are sharks.

Zimbabwe

Plenty of buses travel every day between Lusaka and Harare, via Chirundu – see p82 for details. If you're travelling from Siavonga, take a minibus or charter a car to the border, and walk (or take a shared taxi) across the impressive Kariba Dam to Kariba, from where buses leave daily to Harare. Most travellers cross at Livingstone – see p155 for details.

GETTING AROUND

AIR

The main domestic airports are at Lusaka, Livingstone, Ndola, Kitwe, Mfuwe, Kasama and Kasaba Bay, though dozens of mine air strips cater for chartered planes.

Airlines in Zambia

There are plenty of charter services in Zambia but only one airline offering scheduled flight. **Proflight Zambia** (www.proflight-zambia.com) has filled the domestic gap since Zambian Airways went out of business and is flying regular (up to two or three times daily) from Lusaka to Mfuwe (for South Luangwa National Park), Lower Zambezi, Livingstone (for Victor Falls) and Ndola.

Charter-flight companies cater for guests staying at upmarket lodges/camps in national parks. Charter flights only leave with a minimum number of prebooked passengers and fares are always high, but it's sometimes worth looking around for a last-minute stand-by flight. Check for special deals advertised in *Lowdown* magazine available at bookshops in Lusaka.

BICYCLE

If you plan on cycling around Zambia, do realise that Zambian drivers tend to not give you any room, even if there is no vehicle in the oncoming lane. Save being hit by a car, it is safe to cycle Zambia. Mountain biking is rapidly becoming popular in and around Lusaka. The two best places to purchase mountain bikes are in Lusaka: **CycleMart** (Map pp72-3; ☎ 222062; cnr Chachacha & Malasha Rds; ☉ 8am-5pm Mon-Fri, 8am-1pm Sat) and **Game** (Map pp72-3; Manda Hill Shopping Centre, Great East Rd). Road cyclists will have to bring their own bikes and gear.

BUS & MINIBUS

Distances are long, buses are often slow and many roads are badly potholed, so travelling around Zambia by bus and minibus can

---

DOMESTIC DEPARTURE TAX

The departure tax for domestic flights is US$8. It is *not* included in the price of airline tickets bought in or outside of Zambia, and must be paid at the airport in US dollars.

xhaust even the hardiest of travellers, even
f they *do* like a good butt massage.

All main routes are served by ordinary
ublic buses, which either run on a fill-up-
nd-go basis or have fixed departures (these
re called 'time buses'). 'Express buses' are
aster – often terrifyingly so – and stop
ess, but cost about 15% more. In addition,
everal private companies run comfortable
European-style express buses along the major
outes, eg between Lusaka and Livingstone,
usaka and Chipata, and Lusaka and the
Copperbelt region. These fares cost about
5% more than the ordinary bus fares and
re well worth the extra kwacha. Tickets for
hese buses can often be bought the day
efore. See pp82–3 for more on express
uses zipping around the country.

Many routes are also served by minibuses,
vhich only leave when full – so full that you
night lose all feeling in one butt cheek.
Their fares can be more or less the same
s ordinary buses. In remote areas the
only public transport is often a truck or
ick-up.

CAR & MOTORCYCLE
Bringing Your Own Vehicle

If you're driving into Zambia in a rented
or privately owned car or motorcycle, you
will need a carnet; if you don't have one,
a free Customs Importation Permit will
be issued to you at major borders instead.
You'll also be charged a carbon tax if it's
a non-Zambian registered vehicle, which
just means a bit more paperwork and about
ZK200,000 at the border depending on the
size of your car.

While it is certainly possible to get
around Zambia by car or motorbike, many
sealed roads are in bad condition and
the dirt roads can range from shocking
to impassable, particularly after the rains.
If you haven't driven in Africa before, this
is not the best place to start. We strongly
recommend that you hire a 4WD if
driving anywhere outside Lusaka, and
certainly if you're heading to any of the
national parks or other wilderness areas.
Wearing a seat belt in the front seat is
compulsory.

TRANSPORT IN ZAMBIA

ROAD DISTANCES (km)

Distances are approximate

	Chingola	Chipata	Choma	Kasama	Kitwe	Livingstone	Lusaka	Mansa	Mbala	Mongu	Mpika	Ndola	Sesheke	Siavonga	Solwezi	Victoria Falls
Chingola	---															
Chipata	1040	---														
Choma	720	890	---													
Kasama	960	1475	1225	---												
Kitwe	50	990	670	820	---											
Livingstone	910	1080	190	1345	860	---										
Lusaka	435	605	285	870	385	475	---									
Mansa	875	1400	1150	705	852	1290	790	---								
Mbala	1125	1640	1390	165	1075	1510	1035	870	---							
Mongu	900	1215	900	1480	1480	1085	610	1400	1645	---						
Mpika	750	1265	1015	210	700	1135	660	500	375	1270	---					
Ndola	110	930	610	760	60	800	325	765	1010	935	575	---				
Sesheke	1095	1265	375	1530	1045	185	660	1450	1700	335	1320	990	---			
Siavonga	617	790	410	1055	570	660	185	1000	1220	795	845	510	845	---		
Solwezi	175	1215	900	1035	225	1085	610	1050	1300	1220	860	285	1270	800	---	
Victoria Falls	935	1105	215	470	885	25	475	1290	1535	1110	1160	830	210	685	1110	---

Driving Licence

Foreign licences are fine as long as they are in English, and it doesn't hurt to carry an international driver's licence (also in English).

Fuel & Spare Parts

Diesel costs around ZK5500 per litre and petrol ZK6500. Shortages do occur from time to time. Distances between towns with filling stations are great and fuel is not always available, so fill the tank at every opportunity.

It is advisable to carry at least one spare wheel, as well as a filled jerry can, though petrol is far more volatile than diesel. If you need spare parts, the easiest (and cheapest) vehicle parts to find are those of Toyota and Nissan.

Hire

Cars can be hired from international and Zambian-owned companies in Lusaka, Livingstone, Kitwe and Ndola, but renting is expensive, so consider hiring a car in Malawi and taking it across to Zambia (see p305). Avis, Europcar and Voyagers/ Imperial are at Lusaka airport.

Voyagers/Imperial Car Rental (www.voyagers zambia.com/imperialrates.htm) charges from US$43 per day for the smallest vehicle, plus US$0.32 per kilometre (less per day for longer rental periods). Add to this insurance (from US$26 per day), VAT (17.5%) and petrol. Other companies, such as **4x4 Hire Africa** (www.4x4hireafrica.com), rent old-school Land Rover vehicles, unequipped or fully decked out with everything you would need for a trip to the bush, with prices for an unequipped vehicle starting at about US$120 per day. The best thing about this company is that vehicles come with unlimited kilometres and you can take them across borders, making it easy to nip over to Malawi, Chobe National Park in Botswana (p178) or the Caprivi Strip in Namibia (p179).

Most companies insist that drivers are at least 23 years old and have held a licence for at least five years.

Insurance

Compulsory third-party insurance for Zambia is available at major borders (or the nearest large towns) and costs about US$12 per month. However, it is strongly advised to carry insurance from your own country on top of your Zambian policy.

Road Conditions

While many main stretches of sealed road are OK, beware of the occasional pothole. Sections of main highway however (such as west to Mongu or south to Livingstone) can be in a pretty bad way and rapidly deteriorating with gaping potholes, ridges, dips and very narrow sections that drop steeply off the side into loose gravel. Be wary and alert at all times, and see the boxed text in each Zambian regional chapter describing road conditions in early 2009. Gravel roads vary a lot from pretty good to pretty terrible. Road conditions are probably at their worst soon after the end of the wet season (April, May, June) when many dirt and gravel roads have been washed away or seriously damaged – this is especially the case in and around national parks. Seriously consider travelling by 4WD if using a private vehicle.

Road Rules

Speed limits in and around cities are enforced, though on the open road buses and Land Cruisers fly at speeds of 140kph to 160kph. Beware of vehicles in front of you that signal: if they signal right, it could mean that they are turning, or that there is another vehicle in the oncoming lane. If the vehicle signals left, they are turning or the oncoming lane is clear and you can pass. Or else, it's possible that their signal lights are simply broken.

SPEEDING & SMILING

Speed limits around urban places like Lusaka are signed on the highways. Watch for speed cameras and always stick to the signed limit – Zambia is not a place to speed, even if you do see other vehicles doing it.

At police checkposts (which are very common) smile, say good morning/afternoon, be very polite and take off your sunglasses. A little respect makes a huge difference to the way you'll be treated. Mostly you'll be met with a smile, perhaps asked curiously where you're from, and waved through without a problem.

If you break down, you must place an orange triangle about 6m in front of and behind the vehicle.

HITCHING

As in any other part of the world, hitching is never entirely safe, and we therefore don't recommend it. Travellers who hitch should understand that they are taking a small but potentially serious risk. Despite this general warning, hitching is a common way to get around Zambia. Some drivers, particularly expats, may offer you free lifts, but you should expect to pay for rides with local drivers (normally about the same as the bus fare, depending on the comfort of the vehicle). In such cases, agree on a price beforehand.

LOCAL TRANSPORT

The minibuses that zip around main roads in all cities and larger towns are quick and plentiful. For more comfort, however, taxis are also very good value. They have no meters, so rates are negotiable.

TOURS

Tours and safaris around Zambia invariably focus on the national parks. Since many of these parks are hard to visit without a vehicle, joining a tour might be your only option anyway. Budget-priced operators run scheduled trips, or arrange things on the spot (with enough passengers), and can often be booked through a hostel – try Lusaka Backpackers (p71) in Lusaka or Jollyboys (p156) in Livingstone. Upmarket companies prefer to take bookings in advance, directly or through an agent in Zambia, South Africa or your home country.

Most Zambian tour operators are based in Lusaka and Siavonga, as well as Livingstone. Several companies in Lilongwe, Malawi, may also offer tours to South Luangwa National Park. See p68 for travel agents in Lusaka who can often organise tours, and p125 for budget tours of South Luangwa. Also consider some of these operators:

Barefoot safaris (☎ 0211-707 346; www.barefoot safaris.com) Small group safaris, self-drive, trekking and sailing; covers Zambia, Malawi and surrounding countries.
Kiboko Safaris (☎ 265-01-751226 in Malawi; www.kiboko-safaris.com) Excellent budget camping and lodge safaris in Malawi and South Luangwa, Zambia. Also luxury safaris in Malawi.

Land & Lake Safaris (www.landlake.net) Based in Lilongwe, Malawi, this operator has combined Malawi/Zambia safaris, as well as trips around South and North Luangwa and Victoria Falls. Good budget options available.
Robin Pope Safaris (www.robinpopesafaris.net) One of the most-respected operators in Zambia offering innovative and intrepid tours to destinations such as Kafue and Liuwa Plain, including mobile walking safaris.
Remote Africa Safaris (www.remoteafrica.com) Excellent small operator running safaris in the Luangwa Valley.
Wilderness Safaris (www.wilderness-safaris.com) This company offers a range of tours in all Southern African countries including Zambia and Malawi. In addition to the standard luxury lodge-based tours in remote areas, it offers fly-in safaris and activity-based trips.

TRAIN

The Tazara trains between Kapiri Mposhi and Dar es Salaam in Tanzania (see p196) can also be used for travelling to and from northern Zambia. While the Lusaka–Kitwe service does stop at Kapiri Mposhi, the Lusaka–Kitwe and Tazara trains are not timed to connect with each other, and the domestic and international train terminals are 2km apart.

Zambia's only other railway services are the 'ordinary trains' between Lusaka and Kitwe, via Kapiri Mposhi and Ndola, and the 'express trains' between Lusaka and Livingstone. Refer to the relevant sections for schedules and costs.

Domestic trains are unreliable and slow, so buses are always better. Conditions on domestic trains generally range from slightly dilapidated to ready-for-scrap. Most compartments have no lights or locks, so take a torch and something to secure the door at night.

Tickets for all classes on domestic trains (but not the Tazara service) can be bought up to 30 days in advance.

Classes

On the 'express train' between Lusaka and Livingstone, a 'sleeper' is a compartment for two people; 1st class is a sleeper for four; 2nd (or 'standard') class is a sleeper for six; and 'economy' (or 3rd) class is a seat only. On the 'ordinary train' between Lusaka and Kitwe, 'standard' class is also just a seat. Sometimes the domestic services will only have economy or standard class available – just a seat.

Malawi

Snapshot Malawi

With Tanzania and Zambia's big name national parks and Mozambique's glorious beaches on the doorstep, Malawi has often been left on the sidelines while its neighbours bask in the limelight; and when it has made a splash on the international scene it's usually been for its HIV/AIDS rate or grim poverty statistics, not for the beauty and diversity of the environment or the friendliness of its people. It's a pity, because this small strip of land has serious crowd-pleasing potential.

Slicing through the landscape in a trough formed by the Great Rift Valley is the third-largest lake in Africa – Lake Malawi. A shimmering mass of crystal water, its depths swarm with clouds of vivid cichlid fish and its shores are lined with secret coves, pristine beaches, lively fishing villages and dark, forested hills. Diving, snorkelling and kayaking can all be enjoyed here, and when you're done there's everything from low-key beach huts to glamorous resorts in which to lay your head.

It's not all about the lake, though. Suspended in the clouds in Malawi's deep south are the dramatic peaks of Mt Mulanje, criss-crossed with streams, waterfalls and walking trails. Head north and you'll find the wild wilderness of the Nyika Plateau, where you can hike through rolling grasslands to reach a colonial hilltop town. And while a safari in one of Malawi's parks won't deliver 'Big Five' excitement, you can get up close to some impressive beasts without having to fight with other cars for the privilege.

Malawi is often described as 'Africa for beginners', and true to form its compact size, decent transport links and relative safety make it easy to get around. What's more, the friendly locals and stunning backdrops will ensure that you'll have a fantastic time doing so.

HIGHLIGHTS

- Soaking up the sun in **Lake Malawi's** (p231) private coves, gliding over glassy waters by kayak or diving beneath the surface to discover a world of impossibly brilliant fish
- Wandering past vast granite boulders on the **Viphya Plateau** (p241) and hiking through sweeping valleys in this gorgeous highland area
- Scrambling up the twisted peaks of **Mt Mulanje** (p281), sleeping in mountain huts and admiring the astounding views
- Spotting hippos, crocs and kingfishers on the Shire River in **Liwonde National Park** (p263) and getting up close to elephants
- Escaping to dreamy beaches on **Likoma Island** (p237) and exploring its traditional villages, panoramic walks and the magnificent cathedral

Lilongwe

Lilongwe might be Malawi's capital, but don't come expecting major attractions, great shopping or a happening music scene – compared to many other African capitals, the city is a sleepy backwater. That being said, it has a quiet charm that makes it an enjoyable place to hang out for a day or two. The modern city centre and business hub is a dead loss in terms of atmosphere and activities, but Old Town, where most tourists end up spending their time, has a friendly vibe. There are craft stalls and excellent cafes and restaurants, as well as good bookshops and internet cafes in which to do your onward planning. If you crave action, head for Lilongwe's main market and bus stations for lively streets filled with music, blaring horns and hawkers. The Lilongwe Nature Sanctuary is a welcome green space in between Old Town and City Centre that's home to an admirable new wildlife rehabilitation project. Or check out the tobacco auction floors on the outskirts of town to see Malawi's largest industry in action. Within easy reach of the city are cool forest reserves and a famed pottery workshop at Dedza.

LILONGWE

HIGHLIGHTS

- Get a taste of the wilderness in the city and learn about animal rehabilitation at the **Lilongwe Wildlife Centre** (p208)

- Visit the city's **tobacco auction floors** (p208) for an insight into Malawi's most important export

- Head for the renowned **Dedza Pottery** (p215) to pick up some hand-painted pots and eat a slice of its famous cheesecake

- Hike through the cool evergreen forests of the **Ntchisi Forest Reserve** (p216)

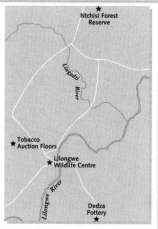

- TELEPHONE CODE: 01   - POPULATION: 669,000   - ELEVATION: 1050M

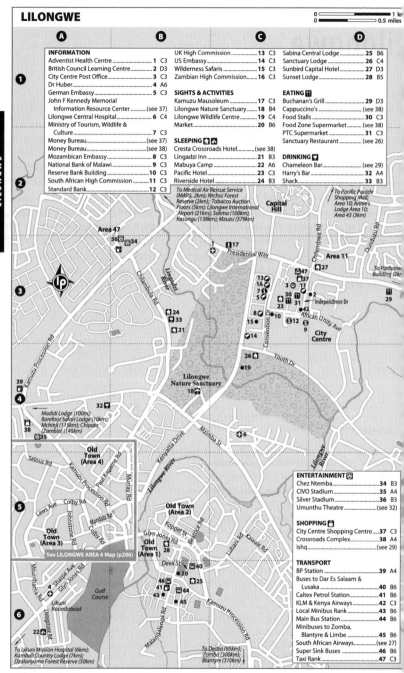

LILONGWE

INFORMATION	
Adventist Health Centre	**1** C3
British Council Learning Centre	**2** D3
City Centre Post Office	**3** C3
Dr Huber	**4** A6
German Embassy	**5** C3
John F Kennedy Memorial Information Resource Center	(see 37)
Lilongwe Central Hospital	**6** C4
Ministry of Tourism, Wildlife & Culture	**7** C3
Money Bureau	(see 37)
Money Bureau	(see 38)
Mozambican Embassy	**8** C3
National Bank of Malawi	**9** C3
Reserve Bank Building	**10** C3
South African High Commission	**11** C3
Standard Bank	**12** C3
UK High Commission	**13** C3
US Embassy	**14** C3
Wilderness Safaris	**15** C3
Zambian High Commission	**16** C3

SIGHTS & ACTIVITIES
Kamuzu Mausoleum	**17** C3
Lilongwe Nature Sanctuary	**18** B4
Lilongwe Wildlife Centre	**19** C4
Market	**20** B6

SLEEPING
Cresta Crossroads Hotel	(see 38)
Lingadzi Inn	**21** B3
Mabuya Camp	**22** A6
Pacific Hotel	**23** C3
Riverside Hotel	**24** B3
Sabina Central Lodge	**25** B6
Sanctuary Lodge	**26** C4
Sunbird Capital Hotel	**27** D3
Sunset Lodge	**28** B5

EATING
Buchanan's Grill	**29** D3
Cappuccino's	(see 38)
Food Stalls	**30** C3
Food Zone Supermarket	(see 38)
PTC Supermarket	**31** C3
Sanctuary Restaurant	(see 26)

DRINKING
Chameleon Bar	(see 29)
Harry's Bar	**32** A4
Shack	**33** B3

ENTERTAINMENT
Chez Ntemba	**34** B3
CIVO Stadium	**35** A4
Silver Stadium	**36** B3
Umunthu Theatre	(see 32)

SHOPPING
City Centre Shopping Centre	**37** C3
Crossroads Complex	**38** A4
Ishq	(see 29)

TRANSPORT
BP Station	**39** A4
Buses to Dar Es Salaam & Lusaka	**40** B6
Caltex Petrol Station	**41** B6
KLM & Kenya Airways	**42** C3
Local Minibus Rank	**43** B6
Main Bus Station	**44** B6
Minibuses to Zomba, Blantyre & Limbe	**45** B6
South African Airways	(see 27)
Super Sink Buses	**46** B6
Taxi Rank	**47** C3

HISTORY

Lilongwe started life as a small village on the banks of the Lilongwe River. The village became a British colonial administrative centre around the turn of the 20th century, after its chief requested protection from belligerent neighbouring ethnic groups. Due to its central location on Africa's main north–south road as well as its position as the terminus of the road from Northern Rhodesia (later Zambia), Lilongwe soon became Malawi's second-largest urban centre, attaining official township status in 1947. In 1968, authorities made the decision to transfer the country's administration from Blantyre and construction of the new city, largely funded by South Africa, began. The new capital was officially declared in 1975, yet the parliament and several ministry buildings remained in the town of Zomba, which had been the political capital since British colonial times. In 1998 the parliament was moved from Zomba to Lilongwe, where it now occupies a modern grandiose palace originally built for former president Dr Hastings Kamuzu Banda.

ORIENTATION

Lilongwe has two centres. City Centre (also called Capital City) has ministries, embassies, some smart hotels, a shopping centre, airline offices, travel agents and several restaurants and cafes. Old Town has a good range of places to stay (including backpackers hostels and campsites), the bus station, the main market, some more tour and travel companies, and a large number of shops. More importantly City Centre is a surprisingly quiet and rather sterile place, whereas Old Town is livelier. The two centres are 3km apart and minibuses frequently run between them.

The heart of City Centre is City Shopping Centre, a collection of office buildings and mini-malls around a circular car park reached from Independence Dr. There are shops, travel agents, banks, a post office and a supermarket. Nearby are the British Council Learning Centre and many embassies. Further out are several ministries, the Kamuzu Mausoleum, a couple of smart hotels and the posh suburbs.

The heart of Old Town is the market on Malangalanga Rd. Just south of the market is the main bus station. Just to the north of the market is Devil St, a narrow road lined with bars and cheap hotels, where you'll also find the departure points for buses headed to Zambia or Tanzania. Malangalanga Rd meets Glyn Jones Rd, the main road to/from Blantyre, lined with cheaper shops selling clothes, material, hardware and so on, running down to the bridge over the Lilongwe River. The streets south of Glyn Jones Rd are called Area 1, and those to the north are called Area 2. On the other side of the bridge is a roundabout. This is Area 3. If you go right at the roundabout, you're on Kamuzu Procession Rd. This is the smart part of Old Town, with more expensive shops, restaurants, cafes, supermarkets, banks and travel agents.

Maps

Survey maps of Malawi and some of its cities are available from the **Department of Surveys Map Sales Office** (Map p206), about 500m south of the roundabout where Glyn Jones Rd meets Kamuzu Procession Rd. Regional and city maps cost MK650; survey maps covering the whole of Malawi cost MK3500. See also p296.

INFORMATION

Bookshops

Bookmart (Map p206; Uplands House, Kamuzu Procession Rd; ⏰ 8.30am-4.30pm Mon-Fri, 8.30am-1pm Sun) Excellent secondhand bookshop with a wide range of recent bestsellers, classics and travel books. It also has a small coffee bar so you can have a latte while you browse. Books cost between MK150 and MK700, depending on their condition.

Central Africana (Map p206; ☎ 01-756317; www.centralafricana.com; Old Town Mall) Has a diverse selection of travel, history and nature books, both new and secondhand. It's a good place to find out-of-print or hard-to-find Malawi guidebooks.

Central Bookshop (Map p206; Nico Shopping Centre) Sells a surprisingly good stock of African literature and local guidebooks.

TBS bookshop (Map p206; Nico Shopping Centre) Sells international and local newspapers and magazines, and some paperback novels.

Emergency

Emergency numbers are as follows:
Ambulance ☎ 998
Fire ☎ 01-757999
Police ☎ 01-753333
Rapid Response Unit ☎ 997

LILONGWE

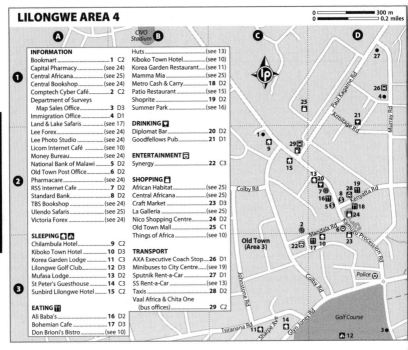

Internet Access

Internet access is readily available in Lilongwe and there are several cheap options both in Old Town and City Centre.

Comptech Cyber Café (Map p206; Mandala Rd; per min MK5) Fast internet connection, printing and photocopying as well as Skype web telephone service.

Licom Internet Café (Map p206; Mandala Rd; per min MK5; ⏰ 7.30am-8pm)

RSS Internet Café (Map p206; Kamuzu Procession Rd; per min MK4.50) Offers quick access.

WI-FI ACCESS

Skyband and Globe hotspots are available throughout the city. For information on charges and locations see p295.

Libraries

The **British Council Learning Centre** (Map p204; ☎ 01-773244; info@britishcouncil.org.mw; ⏰ noon-4pm Mon, 9am-4pm Tue-Thu, 9am-noon Fri), off Independence Dr, and the **John F Kennedy Memorial Information Resource Center** (Map p204; ☎ 01-772222; Old Mutual Bldg, City Centre Shopping Centre; ⏰ 9am-4.30pm Mon-Wed, 9am-noon Thu & Fri) allow nonmembers to read books and magazines in the library, but

not to take them away. Both places also show films on some afternoons and evenings – check their noticeboards for details.

Medical Services

Adventist Health Centre (Map p204; ☎ 01-775456/680; Presidential Way) Good for consultations, plus eye and dental problems.

Dr Huber (Map p204; ☎ 01-750404, 0999-969548; Glyn Jones Rd) Has been highly recommended to us for private consultations, although can be expensive.

Likuni Mission Hospital (off Map p204; ☎ 01-766602/574; Glyn Jones Rd) A better option than Lilongwe Central Hospital, 7km southwest of Old Town, with public wards, private rooms, and some expat European doctors on the staff.

Lilongwe Central Hospital (Map p204; ☎ 01-753555; off Mzimba St) Conditions and facilities are not particularly good here.

Medical Air Rescue Service (MARS; ☎ 01-795018/4967, emergency 01-794242; www.marsmalawi.com; Ufulu Rd, Area 43) MARS clinic with an intensive-care unit and a dentist surgery. It offers laboratory tests for malaria, bilharzia and HIV among others. MARS also has road and air ambulances with staff highly trained in emergency treatment. MARS is linked to Health International and can arrange evacuation to Harare or Jo'burg if things get really serious.

Capital Pharmacy (Map p206; ☎ 01-754294; Nico Shopping Centre; ☻ 8am-5pm Mon-Fri, 8am-1pm Sat & Sun)

Pharmacare (Map p206; ☎ 01-753230; Nico Shopping Centre; 8am-5pm Mon-Fri, 8am-4pm Sat, 8am-1pm Sun)

Money

Money Bureau City Shopping Centre (Map p204; ☎ 01-772239; Centre House Arcade); Crossroads Complex (Map p204; ☎ 01-750789); Nico Shopping Centre (Old Town Map p206; ☎ 01-750659) Has good rates, doesn't charge commission and does cash advances on credit cards.

National Bank of Malawi African Unity Ave (Map p204); Kamuzu Procession Rd (Map p206) You can change money here and get a cash advance on your Visa card. There's a 24-hour ATM that accepts Visa.

Standard Bank African Unity Ave (Map p204); Kamuzu Procession Rd (Map p206) Offers the same facilities as National Bank of Malawi but the ATM also accepts MasterCard and Maestro.

Victoria Forex (Map p206; ☎ 08-825545; Nico Shopping Centre) Offers a similar service to Money Bureau.

Lee Forex (Map p206; ☎ 01-755919; Nico Shopping Centre)

Photography

Lee Photo Studio (Map p206; Nico Shopping Centre; ☻ 7.30am-5pm) Digital printing costs MK80 per photo. A set of passport photos costs MK700. Also sells and prints rolls of film.

Post

City Centre Post Office (Map p204) Located next to City Centre Shopping Centre.

Old Town Post Office (Map p206; Kamuzu Procession Rd)

Telephone & Fax

Many lodges and hotels have phones that their guests can use to make international calls. Several internet cafes also offer an international telephone service or can hook you up to the Skype web telephone service on their computers.

Tourist Information

Ministry of Tourism, Wildlife & Culture (Map p204; ☎ 01-755499; Tourism House off Convention Dr; ☻ 7.30am-5pm Mon-Fri, 8-10am Sat) Information and advice is minimal at this tourist office. For details on tours, flights and hotels you're better off at a travel agency.

Immigration Office (Map p206; ☎ 01-754297; Murray Rd)

Travel Agencies

Barefoot Safaris & Adventure Tours (off Map p204; ☎ 01-707346; www.barefoot-safaris.com; Mandala Rd)

Organises horse riding, hiking, climbing, walking and 4WD safaris throughout Malawi and beyond.

Kiboko Safaris (Map p206; ☎ 01-751226; www.kiboko-safaris.com; Mandala Rd) Specialises in budget camping safaris throughout Malawi and Zambia, although it also has 'luxury' options for softies.

Land & Lake Safaris (Map p206; ☎ 01-757120; www.landlake.net; Mandala Rd) Well-established and knowledgeable company organising tours for all budgets in both Malawi and Zambia.

Ulendo Safaris (Map p206; ☎ 01-754947; www.ulendo.net; Old Town Mall) Organises a variety of tours and safaris in Malawi and Zambia, as well as hotel bookings and flights.

Wilderness Safaris (Map p204; ☎ 01-771393/153; www.wilderness-safaris.com; Bisnowaty Complex, Kenyatta Dr) Excellent operator providing top-end safaris and lodge bookings throughout Southern Africa.

DANGERS & ANNOYANCES

For years muggings were a serious problem around Lilongwe Nature Sanctuary. Though the situation has improved somewhat since the tourist focus shifted to the Lilongwe Wildlife Centre, it's still not wise to walk around the area. If you're visiting the wildlife centre, take a taxi or a minibus.

During the day it's fine to walk everywhere around Old Town and City Centre, although it's much quieter at City Centre at the weekend so you should be on your guard then. At night Malangalanga Rd can be dangerous, and walking to Area 3 is not recommended. The bridge between Area 2 and Area 3 is a favourite haunt for muggers. Always watch out for your things when at the city's main bus station, and if you arrive on a bus after dark take a minibus or taxi to your accommodation. As a general rule it isn't safe to walk around anywhere in the city after dark.

Scams

Bus tickets should only be bought at the bus station; some travellers have been conned out of money by buying tickets on the street when there is no such service. Watch out for people who approach you on the street claiming to work at your hostel/hotel asking to borrow money. They might say that they'll give it back to you later at your hotel but they won't. And they don't work there either.

SIGHTS & ACTIVITIES

The main **market** (Map p204; Malangalanga Rd) near the bus station in Old Town is a pocket of frenetic activity and worth a visit even if

LILONGWE

LILONGWE IN...

Two Days

Start your day with breakfast in one of Old Town's many **cafes** (pp212-13) and take in the gentle buzz of Malawi city life. Then it's time to go shopping. Peruse the jewellery and carvings at the **craft stalls** (p214) outside the post office on Mandala Rd, then off to the city's main **market** (p214) to soak up the lively atmosphere. Feeling hungry? Take a taxi to the Four Seasons Centre on Presidential Way for the best beef the city has to offer at **Buchanan's Grill** (p212), followed by cocktails at the **Chameleon Bar** (p213). If you've any energy left, head west to **Chez Ntemba** (p213), Lilongwe's most dynamic nightclub.

Take it easy on day number two. Take a minibus or taxi out to **Lilongwe Wildlife Centre** (below) to learn about its rehabilitation efforts and to visit the animal enclosures. Then head for the **tobacco auction floors** (below) to see the heart of Malawi's economic life in action. Finish the day with a cool beer at the legendary **Harry's Bar** (p213) and then perhaps take in a band or performance at the next-door **Umunthu Theatre** (p213).

---

you don't want to buy anything. You'll find all manner of things on sale here – bicycle parts, live chickens, vegetables, dustbins, underwear…the list goes on. Be aware, however, that pickpockets operate in the crowds. What's more, some visitors with large bags have been violently robbed so travel light here to avoid unwanted attention and don't bring any valuables, such as a camera, with you. Dozens of little stores line the streets leading up to the market. They all blast out popular Malawian music and sell counterfeit CDs.

For a view of Malawi's economic heart, go to the public gallery overlooking the **tobacco auction floors** (☎ 01-710377; Kenengo Industrial Area; admission free) at the vast Auction Holdings warehouse about 7km north of the city centre, east of the main road towards Kasungu and Mzuzu. This is best reached by taxi, but local minibuses serve the industrial area. Alternatively you can arrange visits with a car and driver/guide through the other companies listed under Travel Agencies (p207). The auction season is April/May to September. See the boxed text, opposite, for more information on this vital commodity.

In between City Centre and Old Town and alongside the Lingadzi River are 180 hectares of wilderness area, otherwise known as the **Lilongwe Nature Sanctuary**. This was once one of the city's most popular attractions, with a number of walking trails winding through indigenous woodland. However, the area became neglected, gained a reputation for theft and muggings, and faced criticism for a lack of animal welfare. Luckily a joint agreement between the Lilongwe Wildlife

Trust and the Department of National Parks and Wildlife is returning the area to its former glory. Though the original natural sanctuary was closed at the time of research the new **Lilongwe Wildlife Centre** (Map p20 ☎ 01-757120; www.lilongwewildlife.org; Kenyatta D adult/child MK840/420; ✆ 8am-4pm Mon-Fri, 8am-noo Sat), an animal rescue and educational facility, is definitely worth a look. The centre is considered by the UK-based Born Free Foundation, among others, to be a safe space for injured animals and for those that have been rescued from the bushmeat an wildlife trades, poorly kept zoos and private collections. The centre's ultimate aim is to rehabilitate the animals for a life back in the wild and it has a strict no breeding, no trade and a non-essential contact policy.

You're not allowed to wander around the centre on your own, but the entry fe includes a tour of the animal enclosures. This isn't a zoo so you aren't guaranteed to see any animals, but you will get to walk through a lovely wilderness area and learn about the centre's aims and animal conservation in Malawi in general. While many of the centre's residents come from Malawi, many are rescued from further afield, including Bella, a one-eyed lion who was rescued from a zoo in Romania.

To get up close to the country's mover and shakers, head to **Parliament Building** (o map p204; Presidential Way), which moved from Zomba in the late 1990s to the ostentatious palace of former president Dr Hastings Kamuzu Banda on the outskirts of Lilongwe At the time of writing, work was under way on a shiny new parliament building nea

Capital Hill, which was scheduled to be completed by 2011.

If you're interested in seeing the final esting place of Malawi's first president Banda, head for the marble and granite **Kamuzu Mausoleum** (Map p204; Presidential Way) n Heroes Acre. Adorned with a huge portrait of Malawi's 'president for life' at he entrance, the mausoleum also houses library and research centre. Construction inished in 2006 at a whopping cost of JS$600,000.

If you're the sporting type, **Lilongwe Golf Club** (right) offers daily membership for JS$10. This allows you to enter the club and use the bar or restaurant. To use the sports acilities there's a small extra charge.

SLEEPING

Lilongwe has a good range of accommodation options. Most budget digs are located in Old Town, which is the most convenient rea of the city to stay due to its eating, drinking and transport facilities.

Budget

All the budget options listed here are in Old Town.

Mabuya Camp (Map p204; 01-754978; www nabuyacamp.com; Livingstone Rd; campsite per person S$4, dm US$6, d & tw US$18;) If you're

looking for Lilongwe's liveliest backpacker spot you've found it. This place buzzes with a happy mixture of solo travellers, overlanders and volunteers relaxing by the pool and in the large shady gardens. There are dorms and a double in the main house as well as chalets and plenty of camping pitches in the garden, and rooms share clean showers set in thatched rondavels. At night the reception doubles up as a small bar, and guests mingle in the lounge or out on the terrace. The food here is pretty good too, with hearty burgers, English breakfasts and fruit smoothies on the menu. If you want to self-cater, however, you can light up one of its barbecues. The only downside is that it's 15 minutes' walk from the centre of Old Town action.

Lilongwe Golf Club (Map p206; 01-753598/118; campsite per person MK800;) A clean, safe and comfortable (hot showers!) option for campers, just off Glyn Jones Rd. Discounts are common for two or more people, and rates include access to the members bar, restaurant and swimming pool.

St Peter's Guesthouse (Map p206; 01-752812, 08-317769; Glyn Jones Rd; r with shared bathroom MK1800) Offers excellent, clean and safe rooms with nets, all of which open onto a courtyard garden. It's quiet and part of the parish so guests should be respectful.

TOBACCO

Tobacco is Malawi's most important cash crop, accounting for more than 60% of the country's export earnings, and Lilongwe is the selling, buying and processing centre of this vital industry. Most activity takes place in the Kenengo Industrial Area on the northern side of Lilongwe, the site of several tobacco-processing factories and the huge and impressive tobacco auction rooms.

A settler called John Buchanan first grew tobacco in Malawi. He planted the crop on his farm near Blantyre in the 1880s. Large-scale tobacco farming started in the area around Lilongwe in the 1920s and has grown steadily in importance ever since. Two types of tobacco are produced in Malawi: 'flue', which is a standard quality leaf, and 'burley', which is of a higher quality and in demand by cigarette manufacturers around the world.

Tobacco is grown on large plantations or by individual farmers on small farms. The leaves are harvested and dried, either naturally in the sun or in a heated drying room, and then brought to Lilongwe for sale (in southern Malawi the crops go to auction in Limbe).

In the auction rooms (called auction 'floors'), auctioneers sell tobacco on behalf of the growers. It's purchased by dealers who resell to the tobacco processors. The tobacco comes onto the floors (the size of several large aircraft hangars) in large bales weighing between 80kg and 100kg and is displayed in long lines. Moisture content determines the value of the leaves: if the tobacco is too dry, the flavour is impaired; if it's too wet, mould will set in and the bale is worthless.

A small proportion of tobacco is made into cigarettes for the local market, but most gets processed in Malawi before being exported to be made into cigarettes abroad. Most processed tobacco goes by road to Durban, South Africa, to be shipped around the world.

Sunset Lodge (Map p204; ☎ 01-724770/18; sunset lodge@globemw.net; Glyn Jones Rd; s/d standard MK2500/3000, superior MK3500/4000, deluxe MK4500/5000) Upstairs in a large building near the bus station, this place has decent rooms, though they are on the small side and the bathrooms could do with a rethink. It's not worth paying the extra for the deluxe rooms unless you are desperate to watch DSTV. If you can, go for a room overlooking the river at the back as these are much quieter.

Sabina Central Lodge (Map p204; ☎ 0888-373172; Kamuzu Procession Rd; r MK2700) The main advantage of staying here is that it's close to the bus and minibus stations if you've got an early morning start. Rooms are large, with TV and fan, and not too noisy considering their location.

ourpick Mufasa Lodge (Map p206; ☎ 0999-071665; Kamuzu Procession Rd, Area 4; dm from US$10, d with bathroom US$35; ▣) This is a fantastic new addition to Lilongwe's budget scene and one that travellers rave about. It may not have a pool or large gardens, but who needs them when you have a balcony with city views, top-notch bathrooms (plenty of changing space in each cubicle so your clothes don't get soggy, and funky glass taps) and a home-away-from-home atmosphere? Rooms range from a large executive room with a four-poster bed to small singles and dorms, and all are decorated with flair (as are the communal areas), with plenty of local craftwork to liven the place up. You can order food or eat your own creations round the huge wooden table in the spotless self-catering kitchen. There's a bar and internet access (Skyband connection planned), and it's right in the centre of Old Town.

Midrange

The following all have restaurants for residents and rates include breakfast, unless otherwise specified.

Barefoot Safari Lodge (off Map 204; ☎ 01-707346; www.barefoot-safaris.com; campsite per person US$9, s/d tent rental US$14/20, s/d/tw chalet US$45/85/85; ▣) A quiet alternative if you'd like to be outside of town with plenty of gardens to hand. There are 6 hectares of the green stuff here and you can opt to stay in chalets or walk-in tents, or to pitch your own tent in the grounds. There's a restaurant and bar and plenty of barbecues if you'd like to make your own dinner. The lodge is 10km out of town on the road towards Mchinji.

Kiboko Town Hotel (Map p206; ☎ 01-751226; www .kiboko-safaris.com; Mandala Rd; s/d from US$48/5 ▣ ⟨⟩) Location-wise, Kiboko can't be bea It's in the heart of Mandala Rd, above th fantastic Don Brioni's Bistro and a mere ski away from Old Town's banks, shops an internet cafes. The rooms aren't bad eith – four-poster beds and comfy bed linen ai complemented with jazzy African prints, an they all have scrupulously clean bathroom The residents bar in particular is gorgeou and seems more suited to a Moroccan ria with its open walls, low seating and open air fireplace. Downstairs is a cafe (open fo breakfast and lunch) serving burgers, sand wiches and yummy Dutch apple pancakes.

Lingadzi Inn (Map p204; ☎ 01-754166; Chilambu Rd; s/d from MK7000/10,500) Perfectly adequat but bland rooms are the name of the gam here – you get satellite TV, 24-hour roo service and the like. On the plus side ther are a couple of large gardens, it's convenier for the Lilongwe Nature Sanctuary, an happening Lilongwe bar, the Shack, is nex door. It's managed by the Malawi Institut of Tourism.

Riverside Hotel (Map p204; ☎ 01-750511; riversio @malawi.netlarge; Chilambula Rd; s/d MK8000/9000) gleaming white lobby full of plush leathe chairs leads to comfortable tiled room with fan, DSTV and tea and coffee facilitie Should you get a hunger on, there's restaurant serving Malawian and India curries and grills.

Chilambula Hotel (Map p206; ☎ 01-751560; Kamuz Procession Rd; r from MK9350; ⟨⟩) Most rooms her open out onto a balcony overlooking th hub of Old Town and have good view over the city. All are large with canopie beds, air-con and fridges, and the executiv rooms in particular are massive and com with sofas, chairs, coffee tables, coffe makers and faux marble bathrooms. It' pretty quiet here though and you migh have the grandfather clock in the resident lounge all to yourself.

Madidi Lodge (off Map p204; ☎ 01-752661; www .madidilodge.com; Area 9; standard s/d US$85/110, maste s/d US$110/128; ▣) An oasis of calm just short walk from Crossroads Complex Wood and brick rooms are decorated wit African artefacts and come with fridge DSTV and safes. The restaurant specialise in producing three-course meals of delight from around the continent.

Korea Garden Lodge (Map p206; ☎ 01-753467/
854/9700; www.kglodge.net; Tsiranana Rd; s/d without
bathroom US$26/28, s/d with bathroom from US$41/52, s/d
executive with air-con from US$73/78; 🖳 🛜 🖳) This
rambling hotel has rooms to suit every budget
from tiny but wallet-friendly 'bronze' rooms,
which share a bathroom, to ensuite executive
rooms with all mod cons. The cheaper you
go the smaller and darker the rooms get, but
they are all spotless with great security. You
also get the advantage of a swimming pool, a
bar and the chance to sample Korean food at
its in-house restaurant.

Annie's Lodge Area 10 (off Map p204; ☎ 01-794572;
www.annieslodge.co.mw; Area 10/285; s/d US$70/80, s/d
executive US$80/90; 🐾 🖳) Popular with aid and
embassy workers, this calm and cool hotel
has a range of plush rooms and apartments,
DSTV and large desks, hidden in serene
gardens.

Top End
Facilities at the following places to stay
include travel and car-hire agents, business
centres, swimming pools, restaurants and bars.

Sanctuary Lodge (Map p204; ☎ 01-775200/1/2; www
thesanctuarylodge.net; campsite per adult/child US$9/6,
s/d incl breakfast from US$125/175; 🖳 🛜 🖳) Just
outside Lilongwe Nature Sanctuary, this
peaceful eco-lodge is encased in 8 hectares
of miombo woodland along the Lingadzi
River, complete with walking trails and
prolific birdlife. Made from environmentally
friendly building materials, Sanctuary
Lodge has cool and quiet stone chalets, with
wide, rustic, wooden beds, clouds of soft
linen and plush bathrooms with massive
showerheads. There's also a campsite with
plenty of braai sites and good hot showers
(there are plans to build a pool, bar and
restaurant just for campers).

Pacific Hotel (Map p204; ☎ 01-776133; reservations
@pacifichotelsmw.com; off Africa Unity Ave, City Centre;
standard s/d MK14,250/16,350, deluxe s/d MK17,100/
19,200; 🐾 🖳 🖳) This new, modern option
makes a suitable alternative to the nearby
Sunbird Capital Hotel. Even the standard
rooms are large, and they're all done up
in calming shades of grey and pale green.
Large windows and ferocious air-con mean
that you feel sealed off from the dust and
heat of the city while still able to look below
and enjoy the activity. The downside compared to the other upmarket hotels is the
lack of gardens.

Sunbird Lilongwe Hotel (Map p206; ☎ 01-756333;
Kamuzu Procession Rd; s/d from US$113/134; 🖳 🛜 🖳)
Set amid sprawling, manicured gardens,
this hotel is well appointed (there's a
business centre, car hire and an Air Malawi
desk) but rather uninspiring. The upside?
Many of the previously tired rooms have
been renovated and have a more modern,
boutique hotel feel.

Sunbird Capital Hotel (Map p204; ☎ 01-773388;
www.sunbirdmalawi.com; Chilembwe Rd; s/d from US$148/
174; 🖳 🛜 🖳) The Capital is popular with
government officials and luxury safari
clients. Step inside the hotel's green confines
and you'll find the requisite gym, pool, restaurants and travel agents to keep guests happy.
Rooms are a different story, however, and
seem to have been left behind in the 1980s.

Kumbali Country Lodge (off Map p204; ☎ 0999-
963402; www.kumbalilodge.com; Nature's Gift Ltd, Capital
Hill Dairy Farm, Area 44; s/d from US$150/180; 🖳 🛜 🖳)
A short drive away from the city centre, in
a gentle rural setting, is a choice of swanky
individual thatched chalets (Madonna has
stayed here on her controversial visits to
Malawi) with beautiful views all the way
to nearby Nkhoma Mountain. This is a
working farm so the food is fantastic and
includes fresh vegetables from the farm
gardens and delicious homemade yoghurts
and cheese. You could easily spend your
entire time here lazing about in your chalet
and in the gardens, but for the more active
there are plenty of nature trails and bird-
spotting opportunities. As for other wildlife?
Hyenas, wild pigs and even leopards have
all been spotted here.

EATING
Lilongwe has a good selection of places to
eat, from cafes serving cheap, local food
(mostly found around Old Town) to stuffy,
European-style places, as well as very good
Indian and Chinese restaurants.

Restaurants
Korea Garden Restaurant (Map p206; ☎ 01-753467;
Tsiranana Rd; starters MK500-700, mains MK1000-2200;
🍽 breakfast, lunch & dinner) Within the Korea
Garden Lodge, this place serves a small
selection of flavoursome Korean favourites,
such as bulgogi and kimchi, alongside the
usual Malawian chicken, chips and *chambo*.

Huts (Map p206; ☎ 01-752912; noon-1.30pm &
6.15-9.30pm Mon-Sat; mains from MK680) Come to

Huts, off Kamuzu Procession Rd, for your fix of tandoori and *dopiaza*. The food here is filling, tasty and good value.

our pick **Don Brioni's Bistro** (Map p206; ☎ 01-756998; Mandala Rd; mains from MK800; ☺ lunch & dinner) Long-time favourite Don Brioni's is a laid-back Italian-style bistro, which fills up with an energetic mix of tourists and locals each evening. You can take a pew in the atmospheric dining room or outside on a candlelit terrace. Food here is excellent and comes in generous portions – you can choose from the main menu or from an always interesting blackboard menu of daily specials. The walls are plastered with customised name plaques for its regular, popular or well-known customers. Ask to see the visitors book – all manner of politicians, journalists and writers have passed through the doors.

Mamma Mia (Map p206; ☎ 01-758362; Old Town Mall; mains from MK1400; ☺ lunch & dinner) The spaghetti and massive pizzas are the main event here, but it also does a good selection of seafood and hearty plates of red meat. Food is served in a slightly dark dining room or on a large covered terrace overlooking the Old Town Mall.

Buchanan's Grill (Map p204; ☎ 01-772846/59; Four Seasons Centre, Presidential Way; mains MK1000-2300; ☺ lunch & dinner Mon-Sat) Sit in the old-fashioned dining room or on a terrace next to a tinkling waterfall and frog ponds at this stylish restaurant within a garden centre. What's on the menu? Great hunks of beef, ribs, schnitzels and juicy burgers. If you've less of a bloodlust there are fish, pasta and salad dishes to keep you happy.

Sanctuary Restaurant (Map p204; ☎ 01-754560; www.thesanctuarylodge.net; meals from MK1300; ☺ lunch & dinner) Based at Sanctuary Lodge, this is a very elegant restaurant with a safari lodge vibe and a large terrace overlooking the lodge swimming pool. Food here is good – from baguettes to chicken to T-bone steaks – and the restaurant is romantically candlelit at night. You can also pop in for a coffee and cake and take it on a picnic table on a grassy lawn underneath the shade of the trees.

Surf n' Turf (off Map p204; ☎ 0999-951000; Pacific Parade Shopping Mall; mains from MK1000; ☺ noon-2pm & 6-11pm Mon-Sat) Another place to fuel the city's meat obsessed, where slabs of beef, chicken and pork are served up to a mostly expat crowd. There's a sunny terrace with

a view, although it's only of Pacific Parad Shopping Mall.

Blue Ginger (off Map p204; ☎ 01-795225; Pacifi Parade Shopping Mall, off Mphonongo Rd; mains MK1200 3000; ☺ noon-2pm & 6-11pm Mon-Sat) Could thi be the best Indian food in Lilongwe? I certainly makes a good effort. Everythin is wonderfully fresh, subtly spiced an beautifully presented in a sleek, glossy dinin room that's perfect for a special night out.

Hotel Restaurants

Most of the midrange and top-end hotel listed earlier have restaurants open t nonguests, where standards and prices ar on a par with the hotel.

Kiboko Town Hotel (Map p206; ☎ 01-75220 Mandala Rd; dishes MK500-1200; ☺ breakfast & lunch Has a courtyard restaurant serving burger toasties, omelettes and a nice selection o savoury Dutch pancakes.

Patio Restaurant (Map p206; ☎ 01-773388; Sunbir Lilongwe Hotel, Kamuzu Procession Rd; light dishes fror US$4; ☺ breakfast & lunch) This is a popula lunchtime destination for business types You can go à la carte or eat from th extensive breakfast and lunch buffets.

Cafes & Quick Eats

Summer Park (Map p206; ☎ 01-755224 (at Ali Baba's, dishes MK400-900; ☺ 7am-10pm) Behind A Baba's. Choose from a small selection o sundaes, milkshakes, burgers and pizzas a the counter and it will be brought out t you in the large garden. Enormous yellow striped awnings provide shade, and there' a constant stream of African pop hits.

Bohemian Cafe (Map p206; ☎ 01-757120; Mandal Rd; snacks from MK450; ☺ 8am-4.30pm Mon-Fri, 9am 2pm Sat) Order at the counter at the bac of Land & Lake Safaris and then sit ou in a cheery vine-covered courtyard with view of the busy street. On offer are bi breakfasts, milkshakes and toasties, as we as treats such as apple pie and ice cream fo those with a sweet tooth. There are plenty o travel magazines and other info on Malaw to browse while you eat.

Ali Baba's (Map p206; ☎ 01-755224; Kamuz Procession Rd; dishes MK500-900; ☺ 8am-9pm Mon-Fri 10am-8pm Sun) This popular fast-food plac dishes up burgers and wraps, as well a sturdier plates of curries and stews.

Cappuccino's (Map p204; Crossroads Comple cappuccino MK280, dishes MK1200-1600; ☺ 7.30am-6pr

Mon-Fri, 8am-6pm Sat) A lunchtime hang-out well-patronised by people working in or nearby Crossroads Complex. There's a small terrace overlooking the mall, a collection of women's and travel magazines for browsing, and a small menu of English breakfasts, salads, wraps and sandwiches, as well as homemade cakes and muffins.

elf-Catering

There are decent supermarkets all over the city. **Shoprite** (Map p206; Kenyatta Rd) in Old Town has the best range and you can buy all sorts of food and even camping supplies. **Metro Cash & Carry** (Map p206; Kenyatta Rd) has more limited and cheaper stock. Near the City Centre Shopping Centre there's a PTC (Map p204) and at the Crossroads Complex there's a Food Zone supermarket (Map p204), which has a good range of food and imported treats.

DRINKING & ENTERTAINMENT
Bars & Nightclubs

If you want to experience a real Lilongwe night out with the locals, head for the area near the Old Town market, which has several bottle stores – these are basic bars that play loud music late into the night. This isn't the kind of place you head out to on your own or without your wits about you, though. Take a streetwise (preferably local) friend and leave the valuables at home.

Synergy (Map p206; Mandala Rd) A lively new club that plays everything from house to Western pop and Congolese rumba and is frequented by a mix of locals, volunteers and backpackers.

Chameleon Bar (Map p204; ☎ 0888-833114; Four Seasons Centre, Presidential Way; ☽ 11am-midnight Mon-Sat, till 10pm Sun) This place is equally popular with Malawians and expats and puts on regular live music and DJ nights, poetry readings and theme parties. Sundays are for laid-back afternoon jazz. It has a great cocktail menu and tables outside at which to enjoy them.

Harry's Bar (Map p204; ☎ 01-757979; off Paul Kagame Rd; ☽ 6pm-late) Harry's is an institution. The owner is a mine of information on the Malawian music scene, and the bar is the place to come if you want to get the low-down on local bands and DJs.

Chez Ntemba (Map p204; off Kamuzu Procession Rd, Area 47; ☽ 6pm-late) Part of the Congolese night-club chain that has branches across Southern

Africa, this is Lilongwe's most fun night out. Hordes of sweaty bodies pack the place out to dance to DJs and live bands with a totally African flavour.

Shack (Map p204; ☎ 0999-962507; Chilambula Rd; ☽ 6pm-late Wed & Fri) Young expats come to this bar in their droves to drink, dance and take part in various theme events (medieval night had just taken place when we visited).

Diplomat Bar (Map p206; ☎ 0888-553492; Kamuzu Procession Rd; ☽ noon-late) Small in stature but big on atmosphere, this pint-sized Old Town bar buzzes with a mixed crowd of expats, travellers and locals at the weekend, when the action often spills out onto the street.

Goodfellows Pub (Map p206; Armitage Rd; ☽ 11.30am-late Mon-Sat) Another lively spot and an expat haven. You can socialise around the pool tables, find a cosy, private corner, or plant a stool at the impressive wooden bar. Standard pub grub is served and it shows UK premiership football matches on the big-screen TV.

Theatre
Umunthu Theatre (Map p204; ☎ 01-757979; www.umunthu.com) Off Paul Kagame Rd, Umunthu is the highlight of Lilongwe's cultural scene. It puts on regular live music, films, club nights and variety shows, showcasing the best of Malawian talent.

Sport
Football matches are played at **CIVO Stadium** (Map p204; Area 9), off Kamuzu Procession Rd, on Sunday, and at the **Silver Stadium** (Map p204; Area 47). Look out for posters or ask local fans for information.

SHOPPING
Malls
City Centre Shopping Centre (Map p204) A collection of buildings off Independence Dr containing shops, travel agents, restaurants, a bank and a post office.

Crossroads Complex (Map p204; Kamuzu Procession Rd) This houses banks, a swanky hotel, minigolf, a variety of upmarket shops, supermarkets and services, and a branch of the South African Steers.

Nico Shopping Centre (Map p206; Kamuzu Procession Rd) Has a bookshop, travel agency, pharmacy and several other shops.

Old Town Mall (Map p206) Off Paul Kagame Rd, this small mall has a couple of bookshops and craft stores as well as the Mamma Mia restaurant.

At the time of writing a new shopping centre was being constructed behind the Nico Shopping Centre and opposite Shoprite. It is due to open in late 2010 and will include a Game supermarket and a Woolworths.

Arts & Crafts

African Habitat (Map p206; ☎ 01-752363; Old Town Mall; ☒ 8.30am-5pm Mon-Fri, 8.30am-1pm Sat) A large craft shop full of sculptures, paintings, bed linen, furniture and books.

Central Africana (Map p206; ☎ 01-756317; www .centralafricana.com; Old Town Mall; ☒ 8.30am-5pm Mon-Fri, 8.30am-1pm Sat) Has an impressive selection of decorative and antique maps well worth framing, old books on every conceivable topic about Malawi and modern guidebooks.

Ishq (Map p204; Four Seasons Centre; ☒ 9am-5.30pm Mon-Sat, 10.30am-4pm Sun) If you've plenty of cash to burn or a house to furnish, come here for stunning pieces of salvaged wood crafted into rustic furniture. It also sells jewellery and clothes.

La Galleria (Map p206; ☎ 01-757742; lacaverna @malawi.net; Old Town Mall; ☒ 9am-4.30pm Mon-Fri, 9am-1pm Sat) Sells sculptures and paintings by well-known Malawian artists (at the time of research it was featuring works by renowned artist David Kelly).

Things of Africa (Map p206; ☎ 0888-964779; Mandala Rd; ☒ 7.30am-5pm Mon-Sat) A souvenir shop selling T-shirts, postcards, jewellery and other crafts.

Markets

To see what Malawians buy, go to the city's main market by the bus station. It's always lively and colourful and is a great place to buy secondhand clothes, although photography is not appreciated.

There's also a craft market (Map p206) outside the Old Town post office, where vendors sell everything from trinket woodcarvings, basketry and jewellery to traditional Malawian chairs. If you go late in the day you're likely to get a better deal.

GETTING THERE & AWAY
Air

For details of flights see p300 and p303. If you're buying a ticket, it's worth trying an agent first (p207) as they offer a wider range of options, charge the same rates as the airlines and sometimes have special deals. Airlines with offices in Lilongwe include the following:

Air Malawi (☎ 01-700811; Lilongwe International Airport)
KLM & Kenya Airways (Map p204; ☎ 01-774227; City Centre)
South African Airways (Map p204; ☎ 01-772242/ 0307; Sunbird Capital Hotel, Chilembwe Rd)

Bus

AXA City Trouper and commuter buses leave from the main bus station where you'll find the AXA ticket office (Map p206), though you can also buy tickets at Postdotnet inside the City Centre PTC, Nico Shopping Centre and at Crossroads Complex.

AXA executive coaches depart from outside the City Centre PTC Supermarket before stopping at the immigration office on Murray Rd and making their way to Blantyre. An executive ticket between the two cities costs MK3100.

Destinations from the main bus station include Mzuzu (MK1200, five hours), Blantyre (MK700 to MK1400, four hours), Kasungu (MK480, two hours), Nkhotakot (MK610, three hours), Nkhata Bay (MK900, five hours), Salima (MK390, one hour), Dedza (MK310, one hour), Mangochi (MK900, 4½ hours) and Monkey Bay (MK1000, six hours).

A number of other bus companies including Coachline and Zimatha, also leave from the main bus station at similar rates and times. Super Sink buses depart from the Caltex Petrol Station between 7am and 8am to Mzuzu (MK1000, six hours).

Long-distance minibuses depart from behind the bus station to nearby destinations such as Zomba (MK1200, four to five hours), Dedza (MK500, 45 minutes to one hour), Mchinji (MK450, 90 minutes), the Zambian border (MK700, two hours), Nchitsi (MK500, 2½ hours), Kasungu (MK600, two hours), Limbe (MK1000, three to four hours), Mangochi (MK1200, four hours) and Nkhotakot (MK1100, three hours).

Vaal Africa (☎ 0999-200086) leaves from the Total petrol station in Old Town on Tuesday and Saturday at 6am, arriving in Johannesburg at 11am the following day (one way MK14,500). **Chita One** (☎ 0999-545453, 0999-022221) leaves on Wednesday and

Sunday at 6am from near the Old Town Mall (one way MK15,500).

Zambia–Botswana Coach (☎ 0999-405340) leaves Tuesday and Friday at 6am arriving in Lusaka at 5pm (MK6000). Kob's Coach leaves the same days, same price, at 5.30am. The Taqwa coach departs from Devil St at 7pm on Saturday, Sunday and Tuesday for the 27-hour journey to Dar Es Salaam (MK8000), continuing on to Nairobi (MK14,000).

GETTING AROUND
To/From the Airport
Lilongwe International Airport is 21km north of the city. A taxi from the airport into town costs MK2000.

The Airport Bus collects passengers from most of the hotels and lodges in town around three hours before a flight departure. The cost is MK1000. You can also pick it up at the airport after arriving.

Public Transport
The most useful local minibus service for visitors is between Old Town and City Centre. From Old Town, local minibuses (marked Area 12) leave from either the bus rank near the market or next to Shoprite. They then head north up Kenyatta Rd, via Youth and Convention Drs or via Independence Dr, to reach City Centre. From City Centre back to Old Town, the bus stop for the return journey is at the northern end of Independence Dr. The fare between the two centres is MK80.

Taxi
The best places to find taxis are the main hotels. There's a rank on Presidential Way, just north of City Centre Shopping Centre. Taxis also congregate outside Shoprite in Old Town. The fare between Old Town and City Centre is about MK1000. Short journeys within City Centre or Old Town cost around MK600. Negotiate a price with the driver first.

AROUND LILONGWE

DZALANYAMA FOREST RESERVE
Dzalanyama is a beautiful forest reserve in a range of hills about 60km by road southwest of Lilongwe. The area is famous for birdwatching, and species include the olive-headed weaver and Stierling's woodpecker.

The only place to stay in the reserve is the **Dzalanyama Forest Lodge** (off Map p204; s/d with shared bathroom US$25/45, whole house US$140), run by Land & Lake Safaris (p207). It's simple and there's only one bathroom and toilet between eight people, but the romantic atmosphere makes up for it. The lodge overlooks a stream and trees brimming with birds and butterflies; at night it's lit up by tons of candles and lanterns. You can spend your days exploring walking trails, mountain biking, birdwatching or simply relaxing. There's no food provided, but if you bring you own provisions there's a cook to prepare meals for you should you choose.

If you don't have your own transport, Land & Lake Safaris arranges transfers to the forest for US$100 per car from Lilongwe, as there's no public transport here. Another option is to take a three-day birdwatching safari, also organised by Land & Lake Safaris, for US$300 per person.

DEDZA
Dedza is a small town 85km southeast of Lilongwe, just off the main road between Lilongwe and Blantyre. The town is one of the highest and coolest places in Malawi, is surrounded by forested hills and sits in the shadow of stately Dedza Mountain. The road south of Dedza skirts the border of Mozambique, revealing on both sides vast plains of rust-red earth and grass, broken by conical granite peaks and a quilt of farmland.

Sights & Activities
There are numerous walks, all with spectacular views, in the **Dedza Mountain Forest Reserve**.

On the northern outskirts of town is **Dedza Pottery** (☎ 01-223069; www.dedzapottery.com; ☽ 7am-5.30pm). Follow the road to the left from town and it's signposted 1km down a dirt road off the main street. It's a pottery workshop and boutique, selling crockery, tiles and garden ceramics all hand painted with colourful illustrations of Malawian life – stay for any length of time in Malawi and you're bound to come across its stuff in tourist hotels and restaurants.

Sleeping & Eating
There are a number of cheap resthouses on Dedza's main street. The best of the bunch is the bright pink **Rainbow Resthouse & Restaurant**

(☎ 01-223062; s/d from MK1000/2000), which has clean rooms, a friendly atmosphere and a restaurant and bar.

Dedza Pottery Lodge (☎ 01-223069; www .nyasalodges.com; per person full board US$56) Has a number of fun, spacious rooms decorated with local art and bright ceramics from the pottery. The rooms all have fridges, which are replenished with soft drinks and beers daily, as well as plenty of tea, coffee and fresh milk. They sit in a large garden and have small terraces from which to enjoy the views.

ourpick Dedza Pottery Restaurant (meals from MK635, desserts from MK330) Mention Dedza Pottery and people in the know will wax lyrical about its cheesecake – and it is indeed a berry-and-cream-laden plate of heaven. But the restaurant doesn't just serve desserts. You can scoff hearty plates of cafe standbys like moussaka and lasagne or go for healthier options like salads (the mountain salad with ginger and green mangoes is particularly recommended). While you eat you can take in views of the pottery garden and the hills beyond, and in the winter there's a log fire to keep you warm.

NTCHISI FOREST RESERVE

This small and rarely visited forest reserve is about 80km north of Lilongwe, near the large village of Ntchisi (*nchee*-see). At the centre of the reserve is Ntchisi Mountain, covered in beautiful evergreen forest, as well as some of the last remaining indigenous rainforest in Malawi, and boasting stunning views of the surrounding area. Birdlife is incredibly varied, and on the mammal side of things you might see blue monkeys, baboons, bush pigs, bushbuck and duikers.

Activities

The folks at **Ntchisi Forest Lodge** can point you to a number of marked trails that you can walk with or without a guide. A popular route is the trail through the forest to the summit of Ntchisi Mountain. It's about 4km away, so allow about three hours for a return walk (more if you enjoy bird watching). You can also hire mountain bikes, visit the nearby villages and meet a local healer or learn how to cook *nsima*, or even take drumming classes.

Sleeping

Ntchisi Forest Lodge (☎ 0999-971748/741967; www .ntchisi.com; campsite per person US$8, half board per adult/ child US$90/60, s supplement US$40; lunch US$5-10;) Originally built as a 'hill station' in 1914 for the colonial district commissioner who came here to escape the heat of his normal base in Nkhotakota. It used to be run by the Department of Forestry, but has now been privatised. There are five bedrooms, a lounge with fireplace, a large terrace, a garden with plenty of comfy chairs and chill out spots, and a restaurant serving delicious locally sourced produce, including herbs and veggies from its garden. Electricity is provided by solar and wind power, evenings are candlelit, and it supports the local community and economy.

This is a very child-friendly place. It can provide babysitters during the day and make special kids meals, and is planning to build a special children's play area.

Getting There & Away

There is no public transport to the lodge, so you'll have to have your own wheels. To get here from Lilongwe, aim north on the M1 and turn right (east) at Mponela on the T350. You will reach a crossroads after about 35km; turn right here towards the village of Dowa, then after another 10km left (north) at a junction to Ntchisi village. About 12km north of this junction (you'll pass through the village of Chindembwe first), a dirt road turns right (east) to the forest reserve; there is a signpost to Ntchisi Forest Lodge.

Northern Malawi

Out of the way and sometimes forgotten, northern Malawi is where ravishing highlands meet hippo-filled swamps, vast mountains loom large over empty beaches, and colonial relics litter pristine islands and hilltop villages. It is Malawi's most sparsely populated region and the first taste many travellers get of this tiny country after making the long journey down from East Africa. For many it's the highpoint of their trip and it's easy to see why.

Hugging the border with Zambia is Nyika National Park – a starkly beautiful wilderness where zebras pose on the skyline, wildflowers tickle the grasses, and pine forests hide leopards and hyenas. Head south a little and the sultry flat woodland and swamps of Vwaza Marsh Wildlife Reserve bring forth huge herds of elephants, antelopes and buffaloes. Sitting within easy striking distance of both of them is Livingstonia, which sucks you into a time warp with its old missionary buildings and quiet, unhurried atmosphere.

This part of Lake Malawi is lined with gleaming coves and pristine beaches, and there's plenty of excellent accommodation in which to enjoy it. Budget travellers will do particularly well here – there's a huge choice of beachfront campsites, waterside huts and backpacker-friendly activities – but other visitors won't go unrewarded either. There's everything here from cosy self-catering lodges to jaw-dropping ecoluxury.

This chapter covers most parts of the Northern Province, from the northern tip of Malawi down to the Mzuzu and Nkhata Bay areas. Places are described roughly from north to south.

HIGHLIGHTS

- Discover **Nyika Plateau's** (p224) grasslands and wildflowers on foot, by bike or on horseback

- Follow in the footsteps of Malawi's early missionaries in the hilltop town of **Livingstonia** (p221)

- Enjoy beachside fun and frolics at popular backpackers' haunt **Nkhata Bay** (p232)

- Take the *Ilala* ferry to **Likoma Island** (p237) to explore remote beaches and visit the incongruous Cathedral of St Peter

- Watch elephants and hippos fight for space at Lake Kazuni at **Vwaza Marsh Wildlife Reserve** (p228)

NORTHERN MALAWI

NORTHERN MALAWI

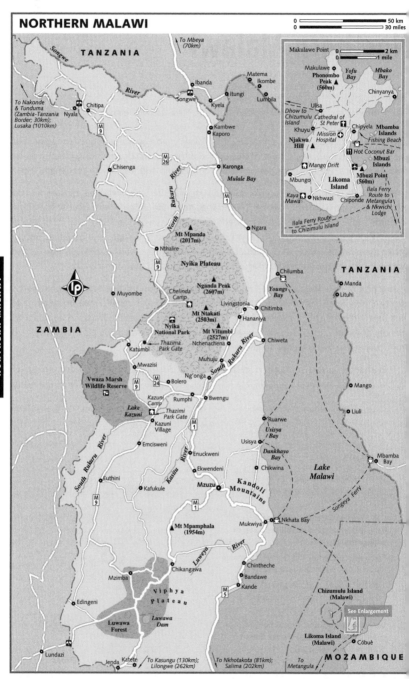

0   50 km
0   30 miles

TANZANIA

To Mbeya
(70km)

Songwe River

Ibanda
Matema
Ikombe
Songwe
Itungi
Kyela
Lumbila

To Nakonde
& Tunduma
(Zambia-Tanzania
Border; 30km);
Lusaka (1010km)
Chitipa
Nyala
M 9

Kambwe
Kaporo

Chisenga
M 26

Karonga

Mulale Bay

M 1

Ngara

Mt Mpanda
(2017m)

Nthalire

Nyika Plateau
M 9

Chilumba

TANZANIA

Manda
Lituhi

Nganda Peak
(2607m)

Muyombe
Chelinda
Camp

Livingstonia
Chitimba

*Youngs
Bay*

Mt Ntakati
(2503m)
Hananiya

ZAMBIA

Nyika
National Park

Mt Vitumbi
(2527m)
Nchenachena
Chiweta

*Thazima
Park Gate*

Katumbi

Muhuju

South Rukuru River

Mwazisi

Ng'onga

Mango

**Vwaza Marsh
Wildlife Reserve**
M 24
M 9
Bolero

Rumphi

Bwengu

Liuli

*Lake
Kazuni*

Kazuni
Camp

Ruarwe

*Usisya
Bay*

*Thazimi
Park Gate*
Kazuni
Village
M 1

Usisya

*Dankhayo
Bay*

Mbamba
Bay

Emcisweni

Enukweni

Chikwina

*Lake
Malawi*

Euthini

Kafukule

Ekwendeni

Mzuzu

**Kandoli
Mountains**

M 1

Mango... Songeya Ferry

Mt Mpamphala
(1954m)

Mukwiya

Nkhata Bay

Mzimba

Chikangawa

Chintheche
Bandawe

*Viphya
Plateau*

Kande

M 5

**Chizumulu Island
(Malawi)**

Edingeni

*Luwawa
Dam*

Luwawa
Forest

See Enlargement

**Likoma Island
(Malawi)**

Lundazi

Cóbuè

Jenda
Katete
To Kasungu (130km);
Lilongwe (262km)
To Nkhotakota (81km);
Salima (202km)
To
Metangula

MOZAMBIQUE

Enlargement

Makulawe Point

0   2 km
0   1 mile

Makulawe
**Phonombo
Peak
(560m)**
*Yofu
Bay*

*Mbako
Bay*

Chinyanya

Ulisa

Dhow to
Chizumulu
Island

Cathedral of
St Peter

Khuyu

Chipyela
**Mbamba
Islands**
Fishing Beach

Mission
Hospital

**Njakwa
Hill**

Hot Coconut Bar

**Mbuzi
Islands**

Mango Drift

**Mbuzi Point
(560m)**

Mbungo

**Likoma
Island**

*Ilala Ferry
Route to
Metangula
& Nkwichi
Lodge*

*Kaya
Mawa*

Nkhwazi

Chiponde

*Ilala Ferry Route
to Chizumulu Island*

KARONGA

In the surrounding dry and dusty country, Karonga is a relaxed little town with wide streets, wandering cattle and shopfronts straight out of a Western; you can almost see the tumbleweed rolling down the street. It's the first place you'll come across if making the journey down from Tanzania and not a bad place to start – you'll be able to check your emails, stock up on cash and have a close encounter with a 100-million-year-old dinosaur.

The town is very spread out – strung out for about 2km along the main street between a roundabout on the north–south road and the lakeshore – which can be tough work with luggage, but there are plenty of bicycle-taxis that will take you anywhere you want to go in town for around MK80.

Information

Karonga has both a Standard Bank and a National Bank of Malawi. There's also an **internet cafe** (per min MK10) at the Cultural & Museum Centre Karonga (below).

Sights & Activities

Cultural & Museum Centre Karonga (CMCK; ☎ 01-362579; www.palaeo.net/cmck; ⏰ 8am-5pm Mon-Sat, 2-5pm Sun) celebrates the numerous fossil discoveries made in these parts, and the skeleton

---

MALAWISAURUS & OTHER ANIMALS

Karonga has the proud title of Malawi's 'fossil district', meaning that it's one of the few places in Africa to have well-preserved remains of dinosaurs and ancient man. More than 1700 animal fossils have been discovered in this area of the Rift Valley, including rhinos, elephants and antelopes. Karonga's most famous discovery is the *Malawisaurus* (Malawi lizard) – a fossilised dino skeleton found 45km south of the town. It's thought that the scaly one lived between 140 million and 100 million years ago during the Cretaceous Period and was a hulking long, 4m high and weighed in at around 11,000kg. Other discoveries in the area include the lower jaw of *Homo rudolfensis*, a 2.5-million-year-old man, and *Paranthropus boisei* (Malema man), a pre-human who also walked the earth 2.5 million years ago. Excavations are still ongoing.

---

of the Malawisaurus (or a copy of it anyway) takes pride of place. Visits are in the form of a guided tour. Following the path of a giant snake along the floor of the museum you'll be taken on a whistle-stop journey of the life of the planet and the Karonga district in particular, from a time when dinosaurs ruled to world to the rise of the mammals to Malawi's fight for independence. There's also some fun stuff along the way: for example, a series of viewfinders, which you can look inside to find a very realistic prehistoric man staring back at you; displays of warriors' dress and smoking pipes from the late 19th century; and colourful wall murals painted by local artists defining the theme of each corner of the museum – from a prehistoric family sitting by the lake to a triumphant Banda waving his fly whip.

Sleeping & Eating

Mufwa Lakeshore Lodge & Camping (☎ 01-362390, 0999-778451; campsite per person MK700, s with/without bathroom MK2500/1200, d with/without bathroom MK3800/2100) A lodge overlooking the lake with a large, green lawn might sound like a good thing but in reality the owners don't make much of it. Bland and basic are the watchwords for the rooms here. Shared facilities are a bit grimy so plump for a room with a bathroom. The property can be difficult to find – there is no identifying sign and it's set back from the road; the turn-off is located between Club Marina and the National Bank of Malawi.

Safari Lodge (☎ 01-362340; s/d/r 12 MK3000/3750/4000) On the road to the lake, this place has spacious rooms but, as with many places in this town, they are a bit run-down. Room 12 costs extra because you're paying for the privilege of air-con but as there's no other difference it's not really worth it. You can get an average meal for around MK750.

Safari Lodge Annex (☎ 01-362340; standard/executive/chalets MK4500/4800/6500) This is Safari Lodge's more attractive and better-endowed sister. There are solid brick chalets here with large bathrooms and separate sitting areas, as well as a pretty garden. Even the standard rooms in the main house have a lot going for them. All rooms have fans and TV. Food is available here too, with snacks costing from MK450 and mains from MK700.

Club Marina (☎ 01-362391, 0999-458657; standard s/d MK5500/6500, superior s/d MK6500/8000) In terms of a nice setting, Club Marina does pretty well – rooms all look inwardly onto a garden and cosy thatched bar, which is a fine place to sink a few beers. Sleeping quarters are just OK though and the bathrooms could do with a refit. Superior rooms are the same size and quality as the standard ones; it's just that they have a TV.

Sumuka Inn (☎ 0999-444816; standard/deluxe/executive MK8500/10,500/12,500, suites from MK15,000) Easily the best digs in Karonga, especially if you're a fan of faux marble and satin – these guys have it in spades. If you really want to lay it on thick go for an executive room and you'll be treated to a huge living and sleeping space, with Louis XIV–style armoires, plush velour bedspreads and marble-look fittings aplenty.

Karonga isn't exactly overflowing with good places to eat. There are a couple of basic cafes around the station, which are much of a muchness, but the nicest place for a bite is probably **Mbande Café** (☺ 8am-5pm Mon-Sat, 2-5pm Sun) at the museum where you can pick up flavoursome traditional food such as chambo, *nsima* and beans.

Getting There & Away

AXA City Trouper buses leave for Lilongwe at 12.30pm (MK2000, 10 hours) from where they continue on to Blantyre (MK2800, 14 hours). Minibuses go to numerous destinations, including Songwe (MK230, 45 minutes) and Mzuzu (MK800, four hours). Taxis to the Tanzanian border go from the main bus station and cost MK500.

If you've got a 4WD you can cross into northern Zambia via Chitipa in northern

Malawi. It's four hours from Karonga to Chitipa on a rough dirt road (there's no public transport but you might be able to get a lift on a truck). After going through customs it is another 80km or four hours' drive to the Zambian border post at Nakonde.

CHITIMBA

Chitimba is a small village near the turn-off to Livingstonia from the main north–south road. Although not much more than a small collection of shops, for travellers the attraction is the long stretch of golden sand and handful of well-placed lodges. It's the perfect place to recharge if you've just done the long trek down from Tanzania or up the big hill to Livingstonia.

Sleeping

There are three places to stay close to the junction with the main road. They can store your gear and arrange a guide if you want to walk up to Livingstonia.

Chitimba Campsite (☎ 0888-387116; www.chitimba.com; campsite per person MK600, dm MK600, stilt chalets with shared bathroom MK2200, d with bathroom MK2800) You'll see the odd cow wandering around this stunning stretch of sand, but they only occasionally interrupt beach volleyball. Now into lobbing things over a net? Then there's a buzzing restaurant and bar right on the water that whips up a mean burger (MK700) and plenty of other tasty treats. At the bar laptops fight for space with beers as overlanders log on to check the news from home. There's tons of space for campers here, as well as dorms and rooms. The en suite doubles are small but cute and covered with bright fabrics (watch out for the low slanted roofs though!) and there are rustic but more spacious twin rooms in reed huts, each with its own little veranda. It can arrange day trips up to Livingstonia for US$25 per person. It is a famous overlanders' spot though, so it can sometimes get pretty rowdy.

Sangilo Sanctuary Lodge (☎ 0999-395203, 0888-392611; www.sangilo.net; campsite per person US$6, d chalets with shared bathroom US$50, d chalets with bathroom US$60) About 8km north of Chitimba, ecofriendly Sangilo is the most upmarket of the lodges hereabouts and has the most striking setting. Handsome chalets have stylish hand-carved beds and perch on the cliffs above a golden bay, making the best of the awesome lake views. At night

---

KARONGA'S WARS

Though it may seem sleepy and uneventful, Karonga has seen its share of excitement in times past. At the end of the 19th century, the African Lakes Corporation waged a private war here against the army of Sultan Mlozi, a powerful Swahili-Arab slave-trader. Later, during WWI, colonial British soldiers, along with their African conscripts, fought off a German invasion from the neighbouring colony of Deutsch Ost-Afrika (later to become Tanzania). It was apparently the only WWI land battle to be fought on Malawian territory. (Another battle took place on the lake – see p259.)

---

ere's nothing to disturb you except for the ound of the waves. Excellent food is served n the outdoor restaurant deck down on e beach (lunch from US$4, dinner from S$12), with a couple of different choices at change daily. The only disappoint-ent is the campsite, which sits behind the wner's house so misses out on the fantastic ews. Call in advance to arrange pick-up om the *Ilala* ferry at Chilumba.

Namiashi Lodge (☎ 0999-421515; s/tw/d MK1500/ 00/4000, 2-bed chalets MK5000) Upkeep is not is resort's strong point. At first it looks as it might not even be open but guests are armly welcomed to its rather rustic rooms nd chalets. At least the setting, bang on the each underneath the shade of some gigantic ees, is pretty gorgeous, and you won't find ny rowdy overland trucks here. Food such s *nsima* and stew (MK400) and chicken urry (MK700) is available. It's about 5km outh of the Livingstonia turn-off.

etting There & Away

minibus or *matola* (pick-up) between hitimba and Mzuzu or Karonga is around 1K600.

IVINGSTONIA

fter two failed attempts at establishing a ission at Cape Maclear and at Bandawe oo many people kept dying from malaria), e Free Church of Scotland moved its ission 900m above the lake to the village f Khondowe. Called Livingstonia after Dr avid Livingstone, the mission was built in 884 under the direction of Dr Robert Laws. he town provides a fascinating glimpse to Malawi's colonial past – most of the ld stone buildings are still around today many of them are used by the local univer-ty). Despite the healthy student population 's a pretty quiet, conservative place and is cohol free. The cool climate, old colonial rchitecture, broad tree-lined streets and unning views at every corner make it erfect place to recover from hard travel in anzania or too much partying on the lake.

ights & Activities

he fascinating **museum** (admission MK250, otos MK100; ☽ 7.30am-5pm) in Stone House he original home of Dr Laws and now a ational monument) tells the story of the uropean arrival in Malawi and the first

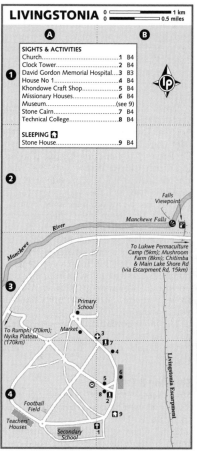

missionaries. Here you can read Dr Laws' letters, peruse black-and-white photos of early missionary life in Livingstonia and browse a collection of Dr Laws' books, in-cluding the old laws of Nyasaland. Also on display is an excellent collection of original magic-lantern slides, an early anaesthesia machine, an old gramophone and the cloak that Dr Laws used to use when he was a moderator.

The nearby mission **church**, dating from 1894, has a beautiful stained-glass window featuring David Livingstone with his sextant, his medicine chest and his two companions, with Lake Malawi in the background. There are services here every Sunday and if you're in town you are welcome to attend.

You might also like to take a look at the **clock tower**. The nearby industrial block was built by the early missionaries as a training centre and is now a **technical college**. The excellent **Khondowe Craft Shop** sells inexpensive carvings and crafts made by local people; all proceeds go directly to the hospital and mission.

Down the road from here are the **David Gordon Memorial Hospital**, once the biggest hospital in Central Africa, and the **stone cairn** marking the place where missionary Dr Robert Laws and his African companion Uriah Chirwa camped in 1894 when they decided to build the mission here. Also nearby is **House No 1**, the original home of Dr Laws before he moved into Stone House.

About 4km from town, the impressive **Manchewe Falls** thunders 125m into the valley below. Follow a small path behind the falls and there's a cave where, as the story goes, local people hid from slave-traders a hundred years ago. Allow an hour for going down and 1½ hours to get back up. Alternatively, if you're walking to/from Chitimba, you can visit on the way.

The more adventurous can also arrange abseiling trips for half a day or longer. For more details contact Mushroom Farm (below).

Sleeping & Eating

Stone House (☎ 01-368223; campsite per person MK600, r with shared bathroom per person MK1400) Built by Dr Robert Laws in the early 20th century and still retaining some original furniture, this is an atmospheric spot. The wood-floor rooms have the feel of a Victorian boarding school and the views from the veranda are superb. Wholesome meals are available (English breakfast MK250, *nsima* and beef stew MK350) and so is a laundry service (MK200).

our pick **Mushroom Farm** (☎ 0999-652485; www .themushroomfarmmalawi.com; campsite per person MK640, tent hire MK800, s/d from MK4000) Drive into this sustainable bush retreat from the Livingstonia road and the views will hit you smack in the face. They're quite simply some of the best in Malawi – you have unobstructed views down over the escarpment and across the lake. Camping spots with their own little fire pit sit right at the cliff edge and there are some gorgeous rooms here too, including a wood-and-thatch

double completely open at the front to take in the views to the max, and a room with traditional cob walls that looks like it could house a hobbit. Want *nasi goreng* for breakfast? You can have it here, as well as noodle soup, pancakes, pasta and other such goodies. Add to that the relaxed vibe and plentiful adventure activities on offer (abseiling, rap jumping) and you could easily spend more time here than you bargained for.

Lukwe Permaculture Camp (☎ 0999-434985, 099 792311; campsites US$5, dm US$10, s/d cabins US$15/2 Located on the northern side of the escarpment road, above the steep zigzags, an hour walk (about 5km) east (downhill) from Livingstonia or about 10km from Chitimba if you're coming up. Thatched cabins s along the edge of the escarpment with dramatic views over Lake Malawi, and there's a chilled lounge with fire pit, comchairs and a friendly atmosphere. The food here is mostly European, serving dishes such as lasagne and pasta, and salad ingredients are all grown here onsite (food should be ordered in advance meals co from MK500 to MK1200). Rooftop camper can also be catered for.

Getting There & Away

From the main north–south road between Karonga and Mzuzu, the road to Livingstonia (known as the Gorode) turns off Chitimba, forcing its way up the escarpment in a series of acute hairpin bend Drivers should attempt this only in a 4W and only if there's been no rain. The road varies between dirt road, very rutted an difficult track, and patches of paved concrete. There's no bus, and you'll wait a very long time if you're hitching.

The alternative is to walk up – it's about 15km, and steep, so it takes around four hours from Chitimba if you follow the road. There are short cuts that can reduce it to less than four hours, but these are even steeper. You can usually pick up a guide at Chitimba Campsite. Take care on this road; isolated incidents of muggings have occurred so it best to check the latest situation before you set off, or take a local guide.

The other way to reach Livingstonia especially if you're coming from the south is to drive up the dirt road from Rumphi for which you'll also need a 4WD. It's also possible to get a truck up this route which aves at 2pm on Tuesdays and Thursdays om outside the PTC Supermarket in umphi and takes about five hours.

A third option is to walk to Livingstonia om the Nyika Plateau (see boxed text 225).

UMPHI

umphi (*rum*-pee) is a small town west of ne main road between Mzuzu and Karonga. Vhile perfectly pleasant, with a circle of ills as a backdrop, the only reason to pass nrough is if you're on your way to Nyika ational Park, Vwaza Marsh Wildlife Reserve r Livingstonia. There are a few basic rest-ouses here as well as supermarkets, a small narket, a petrol station and a bank (though ot with an ATM accepting foreign cards).

leeping & Eating

atunkha Eco-Tourism (☎ 0888-293424; r from MK500) lodge and orphanage 3km out of town. here are simple en suite rondavels here as well as dorms and camping, and all of the profits are used towards the orphanage and other community projects. Activities at the lodge are also community based and guests can visit the orphanage or organise village visits to spend time with the Tumbuka peo-ple. There's a restaurant and bar onsite as well as a small gift shop.

Country Resthouse (☎ 01-372395; s/d from MK800) The best option on the main road, where clean and spacious rooms come with electricity, mosquito nets and fans. It is also the home of Chef's Pride Restaurant, which serves a variety of meals (from MK300) all day, including toasted sandwiches, chicken and beef stews, veggie dishes and curries.

Getting There & Away

Minibuses run to and from Mzuzu (MK400, one hour). Trucks on their way to Chitipa might drop you off at the turning to Chelinda Camp. Minibuses and *matolas* to Kazuni village (from where you can get to

---

HOW NYIKA WAS FORMED

The word *nyika* means 'wilderness', and this particular expanse of high, open wilderness has probably existed in its current form for many centuries. A small population of hunter-gatherers is believed to have inhabited the area more than 3000 years ago, and ancient rock paintings have been found at Fingira Cave, at the southern end of the plateau. When the Bantu people arrived in northern Malawi, most stayed on the plains below the Nyika. The plateau was a place to hunt and smelt iron, but it was never settled in a big way.

The first Europeans to see the Nyika were probably Scottish missionaries, who reached this area in 1894 after it was brought to the attention of the British government by explorer David Livingstone, although it's quite possible that it was seen by Portuguese explorers who were active in the area long before Livingstone came through. The mission station built by the Scottish missionaries, between the Nyika's eastern edge and Lake Malawi, was named Livingstonia and is still a thriving centre today.

Scientists and naturalists who visited Nyika Plateau in the early 20th century recognised the biological importance of the area, and in 1933 measures were taken to protect the stands of juniper trees on the southern part of the plateau from bushfires. In 1948 this section was made into a forest reserve, and at the same time pine plantations were established around Chelinda, near the centre of the plateau.

There were later plans to extend the plantations and develop the area as a source of wood for a proposed pulp mill on Lake Malawi, but access for logging vehicles proved difficult and the scheme was abandoned. Plantations were, however, established on the Viphya Plateau (p241), and plans for a Lake Malawi mill were shelved, although were still occasionally discussed, even as late as the 1990s.

In 1965 the entire upper Nyika Plateau was made a national park, and in 1976 this area was extended further to include the lower slopes of the plateau – an important water-catchment area. This most recent boundary extension included several small settlements, and the people living here were relocated to areas outside the park. When they moved they took the names of their villages with them and now, in the area bordering the park, there are several settlements that share names with valleys and other features inside the park itself.

Vwaza Marsh Wildlife Reserve) should cost around MK500. Most transport leaves from outside the PTC Supermarket.

NYIKA NATIONAL PARK

No, someone hasn't just airlifted some zebras and antelopes and dropped them in Europe; you're still in Southern Africa. But at 1800m above sea level Nyika Plateau, the main attraction of Malawi's 3200 sq km **Nyika National Park** (admission per person US$5, per car US$2; ☉ 6am-6pm), is decidedly different from the rest of Malawi: think the Yorkshire Moors meet the Black Forest. Gently sloping hills, broad valleys and grasslands are met by sporadic pockets of thick pine trees and gin-clear streams; and most mornings

the air is cold and crisp and the silent land scape enveloped in blue mist.

With all that expanse you're likely to hav Nyika to yourself; you won't see many othe tourists here and can quite easily spend th day hiking in the hills without happenin upon another soul – except for the animal that is. Plenty of zebras, bushbucks, reec bucks and roan antelopes (rare elsewhere roam this domain and you may also spo elands, warthogs, klipspringers, jackal, duikers and possibly hyenas and leopard. The landscape is so open that you can spo the wildlife from miles off – and they aren exactly camera shy. In fact the Nyika zebra seem to delight in posing for photos on th skyline. Twitchers should note that mor

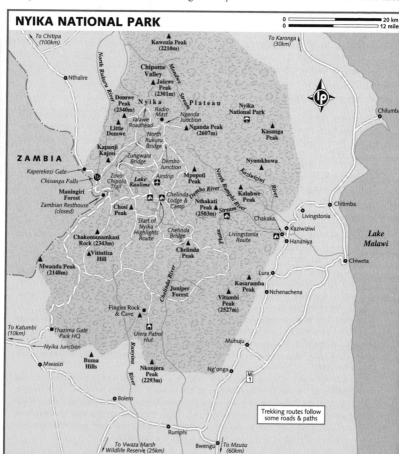

NYIKA NATIONAL PARK

than 400 species of bird have been recorded here, including rarities such as the wattled crane and moustached green-tinkerbirds. And after the wet season the landscape bursts into life in a blaze of wildflowers. There are around 200 species of orchid alone growing on the plateau.

What makes Nyika stand out from the other parks and reserves in Malawi are all the different ways to explore the landscape. Rather than just driving around in a safari vehicle, you can trot over the plains on horseback, take a more energetic route on a mountain bike, ramble through the hills on foot or simply sit down by a stream for a spot of fishing.

It can get surprisingly cold on the Nyika Plateau, especially at night from June to August when frost is not uncommon. Log fires are provided in the chalets and rooms, but bring a warm sleeping bag if you're camping. During dry periods, sectors of the park are burnt to prevent larger fires later in the season. Before setting off for drives or walks, inquire at the park headquarters and avoid areas that are being burnt.

Activities

Changes were afoot in Nyika at the time of research. After the **Nyika Safari Company** lost its tender in 2007, visitors could only stay the night in the park on a mobile safari and Chelinda Lodge had closed down. However, **Wilderness Safaris** (www.wilderness-safaris.com), which also runs the excellent Mvuu

Lodge and Camp in Liwonde National Park, had just won the tender to run the park's tourists concessions. It plans to renovate the existing accommodation and to start up horse riding and biking safaris again, with accommodation reopening in late 2009.

WILDLIFE WATCHING

To appreciate the animals and flowers of Nyika, you can tour the park tracks in your own car (but you'll need a 4WD to access most areas), and by the time this is published you might be able to arrange a guided wildlife-viewing drive at Chelinda Camp. Wildlife viewing is good year round, although in July and August the cold weather means the animals move to lower areas. Birdwatching is particularly good between October and April when migratory birds are on the move.

DAY HIKING

Although you can't enter the park on foot, hiking is allowed once you've checked into camp. There are several spots where you can leave your car and walk for an hour or all day. One of the most popular options is to park at the Jalawe roadhead, north of Chelinda Camp, and then follow the path for 5km to Jalawe Peak. Beyond the summit is a rocky outcrop overlooking the Chipome Valley, a thousand metres below. You can sometimes spot elephants here.

Various paths and tracks wind through the plantation woodland, or across the

---

HIKING & TREKKING ON THE NYIKA PLATEAU

There are a number of long-distance routes available on Nyika. For advice contact **Wilderness Safaris** (www.wilderness-safaris.com) which as of 2009 was in charge of tourist concessions in the park. It should be able to help you with obligatory guides and porters, who have their own sleeping bags, tents, cooking pots and food. You must provide all the equipment and food you need.

When walking in the park you can either follow the set park tracks, paths and wildlife trails or strike out on your own and walk across the trackless grassland. Routes to the peaks and viewpoints on the western and northern escarpments are especially popular. The wilderness trails are not designed to help you get the best animal close-ups with your camera, but rather to show you that animals are part of a wider environment and to help you best enjoy the feeling of freedom and space that Nyika provides.

The only set route on Nyika – and by far the most popular – goes from Chelinda to Livingstonia. It's a hugely rewarding and spectacular walk, crossing east through high grassland then dropping steeply through the wooded escarpment and passing through villages and farmland to reach the old mission station at Livingstonia. This route takes three days. The third night is spent in Livingstonia and on the fourth day you can walk down to Chitimba at the lakeshore. For further information there's a chapter on Malawi in Lonely Planet's *Trekking in East Africa*.

grassland to nearby dams. For longer walks of more than a day, see boxed text p225.

MOUNTAIN BIKING

Nyika's network of dirt roads is ideal for mountain biking. You can base yourself at Chelinda and go for day rides in various directions or camp out overnight (for which you'll need to hire a guide). This is a fun way to cover more ground than you would on foot. Mountain-bike hire should be available again once Wilderness Safaris takes over; otherwise you can bring your own bike in.

HORSE RIDING

Nyika's wide, open landscape lends itself perfectly to horse riding and this is by far the most enjoyable and exhilarating way to experience the plateau. The tussock grass and boggy valley bottoms that can tire hikers are crossed easily by horse, and the extra height means the views are excellent. You can also get much closer to animals such as zebras, elands and roans when on horseback.

Wilderness Safaris plans to reinstate horse safaris once the Chelinda accommodation reopens in late 2009.

FISHING

Some anglers reckon Nyika National Park offers some of the best rainbow trout fishing in Malawi. The best time of year to fish is October and November. Fishing is allowed in the dams near Chelinda Camp (Dam One has the lion's share) and in nearby streams. Only fly fishing is permitted and there's a limit of six fish per rod per day to maintain numbers.

Sleeping

Camping Ground (campsite per person US$10) About 2km from the main Chelinda Camp, this camp is set in a secluded site with vistas of the plateau's rolling hills. The site has permanent security, clean toilets, hot showers, endless firewood and shelters for cooking and eating.

Chelinda Camp (☎ 01-771393; www.wilderness-safaris.com) Chelinda Camp is a series of self-catering stone bungalows tucked into the forest. All of them have huge stone fireplaces, sitting rooms and fully equipped kitchens for self-caterers. The camp was being renovated by Wilderness Safaris at the time of writing.

Chelinda Lodge (☎ 01-771393; www.wilderness-safaris.com) This is a luxury lodge, 1km from

---

MINI-ITINERARIES: NORTHERN MALAWI

Beach frolics, a wilderness area straight out of Scotland, and a hilltop colonial town with its own set of adventure activities.

How Long & How to Get There

Start off in Mzuzu, the northern region's biggest town. It's about six hours on the bus from Lilongwe or four to five hours if you're driving. Or if you're coming from Tanzania, it's the first major town on the highway. Here you can stock up on money, petrol and provisions and head off to do a circuit of northern Malawi's biggest attractions – a day and night in Vwaza Marsh Wildlife Reserve, two nights in Nyika National Park, and a day and night in Livingstonia. If you have your own 4WD you can do this independently, otherwise the easiest way to get through all of that is to organise a mobile safari, perhaps through **Budget Safari** in Nkhata Bay (p233).

After all of that excitement you'll need to chill out, so when you come down the bumpy road from Livingstonia, head for one of the lodges near Chitimba for a couple of days' sunbathing. Then take yourself off to Nkhata Bay for yet more fun in the sun, but this time with more of a party vibe (there are plenty of minibuses from Chitimba if you don't have a car, though you'll probably have to change in Mzuzu). Two or three days here will do, unless you want to stick it out for longer and take a PADI Open Water course at the local dive school.

The *Ilala* ferry is the next port of call. Hop on the ferry (try the 1st-class deck – you can rent a mattress and doze underneath the stars) and head for the islands of Likoma and Chizumulu – there are daily dhow services between the two. Both have accommodation, beautiful beaches and a relaxed, friendly population. The perfect way to finish your trip.

Chelinda Camp. A cluster of log cabins sitting in a clearing of pine trees on the side of a hill, it looks like something out of the pages of a children's storybook. The lodge was undergoing renovations at the time of writing but should be finished by the time this book is published. Roaring fires, luxury bathrooms and gourmet dinners should be the order of the day.

All self-caterers should stock up in either Mzuzu or Rumphi. There's a small shop at Chelinda for National Parks staff but provisions are often basic and supplies sporadic.

Getting There & Away

Despite most maps showing otherwise, there is no road of any sort between Chelinda and Livingstonia or any other town on the eastern side of the plateau. Getting to the park by public transport can be a bit of an ordeal. Wilderness Safaris should be able to offer travellers transfers by road once the Chelinda operation is up and running again.

AIR

Charter flights to Nyika weren't operating at the time of research but might start up again now that Wilderness Safaris has won the park's tourism concession.

BICYCLE

It's possible to bring a mountain bike into Nyika and you can cycle from Thazima (pronounced and sometimes spelt Tazima) Gate to Chelinda, but an early start is recommended due to the distance.

BUS

There are no public buses into the park; the nearest you can get is via the service from Mzuzu to Rumphi (MK250). There you might be able to find a truck or *matola* going to Chitipa to drop you off at the turn-off to Chelinda Camp, but then you'd still have a good 20km to walk.

CAR

The main Thazima Gate is in the southwest of the park, 54km from Rumphi; to Chelinda Camp it's another 55km. The road is dirt after Rumphi and in fair condition as far as Thazima Gate. In the park the tracks are rough and really only suitable for 4WD vehicles or 2WD vehicles with high clearance.

How Much?

There's loads of budget accommodation in northern Malawi, with a good choice of midrange options thrown in and a couple of super luxurious lodges.

Budget

The backpackers beach hot spots are the best places to find cheap accommodation in these parts – Nkhata Bay, Chitimba and Chintheche. You're looking at camping from around US$3, dorms from around US$6 and budget beach huts from around US$10. Livingstonia also has good budget accommodation. All of the backpackers lodges have cafes and bars serving cheap meals and even cheaper beers.

Midrange

Nkhata Bay has some good options for those with a little more cash to splash. Most hostels will have very comfortable rooms with bathrooms from around US$25. There are also a couple of fine midrange alternatives at Chitimba, where rooms go from around US$50.

Top End

The Chintheche Strip and Likoma Island are the places to head for if you really want to max out. There are some outstanding beach resorts here and you can spend anything upwards of US$120 per person for full board, fantastic service and beautiful surroundings.

Tip

Livingstonia is the adventure sports capital of northern Malawi. You can abseil, rap jump or swing over a gorge on a piece of elastic.

Kaperekezi Gate, in the west of the park, is rarely used by travellers. Petrol is available at Chelinda but in limited supply, so it's best to fill up before you enter the park.

VWAZA MARSH WILDLIFE RESERVE

This 1000 sq km reserve is not on the mainstream tourist track (if Malawi even *has* such a thing) and is little talked about, but with its compact size and plentiful buffalo, elephant and hippo population this is a park that shouldn't be overlooked.

The park ranges in appearance from large flat areas of mopane woodland to open swamp and wetlands. The Luwewe River runs through the reserve (draining the marshland) and joins the South Rukuru River (the reserve's southern border), which flows into Lake Kazuni. It joins the Zambian Luangwa ecosystem to the west. A good network of driveable tracks in the reserve is easily explored in a 4WD or high-clearance vehicle; if you're in a 2WD, ask at Kazuni Camp for advice on the condition of the tracks. The best driving route is along the southern edge of the reserve, parallel to the river, heading to Zoro Pools. A better way to witness wildlife is on foot – either around Lake Kazuni or on a longer wilderness trail – but you must be accompanied by a guide.

Like many of Malawi's parks, poachers have hit Vwaza in the past but the animal numbers are still reasonably healthy. As well as a plethora of antelope – puku, impala, roan and kudu, to name a few – there are around 2000 buffaloes and 300 elephants; it's not unusual to see herds of 30 or 40 of them. Vwaza's birdwatching is also excellent. There are some 300 species present here and this is one of the best places in Malawi to see waders, including storks and herons. There are few predators here but occasionally lions and leopards are spotted, as are wild dogs that sometimes pass through from Zambia.

In fact just sitting around Vwaza's main camp will bring plenty of animal sightings. The camp looks over Lake Kazuni (which is inhabited by more than 500 hippos) and on most days you'll see crocodiles lying out in the sun, hippos popping their heads out of the water and a steady parade of animals coming down to the lake to drink. Watched from the safe distance of the camp this is all very exhilarating.

The best time of year to visit is in the dry season; just after the rainy season, the grass is high and you might go away without seeing anything.

Sleeping

The accommodation in the park used to be run by the now defunct Nyika Safari Company. At the time of writing the government had awarded the reserve's tourism concession to a new company, so prices and accommodation were due for an overhaul. Ask on the ground for further information.

Kazuni Camp (campsite per person US$6, s/d chalet with shared bathroom US$10/20) Has simple, rustic chalets with beds, clean sheets and mosquito nets. They are separated by a decent stretch of bush, so you still get a sense of privacy and wilderness while being within a camp; and they're close to the water so that elephants and hippos are frequent night-time visitors. You must bring your own food, and there are cooking stations with barbecues.

Lake Kazuni Safari Camp (huts US$30) Consists of low-key grass and brick en suite chalets in a fantastic position overlooking the flood plains. There's a restaurant sitting underneath the acacia trees. As with Kazuni Camp, this place was in limbo at the time of writing and waiting for a private company to take over the tender from the government.

Getting There & Away

If you're travelling by public transport, first get to Rumphi (reached from Mzuzu by minibus for MK400). From Rumphi there are plenty of *matolas* travelling to and from the Kazuni area and you should be able to get a lift to the main gate for around MK500 to MK700. Otherwise buses and minibuses to Mzimba might drop you at Kazuni village, which is about 1km from the park gate.

By car, head west from Rumphi. Turn left after 10km (Vwaza Marsh Wildlife Reserve is signposted) and continue for about 20km. Where the road swings left over a bridge, go straight on to reach the park gate and camp after 1km.

MZUZU

Mzuzu is the largest town in northern Malawi and serves as the transport hub for the region. Travellers heading to Nkhata Bay, Nyika or Viphya or to and from Tanzania are likely to spend a night or two here on the way and they'll have a pleasant

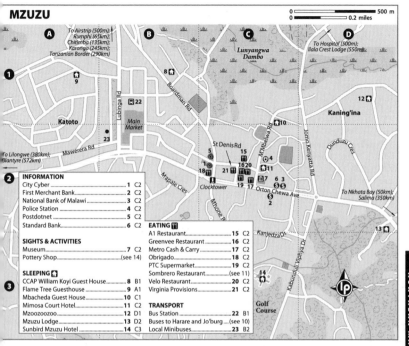

MZUZU

0 — 500 m
0 — 0.2 miles

To Airstrip (500m);
Rumphi (65km);
Chitimba (135km);
Karonga (245km);
Tanzanian Border (290km)

Lunyangwa
Dambo

To Hospital (500m);
Ilala Crest Lodge (550m)

Katoto

Main
Market

Kaning'ina

To Lilongwe (380km);
Blantyre (572km)

Mawerera Rd

Boardman Rd

St Denis Rd

Clocktower

Orton Chewa Ave

To Nkhata Bay (50km);
Salima (350km)

Kanjedza Dr

Golf
Course

Jomo Kenyatta Rd

Dunduzu Cres

Kabundulu viphya Dr

INFORMATION
City Cyber 1 C2
First Merchant Bank 2 C2
National Bank of Malawi 3 C2
Police Station 4 C2
Postdotnet 5 C2
Standard Bank 6 C2

SIGHTS & ACTIVITIES
Museum 7 C2
Pottery Shop .... (see 14)

SLEEPING
CCAP William Koyi Guest House 8 B1
Flame Tree Guesthouse 9 A1
Mbacheda Guest House 10 C1
Mimosa Court Hotel 11 C2
Mzoozoozoo 12 D1
Mzuzu Lodge 13 D2
Sunbird Mzuzu Hotel 14 C3

EATING
A1 Restaurant 15 C2
Greenvee Restaurant 16 C2
Metro Cash & Carry 17 C2
Obrigado 18 C2
PTC Supermarket 19 C2
Sombrero Restaurant .... (see 11)
Velo Restaurant 20 C2
Virginia Provisions 21 C2

TRANSPORT
Bus Station 22 B1
Buses to Harare and Jo'burg .... (see 10)
Local Minibuses 23 B2

stop. Mzuzu feels compact and friendly, its climate is cool and is centred around a long tree-lined avenue. It has banks, shops, a post office, supermarkets, pharmacies, petrol stations and other facilities, which are especially useful if you've come into Malawi from the north.

Information

The National Bank of Malawi, Standard Bank and First Merchant Bank, all on Orton Chewa Ave, exchange travellers cheques and money, and offer credit-card withdrawals. National and Standard Banks have ATMs that accept foreign cards. If you're heading to the lake, cash up here as there is no foreign exchange facility in Nkhata Bay.

Internet access is available at **City Cyber** (per 10min MK100; 8am-5pm Mon-Fri, 8am-4pm Sat) or **Postdotnet** (per 30min MK200 8am-5pm Mon-Fri, 8am-12.30pm Sat), both on Boardman Rd.

Sights & Activities

The **museum** (M'Mbelwa Rd; admission MK100; 7.30am-noon & 1-5pm, tours at 9am, 11am, 1.30pm & 2pm) has displays on the people and the land

of northern Malawi, including the Tumbuka, the Tonga and the Ngoni. Exhibits include traditional hunting implements, musical instruments, and a mock-up of a traditional hut including burning embers and a man cooking food inside. If you're planning to head up to Livingstonia there's an interesting exhibition telling the story of the missionaries' journey.

On the ground floor of the Sunbird Mzuzu Hotel there's a **pottery shop** (01-310622; 9am-4pm) selling mugs, plates and other ceramic goodies from Dedza Pottery (p215) in case you don't have a chance to make it to the workshop itself. It also sells glossy pictorials about Malawi.

Sleeping

Mzoozoozoo (0888-864493; off Jomo Kenyatta Rd; campsites MK300, dm MK800, d MK1400) This is Mzuzu's only hostel and the friendly owners make it a good one. Dorms are in a big timber bungalow, and a stream of activity buzzes around the funky outdoor bar. There's tasty food (dishes MK700) and the place is a mine of information about the locale.

CCAP William Koyi Guest House (☎ 01-931961; Boardman Rd; campsite per person MK350, dm MK500, r with/without bathroom MK2500/950) Quiet and good value, this is a good option for budget travellers and sits in a large sunny garden. The church owns it so it's generally safe and secure, though it also means that there's no booze and you'll have to act in a respectful fashion. Cheap meals are available from MK400 to MK500 and a full English breakfast costs MK250.

Flame Tree Guesthouse (☎ 01-310056, 0999-511423; off Katoto St; campsite per person MK500, s/d incl breakfast MK3000/3800) Budget travellers will live well here. Spotless units centre round a shady garden and all of them have a little piece of veranda to call their own (as well as their own flip-flops in the shower rooms). The neat lounge has DSTV and a book exchange, and if ordered in advance dinner can be served on the veranda. Meals start at around MK800, and include curries, steak and chips, and chicken.

Mbacheda Guest House (M'Mbelwa Rd; s/d with shared bathroom MK750/1500, r with bathroom MK2500) Basic, cheap and friendly, this place has the added advantage of having a bus terminal in its grounds. If you're planning a trip to Johannesburg or Harare, the Danorarea bus goes from here.

Mzuzu Lodge (☎ 01-332097; Orton Chewa Ave; standard s/d MK6000/8000, superior s/d MK7000/10,000, executive s/d MK8500/11,500) If you stay here (and it is in a nice, peaceful location east of town) go for an executive room – newly built, away from the noise of the bar and with all the hotel amenities you could want. Standard rooms on the other hand are next to a noisy bar and are a tad dilapidated.

Ilala Crest Lodge (☎ 01-311834; s/d from MK8000/10,500) The views over the town from here are pretty nice and the rooms aren't bad either. More expensive ones have sitting rooms and verandas with views over the town. If you've less cash to spare you can hole up in a cosy but still functional space. It's about 1.5km northeast of the town centre, just past Mzuzu's hospital.

Mimosa Court Hotel (☎ 01-312833/609; s/d MK8000) This is an excellent midrange choice – large bright corridors open up into scrupulously clean bedrooms, with plenty of wardrobe space, funky art on the walls and cheesy lion-print rugs. The welcome is warm, it's in a great location right in the

centre of town (off M'Mbelwa Rd, behind the museum) and there's also an enjoyable restaurant here.

Sunbird Mzuzu Hotel (☎ 01-332622; www.sunbird malawi.com; s/d from US$96/117; ☒ ☐ ☎) Mzuzu's plushest hotel has large rooms with all the requisite trimmings – deep pile carpets, DSTV, room service. Most rooms are quiet with a view of the town's golf course, and the service is friendly and efficient. Not the most charterful of places but if you want international standards then this is the place to come. It's off Kabunduli Viphya Dr.

Eating

Obrigado (Boardman Rd; snacks from MK50, meals from MK300; ☺ 6am-9pm) Soak up your beer with a mixed plate of samosas and gizzards or tuck into a plate of offal and chips in this large outdoor cafe and beer garden. Fountains, trees and an enormous zebra statue accompany your meals, and at the weekend it puts on live music.

Virginia Provisions (☎ 0999-323335; St Denis Rd; meals MK300-1100; ☺ 6.30am-9pm) The best chill-out spot on the St Denis Rd drag. Sink into a cane chair and enjoy a cool drink while taking in the views of the busy street, or try one of a bewildering array of fried chicken dishes from its menu.

Velo Restaurant (☎ 0999-953667; St Denis Rd; meals MK400-800; ☺ 6.30am-9pm) Chambo and chips and hefty T-bone steaks can be enjoyed here along with a never-ending soundtrack of loud sporting events on TV.

Sombrero Restaurant (☎ 01-312833/608; meals MK500-900; ☺ breakfast, lunch & dinner) The food here has a reputation as some of the best in town and the small sunny terrace and congenial atmosphere make it a fun place for a meal. Steaks, fish and curries are on the menu. It's located at the Mimosa Court Hotel.

A1 Restaurant (St Denis Rd; mains around MK900; ☺ 11.45am-2pm & 6-10pm; ☎ ⓥ) A large selection of vegetarian dishes as well as chicken tikka masala and other Indian restaurant standbys are served within these bright purple, red and blue walls. It also does a good choice of Malawian food.

Greenvee Restaurant (☎ 0888-899666; St Denis Rd; mains from MK600; ☺ 6am-10pm) There's a big veranda from where to watch the street action and a small menu of *nsima*, stew and offal at this friendly little restaurant.

If you're looking for cheap eats there are food stalls around the market and the Mbacheda Guest House (M'Mbelwa Rd). Self-caterers can stock up at the **PTC Supermarket** (Orton Chewa Ave) or the **Metro Cash & Carry** (M'Mbelwa Rd).

Getting There & Away
AXA City Trouper buses go to Lilongwe at 6.30am and 5pm (MK1200, five hours) and local buses leave at 7.30am and 6pm (MK1000, six to seven hours). City Trouper buses also go to Karonga, leaving at 6.30am and 10am

---

WHERE TO ON THE LAKE?

Lake Malawi is the defining feature of this little country's landscape, enticing travellers with its glassy waters, abundance of colourful underwater life and endless saffron beaches. It has often been described as an inland sea and, when trying to spot Mozambique's hazy silhouette on the horizon, it's easy to see why. The lake's enigmatic weather often entertains storms thick enough to rouse 5m waves and intimidating swells, shifting within an hour to flawless blue skies reflected in the water's glassy veneer.

The lakeshore's environment changes starkly from dramatic escarpments in the north to flat, sandy bays in the south. It can be tough figuring out where to go, so the following should help you decide.

The North
The least-developed section of the lake is home to Chitimba Campsite, which serves as a magnet to overland trucks coming in from Tanzania, but if you don't want to party, Sangilo Sanctuary Lodge is your answer or head for the remote and tranquil village of Ruarwe.

Nkhata Bay
Lush hillside framing indented bays makes the landscape reminiscent of the Caribbean (and so is the laid-back vibe). This is above all a beach resort for backpackers, but those in search of a little more comfort will find it too, and the excellent diving, kayaking and socialising will keep them here.

Likoma & Chizumulu Islands
Sublime beaches, unparalleled diving, breathtaking walks, preserved cultures and a beautiful missionary cathedral make these islands a must-see. There's excellent accommodation, from budget beach huts to five-star luxury, and a rare opportunity to immerse yourself in untainted village life.

Chintheche Strip
A secluded collection of camping grounds, lodges and resorts pepper this picturesque stretch of the lake, which is a hop, skip and jump from the wooded hills of the Viphya Plateau.

Senga Bay
The nearest beach paradise to Lilongwe offers a wide range of places to stay, excellent snorkelling and bush walking, and trips to the nearby islands to see giant monitor lizards.

Cape Maclear
Blissful beach vistas, chilled-out resorts and a friendly little village all mix quite happily in Cape Maclear. You could find yourself staying far longer than intended.

Monkey Bay to Mangochi
A smattering of top-end hotels, midrange resorts and budget lodges, many with a few kilometres of private beach and the facilities to keep you from moving far.

(MK800, four hours) and local buses leave to Karonga at noon (MK600, five hours) via Rumphi (MK250) and Chitimba (MK540).

Minibuses go to Lilongwe (MK1300, five hours), Nkhata Bay (MK350, one to two hours), Karonga (MK800, three to four hours), Chitimba (MK700, two hours), Rumphi (MK400, one hour) and the Tanzanian border (MK1200, four hours).

National Bus Company has daily departures to Lilongwe (MK1000), Blantyre (MK2000) and Salima (MK1100).

The **Taqwa bus** (☎ 0999-670468), originating in Lilongwe, travels between Mzuzu and Nairobi on Tuesdays and Sundays (MK15,000) calling at Songwe for the border (MK1500), Mbeya (MK3500) and Dar Es Salaam (MK8000). You should report to the station at 11.30pm for a midnight departure. The bus crosses the border at first light, goes through Mbeya in the morning, gets to Dar Es Salaam late in the afternoon and leaves for Nairobi the next morning.

Danorarea Tours (☎ 0888-639363) leaves from the forecourt of Mbacheda Guest House at 7pm on Fridays, going to Harare (MK7500) and Johannesburg (MK15,000).

NKHATA BAY

Nkhata Bay has quite a different feel from its beachside rivals. Get a little bit out of town and look back at the houses and lodges crawling up the lush hillside above deeply indented bays and you could almost be in St Lucia. The centre of gravity is a small town centre, nestled into a gully with the bay to the west and a gentle rise of dense forest to the east. It's a busy clutch of markets, craft stalls, local activity and wandering visitors.

Strung along the coast from the town centre is a collection of lodges, most secreted in small bays, ranging from backpacker party magnets to laid-back clusters of reed huts on the beach. Most of Nkhata Bay's lodges will provide you with everything you need – food, drink, a beach, entertainment – so it's easy to get so comfortable you never leave their confines. However, patronising local eateries and general meandering are good fun and well worth the extra energy.

Information

There's nowhere to change money so make sure you cash up in Mzuzu or Lilongwe. Alternatively some of the lodges accept credit cards, US currency and traveller cheques for payment. Internet access i available at **Aqua Africa** (☎ 01-352284; www.aqu africa.co.uk; per min MK12; ⏰ 10am-4pm Mon-Sat) an **L-Net Internet Cafe** (per min MK8; ⏰ 7am-5pm Mon Fri, 8am-12.30pm Sat & Sun).

Dangers & Annoyances

Travellers have been attacked and robbe when walking outside the town centre (i particular to and from Chikale Beach), s take extra care when walking this route a it can be quite deserted. Most travellers wil encounter a fair amount of hassle from loca beach boys offering a bewildering amount o services, from beach barbecues to personal ised key rings. If you're not interested, b polite but very firm and they should leave you alone.

Sights & Activities

SWIMMING

On the southern side of Nkhata Bay, **Chikale Beach** is a popular spot for swimming an lazing on the sand, especially at weekends Snorkelling equipment is free for guests a most of the lodges.

KAYAKING

For something more active both **Monke Business** (☎ 01-252365), on Chikale Beach jus next to Njaya Lodge, and **Chimango Tour** (☎ 0999-268595), based at Mayoka Village can organise fully inclusive (meals, kayaks guides and tents) paddling excursions per sonally tailored to your needs from anythin from half a day to a few days down the coas Typical itineraries include idyllic spot along the northern lakeshore such as Usisy and Ruarwe. Chimango Tours also offer trips by catamaran (though in this case tha means two dugout canoes joined by a dec in the middle) and Canadian canoe.

DIVING

Aqua Africa (☎ 01-352284; www.aquaafrica.co.uk offers a number of different diving option from five-day PADI Open Water course for US$310 to casual day dives for US$4 to full-on Dive Master courses for US$50C This place has a stellar reputation and is wel known for its attention to safety and excel lent level of personal attention. Groups ar a maximum of six people and you shoul try to book in advance.

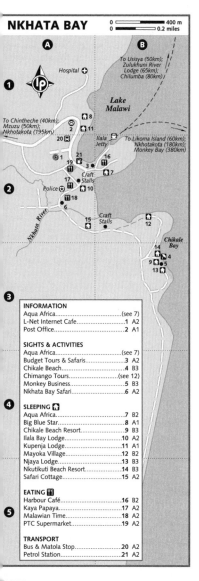

ours
Budget Tours & Safaris (☎ 0999-278903; www.budget safari.com), based at Safari Cottage, organises well-run and interesting safaris around northern Malawi. A five-day safari to Vwaza Marsh Wildlife Reserve, Nyika National Park and Livingstonia costs around US$360, including all meals and camping. For those

who want to explore the region with a bit more flexibility, it can also arrange a 4WD with driver from US$120 per day.

Nkhata Bay Safari (☎ 0999-265064; daviemzungu @yahoo.co.uk; ☻ office 7am-5pm) offers tours to Vwaza, Nyika and Livingstonia as well as further afield to Liwonde National Park and the Zomba Plateau. The average cost is US$80 per person per day all-inclusive. It can arrange bus bookings for Tanzania, cabins for the *Ilala* ferry, flights and lodges. If the office is closed, you can get information about its tours from Njaya Lodge.

Sleeping

Nkhata Bay has several places to stay, all strung out in a line along the road into town and along the lakeshore. All beds at the following have mosquito nets. To get from town to the lodges at Chikale Beach, stay on the dirt road, cross the bridge and then head up the big hill. It's about one to two kilometres, depending on the lodge.

Big Blue Star (☎ 01-352316; s.mccombe@googlemail .com; campsite per person US$3, dm/s/d with shared bathroom US$5/10/20) A large, busy and friendly place near the centre of town, with a touch of the Caribbean running through it. You can either camp or stay in colourful red-, yellow- and green-striped dorms and reed huts. Social life comes courtesy of the lively bar (yes, it plays a lot of reggae), where you can get chatting with one of the many locals who hang out here. There's also a laundry room with TV lounge that shows English premiership football matches.

Kupenja Lodge (☎ 0999-284153; campsites US$3, s/d US$8/15) This place is quiet and relaxed with less of a party vibe than some of the other lodges, but friendly just the same. The stone huts here are pretty basic and not that well soundproofed (you can hear the noise of the town, which can be loud on a weekend night) but they are clean with good views (especially at night when the lake glimmers with the lights of the town) and there's also a very good stretch of beach here. The homemade meals are delicious.

Njaya Lodge (☎ 01-352342; www.njayalodge.com; campsite per person US$7, bandas per person US$12, chalets US$20, family cottages with bathroom per person from US$28) This is the furthest lodge from town and often one of the quietest – once Nkhata Bay's biggest party spot, the crowds have moved on, but that's no bad thing. There's

NORTHERN MALAWI

a lovely selection of accommodation hidden in lush hillside grounds, from en suite chalets at the top of the hill to reed huts to beautiful stone houses right above the water (chalets 1 and 2 share a huge terrace right over the lake waves and a set of stone steps going directly into the water). There's an open restaurant and bar area with Moroccan-style arches and a terrace overlooking the lake. If you've run out of cash it also accepts credit cards.

Mayoka Village (☎ 01-352421; www.mayokavillage .com; campsite per person US$3, dm US$4, traditional mud huts per person US$5, chalets s/d with shared bathroom US$8/16, chalets s/d US$25/50) Probably the most popular lodge in Nkhata Bay and it's easy to see why. There's a rambling collection of chalets and beach huts – some en suite with huge stone baths and broad terraces, and some back-to-basic reed huts down near the water with spotless shared facilities. And there are dorms, mud huts, and plenty of space for campers too. There isn't a stretch of sand to sunbathe on here, but there are plenty of strategically placed sunbathing pods and chairs to lounge on. Life revolves around the buzzing waterfront bar, which serves excellent food and has been the scene of many a raucous party.

Ilala Bay Lodge (☎ 01-352362; s/d MK2000/3000) This place is rather soulless, but could suit if you're looking for hotel-style comforts. There's a range of bland, clean rooms with DSTV, good bathrooms and hot water. There's a restaurant serving Malawian staples and the staff are welcoming.

Aqua Africa (☎ 01-352284; www.aqua-africa.co.uk; tw US$25; 🖳) A good choice if you want to be in town though it might be booked up by people on their dive courses. Neat, secluded and comfortable rooms have balconies overlooking a tiny private beach and the excellent Harbour Cafe is just over the road.

Chikale Beach Resort (☎ 0999-329776, 0888-364337; d/tw MK3500/5000) This place is right next door to Nkutikuti, with a selection of brick chalets grouped around a very nice waterfront bar. The chalets are pretty dark and gloomy on the inside though.

Nkutikuti Beach Resort (☎ 01-352286; s/d/tw MK4500/6000/7500) You'll definitely get away from the backpackers if you come and stay here. Most of the clientele are on conferences or else Malawians or Tanzanians on holiday. The reception is sparkling and

new, but the rooms leave a lot to be desired – it looks like they haven't seen a lick of paint in quite a while. On the plus side some of them are well located along a little ridge right above the water.

Safari Cottage (☎ 0999-278903; www.safa -cottage.com; cottage per day US$65) If you can get a group together (or if you want a whole house to yourself) this is a fantastic self catering option. The cottage sleeps five in three bedrooms, and there's a lounge with TV and stereo, a self-catering kitchen and big, wide veranda with lovely views ou over the lake. There's a daily cleaning service, 24-hour security and you can get you laundry done.

Eating & Drinking

Malawian Time (plate MK350, set meal incl soup & dessert MK750; ⏰ 8am-6pm) This one is different You can order plates (a small selection o different dishes on one platter) or larger se meals of beautifully presented Malawian, Japanese food including croquettes, meatballs with peanuts, and sandwiches. There's an open kitchen at the front of the cafe with a couple of outdoor tables, and the little dining room at the back is half restaurant, half cool craft shop. As well as delicious food it has freshly squeezed juices (MK100) and milkshakes (MK150). It also sells homemade jam (MK480) in a variety of delicious flavours (apple cinnamon, papaya, tea and orange). It can open in the evening if booked in advance.

Kaya Papaya (mains from MK600; ⏰ 7am-late, food served till 9pm) It's hard to miss this bright purple place and if you're in town you should give it a try. Downstairs is a little garden with brightly patterned deckchairs to chill out in and upstairs is an expansive open deck where you can order food and look down on the day-to-day business of the town. The food is pretty tasty and the Thai dishes (for example Thai beef stir-fry and Thai noodle soup) make a good alternative to the norm. There's also a bar here that stays open until the last person leaves.

Harbour Café (light meals from MK600, mains MK900; ⏰ 10am-9pm) Opposite Aqua Africa is this open-air place with views of the lake as well as the village streets. It serves good breakfasts, burgers and baguettes for lunch, and at dinnertime there are daily specials such as lasagne. If you just fancy a snack here are homemade cakes, ice cream and milkshakes.

For self-catering, the **PTC Supermarket** on the main drag is the best bet, although the range is rather limited.

Getting There & Away

All buses and minibuses go from the bus stand on the main road. AXA buses run to Mzuzu (MK300, two hours) and minibuses run to Nkhotakota (MK700, five hours), Chintheche (MK300, one hour) and Mzuzu (MK350, one to two hours). To reach Lilongwe the quickest option is usually to go to Mzuzu and transfer. Many travellers also come or go on the *Ilala* ferry (see p304).

AROUND NKHATA BAY

North of Nkhata Bay, the steep slopes of the Rift Valley escarpment plunge straight down to the lake and there's no room for a road alongside the shore. The isolated villages along this stretch provide a remote experience that is well worth the hike.

Fifteen kilometres north of the village of Usisya is **Zulukhuni River Lodge** (☎ 0999-492774, 995-636701; campsite MK400, dm MK1000, chalets MK1700, stone house MK2500), a gorgeous hideaway barely visible from the water. Stone-and-thatch chalets teeter over the water, backed

by a wild, jungly garden, and there's an impressive bar and restaurant area nestled underneath the curve of a cliff. A troop of fish eagles, kingfishers and otters regularly entertain guests and there are plenty of walks to the nearby river and waterfall to be had. Ask at Kaya Papaya in Nkhata Bay for further details.

The *Ilala* ferry (p304) stops at Ruarwe village, 20 minutes' walk south of the lodge. Alternatively a boat transfer from Nkhata Bay costs around MK2500. You can book this (and the lodge) at Kaya Papaya in Nkhata Bay.

If you're fit, it's possible to walk to Zulukhuni on foot from Usisya, 15km south of Ruarwe. From Mzuzu local *matolas* to Usisya leave at 11am, from where you can walk. It's also possible to walk south from Chitimba Bay. This journey takes two to three days and you should be well prepared with water, food and a tent. The tracks are clear and it's an excellent way to explore the untouched northern shore and visit the many villages along the way. Speak to the lodge before you set out, for an update on track conditions.

CHINTHECHE STRIP

About 40km south of Nkhata Bay, near the unremarkable village of Chintheche, is a beautiful sweep of sand known as the

---

LIVINGSTONIA MARK TWO

If you're visiting one of the lodges on the Chintheche Strip, you should try to visit the **Old Bandawe Mission**, a cavernous church built between 1886 and 1900, which was the short-lived location of the Livingstonia mission (p221). Dr Robert Laws moved the mission north to Bandawe from its original site at Cape Maclear when members of his flock kept falling ill with malaria. Unfortunately, after a few years, the same thing happened at Bandawe, and Dr Laws eventually moved the mission to the cool, malaria-free hillside town of Khondowe, in 1894.

The church is still used regularly today, and if you drop by, the pastor or one of the church elders will be happy to show you around. It is a simple, square building with a series of low steps in a semi-circle facing the altar instead of pews, contrasting sharply with the more European-style church later built at Livingstonia. Admission is free, but donations are welcome.

Perhaps the most interesting thing at Bandawe is the graveyard where several of the early Scottish missionaries are buried. It's some 400m from the church in a hauntingly beautiful spot – their graves silhouetted against the lake and surrounded by a series of low white walls. Our guide was full of stories about the unfortunate people who were laid to rest there. Most of them were young men in their twenties who died of malaria, he told us, and one grave belongs to an unfortunate man who baptised his dog and then died the same day (presumably as a punishment!). A single grave lies outside the wall – apparently this contains the body of a shipwrecked sailor who was not known to be a Christian.

The church is near Makuzi Beach Lodge. Follow the signs to the lodge from the main road and the church is 2.5km down the track.

'Chintheche Strip'. All along it are hotels, lodges and camping grounds to suit all tastes and budgets. They all lie between 2km and 5km east of the main road that runs between Nkhata Bay and Nkhotakota, and usually involve a drive or walk along a dirt track through forest or farmland. If you're travelling by bus, the express services may not stop at every turn-off, but minibuses stop almost anywhere on request. The access roads for the majority of the lodges require 4WD or a high-clearance car, as the tracks are pretty bad.

Activities
DIVING
Aquanuts Dive School (☎ 01-357376, 0888-500420; www.kandebeach.com) based at Kande Beach Resort has an onsite training pool and offers PADI courses, casual dives and PADI scuba refresher courses. It's well run and pays excellent attention to safety and the environment.

HORSE RIDING
A professionally run stable, **Kande Horse** (☎ 0888-500416; www.kandehorse.com) has 28 horses and organises a variety of excursions, from 45-minute rides for children (per person US$12) to all-inclusive packages including four to six hours' riding a day, all meals and rooms at its guest house (per person US$220). Accommodation is in a stone farmhouse at the stables. It is 50km south of Nkhata Bay, just outside the village of Kande, and is well signposted from the road.

YOGA
If you've come to Malawi to find inner peace, this is the place to be. **Makuzi Beach Lodge** (www.makuzibeach.com) has a variety of yoga and meditation retreats on offer. The lodge has its own qualified Sivananda yoga instructor and can offer specially tailored courses including all meals and accommodation. You can also add on a Reiki attunement to the end of your course.

Sleeping
Kande Beach Resort (☎ 01-357376; www.kandebeach.com; campsite per person MK600, dm MK1000, s cabins per person MK1500, beach chalets MK3000, chalets with bathroom MK6000) About 7km from the Makuzi turn-off (55km south of Nkhata Bay), this buzzing and sprawling complex is a popular

stop-off point for overland trucks. Ther are dorms, camping, reed cabins and beach front huts with shared bathrooms, as we as very nice chalets with tree-trunk four posters – unfortunately the latter are se away from the beach behind the overlan truck camping area so you might not hav a peaceful night. There is also a relaxe beach bar and plenty of organised activ ties around the area.

London Lodge (☎ 01-357291; campsite per perso MK800, s/d with bathroom MK1500/2500) Larg thatched cottages are spacious and cool, bu a little dark and ramshackle as is the plac in general. It's on an attractive and quie stretch of beach though and very peacefu There's also a bar and restaurant (dishe around MK800) serving the usual chicke or chambo and chips.

Sambani Lodge (☎ 0888-713857; campsite p person MK1300, s/d/f MK3000/4000/7000) The beach side rooms are breezy and calm, offerin relief from the heat outside. They have ve randas and large windows so you can eve look at the lake view while you're in bec Rates include breakfast.

Makuzi Beach Lodge (☎ 01-357296; www.maku beach.com; full-board per person s/d US$139/119) Thi lodge is seriously good-looking. Cool, pointy hatted chalets are studded around vibran terraced lawns blooming with trees an plants. All have views of the water, roman tic net-swathed four-posters, fans an candles. All this sits in a curved bay shel tered by hills and rocks, and there's a raise bar with balcony and stunning views At night it ups the romance factor wit lantern light and occasional starlit barbecues For activities there's kayaking, snorkellin and fishing. You can find Makuzi Beach b continuing south down the main road pas Chintheche, where you'll reach the turn-of to Bandawe (also called Old Bandawe); it another 3.5km down the track.

Chintheche Inn (☎ 01-771393; www.wilderne -safaris.com; full-board per person US$160, day visitors MK500 This joint is pretty swanky and if you wan to come in and have a look around you' have to get past the bouncers at the gat or pay MK500 for the privilege. Rooms ar kitted out with local artwork, hand-carve chairs and plenty of candles, and open ou onto a private terrace, with your very own path to a beach that looks as if it was freshl combed that morning. The campsite i excellent, with its own bar, tent shelters, and hot, very clean showers.

Ngala Beach Lodge (☎ 01-295359, 0888-192003; www.ngalabeach.com; executive r per person sharing/single occupancy US$60/70, chalets per person sharing/single occupancy US$75/95; 🖳 🛜) Large beachside gardens conceal a selection of huge A-frame chalets with terraces and day beds, decked out in low-key safari chic – African prints, the odd tasteful giraffe statue, that sort of thing. There are hammocks, a wide sweep of sand and plenty of yummy locally sourced food. And best of all, there's an infinity pool. Rates include breakfast and sunset cruise.

Beach House (☎ 0999-960066, 01-876110; house per night US$230) Run by Central Africana of the bookshops' fame (p205), this large colonial house sits backed against sand dunes right by the shores of the lake. There are four bedrooms (the whole house sleeps eight) as well as a huge self-catering kitchen, though there are staff on hand to prepare food should you choose. Continuing with the colonial theme, the house is decorated with old black-and-white photos and maps from back in the days when Malawi was Nyasaland. There's a wraparound terrace and a little orchard at the back where you can pick mangoes and lemons. The house is 2km south of Chintheche. Bookings also available through Jambo Africa (www.jambo -africa.com).

LIKOMA ISLAND

Likoma and Chizumulu Islands are on the Mozambican side of Lake Malawi, but are part of Malawi.

The blissful island of Likoma measures 17 sq km and is home to around 6000 people. Isolation from the mainland has enabled the locals here to maintain their reserved culture, shaped partly by the religious legacy of missionaries but also by the lack of any transient population – international or domestic. These are possibly the friendliest people in Malawi and there is no crime on the island.

Likoma's flat and sandy south is littered with stately baobabs, and offers a constant panoramic view of Mozambique's wild coast only 40km away. In the hilly north, prolific eucalyptus and mango trees compete for views over the vast enormity of the lake. The main drawcard is an abundance of pristine beaches and the activities revolving around them, but there's a healthy dose of other activities, both cultural and physical, to fill several days here. Those looking for wild parties or another beach to conquer will be disappointed, however; Likoma's beauty is its preservation, and both the lodges and locals are happy to keep it that way.

See the map on p218 for details of facilities on Likoma Island.

NORTHERN MALAWI

WORTH THE TRIP: NKWICHI LODGE

OK, so this place on the shores of Lake Malawi may officially be in Mozambique, but most people arrive via Lilongwe and it's a reachable hop over the lake from Likoma Island.

our pick **Nkwichi Lodge** (www.mandawilderness.org; full-board per person from US$290) is barely visible from the shoreline. Seven chalets are tucked deep beneath the trees, so well spaced out from each other that you feel as if you're in your own private wilderness. Each one is special and incorporates the environment around it in innovative ways. There are crooked terraces, huge beds made from old tree trunks, great hulks of rock forming the sides of a room, outdoor baths carved into stone, showerheads emerging from branches and dugout canoes used as tables. It's like honeymooning, Flintstones style. And let's not forget the blinding white coves and brilliant waters, lunches taken under the shade of a 2000-year-old baobab tree and romantic dinners under the stars.

The lodge is totally off grid, using solar power for hot water and sun stoves for cooking. Local farmers provide the fruit and vegetables for the lodge, and it invests heavily in the local community (in fact, it won the award for Africa's Leading Responsible Tourism Company at the World Travel Awards in 2009). Funding from the lodge has contributed to the neighbouring Manda Wilderness project, which is turning 100,000 hectares of Mozambique bush into a community-owned conservation area, and hopefully a future wildlife reserve.

The easiest way to get here is via Likoma Island (above). The folks from Nkwichi will pick you up (by speedboat 40 minutes, dhow 90 minutes, per person one way US$60) from Likoma airport.

Sights

In Chipyela, the huge Anglican **Cathedral of St Peter**, which is said to be the same size as Winchester Cathedral, should not be missed (see boxed text below). You can climb the tower for spectacular views. If you're lucky you might meet the verger who'll happily give you a tour, and you're welcome to join in the service on Sunday morning. Nearby, the neat **market place** contains a few shops and stalls. Down on the lakeshore is a beach where local boats come and go, and the people wash and sell fish. Don't be surprised if some people greet you in Portuguese; traders come here from nearby Mozambique. The *Ilala* ferry stops at another beach about 1km to the south.

Activities

Swimming is a must on Likoma and best on the long stretches of beach in the south, although Yofu Bay in the north is also good. The tropical fish population has been unaffected by the mainland's overfishing, and the **snorkelling** is excellent. For a closer look, Kaya Mawa (right) arranges five-day open water PADI **scuba-diving** courses. The island's compact but diverse area is perfect for **walking** or **mountain biking** – you can bring bikes across on the ferry or hire them from Mango Drift for US$10 per day.

A greater understanding of Chewa culture can be gained by a consultation with Likoma's witch doctor. His clinic is near Khuyu village and you will need to make an appointment. Ask at Kaya Mawa or Mango Drift for further information.

Sleeping & Eating

Mango Drift (☎ 0999-746122; mailmangodrift@gmail .com; campsite per person US$3; dm US$5; s/d chalets with shared bathroom US$10/15) Stone, reed and thatched chalets are basic but have mosquito nets, power points and safes to stash your valuables and staggering views of the lake, spread across a beautiful beach on the western side of the island. There's a bar under a mango tree, and clean, hot showers. Scuba-diving courses can be arranged.

Kaya Mawa (☎ 0999-318359, 0999-318360; www .kayamawa.com; full-board chalets per person US$350) One of Southern Africa's most beautiful luxury lodges, what makes Kaya Mawa special is its design. Chalets are carefully constructed around the rocky bay in which the resort makes its home – there are stone baths, walls made from slabs of existing granite and rock faces used as shower screens. The owners have gone to painstaking lengths to be unobtrusive on both the landscape and local population, and this aim is fully realised. The lodge was

---

LIKOMA MISSIONARIES & THE CATHEDRAL OF ST PETER

European involvement on Likoma Island began in 1882 when members of Universities Mission to Central Africa (UMCA) established a base here. The leaders of the party, Will Johnson and Chauncey Maples, chose the island as protection from attacks from the warlike Ngoni and Yao peoples.

Maples became the first bishop of Likoma, but he died only a few months after being appointed, drowning in the lake off Monkey Bay. Despite the setback, missionary work on the island continued. Between 1903 and 1905 the huge cathedral was built and dedicated to St Peter – appropriately a fisherman. Today it remains one of Malawi's most remarkable buildings.

The cathedral measures over 100m long by 25m wide and has stained-glass windows and elaborate choir stalls carved from soapstone. The crucifix above the altar was carved from wood from the tree where Livingstone's heart was buried in Zambia, and the altar itself sits on what used to be the old slave market back when Likoma was a stopping-off point on the slave route from the interior to the coast.

The cathedral was built at a part of the island called Chipyela, meaning 'Place of Burning', because the early UMCA arrivals had witnessed suspected witches being burnt alive here. The island's main settlement grew up around the cathedral and is still called Chipyela today.

The UMCA missionaries remained on Likoma until the 1940s. During that time they were hard at work – they claimed 100% literacy among the local population at one point. The cathedral fell into disrepair but was restored in the 1970s and 1980s, and local people are understandably very proud of it.

due to close for remodelling at the time of research, to reopen in spring 2010, with refurbished rooms and bathrooms, a suite with its own infinity pool, a four-bed villa and a watersports centre.

Hot Coconut Bar (mains MK200) A popular spot with locals, who are always happy to chat with tourists when they pop in for a drink.

Getting There & Away

Nyassa Air Taxi (☎ 01-761443; www.nyassa.mw) provides charter flights to Likoma. The more of you there are, the cheaper it is per person. For example, a one-way flight from Lilongwe to Likoma Island ranges from US$210 to US$320 per person depending on how many of you there are.

The *Ilala* ferry (p304) stops at Likoma Island twice a week, usually for three to four hours, so even if you're heading elsewhere you might be able to nip ashore to have a quick look at the cathedral (see boxed text, opposite). Check with the captain before you leave the boat. Heading south, the ferry then sails to Metangula on the Mozambican mainland. Local dhows also sail to Cóbuè for MK250.

CHIZUMULU ISLAND

'Chizzie' is smaller than Likoma (and just a few kilometres away) and even more detached from the mainland. Stretches of lucid azure water and white rocky outcrops give this island a Mediterranean flavour, while the backdrop of dry scrub is positively antipodean. The slow and friendly village activity on the perimeter of idyllic beaches, however, is unmistakably Malawian. If you want to visit both islands, transport links make it best to go to Chizumulu first.

Wakwenda Retreat (☎ 0999-348415; campsite US$3.50, dm US$6, r from US$14), smack bang on a postcard-perfect beach, is utter chill-out material. The sizeable bar is constructed around a massive, hollow baobab tree, and there are small wooden chill-out platforms constructed on and around a cluster of boulders in the sand – perfect for sundowners. The shaded lounge area is often the focus of lazy activity such as snorkelling (free gear), card games and goat barbecues. The restaurant (meals from MK500) serves food communal style, so it's easy to get to know the other guests.

The *Ilala* ferry (p304) stops right outside Wakwenda Retreat, so even if you're not staying on the island you can pop over for a drink. There are daily dhow ferries between Likoma and Chizumulu costing around MK200 per person. The trip can take anything from one to three hours depending on the weather; it's an extremely choppy ride when the wind is blowing, and potentially dangerous if a storm comes up. If you're unsure ask at Wakwenda Retreat for advice.

Central Malawi

This small corner of Malawi packs a lot into a small space. First off there are the beaches. Backpackers' Mecca, Cape Maclear, is the first to spring to mind – a sunny peninsula where travellers slip into a daze of snorkelling, sunbathing and laid-back village life. But it's not just backpackers who are seduced by the lake's warm waters – family-friendly resorts dot the coastline and luxury seekers will be rewarded by gorgeous resorts straight out of the pages of a magazine.

A world away in feel, but just a short drive up from the lake, is the Viphya Plateau, a haunting wilderness of mountains, grasslands and mist-shrouded pines that's so beautiful it'll make you forget all about the beach. That not enough for you? Then check out the parks. Nkhotakota Wildlife Reserve and Kasungu National Park had been neglected for many years but now have fine lodges and improved access, and are making strides to increase wildlife stocks and decrease poaching.

To discover more about Malawian culture and history, head for the excellent museum, workshop and gallery at Mua, or visit Nkhotakota and feel a shiver down your spine as you hear tales of the town's involvement in the slave trade.

HIGHLIGHTS

- Make like a beach bum in the country's most laid-back lakeside resort: **Cape Maclear** (p253)
- Hike through cool pine forests and past whaleback boulders on the stunning **Viphya Plateau** (opposite)
- Go hippo-spotting without the crowds at **Kasungu National Park** (p243)
- Throw a pot or two by a beautiful beach at **Nkhotakota Pottery** (p246)
- Delve into Malawi's cultural history at the fascinating **Chamare Museum, Mua** (p252)
- Explore untouched wilderness on foot at the **Nkhotakota Wildlife Reserve** (p247)

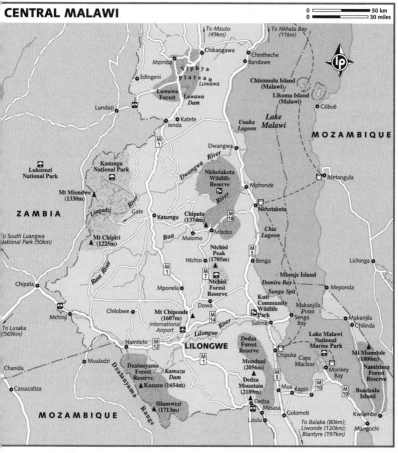

CENTRAL MALAWI

0 — 50 km
0 — 30 miles

IPHYA PLATEAU

he Viphya Plateau forms the spine of
ɛntral and northern Malawi, snaking a
ɔol path through the flat scrubland, dusty
ɔwns and sunny beaches that reign on
ther side. It may be called a plateau, but
ɛere's nothing flat about this part of the
ɔuntry in looks or in atmosphere. Tightly
nit forests give way to gentle valleys
nd rivers, and huge granite domes rise
ɔftly from the earth like sleeping beasts.
idigenous woodland bristles with birds
nd wildflowers, antelope can often be seen,
nd monkeys are regularly spotted darting
ɹrough the trees.

The main route to Mzuzu from Lilongwe
asses through the plateau and much of it

is lined by pine trees, encasing the road in
an eerie silence on misty days (and there
are plenty). When the mist lifts you'll be
rewarded with a line of sweeping grey- and
purple-tinged mountains lining the western
horizon in the distance. If you want to stay
for a few days, there are a few peaceful forest lodges and plenty of hiking, cycling and
rock climbing to be done.

Sights & Activities

Hiking is the main activity here and all of
the accommodations will be able to give
you advice on where the best places are to
roam, though there's a lot to be said for
simply sitting back and taking in the views.
Otherwise, for activity junkies the best

place to head is to Luwawa Forest Lodge (right) where activities organised on the plateau include **rock climbing** (half day per person US$40), **mountain biking** (half day per person US$18), **fishing** (rod hire US$4) and **walking** (guides from US$10). Walking trails include the Luwawa to Chintheche Trail, a two-day hike down to the lakeshore.

Sleeping

Kasito Resthouse (☎ 0888 757342; s/d MK700/1400, whole houses MK4200) There are two charming bungalows here, 50m off the main road. The largest has very clean, well-kept rooms with a bathroom (one of them is self-contained), a kitchen with a wood-burning stove and a fireplace for chilly nights. There is also a smaller annex with two snug rooms with bathrooms. You can choose to self-cater or the friendly caretaker will cook for you. Though the resthouse lacks the views of the lodge, the accommodation itself is in much better condition, and the buildings sit in a fairytale clearing which has picnic tables, piles of logs for cooking and plenty of jumping-off points for long walks. The turn-off to Kasito Resthouse is 200m south of Kasito Lodge on the opposite side of the road.

Kasito Lodge (☎ 0888 757342; per bed MK800) Less than 1km west of the main road between Kasungu and Mzuzu, this is a relaxing place from which to explore the local countryside. There's a good communal lounge with a welcoming fireplace and rocking chairs and a number of sleeping options – you can hire a bed in a room, dormitory style, rent a room in its entirety, or even rent the whole lodge. You'll have to bring all your provisions as there's no food available, but there's a resident housekeeper who can cook for you if you choose. The place has definitely seen better days, but if you don't mind tatty furniture and erratic bathrooms then you'll be fine. The main asset here is the terraced garden where you can picnic or barbecue while taking in stunning views over heather-tinged grasses to the valleys and mountains beyond.

To reach Kasito by car from the south, you continue 27km beyond the Mzimba junction on the main sealed road towards Mzuzu; the lodge is signposted on your left. Coming from the north, you pass a large wood factory at Chikangawa village, and the turn-off to the lodge is a few kilometres beyond here on the right. If you're travelling by bus,

ask the driver to drop you at the junction Kasito Lodge is less than 1km from here.

Luwawa Forest Lodge (☎ 01-991106, 01-34233 www.luwawaforestlodge.com; campsite per person US$ tw/tr with shared bathroom per person US$35, chalets wi breakfast/half board/full board per person US$60/80/8. Set high in the hills, this lodge used t belong to the forestry department but is now privately managed. Comfortable chalet are set in flourishing gardens that includ a sauna, picnic tables and fire pit for sittin around on chilly nights. Guests can self cater but there's also excellent organic foo onsite made with fresh veg from the garde (continental breakfast and packed lunche cost US$6, a hearty three-course lunch US$18 and a three-course dinner US$20 Portions are on the good side of generou but there are plenty of lard-busting activi ties on offer to work it off, including walk ing trails, biking and boating.

There's no public transport to Luwawa, s if you haven't got wheels you'll have to ask th bus driver to drop you at the Luwaw turn-off and then either walk from the mai road or call the lodge for a pick-up. If yo do have a vehicle, the lodge lies 10km east o the main M1 road between Kasungu an Mzuzu and is well signposted. Though th road is rough, you should get by with a high clearance 2WD in the dry season, but in th wet season you'll definitely need a 4WD.

KASUNGU

A fairly large town just off the country main north–south road and about 130k northwest of Lilongwe, Kasungu has nothir much to recommend it, though it's pleasar enough, having a large market and lively at mosphere. The only reason to pass throug is if you're changing transport or stocking u for a visit to Kasungu National Park.

Information

There's a PTC Supermarket, a market an National and Standard Banks with ATM Next to the bus station, you can get reasonab fast internet access at **Internet Sof-Tech Solution** (per min MK10; ☼ 8am-5.30pm Mon-Sat).

Sleeping & Eating

There are a number of bargain-baseme options around the station.

Kasungu Lodge (☎ 0999 646237; s/d MK1000/20C This isn't a bad option if you're stuck

Kasungu for the night. The reasonably large, clean rooms have fans and TVs and are much quieter than many places closer to the town centre. It's on the main road at the southern nd of town just before the BP station and he turning to Lilongwe and Kasungu Naional Park.

Dumisani Motel (☎ 01-253585; s/d/executive MK3500/4500/5900) Despite its unassuming locaion behind the bus station, this is the bestalue joint in town. The rooms are spotless vith cool tiled floors and a nice line in elour throws and satin bedspreads. Execuive rooms are huge and come with the dditional bonus of fridges, sofas and coffee ables. There is a restaurant and bar area ut it's alcohol free, which can be a blessing ome Friday night.

Kasungu Inn (☎ 01-253306; s/d with bath MK5800/200; ❄) Positioned at the northwestern end f town on the road to Mzuzu, this place is t the top end of the price range. Rooms nd bathrooms are large, with the addiional bonus of DSTV and air-conditioning, ut they are poorly lit and thin walls mean hat loud neighbours can be a nuisance. If ou stay at the weekend, make sure you get room on the other side of the quad from he bar, which blares out unnecessarily loud nusic until the small hours.

There are several cheap local restauants on the main street and around the narket, serving meat, beans and *nsima* or hicken and chips. For better quality and more varied menu try the restaurant at he Kasungu Inn. The bar isn't bad for a lrink either, especially if you like cheesy 90s pop music.

ietting There & Away
All buses and minibuses between Mzuzu MK550, three hours) and Lilongwe (MK480, wo hours) come through the town, and here are infrequent *matolas* along the road hrough Nkhotakota Wildlife Reserve to the akeshore (MK500, two to three hours).

KASUNGU NATIONAL PARK
Along the border with Zambia and west of Kasungu town, **Kasungu National Park** (admission er person US$5, per car US$2; ❤ 6am-6pm) sprawls ver 2100 sq km, making it the secondargest park in the country after Nyika. The andscape is formed of gentle hills, miombo voodland, bush and the odd open plain,

interspersed by wide, marshy river courses, called *dambos*, where reeds and grasses grow. A small manmade lake, called the Lifupa Dam, sits at the park's centre.

Poachers have hit the park severely over the past few decades, particularly during the 1980s and 1990s, reducing the once prolific wildlife to a trickle. The park was at one time famous for its elephants, but today it's estimated that only 150 or so remain in the park. If you take a guided drive your chances of spotting them are fairly high, though, especially in the dry season of May to October. You might also see several species of antelope and sometimes buffaloes and zebras. Predators are present in the park but you've a better chance of seeing hyenas, leopards or servals than lions, which are hardly ever seen. If you're staying overnight at the lodge or camp you may well see hippos in the lake and you'll certainly hear them at night. Birdwatchers will be well rewarded here. There are over 300 species, including water, woodland and grassland species.

The park also contains a number of historical sites. These include old iron kilns used by local people in this area before it was made a national park, and some very faint rock paintings that are assumed to be pre-Bantu.

Sights & Activities
All activities in the park revolve around Lifupa Lodge and Camp. You can arrange for a guide to accompany you in your car, rent a safari vehicle and guide, take a walking tour in the early morning, or go fishing in the Lifupa Dam. The dam is also a great spot for birdwatching and if you're feeling lazy you can even indulge from the 1st-floor deck of the main lodge.

By foot or by car, a good place to aim for is Black Rock, about 4km northwest of the lodge, where you can scramble up high and look out over the entire park. The park's other hills include Miondwe, straddling the park boundary and the border with Zambia, and Wangombe (Hill of the Cow), about 23km north of Lifupa Dam.

Sleeping
Lifupa Camp (☎ 0999 768658, 0999 925512; campsite per person US$8, dm US$15, safari tent or bush hut US$25) A 500m walk from the lodge, this is a wonderful spot looking out over swaying

reeds towards the dam, where hippos and elephants are frequent visitors. You can put up your own tent or indulge in the romance of the beautiful but rustic stand-up safari tents and reed huts that are available. There is a large dining area and lounge, a self-catering kitchen, barbecue facilities and clean, shared ablutions.

Lifupa Lodge (☎ 0999 768658, 0999 925512; p person incl breakfast US$80, full board US$110) Dotte throughout the grasses overlooking th Lifupa Dam are a handful of thatched rondavels with sturdy double or twin bed private verandas, hot showers and elec tricity in the evenings. The main lodg is striking, especially the gorgeous uppe

---

MINI-ITINERARIES: CENTRAL MALAWI

Sublime beaches skirt the lakeshore, national parks offer an uncrowded wildlife-watching experience, and in the interior are cool mountains worthy of the Highland fling.

How Long and How to Get There

If you've got your own wheels, head to **Mangochi** (p259) from Lilongwe and spend a few days making your way up the coast, through **Cape Maclear** (p253), **Senga Bay** (p248), and on to **Nkhotakota** (p245). You'll have to limit yourself on public transport – perhaps head straight for Cape Maclear for a couple of days and then bus it up to Nkhotakota via **Monkey Bay** (p253). Then either drive yourself around **Nkhotakota Wildlife Reserve** (p247) for a day (you'll need a 4WD) or arrange a day trip through one of the lakeshore lodges. From here take the road that heads through the reserve and on to **Kasungu** (p242), the jumping-off point for **Kasungu National Park** (p243); a day here is enough to give you a taste. Without wheels you might have to skip this part, as there's no public transport into the park. After you've had your fill of wildlife, head north from Kasungu – the road passes through the **Viphya Plateau** (p241), where you can stop off for a day or two's hiking through the hills. Minibus and bus drivers will drop you off at the turn-off to one for the lodges if you don't have transport.

How Much?

In this part of the country there's something to suit every style and budget, from dirt-cheap campsites to five-star lodges.

Budget

If you're looking for beach frolics on a budget, head for backpackers' favourite, Cape Maclear, where you can camp for around US$4 or bed down in a dorm for around US$10. Both Kasungu National Park and Nkhotakota Wildlife Reserve have camping and budget accommodation from around US$10 per head, and in the Viphya Plateau are a couple of government-run guesthouses where you'll get cheap accommodation (MK700 to MK800) and sublime views.

Midrange

Both Senga Bay and Cape Maclear have some good options for midrange travellers and you can pick up a room for US$50 to US$60. All midrange lodges have restaurants serving a mixture of Malawian and European food.

Top End

The strip of beach between Mangochi and Monkey Bay has a couple of large resort hotels where you'll find a double room from around US$100 and up. Pumulani, a super luxury lodge in Lake Malawi National Park, costs US$450 per person all-inclusive and there's also a top-end lodge in Kasungu National Park (per person US$110 all-inclusive).

Tip

Don't miss a walking safari in Nkhotakota Wildlife Reserve. It's the best way to see the animals.

deck above the main restaurant area, where you can relax in a comfortable chair with a Malawian gin and tonic and watch the sunset, as well as the plentiful elephants, hippos and antelope that visit the dam during the dry season.

Getting There & Away

The park entrance is 40km west of Kasungu town and is signposted off the main Lilongwe to Mzuzu road. The road to the entrance is mostly good quality dirt road – look out for former president Dr Hastings Kamuzu Banda's grandiose palace to the right as you approach the park). From the entrance, it's 21km by the shortest route to Lifupa Lodge for which you'll need a high-clearance car. There's no public transport to the park, so without a car you'd have to hitch from Kasungu – the best place to wait is the turn-off to the park (signposted) near the petrol station on the main road.

NKHOTAKOTA

Though it may seem dull and unassuming, Nkhotakota had a significant and sinister part to play in Malawi's history. In the 1800s the town was home to a huge slave market, set up by Arabic trader Jumbe Salim Bin Abdalla. From here thousands of unfortunate captives were shipped annually across the lake to Tanzania, before being forced to march to the coast. The town still retains a Muslim influence today and you'll see a few Arab relics from slaving times dotted around the town. Nkhotakota is also often described as one of the oldest market towns in Africa.

Today it's strung out over 4km between the busy highway and the lake. Nkhotakota makes a good break in any journey along the lakeshore, but don't expect much action. Nevertheless, the sleepy and quiet pace in the village-like outskirts may be just what's needed after buses and tourist mayhem.

Information

There's a branch of the Commercial Bank of Malawi on the main north–south road, which offers foreign exchange facilities but no credit-card withdrawals. A petrol station and a PTC Supermarket are also on the main road. Buses and minibuses stop at the petrol station. You can get online at the

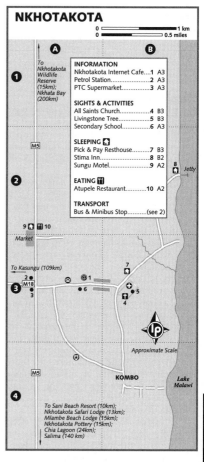

NKHOTAKOTA

0 _____ 1 km
0 _____ 0.5 miles

To Nkhotakota Wildlife Reserve (15km); Nkhata Bay (200km)

INFORMATION
Nkhotakota Internet Cafe....1 A3
Petrol Station......................2 A3
PTC Supermarket................3 A3

SIGHTS & ACTIVITIES
All Saints Church.................4 B3
Livingstone Tree.................5 B3
Secondary School...............6 A3

SLEEPING
Pick & Pay Resthouse..........7 B3
Stima Inn..............................8 B2
Sungu Motel.........................9 A2

EATING
Atupele Restaurant...........10 A2

TRANSPORT
Bus & Minibus Stop..........(see 2)

Market
To Kasungu (109km)
Jetty
Approximate Scale
KOMBO
Lake Malawi

To Sani Beach Resort (10km); Nkhotakota Safari Lodge (13km); Mlambe Beach Lodge (15km); Nkhotakota Pottery (15km); Chia Lagoon (24km); Salima (140 km)

Nkhotakota Internet Cafe (☎ 01-292284; per min MK8; ⏱ 7.30am-4.30pm Mon-Fri, 8am-6pm Sat, 2-6pm Sun), but it's quite small and there's usually a queue. You can hook up your laptop if you have one and it will save you the wait.

Sights & Activities

Things to see include the stone **All Saints Church**, built by missionaries in 1894 – Chauncy Maples, the first bishop of Likoma, is buried here. Church services are still held here and you are welcome to attend if you're in town on a Sunday. The service will be in Chichewa but you can still enjoy the uplifting singing.

In the grounds of the St Anne's Mission Hospital is a large tree called the **Livingstone**

Tree where the explorer David Livingstone camped while leading an expedition to Malawi in the 1860s. When he returned a few years later, he met a local chief called Jumbe, and tried (unsuccessfully) to persuade him to abandon the slave trade.

Sleeping & Eating

Pick & Pay Resthouse (☎ 01-292359; s/d with shared bathroom MK1000/1400) A clean and basic option off the highway. Functional rooms open out onto a mosquito-screened veranda and there's a cafe serving cheap meals for MK200 to MK500.

our pick Sitima Inn (☎ 0999 260005; www.siti mainn.comresort.com; dm per person MK1000, s MK1000-4200, d MK3500-8400) This is easily the best place in town and within convenient staggering distance of the *Ilala* ferry. From the outside, the building looks like part of an old ocean liner, with a couple of old car parts thrown in for good measure. The beautiful interior – with its quirky nautical touches and central courtyard lounge open to the lake breezes – is like a cross between a Moroccan *riad* and an old tugboat. The glimmer of North African promise continues in the gorgeous yet simple rooms, with their warm patterned rugs, sequinned cushions, shimmery gauze shower curtains and gas lanterns for those electricity black-outs. A broad 1st-floor terrace has dreamy views past the swamps to the lake and there's a funky bar decorated with sea dog paraphernalia.

The owners have also made a real effort with the food. Top-notch burgers and steaks are on the menu with more adventurous mains such as crocodile tail in honey balsamic vinegar and chicken breasts in red wine and chocolate (snacks from MK300, mains from MK850).

Sungu Motel (r with breakfast MK2900) Clean spacious rooms are grouped around a courtyard and have fans and good quality bathrooms. There's also a bar and a restaurant that are popular in the evenings.

Atupele Restaurant (mains MK200-500; ☉ 6am-9pm) One of many spots in town for dirt-cheap meals of beans, meat and *nsima* or rice. Conveniently located on the main road.

Getting There & Away

You can get to Nkhotakota by the *Ilala* ferry (p304). AXA buses go to and from Lilongwe (MK610, three hours). The bus will drop you off roughly outside Nkhotakota's Shell petrol station, which is on the highway. Minibuses also leave from here and go to Salima (MK350, two hours) and Nkhata Bay (MK700, four to five hours).

SOUTH OF NKHOTAKOTA

You may like to visit the **Nkhotakota Pottery** (☎ 01-292444), the turn-off for which is signposted 15km south of Nkhotakota town, on the main road. It offers a range of workshops on the fine art of pottery including visits to local potters to see traditional methods. Courses last anything up to two or three weeks (a standard two-week course is priced at US$1300) and include accommodation, food, tuition and excursions to local attractions. Participants are housed in lovely chalets on the beach. If you don't have time for a long course, there is also a workshop where you can make your own pots or decorate some that are already made, and a boutique where you can purchase all manner of colourful hand-painted crockery.

About 24km south of Nkhotakota is the entrance to **Chia Lagoon**, a large bay linked to the main lake by a narrow channel, which is crossed by a bridge near the main road. Local people fish here using large triangular nets on poles.

Sleeping

Nkhotakota Pottery Lodge (☎ 01-751743; www .nyasalodges.com; campsite per person MK1000, dm MK2000, s/d chalets MK6900/8400) Attached to the headquarters of Nkhotakota Pottery, this is the perfect place to indulge your creative side while staying a skip away from a wild, sandy cove. You don't have to be taking a course to stay here but the chalets are often full of potters (and named after them too – rooms don't have numbers, but instead take their names from tales of a certain schoolboy wizard). You also have the option of dorm rooms and camping, and there's an excellent restaurant that provides welcome respite from meat, *nsima* and chips. Both the Pottery Lodge and nearby Safari Lodge (opposite) take credit cards. The lodge is 15km south of town.

Mlambe Beach Lodge (☎ 01-292622, 0999-468458; mlambebeach@yahoo.com; campsite per person MK1365, s/d MK3415/4875, chalets MK9750, house MK19,500) Single and double rooms are fresh and compact with small verandas, mosquito nets, colourful wall murals and views down to the lake. There's also a lovely, large campsite right next to the beach. The airy restaurant (mains around MK1400) is pretty cool too. It's so close to the lake that looking out from your table at high tide it seems as if the water is about to flood in through the dining room's curved arches. Activities on offer include horse riding (per person per hour MK9750). At the time of writing the owners were building chalets and a family house. It's about 100m south of Nkhotakota Pottery.

Sani Beach Resort (☎ 01-292511; www.sanibeach esort.com; s/d from US$25/50) A few kilometres off the main north–south road, 10km south of Nkhotakota town. Simple huts and larger brick-and-thatch chalets sit on a sandy, boulder-strewn beach. There's a great bar with almost 360-degree views, a good restaurant and a relaxed vibe.

Nkhotakota Safari Lodge (☎ 01-751743; www nyasalodges.com; s/d rondavels MK4350/5700, chalets MK6900/8400) A five-minute stroll along the beach from Nkhotakota Pottery (though it also has its own access road, signposted some 2km north of the pottery and 13km south of Nkhotakota), this place makes a wonderfully relaxing getaway. Stay right on the beach either in simple thatched rondavels or in brick chalets decorated with colourful tiles and sinks from the nearby Pottery Lodge, and with private terraces overlooking the sea. The food here is excellent – you specify a time for dinner and it will be all set up and waiting when you arrive. There is a range of tours available here including full-day walking safaris into the park (MK7500 per person), slavery tours of the town (MK5600 per person) and sunset cruises (MK990 per person).

NKHOTAKOTA WILDLIFE RESERVE

West of the main lakeshore road lies the **Nkhotakota Wildlife Reserve** (per person/car US$5/2; 6am-6pm). It consists of 1800 sq km of rough, somewhat inhospitable terrain – dense miombo forests, bush and evergreens – and very few navigable roads. The park has been through hard times. In the 1980s and 1990s it was abandoned to the wiles of poachers because of a lack of funding and plentiful human settlements along its borders. This decline left it difficult to negotiate, with hardly any facilities for visitors, who rarely came to visit anyway.

That's not to say that there isn't any wildlife here that's worth seeing these days. There's a healthy elephant population here, as well as roan and sable antelope, buffaloes, baboons, waterbucks, and even lions and leopards – it's just that wildlife can be difficult to spot because of the dense vegetation and rough terrain. Several large rivers cross the reserve, so the birdlife is also varied and rewarding. There are more than 200 species here including the palm-nut vulture, kingfishers and ground hornbills. The Bua River is excellent for salmon fishing.

Luckily the Department of National Parks and Wildlife is now taking much more of an interest in Nkhotakota. It has recently acquired new vehicles for its anti-poaching scouts and plans to increase this number further. Scout accommodation is being upgraded and in 2009 the government put forward four concessions for ecotourism development, the first of which has been awarded. There are also long-term plans to reintroduce wildlife species that have disappeared over the years, such as the black rhino, and to boost existing populations of elephants, buffaloes and zebras.

Walking is the best way to experience the area, and at least a few hours are needed to spot wildlife. The new wilderness lodge and all of the tourist lodges around Nkhotakota can arrange walking safaris here – you will need to be accompanied by an armed scout.

Sleeping

At the time of research there were two basic campsites in the park, the best of which was **Bua Camp** in a clearing on the banks of the stunning, rocky Bua River, though there were only rudimentary long-drop toilets on offer. The camp is near the eastern boundary of the park and is accessed via the M5 lakeside turn-off, 10km north of Nkhotakota. All the facilities at Nkhotakota Wildlife Reserve are being upgraded, however. The first of the park's eco-concessions was awarded in an area known as Tongole in early 2009, and an upmarket eco-lodge – to be called the **Tongole Wilderness Lodge** (www.tongole.com) – was set to open in 2010. It will sit alongside the Bua River and plans to invest heavily in the local community. A second concession has also recently been awarded and there

---

KUTI COMMUNITY WILDLIFE PARK

Formed from a former government cattle ranch, Kuti Community Wildlife Park consists of 3000 hectares of grasses, woodland and wetland. The park is home to kudu, duiker, bushbuck, genet and civet cats, and bush pig, and the Wildlife Action Group of Malawi, who run the place, have also introduced the giraffe, zebra, nyala, sable, impala, warthog, ostrich…and even three camels (by the time this book is published their mini camel safaris should be up and running!).

The 11 villages around Kuti Ranch are all stakeholders in its development and 50% of the park's revenue is invested in the local community. What's more, they have an environmental education centre that local schoolchildren can visit to learn about the importance of conservation.

You can visit the **wildlife park** (admission per person MK500, per vehicle MK500) for the day or stay the night in their **accommodation** (campsite per person US$3, A-frame chalets US$25). Game walks and game drives cost US$10 per person. Volunteers are welcome with a minimum stay of two weeks – if you're interested, check out www.kuti-malawi.org.

Kuti is located about 1km from the Nkhotakota turn-off, when coming from Lilongwe. The park is signposted and about 5km down the dirt road.

---

are plans to upgrade the park's campsites as well, so watch this space.

Getting There & Away

The turn-off to Bua is 10km north of Nkhotakota town, followed by a rough dirt track. You will need your own wheels to get here. You could also enter the park from the south via the very potholed Nkhotakota–Kasungu road. If you do come this way, look out for the orange sign marking the spot where Patricia Nkhoma, a local woman, was killed by lions in 2002.

SALIMA

The small town of Salima is spread out about 20km from the lake, where the road from Lilongwe meets the main lakeshore road, and is a friendly and low-key place. Traffic is mostly of the two-wheeled variety and centres along a sweeping central boulevard. It's not worth a special visit, however, and is only useful as a place to change transport, stock up on provisions and go to the bank before hitting the lakeshore lodges at Senga Bay.

Chiumbe Executive Lodge (☎ 01-262405; s/d with shared bathroom MK750/1000) Exit the station and this convenient option is signposted directly opposite, up a dirt road. It is pretty basic, with acceptable shared facilities.

Mwambiya Lodge (☎ 01-262314; s/d incl breakfast MK2900/3400) Across the railway line from the bus station, this is probably the best option in Salima. Rooms are large, light and clean, if a little nondescript, and there's a restaurant (meals around MK700) and bar, which plays host to an in-house DJ at the

weekend. At the front of the lodge is a large garden with a pool table and a couple of thatched seating areas.

Half London Lodge (☎ 01-262855; r MK3000) On the way into town opposite the BP station you'll find a warm welcome here, and a handful of sunny rooms opening out onto a small courtyard. The in-house restaurant serves hefty plates of chambo and chips for MK500.

Ubale Forward Restaurant (meals from MK250; ☒ 6am-10pm) Just over the road from the Half London is this charming cafe, plastered with colourful murals of elephants, chickens, crocodiles and even the *Ilala* ferry. Meals include stew and rice, and chambo and chips.

To reach Salima from Lilongwe, it's easiest to take a minibus (MK450, one hour). Minibuses and *matolas* also run frequently between Salima and Senga Bay (MK200, 30 minutes) and less frequently to Nkhata Bay (MK900, six to seven hours) and Mzuzu (MK1000, seven to eight hours). There are also ordinary buses to Mzuzu (MK800, nine hours) via Nkhata Bay (MK700, eight hours).

SENGA BAY

Sitting at the eastern end of a broad peninsula that juts into the lake from Salima, Senga Bay is the closest beach resort to the capital, filling up with city types on balmy weekends. The good points are that it has pretty beaches (though they can get a bit dirty in parts) and a range of accommodation to suit all budgets, from cheap campsites to one of the classiest

SENGA BAY AREA

0 — 3 km
0 — 1.5 miles

...otels in all Malawi. However, the town is very spread out, without a real heart, and it lacks the laid-back village vibe of Cape Maclear or the dramatic indented bays of Nkhata Bay – its two beachside rivals. It can also be difficult to get around – the town's various resorts are spread over a distance of about 10km so without wheels you'll need to make use of local bicycle taxis.

Dangers & Annoyances

Take great care when swimming near the large rocks at the end of the beach at Steps Campsite; you'll find there's a surprisingly strong undertow. Some of the beaches here are flat and reedy – perfect conditions for bilharzia, so get advice from your hotel or lodge to see if it's safe.

Many travellers have complained about persistent hassling from local youths, all wanting to sell souvenirs or arrange boat rides. Be polite and firm in your dealings, and you should be OK.

Sights & Activities

As a break from lazing on the beach, you can go windsurfing or snorkelling, take a boat ride or learn to dive. You could also take a trip out to nearby **Lizard Island** to see its population of giant monitor lizards and its cormorant colony. Many lodges and local guides can arrange this and it should cost about US$30. Alternatively, from Senga Bay town, you can go hiking in the nearby **Senga Hills**. There are a few trails but nothing well established, so they can be hard to follow if the grass is long. But the woodland is beautiful, and the viewpoints overlooking the lake are well worth the effort. It's best to hire a local guide from your hotel to show you the way (and also because there have been isolated incidents of robbery and harassment here). Go early morning or late afternoon: it's cooler, and the light is better for photographs. You might also aim for the **hippo pools** about half an hour's walk up the lakeshore beyond Steps Campsite, or reached by descending the north side of the Senga Hills. Again, a local guide is recommended. The hippos have a reputation for being timid, but aggressive when worried, so take care here.

Birdwatching in the area is excellent, with a good range of habitats in close proximity. You can go into the hills mentioned above, or to the river (where the hippo pools are), which flows to the north of the hills and into the lake through a small marshy area.

If you're looking for souvenirs, there's a strip of **craft stalls** a few kilometres out of Senga Bay, on the Salima road.

About 10km south of Senga Bay is **Stewart Grant's Tropical Fish Farm** (☎ fax 01-263165), which breeds and exports cichlids. If you're genuinely interested you can do a half-hour tour of the farm.

Sleeping

There's a good choice of places to stay in Senga Bay.

Wamwai Beach Lodge (☎ 0888 709999; campsites/dm per person MK300/1500, d or tw MK4500) The wide veranda that wraps around this charming bungalow is a fantastic spot at which to chill and look out at the fishing boats from the local village. Inside are several homely rooms, a fantastic, airy dorm and a dining room – all decked out in plenty of wood and bright local fabrics. Food here is a treat. As well as substantial mains such as chicken curry (MK1300), the baking enthusiast owner whips up fresh goodies daily – if you're hankering after afternoon tea then scones and jam are MK150. Activities can be arranged, including trips to Lizard Island, and they were setting up a PADI dive school at the time of research. They have special rates for backpackers, which include a big breakfast of scones and flapjacks.

Tom's (☎ 01-263017; campsite per person MK500, r MK2000) A vast, shady campsite with spotless showers and toilets, hot water and a barbecue pit. For those who don't fancy being under canvas, they also have a few cheap backpackers rooms. Onsite is Tom's Bar and a small boutique/workshop where you can get your hands on clothes made from traditional Malawian fabric.

Nyama Choma Lodge & Camping (☎ 01-263105; campsite per person MK500, s/d from MK2500/3000) Though not directly on the beach (it's a five-minute walk), this isn't a bad option if you're looking for clean, simple rooms on a budget. There's a pretty thatched bar, you can order food and there's a mellow vibe and mixed clientele. Although there's a campsite here, there isn't much to shield your tent from the scorching sun.

Steps Campsite (campsite per person MK1000) Fantastic little camping spot that combines beautiful views and a clean-white sandy beach with excellent facilities – there's a volleyball pitch; very clean, hot showers; individual power points and round-the-clock security. A raised, circular bar provides the focal point of the campsite and makes a lovely spot for sundowners. Should you get hungry, you can order meals from the Livingstonia Beach Hotel next door. The camp explodes into full party mode at regular full-moon parties.

Cool Runnings (☎ 01-263398, 0999 915173; cool runnings@malawi.net; campsite per person US$4, dm US$8, caravan per person US$10, r with bathroom US$35) An extremely homely and friendly place; small enough to feel cosy and intimate but with enough space to chill out on your own if you choose. It's obvious that a lot of thought has been put into its design, and there are plenty of extra touches that make a stay here memorable – the reading material in the bathrooms, for instance. Each bedroom in the main house is named after a different African country, with corresponding maps and framed snippets of information adorning the walls. Out in the garden, there's room for camping (if you don't have your own tent you can rent one for US$6), as well as a few small, brightly coloured backpackers rooms and an old static caravan for two. The food here is fantastic. Order well in advance and a personally tailored feast will be delivered to you come dinnertime.

Carolina Lake Resort (☎ 01-263220, 0999 338983 r with shared bathroom MK4500, tr MK6000, s/d chalets MK5750/6500) Signposted 3km down a dirt track from the main road, this resort has a loyal following, helped by the charming and friendly service and attractive communal areas, including a large terrace bar by the water, a good restaurant, a sandy volleyball pitch and a lovely quiet stretch of beach. The rather rundown A-Frame chalets and unspectacular rooms let it down, though.

Lakeside Hotel (☎ 01-263400/500; standard executive/superior r MK5500/7500/10,000) On the same dirt road as Carolina Lake Resort, this place has large rooms with TV, fridge and fan and massive verandas (each with its own bench) overlooking the garden and out to the lake. There is a restaurant serving burgers, chicken and Chinese meals from MK800. It's an attractive spot but feels a little soulless.

our pick Safari Beach Lodge (☎ 01-263143, 0999 365494; www.safaribeachlodge.net; s/d MK11,900/16,100 🌐 📶) It all starts off well – there are large modern rooms with TV in the main building, as well as a great restaurant and a large veranda with comfy cane chairs – but the best is yet to come. A quick scramble up the hill reveals a row of gorgeous stone huts (and one safari tent), which perch on the side of the cliff. They all have wide balconies overlooking the lake, with outstanding views, simple interiors, and separate, open-air bamboo and rock showers (warning: keep the loo paper in your hut or the local baboons will steal it). In front of the main lodge, a grassy lawn bursts with flowers and trees, and there are plenty of chill-out spots, including a rock-shrouded perch overlooking the small swimming pool, and a table right at the cliff's edge – a perfect sundowner spot. Follow a path down to a private beach where you'll find kayaks and snorkels and a swing for two – it's a perfect spot for their regular Saturday barbecues. The lodge is 1km off the main road; turn off just before the gates to the Sunbird Livingstonia Beach Hotel.

Mpatsa Beach Lodge (mpatsalodge@mpatsa.com; s/d/tw MK13,000/16,000/18,000; ⊠) This is a new hotel next door to the Carolina Lake Resort. It's a white, two-storey building with a number of rooms opening out onto a large communal veranda, with views over a grassy lawn down to the beach. Rooms have a few quirky touches such as bathrooms hidden behind wardrobes.

Sunbird Livingstonia Beach Hotel (☎ 01-263222/444; www.sunbirdmalawi.com; s/d from US$107/129; ⊠) Originally built back in the 1920s, this was once a favourite haunt for fancy colonial balls and banquets, before falling into disrepair and disrepute. These days it's pristine and gorgeous, and once again injects a touch of glamour into Senga Bay. A vast selection of rooms and chalets sit along a perfect stretch of beach that is only broken up by the occasional, perfectly coordinated beach lounge. Superior rooms have large patios with steps down to the beach, while the deluxe chalets are huge, high-ceilinged affairs with uninterrupted lake views.

Eating & Drinking

Tom's Bar (⊠ 8am-late) Popular little spot with both locals and visitors for a cold beer. It closes when the last person leaves.

Red Zebra Cafe (waffles MK450, mains MK850-1200; ⊠ 7am-10.30pm) Black-and-white pictures of rock legends and an eclectic soundtrack of chilled summer tunes set the scene here, and if you tire of lounging on the beach, a table on the veranda of this vibey cafe is

a good alternative. Daily offerings are scribbled on the blackboard and include grills, stews, curries and waffles. Things kick off on weekend evenings and live bands occasionally put in an appearance.

Getting There & Away

First get to Salima (for details see p248). From there, local pick-ups run to Senga Bay (MK200), dropping you in the main street. If you want a lift all the way to Steps Campsite, negotiate an extra fee with the driver. If you're travelling to/from Cape Maclear, consider chartering a boat; it's not too expensive (around US$180) if you get a group together, it's good fun and it saves one hell of a trip on the bus.

MUA

Wedged between Salima and Balaka, Mua is a small town that's famous for a not-so-small mission. Built at the beginning of the 20th century by Catholic 'white fathers', Mua Mission houses a school, a hospital and the fascinating Kungoni Centre of Culture and Art. Established over thirty years ago, the centre is dedicated to breeding greater understanding of Malawi's culture and history among tourists and Malawians alike.

MALAWI'S LAKE OF STARS

Since 2004, Malawi's sandy shores have been regularly rocking to the sound of Malawi's greatest pop acts and a smattering of international DJs. Organised by a British club promoter who fell in love with Malawi while working on a gap year, the three-day Malawi Lake of Stars Festival takes place every September/October at different locations by the lake; in 2009 it took place at Sunbird Nkopola Lodge (p258). The aim is to raise funds for local charities, as well as to boost the profile of Malawian music and have loads of fun. Think miniature Glastonbury with heat and flip-flops instead of mud and wellies. All kinds of acts have taken to the stage, from Malawian reggae superstars the Black Missionaries, to up-and-coming African hip-hop stars, to British folk musicians. The event attracted over 3000 people in 2008 and it looks set to get even bigger. For further info visit www.lakeofstars.org.

Sights & Activities

The **Kungoni Centre of Culture and Art** (☎ 01-262706; www.kungoni.org; ☷ 7.30am-4pm Mon-Sat) is made up of several different workshops and exhibitions. Set up in 1976 by a Canadian, Father Claude Boucher (who still directs the centre), it has developed into an important focal point for cultural information and training.

If you only visit one thing here, make it the **Chamare Museum** (☷ 7.30am-4pm Mon-Sat). It has three exhibition rooms, beautifully decorated with vibrant murals depicting scenes from Malawian history. The three rooms concentrate on the three main cultural groups of the region (Chewa, Ngoni and Yao) and their approach to traditional beliefs, with fascinating exhibits from rituals and rites of passage, including a huge collection of Gule Wamkulu masks (below). A guide is included in the entrance fee; the tour takes at least an hour and costs MK900.

The **carving workshop** – an open-air hut near the museum – also makes an interesting visit. You can watch the talented artists go to work on blocks of wood (only obtained through environmentally sustainable means), carving them into exquisite sculptures. The workshop also operates as a training centre where the experienced carvers train new recruits. They also run sporadic courses on Malawian history and culture, and there are frequent perform-

ances of dances and songs from the Chewa, Ngoni and Yao cultures. Contact the centre for further details.

The **Kungoni Art Gallery** (admission MK300) showcases woodcarvings and other artwork, such as painting and embroidery. Proceeds from the sale of these go to help the local community.

For people with a genuine interest in learning more about Malawian history and culture there's the **Kafukufuku Research Centre** (per day MK600) where you can delve into photographs, books and research papers. The centre also runs sporadic courses on Malawian culture, history, art and language. They include a visit to the museum, group participation, videos and free access to the library. Contact them for further information (☎ 01-262706; www.kungoni.org).

Sleeping & Eating

Namalikhate Hostel (☎ 01-262706; s/d MK5000/7000) For overnight stays this is a gorgeous place, just a short walk up the hill from the mission itself. Guests are put up in chalets, each bearing a distinctive carved mask outside which denotes the theme of the decor inside. They are all nicely decked out and full of local features, such as carved mirrors and hand-dyed fabrics. Each has a small veranda. Outside, a thatched open-air lounge area along the river looks out past a mini gorge to the local village – from

---

GULE WAMKULU

Performed at funerals, major celebrations and male initiation ceremonies, Gule Wamkulu or 'Great Dance' is the most popular dance among the Chewa. It can't be performed by just anyone; only members of a secret society, sometimes called the Nyau brotherhood, are allowed to participate. Dancers perform clad in magnificent costumes and brightly painted masks made from cloth, animal skins, wood and straw. Each dancer represents a particular character (there are more than 150 Gule Wamkulu characters) – a wild animal, perhaps, or an ancestral spirit, sometimes even a modern object like a car or a plane. Each character has its own meaning – for example lions represent strength and power and often appear at the funeral of a chief.

Supported by an entourage of drummers and singers, the dancers achieve a state through which they can summon up the spirits of animals or dead relatives. As the drumbeats quicken, they perform dances and movement with incredible energy and precision. Some of this is pure entertainment, some of it is a means of passing on messages from ancestral spirits, and some of it aims to scare the audience – as a moral lesson or a warning. Through acting out mischievous deeds, the Gule Wamkulu characters are showing the audience, as representatives of the spirit world, how not to behave.

There are both individual and group performances and they take place during the day and at night – when the audience watches from afar. The dance is widespread in central and southern Malawi and is also performed in Zambia's Eastern Province and the Tete province of Mozambique.

here steps go down to a stunning open-air dining area (MK1200 for meals).

Getting There & Away

Mua is about 50km south of Salima on the road to Balaka. The Mua Mission is about 1km from the main road and is clearly signposted.

MONKEY BAY

This small town is a port and ship repair centre hidden behind the Cape Maclear headland. Monkey Bay itself isn't particularly interesting but there are a couple of good places to stay should you end up here for a night or two. And you might well do if travelling by the *Ilala* ferry – this is one of the stop-off points. Monkey Bay also has a market and a PTC Supermarket, but no ATM or money exchange.

Sleeping

Mufasa Rustic Camp (☎ 0999 258959; campsite per person MK450) At just 400m from the Harbour this beautiful beach spot is perfect for backpackers. It is basic, hence the name, but will offer hot showers, camping and rooms, though it will be electricity free. The owners will arrange pick-ups from the *Ilala* ferry by tuk-tuk, and they also plan to do boat transfers to Cape Maclear.

Zawadi Resthouse (☎ 01-587232; s/d with shared bathroom MK500/600) On the main road, Zawadi offers rooms grouped around a sandy courtyard with clean showers, toilets and fan. It is conveniently located but can be a little noisy.

Venice Beach Backpackers (campsite per person MK500, dm MK1120, s/d with shared bathroom MK2400/3200, chalets MK4000) This place is about 1.5km from the main road and it's a great alternative to the lodges at Cape Maclear. There's a very clean stretch of beach, a chilled beach bar and a two-storey thatched building housing a selection of dorms and doubles as well as a top-floor viewing deck with plenty of hammocks. There are also a couple of chalets next to the main building. You can buy good meals here (snacks MK400, dinner and lunch MK850).

Getting There & Away

From Lilongwe, AXA buses go to Monkey Bay, usually via Mua and the southern lakeshore (MK1000, four hours). From Lilongwe

you're probably better off going by minibus to Salima (MK450, one hour), from where you might find a minibus or *matola* going direct to Monkey Bay.

It's much easier to reach Monkey Bay from Blantyre on the ordinary bus that travels via Liwonde and Mangochi (MK890, five to six hours). A quicker option is to go by minibus (MK1000, four to five hours), but you'll need to leave early in the morning and you might have to change at Mangochi. Many travellers also use the *Ilala* ferry to travel up and down the country to or from Monkey Bay (p304).

From Monkey Bay, a *matola* ride to Cape Maclear should cost MK300. Although not far away, it can take forever to get there and you could have to wait hours for a *matola* departure. To Mangochi, a minibus costs around MK450 and the AXA bus MK250.

CAPE MACLEAR

Cape Maclear – a long piece of golden beach shielded by granite hills and thick green bush – sits on a scenic jut of land at the southern end of Lake Malawi, with the alluring Domwe and Thumbi Islands anchored offshore in a glassy blue bay. It's one of Southern Africa's legendary backpackers' hang-outs and the kind of place where plans are forgotten as you sink into a daily rhythm of sunbathing, snorkelling, hanging out in the local village and socialising with newfound friends. There are plenty of sleeping options here to keep all sorts happy – from reed huts and tents on the beach to upmarket lodges serving fine French cuisine. It also feels incredibly friendly – the various accommodations exist in and around Chembe village and a stroll down the sand leads to encounters with fishermen in dugout canoes, local kids and women doing their washing, as well as sunbathing backpackers. If you tire of the day-to-day grind of dozing in the sun, there's plenty of hiking, sailing and snorkelling fun to be had out there.

Dangers & Annoyances

Scams to watch out for at Cape Maclear include the boys who take money in advance for a boat ride or barbecue and then disappear, or who take you on a boat then go through your day-pack while you're snorkelling. Real robberies do occasionally happen on the beach or surrounding hills;

CENTRAL MALAWI

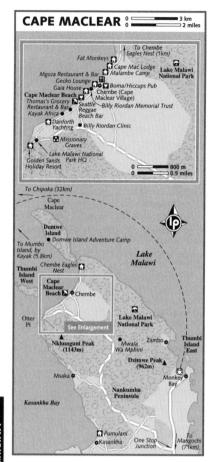

CAPE MACLEAR

violence is very unlikely, but don't carry anything valuable. Travellers sometimes receive hassle from beach boys selling boat trips or barbecues. If you're not interested a firm 'No' will usually suffice.

Information

The **Billy Riordan Clinic** dispenses bilharzia medicine daily at 4.30pm for MK3000. Regular consultation times for minor complaints are 8am to noon and 2pm to 4pm Monday to Friday for a fee of MK8500. Emergency hours are 10am to noon and 3pm to 4pm on Saturday and Sunday.

Skyband has come to Cape Maclear so most of the lodges have wi-fi and many will lend you a laptop to check your emails.

Sights

Much of the area around Cape Maclear including several offshore islands, is part of **Lake Malawi National Park** (admission per person/car US$5/1), one of the few freshwater aquatic parks in Africa, and designated a Unesco World Heritage Site back in 1986. The park headquarters are just inside the gate, where you'll also find a visitor centre which doubles as a small **museum and aquarium** (7.30am-noon & 1-5pm Mon-Sat, 10am-noon & 1-4pm Sun).

The aquarium isn't exactly brimming over with marine life and is more like a little information centre, with explanatory panels about the lake life overshadowing the one functioning tank with its few fish and solitary turtle. The museum charts the area's history and you'll be offered a guided tour. It's interesting to hear the guide paint a picture of a time when hyenas and leopards prowled the shore and the lake was inhabited by crocodiles! The museum also provides a good back-story on Livingstone's first mission if you're off to visit the nearby missionary graves.

Just before the entrance gate to the National Park is a sign pointing to a path which leads towards the hills overlooking the bay. A few hundred metres up here is a small group of **missionary graves**, marking the last resting place of the missionaries who attempted to establish the first Livingstonia Mission here in 1875.

Activities

The Cape Maclear Tour Guides Association is a membership organisation for the area's guides. Its aim is to make sure that business is fairly distributed among registered guides and that tourists do not experience hassle from touts. All registered guides work to a set price list, and your accommodation should be able to arrange a guide for any activities you wish to do.

SNORKELLING

Guides registered with the Cape Maclear Tour Guides Association can organise a number of half- and full-day trips involving snorkelling. For example, trips to **Thumbi Island West** will cost around US$30 per person including food, snorkel hire, park fees and fish eagle feeding.

If you prefer to go snorkelling on your own, many places rent gear (rates start at about US$5, but check the quality of your

CICHLID FISH

There are around 500 species of fish in Lake Malawi. Most of these are of the family *Cichlidae* – the largest family of fish in Africa – and 99% of these cichlids are endemic to the lake. Chambo, familiar to anyone who has eaten in a restaurant in Malawi, are one type of cichlid. Others include the small *utaka*, which move in big shoals and are caught by fishermen at night. But Lake Malawi is most famous for the small and colourful *mbuna*, of which there are many species. As well as being attractive to snorkellers and divers, *mbuna* are popular with aquariums, and for scientists they provide a fascinating insight into the process of evolution. *Mbuna* identification and classification is an ongoing process and it is thought that many species of *mbuna* remain undiscovered.

Cichlids have evolved over the millennia from one common species into many hundreds, yet they have continued to coexist. This has been achieved by different species developing different ways of feeding. Chambo eat phytoplankton, which they filter out of the water through their mouths, whereas *mbuna* have different methods of feeding. Some have developed special teeth to help them scrape algae off the rocks; there are also 'snail eaters' with strong flat teeth, perfect for crushing shells; and 'sand diggers', which filter insects and small animals out of the sand.

Also interesting is the cichlid breeding process. The male attracts the female with his bright colours and, if suitably impressed, she lays eggs, which she immediately takes in her mouth for protection. The male has a pattern near his tail resembling the eggs, which the female tries to pick up, at which point the male releases his sperm into the water, which the female invariably inhales. This process is repeated until all or most of the eggs are fertilised. The female keeps the eggs in her mouth, and when they become baby fish, they stay there for protection. They emerge only to feed, but at the slightest sign of danger, the mother opens her mouth and the young swim straight back in.

mask). **Otter Point**, less than 1km beyond the Golden Sands holiday resort, is a small rocky peninsula and nearby islet that is popular with snorkellers and even more so with fish. You may even see otters here.

DIVING

For diving, go to **Kayak Africa** (☎ 0999 942661; www.kayakafrica.net) or Danforth Yachting (below). Both offer PADI Open Water courses for around US$300, as well as casual dives for experienced divers.

KAYAKING

If you prefer to stay on top of the water, several of the lodges rent out kayaks. For a longer expedition, Kayak Africa (above) is worth a look if you have the cash. You can arrange to kayak out to one of their beautiful camps on Domwe and Mumbo Islands, or even between them. The cost includes accommodation, good meals, hot showers, snorkel gear and park fees. See p256 for the details.

BOAT TRIPS

Yet another option is sailing on a yacht with **Danforth Yachting** (☎ 0999 960077; www.danforth yachting.com). A sunset cruise around Cape Maclear aboard the *Mufasa* costs US$25 per person (minimum six people required); a full-day island-hopping cruise costs US$75 per person (minimum four people), including lunch; and an overnight cruise including all meals, as well as snorkelling and fishing equipment, costs US$200 per person (minimum four people). The owners also have exquisite accommodation (p257).

Guides registered with the Cape Maclear Tour Guides Association can arrange a number of boat trips to Thumbi Islands and Otter Point from US$25 per person. Sunset Booze cruises are also popular and cost around US$15 per person (not including drinks).

HIKING

There's a good range of hikes and walks in the hills that form a horseshoe around the plain behind the village and the beach. You can go alone or arrange a guide, either from the village, your lodge or at the national park headquarters. The park's rate for a guide is US$10 to US$15 per person for a full-day trip. The main path starts by

CENTRAL MALAWI

the missionary graves and leads up through woodland to a col below **Nkhunguni Peak**, the highest on the Nankumba peninsula, with great views over Cape Maclear, the lake and surrounding islands. It's six hours' return to the summit; plenty of water and a good sun hat are essential.

Another interesting place to visit on foot is **Mwala Wa Mphini** (Rock of the Tribal Face Scars), which is just off the main dirt road into Cape Maclear, about 5km from the park headquarters. This huge boulder is covered in lines and patterns that seem to have been gouged out by long-forgotten artists, but are simply a natural geological formation.

If you want a longer walk, a small lakeside path leads southwest from Otter Point, through woodland above the shore, for about 4km to a small fishing village called **Msaka**, which has a small bar/shop serving cold drinks. From here a track leads inland (west) to meet the main dirt road between Cape Maclear and Monkey Bay. Turn left and head back towards Cape Maclear, passing Mwala Wa Mphini on the way. The whole circuit is about 16km and takes four to five hours.

VOLUNTEERING
Billy Riordan Memorial Trust (www.billysmalawi project.org) was set up in memory of a young man, Billy Riordan, who sadly drowned in the lake in 1999. The trust has established a clinic and provides medical care in the area. The trust needs medical volunteers (doctors, dentists, nurses, lab technicians). Work in administration, agriculture and horticulture is also available. They prefer volunteers who can commit for a minimum of four months.

Sleeping
Golden Sands Holiday Resort (campsite per person MK500, 1-/2-/3-person rondavels MK800/900/1000) The crumbling main building barely reveals a hint of the Golden Sands' history. Built at the turn of the century, it was subsequently given to Queen Elizabeth

II as a gift and remained regularly in use until it was left to rot after independence. Now accommodation consists of camping or run-down rondavels in the grounds. The main advantage of staying here is that it's quiet and away from the bustle in the village, but you have to be prepared to rough it. Golden Sands sits at the far western end of the beach, a little past Lake Malawi National Park Headquarters. You will have to pay park fees to stay here because it is inside the park.

Malambe Camp (☎ 0999 258959; campsite per person MK450, dm MK700, standing tent MK800, huts MK1000) Choose from simple huts constructed from reed mats, permanent tents (with proper beds inside) or a large, light reed dorm. There's also space for camping, spotless showers and toilets, a self-catering kitchen, barbecues and a bar, and an area with plenty of loungers and a funky sofa bed.

Mgoza restaurant & bar (r MK1000) This is principally a bar and restaurant but there are a few great value rooms on the property. They all have huge beds swathed in mosquito nets, small terraces and spotless en suite showers and toilets screened off from the room with colourful fabric.

Fat Monkeys (campsite per person MK500, dm/d MK1000/3500; ⌨ 🖥) This is a rambling spot about 1km east of the village centre with a wide variety of rooms. There's a dorm, spacious and airy double rooms, a massive camping area with plenty of parking and a large bar right by the water. It's a lively place and popular with car campers.

ourpick **Gecko Lounge** (☎ 01-599188 or 0999 787322; www.geckolounge.net; dm US$10, d US$55 self-catering chalets US$80; 🖥 🛜) Gecko is one of the best places to stay in Cape Maclear and has grown considerably over the past couple of years. Jaunty orange thatched huts contain a dorm, double rooms and self-catering units, all with solid, comfortable beds, fans, mosquito nets and safes that are large enough to stash all your valuables and more. Hammocks and cane pods swing from the trees, and there's a lovely bar/lounge right on the water that hosts regular parties and live music. You can hire a laptop to check your emails (MK200 for 30 minutes), rent kayaks and snorkelling gear or hire DVD players and DVDs to watch in the comfort of your own room.

Chembe Eagles Nest (☎ 0999 960628, 0999 966507; www.chembenest.com; campsites US$10, cottages & safari tents per person incl dinner, bed & breakfast US$60; ▯ ☎ ▣) At the far northern end of Cape Maclear Beach, this lodge sits in an idyllic spot on a beautiful and very clean broad stretch of private beach, strewn with palm trees and shaded tables, and nestled against the side of the hills. Accommodation consists of airy brick-and-thatch chalets with wooden four posters and spacious verandas.

Cape Mac Lodge (☎ 0999 621279; rogerl@africa online.net; s/d US$90/150; ▯ ☎) Upmarket digs in the heart of the action, with cool tiled rooms with large beds, plush bathrooms, cool tile floors and terraces with views out to the lake. It also has a restaurant, Froggies, which serves excellent French cuisine. There's a pool and a whirlpool.

Danforth Yachting (☎ 0999 960077/770; www danforthyachting.com; full-board per person US$125; ▯ ☎) Come here for glamour, nautical style. Nights are spent in seriously sexy rooms decked out in maritime shades of blue and green, and days can be spent making like a millionaire on their swanky yacht, *Mufasa*, or perhaps enjoying a spot of champagne in their infinity pool. There's also a bar, restaurant and outdoor lounge area in front of a stretch of rich grass with prime views of the lake.

ourpick Kayak Africa (☎ contact via Wilderness Safaris or +27-21 7831955; www.kayakafrica.net) Tour operator Kayak Africa own the following two incredibly romantic lodges just off-shore Cape Maclear on deserted Domwe and Mumbo Islands.

Domwe Island Adventure Camp (per person incl kayak & snorkelling gear US$50) This is the smaller and more rustic of the two lodges. It's self-catering, with furnished safari tents, shared eco-showers and toilets, as well as a bar and a beautiful staggered dining area, open to the elements and set among boulders.

Mumbo Camp (per person incl meals, kayak & snorkelling gear US$180) Has en suite walk-in tents on wooden platforms, tucked beneath trees and above rocks, with spacious decks and astounding views. Most people choose to get to the island by kayak, from the Kayak Africa reception in Cape Maclear – the camp staff will bring along your stuff in a separate boat. It would be perfectly acceptable to just laze around on the hammocks and decks of the camps and indulge in that castaway feeling, but there are kayaks, snorkels and scuba lessons to be had should you choose.

Eating & Drinking

Popular with travellers are beach barbecues arranged by local guides. A chicken or fish barbecue accompanied by drummers costs around US$10 per person and can be arranged by your lodge or just ask around the village.

Thomas's Grocery Restaurant and Bar (dishes from MK400) This is a great local eatery if you want to leave the confines of your lodge. Meals are the usual fish or chicken and chips or *nsima* with the odd nod to backpackers in the way of pasta and burgers. The outdoor bench seating is the perfect spot to watch the village operate around you.

Boma/Hiccups Pub (☯ noon-late; dishes MK700-1000) Sit in a window seat or at tables out on the street to watch the village action; enjoy tasty food in the courtyard restaurant at the back; or pull up a bar stool at the English-style bar (look out for the pirate-themed quotations). There's also a DJ booth up in the eaves and a 1st-floor dance floor that gets packed at the weekends.

Mgoza Restaurant and Bar (☯ 10am-late; dishes MK700-1000) This is a relaxed spot for a beer or a cocktail. The inside bar has slinky, low, Moroccan-style seating and a picture window looking out towards the lake. Outside are a number of cosy seats in the grass and upstairs there's a viewing deck perfect for sundowners. They also serve bar meals.

Gecko Lounge (dishes around MK800-1000) The restaurant at Gecko is a good place to drop in for a meal by the water. They are well known for their pizzas (from MK900), which have an eclectic range of toppings, from fish to mango. You can get your pizzas to go for an extra MK100.

Seattle Reggae Beach Bar (☯ 11am-late) A little shack on the beach with cheap beers and spirits and (of course) a reggae soundtrack. It gets raucous at the weekends and is a good place to come if you fancy hanging out with a local crowd.

CENTRAL MALAWI

Getting There & Away

By public transport, first get to Monkey Bay, from where a *matola* should cost MK300. If you're driving from Mangochi, the dirt road to Cape Maclear (signposted) turns west off the main road, about 5km before Monkey Bay. Be warned, however: it's a bumpy ride and unless you're in a 4WD or high-clearance vehicle, it'll be slow going.

From Cape Maclear, if you're heading for Senga Bay, ask around about chartering a boat. It will cost around US$180, but it's not bad when split between four to six people and much better than the long, hard bus ride. *Matolas* leave for Monkey Bay from around 6am, on a fill-up-and-go basis, and take about an hour (MK300). From there you can get onward transport.

MONKEY BAY TO MANGOCHI

From Monkey Bay the main road runs south to Mangochi. Along this stretch of lake are several places to stay, catering for all tastes and budgets. All the following are signposted off the main road.

Palm Beach Leisure Resort (☎ 0999 943050, 0999 912726; www.palmbeach-mw.com; campsite per person MK1000, s/d/self-catering chalets MK8000/11,200/16,000) Located 8km north of Mangochi, this is a pleasant resort with chalets dotted around large grassy grounds, right by the shores of the lake. The chalets have thatched roofs, vaulted ceilings and stained-glass windows that were handmade by the owner. All kinds of renovations are planned, including a new campsite and bathrooms and budget A-Frames for backpackers. Activities on offer include booze cruises, kayaking, sailing and water-skiing, and there's a good restaurant.

Sun 'n' Sand Holiday Resort (☎ 01-594550; www.sunnsand-malawi.com; permanent tents s/d US$22/35, s/d from US$75/107; ✷ 🖥) This is a huge resort with over 100 rooms spread out over a large area (and a small, sad-looking zoo), so just getting around is a bit of a trek. Rooms are simple with DSTV and air-con but could do with a paint and polish. There's also a camping village with its own beach bar and several permanent tents under thatched shades. While large and well equipped it all feels a little bit soulless. It's signposted 25km south of Monkey Bay.

Norman Carr Cottage (☎ 0999-207506, 0888-355357; www.normancarrcottage.com; per person sharing US$80, s US$110; ✷) Unlike some of the big chain hotels along this stretch of coast, Norman Carr Cottage manages to be low key and full of character as well as luxurious. Six suites and a family cottage have massive handmade king-sized beds, small living areas and open-air garden showers. The beach and gardens are full of hanging chairs and sun beds and there's a beachside pool and whirlpool – a perfect setting to indulge in that Malawian gin and tonic. Food is great (the English breakfast comes particularly recommended) and rates include all activities and food so you can snorkel to your heart's content. It is about 15km south of Monkey Bay.

Sunbird Nkopola Lodge (☎ 01-580444; www.sunbirdmalawi.com/nkopola; s/d US$100/121; ✷)

MALAWI C'EST CHIC

ourpick Pumulani (☎ 216 246 090; www.pumulani.com; all-inclusive rate per person US$450) Malawi may be all the rage with backpackers, but what is there for softies? Opened in 2008, Pumulani is a ridiculously stylish lakeside lodge inside Lake Malawi National Park, with an outstanding hillside setting worthy of a ton of glossy spreads. Designed by a fancy architect, the rooms blend in beautifully with the stunning scenery that surrounds them – that means curved lines, grass roofs and interiors inspired by nature. Rooms have plenty of huge windows to let in the light, views of the surrounding forest and lake, and massive wooden terraces from where to gaze at the clear waters and sweep of golden sand below. Colossal bathrooms include slipper baths strategically placed so you can gaze out at the view. Food is amazing and all sorts of private dinners can be arranged, including candlelit barbecues on the beach underneath the stars. Yes, it's expensive, but a number of activities are included in the price, including snorkelling, fishing and trips on their romantic old traditional wooden dhow.

Other touches of luxury in Malawi? How about **Kaya Mawa** (p238) where you can step directly from the terrace of your rustic-luxury rock-hewn bungalow into the crystal waters of the lake, or **Mvuu Wilderness Lodge** (p265) for 'camping' with a sky-high romance quotient.

HMS *GUENDOLIN*

HMS *Guendolin* was a military boat, made in Britain and assembled in Mangochi in 1899. At 340 tonnes, it was for many years the largest boat on the lake and had a top speed of 12 knots. It also had two powerful guns on board. Such a show of strength was thought necessary by the colonial authorities in order to deter slave-traders who crossed the lake in dhows with their human cargo, but also because colonial rivals Germany and Portugal had territory facing Lake Malawi and were believed to want to increase their influence in the region.

The Germans also had a gunboat, called *Herman von Wissemann*, but despite the friction between their two governments, the captains of the two ships were apparently great friends and would often meet at various points around the lake to drink beer and shoot the breeze.

When WWI was declared in 1914, the *Guendolin* was ordered to destroy the German boat. The British captain knew where the *von Wissemann* would be, as he and the German captain had previously arranged a rendezvous.

But the German captain wasn't aware that war had erupted, and his ship was completely unprepared. The *Guendolin* steamed in close, then bombed the *von Wissemann* and rendered it unuseable. The German captain and crew were then informed of the commencement of hostilities and taken prisoner. This rather unsporting event happened to be the first British naval victory of WWI and Lake Malawi's only recorded battle at sea.

In 1940 the *Guendolin* was converted to a passenger ship, and one of the guns was set up as a memorial in Mangochi, near the clock tower (below). Some years later the ship was scrapped. All that remains today is the gun; the compass and the ship's bell are on display at the museum.

Located about 18km north of Mangochi, accommodation here ranges from an excellent campsite to large rooms for families. Rooms are clean and well equipped and most open out onto private patios with views of the beach. The campsite is separate with its own clean hot showers and toilets as well as a smattering of chalets with a bathroom. Onsite facilities include a swimming pool, volleyball court and even a bird sanctuary. They can also organise a range of excursions around the area.

Club Makokola (☎ 01-580244/445/469; www .clubmak.com; s/d from MK17,900/26,400; 🏊) Club Mak (as it is known) is one of the country's most famous resorts and certainly the plushest along this strip. Even the entrance is grand: huge security gates open onto a grand, flower-lined drive leading to the reception. All chalets are a short stroll to the pristine beach and some are right next to the water. Decor is understated ethnic chic and includes hand-carved tables and wooden lamps, Malawian art and painted ceramic sinks. There are a huge amount of facilities here – including two tennis courts, two swimming pools and a mini soccer pitch – and a large range of activities on offer, from sailing to golf. It has its own airstrip.

MANGOCHI

Mangochi lies near the southern end of Lake Malawi, strung out between the main lakeshore road and the Shire River. The town was once an important slave market, and then an administrative centre in colonial days, when it was known as Fort Johnston. Facilities include several shops, supermarkets, a post office and National and Standard Banks with ATMs.

Sights & Activities

The excellent **Lake Malawi Museum** (admission MK200; ☒ 7.30am-5pm Mon-Sat) houses ethnographic, environmental and historical exhibits, telling the history of the lake. There's also a replica of the foredeck and bridge of the old gunboat HMS *Guendolin* (see boxed text above). To get here, turn right at the clock tower, by the waterfront.

On the waterfront is the **Queen Victoria Clock Tower**, built in 1901 in memory of the queen. Just behind it is the squat stone **MV Vipya Memorial**, dedicated to the 145 passengers and crew who died when the *Viphya* sank on 30 July 1946. Next to that stands the **6PR Hotchkiss Gun** that stood on the *Guendolin* Patrol Gun Boat from 1889 to 1940.

Sleeping

Mawunde Lodge (☎ 01-594051; r with shared bathroom from MK300; r MK1500) Near the bus station, this place has very cheap and basic rooms with shared showers and squat toilets. It's best to go for the rooms with their own bathroom, which also have fan and TV and are brighter and cleaner than the shared-facility rooms.

Holiday Hotel (☎ 01-594789; s/d with shared bathroom MK1000/1500, s/d MK1800/3200) This large hotel, located conveniently near the bus station, has a collection of basic, mostly clean rooms with fans and mosquito nets. It's a bit claustrophobic and depressing though, and there's a noisy bar.

RG PAC Motel (☎ 01-594789; s/d MK4000/5000) The newest hotel in town has clean rooms with enormous TVs and fans, clustered around a large courtyard. There's a slight Fawlty Towers element here though, as despite being brand new the rooms have niggles such as wobbly sinks, sockets that don't work and windows that don't fit properly. Still, the management is very helpful and there's a good restaurant where you can sit out underneath trees and a hanging trellis. It's alcohol free, though. The motel is on the Mongochi to Monkey Bay road, just before the turning to Mangochi's town centre.

Villa Tafika Lodge (☎ 01-593544; www.villa tafika.com; standard/classic/river view/ste 5950/7000/10,950/14,500; ✵) Without a doubt the best place to stay in town, and the best located – right by the clock tower overlooking the river. The villa was built in 1895 and was the house of EL Rhoades, the commander of the gunboat *Guendolin*. The best rooms are in the original villa – they are large, with four-poster beds draped with mosquito nets, and rocking chairs. The river view room, right at the top of the house, has an elegant balcony from where you can survey the town. All around the house are old black-and-white pictures of the house in times past, as well as framed information panels telling the house's history and the story of Mr Rhoades. A new wing contains standard rooms that are perfectly comfortable, if not as atmospheric (though watch out for the steep metal steps!).

Eating & Drinking

All around the bus station are cheap cafes selling beans and *nsima* or stews for around MK300. The best places to eat are at the hotels: RG PAC Motel's restaurant serves Malawian favourites (from MK700) in a pretty courtyard setting, and Villa Tafika has outdoor dining where you can eat grills (MK1200) with a view of the clock tower.

Getting There & Away

All buses between Blantyre and Monkey Bay stop in Mangochi. There are minibuses to/from Liwonde (MK450), Ulongwe, for Liwonde National Park (MK350), Blantyre (MK950) and the Mozambican border at Chiponde (MK800). For border crossing information, see p302.

CENTRAL MALAWI

Southern Malawi

This is the most developed and densely populated part of Malawi, home to the country's commercial capital and two of its major industries – sugar and tea. Southern Malawi also receives the highest proportion of foreign visitors, in most part drawn by the chance to scale mountains and watch wildlife in an incredibly beautiful and diverse landscape.

To the east, resting on the border with Mozambique, cool, mist-shrouded Mt Mulanje, Malawi's highest peak, dominates the skyline, reached by a beautiful drive through vibrantly green tea estates that line the valley below. A short way north is the Zomba Plateau, a stunning highland area straight out of a fairytale. Safari lovers can get their kicks at the country's best national park – Liwonde – where you can get up close to elephants, hippos, rhinos and crocodiles, and spend the night in tented luxury without the crowds of Southern Africa's more famous parks. Need big city action? Make for Blantyre, the country's most dynamic city, for restaurants, bars and a friendly, welcoming vibe.

Despite the burgeoning population, this part of Malawi can still feel as if it's wild and untrammelled. Head into the deep south through the thick heat of the Shire Valley, past the cane fields and sugar-industry towns, and you'll find three little-visited nature reserves, which, while not overflowing with the stars of the safari scene, are steeped in romantic wilderness atmosphere.

HIGHLIGHTS

- ▪ Spend a few days hiking the craggy peaks of **Mt Mulanje** (p281)
- ▪ Glide past hippos and crocodiles in a dugout canoe at **Liwonde National Park** (p263)
- ▪ Wander through misty pockets of pine forest at the **Zomba Plateau** (p267)
- ▪ Drive through bright green tea fields and spend the night in an old planter's home at the **tea estates** (p286) near Mulanje
- ▪ Go elephant tracking and sleep under luxury canvas at the **Majete Wildlife Reserve** (p287)
- ▪ Spend some alone time with nature at the little-visited wilderness of **Mwabvi Wildlife Reserve** (p289)

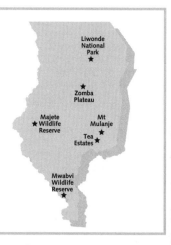

SOUTHERN MALAWI

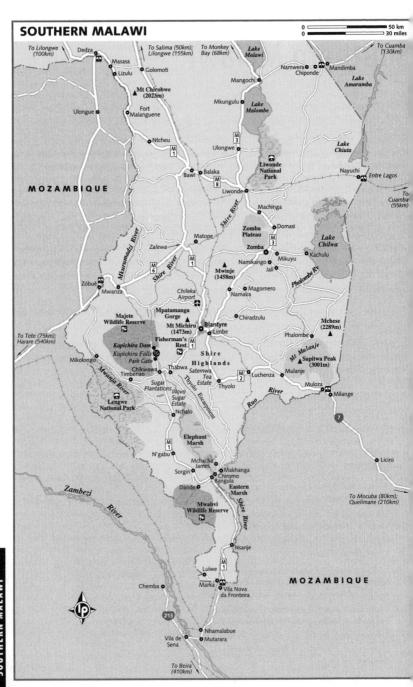

| 0 | | 50 km |
| 0 | | 30 miles |

To Lilongwe (100km)
Dedza
Masasa
Lizulu
Golomoti
To Salima (50km); Lilongwe (155km)
To Monkey Bay (68km)
Lake Malawi
Namwera
Chiponde
Mandimba
To Cuamba (130km)
Lake Amaramba
Mangochi
Mt Chirobwe (2023m)
Mkungulu
Lake Malombe
Fort Malanguene
Ulongue
Ntcheu
M1
Ulongwe
M3
Lake Chiuta
Nayuchi
Entre Lagos

MOZAMBIQUE
Bawi
Balaka
M8
Liwonde
Liwonde National Park
Machinga
To Cuamba (55km)

Mkurumadzi River
Zalewa
Matope
Shire River
Zomba Plateau
Domasi
Zomba
M3
Lake Chilwa
Kachulu

Zóbuè
Mwanza
M6
Shire River
M1
Mwinje (1458m)
Namikango
Mikuyu
Jali
Phalombe Rv

Majete Wildlife Reserve
Chileka Airport
Magornero
Namaka
Mchese (2289m)

To Tete (75km); Harare (540km)
Mpatamanga Gorge
Mt Michiru (1473m)
Blantyre
Limbe
Chiradzulu
Phalombe

Fisherman's Rest
M1
Mt Mulanje
Sapitwa Peak (3001m)

Kapichira Dam
Kapichira Falls
Park Gate
Shire Highlands
Mulanje
Muloza
Milange

Mikolongo
Chikwawa
Timbenao
Thabwa
Satemwa Tea Estate
M2
Luchenza
Muloza
Ruo River

Mwanja River
Sugar Plantations
Illovo Sugar Estate
Thyolo Escarpment
Thyolo

Lengwe National Park
Nchalo

M1
N'gabu
Elephant Marsh

Mchacha James
Sorgin
Makhanga
Chiromo
Bangula
Eastern Marsh

Zambezi River
Dande
Mwabvi Wildlife Reserve

To Mocuba (80km); Quelimane (210km)
Liciro

Shire River
Nsanje

M1
Lulwe
Chemba
Marka
Vila Nova da Fronteira
MOZAMBIQUE

213
Nhamalabue
Vila de Sena
Mutarara

To Beira (410km)

LIWONDE

Straddling the Shire River, the small town of Liwonde is one of the gateways to Liwonde National Park. The river divides the town in two; to the east you'll find the main bus stations, the market, supermarkets and the train station. West of the river are several tourist lodges. The only reason most visitors pass through Liwonde is as a stopover on the way into the park, but it can be a pleasant place to spend the night. Stay along the river for a view of fishermen in traditional dugouts and reed-lined shores twitching with birdlife, all set to a soundtrack of grunting hippos.

Sleeping

Shire Camp (☎ 0884-327794; campsite per person MK1000, chalets incl breakfast MK3500) An excellent budget choice with a fabulous setting bang on the river. You can either pitch a tent in their campsite or bed down in one of their kooky thatched chalets, complete with fan, nets and veranda. A nice touch is the semi-open roofs at the back (screened so no beasties can get in) allowing you to see the tops of the trees from the bathroom. Another plus is their open-air riverside restaurant (meals from MK300) with tables lined up mere feet from the river – a great spot for sundowners (beers MK150). Shire Camp is on the river's north bank. Take the dirt road on the right just before the National Bank.

Sun Village Lodge (☎ 01-542330; s/d MK2915/5330) On the northern side of town, opposite the National Bank, Sun Village is certainly well located and the setting is nice enough, with rooms grouped around a pretty garden square. The rooms are quite run-down though and their condition varies greatly so ask to see a few before choosing.

Warthogs Wallow (☎ 01-542426; r with fan MK3000) The upside? This hotel is set right along the south bank of the river, with strategically placed thatched drinking areas and a raised turreted bar perfect for hippo spotting. The downside? The grounds are dusty and neglected, and the rooms could do with a serious revamp. There's a choice between ground-floor or 1st-floor rooms with a fan, nets and screened verandas, set in two-storey buildings throughout the grounds. Plump for a top-floor room as they have vaulted ceilings and views.

Shire Lodge (☎ 01-542277; s/d MK4500/5500; ⚄) Owned by the same people who run Hippo View Lodge, and just a short hop down the road, this large plot houses 18 chalets with large double beds and small terraces. Peeling paint and tatty bedspreads make them seem a little worn, but renovations were due to begin at the end of 2009, including the construction of a brand-new complex of 20 bedrooms.

Liwonde Motel (☎ 01-542338; standard/superior r MK4500/5700) This place has a handful of well-kept rooms opening out onto a bright courtyard. All of the rooms have fans and DSTV, and the superior rooms have bigger bathrooms and sitting areas featuring natty brown sofas straight out of the '80s. There's a bar here including a thatched gazebo for shaded boozing. It's in the town centre next to the market.

Hippo View Lodge (☎ 01-542822 or 542255; www .hippoviewlodge.com; superior s/d MK8900/13,800, VIP s/d MK11,400/17,300, family chalet MK35,000; ⚄ ▣ 🛜) Turn right down the dirt road just before the National Bank and look out for the two hippos flanking the road just before the entrance. Set in sprawling, flower-filled grounds right next to the river this is the classiest and best-equipped joint in town. All of the rooms are spacious, with air-con, DSTV, tea and coffee facilities and small seating areas. Superior rooms lead off communal balconies while the VIP rooms have private patios (not to mention swish dressing areas in the rooms themselves). At the restaurant you can dine to the tinkling of fountains, under canopies propped up by faux pillars. Should you wish to get out on the water, a wide range of boat trips is available.

Getting There & Away

Lakeshore AXA buses pass by Liwonde on their way up to Mangochi but most drop off passengers at the turn-off and not in the town itself, so you're better off using a minibus, which run regularly from Zomba (MK250, 45 minutes), Limbe (MK500, three hours) and Mangochi (MK450, two hours). You can also get a minibus to the Mozambique border at Nayuchi (MK850, 2½ to three hours).

LIWONDE NATIONAL PARK

Though small in stature **Liwonde National Park** (admission per person/car US$5/2) tops the list for visitor numbers and is Malawi's number one wildlife destination. While it can't rival the parks of neighbouring Zambia for big game excitement, Liwonde is still a beautiful and exciting place to visit with all the romantic safari atmosphere you'll ever need. Unless you are looking to tick off the big five, you won't be disappointed.

The Shire River dominates the 548 sq km park – a wide, meandering stretch lined by thick undergrowth and tall, statuesque palms. Surrounding it are flood plains, woodland and parched scrub. Unsurprising then, that the park is prime hippo- and croc-spotting territory, and you shouldn't let a trip here pass you by without canoeing on the river. Gliding silently past hippos, waterbirds and massive Nile crocodiles sunning themselves on riverbanks is a thrilling, if sometimes disconcerting, experience. Waterbucks are also common near the water, while beautiful sable and roan antelopes, zebras and elands populate the surreal flood plains in the east. Night drives can reveal spotted genets, bushbabies, scrub hares, side-striped jackals and even spotted hyenas. The main event here though is the elephants – there are over 600 in Liwonde.

LIWONDE RHINO SANCTUARY

The **rhino sanctuary** (admission US$3) is a fenced-off area within the park that was developed with the purpose of breeding rare black rhinos. It has since been expanded to protect a number of mammal species from poaching. At the time of research 10 black rhinos were living in the enclosure along with populations of Lichtenstein's hartebeest, Cape buffalo, Burchell's zebra, eland and roan antelope. You can go on nature drives here and all funds are put back into conservation projects. Over time, a number of animals have been released back into Liwonde or taken to nearby Majete Wildlife Reserve.

The combination of rich riverine, mopane and grassland habitats means that birdlife here is very varied. There are more than 400 of Malawi's 650 species here including Pel's fishing owl, African skimmer and brown-breasted barbet, and it's the only place in the country you'll find Lillian's lovebird. October to January is particularly interesting as it brings migratory birds such as Böhm's bee-eaters to the park.

Activities

If you have your own 4WD or high-clearance vehicle you can tour the park's network of tracks (although many close in the wet season and vary from year to year, so check the situation with the camp). If you're staying at Mvuu Wilderness Lodge (opposite) then game drives are included in your accommodation rate. For those on a budget, Chinguni Hills Lodge (opposite) offers walking safaris (per person US$15), boating safaris (per person US$25) and day and night drives (per person US$20). Alternatively, game drives can be arranged at Mvuu Camp. If you can't stay in the park, Hippo View Lodge (p263) in Liwonde town, operates wildlife-viewing boat trips along the Shire River.

Sleeping

Places to stay in Liwonde remain open all year – you can reach them by boat even if rain closes some of the park tracks.

Njobvu Cultural Village (☎ 0888-623530 or through Mvuu Camp reception 01-542135; www.njobvuvillage.com;

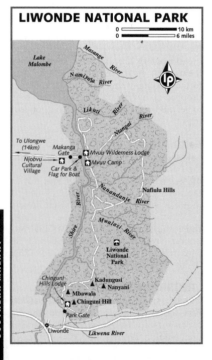

LIWONDE NATIONAL PARK

0 ———————— 10 km
0 ———————— 6 miles

Lake Malombe

Masanje River

Namwela River

Likuzi River

River

Ntangai River

To Ulongwe (14km)

Makanga Gate

Mvuu Wilderness Lodge

Njobvu Cultural Village

Car Park & Flag for Boat

Mvuu Camp

Nanandanje River

Nafiulu Hills

Shire River

Mwalasi River

Liwonde National Park

Chinguni Hills Lodge

Kadungusi

Nanyani

Mbawala

Chinguni Hill

Park Gate

Liwonde

Likwena River

accommodation only per person US$6, full-board & activities per person US$30) Sitting near the park's Makanga Gate, Njobvu offers visitors a rare opportunity to stay in a traditional Malawian village, sleeping in traditional mud-brick huts (with or without a mattress – your choice!). During the day you are invited to take part in the villagers' daily lives, visiting traditional doctors, visiting the village school, learning how to pound cassava, and eating traditional food like *nshima* and pumpkin, or *thobwa*, the locally brewed beer. All proceeds go directly to the community.

Mvuu Camp (☎ 01-542135; campsite per person US$10, full-board chalets per person US$250; 🔊) Managed by Wilderness Safaris (p207) this camp is deep in the northern part of the park on the banks of the river. Stone chalets have tented roofs, swish interiors and verandas overlooking the river, and the small campsite has spotless ablution blocks and self-catering facilities, including utensils. Alternatively, you can eat at the open-plan thatched restaurant; the food is fantastic. There's also a bar and lounge area with wide lake views and a swimming pool, which even has helpful steps for hippos to get in and out. They wander around the camp at night, as do elephants.

Mvuu Wilderness Lodge (full-board chalets per person US$400; 🔊) A short distance upriver from Mvuu Camp (and also managed by Wilderness Safaris), this intimate lodge is full of romantic bush atmosphere. Sumptuous safari tents have huge beds covered with billowing mosquito nets, and semi-open roofs and bathrooms (screened-in though) so you can look out at the sky. Private balconies overlook a water hole where there are plenty of birds and wildlife. There's a small swimming pool, a restaurant serving excellent food and a raised lounge area overlooking the lagoon. Need room service? Beat on the in-room drum. Rates include park fees and all wildlife drives, boat rides and bird walks.

Getting There & Away

The main park gate is 6km east of Liwonde town. There's no public transport beyond here, though ask around and you might be able to find a *matola* (pick-up) to take you as far as Chinguni Hills for around MK300. From the gate to Mvuu Camp is 28km along the park track (closed in the wet season); a 4WD vehicle is recommended for this route.

Another way in for vehicles is via the dirt road (open all year) from Ulongwe, a village between Liwonde town and Mangochi. This leads for 14km through local villages to the western boundary. A few kilometres inside the park is a car park and boat jetty, where a watchman hoists a flag to arrange a boat from Mvuu Camp to come and collect you. This service is free if you're staying at the camp.

Alternatively, if you make a booking in advance for Mvuu Camp through Wilderness Safaris in Lilongwe (p207) the camp can arrange a boat transfer from Liwonde town for US$100.

CHIFUNDO ARTISANS NETWORK

If you're near the large market town of **Balaka**, pay a visit to the **Chifundo Artisans Network** (☎ 0888-365960; 🕐 8am-4pm daily, tours Mon-Fri) a craft studio and community initiative that employs (and trains) some 40 local people to make a range of different crafts, from Malawian dolls to colourful hand-painted textiles, to handmade recycled paper. You can visit the studio and afterwards buy some of the products at the onsite store; there's also a small cafe here. To get here stay on the road past Balaka – Chifundo is signposted behind the mission church. If you don't have wheels, first get to Balaka and then take a bicycle taxi to 4 Ways Bottle store, from where you can walk (again, there are signs).

For those without wheels, the best option is to get any bus or minibus between Liwonde town and Mangochi and get off at Ulongwe (make sure you say this clearly, otherwise the driver will think you want to go to Lilongwe). In Ulongwe local boys wait by the bus stop and will sometimes take you by bicycle to the park gates or to the banks of the river just outside it from where you can arrange to be picked up (MK600). They usually won't take you into the park itself (they don't want to risk coming across any elephants!). If you've got a lot of luggage there may be an extra charge or you may need two bikes. The ride takes about an hour, and you should leave with plenty of time before dusk.

ZOMBA

Zomba makes a welcome change from some of Malawi's other big cities. Lying in the shadow of the Zomba Plateau, natural beauty is abundant, and the town is also rich in history. The capital of Malawi from 1891 until the mid-1970s, Zomba's colonial heritage is still much in evidence. It is home to wide, tree-lined streets, and clambering up the town's gently sloping hills are a number of faded old colonial beauties, including the impressive State House. East of the main road is the town's friendly commercial centre. There's a lively market, banks, bureaux de change, internet cafes and a couple of decent eateries.

Information

Internet access is available at **Global Links Suppliers** (per min MK5; 7.30am-5pm Mon-Sat) opposite the market. There are Standard, National and First Merchant Banks in the town. If you need to change money, **Cashpoint Forex Bureau** (7.30am-5pm Mon-Fri, 8am-noon Sat) has reasonable rates. For supplies, there's a Shoprite, a PTC and a Metro Cash & Carry.

Sleeping

Municipality of Zomba Resthouse (r with shared bathroom MK500, d MK650) A bargain-bucket place close to the bus station, this option is only worth it if you need somewhere very cheap and close to public transport as the standard is pretty basic.

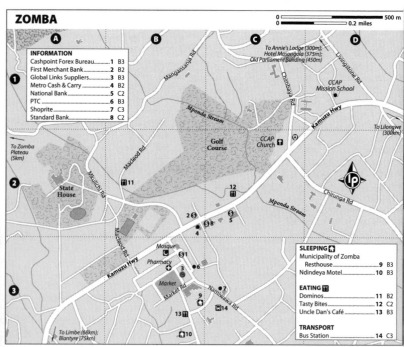

ZOMBA

	0 ⊢━━━━━┥ 500 m
	0 ⊢━━━━━┥ 0.2 miles

INFORMATION
Cashpoint Forex Bureau.........1 B3
First Merchant Bank................2 B2
Global Links Suppliers............3 B3
Metro Cash & Carry.................4 B2
National Bank...........................5 C2
PTC..6 B3
Shoprite....................................7 C3
Standard Bank.........................8 C2

To Annie's Lodge (300m);
Hotel Masongola (375m);
Old Parliament Building (450m)

SLEEPING
Municipality of Zomba
  Resthouse............................9 B3
Ndindeya Motel.....................10 B3

EATING
Dominos.................................11 B2
Tasty Bites.............................12 C2
Uncle Dan's Café...................13 B3

TRANSPORT
Bus Station............................14 C3

SOUTHERN MALAWI

Ndindeya Motel (☎ 01-525558; s/d MK1850/2350, ecutive r MK2950) A good budget option right in ue heart of the action and a short walk from ue bus station. Rooms are large, spread out cross two rambling bright buildings and all rates include breakfast. The executive ooms are the most spacious, and have small ounge areas, but they are also closest to the ar so noise can be a factor.

Annie's Lodge (Map p268; ☎ 01-527002; Livingstone l; standard/superior r MK6995/8995, executive r MK11,995, t MK16,995; 🖥 🛜) The most gracious of omba's hotels. Scattered along a hillside a jumble of white colonial buildings ith green corrugated iron roofs and wide erandas. Faded colonial glamour may be ue name of the game outside, but inside the ooms are perfectly modern, with DSTV, ir-con and large bathrooms. The executive ooms are housed in a new wing and sit the top of the plot; what they lack in ld-fashioned charm, they make up for in reat views.

Hotel Masongola (Map p268; ☎ 01-524688; vingstone Rd; hotelmasongola@clcom.net; s/d from S$40/75) Another colonial leftover, this hotel as once the house of Malawi's first governor. Iowever, the transition from colonial house hotel hasn't been as successful as Annie's odge. The rooms in the old buildings look ather faded and are expensive for what you et, and there's an unsightly modern wing ttached. There are lovely gardens at the ack of the property though, which make nice sundowner spot, and the restaurant erves tasty portions of grilled meats.

ating

here are plenty of cheap hole-in-the-wall laces around the bus station where you an pick up plates of chicken and *nshima* r chips for around MK200.

Dominos (Macleod Rd; meals from MK600; pizzas from K700; 🕙 10am-midnight daily) Overlooking the own's golf course, this open-air bar and estaurant is fun, friendly and a good place meet locals. A menu of Malawian staples nd pizzas is available, and they show all nanner of sporting events on their big-creen TV. Should you fancy a manicure to along with your beer: there's an on-site eauty parlour (open 9am to 6pm).

Uncle Dan's Café (☎ 01-527114; dishes from MK400; 🕙 7.30am-6pm Mon-Fri, 7.30am-7pm Sat, 8.30am-4.30pm un) Good value and deservedly popular with travellers, this little cafe serves up fantastic homemade burgers and pasta dishes. It's also worth popping in at teatime – tea and cocoa with fresh-baked cookies and cakes costs MK500. Look for the sign saying 'Aaron & Lisa Pizzeria' – Uncle Dan's is inside.

Tasty Bites (Kamuzu Hwy; dishes from MK500; 🕙 8am-8pm Wed-Mon) Curry addicts will be well looked after here. Flavoursome Pakistani curries, shawarmas, samosas and Indian tea are all on the menu, along with more standard meals such as burgers and steaks. The large dining room has a notice board with information about the local area and beyond, and there are a couple of tables for outside dining (though the view is of the car park and a main road). The sweet-toothed can munch on one of the sinful-looking cupcakes from the counter at the front.

Getting There & Away

Zomba is on a main route between Lilongwe and Blantyre. The bus station is in the town centre, off Namiwawa Rd. AXA buses run to/from Zomba and Lilongwe (MK1000, five to six hours), Blantyre (MK350, 1½ to two hours), Liwonde (MK200, one hour) and Nkhata Bay (MK1720) via Mangochi (MK700).

Minibuses go every hour or so to Limbe (MK390, one hour) and also head to Lilongwe (MK1200, four to five hours) Liwonde (MK250, 45 minutes) and Mangochi (MK800).

ZOMBA PLATEAU

A huge slab of mountain rising some 1800m behind Zomba town, Zomba Plateau is a gorgeous highland paradise – Malawi style. Criss-crossed by streams, lakes and tumbling waterfalls, and covered in pine forest and patches of woodland, you half expect Little Red Riding Hood to come skipping out from between the trees – except here she'd be hiding from leopards, not the Big Bad Wolf.

The plateau can be explored on tracks by car, or on foot on the numerous winding paths and trails that ring and cross the mountain, and if you walk along the edge of the escarpment you'll take in magnificent views across the plains towards Lake Chilwa or out towards Mulanje. The plateau is divided into two halves by the Domasi

Valley. The southern half has a road to the top, a hotel (the landmark Ku Chawe Inn), a camping ground, several picnic places and a network of driveable tracks and hiking paths.

Zomba Plateau is known as a hotspot for birds, with mountain wagtail and Bertram's weaver among the species found here; mammals also make the plateau their home, including bushbucks, vervet monkeys and even the occasional leopard.

Sights & Activities

A few kilometres from Ku Chawe Inn are the **Mandala Falls**, not as impressive as they used to be since the Mulunguzi Dam was significantly enlarged in 1999. A nature trail

runs from the Forest Campsite past the da and on to Mandala Falls. From here you ca hike through some beautiful indigenou forest and a trout farm, to **Williams Fal** another fairly impressive cascade.

A popular place to visit is **Chingwe's Hole** c the western side of the plateau. Accordir to local rumour, the hole was said to lea to the bottom of the Rift Valley and, i days of old, local chiefs would throw the enemies down there. The rumours are mor impressive than the actual sight though, bu it's worth a visit for the short nature tra that starts here and the stunning view looking westward over the Shire Valley.

For even more impressive views, hea for the eastern side of the plateau, whei

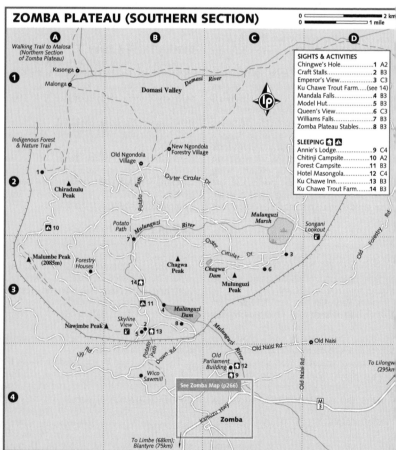

ZOMBA PLATEAU (SOUTHERN SECTION)

0 ——————— 2 km
0 ——————— 1 mile

SIGHTS & ACTIVITIES
Chingwe's Hole.................1 A2
Craft Stalls.......................2 B3
Emperor's View................3 C3
Ku Chawe Trout Farm.....(see 14)
Mandala Falls...................4 B3
Model Hut.........................5 B3
Queen's View....................6 C3
Williams Falls....................7 B3
Zomba Plateau Stables.......8 B3

SLEEPING
Annie's Lodge....................9 C4
Chitinji Campsite...............10 A2
Forest Campsite................11 B3
Hotel Masongola..............12 C4
Ku Chawe Inn...................13 B3
Ku Chawe Trout Farm.......14 B3

SOUTHERN MALAWI

Queen's View (named after Queen Elizabeth, wife of King George VI, who visited Zomba in 1957) and **Emperor's View** (after Emperor Haile Selassie of Ethiopia, who visited in 1964) overlook Zomba town and out towards Mulanje.

Should the urge to shop grab you there are a number of **craft stalls** just outside the Ku Chawe Inn.

HIKING ON THE ZOMBA PLATEAU
The southern half of the plateau is ideal for hiking. The network of tracks and paths can be confusing though, so for more help with orientation there's a 3D map of the plateau in the **Model Hut**.

For detailed information on hiking routes on the southern half of the plateau the now out of print *Zomba Mountain: A Walker's Guide,* by Martin Cundy, is useful and should be available in bookshops in Blantyre.

Keen hikers may find the northern half of the plateau more interesting. There are few tracks here and no pine plantations – the landscape is similar to that of Mt Mulanje and Nyika Plateau.

It's recommended either to walk in a group or to use a guide when hiking, as there are occasional muggings on the plateau. There are guides registered with the Ministry of Forestry, Fisheries and Environmental Affairs based at the Model Hut, who charge around US$20 per day, although the rate is open to negotiation as there's no set price. More expensive guides are also available from the Ku Chawe Inn.

HORSE RIDING
You can arrange horse-riding excursions with **Zomba Plateau Stables** (☎ 0888-714445/3;

maggieparsons@iwayafrica.com; per person per hour MK4000) for anything from an hour to five to six hours. They're located opposite the Mulunguzi Dam.

FISHING
The plateau's streams and lakes are stocked with rainbow trout but it can difficult for anglers to get a fishing permit, which you'll have to arrange in advance (contact the Angling Society of Malawi for further information at www.anglingmalawi.org). You're better off heading for the **Ku Chawe Trout Farm** (admission per person/car MK120/50). It charges an entry fee for day visitors and you can fish in the trout ponds for MK1000 per kilo of fish you catch.

Sleeping & Eating
There are no shops on the plateau so campers and self-caterers should bring everything they need up from Zomba town. If all else fails though, you'll find a number of stalls between the Ku Chawe Inn and the Forest Campsite, and on the road up to the plateau itself, selling fresh vegetables as well as delicious fresh raspberries and strawberries.

Forest Campsite (campsite per person MK400) An aptly named spot with toilets and wood-fired hot showers all among large pine trees. It's fantastic in the sunshine but feels a bit spooky on misty days – and of those there are plenty.

Chitinji Campsite (campsite per person MK500, r per person MK700) Near Malumbe Peak in the west, this isn't the place to come if you're looking for lots of facilities, and you'll need at 4WD to cope with the very bumpy track to get here, but the trek is well worth it. You'll be rewarded with wild terraced gardens

---

THE POTATO PATH
The Potato Path is the most popular hike; it's a direct route from town leading all the way up to the plateau. To find the path, head up the main road from town leading up to the plateau and look for the signpost – it's at a sharp bend in the road some 2km from Zomba town. The path climbs steeply through woodland to reach the plateau near Ku Chawe Inn.

From near Ku Chawe Inn, the Potato Path then goes straight across the southern half of the plateau, sometimes using the park tracks, sometimes using narrow short cuts, and leads eventually to Old Ngondola Village, from where it descends quite steeply into the Domasi Valley.

The Domasi Valley is well known for its fertile soil, plentiful water and good farming conditions, so here the local people grow vegetables (especially potatoes) and take them along the Potato Path (hence the name) down to Zomba town to sell in the market.

Allow two to three hours for the ascent, and about 1½ hours coming down.

and camping spots among the trees, with nothing to disturb you except for the sound of gentle rushing water. It's pretty cold up here but, if you can take it, you'll emerge from your tent in the morning to a sublime view out over a valley of pines, framed by sweeping, wildflower-dusted hills. For those that need more warmth, there's a basic stone hut with a couple of rooms, though you should bring bedding with you. On the practical side, the stone hut has shared showers and toilets (also used by the campers), and there are barbecue facilities and a washing-up spot.

Ku Chawe Trout Farm (☎ 01-525271/0888-638524; campsite per person MK600, r with shared bathroom MK1600, self-contained r MK2000, 4-bed self-contained chalets MK5000) The most convenient self-catering spot on the mountain has the option of basic rooms in small stone cottages or, better still, wooden hillbilly cabins with basic bathrooms, little kitchenettes (with a gas camping stove and no fridge) and balconies equipped with rocking chairs to take in the views of the plateau. There's also a large grassy campsite with sheltered dining spots, barbecue facilities and a small river rushing past. There are toilets at the campsite, but showers are located behind the cottages on other side of the complex so it's a bit of a trek in the mornings.

our pick Ku Chawe Inn (☎ 01-514237; superior/deluxe r US$80/110; 🖳) Perched on the hillside like a mist-cloaked Tuscan palace, surrounded by lively terraced gardens full of gorgeous trees and flowers, and blessed with marvellous views over the plateau and all the way over to Lake Chilwa, the rambling, redbrick Ku Chawe Inn is by far the nicest place to stay around these parts. After a hard day of hiking or biking (cycles MK300 an hour), or sitting in a comfy car (jeep trips US$70 for three hours) you can head back to your room, sink into a comfy chair and enjoy the view from massive, almost floor-to-ceiling windows, perhaps toasting your feet by the warmth of the stone fireplace.

Getting There & Away

A sealed road leads steeply up the escarpment from Zomba town to the top of the plateau (about 4km). After passing the Wico Sawmill, a two-way sealed road known as the Down Rd, veers east and continues for another 2km before turning

into a dirt track. Up Rd is now open only to walkers.

There's no bus up to the plateau but local people hitch by the junction on the main street in Zomba town near the PTC supermarket. Alternatively, you can take a taxi (negotiable from around MK1500). If this is beyond your means, get a taxi part way through the suburbs, say as far as Wico Sawmill, then simply walk up the Up Rd. Alternatively, you can walk all the way from Zomba town to the plateau via the road or on the Potato Path (p269).

BLANTYRE & LIMBE

Welcome to Malawi's most populous city – and the country's commercial and industrial hub. Compared to most major Southern African cities Blantyre is pretty sleepy, but in Malawian terms it's positively buzzing. During the week the city streets are alive with activity as office workers, hawkers and shopkeepers go about their business. It has the best and most diverse choice of restaurants in the country, several happening bars and cultural centres, a charming national museum, a fascinating library and archives where you can get to grips with the country's history. Add to that numerous tour operators, banks, internet cafes and other practicalities, and Blantyre makes a pleasant stopover as well as a place to get things done.

To the east Blantyre joins its more sedate sister city of Limbe, which is only of interest to travellers for its minibus station and grand old mission church. Unless stated otherwise, every address in this section is in Blantyre rather than Limbe.

History

Blantyre is the oldest settlement in Malawi and the oldest urban centre in Southern Africa. It was founded in 1876 by missionaries from the Church of Scotland, and is named after Blantyre in South Lanarkshire, Scotland, where David Livingstone was born. After attaining municipality status in 1895, Blantyre quickly gained a reputation as a commercial centre because of its place at the heart of the region's ivory trade. Neighbouring Limbe sprang up at the beginning of the 20th century after the Shire Highlands Railway Company headquarters were established there, experiencing

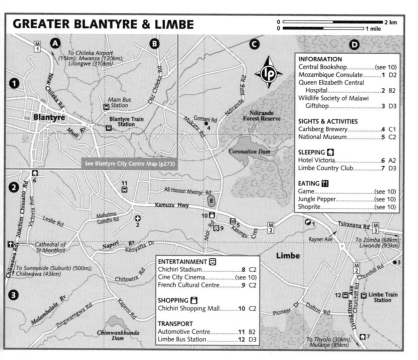

GREATER BLANTYRE & LIMBE

INFORMATION
Central Bookshop...............(see 10)
Mozambique Consulate..........1 D2
Queen Elizabeth Central
    Hospital............................2 B2
Wildlife Society of Malawi
    Giftshop...........................3 D3

SIGHTS & ACTIVITIES
Carlsberg Brewery.................4 C1
National Museum.................5 C2

SLEEPING
Hotel Victoria.......................6 A2
Limbe Country Club.............7 D3

EATING
Game.................................(see 10)
Jungle Pepper....................(see 10)
Shoprite.............................(see 10)

ENTERTAINMENT
Chichiri Stadium....................8 C2
Cine City Cinema...............(see 10)
French Cultural Centre...........9 C2

SHOPPING
Chichiri Shopping Mall.........10 C2

TRANSPORT
Automotive Centre...............11 B2
Limbe Bus Station................12 D3

a boom as more and more people moved to the easily accessible town. In 1956 the two merged to become one city.

Orientation

Despite the sprawling suburbs and townships surrounding Blantyre, the city centre is very compact, with most places of importance to travellers within easy walking distance. Central Blantyre's main street is Victoria Ave; along here are several large shops, the tourist office, the map sales office, banks, bureaux de change and travel agents. To the east is Haile Selassie Rd, which contains many smaller shops. At the northern end of Victoria Ave is the landmark Sunbird Mount Soche Hotel.

East of Sunbird Mount Soche Hotel is a major traffic roundabout, from where the main road north leads to the airport, Mwanza and Lilongwe. This road has no official name but is known as New Chileka Rd. Approximately 500m further east is another roundabout, with a small clock on a concrete pedestal in the middle: from here Chileka Rd leads north to the bus station

and outer suburbs; and Chipembere Hwy, heading south, turns into the Kamuzu Hwy, which veers east towards Limbe and, ultimately, Zomba, Mulanje and Liwonde.

MAPS

Survey maps of Blantyre and the surrounding area are available from the **Department of Surveys Map Sales Office** (Map p273; Victoria Ave). Regional and city maps cost MK650; survey maps covering the whole of Malawi cost MK3500.

Information

BOOKSHOPS

Central Africana Bookshop (Map p273; ☎ 01-876110; Uta Waleza Centre, Kidney Cres; centralafricana@africa -online.net) The main attraction here is the broad selection of antiquarian books (there are plenty of leather-bound tomes covering topics from history to Southern African birdlife) but they also have a selection of old colonial maps, up-to-date travel guides, maps and glossy pictorials.

Central Bookshop (Map above; ☎ 01-872191; Chichiri Shopping Mall) This place stocks a selection of books, maps and magazines including guides to Malawi, trashy bonk-busters and a good selection of children's books.

Wildlife Society of Malawi Giftshop (Map p271; Churchill Rd, Limbe) At the Heritage Centre. Specialises in books about natural history and national parks.

CULTURAL CENTRES
French Cultural Centre (Map p271; ☎ 01-871250; cnr Moi Rd & Kasungu Cres; ☻ 8am-noon & 2-5.30pm Mon-Fri, 8am-noon Sat) Has a library and resource centre and offers a variety of classes, from French language to yoga to Chichewa. The centre also puts on regular live music, theatre and film screenings.

EMERGENCY
Ambulance ☎ 998
Fire ☎ 01-971999
Police ☎ 01-823333
Rapid Response Unit ☎ 997

INTERNET ACCESS
You will find plenty of internet bureaus in Blantyre. Skyband and Globe wi-fi hotspots are available throughout the city. For information on charges and locations see p295.
E Centre Internet Café (Map opposite; cnr Victoria Ave & Independence Dr; per min MK4.50; ☻ 8am-5pm Mon-Sat, 9am-4pm Sun) Reasonable speed internet access. You can munch on homemade banana muffins (MK50) while you surf.
Icon Internet Café (Map opposite; off Livingstone Ave; per min MK5; ☻ 8.30am-6pm Mon-Sat, 10am-5pm Sun) High-speed internet access.

MEDICAL SERVICES
One Stop Pharmacy (Map opposite; Chilembwe Rd; ☻ 8am-6pm Mon-Fri, 9am-2pm Sat) Well-stocked pharmacy that's a member of the national chain.
Mwaiwathu Private Hospital (Map opposite; ☎ 01-822999; Chileka Rd; ☻ 24hr) For private medical consultations or blood tests, this hospital, east of the city centre, is good. A consultation is US$10; all drugs and treatment are extra.
Queen Elizabeth Central Hospital (Map p271; ☎ 01-874333; ☻ 24hr) The malaria test centre at this government-run hospital, off Chipembere Hwy, charges US$10 for a malaria test. Ask for directions as the test centre is hard to find.
Seventh Day Adventist Clinic (Map opposite; ☎ 01-820006; Kabula Hill) For medical or dental problems, this clinic charges US$10 for a doctor's consultation and US$10 for a malaria test.

MONEY
There are a couple of branches of the National Bank of Malawi and one branch of Standard Bank on Victoria Ave. They all change cash and travellers cheques and have 24-hour ATMs. Standard accepts a number of foreign cards including Visa, MasterCard, Cirrus and Maestro. National Bank only accepts Visa.
Victoria Forex Bureau (Map opposite; ☎ 01-821026; www.victoriaforex.com) usually has more competitive rates and charges no commission. You can get a speedy cash advance on your credit card here for a fee of MK500.

POST
Post office (Map opposite; Glyn Jones Rd; ☻ 7.30am-4.30pm Mon-Fri, 8am-10am Sat) Has poste restante and EMS express mail.

TELEPHONE
There are several small phone bureaus around the main bus station and on Glyn Jones Rd outside the Sunbird Mount Soche Hotel from which you can make national calls from MK25.

TOURIST INFORMATION
Immigration office (Map opposite; Government Complex, Victoria Ave) If you need to extend your visa, Blantyre has an immigration office.
Tourist office (Map opposite; ☎ Regional Tourism officer 0888-304362; Government Complex, Victoria Ave; ☻ 7.30am-5pm Mon-Fri) This small office in the Department of Tourism stocks a few leaflets, sells maps of Malawi (MK500) and can offer enthusiastic, though not always that helpful, advice. It's on the 2nd floor.

TRAVEL AGENCIES
Jambo Africa (Map opposite; ☎ 01-823709/835356; www.jambo-africa.com; Sunbird Mount Soche Hotel, Glyn Jones Rd) Offers a wide range of tours and services including day tours in and around Blantyre. A Blantyre cultural tour costs US$75 per person, a day trip to Mua Mission costs US$175 per person, and three-day hiking tours of Mt Mulanje cost US$370 per person. They can also arrange accommodation bookings around the country, car hire, and air and road transfers.
Ulendo Safaris (Map opposite; ☎ 01-820752; www.ulendo.net; 3rd fl, Livingstone Towers, Glyn Jones Rd) Booking agents for Kenya Airways and South African Airways, and offers car hire, transfers and tours. They also own a couple of luxury lodges in Lilongwe and the Satemwa Tea Estate.
Soche Tours and Travel (Map opposite; ☎ 01-820777; www.sochetours.mw; Chayamba Bldg, Victoria Ave) Car hire, transfers, local and international flight bookings, as well as tours of Blantyre and the region.

Dangers & Annoyances
It's not safe to walk around the city alone at night – in particular, there have been reports of muggings on travellers walking

BLANTYRE CITY CENTRE

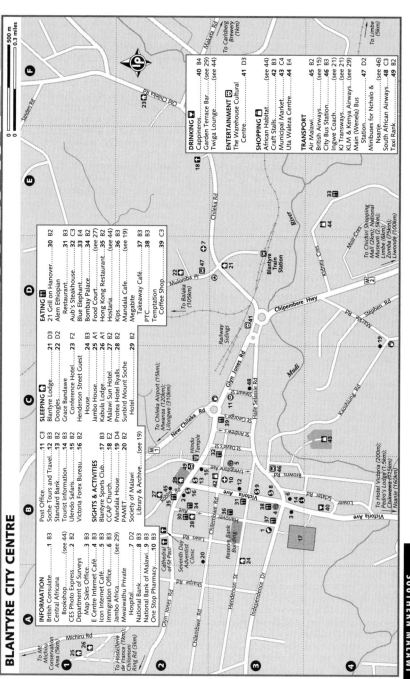

INFORMATION
British Consulate............................1	B3
Central Africana	
Bookshop................................(see 44)	
CES Photo Express...........................2	B2
Department of Surveys	
Map Sales Office........................3	B3
E Centre Internet Café.....................4	B3
Icon Internet Café............................5	B3
Immigration Office...........................6	B3
Jambo Africa..............................(see 29)	
Mwaiwathu Private	
Hospital.....................................7	D2
National Bank...................................8	B3
National Bank of Malawi...................9	B3
One Stop Pharmacy........................10	B3
Post Office......................................11	C3
Soche Tours and Travel..................12	B3
Standard Bank................................13	B2
Tourist Information.........................14	B3
Ulendo Safaris...............................15	B2
Victoria Forex Bureau.....................16	B2

SIGHTS & ACTIVITIES
Blantyre Sports Club.......................17	B3
CCAP Church..................................18	E2
Mandala House...............................19	D4
Society of Malawi	
Library & Archive......................20	B2

SLEEPING
Blantyre Lodge...............................21	D3
Doogles...22	D2
Grace Bandawe	
Conference Hotel.....................23	F2
Henderson Street Guest	
House.....................................24	B3
Jambo House..................................25	A1
Kabula Lodge.................................26	A1
Malawi Sun Hotel...........................27	B2
Protea Hotel Ryalls.........................28	B2
Sunbird Mount Soche	
Hotel.....................................29	B2

EATING
21 Grill on Hanover.......................30	B2
Alem Ethiopian	
Restaurant...............................31	B3
Aub's Steakhouse...........................32	C3
Blue Elephant.................................33	E4
Bombay Palace...............................34	B2
Food Court................................(see 27)	
Hong Kong Restaurant...................35	B2
Hostaria....................................(see 44)	
Kips...36	B3
Mandala Cafe............................(see 19)	
Megabite	
Takeaway Café........................37	B3
PTC...38	B3
Temptation	
Coffee Shop............................39	C3

DRINKING
Cappineros.....................................40	B4
Garden Terrace Bar.....................(see 29)	
Twiga Lounge..........................(see 44)	

ENTERTAINMENT
The Warehouse Cultural	
Centre....................................41	D3

SHOPPING
African Habitat..........................(see 44)	
Craft Stalls.....................................42	B3
Municipal Market...........................43	C4
Uta Waleza Centre.........................44	E4

TRANSPORT
Air Malawi......................................45	B2
British Airways...........................(see 15)	
City Bus Station.............................46	B3
Ingwe Coach............................(see 21)	
KJ Transways.............................(see 21)	
KLM & Kenya Airways................(see 29)	
Main (Wenela) Bus	
Station...................................47	D2
Minibuses for Nchalo &	
Nsanje.................................(see 46)	
South African Airways....................48	C3
Taxi Rank.......................................49	B2

in between Doogles and the city after dark. Always use a taxi after dark. You should also watch out for your valuables when using the busy bus and minibus stations at Blantyre and Limbe.

Sights & Activities

Blantyre's most magnificent building is the red-brick **CCAP Church** (Map p273), officially called St Michael and All Angels Church. The original church was a simple affair, built by Scottish missionary Reverend DC Scott in 1882. It wasn't built to last, however, and in 1888 the missionaries – none of whom had any experience in construction – started work on a new, more impressive church, using only local handmade bricks and wood. It's an impressive feat of elaborate brickwork moulded into arches, buttresses, columns and towers, topped with a grand basilica dome. Inside the church you'll find a number of memorials to people who died during the Mission's early years.

Set-up in the 1990s, **PAMET** (Map p273; ☎ 01-823895; www.pamet.org.mw; 10 Chilembwe Rd; ☒ 10am-5pm Mon-Fri) – the Paper Making Education Trust – started out by training schools to recycle paper to make their own teaching materials. Today, they have a workshop and shop selling stationery, books, photo albums and greetings cards made from a range of different materials including banana bark, recycled paper and even elephant dung. For MK200 you can take a tour of their workshop to see how it's all done.

Malawi's **National Museum** (Map p271; Kasungu Cres; admission MK200; ☒ 7.30am-5pm) is of the small and dusty variety, with a number of not particularly well laid out exhibits documenting the country's wildlife, human evolution and involvement in the slave trade, among other topics. There are some gems here though, including a royal ceremonial stool dating back to the 16th century, and a fascinating display on Gule Wamkulu – an important traditional dance for the Chewa (p252). Lying in the museum grounds are a number of beautiful, rusty relics of Malawi's bygone transport age including an old locomotive dating back to 1904, a decrepit City of Blantyre fire engine and an old Nyasaland Bus.

The museum is midway between Blantyre and Limbe, a 500m walk from the Chichiri Shopping Mall. Take a minibus headed for

Limbe and ask to be let off at the museum. Otherwise a taxi will cost around MK1000.

Beer monsters can head for the **Carlsberg Brewery** (Map p271; ☎ 01-870022; Gomani Rd), east of the centre. Every Wednesday at 2.30pm, the brewery lays on free tours, which have to be booked in advance. You'll be told all about the brewing process after which you'll be rewarded with a free tasting session. Some places to stay in Blantyre will arrange transport here. Alternatively, you can walk or get a taxi.

Mandala House (Map p273; ☎ 01-871932; off Kaoshiung Rd; ☒ 8.30am-4.30pm Mon-Fri, 8.30am-1pm Sat) is the oldest building standing in Malawi and was built back in 1882 as a home for the managers of the Mandala Trading Company. It's a quietly grand colonial house, encased in wraparound verandas and set in lovely gardens. Inside the house is a cafe (p273), an art gallery and the **Society of Malawi Library & Archive** (☒ 9am-noon Mon-Fri, 6-7.30pm Thu), which contains a vast number of journals, books and photographs, some dating as far back as the 19th century. You could easily while away a spare afternoon perusing old volumes on politics, history, exploration and wildlife.

To enjoy the country club vibe colonial style head for the **Blantyre Sports Club** (Map p273; ☎ 01-821172/835095; Victoria Ave/Independence Dr), which dates back to 1896. It offers daily membership for MK1200, which allows you to enter the club and use the bar and restaurant (there's a good buffet on Sunday lunchtimes for MK1000 per person). This enables you to use the pool (MK350), to play squash or tennis (MK230) or to play a round of golf (nine holes MK500). Equipment can be hired.

Sleeping

There are a couple of decent options for budget travellers as well as an excellent choice of midrange and top-end accommodation. Most are located near the city centre, though a couple of the budget options are near the main bus station.

BUDGET

Doogles (Map p273; ☎ 01-821128; Mulomba Pl; campsite per person US$5, dm US$8, chalets with shared bathroom US$20, d US$25; ☐) Backpackers can pitch their tents here, and there's also room for a few trucks and cars with tents. The rooms and dorms are decent enough but some of the chalets are looking a little rough, and it's not the most friendly of places. The bar is open to the general public and is always lively – fine if you want to party, not so good if you want to relax or get some sleep.

Limbe Country Club (Map p271; ☎ 01-841145; Livingstone Ave, Limbe; camping per person MK1000) An alternative for those with wheels. Here you can park and camp on the edge of the playing fields. Rates include club membership, so you can use the showers and restaurant inside.

Kabula Lodge (Map p273; ☎ 01-821216; www .kabulalodge.co.mw; Kabula Hill; dm/s/d with shared bathroom US$10/15/30, r with bathroom US$40; 🖥 🛜) In a quiet suburb northwest of the city centre, off Michiru Rd, this is a homely spot with a selection of spotless dorms, singles and doubles, and it's very popular with long-stay volunteers. There's a TV lounge and a self-catering kitchen, or tasty meals can be prepared if given enough advance notice. Rates include breakfast. Best of all though are the magical views over the hills from the wraparound veranda.

Blantyre Lodge (Map p273; ☎ 01-834460; Chileka Rd; s/d from MK3500/5000; 🚗) This large hotel near the bus station has secure, bright rooms with TV, air-con and spic-and-span bathrooms. They usually have space so it's a good option for early morning bus takers. There can be a bit of noise from the street at night though.

Henderson Street Guest House (Map p273; ☎ 01-823474/794572; 19 Henderson St; r from MK4650) A relaxing and cosy guesthouse shielded from the street by a peaceful, flower-filled garden. The rooms are all in good nick and have spacious bathrooms and DSTV. Rates include a huge breakfast.

Grace Bandawe Conference Hotel (Map p273; ☎ 01-834267; Old Chileka Rd; s/d/ste MK4200/5400/6000) Set in large gardens away from the noise of the city, this is a popular place for conferences and is more Malawian in flavour then some of the other budget places in town. Rooms are very clean and brightened up by shiny bedspreads and lace curtains. There's a lounge where you can watch DSTV and meals are available (three-course meal MK1550).

MIDRANGE & TOP END
Hostellerie de France (off Map p273; ☎ 01-869626; www.hostellerie-de-france.com; cnr Chilomoni Ring Rd & Kazuni Cl; studio from US$40, r from US$50, apt from

US$100; 🖥 🛜 🖼) You'll find everything you need here, from dorms, to executive doubles to apartments and studios, and there are discounts for long stayers. The swimming pool (and attached Jacuzzi!) looks out across the valley to Mt Ndirande and there's a restaurant with a pretty sophisticated menu (garlic mussels, goose-liver pâté, rabbit in white wine and mustard) and excellent French wines. They can also organise great-value car rental.

Jambo House (Map p273; ☎ 01-823709; www .jambo-africa.com; Kabula Hill; s with/without bathroom US$55/50, d with/without bathroom US$90/80; 🖥 🛜 🖼) Owned by Jambo Africa and popular with long stayers, this little house has a large, comfortable lounge, swimming pool and top views of Mt Ndirande. The rooms are a bit of a let down though, and the bathrooms in particular are showing signs of wear – it's pretty overpriced for what you get. You can help yourself to drinks from the honesty bar and, if you order in advance, the staff will cook you a meal and serve it in the dining area or in your room. But be warned, even with advance notice the service can be excruciatingly slow. All prices include a very hearty breakfast.

Pedro's Lodge (off Map p273; ☎ 01-833430; www .pedroslodge.com; 9 Smythe Rd, Sunnyside; s/d US$70/100; 🖼 🖥 🛜 🖼) Book in advance to stay at this small, family-run guesthouse where you'll immediately feel welcome. Eight clean, comfortable rooms with DSTV look out onto a small swimming pool and lush green lawn. The cosy restaurant is reminiscent of a Parisian bistro and serves really delicious meals.

Malawi Sun Hotel (Map p273; ☎ 01-824808; Robins Rd; s/d from US$100/120; 🖼 🖥 🛜) A self-confessed 'safari-style' joint that houses its rooms in two-storey blocks or small chalets and decks them out with solid wooden beds, animal-print chairs and curtains. It makes use of beautiful views over the surrounding hills with several strategically placed benches and an open lounge complete with balcony. The on-site Aamari restaurant serves everything from pasta and curries to beef stew and *nshima* (mains MK750 to MK2800) and there's also a fast-food court. At the time of writing they were constructing a new swimming pool and bar area.

Hotel Victoria (off Map p273; ☎ 01-823500; www .hotelvictoriamw.com; Victoria Ave; s/d US$120/150, ste from

US$150; 🛏 💻 🅿) Another top-end choice, this place looks rather like a Travelodge from the outside but things improve once inside. Rooms are relatively spacious with floral-themed furnishings, crisp linen and good bathrooms.

Sunbird Moche Soche Hotel (Map p273; ☎ 01-620588; mountsoche@sunbirdmalawi.com; Glyn Jones Rd; s/d US$140/170; 🛏 💻 🛜 🅿) This is a popular business hotel and is bursting with the requisite facilities. It's perhaps not such a good deal for tourists though; the rooms are looking rather tired and aren't great value. If you do stay, plump for a room at a back: they have balconies with grand views over the hills.

Protea Hotel Ryalls (Map p273; ☎ 01-820955; ryalls@proteamalawi.com; 2 Hanover Ave; s/d US$215/245; 💻 🛜 🅿) Ryalls is the oldest established hotel in Malawi. It opened in 1922 and was a legendary stop for travellers on the Cape-to-Cairo route. The hotel has since grown and there's a less atmospheric new wing, but the original building has been renovated with old-fashioned flair and the plush rooms and communal areas are full of black-and-white photographs telling tales of old. They also run the superb 21 Grill on Hanover next door.

Eating

Blantyre has a good selection of places to eat to suit all budgets, and the widest variety available in Malawi.

RESTAURANTS

Alem Ethiopian Restaurant (Map p273; ☎ 01-822529; Victoria Ave; dishes MK300-800; 🕐 8am-5pm Mon-Sat) Delicious *injera* (sour millet pancake) and *doro wot* (chicken with hot pepper sauce) are on the menu here, but you can also have a plate of bland old chicken and chips or beef stew if you so desire.

Blue Elephant (Map p273; ☎ 0999-965850; Kidney Cres, Ginnery Cnr; mains from MK950; 🕐 noon-late) Very popular pub and restaurant with both the expat and Malawian crowd. Solid food such as baked potatoes, burgers and apple pie is available all day long; after you've eaten you could stay on to listen to one of the local bands that plays regularly or for the Saturday night disco.

Hong Kong Restaurant (Map p273; ☎ 01-820859; Robins Rd; mains MK700-1200; 🕐 noon-2pm & 6-10pm Tue-Sun) This popular restaurant sits in a

large red-and-white, pagoda-style building within a large car park. The theme continues within – large Chinese lanterns hang from an elaborately carved, red wooden ceiling, and there are a couple of elegant private rooms. Food is good, and comes in generous portions – alongside the usual sweet and sour and spring rolls you'll find chicken with peanuts and whole chillies, and fried chicken gizzards.

Hostaria (Map p273; ☎ 0888 282828; Uta Waleza Centre, Kidney Cres; mains from MK1200; 🕐 noon-2pm & 7-9.30pm Mon-Sat) Yummy home made pastas and pizzas are on the menu at this well loved Italian restaurant as well daily chalkboard meat and fish specials. The decor is pretty sweet too, with high ceilings, a mezzanine floor and funky chandeliers made out of coke bottles.

ourpick Mandala Cafe (Map p273; Mackie Rd; light meals MK1200; 🕐 8.30am-4.30pm Mon-Fri, 8.30am-12.30pm Sat; 🛜) Sit on a breezy stone terrace or in the garden at a table fashioned from a tree trunk in the grounds of Mandala House (p274) at this chilled cafe. There are swings and a see-saw to keep the kids happy, a selection of tourist leaflets and magazines to browse, and a speedy wi-fi hotspot. Regulars love the freshly brewed coffee, iced tea and homemade 'cakes of the day' (MK500), but you can also get savoury snacks and main meals.

Bombay Palace (Map p273; ☎ 0888-400400/600600, Hanover Ave; mains MK1200-2000; 🕐 noon-1.45pm Tue-Sun, 6.30-10pm daily; 🛜) Head here for fresh, delicately spiced Indian food – the best in town. Dishes such as sizzling mutton and chicken lollipops (deep-fried chicken with chilli and garlic) are served in a chic dining room lined with Indian paintings.

Aub's Steakhouse (Map p273; ☎ 0999-960628/ 966507; Livingstonia Bldg, Chilembwe Rd; mains MK1750-2300; 🕐 noon-2pm & 7-10pm Mon-Sat; 💻 🛜) Hankering after a huge hunk of dead cow or some finger lickin' ribs? Mosey on down here and you'll be rewarded with a meat-, cheese- and carb-laden menu, all served up in the shadow of cowboy hat, saddle and horseshoe-adorned walls. For the faint-hearted there are 'ladies' or 'low-carb' portions. There's also a cartoon-themed children's play area.

21 Grill on Hanover (Map p273; ☎ 01-820955; Protea Hotel Ryalls; Hanover Ave; mains around MK2900; 🕐 noon-2pm & 6.30-10pm) Folks say this is the poshest restaurant in Blantyre (or, as the staff like to boast, in the whole of Malawi) and it's hard to disagree. The restaurant is all soft upholstered chairs, book-lined walls and leather armchairs, and gentle piano music accompanies your excellent grilled meats and seafood. It feels a little as if you're secreted away in some traditional, exclusive gentleman's club. You'll have to pay for the privilege though.

FOOD STALLS & CAFES
Kips (Map p273; ☎ 01-635247; Hanover Ave; breakfast MK300, dishes MK200-1000; ☺ 7am-10pm Sun-Thu, 8am-midnight Fri & Sat) Kips dishes up a real mix of pizzas, burgers, fish, steak, Malawian and Indian meals. It's clean and deservedly popular with locals.

Temptation Coffee Shop (Map p273; Glyn Jones Rd; dishes MK300-400; ☺ 8.30am-6pm) You can pick up a samosa from behind the counter or take a seat for frothy milkshakes, coffee or main meals of *nshima* and stew, fish and chips, and the odd curry. Clean, friendly and good value.

Megabite Takeaway Café (Map p273; ☎ 01-824221; Independence Dr; dishes MK300-500; ☺ 11am-9pm) This courtyard cafe brings a bit of the countryside into the city with plants and tree trunks mixing with the plastic tables. Eat healthy plates of stew or fried *chambo* and chips, play a game of pool (MK100 per game) or just pop in for a drink. There are plans to extend the opening hours to midnight.

Food Court (Map p273; Malawi Sun Hotel, Robins Rd; dishes around MK500; ☺ 10am-10pm) A popular collection of fast-food outlets grouped round a raised patio with fabulous views over the hills. Choices include Blue Savannah, which serves fried chicken, shawarmas, burgers and salads for around MK500, or ice-cream parlour Scoops and Shakes, where can get your favourite chocolate bar whizzed into a milkshake for MK550.

Jungle Pepper (Map p271; ☎ 0888-826229, 0999-826229; www.junglepepperpizza.com; pizzas MK1100-1400; ☺ 10.30am-2.30pm & 4.30-8.30pm) This popular take-away pizza shop shares a big shaded courtyard at the Chichiri Shopping Mall with a number of other fast-food joints. Toppings veer toward the exotic, such as peri peri and mango chicken. You can also buy pizza by the slice for MK400.

SELF-CATERING
The main **PTC** (Map p273; Victoria Ave) Supermarket sells food and other goods, much of it imported from South Africa or Europe and

sold at similar prices. There are also huge **Shoprite** (Map p271; Chichiri Shopping Cente, Kamuzu Hwy) and **Game** (Map p271; Chichiri Shopping Cente, Kamuzu Hwy) supermarkets a few kilometres out of town.

Drinking
Cappineros (Map p273; ☎ 0999-939260; Victoria Ave) A lively, friendly pub with a large beer garden that puts on regular music and themed events. You can play pool here or watch big-name sports, and solid grub is available. It's next to the Kairo International Casino. Look for the sign – it's down the drive.

Twiga Lounge (Map p273; ☎ 0999-966507; Uta Waleza Centre, Kidney Cres) This bar and nightclub is popular with young expats and Malawian professionals who come here to down cocktails and dance to the country's top DJs. Regular theme nights include School Disco.

Garden Terrace Bar (Map p273; Sunbird Mount Soche Hotel) Catering to a more sophisticated market, its tranquil surrounds are appealing. At the same hotel, the Sportsman's Bar is favoured by local businessmen and other movers and shakers.

Entertainment
Warehouse Cultural Centre (Map p273; www .thewarehouse-malawi.net) Wedged between the railway line and a major roundabout, this former depot now consists of a soundproofed theatre, cafe and bar. It's one of the country's most exciting venues and a staunch supporter of Malawian music, art, dance, theatre and literature. The owners organise a diverse timetable including regular poetry readings, comedy shows, screenings, writing workshops and live-music events featuring the best Malawian music has to offer.

French Cultural Centre (Map p271; ☎ 01-871250; direction@ccfmw.org; cnr Moi Rd & Kasungu Cres; ☺ 8am-noon & 2-5.30pm Mon-Fri, 8am-noon Sat) The centre has an excellent and varied programme of concerts, plays and readings.

Cine City Cinema (Map p271; ☎ 01-912873; Chichiri Shopping Cente; tickets MK1000 Mon-Thu, MK1200 Fri-Sun; ☺ closed Tue) Big-name films are shown at 5.30pm and 8pm daily with an extra 2.30pm showing at the weekend. It's in the basement of the Chichiri Shopping Mall, underneath Game supermarket.

Both the Blantyre Sports Club and the Limbe Country Club feature regular live music. Occasional live music is played at both the Sunbird Mount Soche Hotel and Protea Hotel Ryalls.

Blantyre's main sports venue is the **Chichiri Stadium** (Map p271, off Makata Rd) between the city centre and Limbe. This is also Malawi's national stadium; international football and other events are held here. There's no regular programme but matches are advertised in the newspaper and on billboards around town.

Shopping

There are a number of **craft stalls** on Chilembwe Rd. The work on sale is excellent and browsing is refreshingly hassle free. The more chaotic **Municipal Market** (Map p273; Kaoshiung Rd) is also worth a visit. For high-end craft hunters, **African Habitat** (Map p273; ☎ 01873642; Uta Waleza Shopping Centre, Kidney Cres; ⏰ 7.30am-4.30pm Mon-Fri, 8am-noon Sat) is a good bet – it's a cavernous boutique crammed full of furniture, jewellery, sculpture, art, textiles and books. Two kilometres out of town is the **Chichiri Shopping Mall** (Map p271; Kamuzu Hwy), which has bookshops, pharmacies, boutiques and large Shoprite and Game supermarkets.

For buying print film, getting digital photos printed or passport photos taken, there is **CES Photo Express** (Map p273; Glyn Jones Rd; ⏰ 7.30am-5pm Mon-Fri, 8am-1pm Sat).

Getting There & Away
AIR
Blantyre's Chileka airport is about 15km north of the city centre. For details on the airport and flights to/from Blantyre see p300 and p303. Airline offices in Blantyre include:
Air Malawi (Map p273; ☎ 01-820811; Robins Rd; 7.30am-4.30pm Mon-Fri, 8am-noon Sat)
British Airways (Map p273; ☎ 01-824333/519; Livingstone Towers, Glyn Jones Rd)
KLM & Kenya Airways (Map p273; ☎ 01-824524; Sunbird Mount Soche Hotel)
South African Airways (Map p273; ☎ 01-820627; Nico House, Stewart St)

BUS & MINIBUS
Blantyre's main bus station for long-distance buses is Wenela Bus Station (Map p273; Mulomba Pl), east of the centre. National Bus Company and AXA City Trouper buses run from here to Lilongwe (MK1200, four hours) Mzuzu (MK2000, nine to 10 hours), Monkey Bay (MK890,

five to six hours) via Zomba (MK350, 1½ to two hours) and Mangochi (MK650, four to five hours), Mulanje (MK400, 1½ hours) and Karonga (MK2800, 14 hours).

AXA Executive coaches depart from the **Automotive Centre** (Map p271; Ginnery Cnr), where you'll also find their ticket office, and call at the Chichiri Shopping Mall and the car park outside Blantyre Lodge (near the main bus station) before departing the city. They leave twice daily to Lilongwe (MK3100, four hours).

Long-distance minibuses go from the bus station in Limbe; most leave on a fill-up-and-go basis. It's often quicker to get a local minibus to Limbe bus station and then a long-distance bus or 'half-bus' from there rather than wait for AXA or other bus services in Blantyre. Routes include Zomba (MK390, one hour), Mulanje (MK450, 1¼ hours), Mangochi (MK950) and the border at Muloza (MK750, 1½ hours).

Long-distance minibuses to the Lower Shire including Nchalo (MK400, two hours) and Nsanje (MK850, four hours) leave from the City Bus Station near Victoria Ave in Blantyre.

The car park next to Blantyre Lodge is the pick-up and drop-off point for long-distance bus companies headed for Jo'burg. **Ingwe Coach** (☎ 01-822313) goes to Jo'burg at 8.30am on Tuesday and Sunday (MK15,000, 25 hours). **KJ Transways** (☎ 01-914017) leaves for Jo'burg on Tuesday and Saturday at 7am (MK13,500, 25 hours).

TRAIN
For information on trains that stop at Blantyre and Limbe, see p302 and p306.

Getting Around
TO/FROM THE AIRPORT
A taxi from the airport to the city costs around MK2000, but agree on a price with the driver first. The price can be negotiated down a bit if you're going from the city to the airport. If your budget doesn't include taxis, frequent local buses between the City Bus Station and Chileka Township pass the airport gate. The fare is MK100.

BUS
Blantyre is a compact city, so it's unlikely you'll need to use public transport to get around, apart from the minibuses that

shuttle along Chipembere Hwy between Blantyre city centre bus station and Limbe bus station. The one-way fare is MK80.

TAXI
You can find private-hire taxis at the Sunbird Mount Soche Hotel or at the bus stations. A taxi across the city centre costs around MK500; between the centre and the main bus station costs from MK600; and from Blantyre to Limbe costs around MK1200.

AROUND BLANTYRE
Blantyre is surrounded by three 'mountains' – Michiru, Soche and Ndirande – all actually large hills that can be hiked to the summit. Some hikers have been attacked on **Mt Ndirande**, so you should only go here with a guide. You should be able to arrange this at your accommodation for around MK1000 per day. The path up **Mt Soche** starts at Soche Secondary School.

Mt Michiru Conservation Area
If you have a day to spare you could head for the nature trails at **Mt Michiru** (admission per person/car MK50/200), 8km northwest of the city. It's good for birdwatching, with over 400 species recorded here, and resident animals include monkeys, klipspringers and even leopards, though you're unlikely to see any of them. It's still a pleasant place to spend a few hours, however, with beautiful views all around. Particularly lovely is the picnic

area overlooking the city, with seats carved out of the rock on a bluff at the edge of the mountain. You might also notice a huge cross on the side of the hill – the Way of the Cross Roman Catholics march up the mountain on a pilgrimage every Easter.

To reach the **visitor centre** (where the trails start), take Kabula Hill Rd from the city and Michiru Rd through a select suburb and then a township. At the end of the sealed road (3km from Blantyre) a dirt road leads along the eastern foot of the mountain. Take the left turn signposted 'nature trails', which leads you to a green gate from where you'll be directed to the reception further up the hill. After you've paid the entry fees they can give you a map or will arrange a guide for you at no extra charge (though a tip of about MK200 is appropriate). There's no public transport, but you could get a taxi as far as the driver is prepared to go along the dirt road – that won't get you very far though – the road is terrible, especially after the rains, and much better attempted in a 4WD. What's more, there are very few visitors so you'd have trouble getting a lift back.

Fisherman's Rest
Fisherman's Rest (☎ 0888-836753; www.fishermans rest.net; adult/child MK300/150) is a nature reserve, lodge and cafe, and makes a good place to stop off on the way down to the Lower Shire or as a day trip from Blantyre. The reserve is open from sunrise to sunset and has several attractive nature trails; although

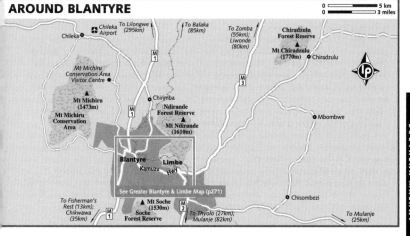

AROUND BLANTYRE

0 — 5 km
0 — 3 miles

Chileka ◯ Chileka Airport To Lilongwe (295km)
To Balaka (85km)
To Zomba (55km); Liwonde (80km)
Chiradzulu Forest Reserve
▲ Mt Chiradzulu (1770m) ◯ Chiradzulu

Mt Michiru Conservation Area Visitor Centre ●

M1

M3

▲ Mt Michiru (1473m)
Mt Michiru Conservation Area

◯ Chirimba
Ndirande Forest Reserve
M1
▲ Mt Ndirande (1610m)

◯ Mbombwe

Blantyre ◆— Limbe
Kamuzu Hwy

See Greater Blantyre & Limbe Map (p271)

◯ Chisombezi

To Fisherman's Rest (13km); Chikwawa (35km)
▲ Mt Soche (1530m)
M1 Soche Forest Reserve
M2 To Thyolo (27km); Mulanje (82km)

To Mulanje (25km)

you're not likely to see many animals other than a few antelopes, the surroundings are beautiful and the views out over the Rift Valley awesome.

SLEEPING & EATING

If you want to stay the night there's a cosy **lodge** (per night US$180 plus per person supplement of US$25, dinner US$15) sleeping six that can be rented out in its entirety. It has three bedrooms, a farmhouse-style kitchen and a fantastic lounge area complete with huge stone fireplace. It's set in an acre of gardens. Inside the reserve itself is the **Woodland Cottage** (per person US$40) with en suite rooms and a family apartment opening out onto a veranda. For those with a more rustic bent, hidden deep in the bush are wooden stilted **bush camp hides** (per person US$40) with twin beds, private bathroom facilities and stunning views over the valley from their verandas.

Below the lodge is the **Old Mill Tea House** (snacks from MK100, meals from MK750; ☎ 9am-6pm). You can sit on the cafe's veranda or take a pew on a table and chairs made from old tree trunks to sample delicious homemade soups and cakes, as well as substantial meals such as Thai curries and lasagne. When you're done you can swing on an old tyre, climb up the tree house, wander the terraced gardens or just soak up the view. If you don't want to eat at the cafe you can bring your own picnic for MK500/250 per adult/child. Entry to th nature reserve is free for customers, an homely accommodation is available at th Tea House for US$40 per person per nigh including breakfast (though unfortunatel none of the rooms have views).

MULANJE

Hear 'Mulanje' and most travellers wil automatically think of the mountain – an indeed this lively small town sits right i its shadow. However, Mulanje is also at th centre of the country's tea-growing industr and the surrounding slopes and fields are covered with vivid green tea leaves. Ther are two parts to Mulanje. If coming from th direction of Blantyre, which most traveller are, you'll first hit the **Chitakale Trading Centre** (where the dirt road to Likhubula turns of the main sealed Blantyre–Mulanje road) Here you'll find the Mulanje Infocentre, PTC and two petrol stations. Continue fo 2km to Mulanje town where you'll find the main bus station, hotels and banks.

Sleeping

Council Resthouse (r with/without bathroom MK500/300 Close to the bus station, Council Resthouse is bargain basement in price and quality.

MALAWI'S CUP OF TEA

South and east of Blantyre, on the rolling hills of the Shire Highlands, the climate is ideal for growing tea, and the area is covered with plantations (or 'estates'). The first tea bushes were imported from India during the early days of the Nyasaland colony, and the tea production quickly became a major industry. It's now a major export crop (along with tobacco and sugar), providing thousands of people with jobs.

As you travel along the main road between Limbe and Mulanje, the hills on either side are covered with a patchwork of vibrant green tea fields dotted with dense pockets of deep-green pine and palms. The tea-pickers (men and women) work methodically through the lines of bushes, picking just a few leaves and a bud from the top of each and throwing them into large baskets on their backs. At the end of each shift the baskets are taken to a collection area where they are weighed and each worker's wages are calculated. The leaves are then transported to a tea factory where they are trimmed and dried before being packed in bags and boxes ready for export. A small proportion of low-quality tea stays within the country to be sold locally.

If you have a genuine interest in tea production it may be possible to arrange a tour of an estate and factory. There is no established set-up; you simply call the estate and ask a senior manager if it's possible to visit. You'll probably need your own vehicle, or have to take a taxi, as most estate offices are off the main road and difficult to reach by public transport. The best place to start with is **Satemwa Tea Estate** (☎ 01-473233/500; www.satemwa.com) near the small town of Thyolo (*cho*-low) on the main road between Limbe and Mulanje. Otherwise the Mulanje Infocentre (p282) at the Chitakale Trading Centre can organise tours of local estates.

Mulanje Motel (☎ 01-466245; r with/without bathroom MK800/550) Heading closer to Likhubula on the main road, Mulanje Motel is a much better budget option.

Mulanje View (☎ 01-466348; s/d with shared bathroom MK1000/2000, r with bathroom MK2500). Small cell-like rooms share spotless ablutions at this rambling place opposite the Mulanje Mountain Conservation Trust. To maximise your space go for one of the self-contained room, which are marginally bigger. There is a bar/restaurant (serving plates of the usual *nshima* and meat for around MK450) and the garden is dotted with little thatched gazebos for chilling out in.

Limbani Lodge (☎ 01-466390; standard r MK1000, VIP s/d MK3000/3500) While the standard rooms are poky, miserable and hidden down a long, dark corridor, VIP rooms are light, with plenty of space and small kitchenettes. They are clustered around a sandy courtyard with dramatic mountain views as a backdrop. Take the turning opposite the bus station near the school for the blind.

Kara O' Mula (☎ 01-466515; www.karaomula.com; s/d MK5850/7600, executive s/d MK7050/8800; ☙) Hidden up a dirt road at the foot of the mountain, Kara O' Mula – with its leafy grounds, large swimming pool (fed by fresh water from a small waterfall) and wide terrace restaurant – is a perfect place to relax after a hard day's hiking. Rooms in the main building are perfectly pleasant but best are the wood chalets just up the hill, which have bamboo four-poster beds, wooden log shelves and vaulted thatch ceilings. Very good meals are available from MK1100 and there are two bars, one by the pool and one log cabin–style affair right by the restaurant.

Getting There & Away

AXA buses go to/from Blantyre (MK400, 1½ hours), as do minibuses (MK450, 1¼ hours). If you're heading for the border with Mozambique, minibuses and *matolas* run to Muloza (MK300, 30 minutes). For more border crossing information, see p302.

MT MULANJE

A huge hulk of twisted granite rising majestically from the surrounding plains, Mt Mulanje (also called the Mulanje Plateau) towers over 3000m high. All over the mountain are dense green valleys and rivers that drop from sheer cliffs to form dazzling waterfalls. The locals call it the 'Island in the Sky' and on misty days (and there are many of those) it's easy to see why – the mountain is shrouded in a cotton-wool haze, and its highest peaks burst through the cloud to touch the heavens.

Mulanje measures about 30km from west to east and 25km from north to south, with an area of at least 600 sq km. On its north-eastern corner is the outlier Mchese Mountain, separated from the main massif by the Fort Lister Gap. The massif is composed of several bowl-shaped river basins, separated by rocky peaks and ridges. The highest peak is Sapitwa (3001m), the highest point in Malawi and in all Southern Africa north of the Drakensberg. There are other peaks on the massif above 2500m and you can reach most of the summits without technical climbing.

The mountain's lower slopes are covered in pine, eucalyptus and miombo woodland. Get a little higher and you'll find wild moorland crowned with a healthy scattering of wildflowers. Of particular note is the endemic Mulanje cedar, which can grow up to 40m high. There's plenty of wildlife on the mountain too – pint-sized antelopes called klipspringers, vervet monkeys and rock hyraxes are all seen regularly, and birdlife includes black eagles, buzzards and kestrels.

Some people come to the base of the mountain just for a day visit, but the stunning scenery, easy access, clear paths and well-maintained huts make Mulanje a fine hiking area and many travellers spend at least a few days here.

MALAWI'S ADVENTURE SPORT

Taking place July each year, the **Mt Mulanje Porters' Race** follows a gruelling, rocky route over the country's highest peak. When it first got going more than 10 years ago it was only open to porters and guides, but these days anyone can take part. Starting at the Likhubula Forestry Office, participants run up 25km of rugged terrain to the Chambe and Lichenya Plateaus and then back again, reaching 2500m above sea level at the highest point of the race. In 2009 around 450 people took part, and the fastest completion time was a staggering two hours and five minutes. If you think you can handle it, see www.mountmulanje.org.mw.

SOUTHERN MALAWI

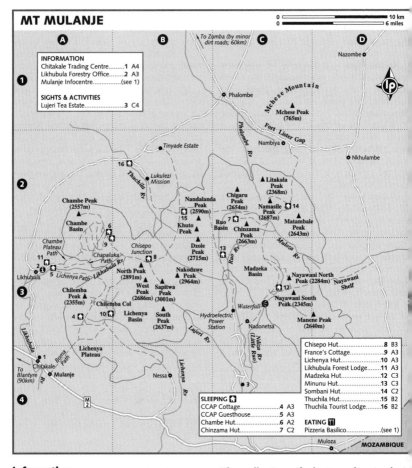

MT MULANJE

0 ——————— 10 km
0 ——————— 6 miles

INFORMATION
Chitakale Trading Centre.........**1** A4
Likhubula Forestry Office........**2** A3
Mulanje Infocentre................(see 1)

SIGHTS & ACTIVITIES
Lujeri Tea Estate.....................**3** C4

Chisepo Hut.......................**8** B3
France's Cottage..................**9** A3
Lichenya Hut.....................**10** A3
Likhubula Forest Lodge.......**11** A3
Madzeka Hut.....................**12** C3
Minunu Hut.......................**13** C3
Sombani Hut......................**14** C2
Thuchila Hut.....................**15** B2
Thuchila Tourist Lodge........**16** B2

SLEEPING
CCAP Cottage.....................**4** A3
CCAP Guesthouse................**5** A3
Chambe Hut........................**6** A2
Chinzama Hut.....................**7** C2

EATING
Pizzeria Basilico..................(see 1)

Information
Hiking on Mt Mulanje is controlled by the **Likhubula Forestry Office** (PO Box 50, Mulanje; 7.30am-noon & 1-5pm), at the small village of Likhubula, about 15km north of Mulanje town. Entry fees are MK100 per person; vehicle entry fee costs MK200 and the forestry office car park is MK100 a day. The friendly and helpful staff can arrange guides and porters from an official list. You must register here and make reservations for the mountain huts (you can also call or write in advance). Camping is permitted only near huts and only when they're full. Open fires are not allowed – this is especially important during the latter part of the dry season when there is a serious fire risk.

The collecting of plants and animals is forbidden.

Also good for information is the **Mulanje Infocentre** (☎ 01-466466/506, infomulanje@malawi.net) based at Chitakale Trading Centre, on the corner of Phalombe Rd. It's set up to give travellers all pertinent information about hiking on the mountain and carries a good selection of books and maps. They also rent out sleeping bags (per day MK500), thermal sleeping pads (per day MK250) and tents (per day MK700). They can also arrange mountain guides and porters. Tours to the nearby Dziwe la Nkhalamba waterfall (MK1300) and to the Lujeri and Mulli Brothers tea estates (per person US$15) are also arranged. They told us that

CHAMBE–LICHENYA LOOP

This short but beautiful route is not an officially named trail, but we give it this title and recommend it for a good taste of Mulanje if you haven't got time for a traverse of the whole massif. It starts and finishes at Likhubula Forestry Office, and takes three days and two nights, but it could be shortened to two days.

Likhubula Forestry Office to Chambe Hut

This stage is the same as the first stage of the Mulanje traverse (p284).

Chambe Hut to Lichenya Basin

This stage is four to five hours. Heading east from Chambe Hut (towards Thuchila), turn right at a junction about 1½ hours from Chambe Hut to reach the Lichenya Basin, and either the CCAP Cottage or Lichenya Hut.

Lichenya Basin to Likhubula Forestry Office

This stage is four to five hours. Go across a col to the east of Chilemba Peak (you could sidetrack up here for fine views – allow two hours return) then descend through beautiful forest to eventually reach Likhubula.

there are plans to develop rock climbing and abseiling tours on the mountain in the near future.

There is nowhere to buy food on Mt Mulanje so you must carry all you need. At Likhubula there's a small market, but you're better off getting supplies at Chitakale, which has shops, stalls and a small supermarket, or in Blantyre.

GUIDEBOOKS & MAPS

The *Guide to Mulanje Massif,* by Frank Eastwood, has information on ascent routes and main peaks plus a large section on rock climbing, but nothing on the routes between huts.

If you need detailed maps, the Department of Surveys prints a map of the mountain at 1:40,000, which shows most of the paths and huts. The 1:30,000 *Tourist Map of Mulanje* covers a similar area, overprinted with extra information for hikers. Both these maps cost MK650 and are usually available from the Department of Surveys Map Sales Offices in Lilongwe (p205) and Blantyre (p271), but stocks occasionally run dry.

GUIDES & PORTERS

Porters are not obligatory but they make the hiking easier, especially for the first day's steep hike from the Likhubula Forestry Office. Guides are definitely recommended to help you through the maze of paths.

As you arrive in Likhubula (or Mulanje town) you'll no doubt be approached by hopeful locals looking for work, but you should arrange guides and porters only at Likhubula as the forest station keeps a registered list, which works on a rotation system. Some porters are not on the list but are 'cleared' by the office staff.

There is a standard charge of around MK1000 per day per porter and MK1300 per guide (regardless of group size). The total fee for the whole trip should be agreed before departure and put in writing. Fees are paid at the end of the trip but porters are expected to provide their own food, so about 25% may be required in advance. You may want to tip your porters and guides if the service has been good; a rule of thumb is to pay something around an extra day's wage for every three to five days. The maximum weight each porter can carry is 18kg.

HIKING ROUTES

There are about six main routes up and down Mulanje. The three main ascent routes go from Likhubula: the Chambe Plateau Path (also called the Skyline Path), the Chapaluka Path and the Lichenya Path. Other routes, more often used for the descent, are: Thuchila (*chu*-chila) Hut to Lukulezi Mission; Sombani Hut to Fort Lister Gap; and Minunu Hut to the Lujeri Tea Estate.

SOUTHERN MALAWI

Once you're on the massif, a network of paths links the huts and peaks, and many different permutations are possible; we outline some choices in the boxed text below. Be warned that some of the routes are impassable or otherwise dangerous. The route from Madzeka Hut to Lujeri is very steep, for example, as are the Boma Path and the path from Lichenya to Nessa on the southwestern side of Mulanje.

As a rough guide, it takes anything from two to six hours to hike between one hut and the next, which means you can walk in the morning, dump your kit, then go out to explore a nearby peak or valley in the afternoon.

A MULANJE TRAVERSE

There are many ways to traverse the Mulanje massif. The route we describe briefly here, from Likhubula to Fort Lister Gap, is one of several options, although it seems to be the most popular. It can be done in four days, but there are several variations that can extend this period and plenty of opportunities for sidetracking.

Likhubula Forestry Office to Chambe Hut

There are two options: the Chambe Plateau Path, which is short and steep (two to four hours), and the Chapaluka Path (3½ to five hours), which is less steep and more scenic. From the hut veranda, there are good views of the southeastern face of Chambe Peak (2557m), but if you fancy reaching the summit of this spectacular peak, from Chambe Hut it will take you five to seven hours to get to the top and back. The ascent is stiff and the paths are vague, so you may need a guide. About two to 2½ hours from the hut, you reach a large cairn on a broad, level part of the ridge at the foot of the main face. You might be happy with reaching this point, which offers excellent views over the Chambe Basin to the escarpment edge and the plains far below.

Chambe Hut to Chisepo or Thuchila Hut

This route is 12km (five to six hours). About two hours from Chambe, you reach Chisepo Junction, where a path leads up to the summit of Sapitwa Peak (3001m). You can hike to the summit of Sapitwa but it's a toughie – not surprisingly, perhaps, Sapitwa means 'Don't Go There' in the local language – and the upper section involves some tricky scrambling among large boulders and dense vegetation. From Chisepo Junction you should allow three to five hours for the ascent, plus two to four for the descent. You can then either spend the night at Chisepo Hut or push on through to either Chambe or Thuchila Hut. If you're short of time, you can do a shorter loop by descending from Thuchila Hut to Lukulezi Mission, then hiking or catching a *matola* back to Likhubula.

Thuchila Hut to Sombani Hut

This stage (12km, four to five hours) takes you across a small col and down into the Ruo Basin. About two hours from Thuchila Hut, you reach Chinzama Hut, where you can stop if you want an easy day. The large mountain directly opposite Sombani Hut is Namasile (2687m), which takes about three hours to ascend, plus two hours on the descent. The path is steep and strenuous in places, spiralling round the northern side of the mountain to approach the summit from the west. A guide is recommended unless you're competent on vague paths in bad weather.

Sombani Hut to Fort Lister Gap

This stage (5km, three hours) is all downhill, with great views over the surrounding plains. There are a lot of forks, so a guide is useful to show you the way, otherwise, at every fork keep going down. For the last section you follow a dirt track, past Fort Lister Forest Station, from where it's another 8km along the dirt road to Phalombe village. There's little or no traffic, so you'll have to hike (about two hours), but it's pleasant enough. Most porters include this stretch in the fee you pay for the final day.

From Phalombe there are one or two buses a day back to Likhubula or Mulanje (MK200, one hour) and there should be plenty of *matola* (MK250).

Dangers & Annoyances

Hikers should remember that Mulanje is a big mountain with notoriously unpredictable weather. After periods of heavy rain, streams can become swollen and impassable – do not try to cross them! Wait until the flood subsides (sometimes after a few hours) or adjust your route to cross in safety further upstream. Also, be aware that much of the mountain's granite surface can become very slippery and dangerous when wet. Even during the dry season, it's not uncommon to get rain, cold winds and thick mists, which make it easy to get lost. Between May and August, periods of low cloud and drizzle (called *chiperone*) can last several days, and temperatures drop below freezing. Always carry a map, a compass and warm and waterproof clothing should the weather change, or you risk suffering from severe exposure. Never set out on a climb alone and always tell someone where you're going and when you plan to return.

Sleeping

BELOW THE MOUNTAIN

CCAP Guesthouse (campsite per person MK800, chalets per person MK2000) The CCAP Mission, after the reserve gates, has cosy rooms, self-catering chalets and camping.

Likhubula Forest Lodge (☎ 01-467737; campsite per person MK900, s with/without bathroom incl breakfast MK5800/5000, d with/without bathroom incl breakfast MK8200/7300, s with/without bathroom half board MK7700/6800, d with/without bathroom half board MK11,800/10,800, whole lodge MK36,000) At Likhubula, also after the reserve gates, this lodge has simple, clean rooms including two en suite, a terrace with pretty views and a cosy lounge with a fireplace and rocking chairs – perfect for a few hours playing the lodge copy of Scrabble or browsing the shelf of old books and magazines. There's a separate annex with its own small veranda.

Thuchila Tourist Lodge (☎ 0888-188607/400231; thuchilatlodge@africa-online.net; r with bathroom from MK5500, r with bathroom and TV from MK7500) Twenty kilometres past Likhubula on the road to Phalombe, this is another convenient spot for starting or finishing a climb up the mountain, at the base of the path to Thuchila Hut. There are rooms with shared bathroom as well as a few self-contained units, all housed in pretty red brick and timber bungalows. There's a large garden,

---

---

beautiful views and a restaurant and bar serving filling Malawian meals.

ON THE MOUNTAIN

Forestry huts (campsites per adult/child MK400/200, huts per adult/child MK700/350) On Mulanje are eight forestry huts: Chambe, Chisepo, Lichenya, Thuchila, Chinzama, Minunu, Madzeka and Sombani. Each is equipped with benches, tables and open fires with plenty of wood. Some have sleeping platforms (no mattresses); in others you just sleep on the floor. You provide your own food, cooking gear, candles, sleeping bag and stove (although you can cook on the fire). A caretaker chops wood, lights fires and brings water, for which a small tip should be paid.

Payments must be made at Likhubula Forestry Office – show your receipt to the hut caretaker. Camping is permitted near the huts when there are no more beds. Some huts may be full at weekends, but you can normally adjust your route around this.

CCAP Cottage (beds MK700) On the Lichenya Plateau, this is similar to the forestry huts but there are utensils in the kitchen, plus mattresses and blankets. You can make reservations at the CCAP Mission in Likhubula.

France's Cottage (beds MK700) A more comfortable option than the huts, this small

SOUTHERN MALAWI

two-bedroom cottage sleeps six and comes with a living room complete with cooking fireplace. There are two single beds and two bunk beds. It's in the Chambe basin near the Chambe hut. Ask at the Likhubula Forestry Office or contact the Mountain Club of Malawi (www.mcm.org.mw) for further information.

Eating

BELOW THE MOUNTAIN

Pizzeria Basilico (☎ 0888-878830; small/large pizzas from MK700/1050) Underneath Mulanje Info-centre this place has a breezy terrace overlooking the street and serves an excellent selection of wood-fired pizzas (you can see them rolling the dough before your very eyes) as well as a range of pastas and grills.

Getting There & Away

See p278 and p281 for information on buses between Blantyre and Mulanje town. The dirt road to Likhubula turns off the main sealed Blantyre–Mulanje road at Chitakale, about 2km west of the centre of Mulanje town – follow the signpost to Phalombe.

If you're coming from Blantyre on the bus, ask to be dropped at Chitakale. From here, irregular *matola* run to Likhubula (MK150). If you're in a group, you can hire the whole *matola* to Likhubula for around MK1000. Alternatively, you can walk (10km, two to three hours); it's a pleasant hike with good views of the southwestern face of Mulanje on your right.

LOWER SHIRE

This is one of the least visited areas of the country – a baking stretch of flat plains, swampland, sugar cane and maize fields, where the Shire River makes its final journey before plunging into the great Zambezi. Coming from the north, the main road spirals sharply downwards – affording breathtakingly beautiful views out towards Mozambique – to meet the dense heat of the valley below, quite a shock if you've arrived from the relatively cool and green surrounds of Blantyre.

A small strip of territory it may be, but there's a lot to see here, including three wilderness areas and a vast tract of

---

LIVING LIKE A PLANTER

A couple of days acting like the big boss and sinking G&Ts on the veranda of a beautiful old planter's home makes an atmospheric start (or end) to a hike up the mountain. Here are some of our suggestions:

■ The **Lujeri Tea Estate** (☎ 01-460266/460243) sits at the base of Mt Mulanje between Mulanje town and Muloza and is reached by a winding dirt road that makes its way up past estate workers' houses, avenues of tall pines and acres of bright green tea. After the main gates you'll reach the **Lujeri Guest House** (s/d US$60/80, whole house US$190, sleeps 10; ☒), a quaint old planters' home with high ceilings, a wide cool veranda, chintzy central lounge with fireplace, and a small swimming pool shaded by trees and moss-covered rocks. A stay at neighbouring **Lujeri Lodge** (whole house US$200, sleeps 10; ☒), a larger and grander version of the Guest House, is like stepping back in time. It's a classic colonial tin-roofed affair; you can almost hear the tinkling of laughter and jazz piano as you're lounging on the enormous wraparound veranda. The gardens are an explosion of lush plants and flowers and there's a large swimming pool and miniature tennis court should you wish to be active. The staff at both lodges can direct you to beautiful walks in the shadow of the mountain.

■ Stunning **Huntingdon House** (☎ 01-794555; s/d full board from US$275/300) sits on the Satemwa Tea Estate near the small town of Thyolo. Built in 1928, this rambling old house has been recently renovated and is dripping with history and old-fashioned charm. There are five beautiful suites here (including one created from the old family chapel) and each has a story to tell. Horse riding, biking and walking trails are all available here and in the evenings amazing silver service meals are served, perhaps accompanied by a tale or two about the old days courtesy of the owners – descendents of the original planters. The lodge is bookable through Ulendo Safaris in Blantyre. Also on the estate are two self-catering properties – Chawani Bungalow and Magara Lodge, which were being upgraded at the time of writing.

swampland, so it's a shame that it's often overlooked. Things are slowly improving, however, and with better facilities and animal numbers on the rise, more and more people are visiting this tiny corner of the country.

Majete Wildlife Reserve

Majete Wildlife Reserve (www.majete.org; adult/child MK2000/1000, vehicle MK200, maps MK100) is a beautiful wilderness area of hilly miombo woodland and savannah, hugging the west bank of the Shire River. Years of poaching in the 1980s and 1990s left the park depleted and dilapidated, but since it was taken over by African Parks (www.africanparks -conservation.com) in 2003, things have been looking up. A perimeter fence has been erected around the whole reserve and accommodation and roads have been upgraded.

There are now over 4000 animals in Majete, most translocated from other parks in Malawi and elsewhere in Southern Africa, including zebras, antelopes, black rhinos, buffaloes and over 140 elephants. There are plenty of hippos in the river and the park is also known for its rich birdlife. In the long term it's hoped that Majete will become a 'big five' park. Come now and you'll be able to enjoy it in peace.

SIGHTS & ACTIVITIES

There are 250km of tracks in the park, and you'll need a high-clearance car to get around – a 4WD is strongly recommended, especially during the wet season. The two main routes here are the Mkurumadzi Rd, which runs parallel to the Shire River (although not near enough for you to see it from the track) and Namitsempha Rd, heading west from the entrance. Along Mkurumadzi Rd, just past the park entrance, are the grand Kapichira Falls, which David Livingstone failed to cross on one of his expeditions back in 1859; further on is Mvuu Spot, a small hide from where you can watch hippos frolicking in the river.

If you'd rather your activities were organised there is plenty on offer, including bush walks (per person MK1500), game drives (per person MK3500) and, for the brave, elephant tracking on foot (per person MK3500). You can also opt to have a scout join you in your own car (MK2000).

At the entrance to the park is a small open-air **heritage centre and gift shop** featuring a display of art and craftwork made in and around Majete by local people. There's also a little museum with displays on the region's history and natural heritage as well as information on conservation projects in the surrounding communities. You can buy cold soft drinks and beers here, and there's a wooden deck where you can sit and look out into the bush.

SLEEPING

There are two places to stay in the reserve currently, an upmarket bush camp and a community campsite. In the future, African Parks plans to introduce bush camping, where guests will be able to go deep into the bush with armed scouts and spend a night out in the wilderness.

Community Campsite (campsite per person MK700, s/d shelter MK500/700) Just built at the time of writing, it's a peaceful place with spotless kitchen and barbecue facilities, ample firewood and a small bar with cold drinks, toilet paper, matches, and other essentials for sale. There are also a couple of raised thatched camping platforms reached by ladder, with dynamite views out over the park. To get here turn left just before the heritage centre.

Thawale Camp (full-/half-board bush tent per person from MK9850/8750, s supplement MK1650) A beautiful upmarket bush camp about 3km from the reserve's main entrance. Each safari tent is set on a raised wooden platform in the bush, with small verandas and gorgeous bathrooms at the back, complete with deep baths, stone sinks and loos with a view. They're also well spaced out so you really get the sense that you're in the middle of nowhere. There's a central lodge for meals (the food is excellent) with plenty of comfortable chairs to sink into, safari books for browsing and a stone terrace with outdoor fire pit. The camp isn't fenced so expect regular visits from elephants, buffaloes and other creatures.

GETTING THERE & AWAY

Majete lies west of the Shire River, some 70km southwest of Blantyre. Follow the road to Chikwawa from where signs will direct you to the reserve. By public transport, the nearest you can get is Chikwawa.

SOUTHERN MALAWI

Lengwe National Park

Lengwe is Malawi's southernmost park. It's flat and arid with plenty of driveable tracks (yes, some are even manageable with a 2WD!) among mixed woodland and grassy *dambo* (wetlands). The sparse vegetation means that animal viewing is good here; in the dry season animals congregate around the park's few permanent watering holes. Mammals include nyalas (at the northern limit of their distribution in Africa), bushbucks, impalas, duikers, kudus, warthogs and buffaloes. There's also a large and varied bird population. The park has several walking trails and 'hides' overlooking the watering holes, where you can watch the animals come and graze. There's one within five minutes' walk of the lodge.

ACTIVITIES

The lodge can organise a wide range of activities in the park such as game drives (per person US$25), walking safaris (per person US$12) and evening tours to Ndankwera Cultural Village where you'll be fed and entertained for US$35 per person (minimum four people). They also arrange a number of boat trips including fishing trips and full-day excursions to Elephant Marsh (per person US$175).

At the park entrance is a small gift shop selling woven rugs and bags as well as locally made produce such as Lengwe peanut butter and baobab jam. At the time of research, construction was underway on a heritage centre and museum next door to the gift shop.

SLEEPING

Nyala Lodge (bookings through Jambo Africa; ☎ 01-823709,www.jambo-africa.com; s/d incl breakfast per person US$80/70, half-board per person s/d US$90/80, full-board per person s/d US$125/115) A fully functioning lodge in a clearing in the bush, but there isn't a particularly great view from here and it lacks some of that romantic safari atmosphere. Very large thatched chalets have verandas and spacious bathrooms, there's a central lounge and bar, and hammocks and chairs dotted throughout the grounds. For those on a budget there is a separate **campsite** (campsite per person US$6, chalets per person US$30) and budget chalets for self-caterers.

GETTING THERE & AWAY

By car, take the main road from Blantyre south towards Nsanje. By public transport, take a bus from Blantyre to Nchalo or Nsanje. About 20km from the Shire Bridge a signpost indicates Lengwe National Park to the right. The park entrance is another 10km to the west through sugarcane plantations.

Nchalo

If you want to sleep outside the park the nearest you'll get is the sugar-industry town of Nchalo, home to the **Ilovo Sugar Estate** (coming from Blantyre turn left after the Total station). It is like a miniature kingdom with schools, hospital, an airfield, company housing and a golf course. The reason to visit is the **Ilovo Sports Club** (☎ 01-425200; s/d full-board MK9850/14,900), 8km east of Nchalo, which has a good restaurant, chalets and rooms overlooking the river; it's right by the sugar estate golf course. The rooms are no-frills affairs and rather overpriced, but that's what you get for being in the estate's 'senior staff' section. There is also the downmarket **Shire Club** (☎ 01-425200; r with shared bathroom MK1600) or the estate's 'junior staff' section, which has a shop, very basic rooms and a noisy bar. If you don't want to stay on the estate, some 500 metres north of town is the **Kukhala Motel** (☎ 01-424424; r from MK2000). It has decent, clean rooms (plump for a more expensive one as the cheaper rooms are like prison cells) and a restaurant and bar here serving basic meals of chicken and chips (meals MK400 to MK500).

Elephant Marsh

The Elephant Marsh is a large area of seasonally flooded plain on the Shire River about 30km downstream from Chikwawa, just south of the vast Ilovo Sugar Estate. Despite the name, there are no elephants here any more, although vast herds inhabited the area less than 100 years ago. Some hippos and crocodiles occur in quiet areas, but the main draw is the spectacular selection of birds. This is one of the best **birdwatching** areas in Malawi; you'll see a number of rare waders here. Even if you're not a fan of our feathered friends, it's worth considering a visit here simply to sample this peaceful and very unusual landscape, and spend a morning or so floating on the ly-studded waters past baobabs and stately palm trees.

As mornings and evenings are the best times to see birds (it's also not so hot), travellers without wheels may find it convenient to stay overnight in the village of Bangula, which has a council rest house. If you have a car, you could stay in Nchalo.

GETTING THERE & AWAY

The only way to see the marsh properly is by boat. The usual way of doing this is to hire a boatman and his dugout canoe at a small village called Mchacha James on the east side of the marsh, about 7km from Makhanga.

If you're driving, head southwest of Blantyre for 30km and turn left (east) at Thabwa (the bottom of the escarpment). Makhanga is another 65km or so further south, following the Thyolo Escarpment. From Makhanga, head north towards Muona village. After 2.5km a dirt track leads west for 4.5km through villages and small fields to Mchacha James. This route is not signposted so ask for directions – it may be worth arranging a local guide in Makhanga. During the rains it sometimes isn't possible to cross the bridge to Mchacha James. You can probably get a boat across and then walk but you might not want to leave your car unattended.

If you're without wheels, take the bus from Blantyre that travels to Nchalo and Nsanje. You can get a *matola* from either of these towns to Makhanga. Alternatively, you can get off this bus at Bangula and then take a *matola* through Chiromo to Makhanga. From Makhanga, you can walk (it's a good hour), take a bicycle taxi or charter a *matola* to Mchacha James.

Nyala Lodge (opposite) arranges day trips to the Elephant Marsh, as does Jambo Africa (p272) in Blantyre.

Mwabvi Wildlife Reserve

Sitting at the country's southernmost tip, Mwabvi (admission per person/car MK750/300) is the smallest, most remote and least accessible of Malawi's game reserves. As with many of the country's other wilderness areas, Mwabvi has been severely hit by poachers in the past, and wildlife stocks have been diminished, though species here do include buffaloes, kudus, sable antelopes, bushpigs,

---

MWABVI: WHAT'S IN A NAME

Mwabvi Wildlife Reserve is named after the river that runs through it and also after the endangered Mwabvi tree, only one of which remains in the park (ask one of the wardens to direct you to it – it's clearly marked). The root and bark of the tree is poisonous and, as the story goes, in olden days was used as a measure against witchcraft. If suspicious, supernatural events were taking place in the local village, the elders would pound up the roots of a Mwabvi tree, make it into a powerful drink, line up the villagers and force them one by one to drink... The innocent would instantly regurgitate the concoction, but the perpetrators of the dastardly deeds would suffer a painful death.

---

bushbucks and a handful of leopards. In Mwabvi, though, it doesn't seem to matter. The magic of coming here is its very isolation and its untouched wilderness atmosphere. The scenery is gorgeous too – gentle wooded hills sit alongside sweeping boulders and clear streams tumble though steep rocky gorges. Get up high and you'll be rewarded with spectacular views over the Shire and Zambezi Rivers.

Project African Wilderness (www.projectafrican wilderness.com) has taken over the management of the reserve with the aim of protecting and restoring it. Two new camps have already been built, there are plans to start fencing Mwabvi's borders in 2010, and new wildlife species will be introduced.

ACTIVITIES

At the main gates you can pay for a guide to accompany you in your car (US$2), organise a walking safari (per person US$10), game drive (per person US$15) or visit a local village on a cultural tour (per person US$5).

SLEEPING

There are two places to stay in Mwabvi, one inside and one outside the park. To make a booking at either one contact **Project African Wilderness** (☎ 01-707346; barefoot@projectafrican wilderness.com).

Chipembere Camp (campsite per person US$5; dm per person US$15) It's a shady campsite with spotless ablutions and an airy dorm with

PATRICK JERE, WILDLIFE SCOUT

How long have you worked as a scout at Mwabvi? For four years. Before that I was a scout at Liwonde National Park for 10 years.

What did you have to do to become a scout? I had six months of training, including how to use guns, how to read park maps and how to track game.

What are your main duties as a scout? I take tourists around the park to show them the animals. But most of the time I work patrolling the park, to protect the animals and the plants from poachers. I also work as a government hunter. I go into the villages to kill animals that are bothering the people. For example, sometimes hippos eat the villagers' maize crops and crocodiles kill the villagers.

So has poaching been a big problem in the park? Yes, there used to be lions and black rhinos here, but the poachers killed all of them. There are a lot of poachers who come to the park from Mozambique. It was particularly badly during the war when refugees came from Mozambique and killed a lot of the game here. These days the poachers mostly kill buffaloes, which they use for its meat.

The park is quite isolated; what are visitor numbers like here? We see very few visitors at the moment because the park is underdeveloped and there isn't much game. Project African Wilderness is now developing the park. The park will be fenced off in 2010; they will reintroduce animals, for example, bringing in black rhino and blue wildebeest from South Africa and chimps from the DRC.

Patrick Jere is a wildlife scout at Mwabvi Wildlife Reserve

large, mosquito-screened windows and a small book library. There are barbecue and kitchen facilities here. About 500m before you come to the main gate is a crossroads. Take the right-hand fork signposted Chipembere Camp.

our pick **Migudu Camp** (campsite per person US$15) This is a beautiful location inside the reserve with six camping spots well spread out among the bush, each with its own barbecue and viewing point. Site number 3, hugged by a large grey and purple boulder, is the most picturesque. There's a walking trail from the campsite as well as two-storey game viewing deck with awe-inspiring views all the way over to the mountains that

border the reserve and into Mozambique. At the time of writing you could only self-cater by barbecue, but they are building a kitchen and reception area and you will be able to buy cold drinks.

GETTING THERE & AWAY
Access is possible only with a 4WD. The reserve office is reached from the main road between Chikwawa and Nsanje, 8km off the main road just east of the village of Sorgin, and about 10km west of Bangula. To get here it's a pleasant drive through millet fields and past villages and it is well signposted. It's not possible to get here by public transport.

Malawi Directory

ACCOMMODATION

Malawi has long been a popular destination for backpackers who will find a good range of suitable accommodation across the country. These days midrange and top-end travellers are also well catered for. There are plenty of comfortable tourist lodges, as well as the odd luxury beach or safari lodge.

Budget

At the budget end of the price range, in almost every town there is a council or government resthouse. Prices vary from as little as US$2 up to around US$8 for a double, but conditions are generally spartan to say the least and downright disgusting at worst. In national

parks and along the lakeshore, many places offer camping as well as self-catering chalets or cabins. Camping costs from around US$3 to US$10, depending on whether you're presented with long-drop toilets and bucket showers, or well-equipped affairs with hot showers and power points.

You'll find backpacker hostels all over the country, in the major cities as well as at popular lakeshore destinations such as Cape Maclear and Nkhata Bay. Prices range from US$5 to US$10 for a dorm up to about US$10 to US$15 per person for a double or triple with shared facilities and around US$30 for an en suite room. Camping is usually about US$3 to US$5.

Midrange

Midrange hotels and lodges start from about US$30 up to US$80 for a double, including taxes, usually with private bathroom and breakfast, sometimes with air-con. Additionally, some backpackers lodges have stylish en suite options for around US$30 to US$50 for a double. Often, the quality of service at small midrange tourists' lodges is just as good or even better (and more personal) than that at the expensive big hotels.

Top End

Standard top-end hotels in the big cities and at beach resorts range from US$100 to US$250 for a double room, with in-room facilities such as private bathroom, TV, air-con and telephone, and hotel facilities such as swimming pools, tennis courts and organised activities. The price normally includes taxes and breakfast. Then there are the exclusive beach hotels and safari lodges,

---

BOOK ACCOMMODATION ONLINE

For more accommodation reviews and recommendations by Lonely Planet authors, check out www.lonelyplanet.com/hotels. You'll find the true, insider lowdown on the best places to stay. Reviews are thorough and independent. Best of all, you can book online.

PRACTICALITIES

■ Malawi's main **newspapers** are the *Daily Times,* the *Malawi News* and *The Nation. The Chronicle* is a smaller publication but with a strong independent voice.

■ Malawi's national **radio station**, the Malawi Broadcasting Corporation, combines music, news and chat shows in English, Chichewa and some other local languages. International news is brief but wide-ranging. Commercial stations include Capital FM, providing a steady stream of international and Malawian hits as well as local and international news.

■ **TV Malawi** was launched in 1999 and consists mostly of imported programmes, news, regional music videos and religious programmes. International satellite channels are available in most midrange and top-end hotels.

---

which charge anything from US$100 to US$450 per person, per night, though this usually includes all meals and some activities.

ACTIVITIES

Malawi provides a wide range of activities for travellers. Lake Malawi is the main destination so diving and snorkelling are particularly popular.

Birdwatching

Malawi is a great destination for birding with almost 650 species recorded here. The best place to start is the national parks. Liwonde (p263) is an excellent spot, with particularly good birdlife along the river, and the forests in Nyika (p224) are also good. For water birds, Elephant Marsh (p288) in Malawi's far south is your surest bet. Land & Lake Safaris (www.landlake.net, p207) Lilongwe can organise birdwatching tours around the country, as can Budget Safari (www.budget-safari.com, p233) in Nkhata Bay.

Diving & Snorkelling

Lake Malawi's population of colourful fish (p255) attracts travellers to come scuba diving. The lake is reckoned by experts to be among the best freshwater diving areas in the world and one of the cheapest places to learn how to dive. The water is warm and (depending on season) visibility and weather conditions are usually good. Places where you can hire scuba gear and take a PADI Open Water course include Nkhata Bay (p232), Cape Maclear (pp254–5), Likoma Island (p238) and Senga Bay (p249).

If you don't want to dive you can still have fun with the fish. Gear for snorkelling can be hired from most dive centres, and most lakeside hotels rent snorkelling equipment.

Other Watersports

Many of the more upmarket places along the lake have facilities for water-skiing or windsurfing. You can also go sailing, or join luxurious 'sail safaris' where everything is done for you – Danforth Yachting (p255) and Pumulani (p258) on the southern lakeshore can both organise this for you. Kayaking is available at Cape Maclear (p255) and Nkhata Bay (p232) and at many of the lodges that dot the lakeshore.

Fishing

You can go fishing in Lake Malawi for *mpasa* (also called lake salmon), *ncheni* (lake tiger), *sungwa* (a type of perch), *kampango* or *vundu* (both catfish). There are trout in streams on Nyika, Zomba and Mulanje Plateaus, and tigerfish can be hooked in the Lower Shire River. Anglers can contact the Angling Society of Malawi (www.anglingmalawi .com) for further details.

Hiking

The main areas for hiking are Nyika (p225) and Mulanje. Other areas include Zomba (p269), and various smaller peaks around Blantyre. Mulanje is Malawi's main rock-climbing area, with some spectacular routes, although local climbers also visit smaller crags and outcrops. Rock climbing can also be arranged in Livingstonia and in the Viphya Plateau (p241).

The Mountain Club of Malawi (www.mcm .org.mw) provides a wealth of information about hiking on Mt Mulanje.

Horse Riding

Malawi's biggest horse riding destination is the Nyika Plateau – the huge open landscape lends itself perfectly to exploration on horseback. At the time of research there hadn't been any horse riding on the plateau for quite a while, but a new company has bought up the tourist concessions in Nyika so tours should be available again by the time this book is published. There's also a stables on the Zomba Plateau that can arrange short rides, and horse riding is also popular at Kande Beach near Chintheche.

Cycling

Several of the lakeshore lodges will hire out mountain bikes, usually for about US$10 a day. Areas that are great for mountain biking include Nyika National Park (p224) – with its hilly landscape and good network of dirt tracks – and the Viphya Plateau (p241). You should be able to hire bikes at both these destinations.

BUSINESS HOURS

Offices and shops in the main towns are usually open from 8am to 5pm weekdays, with an hour for lunch between noon and 1pm. Many shops are also open Saturday morning. In smaller towns, shops and stalls are open most days, but keep informal hours. Bank hours are usually from 8am to 3.30pm weekdays. Post and telephone offices are generally open from 7.30am to 5pm weekdays, sometimes with a break for lunch. In Blantyre and Lilongwe, they also open Saturday morning.

CHILDREN

There are few formal facilities for children in Malawi; however, Malawi is generally a safe and friendly place for children to visit. Older kids will love the many outdoor activities that Malawi has to offer and many of the lodges in Malawi's wilderness areas and beaches are geared towards families.

Most of the big international hotels in Blantyre and Lilongwe can provide babysitting services, family rooms and cots for babies, as can several of the tourist lodges up and down the coast. Similarly, many of the big city restaurants frequented by expats and tourists will be able to provide high chairs. Disposable nappies and formula are widely available in supermarkets and speciality shops in Lilongwe, Blantyre and Mzuzu but can be difficult to find elsewhere.

For more information about surviving on the road with kids, check out Lonely Planet's *Travel With Children* by Brigitte Barta.

CLIMATE CHARTS

Malawi has a tropical climate with a number of regional variations. The country's steamiest areas are the Shire Valley and Lake Malawi. Malawi's highland regions include Nyika, Mulanje and Dedza and can be very cold at certain times of the year, especially at night. The hot rainy season kicks in between November and March.

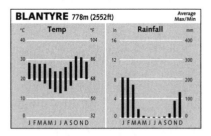

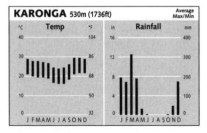

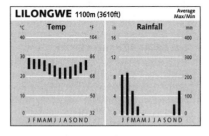

CUSTOMS REGULATIONS

Like any country, Malawi doesn't allow travellers to import weapons, explosives or narcotics. Plants and seeds, livestock and live insects or snails are also prohibited. It is illegal to take products made from endangered animals or plants out of the country. A yellow fever certificate is required from people arriving from an infected area.

DANGERS & ANNOYANCES
Crime
Malawi was once one of the safest countries in the world for independent travellers, but in recent years incidences of robberies or muggings have increased. However, incidents are still rare compared with other countries, and violence is not the norm. Some safety advice is given in the Lilongwe and Blantyre sections. There have also been robberies at popular lakeshore areas such as Cape Maclear and Nkhata Bay, but here violence is very rare.

Scams to be aware of if you're buying curios are the eager young men who offer to wrap your purchase in paper and cardboard, then want more for this job than you paid for the carving. Also on the economic front, beware of locals asking you to break a US$100 bill into US$10 bills and US$20 bills. Naturally, the US$100 bill is a fake.

Wildlife
Potential dangers at Lake Malawi include encountering a hippo or crocodile, but for travellers the chances of being attacked are extremely remote. Crocodiles tend to be very wary of humans and are generally only found in quiet vegetated areas around river mouths, although they may sometimes be washed into the lake by floodwater. Therefore you should be careful if you're walking along the lakeshore and have to wade a river. Popular tourist beaches are safe, although, just to be sure, you should seek local advice before diving in. The most dangerous animals in Malawi are the mosquitoes that transmit malaria.

EMBASSIES & CONSULATES
Malawian Embassies & Consulates
Malawi has diplomatic missions in the following African countries: Kenya, Mozambique, South Africa, Tanzania, Zambia and Zimbabwe. Other Malawaian embassies/high commissions around the world:
Canada (☎ 613-236 8931; 7 Clemow Ave, Ottawa, Ontario K1S 2A9)
France (☎ 01 4070 1846; 20 Rue Euler, 75008 Paris)
Germany (☎ 49 30 8413 540; Westfalische Strasse 86, 10709 Berlin)
South Africa (☎ 27 12 430 9900; 770 Government Ave, Hatfield 0082, Pretoria)
Tanzania (☎ 255 22 266 6248 or 266 6284; 38 Ali Hassan Mwinyi Rd, Dar es Salaam)
UK (☎ 44 208 455 5624; 70 Winnington Rd, London N2 0TX)
USA (☎ 202-797 1007; 2408 Massachusetts Ave NW, Washington DC 20008)

Although Malawi has no high commission in Australia, it is represented by the **Consular Office, Australian Department of Foreign Affairs and Trade** (☎ 02-6261 3305; John McEwen Cres, Barton, ACT 2600).

Embassies & Consulates in Malawi
The following countries have diplomatic representation in Malawi:
Germany (☎ 01-772555; Convention Dr, City Centre, Lilongwe)

THE GREAT BILHARZIA STORY

Bilharzia (or schistosomiasis) is a disease that occurs all over Africa. It is transmitted by minute worms carried by infected humans and water snails. Both 'hosts' need to be present for the worms to transmit the disease. Bilharzia can be contracted if you swim or paddle in the lakes, ponds or any shallow water, especially near villages or where reeds grow.

Although parts of the lake might be very low risk, in other areas – including some popular tourist destinations – you undoubtedly have a risk of contracting bilharzia. There's no need to panic, and no reason to avoid coming to the lake – but you should be aware of the risk.

If you do decide to swim, and you do contract bilharzia, you might suffer from some symptoms almost immediately, in which case you should seek treatment fast. But usually symptoms do not show until the disease is well established – and this can be weeks or months after exposure. Long-term effects can be very harmful so it is *essential* that you have a check-up for the disease when you get home or reach a place with good medical services. Be sure your doctor is familiar with bilharzia, and be aware that the disease may have a long incubation period and may not be initially apparent, so you might need more than one test. For more information see *Health* (p310).

Mozambique Embassy (☎ 01-774100; Convention Dr, City Centre, Lilongwe); Consulate (☎ 01-843189; 1st fl Celtel Bldg, Rayner Ave, Limbe)

South Africa (☎ 01-773722, sahe@malawi.net; Kang'ombe Bldg, City Centre, Lilongwe)

UK High Commission (☎ 01-772400; off Kenyatta Rd, City Centre, Lilongwe); Consulate (Hanover Ave, Blantyre)

USA (☎ 01-773166; Convention Dr, City Centre, Lilongwe)

Zambia (☎ 01-772590; Convention Dr, City Centre, Lilongwe)

FESTIVALS & EVENTS

The Malawi Lake of Stars Music Festival (www.lakeofstarsfestival.co.uk) takes place each October in Senga Bay and attracts live music acts from around Africa and the UK. It lasts for three days and proceeds go to charity.

GAY & LESBIAN TRAVELLERS

Male and female homosexuality is illegal in Malawi. On top of this, the people of Malawi are conservative in their attitudes towards gays and lesbians, and gay sexual relationships are culturally taboo – although some homosexual activity, especially among younger men, does occur. In most places, open displays of affection are generally frowned upon, whatever your orientation, and show insensitivity to local feelings.

HOLIDAYS

Public holidays in Malawi:

New Year's Day 1 January
John Chilembwe Day 15 January
Martyrs' Day 3 March
Easter March/April – Good Friday, Holy Saturday and Easter Monday
Labour Day 1 May
Freedom Day 14 June
Republic Day 6 July
Mother's Day October – second Monday
Christmas Day 25 December
Boxing Day 26 December

When one of these dates falls on a weekend, normally the following Monday is a public holiday. Islamic holidays are also observed throughout Malawi by the Muslim population.

INSURANCE

A travel insurance policy that covers theft, property loss and medical expenses is essential. There is a wide variety of insurance policies available, and it's wise to check with a reliable travel agent to find out which is the best policy for Malawi.

When buying your travel insurance *always* check the small print – some policies specifically exclude 'dangerous activities' that could be anything from scuba diving to horse riding. You should also check whether the medical coverage is on a pay first, claim later basis; if this is the case, keep all documents relating to any medical treatment. You should also make sure that your medical coverage includes the cost of medical evacuation.

Worldwide travel insurance is available at www.lonelyplanet.com/travel_services. You can buy, extend and claim online anytime – even if you're already on the road.

INTERNET ACCESS

You'll find several internet cafes in Lilongwe (p206), Blantyre (p272) and Mzuzu (p229) and most towns will usually have somewhere to check your emails even if it is expensive and slow. The introduction of wireless broadband services by Skyband and Globe has made a huge difference. Many hotels and restaurants in Lilongwe, Blantyre and Mzuzu have wi-fi connections, as do quite a few tourist hotels around the country. To get online, you must buy a prepaid voucher, which in theory you can buy at any wi-fi hotspot, though places often run out. Skyband vouchers cost MK600 for one hour, MK2000 for five hours and MK8000 for a week's unlimited usage. Globe vouchers cost MK200 for 30 minutes and MK500 for an hour. For a comprehensive list of establishments offering wi-fi services visit www.skybandhotspots.com for Skyband or www.globemw.net for Globe.

MALAWI DIRECTORY

LEGAL MATTERS

Marijuana or cannabis (also known locally as 'Malawi gold', 'Malawi black' or *chamba)* can be bought in many parts of Malawi, especially in some lakeshore resorts frequented by younger travellers. Buying, selling, possession and use are all serious offences in Malawi, attracting anything from a very high fine (several thousand dollars) to a maximum penalty of life imprisonment. Tourists caught may be fined and then deported, or even jailed. Some dealers are police informers, and in government crackdowns the police have been known to raid hostels and campsites. These days most hostels and campsites will not allow you to smoke openly.

MAPS

Useful maps, available in local bookshops, include the government-produced *Malawi* (1:1,000,000), showing shaded relief features and most roads, and the *Malawi Road & Tourist Map* (same scale), showing all main roads, some minor roads and national parks (but no relief) plus street maps of the main towns.

For more detail, government survey maps (1:50,000 and 1:250,000) are available from the Department of Surveys Map Sales Offices in Blantyre and Lilongwe. Specific maps and guidebooks on national parks and hiking areas are detailed under the listings for those areas.

MONEY

Malawi's unit of currency is the Malawi kwacha (MK). This is divided into 100 tambala (t).

Bank notes include MK200, MK100, MK50, MK20, MK10 and MK5. Coins are MK1, 50t, 20t, 10t, 5t and 1t, although the small tambala coins are virtually worthless.

At big hotels and other places that actually quote in US dollars you can pay in hard currency or kwacha at the prevailing exchange rate.

ATMs

Standard and National Banks are the best bet for foreigners wishing to draw money out of their home account. Standard Bank accepts foreign Visa, MasterCard, Cirrus and Maestro cards at their ATMs. National Bank ATMs only take foreign Visa cards at present. ATMs are found in most cities

and towns including Lilongwe, Blantyre, Mzuzu, Karonga, Liwonde, Salima, Mangochi, Kasungu and Zomba.

On busy weekdays there can be huge queues at the big city ATMs (Old Town in Lilongwe is particularly bad) and ATMs often run out of money or are suddenly closed for maintenance. Several travellers have reported having their cards swallowed up by the machines so it's a good idea to have a back-up card.

Black Market

There's no real black market in Malawi. You may get one or two kwacha more for your dollar on the street, but the chances of robberies or cons (or fake US$50 and US$100 bills) means that the risk is not really worth taking compared to going to a bank or bureau de change.

Credit Cards

You can get cash with a Visa card at Standard Bank and the National Bank of Malawi in Blantyre and Lilongwe. The charge is around US$5 and it can take several hours. You're best off going to a foreign exchange bureau that will provide the same service for around US$3 and transactions are completed on the spot.

You can use Visa cards at some but not all of the large hotels and top-end restaurants (be warned that this may add a 5% to 10% surcharge to your bill). It seems even harder to use a MasterCard. If you usually rely on plastic, you're better off using it to draw out cash and paying with that.

Tipping

Tipping is not generally expected in Malawi, as many restaurants and services will add on a service charge to your bill.

Travellers Cheques

You can change travellers cheques at most major banks and bureaux de change, although you will need to show them the original purchase receipt. You can sometimes use travellers cheques to pay at large hotels and lodges.

PHOTOGRAPHY & VIDEO

Some internet cafes in Blantyre and Lilongwe will burn CDs or DVDs from digital images using card readers or USB connections, and photo studios will make digital prints of your photos for around MK80 per image. Print film processing is also available in the major cities and is pretty reasonable, with most places charging around MK1000 for a roll.

The usual rules apply for photographing people; don't push cameras into people's faces and ask beforehand if they mind having their photo taken. In rural areas you will often find children keen to get in front of the lens and see themselves displayed on your LCD screen. People might ask you if you'll send them a copy of the photo you've taken of them. If you agree, remember to follow up on your promise.

POST

Post in and out of Malawi is a bit hit and miss. Some letters get from Lilongwe to London in three days, others take three weeks. Mail from Lilongwe or Blantyre to Cape Town often takes a month. In rural areas, the post can be very slow. Post offices in Blantyre and Lilongwe have poste restante services.

To African destinations, letters less than 10g and postcards cost MK80. To Europe, India, Pakistan and the Middle East it's MK150 and to the Americas, Japan or Australasia postage is MK200. It's quicker (and probably more reliable) to use the EMS Speedpost service at post offices. Letters up to 500g cost MK750 to Europe and MK1000 to Australia and the USA.

Airmail parcel rates used to be famously cheap, allowing you to send home large woodcarvings at a low price. It now costs about MK2000 plus MK500 per kilo to send items outside Africa. Surface mail is cheaper.

SHOPPING

You can find all kinds of curios and souvenirs for sale in Malawi, including animals and figures carved from wood, ornaments such as bowls and chess-sets, and the very popular 'chief's chair', which is a three-legged stool made from two pieces of wood, with a high back decorated with pictures.

You will also see objects made from grass and palm leaves, such as baskets and boxes, or intricate models of cars and lorries. Contemporary soapstone carvings, paintings, clay pots and figures, and malachite jewellery are also available.

There are craft stalls aimed at tourists in both Blantyre and Lilongwe as well as in the country's more popular tourist areas. Much of it is stuff that's been banged out in a hurry but if you look hard you'll also find some excellent quality works in wood and stone. Prices are usually not fixed, so you have to bargain, but if you prefer not to, there are craft shops in Blantyre and Lilongwe that use price-tags, though they are generally more expensive.

In markets all over Malawi you can buy *chitenjes,* sheets of brightly coloured cloth that local women use as wraps, cloaks, scarves and baby carriers. They make nice souvenirs and practical items for women travelling, particularly if you'll be travelling in rural areas where you need to cover up.

Bargaining

At craft and curio stalls, where items are specifically for tourists, bargaining is very much expected, but it's impossible to say how far you should try and lower the price. Some vendors might initially ask for double the price they're willing to accept, some more, some less. The best thing to do is to ask other travellers what they've paid for similar items, and visit several different other stalls beforehand, so you can get an idea of what a fair price should be. Decide what you want to pay or go by what others have told you they've paid and make a lower offer. This will usually be rejected but you can then haggle with the vendor until you arrive at a mutually agreeable price. Try not to have the attitude that people are trying to rip you off. If the price seems fair and affordable to you, there's no point in bargaining someone down just for the sake of it.

SOLO TRAVELLERS

Solo travellers will get along just fine in Malawi. You might attract a little attention in rural areas, especially if you're a woman but other than that people will barely notice you. Of course, solo travellers should be more careful at busy bus stations (no one else to watch out for your stuff) and when walking around in isolated areas or at night (this especially applies to solo women who should apply extreme caution). If you want to check out the bars in a major city it's much easier and safer to go with a group.

Cost is also an issue for solo travellers. A single room is usually more than half the price of a double or twin room, and many of the more upmarket, full-board lodges and safari companies apply a single person supplement.

TELEPHONE

International calls (to destinations outside Africa) from public phone offices cost around MK500 per minute. The international code for Malawi if you're dialling from abroad is ☎ 265.

Telephone calls within Malawi are inexpensive, around MK50 per minute depending on the distance, and the network between main cities is reliable, although the lines to outlying areas are often not working. Calls to mobiles within Malawi cost around MK70 per minute.

Mobile Phones

Mobile phones are in use everywhere in Malawi. Mobile phone prefixes are ☎ 0888 or ☎ 0999 and the two major networks are TNM and Zain. Sim cards are readily available and the most convenient way to buy them is from one of the many vendors on the streets, usually clad in the bright colours of their network provider. They cost around MK700 and include a small amount of airtime. You can buy top-up cards from street vendors, at supermarkets, internet cafes and petrol stations and they cost anything from MK35 to MK2800 depending on how much airtime you need.

Phone Codes

Malawi does not have area codes, but all landline numbers begin with ☎ 01, so whatever number you dial within the country will have eight digits. Numbers starting with 7 are on the Lilongwe exchange; those starting with 8 are in Blantyre; 5 is around Zomba; 4 is the south; 3 is the north; and 2 is the Salima area.

TIME

Malawi is two hours ahead of Greenwich Mean Time (GMT/UTC). The country does not have daylight saving time. When it's noon in Malawi, it's 2am in Los Angeles, 5am in New York, 10am in London, 8pm in Sydney and 10pm in Auckland.

TOILETS

There are two main types of toilet in Malawi: the Western style, with a toilet bowl and seat; and the African style, which is a hole in the floor, over which you squat. Standards of both can vary tremendously, from pristine to nauseating. In towns and cities, especially in cafes, restaurants and hotels frequented by foreigners, toilets are generally of the Western variety, although public toilets in bus stations and at local bars will probably be a squat job.

In rural areas squat toilets are built over a deep hole in the ground. These are called 'long-drops', and the waste matter just fades away naturally, as long as the hole isn't filled with too much other rubbish (such as paper or synthetic materials, including tampons – these should be disposed of separately).

TOURIST INFORMATION

There are tourist information offices in Blantyre and Lilongwe but you're much better off asking for advice from your hostel or hotel, or from a travel agency. Outside Malawi, tourism promotion is handled by UK-based **Malawi Tourism** (☎ 0115-982 1903; fax 0115-981 9418; www.malawitourism.com), which responds to inquiries from all over the world.

TRAVELLERS WITH DISABILITIES

People who don't walk will not have an easy time in Malawi. Even though there are more disabled people per head of population here than in the West, there are very few facilities. A few official buildings are constructed with ramps and lifts – but not many, and probably not the ones you want to visit. Some major hotels in the cities also have ramps and/or lifts, but again not many.

VISAS

Visas are not required by citizens of Commonwealth countries, the USA and most European nations. On entering the country you'll be granted 30-day entry, which can then be easily extended at immigration offices in Blantyre or Lilongwe. The process is straightforward and free.

VOLUNTEERING

There are numerous volunteer opportunities in Malawi. While travelling here you'll no doubt meet plenty of people working with

Peace Corps or VSO, as well as young people volunteering via major Western volunteer organisations, usually on a gap year. A good initial contact is Volunteer Abroad (www.volunteerabroad.com), which has listings of current volunteer options in Malawi. Otherwise, local grassroots opportunities include the following:

Ripple Africa (www.rippleafrica.org) recruits volunteer teachers, doctors, nurses and environmental workers for a number of projects based in Nkhata Bay district.

Billy Riordan Memorial Trust (www.billysmalawiproject.org) has established a clinic in Cape Maclear and provides medical care in the area. The trust needs medical volunteers (doctors, dentists, nurses, lab technicians).

Wildlife Action Group (www.wag-malawi.org) invites volunteers to assist in the management and maintenance of the Thuma Forest Reserve.

Butterfly Space (www.butterfly-space.com) is involved in a number of projects in Nkhata Bay, including a nursery and a community resource centre and would like volunteers that can devote more than a few weeks and get involved with the local community.

WOMEN TRAVELLERS

Malawi is generally a safe destination for women travelling alone or with other women and you should receive few problems. It's possible that you'll receive unwanted attention from men, but not any more than you might in other parts of the world. In fact, many women travellers report that, compared to North Africa, South America and numerous Western countries, Malawi feels relatively safe and unthreatening.

If you do receive hassle from men, firmly decline their advances and you'll usually be left alone. If you want to go out at night apply the same common sense that you would at home. Don't wander around on your own in poorly lit or deserted areas and don't get too drunk.

What you wear may greatly influence how you're treated. Malawian women dress conservatively, in traditional or Western clothes, so when a visitor wears something significantly different from the norm, she will draw attention. In the minds of some men, revealing too much flesh will be seen as provocative. In general, use your common sense, look at what other women are wearing and follow suit. Keep most of your legs covered, at least to below the knee. Wearing short shorts or a bikini might be acceptable on the beach in tourist areas but not elsewhere.

Transport in Malawi

TRANSPORT IN MALAWI

GETTING THERE & AWAY

The main way to get to Malawi is by land or air. Overland, travellers might enter the country from Zambia, Mozambique or Tanzania. Boats also bring travellers over Lake Malawi from Mozambique. There are no direct flights to Malawi from Europe or the United States. The easiest way to reach the country by air is via Kenya, Ethiopia or South Africa. Flights, tours and rail tickets can be booked online at www.lonelyplanet .com/travel_services.

ENTERING MALAWI

Entering Malawi is a simple, straightforward process. You must present a passport with at least six months of validity remaining, and should be in possession of an onward or return ticket, though this is seldom checked. Tourists are generally given a 30-day stay, extendable once you're in the country.

AIR
Airports & Airlines

Kamuzu International Airport (LLW; ☎ 700766), 19km north of Lilongwe city centre, handles the majority of international flights. Flights from South Africa, Kenya,

Zambia and Tanzania also land in Blantyre at **Chileka International Airport** (BLZ; ☎ 694244). The country's national carrier is **Air Malawi**, which operates a number of internal and regional flights.

AIRLINES FLYING TO/FROM MALAWI

Air Malawi (airline code QM; ☎ 01-265 820811 or 773680; www.airmalawi.com) has a decent regional network, with flights heading to Dar Es Salaam, Johannesburg, Nairobi, Lusaka and Harare from Blantyre and Lilongwe.

South African Airways (airline code SA; ☎ 01-265 1 620617/772242; www.flysaa.com) flies twice weekly between Blantyre and Johannesburg, and five times weekly between Lilongwe and Johannesburg (with connections to Durban, Cape Town etc).

Kenya Airways (airline code KQ; ☎ 01-774 227/624/ 524; www.kenya-airways.com) flies four times a week to/ from Nairobi and six times a week to/from Lusaka.

Ethiopian Airways (airline code ET; ☎ 01-771002 or 771308; www.flyethiopian.com) flies four times a week from Addis Ababa.

Tickets

It's always worth shopping around when buying tickets and as a general rule buying direct from the airline is usually more expensive. Airline websites and ticket-booking sites on the internet are good places to start looking for a flight to Malawi. Try the following services:

Opodo (www.opodo.com) This website can book tickets to a variety of locations.

Lonely Planet (www.lonelyplanet.com) Use the Trip Planner service to book multistop trips.

THINGS CHANGE...

The information in this chapter is particularly vulnerable to change. Check directly with the airline or a travel agency to make sure you understand how a fare (and a ticket you may buy) works and be aware of the security requirements for international travel. Shop carefully. The details given in this chapter should be regarded as pointers and are not a substitute for your own careful, up-to-date research.

AFRICA

There are direct flights to Malawi from Ethiopia, Kenya, South Africa and Zambia. Sample high season one-way/return fares are about US$550/730 from Nairobi, US$350/400 from Johannesburg, US$750/900 from Addis Ababa and US$400/450 from Lusaka.

AUSTRALIA & NEW ZEALAND

The cheapest way to get to Malawi from Australia or New Zealand is usually via Johannesburg. High season return fares from Sydney start at about A$2800. Well-known agencies for cheap fares include:

Flight Centre (☎ 133 133 using local area code; www
.flightcentre.com.au). Offices throughout Australia.

STA Travel (☎ 1300 733035; www.statravel.com.au)
Offices in all major cities and on university campuses.

CONTINENTAL EUROPE

There are no direct flights to Malawi from Europe, but you can fly to Malawi via South Africa, Ethiopia or Kenya. High season return fares start at around €900.

Recommended travel agents in France are:

Nouvelles Frontières (☎ 08 25 00 07 47; www
.nouvelles-frontieres.fr)

Voyageurs du Monde (☎ 01 40 15 11 15; www.vdm
.com)

Recommended agencies with branches in Germany:

Just Travel (☎ 089-747 33 30; www.justtravel.de)
STA Travel (☎ 0180-545 64 22; www.statravel.de)

From other countries in Europe try the following agencies:

Airfair (☎ 0206-20 51 21; www.airfair.nl; Netherlands)
Barcelo Viajes (☎ 902 200 400; www.barceloviajes
.com; Spain)
CTS Viaggi (☎ 06 441 1166; www.cts.it; Italy)
SSR Voyages (☎ 058 450 4020; www.ssr.ch;
Switzerland)

UK & IRELAND

To get to Malawi from the UK and Ireland your best bet is to fly via Addis Ababa, Nairobi or Johannesburg. Return flights in high season start at around £600. You could also fly direct to Lusaka (£700) and make your way overland (see p302).

Popular travel agencies in the UK include:
North-South Travel (☎ 01245-608291; www.north
southtravel.co.uk) Part of this agency's profits go to projects in the developing world.

TRANSPORT IN MALAWI

CLIMATE CHANGE & TRAVEL

Climate change is a serious threat to the ecosystems that humans rely upon, and air travel is the fastest-growing contributor to the problem. Lonely Planet regards travel, overall, as a global benefit, but believes we all have a responsibility to limit our personal impact on global warming.

Flying & Climate Change

Pretty much every form of motor travel generates CO_2 (the main cause of human-induced climate change) but planes are far and away the worst offenders, not just because of the sheer distances they allow us to travel, but because they release greenhouse gases high into the atmosphere. The statistics are frightening: two people taking a return flight between Europe and the US will contribute as much to climate change as an average household's gas and electricity consumption over a whole year.

Carbon Offset Schemes

Climatecare.org and other websites use 'carbon calculators' that allow jetsetters to offset the greenhouse gases they are responsible for with contributions to energy-saving projects and other climate-friendly initiatives in the developing world – including projects in India, Honduras, Kazakhstan and Uganda.

Lonely Planet, together with Rough Guides and other concerned partners in the travel industry, supports the carbon offset scheme run by climatecare.org. Lonely Planet offsets all of its staff and author travel.

For more information check out our website: lonelyplanet.com.

STA Travel (☎ 0871-230 0040; www.statravel.co.uk)
Trailfinders (☎ 0845-058 5858; www.trailfinders.co.uk)
Travel Bag (☎ 0871-703 4698; www.travelbag.co.uk)

USA & CANADA

Flights to Malawi from the USA and Canada will typically make two stops: the first in London or Paris and another in Southern or Eastern Africa before reaching Malawi. A typical return flight in high season from New York costs from $1400; $2000 from Los Angeles.

Useful options in the USA include:
STA Travel (☎ 1-800 781 4040; www.statravel.com)

Useful options in Canada include:
Flight Centre (☎ 1-877 967 5302; www.flightcentre.ca)

LAND
Bus

It is possible to cross into Malawi by bus from Tanzania, Zambia and South Africa and there are direct services from Johannesburg, Dar Es Salaam, Nairobi and Lusaka to Blantyre and Lilongwe. When crossing the border you will have to get off the bus to pass through customs and pay for your visa.

Car & Motorcycle

You will need a valid *carnet de passage* for your car, which will require entry/exit stamps when entering/leaving the country, as well as full car registration details and insurance documents, and you will have to pay US$20 road tax. If you don't have a carnet you will need to purchase a temporary import permit for US$3 and compulsory third-party insurance costs US$25 for a month. You won't find fuel or supplies at the borders themselves so take enough to continue to the nearest town. For more information on getting around by car see p305.

MOZAMBIQUE
South

The quickest way to reach Mozambique south of the Zambezi is to take a minibus to the Mozambican border crossing at Zóbuè (*zob*-way; MK500) and then a minibus to Tete (US$2), from where buses go to Beira and Maputo. You could also get a Blantyre–Harare bus to drop you at Tete and then get a bus to Beira or Maputo.

Central

If you are heading for central Mozambique, there are several buses per day from Blantyre to Nsanje (MK850), or all the way to the Malawian border at Marka (*ma*-ra-ka; MK900). It's a few kilometres between the border crossings – you can walk or take a bicycle taxi – and you can change money on the Mozambique side. From here pick-ups go to Mutarara, Nhamilabue and Vila de Sena.

North

There are three border crossings from Malawi into northern Mozambique: Muloza, from where you can reach Mocuba in Mozambique, and Nayuchi and Chiponde, both of which lead to Cuamba in Mozambique.

Regular buses run from Blantyre, via Mulanje, to Muloza (MK750). From here, you walk 1km to the Mozambican border crossing at Milange, from where it's another few kilometres into Milange *vila* (town) itself. From Milange there's usually a *chapa* (pick-up or converted minibus) or truck about every other day in the dry season to Mocuba, where you can find transport on to Quelimane or Nampula.

Further north, minibuses and *matolas* run a few times per day between Mangochi and the border crossing at Chiponde (MK800). It's then 7km to the Mozambican border crossing at Mandimba and the best way to get there is by bicycle taxi (US$2). Mandimba has a couple of *pensãos*, and there's at least one vehicle daily, usually a truck, between here and Cuamba (US$4).

The third option is to go by minibus or passenger train from Liwonde to the border at Nayuchi (MK850). You can then take a *chapa* from the Mozambican side of the border to Cuamba.

Boat

The Lake Malawi ferry *Ilala* (p304) stops at Metangula on the Mozambican mainland. If you're planning a visit you must get a visa in advance and make sure to get your passport stamped at Malawian immigration on Likoma Island or in Nkhata Bay.

Train

If you're heading to northern Mozambique, a passenger train departs from Limbe on Wednesdays at 7am, travelling via Balaka and Liwonde to the border at Nayuchi. The fare from Limbe to Nayuchi is US$3.30, but it's more popular to get on at Liwonde, from where it costs US$2. From Nayuchi (where there are moneychangers) you can walk to Entre Lagos, and then get a *chapa* to Cuamba.

SOUTH AFRICA
There are a number of bus companies running services from Lilongwe and Blantyre to Johannesburg. **Vaal Africa** (☎ 0999-200086) operates a service between Lilongwe and Johannesburg on Tuesdays and Saturdays for MK14,500. **Chita One** (☎ 01-622313, 829879) runs services to Johannesburg on Wednesdays and Sundays for MK15,000. From Blantyre, try **Ingwe Coach** (☎ 01-822313, Tue & Sun, MK15,000). Buses from Lilongwe leave from outside the petrol station on Paul Kagame Rd in Old Town. In Blantyre, most Johannesburg-bound buses depart from the car park outside Blantyre Lodge.

TANZANIA
If you want to go the whole way between Lilongwe and Dar es Salaam, three buses a week (Tuesday, Saturday and Sunday) depart from Devil St in Lilongwe. There's a ticket office where you can book; fares are MK8000 or MK14,000 if you continue on to Nairobi. These buses also pick up and drop off in Mzuzu and Mbeya (Tanzania) and are handy for going between northern Malawi and southern Tanzania.

If you're going in stages, buses and minibuses run between Mzuzu and Karonga (MK800, three to four hours), from where you can get a taxi to the Songwe border crossing (MK500). It's 200m across the bridge to the Tanzanian border crossing.

Once you're on the Tanzanian side of the border, minibuses and bicycle taxis travel the 5km distance to Kyela, from where you can get a bus to Dar es Salaam. You can change money with the bicycle-taxi boys but beware of scams.

ZAMBIA
There are four direct buses per week (two on Tuesday and two on Friday) between Lilongwe and Lusaka (MK6000), also departing from Devil St – the journey takes at least 12 hours. Regular minibuses run between Lilongwe and Mchinji (MK400).

From here, it's 12km to the border. Local shared taxis shuttle between Mchinji and the border post for around MK200 per person, or MK1000 for the whole car.

From the Zambian side of the border crossing, shared taxis run to Chipata (US$2), which is about 30km west of the border, from where you can reach Lusaka or South Luangwa National Park (p128).

If you've got a 4WD you can cross into Northern Zambia via Chitipa in northern Malawi. It's four hours from Karonga to Chitipa on a rough dirt road, and then the Malawian border post is 5km out of town. After going through customs it is another 80km or four hours' drive to the Zambian border post at Nakonde.

GETTING AROUND

You can travel around Malawi by air, road, rail or boat. Compared to other countries in the region, distances between major centres are quite short, and generally roads and public transport systems are quite good, making independent travel fairly straightforward.

AIR
For domestic flights, departure tax is US$5.

Airlines in Malawi
Air Malawi (☎ 01-772123, 753181, 788415; www.air malawi.com) Air Malawi's domestic schedule has diminished somewhat and the airline currently only operates regular flights between Lilongwe and Blantyre (MK12,000 one way). Air Malawi's booking system is not always reliable, so be prepared for lost reservations or double bookings.
Nyassa Air Taxi (☎ 01-761443; www.nyassa.mw) Provides charter flights to airstrips around the country, and to Mfuwe in Zambia in five- and seven-seater aircraft. The more of you there are the cheaper it is per person. For example, a one-way flight from Lilongwe to Likoma Island ranges between US$320 and US$210 per person depending on how many of you there are.

BICYCLE
Bicycles are available for hire at many lodges throughout Malawi at a cost of around US$10 per day. You can also hire bicycles or arrange mountain-bike tours through Land & Lake Safaris (p207).

BOAT

The *Ilala ferry* (☎ 01-587311; ilala@malawi.net) chugs passengers and cargo up and down Lake Malawi once a week in each direction. Travelling between Monkey Bay in the south and Chilumba in the north, it makes 12 stops at lakeside villages and towns in between. (You can get to the Mozambican mainland via the *Ilala;* p302.) Many travellers rate this journey as a highlight of the country, although there are occasionally nasty storms. If you're unlucky, be prepared for some pitching and rolling.

The whole trip, from one end of the line to the other, takes about three days. The official schedules are detailed in the table below (only selected ports are shown).

Northbound port	Arrival	Departure
Monkey Bay	–	10am (Fri)
Chipoka	1pm, 4pm (Fri)	
Nkhotakota	12am, 2am (Sat)	
Metangula	6am, 8am (Sat)	
Likoma Island	1.30pm	6pm (Sat)
Nkhata Bay	1am, 5am (Sun)	
Ruarwe	10.15am	11.15am (Sun)
Chilumba	5pm (Sun)	–

Southbound port	Arrival	Departure
Chilumba	–	1am (Mon)
Ruarwe	6.45am	8am (Mon)
Nkhata Bay	12.45pm	8pm (Mon)
Likoma Island	3.15am	6.15am (Tue)
Metangula	noon	2.00pm (Tue)
Nkhotakota	5.30pm	7.30pm (Tue)
Chipoka	3.30am	7.30am (Wed)
Monkey Bay	10.30am (Wed)	–

The *Ilala* has three classes. Cabin Class was once luxurious and the cabins are still in reasonable condition. The spacious 1st Class deck is most popular with travellers, due largely to the sociable bar, around which you are likely to meet a new soulmate or two. There are also seats, a shaded area and mattresses for hire (MK500) in case you're doing the long-haul journey. Economy covers the entire lower deck and is dark and crowded, and engine fumes permeate from below.

Cabin Class and First Class passengers can dine in the ferry's restaurant, where a beef curry, *peri-peri* chicken or meal of similar standard costs about MK800. Food is also served from a galley on the Economy deck;

a meal of beans, rice and vegetables costs under MK150.

Reservations are usually required for Cabin Class. For other classes, tickets are sold only when the boat is sighted.

SAMPLE ROUTES & FARES

All of the following sample fares are from Nkhata Bay.

Destination	Cabin (US$)	1st Class (US$)	Economy (US$)
Likoma Island	52	20	7
Metangula	92	50	12
Ruarwe	46	19	6
Monkey Bay	141	82	18

When the *Ilala* stops at lakeside towns or villages, the water is too shallow for it to come close; the lifeboat is used to ferry passengers ashore. On its southbound journey, the *Ilala* docks at Nkhata Bay for seven hours and traders come aboard, selling food, drinks and newspapers.

BUS & MINIBUS

Bus

Malawi's main bus company is **AXA Coach Services** (☎ 01-876000; agma@agmaholdings.net). AXA operates three different classes. Coaches are the best and the most expensive. It's a luxury non-stop service with air-con, toilet, comfortable **AXA Executive** reclining seats, snacks and fresh coffee, good drivers and even an on-board magazine. Services operate between Blantyre and Lilongwe twice a day (pp214 & 278) from special departure points in each city (not the main bus stations).

AXA Luxury Coach and City Trouper services are the next in line. These buses have air-con and reclining seats as well as TVs, but don't have toilets. They ply the route between Blantyre and Karonga, stopping at all the main towns with limited stops elsewhere.

Lastly there are the country commuter buses. These buses have the most extensive network but they are also the slowest as they stop all over the place. Commuter buses are handy for backpackers as they cover the lakeshore route.

There are several other private bus companies that operate around Malawi, including **Coachline** and **Zimatha**. Some of these operate on a fill-up-and-go basis. Fares are about the same as AXA City Trouper services. If you're headed for Mzuzu another alternative is the comfortable **Super Sink Bus** between Lilongwe and Mzuzu. There's one daily service in the early morning.

There are also local minibus services around towns and to outlying villages, or along the roads that the big buses can't manage. (In Malawi vehicles with about 30 seats are called 'half-buses' to distinguish them from big buses and minibuses.) All of these operate on a fill-up-and-go basis.

In rural areas, the frequency of buses and minibuses drops dramatically – sometimes to nothing. In cases like this, the 'bus' is often a truck or pick-up, with people just piled in the back. In Malawi this is called a *matola*.

Reservations

You can buy a ticket in advance for AXA Executive, Luxury Coach and City Trouper services, all of which have set departure times. They have offices at the main bus stations and departure points or you can also buy tickets at branches of **Postdotnet** (postdotnetmw.com) (post, internet and business centres found in Malawi's major towns). A week's notice is sometimes needed for the Executive coach, particularly for Friday and Sunday services.

CAR & MOTORCYCLE

The majority of main routes are mostly good quality sealed roads, though off the main routes roads are sometimes potholed, making driving slow, difficult and dangerous. Secondary roads are usually graded dirt. Some are well maintained and easy to drive on in a normal car; others are very bad, especially after rain, and slow even with a 4WD. Rural routes are not so good, and after heavy rain are often impassable, sometimes for weeks. Several of the lodges along the lakeshore have poor access roads that need a 4WD and you'd be much better off with one for getting to the more out of the way lodges in Nkhata Bay or Cape Maclear. The same goes for the country's national parks and wildlife reserves.

Bring Your Own Vehicle

If you're bringing a car into Malawi from any other country without a carnet, a temporary import permit costs US$3 (payable in kwacha) and compulsory third-party insurance is US$25 for one month. There's also a US$20 road tax fee – you must produce the documentation for this if you are driving the car out. When you leave Malawi, a permit handling fee of US$5 is payable. Receipts are issued.

Driving Licence

You need a full driving licence (international driving licence is not necessary), and are normally required to be at least 23 years old and have two years' driving experience.

Fuel & Spare Parts

Fuel costs around MK210 per litre for petrol and MK199 per litre for diesel. Supplies are usually reliable and distances between towns with filling stations are not long in Malawi, so you rarely need to worry about running dry. Spare parts are available in Lilongwe, Blantyre and Mzuzu.

Hire

Most car-hire companies are based in Blantyre and Lilongwe. Those with offices in more than one city can arrange pick-up-drop-off deals. International names include Avis, and there are several independent outfits. You should shop around as companies often have special deals and some will negotiate. You can also hire a car through a travel agent – they may have access to special deals. Whoever you hire from, be prepared for a car that is not up to Western standards. Check the tyres and as much else as you can. If anything is worn or broken, demand repairs or a discount.

Self-drive rates for a small car with unlimited mileage start at around US$50 per day. For a 4WD you're looking at around US$150 per day. To this add 17.5% government tax, plus another US$3 to US$7 a day for insurance. There will usually be a fee of about 5% for using a credit card. Also, most companies will quote you in dollars but if you pay by card they'll have to exchange this into kwacha first – usually at a hugely unfavourable rate.

If you'd rather not drive yourself, most companies will arrange a driver for you at a cost of around US$45 a day.

Rental companies in Malawi include the following:

Avis (☎ in Lilongwe 01-756103, 756105, in Blantyre 692368) Also has offices at Lilongwe and Blantyre airports and at some large hotels.

Sputnik Car Hire (☎ 01-761563; www.sputnik-car -hire.mw; Lilongwe)
SS Rent A Car (☎ in Lilongwe 01-751478, in Blantyre 01-822836; www.ssrentacar.com)

Insurance
Third-party insurance is a requirement for all drivers, but this can be arranged through car-hire companies or purchased at border posts.

Road Rules
Malawians drive on the left. Seat belts are compulsory. Speed limits are 80km per hour on main roads and 60km in built-up areas.

TOURS
Several companies organise tours around the country, ranging from a few days to three weeks. Trips into Zambia or Mozambique are also available, although Malawi's safari scene is much smaller than, say, South Africa's or Zimbabwe's. Tours may be 'mobile' (ie moving from camp to camp every few days) or based in one place, with excursions each day. Most are vehicle based, although some outfits also organise walking trips, horseback safaris, or boating on the lake. Tours normally include transport, accommodation and food, but prices vary considerably according to standards – from budget to luxury. There are only a few budget companies that can arrange tours on the spot – most prefer advance bookings, although sometimes a couple of days is enough. Budget tours are usually around US$50 per day. Most midrange and top-end companies also need advance bookings, and charge from US$80 per person per day, easily climbing to US$200 per day or more.

The following is a list of major tour operators in Malawi, with a variety of budgets to suit most pockets.

Barefoot Safaris (☎ 01-707346; www.barefoot-safaris .com) Offers midrange tours, mostly geared towards wildlife watching in Malawi, Zambia and Tanzania. Tours are in a vehicle or on foot and it can also tailor individual safaris. Whether you're walking or viewing, tours cost from around US$100 per person per day and include all meals and accommodation.

Jambo-Africa (☎ 01-823709; www.jambo-africa.com) Based at the Mount Soche Hotel in Blantyre. On most of their tours you'll stay in lodge accommodation so they are on the pricey side. A three-day tour to Lengwe National Park costs US$500 per person and Mt Mulanje hiking packages cost from US$370 for three days.

Land & Lake Safaris (☎ 09-942661; www.kayak africa.net) An excellent company running tours to suit all budgets from three-day camping safaris in South Luangwa (per person US$375) to a luxury 11-day extravaganza combining South Luangwa with sailing on Lake Malawi (per person US$2500). It also runs specialised birdwatching tours and hiking tours.

Kiboko Safaris (☎ 01-751226; www.kiboko-safaris.com) These guys are the best option for budget trips, with a range of wallet-friendly camping tours on offer, including week-long tours of southern or northern Malawi, trips to South Luangwa and Victoria Falls, and a 15-day East Africa Odyssey. Prices start at around US$70 for budget camping tours and US$120 for a more comfortable tour staying in chalets.

Budget Safaris (☎ 0999-278903; www.budget-safari .com; Nkhata Bay) Organises a wide range of individually tailored tours all around Malawi and Zambia (you can choose whether to camp or stay in comfortable lodges). Prices start at around US$360 per person for a five-day tour of Vwaza and Nyika. It also offers birdwatching tours and car rental.

Wilderness Safaris (☎ 01-771393; www.wilderness -safaris.com; Bisnowaty Service Centre, Kenyatta Rd, Lilongwe) Operates all accommodation and facilities in Liwonde National Park and has recently acquired the concession for Nyika National Park. It can also arrange flights, air charters, car hire and mid- to top-end safaris to South Luangwa National Park in Zambia.

TRAIN
Trains run every Wednesday between Blantyre and Balaka (MK500), but passengers rarely use them as road transport on this route is quicker and cheaper. The service of most use to travellers is the twice-weekly train service (Tuesdays and Saturdays) between Limbe and the Mozambican border at Nsanje (MK800).

Central East African Railways took over the running of the railway in 2008. A US$7 million investment hopes to revitalise the railway and extend it to link up with Chipata in Zambia.

Health Dr Caroline Evans

CONTENTS

Africa certainly has an impressive selection of tropical diseases on offer, but you're much more likely to get a bout of diarrhoea, a cold or an infected mosquito bite than an exotic disease. As long as you stay up to date with your vaccinations and take some basic preventive measures, you'd have to be pretty unlucky to succumb to most of the health hazards covered in this chapter.

BEFORE YOU GO

H1N1

The H1N1 virus (commonly referred to as 'Swine Flu') was given a 'Phase 6' rating by the World Health Organization in June 2009. A 'Phase 6' alert means the virus is now considered a global pandemic. Like most countries, Zambia and Malawi have been affected. As of October 2009, the virus was widespread geographically but the number of cases were relatively low, as was the severity.

At press time, airport staff in some countries were screening arriving passengers for symptoms of the H1N1 flu. Check with the embassy of the country you're visiting to see if they have imposed any travel restrictions. It's best not to travel if you have flu-like symptoms of any sort.

For the latest information, check with the World Health Organization (www.who.int/en).

Before you go get a check-up at your dentist, and from your doctor if you have any regular medication or chronic illness, eg high blood pressure or asthma. You should also organise spare contact lenses and glasses (and take your optical prescription with you); get a first aid and medical kit together; and arrange necessary vaccinations.

Many vaccines don't take effect until two weeks after you've been inoculated, so visit a doctor six to eight weeks before departure. Ask your doctor for an International Certificate of Vaccination (otherwise known as the yellow booklet), which will list all the vaccinations you've received. This is mandatory for the African countries that require proof of yellow fever vaccination upon entry, but it's a good idea to carry it anyway, wherever you travel. Those heading off to very remote areas might like to do a first aid course (contact the Red Cross or St John's Ambulance).

Bring any medications in their original containers, clearly labelled, together with a signed and dated letter from your physician describing all medical conditions and medications.

INSURANCE

Find out whether your insurance plan will make payments directly to providers or will reimburse you later for overseas health expenditures. It's vital to ensure that your travel insurance will cover the emergency transport required to get you to a hospital in a major city, to better medical facilities elsewhere in Africa, or all the way home, by air and with a medical attendant if necessary.

RECOMMENDED VACCINATIONS

The **World Health Organization** (www.who.int/en/) recommends that all travellers be covered for diphtheria, tetanus, measles, mumps, rubella and polio, as well as for hepatitis B, regardless of their destination.

The following vaccinations are recommended by the **Centers for Disease Control and Prevention** (CDC; www.cdc.gov) for all parts of Africa: hepatitis A, hepatitis B, meningococcal meningitis, rabies and typhoid, and boosters for tetanus, diphtheria and measles.

Yellow fever is not necessarily recommended for all parts of Africa, although the certificate is an entry requirement for many countries (see p311).

MEDICAL CHECKLIST

It is a very good idea to carry a medical and first aid kit with you when travelling, to help yourself in the case of minor illness or injury. You should consider packing the following items:

- Antibiotics (prescription only), eg ciprofloxacin (Ciproxin) or norfloxacin (Utinor)
- Antidiarrhoeal drugs (eg loperamide)
- Acetaminophen (paracetamol) or aspirin
- Anti-inflammatory drugs (eg ibuprofen)
- Antihistamines (for hayfever and allergic reactions)
- Antibacterial ointment (eg Bactroban) for cuts and abrasions (prescription only)
- Antimalaria pills
- Steroid cream, such as hydrocortisone (for allergic rashes)
- Bandages, gauze, gauze rolls
- Adhesive or paper tape
- Scissors, safety pins, tweezers
- Thermometer
- Pocket knife
- DEET-containing insect repellent for the skin
- Permethrin-containing insect spray for clothing, tents, and bed nets
- Sun block
- Oral rehydration salts
- Iodine tablets (for water purification)
- Syringes and sterile needles
- Acetazolamide (Diamox) for altitude sickness (prescription only)
- Sterile needles, syringes and fluids if travelling to remote areas

If you are travelling through a malarial area – particularly an area where falciparum malaria predominates – consider taking a self-diagnostic kit that can identify malaria in the blood from a finger prick.

INTERNET RESOURCES

There is a wealth of travel health advice on the internet. The WHO publishes a superb book called *International Travel and Health* which is revised annually and is available online at no cost at www.who.int/ith/. Other websites of general interest are: MD Travel Health at www.mdtravelhealth.com, which provides complete travel health recommendations for every country, updated daily (also at no cost); the CDC at www.cdc.gov; and Fit for Travel at www.fitfortravel.scot.nhs.uk, which has up-to-date information about outbreaks and is very user-friendly.

It's also a good idea to consult your government's travel health website before departure, if one is available.

IN AFRICA

AVAILABILITY & COST OF HEALTH CARE

Health care in Africa is varied: it can be excellent in the major cities, which generally have well-trained doctors and nurses, but it is often patchy off the beaten track. Medicine and even sterile dressings and intravenous fluids might need to be purchased from a local pharmacy by patients or their relatives. The standard of dental care is equally variable, and there is an increased risk of hepatitis B and HIV transmission via poorly sterilised equipment. Generally, public hospitals in Africa offer the cheapest service, but will have the least up-to-date equipment and medications; mission hospitals often have more reasonable facilities; and private hospitals and clinics are more expensive but tend to have more advanced drugs and equipment and better trained medical staff.

It is strongly recommended that all drugs for chronic diseases be brought from home. Also, the availability and efficacy of condoms cannot be relied upon – bring all the contraception you'll need.

There is a high risk of contracting HIV from infected blood if you receive a transfusion in Africa. The **Blood Care Foundation** (www.bloodcare.org.uk) is a useful source of safe, screened blood, which can be transported to any part of the world within 24 hours.

INFECTIOUS DISEASES

While not an exhaustive list, some precautions against these most common traveller ailments can go a long way.

Diphtheria

Diphtheria is spread through close respiratory contact. It usually causes a temperature and a severe sore throat. Sometimes a membrane forms across the throat resulting in the need for a tracheostomy to prevent suffocation. Vaccination is recommended for those likely to be in close contact with the local population in infected areas. More important for long stays than for short-term trips.

Hepatitis A

Hepatitis A is spread through contaminated food (particularly shellfish) and water. It causes jaundice and, although it is rarely fatal, it can cause prolonged lethargy and delayed recovery. The first symptoms include dark urine and a yellow colour to the whites of the eyes. Sometimes a fever and abdominal pain might be present. Hepatitis A vaccine is given as an injection: a single dose will give protection for up to a year.

Hepatitis B

Hepatitis B is spread through infected blood, contaminated needles and sexual intercourse. It affects the liver, causing jaundice and occasionally results in liver failure. Most people recover completely, but some people become chronic carriers of the virus, which can lead eventually to cirrhosis or liver cancer. Those visiting high-risk areas for long periods, or those with increased social or occupational risk, should be immunised.

HIV

Human immunodeficiency virus (HIV), the virus that causes acquired immune deficiency syndrome (AIDS), is an enormous problem throughout Africa. The virus is spread through infected blood and blood products, by sexual intercourse with an infected partner and from an infected mother to her baby during childbirth and breastfeeding. It can be spread through 'blood to blood' contacts, such as with contaminated instruments during medical, dental, acupuncture and other body-piercing procedures, and through sharing of intravenous needles. At present there is no cure. If you think you might have been infected with HIV, a blood test is necessary; a three-month gap after exposure and before testing is required to allow antibodies to appear in the blood.

Malaria

The disease is caused by a parasite in the bloodstream spread via the bite of the female Anopheles mosquito. Unlike most other diseases regularly encountered by travellers, there is no vaccination against malaria (yet). However, several different drugs are used to prevent malaria, and new ones are in the pipeline. Up-to-date advice from a travel health clinic is essential as some medication is more suitable for some travellers than others.

Malaria can present in several ways. The early stages include headaches, fevers, generalised aches and pains, and malaise, which could be mistaken for flu. Other symptoms can include abdominal pain, diarrhoea and a cough. Anyone who develops a fever in a malarial area should assume malarial infection until a blood test proves negative, even if you have been taking antimalarial medication. If not treated, the next stage could develop within 24 hours, particularly if falciparum malaria is the parasite: jaundice, then reduced consciousness and coma (also known as cerebral malaria) followed by death. Treatment in hospital is essential, and the death rate might still be as high as 10% even in the best intensive-care facilities.

Be obsessive about avoiding mosquito bites. Use nets and insect repellent, and report any fever or flu-like symptoms to a doctor as soon as possible.

If you are planning a journey through a malarial area, particularly one in which the falciparum type predominates, consider taking standby treatment. Emergency standby treatment should be seen as emergency treatment aimed at saving the patient's life and not as routine self-medication. It should be used only if you will be far from medical facilities and have been advised about the symptoms of malaria and how to use the medication. Medical advice should be sought as soon as possible to confirm whether the treatment has been successful. The type of standby treatment used will depend on local conditions, such as drug resistance, and on what antimalarial drugs were being used before standby treatment. This is worthwhile because you want to avoid contracting a particularly serious form such as cerebral malaria, which affects the brain and central nervous system and can be fatal in 24 hours. As mentioned on p308, self-diagnostic kits, which can identify malaria in the blood from a finger prick, are also available in the West.

HEALTH

The risks from malaria to both mother and fetus during pregnancy are considerable. Unless good medical care can be guaranteed, travel throughout Africa when pregnant – particularly to malarial areas – should be discouraged unless essential.

Meningococcal Meningitis

Meningococcal infection is spread through close respiratory contact and is more likely in crowded situations, such as dormitories, buses and clubs. Infection is uncommon in travellers. Vaccination is recommended for long stays and is especially important towards the end of the dry season, which varies across the continent. Symptoms include a fever, severe headache, neck stiffness and a red rash. Immediate medical treatment is necessary.

Poliomyelitis

This is generally spread through contaminated food and water. It is one of the vaccines given in childhood and should be boosted every 10 years, either orally (a drop on the tongue) or as an injection. Polio can be carried asymptomatically (ie showing no symptoms) and could cause a transient fever. In rare cases it causes weakness or paralysis of one or more muscles, which might be permanent.

Rabies

Rabies is spread by receiving the bites or licks of an infected animal on broken skin. It is always fatal once the clinical symptoms start (which might be up to several months after an infected bite), so post-bite vaccination should be given as soon as possible. Post-bite vaccination (whether or not you've been vaccinated before the bite) prevents the virus from spreading to the central nervous system. Animal handlers should be vaccinated, as should those travelling to remote areas where a reliable source of post-bite vaccine is not available within 24 hours. Three preventive injections are needed over a month. If you have not been vaccinated you will need a course of five injections starting 24 hours or as soon as possible after the injury. If you have been vaccinated, you will need fewer post-bite injections, and have more time to seek medical help.

Schistosomiasis (Bilharzia)

This disease is spread by flukes (minute worms) that are carried by a species of freshwater snail. The flukes are carried inside the snail, which sheds them into slow-moving or still water. The parasites penetrate human skin during paddling or swimming and then migrate to the bladder or bowel. They are passed out via stool or urine and could contaminate fresh water, where the cycle starts again. Avoid paddling or swimming in suspect freshwater lakes or slow-running rivers. There might be no symptoms. There might be a transient fever and rash, and advanced cases might have blood in the stool or in the urine. A blood test can detect antibodies if you might have been exposed, and treatment is then possible in specialist travel or infectious disease clinics. If left untreated the infection could cause kidney failure or permanent bowel damage. It is not possible for you to infect others. Self-treatment: none.

Tuberculosis (TB)

TB is spread through close respiratory contact and occasionally through infected milk or milk products. BCG vaccination is recommended for those likely to be mixing closely with the local population, although it gives only moderate protection against TB. It is more important for long stays than for short-term stays. Inoculation with the BCG vaccine is not available in all countries but is given routinely to many children in developing countries. The vaccination causes a small permanent scar at the site of injection and is usually given in a specialised chest clinic. It is a live vaccine and should not be given to pregnant women or immunocompromised individuals.

TB can be asymptomatic, only being picked up on a routine chest X-ray. Alternatively, it can cause a cough, weight loss or fever, sometimes months or even years after exposure.

Typhoid

This is spread through food or water contaminated by infected human faeces. The first symptom is usually a fever or a pink rash on the abdomen. Sometimes septicaemia (blood poisoning) can occur. A typhoid vaccine (typhim Vi, typherix) will give protection for three years. In some countries, the oral vaccine Vivotif is also available. Antibiotics are usually given as treatment, and death is rare unless septicaemia occurs.

Yellow Fever

Travellers should carry a certificate as evidence of vaccination if they have recently been in an infected country, to avoid any possible difficulties with immigration. For a full list of these countries, visit the websites of the **CDC** (www.cdc.gov/travel/blusheet.htm) or the **WHO** (www.who.int/wer/). There is always the possibility that a traveller without a legally required, up-to-date certificate will be vaccinated and detained in isolation at the port of arrival for up to 10 days, or possibly repatriated.

Yellow fever is spread by infected mosquitoes. Symptoms range from a flu-like illness to severe hepatitis (liver inflammation), jaundice and death. The yellow fever vaccination must be given at a designated clinic and is valid for 10 years. It is a live vaccine and must not be given to immunocompromised or pregnant travellers.

TRAVELLERS' DIARRHOEA

It's very likely that you will get diarrhoea while travelling in Africa. It's the most common travel-related illness – figures suggest that at least half of all travellers to Africa will get diarrhoea at some stage. Sometimes dietary changes, such as increased spices or oils, are the cause. To help prevent diarrhoea, avoid tap water unless you're sure it's safe to drink (see p312). You should also only eat fresh fruits or vegetables if cooked or peeled, and be wary of dairy products that might contain unpasteurised milk. Although freshly cooked food can often be a safe option, plates or serving utensils might be dirty, so you should be highly selective when eating food from street vendors (make sure that cooked food is piping hot all the way through). If you develop diarrhoea, be sure to drink plenty of fluids, preferably an oral rehydration solution containing water (lots), and some salt and sugar. If you start having more than four or five stools a day, you should start taking an antibiotic (usually a quinoline drug such as ciprofloxacin or norfloxacin) and an antidiarrhoeal agent (such as loperamide) if you are not within easy reach of a toilet. If diarrhoea is bloody, persists for more than 72 hours or is accompanied by fever, shaking chills or severe abdominal pain, you should seek medical attention.

Amoebic Dysentery

Contracted by eating contaminated food and water, amoebic dysentery causes blood and mucus in the faeces. It can be relatively mild and tends to come on gradually, but seek medical advice if you think you have the illness as it won't clear up without treatment (which is with specific antibiotics).

Giardiasis

This, like amoebic dysentery, is also caused by ingesting contaminated food or water. The illness usually appears a week or more after you have been exposed to the offending parasite. Giardiasis might cause only a short-lived bout of typical travellers' diarrhoea, but it can also cause persistent diarrhoea. Ideally, seek medical advice if you suspect you have giardiasis, but if you are in a remote area you could start a course of antibiotics.

ENVIRONMENTAL HAZARDS
Heat Exhaustion

This condition occurs following heavy sweating and excessive fluid loss with inadequate replacement of fluids and salt, and is particularly common in hot climates when taking unaccustomed exercise before full acclimatisation. Symptoms include headache, dizziness and tiredness. Dehydration is already happening by the time you feel thirsty – aim to drink sufficient water to produce pale, diluted urine. Self-treatment: fluid replacement with water and/or fruit juice, and cooling by cold water and fans. The treatment of the salt-loss component consists of consuming salty fluids, as in soup, and adding a little more table salt to foods than usual.

Heatstroke

Heat exhaustion is a precursor to the much more serious condition of heatstroke. In this case there is damage to the sweating mechanism, with an excessive rise in body temperature; irrational and hyperactive behaviour; and eventually loss of consciousness then death. Rapid cooling by spraying the body with water and fanning is ideal. Emergency fluid and electrolyte replacement is usually also required by intravenous drip.

HEALTH

Insect Bites & Stings

Mosquitoes might not always carry malaria or dengue fever, but they (and other insects) can cause irritation and infected bites. To avoid these, take the same precautions as you would for avoiding malaria (see p309). Use DEET-based insect repellents.

Bee and wasp stings cause real problems only to those who have a severe allergy to the stings (anaphylaxis.) If you are one of these people, carry an 'epipen' – an adrenaline (epinephrine) injection, which could save your life.

Scorpions are frequently found in arid or dry climates. They give a painful bite that is sometimes life-threatening. If bitten by a scorpion, take a painkiller. Medical treatment should be sought if collapse occurs.

Bed bugs are often found in hostels and cheap hotels. They lead to very itchy, lumpy bites. Spraying the mattress with crawling insect killer after changing bedding will get rid of them.

Scabies is also frequently found in cheap accommodation. These tiny mites live in the skin, particularly between the fingers. They cause an intensely itchy rash. The itch is easily treated with malathion and permethrin lotion from a pharmacy; other members of the household also need treating to avoid spreading scabies, even if they do not show any symptoms.

Snake Bites

Avoid getting bitten! Do not walk barefoot, or stick your hand into holes or cracks. However, 50% of those bitten by venomous snakes are not actually injected with poison. If bitten by a snake, immobilise the bitten limb with a splint (such as a stick) and apply a bandage over the site, with firm pressure. Do not apply a tourniquet, or cut or suck the bite. Get medical help as soon as possible so antivenom can be given if needed.

Water

Never drink tap water unless it has been boiled, filtered or chemically disinfected (such as with iodine tablets). Never drink from streams, rivers and lakes. It's also best to avoid drinking from pumps and wells – some do bring pure water to the surface, but the presence of animals can still contaminate supplies.

TRADITIONAL MEDICINE

At least 80% of the African population relies on traditional medicine, often because conventional Western-style medicine is too expensive, because of prevailing cultural attitudes and beliefs, or simply because in some cases it works. Although some African remedies seem to work on malaria, sickle cell anaemia, high blood pressure and some AIDS symptoms, most African healers learn their art by apprenticeship, so education is inconsistent and unregulated.

HEALTH

Language

CONTENTS

MALAWI

English is the official language in Malawi and is widely spoken. Chichewa, one of the many languages in Malawi, is used throughout the country as a common tongue.

CHICHEWA

Chichewa is a complex language so one single word cannot always be given for its English equivalent. The most common form is given here, but keep in mind when using this that you may not be speaking 'proper' Chichewa. Importantly, though, you'll be understood, and locals will be pleased to hear a visitor using their language.

Basics

Mazungu means 'white person', but is not derogatory. *Bambo* literally means 'father' but is a polite way to address any Malawian man. The female equivalent is *Amai* or *Mai*. Chichewa speakers talking together will normally use English for numbers and prices. Similarly, time is nearly always expressed in English.

Hello.	*Moni.*
Please.	*Chonde.*
Thank you.	*Zikomo.*
Excuse me.	*Zikomo.*
Good./Fine./OK.	*Chabwino.*
Good night.	*Gonani bwino.*
How are you?	*Muli bwanji?*
I'm fine.	*Ndili bwino.*
Goodbye. (to person staying)	*Tsala bwino.* (lit: 'stay well')
Goodbye. (to person leaving)	*Pitani bwino.* (lit: 'go well')
What's your name?	*Dzina lako ndani?*
Yes./No.	*Inde./Iyayi.*
I don't understand.	*Sindikunva.*
How much?	*Ntengo bwanji?*
I want ...	*Ndifuna ...*
I don't want ...	*Sindifuna ...*
today	*lero*
tomorrow (early)	*m'mara*
tomorrow	*mara*
yesterday	*dzulo*
Women	*Akazi*
Men	*Akuma*
to eat	*kudya*
to sleep	*kugona*
to buy	*kugula*

Food & Drink

Please bring me ...	*Mundi passe ...*
bread	*buledi*
chicken	*nkhuku*
coffee	*khofi*
eggs	*mazira*
fish	*somba*
fruit (one)	*chipasso*
fruits (many)	*zipasso*
lake perch	*chambo*
meat	*nyama*
milk	*mkaka*
potatoes	*batata*
tea	*ti*
vegetables	*mquani*
water	*mazi*

In restaurants *nsima* is a maize porridge with a sauce of meat, beans or vegetables.

ZAMBIA

English is the official language and is widely spoken. Of the scores of languages spoken in Zambia, the main four are covered in this chapter: Bemba, Lozi, Nyanja and Tonga.

Zambians place much emphasis on the relationship between speakers and it's very important to use the correct forms of address, particularly with the Lozi. There are often two different ways to say 'you' and to greet people, depending on their social status. The informal mode is used for children, friends and peers. The polite mode is used for strangers, elders and adults of equal or higher status. The following phrases include the abbreviations 'inf' for informal and 'pol' for polite where required.

BEMBA

Bemba is spoken very widely in Lusaka and in the Central, Copperbelt, Luapula and Northern Provinces. When addressing elders, add *bashikulu* (grandfather) for a man and *bamama* (grandmother) for a woman. You can generally get by using English numbers for prices and times.

Greetings & Civilities

Hello.	*Muli shani.*
Greetings!	*Uli shani?* (inf)
	Mwapolenipo mukwai! (pol)
Goodbye.	*Shalapo.* (inf)
	Shalenipo mukwai. (pol)
Good morning.	*Wabuka shani?* (inf)
	Mwashibukeni?/
	Mwabuka shani? (pol)
Good evening.	*Icungulupo/*
	Mwatushenipo mukwai.
Good night.	*Icungulopo.*
How are you?	*Uli shani?* (inf)/
	Muli shani? (pol)
I'm fine.	*Ndifye bwino.*
Good./Fine./OK.	*Chawama./Chilifye./Chisuma./*
	Chilifye bwino.
Please.	*Mukwai.*
Thank you./	*Natasha/Natotela/Banjeleleko.*
Excuse me.	

Useful Words & Phrases

Yes.	*Ee./Ee mukwai.*
No.	*Awe./Teifyo.*
I don't understand.	*Nshumfwile bwino.*
What's your name?	*Niwe nani ishina?* (inf)
	Nimwe banani ishina? (pol)
My name is ...	*Ishina lyandi ni ne ...*
How much?	*Shinga/Nishinga?*
Toilets	*Ifimbusu*
Men	*Baume*
Women	*Banakashi*
today	*lelo*

tomorrow (early)	*mailo ulucelo*
tomorrow	*mailo*
yesterday	*mailo yafumineko*

Food & Drink

Please bring me ...	*Ndetele niko ...*
bananas	*nkonde*
beans	*cilemba*
beer	*bwalwa*
bread	*umukate*
cassava	*kalundwe*
chicken	*inkoko*
coffee	*kofi*
eggs	*amani*
fish	*isabi*
fruit (one/many)	*icisabo/ifisabo*
meat	*inama*
milk	*umukaka*
mushrooms	*ubowa*
oranges	*amachungwa*
peanuts	*mbalala*
potatoes	*ifyumbu*
tea	*chai*
vegetables	*umusalu*
water	*amenshi*
drinking water	*amenshi yakunwa*

Amasuku is a very sweet wild fruit; *ifungo* or *lufungo* is a wild-plum-like fruit.

LOZI

Lozi is spoken mainly in Western Province. If greeting royalty or aristocrats, use *Ba lumele Malozi, sha.* English numbers are usually used to express time.

Greetings & Civilities

Hello.	*Eeni, sha.* (general greeting)
	Lumela. (inf)
	Mu lumeleng' sha. (pol)
Goodbye.	*Musiale (foo/hande/sinde).* (pol)
	Siala (foo/hande/sinde). (inf)
Good morning.	*U zuhile.* (inf)/
	Mu zuhile. (pol)
Good afternoon/	*Ki manzibuana./U tozi.* (inf)
evening.	*Mu tozi.* (pol)
Good night.	*Ki busihu.*
How are you?	*U cwang'?/W'a pila?/*
	W'a zuha? (inf)
	Mu cwang'?/Mw'a pila?/
	Mw'a zuha? (pol)
I'm fine.	*N'i teng'/N'a pila/N'a zuha.*
Please.	*Sha.* (pol)
Thank you (very much).	*N'itumezi (hahulu).*

Excuse me.	*Ni swalele.* (inf)
	Mu ni swalele. (pol)
Good./Fine.	*Ki hande.*
OK.	*Ku lukile.*

Useful Words & Phrases

Yes.	*Ee.* (inf)/
	Eeni. (pol – add *sha* at
	the end for Sir/Madam)
No.	*Awa.* (inf)
	Batili. (pol)
I don't understand.	*Ha ni utwi.*
What's your name?	*Libizo la hao ki wena*
	mang'? (inf)
	Libizo la mina ki mina
	bo mang'? (pol)
My name is ...	*K'i na ...*
How much?	*Ki bukai?*

Toilets	*Bimbuzi/Limbuzi*
Men	*Banna*
Women	*Basali*

today	*kachenu*
tomorrow (early)	*kamuso kakusasasa/ka mamiso*
tomorrow	*kamuso*
yesterday	*mabani*

Food & Drink

Use *Ndate* (sir) or *Ma* (madam) to denote 'please'.

Please bring me ...	*Ndate/Ma, ha mu ni fe ...*
banana/s	*likonde/makonde*
beans	*manawa*
beef	*nama ya komu*
beer	*bucwala/mutoho*
bread	*sinkwa*
chicken	*kuhu*
coffee	*kofi*
egg/s	*lii/mai*
fish	*tapi*
food	*licho/sicho*
freshwater bream	*papati*
fruit (one)	*tolwana*
fruit (many)	*litolwana*
gravy	*mulo*
meat	*nama*
milk	*mabisi*
mushrooms	*mbowa*
peanuts/cashews	*ndongo*
pork	*nama ya kulube*
potatoes	*makwili*
rice	*raisi*
salt	*lizwai*

tea	*tii*
vegetable/s	*miloho/muloho*
water	*mezi*
drinking water	*mezi a kunwa*

Some local foods and dishes:

maheu	nonalcoholic fermented porridge
mala	intestines
munati	sweet
mushwati	large sugar cane
nswe	small sugar cane
shombo	cassava leaf vegetable

Numbers

1	*il'ingw'i*
2	*z'e peli* or *bubeli*
3	*z'e t'alu* or *bulalu*
4	*z'e ne* or *bune*
5	*z'e keta-lizoho*

NYANJA

Nyanja is widely spoken in Lusaka and in Central and Eastern Provinces. You can generally get by using English numbers for prices and times.

Greetings & Civilities

Hello.	*Bwanji.*
Good morning.	*Mwauka bwanji.*
Good afternoon.	*Mwachoma bwanji.*
Good night.	*Gonani bwino.*
Goodbye.	*Pitani bwino/salani bwino.*
How are you?	*Uli bwanji?* (inf)
	Muli bwanji? (pol)
I'm fine.	*Ndili bwino.*
Thank you./	*Zikomo.*
Excuse me.	
Thank you very much.	*Zikomo kwambiri.*
Good./Fine./OK.	*Chabwino.*

Useful Words & Phrases

Yes./No.	*Inde./Iyai.*
I don't understand.	*Sindimvera.*
What's your name?	*Dzina ianu ndani?*
My name is ...	*Dzina ianga ndine ...*
How much?	*Ndizingati?*

Toilets	*Chimbuzi*
Men	*Amuna*
Women	*Akazi*

today	*lelo*
tomorrow (early)	*m'mawa*
tomorrow	*mawa*
yesterday	*dzulo*

Food & Drink

Please bring me ...	*Ndifuna kukhala ndi ...*
beans	*kaela*
beef	*nyama ya ng'ombe*
beer	*mowa*
bread	*buledi*
chicken	*nkuku*
coffee	*khofi*
eggs	*ma egesi*
fish	*nsomba*
fruit (one/many)	*cipatso/zipatso*
meat	*nyama*
milk	*mukaka*
pork	*nyama ya nkumba*
potatoes	*mapotato*
sweet potato	*kandolo*
tea	*tiyi*
vegetables	*mbeu zaziwisi*
water	*mandzi*
drinking water	*mandzi yo kumwa*

TONGA

Tonga is spoken mainly in Southern Province. You can generally get by using English numbers for prices and time.

Greetings & Civilities

Hello.	*Wabonwa/Wapona.* (inf)
	Mwabonwa/Mwpona. (pol)
Goodbye.	*Muchale kabotu.*
Good morning.	*Mwabuka kabotu.*
Good evening.	*Kwa siya.*
Good night.	*Kusiye kabotu.*
How are you?	*Muli buti?*
I'm fine.	*Ndi kabotu.*
Please.	*Ndalomba.*
Thank you./	*Amuninjatile.*
Excuse me.	
Thank you very much.	*Twalumba kapati.*
Good./Fine./OK.	*Mbubo.*
What's your name?	*Ndiweni izyina?*
My name is ...	*Izyina iyangu ndime ...*

Useful Words & Phrases

Yes.	*Ee.*
No.	*Pepe.*

I don't understand.	*Tandileteleli.*
How much?	*Mali nzi?*

Toilets	*Chimbuzi*
Men	*Ba lumi/Mulombwana*
Women	*Ba kaintu*

today	*tunu*
tomorrow	*chifumo*
yesterday	*ijilo*

Food & Drink

Please bring me ...	*Mu ndetele ...*
beans	*bunyanga*
beef	*nyama ya ng'ombe*
beer	*bukoko*
bread	*chinkwa*
chicken	*nkuku*
coffee	*nofi*
eggs	*ma gee*
fish	*inswi*
meat	*nyama*
milk	*mukupa*
onion	*hangisi*
potatoes	*mapotato*
pumpkin leaves	*lungu*
rice	*laisi*
sweet potato	*chibwali*
tea	*tii*
tomatoes	*lunkomba*
vegetables	*cisu mani*
water	*menda*
drinking water	*menda a kumwa*

Numbers

1	*komwe*
2	*tobilo*
3	*totatwe*
4	*tone*
5	*tosanwe*

Glossary

Although English is widely spoken in Zambia and Malawi, native speakers from Australasia, North America and the UK will notice many words that have developed different meanings locally. There are also many unusual terms that have been borrowed from Afrikaans, Portuguese or indigenous languages. This Glossary includes many of these particular 'Afro-English' words, as well as other general terms and abbreviations that may not be understood.

In African English, repetition for emphasis is common: something that burnt you would be 'hot hot'; fields after the rains are 'green green'; a crowded minibus with no more room is 'full full', and so on.

For useful words and phrases in local languages, see p313.

ablutions block – found at camping grounds and caravan parks: a building that contains toilets, showers and a washing-up area; also known as an amenities block

af – derogatory reference to a black person, as bad as 'nigger' or 'abo'

animist – a system of belief in the existence of the human soul, and in spirits that inhabit or are represented by natural objects and phenomena, which have the power to influence human life for good or ill

baas – boss; subservient address reserved mainly for white males

baixa – commercial area

bakkie – utility or pick-up truck (pronounced bucky)

bilharzia – water-borne disease caused by blood flukes (parasitic flatworms) that are transmitted by freshwater snails

biltong – a chewy dried meat that can be anything from beef to kudu or ostrich

boerewors – Afrikaner farmers' sausage of varying quality

boma – a local word for 'town' in Zambia and Malawi, and some other countries, but elsewhere in East Africa it means 'fortified stockade'; may be derived from the colonial term BOMA (British Overseas Military Administration), applied to any government building, such as offices or forts

braai – a barbecue; a Southern African institution, particularly among whites

buck or **bok** – any kind of antelope

buhobe – staple made from maize, millet or cassava flour (Lozi)

bundu – the bush, the wilderness

bushcamp – a small and exclusive place to stay deep in a national park, usually dismantled in the wet season, then rebuilt next dry season

busunso – any sauce used with buhobe

camp (noun) – a place to stay, but not necessarily one that entails 'camping', or even budget accommodation; throughout Africa, many places with 'camp' in the name are upmarket establishments – effectively small hotels in national parks but retaining the feel of being out in the bush

CBD – Central Business District; this rather scientific-sounding abbreviation is commonly used where other English speakers might say city centre or downtown area

cell phone – mobile phone (wireless)

chambo – a fish of the tilapia family, commonly eaten in Malawi

chapa – converted passenger truck or minivan (Malawi)

chibuku – local style mass-produced beer, stored in tanks and served in buckets, or available in takeaway cartons (mostly in Malawi) and plastic bottles known as scuds.

chiperone – damp misty weather that affects southern Malawi

chitenje – multicoloured piece of material used as a scarf and sarong

dagga – (pronounced da-kha) Southern African term for marijuana

dambo – area of grass, reeds or swamp alongside a river course

dassies – herbivorous gopher-like mammals of two species: Procavia capensis, also called the rock hyrax, and Dendrohyrax arborea or tree hyrax; these are not rodents but thought to be the closest living relatives of the elephant

dhow – Arabic sailing vessel that dates from ancient times

difaqane – forced migration by several Southern African ethnic groups in the face of Zulu aggression; also known as mfecane

djembe – a type of hand drum

donga – steep-sided gully caused by soil erosion

donkey boiler – it may sound cruel, but this has nothing to do with donkeys; it's a water tank positioned over a fire and used to heat water for showers and other purposes

drift – a river ford; most are normally dry

euphorbia – several species of cactus-like succulents that are endemic in Southern Africa

flotty – a hat for canoe safaris, with a chin-strap and a bit of cork in a zippered pocket to ensure that it floats in case of a capsize

4WD – four-wheel drive; locally called 4x4

fynbos – fine bush, primarily proteas, heaths and ericas

game – formerly used for any animal hunted, now applies to all large, four-footed creatures

gap it – make a quick exit; often refers to emigration from troubled African countries

GMA – Game Management Area

igini – magic charm used by witches; other magic charms are also known as *inkuwa*

ilya – a delicacy of very thin corn porridge mixed with yoghurt and sugar (Lozi)

inselberg – isolated ranges and hills; literally 'island mountains'

Izzit? – rhetorical question that most closely translates as 'Really?' and used without regard to gender, person or number of subjects; therefore, may also mean 'Is it?', 'Are you?', 'Is he?', 'Are they?', 'Is she?', 'Are we?' , etc; also 'How izzit?', for 'How's it going?'

jesse – dense, thorny scrub, normally impenetrable to humans

jol – party, both verb and noun

just now – refers to some time in the future but implies a certain degree of imminence; it could be half an hour from now or two days from now

kalindula – modern Zambian style of music involving a blend of Congolese rumba and more gentle indigenous sounds

kampango – catfish (Malawi)

kankobele – thumb piano; consists of narrow iron keys mounted in rows on a wooden sound board

kapenta – an anchovy-like fish (*Limnothrissa mioda*) caught in Lake Kariba

KK – popular nickname for Kenneth Kaunda (not derogatory)

kotu – king's court (Zambia)

kwacha – Zambian and Malawian currency

kwasa kwasa – Congo-style rumba music

litunga – king (Zambia)

LMS – London Missionary Society

lodge – generally like a camp, ie remote and exclusive, but larger and with more permanent features

lupembe – wind instrument made from animal horn

lutindzi – type of grass

mabele – sorghum

makishi – a dance performed in Zambia featuring male dancers wearing masks of stylised human faces and with grass skirts and anklets

Malawi shandy – nonalcoholic drink made from ginger beer, Angostura bitters, orange or lemon slices, soda and ice

mapiko – masked dance of the Makonde people

marimba – African xylophone, made from strips of resonant wood with various-sized gourds for sound boxes

mataku – watermelon wine

matola – pick-up or van carrying passengers (Malawi)

mbira – thumb piano; consists of five to 24 narrow iron keys mounted in rows on a wooden sound board

mealie meal or **mielie pap** – maize porridge, a dietary staple throughout the region

mielies – cobs of maize

mfecane – see *difaqane*

miombo – dry, open woodland, also called *Brachystegia* woodland; comprises mainly mopane and acacia *bushveld*

mokoro (plural **mekoro**) – dugout canoe; propelled by a well-balanced poler who stands in the stern

mopane worms – the caterpillar of the moth *Gonimbrasia belina*, eaten as a local delicacy throughout the region

mpasa – lake salmon (Malawi)

mujejeje – rocks that resonate when struck

murunge – see *muzungu*

muti – traditional medicine

muzungu – white person

nalikwanda – huge wooden canoe that is painted with black and white stripes and carries the *litunga*

ncheni – lake tiger fish (Malawi)

nganga – fortune teller

now now – definitely not now, but sometime sooner than 'just now'

nshima – filling maize porridge-like substance eaten in Zambia; spelled *nsima* in Malawi

pan – dry, flat area of grassland or salt, often a seasonal lake-bed

participation safari – an inexpensive safari in which clients pitch their own tents, pack the vehicle and share cooking duties

Pedicle, the – the tongue of Democratic Republic of Congo territory that almost divides Zambia into two

peg – milepost

photographic safari – safari in which participants carry cameras rather than guns

pint – small bottle of beer or can of oil (or similar), usually around 300ml to 375ml (not necessarily equal to a British or US pint)

piri-piri or **peri-peri** – very hot pepper sauce of Portuguese/Angolan origin; the basis for the Nando's chain's chicken concoctions

potjie – (pronounced *poy*-kee) a three-legged pot used to make stew over an open fire; also refers both to the stew itself and to a gathering at which the stew forms the main dish

relish – sauce of meat, vegetables, beans etc, eaten with boiled *mielie* meal (*nsima*, *nshima* etc)
robot – no, not R2D2 – it's just a traffic light
rondavel – round, African-style hut
rooibos – literally 'red bush' in Afrikaans; herbal tea that reputedly has therapeutic qualities

sangoma – witchdoctor; herbalist
slasher – hand tool with a curved blade used to cut grass or crops, hence 'to slash' means 'to cut grass'
squaredavel – see *rondavel* and work out the rest
sungwa – a type of perch (Malawi)

tackies – trainers, tennis shoes, gym shoes
tambo – fermented millet and sugar drink
toasties – toasted sandwiches

township – indigenous suburb, typically a high-density black residential area
UTC – Universal Time Coordinate (formerly GMT); the time at the prime meridian at Greenwich, UK

van der Merwe – archetypal Boer country bumpkin who is the butt of jokes throughout Southern Africa
veld – open grassland (pronounced felt), normally in plateau regions; lowveld, highveld, bushveld, strandveld, panveld
vlei – (pronounced flay) any low open landscape, sometimes marshy

watu – dugout canoe used in western Zambia

zol – see *dagga*

The Authors

ALAN MURPHY
Coordinating Author

Alan remembers falling under Southern Africa's ambient spell after bouncing around in the rear of a bakkie on the way from Johannesburg airport in 1999. Since then he's been back four times working for Lonely Planet, including this trip to Zambia. Whether watching elephants crossing a river, tracking lions in the bush, glimpsing elusive wild dogs or chuckling at the clownish behaviour of curious baboons, he finds wildlife watching exhilarating. Perhaps the logistical difficulties of getting around Zambia hit home though when he got told: 'go down the track and then take a right at the turn-off where the sign has fallen down'. This trip was one big adventure, made even more enjoyable by a 4WD named Bessie and a travelling companion named Smitzy. Alan wrote the Zambia & Malawi Highlights, Colour Itineraries, Destination Zambia & Malawi, Getting Started, Itineraries, History and Grassroots Development chapters, plus the Zambian chapters (except for Northern Zambia).

NANA LUCKHAM

Born in Tanzania to a Ghanaian mother and an English father, Nana started life criss-crossing Africa by plane and bumping along the roughest of roads. She first made it to Southern Africa in 1994 when she spent six months living in Zimbabwe. After several years as an editor and a United Nations press officer, she got into travel writing full time and has hauled her backpack all over Africa researching guidebooks to destinations such as Algeria, Kenya, South Africa and Benin. She was thrilled to return to Malawi (the scene of her very first Lonely Planet assignment) for this book. Nana wrote the Culture, Environment, Northern Zambia and Malawi chapters and contributed to the Highlights and Itineraries chapters.

CONTRIBUTING AUTHOR

Nicola Simmonds has worked in and backpacked around Indonesia, India, Sri Lanka, Europe, Japan, Central and South America. Having then lived in Angola and Zimbabwe for seven years (with her husband and, eventually, three kids), mastering water shortages, African bureaucracy and out-of-control economies, covering Zimbabwe post 'dollarisation' was nothing but joy. She has just spent a year in Sri Lanka and is currently figuring out where to go next. Nicola wrote the Victoria Falls chapter.

LONELY PLANET AUTHORS

Why is our travel information the best in the world? It's simple: our authors are passionate, dedicated travellers. They don't take freebies in exchange for positive coverage so you can be sure the advice you're given is impartial. They travel widely to all the popular spots, and off the beaten track. They don't research using just the internet or phone. They discover new places not included in any other guidebook. They personally visit thousands of hotels, restaurants, palaces, trails, galleries, temples and more. They speak with dozens of locals every day to make sure you get the kind of insider knowledge only a local could tell you. They take pride in getting all the details right, and in telling it how it is. Think you can do it? Find out how at **lonelyplanet.com**.

Behind the Scenes

THIS BOOK

Zambia & Malawi was researched and written by
Alan Murphy and Nana Luckham. The Victoria
Falls chapter was written by Nicola Simmonds.
The Health chapter was written by Dr Caroline
Evans. This guidebook was commissioned in
Lonely Planet's Melbourne office, edited and laid
out by Cambridge Publishing Management, UK,
and produced by the following:

Commissioning Editors Stefanie Di Trocchio, Tashi
Wheeler
Coordinating Editor Catherine Burch
Coordinating Cartographer Sam Sayer
Coordinating Layout Designer Paul Queripel
Managing Editors Melanie Dankel, Brigitte Ellemore
Managing Cartographers Shahara Ahmed, Adrian
Persoglia
Managing Layout Designer Sally Darmody
Assisting Editors Michala Green, Scarlett O'Hara,
Emma Sangster, Ceinwen Sinclair, Kelly Walker
Assisting Cartographers Chris Lee Ack, Ross Butler,
Dennis Capparelli
Assisting Layout Designer Trevor Double
Cover Research Naomi Parker, lonelyplanetimages
.com
Internal Image Research Jane Hart,
lonelyplanetimages.com
Indexer Marie Lorimer

Project Manager Melanie Dankel
Language Content Annelies Mertens, Laura Crawford

Thanks to Imogen Bannister, Chris Girdler, Michelle
Glynn, Martin Heng, Katie Lynch

THANKS
ALAN MURPHY
Firstly I'd like to thank Smitzy, my friend and travelling companion – his curiosity, incisive observations on the road and help with research were
invaluable. Francis, a reliable taxi driver in Lusaka,
was a great help. Thanks to Elke at Tikondane for
helping me understand village life. Thanks to the
authors of the Botswana and Namibia chapters of
the latest Lonely Planet *Southern Africa* guide who
provided text. I'd also like to acknowledge David
Else's Lonely Planet *Zambia* guide, which was a
great resource for this new book. Lastly, thanks
to the Zambian people we met who were warm,
friendly and unfailingly helpful.

NANA LUCKHAM
At Lonely Planet my thanks go to Tashi Wheeler,
Will Gourlay, Stefanie Di Trocchio and my co-author
Alan Murphy. In London, thanks as ever to Patrick
Smith for his pre-departure advice and contacts.
Thanks also to Gilbert at Njaya Lodge in Nkhata

THE LONELY PLANET STORY

Fresh from an epic journey across Europe, Asia and Australia in 1972, Tony and Maureen Wheeler
sat at their kitchen table stapling together notes. The first Lonely Planet guidebook, *Across Asia
on the Cheap*, was born.

Travellers snapped up the guides. Inspired by their success, the Wheelers began publishing
books to Southeast Asia, India and beyond. Demand was prodigious, and the Wheelers expanded
the business rapidly to keep up. Over the years, Lonely Planet extended its coverage to every
country and into the virtual world via lonelyplanet.com and the Thorn Tree message board.

As Lonely Planet became a globally loved brand, Tony and Maureen received several offers for
the company. But it wasn't until 2007 that they found a partner whom they trusted to remain true
to the company's principles of travelling widely, treading lightly and giving sustainably. In October
of that year, BBC Worldwide acquired a 75% share in the company, pledging to uphold Lonely
Planet's commitment to independent travel, trustworthy advice and editorial independence.

Today, Lonely Planet has offices in Melbourne, London and Oakland, with over 500 staff members and 300 authors. Tony and Maureen are still actively involved with Lonely Planet. They're
travelling more often than ever, and they're devoting their spare time to charitable projects. And
the company is still driven by the philosophy of *Across Asia on the Cheap*: 'All you've got to do
is decide to go and the hardest part is over. So go!'

Bay, Patrick Jere at Mwabvi Wildlife Reserve, Ackson Kasonde for driving me around southern Malawi, and to Patrick and Jona from Budget Safari for their kindness, good humour and company in northern Malawi and Zambia.

ACKNOWLEDGMENTS

Many thanks to the following for the use of their content:

Globe on title page ©Mountain High Maps 1993 Digital Wisdom, Inc.

All internal photographs by Lonely Planet Images, and by David Else p8 (#6), p11 (#6 & #7); Michael Gebicki p6 (#1), p9 (#2); Dennis Jones p6 (#4); Andrew MacColl p12; Carol Polich p9 (#1); Andy Rouse p7 (#3); Ray Tipper p5; Ariadne Van Zandbergen p7 (#2 & #5), p8 (#5), p10. All images are the copyright of the photographers unless otherwise indicated. Many of the images in this guide are available for licensing from Lonely Planet Images: lonelyplanetimages.com

BEHIND THE SCENES

Index

INDEX

INDEX

GreenDex

It seems like everyone's going green these days, but how can you know which businesses are actually eco-friendly, and which are simply jumping on the eco/sustainable bandwagon? Many lodges and camps in and around national parks claim to be involved in conservation activities, and indeed many of them are – helping, for example, to support important practices such as anti-poaching measures.

The following tours, attractions and accommodation choices have all been selected by Lonely Planet authors because they demonstrate an active sustainable-tourism policy. Many are involved in conservation or environmental activism, some are owned and operated by local Zambians, and some are genuine cultural experiences, thereby helping to promote, maintain and preserve local identity and culture.

We want to keep developing our sustainable tourism content. If you think we've omitted someone who should be listed here, or if you disagree with our choices, email us at www.lonelyplanet.com/feedback and set us straight for next time. For more information about sustainable tourism and Lonely Planet, see www.lonelyplanet.com/responsibletravel

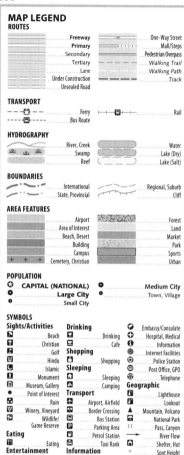

MAP LEGEND

ROUTES

Freeway	One-Way Street
Primary	Mall/Steps
Secondary	Pedestrian Overpass
Tertiary	Walking Trail
Lane	Walking Path
Under Construction	Track
Unsealed Road	

TRANSPORT

Ferry	Rail
Bus Route	

HYDROGRAPHY

River, Creek	Water
Swamp	Lake (Dry)
Reef	Lake (Salt)

BOUNDARIES

International	Regional, Suburb
State, Provincial	Cliff

AREA FEATURES

Airport	Forest
Area of Interest	Land
Beach, Desert	Market
Building	Park
Campus	Sports
Cemetery, Christian	Urban

POPULATION

CAPITAL (NATIONAL)	Medium City
Large City	Town, Village
Small City	

SYMBOLS

Sights/Activities
- Beach
- Christian
- Golf
- Hindu
- Islamic
- Monument
- Museum, Gallery
- Point of Interest
- Ruin
- Winery, Vineyard
- Wildlife/Game Reserve

Eating
- Eating

Entertainment
- Entertainment

Drinking
- Drinking
- Cafe

Shopping
- Shopping

Sleeping
- Sleeping
- Camping

Transport
- Airport, Airfield
- Border Crossing
- Bus Station
- Parking Area
- Petrol Station
- Taxi Rank

Information
- Bank, ATM

- Embassy/Consulate
- Hospital, Medical
- Information
- Internet Facilities
- Police Station
- Post Office, GPO
- Telephone

Geographic
- Lighthouse
- Lookout
- Mountain, Volcano
- National Park
- Pass, Canyon
- River Flow
- Shelter, Hut
- Spot Height
- Waterfall

LONELY PLANET OFFICES

Australia
Head Office
Locked Bag 1, Footscray, Victoria 3011
☎ 03 8379 8000, fax 03 8379 8111
talk2us@lonelyplanet.com.au

USA
150 Linden St, Oakland, CA 94607
☎ 510 250 6400, toll free 800 275 8555
fax 510 893 8572
info@lonelyplanet.com

UK
2nd fl, 186 City Rd,
London EC1V 2NT
☎ 020 7106 2100, fax 020 7106 2101
go@lonelyplanet.co.uk

Published by Lonely Planet Publications Pty Ltd
ABN 36 005 607 983